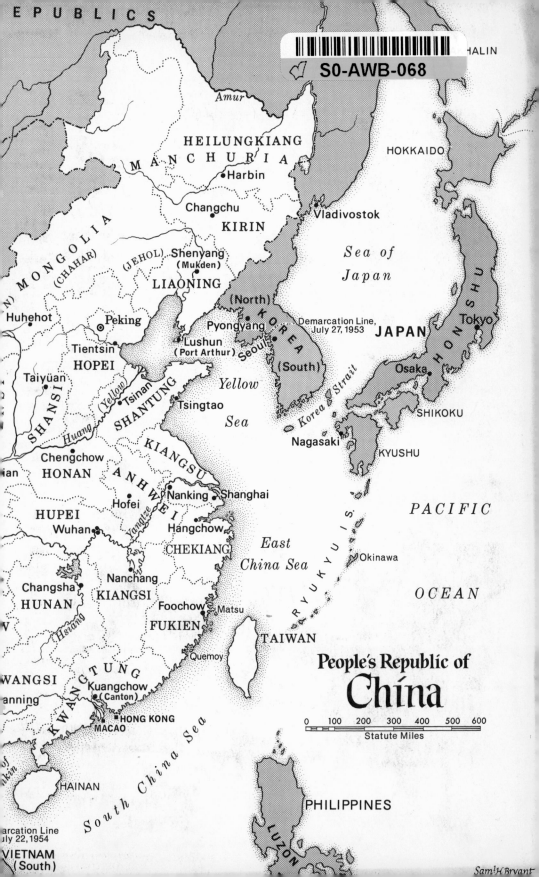

EPUBLICS

S0-AWB-068

HALIN

Amur

HEILUNGKIANG

M A N C H U R I A

HOKKAIDO

• Harbin

Changchu•

KIRIN

• Vladivostok

Sea of Japan

M O N G O L I A
(CHAHAR)

(JEHOL)

Shenyang
(Mukden)•

LIAONING

(North)

Huhehot•

⊙ Peking

• Tientsin

HOPEI

• Lushun
(Port Arthur)

K
O
R
E
A

Demarcation Line,
July 27, 1953

JAPAN

H
O
N
S
H
U

• Tokyo

Pyongyang•

Seoul•

Taiyüan•

SHANSI

(Yellow)

•Tsinan

SHANTUNG

Huang

(South)

Osaka•

Yellow

Korea Strait

SHIKOKU

Tsingtao•

Sea

KIANGSU

Chengchow•

HONAN

A N H W E I

Nagasaki•

KYUSHU

Nanking•

•Shanghai

PACIFIC

ian

Hofei•

HUPEI

Wuhan•

Yangtze

Hangchow•

CHEKIANG

*East
China Sea*

OCEAN

Changsha•

HUNAN

Nanchang•

KIANGSI

Hsiang

Foochow•

FUKIEN

Matsu•

Okinawa

R
Y
U
K
Y
U

I
s.

•Quemoy

TAIWAN

WANGSI

anning

K W A N G T U N G

Kuangchow
(Canton)•

People's Republic of
China

HONG KONG

MACAO•

0   100   200   300   400   500   600

Statute Miles

South China Sea

HAINAN

PHILIPPINES

arcation Line
ly 22, 1954

VIETNAM
(South)

LUZON

Sam H Bryant

HAN, Suyin, pseud. **The morning deluge; Mao Tsetung and the Chinese revolution, 1893–1954.** Little, Brown, 1972. 571p il map 72-4816. 12.95. ISBN 0-316-34289-0

CHOICE   FEB. '73

History, Geography & Travel

Asia & Oceania

Scholar, doctor, authoress, Han Suyin, who has made 16 visits to the People's Republic of China, is a knowledgeable observer of developments in that country. Readers can look forward to her second volume (in preparation) which will deal with the post-1950 transformation of China. The book, though very provocative, suffers from its ambitious attempt at a history of revolutionary China and a biography of Mao. Han's dilemma, however, is appreciated, because she finds it impossible to write one without the other. From an academic point of view, this book adds little new information on Mao's revolutionary career, which has been well elucidated. Nonetheless, it invites comparison with Edgar Snow's monumental *Red star over China* (rev. ed.; CHOICE, Nov. 1968) and *Red China today* (rev. ed. 1971) because of her extensive interviews with people who appeared in Mao's life, interviews which have eluded many otherwise well-documented works. Readers with no historical background in China may find the book difficult, and readers with no appreciation of the Chinese nationalistic aspirations may find it objectionable. Han hints at the infallability of Mao, an obvious partiality which she finally explains on page 380. There are

BOOKS BY HAN SUYIN

DESTINATION CHUNGKING

A MANY-SPLENDORED THING

AND THE RAIN MY DRINK

THE MOUNTAIN IS YOUNG

CAST BUT ONE SHADOW

WINTER LOVE

TWO LOVES

THE FOUR FACES

THE CRIPPLED TREE

A MORTAL FLOWER

CHINA IN THE YEAR TWO THOUSAND AND ONE

BIRDLESS SUMMER

ASIA TODAY

THE MORNING DELUGE

THE
MORNING DELUGE

A child of two cultures, daughter of a Chinese engineer and a Belgian from the Denis family, Han Suyin was born in China at a railway station in September 1917. Since then she has lived, worked and studied in many countries, attending Yenching University, Brussels University, and receiving her M.D. in England in 1948; but she has always returned to China. From 1939 to 1942 she lived in Chungking, serving as a midwife and working with an American missionary doctor, work which served as the basis for her first book, DESTINATION CHUNGKING. Since then, Han Suyin has written eleven other books, including A MANY-SPLENDORED THING, AND THE RAIN MY DRINK, THE MOUNTAIN IS YOUNG, TWO LOVES, THE FOUR FACES, and three volumes of her autobiography, THE CRIPPLED TREE, A MORTAL FLOWER and BIRDLESS SUMMER. She has also lectured and traveled in twenty-five countries and worked as a doctor in Hong Kong, Singapore, and in Malaya during the guerilla emergency. From 1956 to 1972 Dr. Han has spent part of each year in China, systematically following the Chinese Revolution as it has evolved, including the Cultural Revolution, most recently touring the Silk Road and Sinkiang Province and the border regions between China and the U.S.S.R., tracing the Long March and interviewing many survivors. THE MORNING DELUGE is the result of these fifteen years of research, travel and personal interviews, and of a basic understanding of the physical factors and the emotional and cultural components of the Chinese Revolution which make it understandable in all its aspects to the rest of the world.

THE
MORNING DELUGE

MAO TSETUNG AND THE
CHINESE REVOLUTION

1893-1954

by HAN SUYIN

LITTLE, BROWN AND COMPANY · BOSTON · TORONTO

FIRST EDITION

T 10/72

The author is grateful to Lois Wheeler Snow and Grove Press, Inc. for permission to include excerpts from the first revised and enlarged edition of RED STAR OVER CHINA by Edgar Snow. Copyright 1938, 1944 by Random House, Inc. Copyright © 1968 by Edgar Snow. Copyright © 1961 by John K. Fairbank.

Library of Congress Cataloging in Publication Data

Han, Suyin, pseud.
  The morning deluge.

  Includes bibliographical references.
  1. Mao, Tsê-tung, 1893–   2.   Communism
—China. I. Title.
DS778.M3H35   951.05'092'4 [B]   72-4816
ISBN 0-316-34289-0

Published simultaneously in Canada
by Little, Brown & Company (Canada) Limited

PRINTED IN THE UNITED STATES OF AMERICA

The life of Chairman Mao is in essence the history of new China. Rare are instances when an individual makes such a profound impact on a nation's history.

HAILE SELASSIE
in Peking,
October 6, 1971

Author's Note

For this book I am indebted to an extent which cannot be repaid, first to the memory of the millions of peasants and workers of China who died for the Revolution, and whose children today walk as men in full dignity towards the building of their own future. I am also indebted to many many friends, both in China and elsewhere, in particular to the late Edgar Snow, who gave me so much time and also allowed me to read and to utilize so much of his material. There are also many American writers, scrupulously fair, to whom I am greatly indebted for their contribution to truth.

I am also grateful and wish to thank Madame Teng Ying-chao, the wife of His Excellency Premier Chou En-lai, for having fired my imagination with a single sentence, and thus planted the seed of this book, almost sixteen years ago. In a talk with her in June 1956, she compared the people of China to a great ocean, and the leaders (such as herself) to the white froth on the wavetops, born of them, carried by them, forever renascent, but nonexistent without the ocean. This image I never forgot. I thought then of Chairman Mao as both the child and the leader of the Revolution, the nation-man and also the man-ocean, the student of his people as well as their teacher; the one who represents and articulates their genius and also is most indebted to that genius; the builder of a New China and the destroyer of that worst of all Chinese traditions: submission and obedience to the ruler.

The sources for this book include not only the usual representative material published concerning China, but also numerous personal interviews and talks, and the frequent journeys of the author to China over the last sixteen years, together with consultation of documents, newspaper reprints, and other sources in many museums in China today, and visits to several of the old Red bases, such as Juichin and Chingkangshan, mentioned in the book.

The author reiterates her gratitude to scholars and researchers in Chinese studies, including many whose works have not yet been published. She is also indebted to the late Anna Louise Strong, that magnificent and courageous American writer, for her help and advice; to Dr. Ma Hai-teh (George Hatem) and to Mr. Rewi Alley, at present both in China; to the distinguished French economists Madame Helene Marchisio and Dr. Charles Bettelheim, and to numerous other persons throughout the world whose many years of association with China and study of Chinese problems have helped her in evaluating the sometimes contradictory material at her disposal. But the main sources still remain the interviews with hundreds of Chinese workers, peasants, soldiers, Long Marchers and others throughout the vast land of China who participated in these events and whose eyewitness accounts often contradicted certain material published in the Western world which has acquired validity by constant repetition. The author hopes that the new material and views in this book will bring a fresh understanding of the development of the Chinese Revolution.

HAN SUYIN

Contents

Maps and Illustrations

THE
MORNING DELUGE

Prologue

When Emperor Haile Selassie of Ethiopia visited the People's Republic of China in October 1971, he had this to say: "Today no one refers to China without mentioning its great leader, Chairman Mao Tsetung. The life history of Chairman Mao is in essence the history of New China. Rare are instances when an individual makes such a profound impact on a nation's history."

It is essentially in this spirit that *The Morning Deluge* has been written. It is not meant to be the biography of a single hero, a genius, a Caesar in absolute authority, a superman above the crowd, manipulating people and events. It is to give, through episodes of Chairman Mao's life and especially through his development as a revolutionary and as a thinker, the story of the Chinese Revolution.

This book is not an officially sponsored book. It is entirely the author's responsibility. No approval has been sought, but I am grateful to the Chinese government for allowing me numerous interviews with people who went through the Revolution, who made the Long March, who lived these events. Ordinary people, whose testimony is precious.

The heroic view of an individual fashioning history at will, wreaking his fancies upon helpless millions, exacting absolute obedience, has guided many a so-called biography of Chairman Mao. Nothing could be further from the truth. Many historical events have been described according to the testimony of Communist Party renegades or Kuomintang sources. I have examined them and compared them with other sources, and in many instances have found them fanciful. There are also many so-called secret documents, procured by means which are not explained and purporting to represent official pronouncements. These have also been examined; only in certain cases, when certain sentences used were also heard in China, have these been mentioned, with due caution.

The Chinese Revolution brought forth its leader in Mao Tsetung; Mao Tsetung shaped the Chinese Revolution. This dialectical link, symbiosis between a man's life and the Revolution to which he has given his life, makes it impossible to write of the one without the other. Mao Tsetung has embodied the aspirations, needs, and desires of his nation and of his people; their will to revolt, to end exploitation, misery, injustice; to free themselves and become masters of their own destiny. Not a single day has Mao Tsetung departed from this goal, and he has always gone back to the peasants and workers, the downtrodden of his land, to learn from them, with magnificent humility. The source of his creative power, as he will say himself, is the boundless creative power of the masses, who topple empires and transform the earth. He found his own people with limitless enthusiasm for revolution, and unhesitatingly gave all of himself to it, and hence became their leader, the nation-man.

Because the development of a man is the process by which his ideas are formed, it is also impossible to describe the Chinese Revolution without studying the thinking of Chairman Mao. Mao Tsetung Thought was developed in this great forward movement, this overwhelming tide which has brought, with a speed unparalleled in history, one quarter of humanity into the modern age and into its own future. Not only did he formulate and develop the ideas which would make action possible, but he has also documented them, and this scientific study of the relation between theory and practice, between idea and action, makes his thinking of world importance today.

Mao Tsetung's grasp of the future, his vision of man's true role on earth, has given him a place as a world figure. His creative genius has come from this constant return to the people, resisting all attempts to elevate himself above them. Much has been said about the "personality cult"; I have seen true, genuine love and admiration from the ordinary people of China for Mao Tsetung. The personality cult evolved round him by city bureaucrats he has done his best to put down, withdrawing himself as a person, giving to the people all homage for the Revolution. Only the people are the heroes of history; only they make it. It is in this spirit, not elevating Mao as a genius, but showing him as a man, in a constant search for truth, for reality, that this book has been written.

Chairman Mao was born when China was crumbling, in misery

and degradation and despair, halfway in that span of one hundred and nine years known as China's semi-feudal semi-colonial period. Since 1840, the time of the first Opium War made upon China by Great Britain to force the drug upon the Chinese people, China's story had been one of swift ruin. The ruin was not only material, with the Western colonial powers exploiting China at the point of the gun, forcing upon her unequal treaties, burning the palaces of Peking, massacring inhabitants at will, exacting huge sums of "indemnity" for wars made upon her; it was also spiritual. None of the old values and traditions could stem this tide of destruction, and when Mao Tsetung was born China's revolution had already begun. Great peasant revolts had taken place; his childhood was pinpointed with famines and devastation and revolts. Already that great and noble revolutionary of the early twentieth century, Dr. Sun Yatsen, had begun to lead those who, in the first surge of revolt, sought to make the Chinese people free.

Although far removed from the centers of revolt, in the deep countryside, a farmer's child, Mao Tsetung was plunged into the turmoil of his generation. So swift were the changes that took place that Mao's life is a recapitulation of what his generation says, that they have lived through many ages in their country's history. In these changes Mao Tsetung participated, and when others gave up, gave in, gave way to despair, he went on, undaunted, unfaltering. Perhaps his greatest moment was in 1927, when all seemed lost, and when Mao rallied, persuaded, exhorted a band of heroic peasants and workers to continue, and with them ascended his eagle's nest, a forbidding mountain, there to forge a new Army, a new Party, and to nurse back to life the Revolution which seemed drowned in blood.

This enormous faith in the future was not an abstract belief; it was a staunch confidence in the strength and power of *people,* in their heroism and their courage. As the artist sees beyond the surface and seeks the essence of truth in all things, Mao Tsetung is the artist of the Revolution, seeing hope and joy and power where others only saw weakness, ignorance, slavery. Because he had the eyes of love, because he is bone of the bone, flesh of the flesh of the Chinese peasants and workers, he had that true greatness which is humility; and humility led him to a total faith in the millions. Revolution is made with passion and guts and vision and everything that one has or is, and so is artistic creation. If this book is said to be pro-Mao Tsetung, the answer is that it is. For there cannot be a true attempt to picture the story of a revolution if one does not also describe the faith and the steadfastness, beyond all practical considerations, which animate it.

Of Mao Tsetung can be said what Thomas Traherne wrote: "Strange is the vigor in a brave man's soul. His courage fits him for all attempts, makes him the bulwark and defense of his being and of his country." Mao Tsetung's repose and security were not in himself, but always in the hearts of his countrymen, from whom he strove to cast out fear, from whom he called forth boldness and initiative.

And because Mao Tsetung gave the Chinese people that liberation of the mind which is true liberty, there is far greater hope in the world that all the peoples on earth may achieve true brotherhood.

PART I

1

Childhood

Mao Tsetung was born on December 26, 1893, in the village of Shaoshan Chung, one of a scattered group of clan villages in the fertile valley of Shaoshan, Hunan province. The nearest town, twenty-two miles away, is the district town of Hsiangtan, so named because of the beautiful, winding Hsiang river, which flows from southwest China through three provinces into the spongy meander of lakes and tributaries which forms the middle basin of the Yangtze river. The Hsiang connects the district with Changsha, the turbulent, steamy capital of Hunan province; with Wuhan, the triple metropolis * upon the Yangtze; and with the ocean port of Shanghai. Cargo boats of three to five thousand tons ply its waters bringing pork and bristle, rice and salt; the old imperial highway from the southernmost city of Canton, now called Kuangchow, † ran through the district to Peking bearing tribute and couriers and silk; in the early 1900's a railway would be built along the road.

The district where Mao was born was therefore a natural crossroads for commerce, and a wealthy agricultural area. It was also a strategic region, for no travel either in peace or in war could avoid this heart province of China; east to west, south to north, the province commanded the roads and the rivers. The Hunan people were renowned for their acumen, enterprise and energy; their peasant traders sustained far-reaching commercial links throughout the country. In the late nineteenth and early twentieth centuries Hunan was also a center of intellectual accomplishment, and hence of dissidence and revolt; it fostered the best scholars in China, it also boasted a

---

* Hankow, Hanyang, Wuchang are the names of the three cities which form Wuhan.
† A name we shall use in this book, since modern Chinese detest the name Canton, with its old colonial flavor.

plethora of militarists. Both the generals who helped the crumbling Manchu dynasty and the revolutionaries who brought it down found their recruits in Hunan. Throughout the nineteenth century Hunan had been on the highway of internecine warfare. The great Taiping peasant uprising (1850 to 1864) had found here its millions of valorous warriors; for despite the fertility of the province and the unrelenting labor of its inhabitants, it was a region of peasants impoverished by landlords and exorbitant taxation. The Taiping revolt was put down with enormous slaughter; the peasantry went back to squalid oppression. But the memory of rebellion was strong in the villages of Hunan, and the 1911 Revolution to come was already in embryo in the schools of the capital city, Changsha, when Mao was born.

Today Shaoshan Chung, Mao's birthplace, is a medium-sized brigade,* part of a commune, with 708 families. The majority of the families are still named Mao.† The clan house remains, now turned into a museum. Shaoshan today receives a million visitors annually. In 1963, 30,000 people visited it; in 1964, 70,000; in 1965, 205,-000. In 1966, the midyear had already seen over 310,000 pilgrims. On a day in July 1966, I saw delegations of peasants, some from far-off Tibet and Singkiang, walking up the pathways, holding banners and portraits of Chairman Mao Tsetung. In 1971, up to 10,000 visitors a day streamed in orderly files to visit the house where he was born. Today the clay brick farmhouse with its two wings, one roofed with tile and one with rice stalk thatch, with its pathway winding between lotus ponds, is as familiar to 800 million Chinese as their own homes.

The farmhouse grew from an original mud-walled shack with a low-pitched thatch roof, which Mao Tsetung's grandfather, a poor peasant crushed by debt, erected in 1878. Mao Tsetung's father, Mao Jen-shen, was then a wiry eight-year-old, hard-working in the fields. He had very little schooling, for at sixteen he enrolled in the imperial army as a soldier to pay off his father's debts. After seven years, and incredible self-denial, he had saved enough from his soldier's pittance to buy back the small piece of land (about half an acre) which the elder Mao had lost to a landlord. Mao Jen-shen gradually improved the farmhouse, chiefly after 1903, when he ac-

---

* A brigade is a section of a commune, and consists of several production teams.

† Among the families living there, eight are of revolutionary martyrs, 123 of Army men and Communist cadres.

Birthplace of Mao Tsetung in Shaoshan, Hunan province. In front, one of the lotus ponds where he learned to swim.

quired another one and a half acres and thus became, in the classification established later by his son, a lower middle peasant.

Two families * lived in this house, one in each wing, connected by a central hall in which, facing the entrance, was recessed a wooden ancestors' shelf. As Mao Jen-shen grew from poor to middle peasant he added rooms to his wing, and two years before his death in January 1920 was able to afford a tile roof, though the floor remained of beaten earth. The other family could not afford a tile roof. The present government has maintained the house exactly as it was.

Mao Jen-shen was inordinately hard-working, frugal and tenacious. His bitter youth stunted him physically; the photographs show him early emaciated; he died at fifty of typhoid fever. To accomplish what he did, buy back the land his father had lost, establish a family, and reach comparative comfort, he worked unceasingly, never sparing himself nor his sons. An urge to better himself drove him relentlessly; he was harsh towards his family and his eldest son, who early opposed him. He put his children to labor in the fields as soon as they were out of the toddling stage. He became the kind of man who lies sleepless worrying over the harvest, and forever reproved his family for waste and idleness. Mao Tsetung was not brought up as a rich peasant's son but as the son of a poor peasant driven by the memory of hunger and want. At sixteen, Mao only ate one egg a month, and he saw meat three or four times a year.

Biographers have made much of the father-son relationship in Mao's life. This is because, in the only record we have which is Mao's own about his childhood,† he starts on this aspect of family life and goes on about it at length. He makes no attempt to hide his feelings of revulsion against his father. This relationship has therefore been described as abnormal, based on hatred, an Oedipus complex; Mao's achievements have been explained away as founded on this childhood frustration.

But the father-son relationship in Mao's family was not abnormal. On the contrary, it was a prevailing and prevalent feature of the times, as any scanning of the novels and literature of that period will reveal. This resentment, this generation ditch, is found in the lives of almost every one of the revolutionaries whose childhood fell within

* Some biographers report that the other family was named Tsou. There was a Tsou family who moved into the house, but the ownership changed hands four times.

† See Edgar Snow *Red Star Over China* (1937, first revised and enlarged edition New York 1968), part IV, from which quotations from Mao are used throughout this book.

the 1890's to 1920's period. It was not a private but a public feature, a definite social phenomenon, just as today in the United States the generation gap cannot be explained in terms of Freudian psychology or of family relationships alone. Mao's contemporaries, and the generation to follow his, looked upon family rebellion as the first step in a general revolt against society, against Confucian tradition; it was a part of the search for new values, for a new order in the making.

In Mao's case, it was not trivial quarrels about food, or work, or study which would motivate his disagreements with his father. It would be something more basic: his identification with his downtrodden mother, with the laborer his father hired, with his siblings, against authoritarianism and absolute patriarchial rule.

Mao Jen-shen was not a wicked man, but he belonged to his own generation; he had labored and toiled to bring his family a modicum of security, and he did not understand why his eldest son should want to thwart his wishes. All he wanted was that he should be thrifty, hard-working, obedient, raise a family and the family status, in traditional style. All he knew was that the child was headstrong, almost impossibly self-willed, a dreamer; and yet it was he who had to give in, more often than not, and he did not know what strange power his son had. In his harsh manner, he not only loved his son, he was also nonplussed and unwillingly fascinated. This love of his, however, could only be expressed in roughness, in scolding, because that was the way the older generation treated the young ones in those days, when to disparage one's children and wife was a part of traditional courtesy.

There is no "autobiography" of Mao save what he told Edgar Snow in 1936. Biographies by Chinese or Westerners (egregious admirers or virulent haters) are often rehashes based on hearsay. Today, with time and reverence, it is almost impossible to get a non-hagiographic account of Mao's childhood days. Childhood tales may endear, but do not inform. His own spontaneous descriptions show that he belonged to the rebellious generation which would effect the long overdue changes for which China was ripe. Mao's rebellion was always an explicit one, a lucid, conscious affirmation, linking his acts of revolt to a general, and generational, social context. He carried his young rage of change with him wherever he went.

Physically, Mao grew tall and strong, taller and more robust than most boys of his age. His passion for water, an original trait, developed early. He taught himself to swim when he was six years old. Outside the farmhouse were two ponds where the children splashed in the hot summer; in them lotuses were grown, for food. Swimming became for him not only a physical experience but an exhilarating mental release. There is a connection in Mao between this addiction to swimming and the decisive movements of his mind. Sixty years later, on July 16, 1966, Mao Tsetung would swim the Yangtze river at Wuhan the day before returning to Peking to lead the Great Proletarian Cultural Revolution. The act was symbolic; for the Cultural Revolution would be a flood, sweeping away many accepted symbols, renewing the freshness of revolution, renewing his own youthful exploits through yet another generation of rebels.

In 1962, one summer day in Peking, Mao Tsetung went swimming in the newly built reservoirs of the Ming tombs * together with Liu Shao-chi, at that time President of the Republic. The great struggle between the two as to the policy to follow in building the Chinese state had already begun; they would soon clash in enmity. Besides being a fellow Hunanese, for he was born in a village not far from Mao's own, in 1898, Liu was regarded as Mao's successor and his intimate friend. When they emerged to dry themselves in the sun, young swimmers crowded around Mao, who spoke with them, but Liu did not say a word.

In September 1959, Mao Tsetung went to inspect the large Miyun reservoir and its hydroelectric plant, thirty-seven miles from Peking. He then had a swim, lasting forty minutes, in the hill-surrounded man-made lake. One is tempted to associate Mao's swim in that cold autumn to the problems then facing China. For at the time Mao was in a minority, power taken from him; before him loomed the Sino-Soviet conflict, the abrupt tearing up of the agreements made between the USSR and China by Khrushchev. Khrushchev was at Camp David conferring with Eisenhower; the USSR was backing the Indian side of the Sino-Indian border dispute. All this spelled danger to the Revolution. Mao swam in the ice-cold water for forty minutes and came out smiling, his mind made up.

Again, on July 16, 1971, anniversary of Mao's swim in the Yangtze † which started the Cultural Revolution, when all over China millions were plunging in lakes and rivers and the sea in commemoration, another Mao decision would be broadcast. Presi-

* Built by student volunteers in 1958–1959.
† From the age of sixty-three to seventy-three (1956–1966), Mao Tsetung swam the Yangtze river eight times at its widest point — about four miles back and forth.

dent Nixon had asked to come to China, and he had been invited. Why was this date chosen? Coincidence perhaps.

From the childhood lotus pond to the tidal bore of the Revolution there is, in Mao's language, the vivid imagery of water in its sweetness and its strength, in its life-giving passion and its irresistible forward movement. He has reshaped the Chinese language in terms of tides, waves, crests, seas, water, the flood. "That man . . . he's an ocean," said Edgar Snow to me in January 1971 after his last interview with Mao Tsetung. Unrelenting as flood, as water, the Revolution is Mao's whole being, thought and action. He merges with the moving tide within the ocean body of the Chinese Revolution. It is impossible to separate them. The one is the other.

The valley of Shaoshan is called Hibiscus Land, because of its beauty. From the fields which once belonged to Mao Tsetung's father (dispersed patches, not one larger than a quarter-acre) a hill range is seen, and one prominence is striking — a cone 1,700 feet high with a small Buddhist monastery atop. Mao's mother used to go there, climbing the stone paths on her bound feet. The young boy went with her, to stare without reverence at the dim smoke-wreathed figures of gilded clay.

At the age of six, Mao Tsetung, up before dawn, worked in the fields. As the night mists withdrew, he would see the first rays of the sun fingering the blue hills, inching above them; the light would dazzle him and the rice-heavy plain around him. Feet in the mud, head wrapped in sunlight, the little boy who would one day be called the great Red Sun felt his soul widen, and he would raise his arms to catch the sun upon all of his skin. Among those hills he had lost himself once for three days, running away from a teacher who beat him. Hills, mountains would become his refuge and strength in years to come, cradle his growing thoughts. The highlands of his mind were reached in strain and suffering among the mountains of his country.

"In times past the legendary emperor Shun came to Shaoshan, and pleased with the green prolific plain, sparkling its water meanders, he climbed the hills, sat on a pleasant crest and began to sing. A musical instrument was devised by him here to partner his singing, hence the name Shao music, peculiar to the region; and Shaoshan, musical mountain. The birds of the air, enthralled by Shun's melody, flocked here, among them phoenixes; they stayed, paired and nested. Hence Shaoshan is known as the birthplace of phoenixes; great men doing great deeds." Every child in the district knows the legend, and Phoenix Hill is the name of the cone-shaped height Mao climbed so often.*

Mao Tsetung, a small boy bending over the rice shoots in the dawn, watched the sun rise, heard echoes of Shun's music as the land round him stirred into life. And every day was marvel, the first day of the world.

> *So deep the night, so slow to break the crimson dawn;*
> *Demons and ghouls held sway so many centuries,*
> *Like desert sand, our hapless downtrodden people,*
> *Then the cock crowed.*
> *And suddenly all under heaven clear in the light*
> *And from Khotan to ocean sounds of music,*
> *Setting the poet's mind aglow with dreams . . .†*

The young Mao would go up, up, climbing the hills, walking for hours. He would in years to come climb higher mountains and feel the sky just "three foot three above me." ‡ He would sing: "How beautiful your mountains and rivers, O my country." But in the vulnerable years of childhood it was a beauty spoiled, wracked by misery and want, tyranny and exploitation. Of this he was conscious very early. The peasants of Hunan, of China, had a long tradition of revolt, and Mao was born a rebel, in a rebellious land.

The work Mao did as a child was not light; he labored long hours weeding, watering the buffalo and currying it, gathering wood for charcoal and manure from the pigsties, picking beans, after the paddy harvest going over the field for spare stalks. He grew tall and thin, his father grumbled at his ravenous appetite. At seven he was sent to the village primary school of Nan An, run by an old-type teacher, well thought of because he beat his pupils mercilessly. No teacher was reckoned worthy unless he showed severity to the children in his care. Each child, to recite his lessons, would leave his desk, stand in front of the teacher's desk, then promptly turn his back to him and recite. Mao refused to stand up. "If you can hear me well and sit, why should I stand up to recite?" he said. And clung to his desk and stool. The teacher was pale with fury. Never in a thousand years had this custom been challenged. He ordered the

---

* Interviews (1964 and 1971) with the head of the revolutionary committee of the Shaoshan museum.

† Poem by Mao Tsetung.

‡ See poem page 291.

seven-year-old to stand before his desk, but Mao dragged his stool with him and sat himself next to the teacher. The teacher then tried to heave him upright. Mao got up and left the school, and lost himself for three days in the hills. His distraught parents were overjoyed when he was found, and after that he was not beaten in school. "The result of my act of protest impressed me. . . . It was a successful 'strike.' " From this episode, Mao would go on; in each school he would attend Mao would lead student revolts, to reform teachers whose conduct he thought unbecoming. "Why should not one go to sleep during a boring lecture?" Mao would say in 1967, to the delight of another generation of young rebels.

Mao Tsetung's passion for reading began as soon as he could read tolerably. His best-loved books were romances, stories of rebellion and adventure. He did not like the classics, though he memorized them easily. Mao read those romances at school, covering them with a classic, and at home, between spells of work, under a tree in the hot noons. *Water Margin, Revolt Against the Tang, Travels in the West,* and *Three Kingdoms* had been banned by the Manchu dynasty a century previously as pernicious, because they were historical memories, in fiction form, of revolt against tyranny. Peddlers would bring them from home to home, every child knew by heart their episodes and heroes; they were read till their pages were worn through, in spite of the edicts. In his room, Mao covered the door connecting his room to his parents' bedroom with a blanket so that no light shone through the chinks and read, by the light of an oil wick, the night through.* More than half a century later he still reads a book a day or more, underlining passages he finds interesting for his wife Chiang Ching to read.

Mao Tsetung's characteristics as a child were a passion for justice, an uncommon propensity for arguing, an unequaled stubbornness when he thought he was right. Mao never lost this childhood quality. But all childhood episodes are to be handled with caution, for they project the image of a young saint. He was above all true to himself; whatever he thought he would immediately translate into action, regardless of admonition. This urge for "seeing if it works" denotes a scientific spirit, uncommon in a medieval environment, with accepted values untried by experiment. "Knowledge is the beginning of action and action is the accomplishment of knowledge,"

---

* The countryside of Shaoshan only acquired electric light in 1966. Until then Hunan peasants used vegetable oil in which wicks were dipped.

the philosopher Wang Yang-ming had proclaimed, and thus Mao acted. In Mao's mind the heroes of romantic tales were real people he longed to emulate, not dead images to be smothered in incense and forgotten. He was willing to endure unpleasantness to help others if he thought their cause was right, and this "righting of wrongs" instinct, so deep in him, would give him throughout his life a kind of candor, an innocence almost naïve. Thus he would save some old woman's crop from a storm before saving his own family's grain, and explain that it was the only thing to do, since she needed the grain more than his father did; he would give his warm gown to a poor student and go home shivering. For all these things he was scolded and punished. But his mother understood him well, for she too was generous of spirit, ever ready to share what she had.

"She pitied the poor and often gave them rice when they came to ask for it during famines. But she could not do so when my father was present. . . . We had many quarrels in my home over this question. There were two 'parties' in the family. One was my father, the Ruling Power. The Opposition was made up of myself, my mother, my brother, and sometimes even the laborer. . . . The dialectical struggle in our family was constantly developing." Thus Mao described the family scene, and the mother whom he venerated. Mao's mother, Wen Chi-mei, came from Hsiang Hsiang, a county sixteen miles from Shaoshan. As is the custom in peasant China among the poor, she was older than his father when they were married. She died of tuberculous lymphadenitis in October 1918. Mao Tsetung loved her very deeply; he wrote about her and spoke of her with deep emotion, even decades after her death.

Beside Mao Tsetung, Wen Chi-mei bore two other sons, Mao Tse-min, born in 1896, and Mao Tse-tan, born in 1905. Both of them seem to have been passionately devoted to their elder brother and followed him during all the years of their lives. So did his adopted sister, Mao Tse-chien, born in 1905 in another family of the Mao clan. "After the death of the Chairman's parents the family became far more revolutionary," the director of the Shaoshan museum said to me in 1966, indicating the restraint imposed upon the young by the parents. It seems certain that in the necessary process of asserting his personality, Mao earned the admiration of many of the young in his village. Later, in the 1920's, it was there he would found his first peasant Communist Party branch, drawing upon his own kin. They followed him and laid down their lives for the Revolution.

This early training in contradiction within a family, this "dialectical struggle" which lay beneath the "harmony and unity" vermilion paper slogans, the façade of valedictory eulogies of family filial piety, pasted at New Year on both sides of the shelf upon which stood the ancestors' tablets, Mao would see as the start of his own revolt against society. His knowledge of the classics, quick-witted use of sententious phrases and quotations, became "a powerful argument of my own for debating with my father on his own ground." Thus, by using the moralistic lore of the revered ancients, he bolstered his sense of outrage against the hypocrisy of tradition. Daring to argue was in itself a break against filial piety. No son was supposed ever to talk back to his father * ; but Mao Tsetung spoke with such fire, raged with such logic, persisted with such eloquence, that the peasants of Hunan, always a good audience, were delighted and impressed, and would go round repeating the young boy's catchy phrases. Even his father, torn between anger and grudging admiration and pride, would nearly always give in.

The times were of change. In peasant Shaoshan, ensconced in its green valley, seemingly sleepy, the incipient revolution disturbed the elders. The 1900 uprising of the Righteous Fists against massive foreign exploitation was essentially a peasant revolt.† It had opened a new era of resistance, although this was not noticeable at the time. It had dealt a death blow to the odious and idiotic tyranny of the Manchu dynasty, already bankrupt under the burden of foreign debt imposed by the Western powers and Japan. It was a violent demonstration against their pillage of China. This revolt was a landmark in China's contemporary history, precursor of the revolutions to come, but it was put down by the combined forces of the European powers and Japan.‡

When Mao was ten years old there were foreign garrisons in every main city, including Changsha, the capital of Hunan province; gunboats (British and American) patrolled the lakes and waterways of Middle China, sailed down the Hsiang river, or rode the high waters of the Yangtze up to Szechuan, deep in the interior. Foreign power protected and supported the captive Manchu imperial government, now become the main safeguard of foreign interests against seething

* Even today in India, young people in their twenties complain that they are never allowed to "talk back." This happens even in well-educated families.

† Also known as the Boxer Rebellion, it was at first an antidynastic movement, but was turned by the Manchu dynasty into an antiforeign movement. See Victor W. Purcell *The Boxer Uprising* (Cambridge, England, 1963).

‡ Great Britain, France, Germany, Italy, Belgium, United States, Russia, Japan.

popular revolt. Mao Tsetung's grandfather, who lived till 1908, was incensed at the thought of a British garrison in Changsha, was aware of the humiliating indemnities and concessions imposed upon China by the victorious Western powers. The old man was no revolutionary, but he was a patriot.

Educational reforms were proclaimed in 1901 and 1902, and in 1906 a program of "new" primary schools and modern institutions of higher learning was drawn up by the Manchu imperial dynasty, but little was done. However, schools of "new learning" * were organized, and subsidized chiefly by merchants' guilds, overseas Chinese, and landlords. Mercantile society wanted reforms in education for its children. The Chinese have always excelled at promoting schemes for the self-interest of a guild, clan or other association based on local or provincial membership, and now clans, guilds and societies took over when the Manchu empire crumbled. Though the schools were ostensibly government-supported, most were run on private contribution. This practice was prevalent in Hunan, Hupei and the coastal provinces, where the influence of the merchant class and intellectuals "newly returned" from abroad, especially Japan,† was strong. Thus, very quickly, institutions grew up which became training grounds for dissent and rebellion. Hunan's capital, Changsha, was such a focus.

Some of these new schools were set up in temples, and the clay gods were boarded up, to turn the prayer halls into classrooms. Mao Tsetung, like Sun Yatsen before him, was naturally irreverent towards clay deities, and his Buddhist mother could not convince him of their superhuman attributes. This agnosticism was of his age and his generation, for Sun Yatsen, too, had battled against images of veneration.

In 1906 occurred an event which was to mark Mao Tsetung deeply. Famine, one of the great recurrent famines of China, due to floods, stalked the provinces of Hupei and Hunan, coincident with the Russo-Japanese war (1904–1905), which was fought on Chinese soil, in Manchuria. The war helped to fire patriotism among Chinese students in Japan. It was due to the designs the Russian and Nippon empires both had on Manchuria, and it was the first time Mao's gen-

* "New learning" meant learning history, geography, mathematics and the natural sciences, instead of learning only the classics. But the teaching of the classics continued as part of Chinese language teaching.
† The practice of sending Chinese students abroad also started in the 1890's, but accelerated after the defeat of the Boxer uprising in 1901.

Peking, 1900, after the Righteous Fists (Boxer) Uprising was put down by foreign troops. Above, the partially destroyed Chien Men gate; below, U.S. Marines march in the city.

eration saw a white and predatory power beaten by an Asian one, similarly predatory. At the same time as the war and famine, Sun Yatsen, the revolutionary of those decades, launched yet another insurrection to overthrow the Manchus and establish a republic in China. Seven such attempts were made by Sun Yatsen between 1906 and 1908. They all failed; nevertheless they sustained and inspired a generation of intellectuals with the necessity for revolt. The unquenchable Sun Yatsen, to whom Mao renders full praise, was never disheartened by defeat. "Let's try again" was his constant retort to those who were disheartened. The Revolution of 1911, the overthrow of the Manchu dynasty in China, and the establishment of a republic were all due to this indomitable leader from Kwangtung, who devoted his life to try to restore to China her independence and her sovereignty, whose dream was to establish in China a system of parliamentary democracy as in the West.* Today his portrait, facing Mao Tsetung's, hangs in the great Red Square of Peking on October 1, anniversary of the triumph of the Revolution. And in 1906 it was, indirectly, because of him that the boy Mao got his first sharp memory of revolt beyond the confines of the family circle.

The Hunan insurrection of 1906 was launched by Huang Hsing, a Hunanese, member of Sun Yatsen's revolutionary organization the Tung Meng Hui (then sited in Japan). Its particular feature was that the uprising began in the coal mines of Pinghsiang and in Liuyang, where the famine was particularly severely felt. The leaders of the peasant secret societies † cooperated with Sun Yatsen's revolutionaries, and a march on Changsha, the provincial capital, was organized in which thousands of miners, peasants, and the local soldiery took part. On the way the hungry marchers raided the grain stores of the landlords. Again the old Taiping ‡ cry went up: "Share the land!" This uprising created so much excitement that many Chinese students in Japan came home to join the Hunan insurrection. The people of Changsha, who were starving, sent a delegation to beg for relief to the governor of the province, but he replied, "Why haven't you got any grain? I always have enough!" The citizens then rioted, at-

* See Bernard Martin *Strange Vigour: A Biography of Sun Yat-sen* (London 1944).

† Secret societies at first emanated from peasant revolts against Manchu rule, though later many degenerated into Chinese mafias. In Hunan, Szechuan, the secret societies were particularly strong among boatmen, peddlers, petty craftsmen and the peasantry.

‡ The Taiping peasant uprising (1850–1864), most famous of all China's many peasant uprisings, was also put down with the help of foreign powers.

tacked the governor's official quarters, and raided the rice barns of hoarders. Both in city and countryside the revolt spread. Six thousand miners at the Anyuan coal mines (where later Mao Tsetung was to establish the first Communist Party cell of Hunan) picketed the administrative offices of the mines; they were joined by the local peasants, waving banners inscribed "Share the land." The whole province became involved; a movement so widespread was already more than an antidynastic uprising, it threatened social revolution. Seriously alarmed, the military governor sent three provincial armies to cut down the unarmed peasants and miners. Members of Sun Yatsen's party were caught and executed. The heads of the slaughtered adorned the city gates and remained exhibited till the New Year.

Mao Tsetung heard of this event from some bean merchants fleeing from Changsha, who came through Shaoshan and told the story to the head of the Mao clan; the children crowded round, shoving each other to catch a word. While the elders commiserated with the merchants, the young at school discussed it; but their sympathies were for Huang Hsing and his colleagues, who became heroes for Mao Tsetung, then a vulnerable twelve years old. This event shows that already, even without knowing why, the young were opposed to their parents' opinions and reactions. "Most of the other students sympathized with the 'insurrectionists,' " Mao notes, "but from an observer's point of view. They did not understand that it had any relation to their own lives. . . . I never forgot it." And this was the essential difference. Thirty years later Mao was to look upon this incident as part of his life as a revolutionary. "I felt that there with the rebels were ordinary people like my own family and I deeply resented the injustice of the treatment given to them."

The child Mao Tsetung thus spanned a world in turmoil, between the crumbling tyranny of an old feudal empire and an unknown future which could only be brought to birth by the mass uprisings of the exploited against their exploiters. Little did he then know how much he would give of himself in shaping that future, but all his generation, like him, were sensitized to injustice and exploitation. They already reacted to events in diametrically opposite ways to their parents.

In that same year the fledgling rebel was told by his father that he had studied enough, and must work on the land and keep his father's account books. Mao Jen-shen now had 15 mous of land * and

* Six mous equal an acre.

needed the extra labor of his son. Later, he would acquire yet another 7 mous of land and would need a hired "labor-hand" to till the additional crops. The field laborer was paid one Chinese dollar * a month, which under conditions at that time in China was almost generous. Mao received no money from his father for his work, and at thirteen he was doing man's work in the fields and also keeping accounts for his father's small grain trade. Another incident then occurred, in Shaoshan itself, which would mark him for life.

One of the local landlords came into conflict with some of his peasant tenants over rent payments. The peasants were members of the Kelao, the Elder Brother secret society, the most widespread among the peasantry in Hunan, Szechuan and Hupei. Sun Yatsen's organization relied much on this particular Kelao society for armed insurrection and for the smuggling of weapons. In various popular movements, such as the railway dispute in Szechuan,† the Kelao would play a prominent part, and thus participate in China's Revolution of 1911.

The landlord won the lawsuit against his tenants by the usual bribery of the magistrate; his tenants rioted, but were then hunted down by the military governor's troops and fled to a local mountain, the Liu Shan. This withdrawal to a mountain stronghold was a traditional feature of peasant uprisings, celebrated in historical romances. The "bandits," as they were now called, were captured and their leader, Pang the Millstone Maker, beheaded. Once again Mao felt that heroic deeds of the past had been re-enacted in actual, solid events affecting his own county, his own village. Once again he saw the incident not as something apart from himself, but as an intimate personal concern. Injustice! Injustice! Would no one rise against this monstrous betrayal of virtue? History then began to appear to him as a grand tradition of righteousness, of rebellion in a just cause against tyrants and exploiters. From that time dates Mao's almost compulsory sense of identification with the downtrodden, the persecuted.

The Chinese are traditionally history-minded, Chinese memory being both specific and historical. Even in these childhood years Mao's conception of events and his relation to them is historical; it is not abstract, self-centered, alienated. This historicity he was to develop through the years, but it is inherent in his makeup. For him no

* At that time worth 25 to 30 cents.

† See Han Suyin *The Crippled Tree* (New York 1965) for an account of the railway movement in Szechuan, one of the factors that sparked the 1911 Revolution.

breach could exist between past and present, only a continuity. And he also had, like so many Chinese peasants, an excellent memory. Most Chinese can recall the names of at least several hundred personages, dating from 800 B.C. through Chinese history; not only names, but their relationships, deeds and words. Chinese fiction is fictionalized history, with no attempt to disguise the fact. Tales of strategy and tactics, of how battles are won and political schemes concocted, are the backbone of the romances which Mao and millions of other Chinese little boys loved and continue to love. But where Mao would be different would be in his identification with revolt, especially with peasant acts of rebellion. His mind was scientific. It reasoned naturally from cause to effect, and it reasoned that if such evil things happened, then there was something wrong with the system which allowed them.

There was at the time a "radical" teacher at a local school whose talk greatly influenced Mao; also, a political pamphlet fell in his hands opening with the sentence: "Alas, China will be subjugated!" "After I read this I . . . began to realize that it was the duty of all the people to help save it" (the country), said Mao. And so, his imagination nourished by the sporadic revolts round him, committed to be more than an observer by the intensity of his feelings, he now made the leap from individual to nationwide injustice. Already he felt himself part of his country's history, history a part of himself.

Very soon after, once again famine came to the district. The winter rice was exhausted, and the poor farmers asked help of the well-to-do and began a movement, "Let's eat at the Big House," meaning the landlords' granaries. But the rich were exporting their rice to the city. One consignment belonging to Mao Tsetung's father, who was now running a grain trade, was seized by the poor villagers. Mao sided with them against his father, whose "wrath was boundless." At the same time Mao felt that the method used by the peasantry, of raiding the grain, was wrong, because it did not solve the fundamental poverty and exploitation of the needy. He spent hours, weeks, months turning all this over in his mind. Knowing his father wrong, at the same time aware that the poor, in the end, would still be punished, he lay awake, tossing in his bed, wondering where was truth, and justice, and what was the meaning of all the misery, the beastliness, the suffering.

And so Mao Tsetung irritated his father, not only because of his reading habits, but because he was dreamy, withdrawn, and demanded to go to school again. He was a hefty fifteen years old, as tall and big as a man, carrying on his shoulders two heavy manure baskets, doing the work of "one man and a half." He must be married, thought Mao Jen-shen. Marriage was the cure for intractability, dreaminess, moodiness. Marriage, children would sober Mao Tsetung.

But Mao, his work done, would take his two books (*Water Margin* and *Three Kingdoms*) to a place under a tree, behind an ancient grave. "Frequently he arrived at a state bordering ecstasy as he followed the lives and adventures, the scheming and the strategies of his favorite heroes," writes Siao Yu, one of his hostile biographers.* Mao strenuously objected to being married against his will. But Mao Jen-shen arranged the ceremony, which was performed in 1908. Mao refused to have anything to do with the girl. Such was the scandal and the shame (for the bride's family) of Mao's refusal to consummate the marriage that to this day no one in Shaoshan will reveal the name of the bride's clan. All we know is that she was older than he by the customary four or five years, and "comely."

This experience, and Mao's devotion to his mother, probably started him on his lifelong campaign for the liberation of women; his indignation at the shameful treatment of women in China was to become an integral part of his resolve to change the world. Mao Tsetung's mother was a very good-looking woman with the same stubborn streak, a great power of self-control, and "wholly illiterate" as her son tells us. He looks astonishingly like her, so much so that in his youth, photographs of Mao Tsetung, especially when his hair was long (and he seldom had enough money for a haircut), are almost feminine, with the same large dreamy eyes, the high forehead and great shock of hair, the sensitive firm mouth, the attractive smile. Mao Tsetung grew to be six feet, and very handsome. Madame Liu Ying † tells of seeing him often when he was in Changsha. "He was so tall and so good-looking, people stopped talking to watch him. And he was always so calm." The likeness to his mother is still visible today, especially when he smiles or talks, looking very much like the photograph of her, round-faced and large-eyed, taken in 1906 or 1907, and hanging on the wall of his parents' bedroom in the Shaoshan home.

Mao Tsetung seems to have entertained good relations with his mother's family, who helped him once or twice with small loans.

* Siao Yu *Mao Tsetung and I Were Beggars* (Syracuse, N.Y., 1959).
† Interviewed by the author. Madame Liu was an acquaintance of Mao's wife Yang Kai-hui, whom he was to marry in 1921.

Perhaps it is in memory of his mother that Mao Tsetung coined this beautiful sentence: "Woman carries half of Heaven upon her shoulders" (half the responsibility of the world is hers).

The years 1908 to 1911 were turbulent. Everywhere widespread, fierce rebellions erupted. Sun Yatsen's revolutionary movement was now followed all over China. Armed insurrection became increasingly frequent; students, now become radical teachers, taught in the schools of "new learning" and spread the sentiment of national independence to the student body. They denounced the Manchu dynasty, denounced traditions; the pupils imbibed revolt as part of the curriculum. The writings of Confucius were attacked; and as in every age of revolt, the incomprehension between the generations grew. The young knew that no adult could tell what the future would be; they were thrown upon themselves, the future theirs to fashion; but how? No classics, no ancient wisdom could guide them any longer. Only dissent, only revolt was a signpost to becoming. A total revolt against feudal society was in the making, though it appeared impossible at the time that 2,500 years of feudal tradition and the social system it had engendered would so swiftly succumb.

Carrying his baskets of manure, digging furrows, planting rice, giving away his clothes to needy strangers, Mao Tsetung was tormented by a need to participate in this half-sensed cataclysm and resurrection in which his father's world would disappear and a new world would emerge.

Shortly after his marriage (possibly spurred by resentment at the coercion thus imposed on him) Mao Tsetung left Shaoshan to stay with a friend, an unemployed law student, in Hsiangtan. He walked to Hsiangtan, with some rice packed in a small pouch, and stayed there, reading, arguing, meeting radicals; perhaps his mother helped, secretly, with a little money. Then as usual his father called him back and Mao Tsetung returned home. But he returned more rooted in revolt than ever, more dedicated to a search for truth, more determined to "learn from all sources." In his life he would make many friends, seek out many teachers. Ideas were always to stir him; he would pounce on them, grow tremendously excited. Then he would start to re-examine, to test the idea by doing; this would reveal a flaw and Mao Tsetung would once again search, listen, learn, read, try. In this quest he would go through many a metamorphosis, but his purpose would remain a search for truth, for reality, for valid principles to be translated into action. "I began to realize that it was the duty of all the people to help to save . . . my country." Many years later he would say: "National liberation, a consciousness of national independence, is always the first step in any revolution; it is the first emotion in any revolutionary." It was this emotion which possessed him now, fired him with the desire to study.

The full-fledged rebel develops by fits and starts. All the ingredients for the questioning of every tradition, tenet, value were present when Mao Tsetung passed from childhood to adolescence to young manhood. The age bred revolutionaries. A total involvement and concern with national affairs was considered "normal" by the young students and teenagers then — though not by their elders. Already students had led great demonstrations against the shameful treaty of Shimonoseki (1893), marking the end of the war with Japan, and China's defeat. In 1905, Chinese students had organized a boycott and protested against American immigration policies, discriminatory against Chinese. The young Mao Tsetung was brought, during his stay at Hsiangtan, in contact with problems not only of local interest but of national dimensions. He noticed that in all the books he had read there was nothing about the "peasantry," while around him peasants rose in revolt, assaulted rice hoarders, and demanded land for the landless. The savagery of the repressions against the peasants was accepted by teachers and the intelligentsia. They were concerned but not personally involved. Why did they not feel personally involved? Mao was to struggle with this problem of personal involvement for many a year. It was to remain for him the touchstone of revolutionary advance: total identification with the exploited.

But Mao took longer to make up his mind than others because of a thoroughness, a perfectionism which marked even his labor in the fields. He progressed slowly, but he went further than his contemporaries. The story is told of Mao and another child picking beans. His father berated him when the other child had finished his rows long before Mao Tsetung, who still plodded with half his rows unfinished — until his father looked at Mao's basket, which was as full as the other. He had left no bean unplucked. And so it would be with his career as a revolutionary.

When Mao Tsetung returned home from Hsiangtan once more to plow and to plant and to reap in his father's fields and to do bookkeeping for his father's grain trade accounts, Mao Jen-shen suggested his son be apprenticed at Hsiangtan to a rice dealer, a business partner of his. Hsiangtan being a "radical" place, Mao thought at first that he could study in his spare time, reading at night as he did at home, while being an apprentice by day. But the choice, finally, was another school. Which to Mao meant political involvement, knowledge and action.

Mao had heard through relatives of his mother's of a "modern education school" in Hsiang Hsiang, where his mother's relatives lived. "My father finally agreed to let me enter, after friends had argued to him that this 'advanced' education would increase my earning powers." Thus Mao said, wryly, of the consent he finally wrung from the older man. The year was 1910, and he was sixteen years old.

2

Youth and School Years

Mao Tsetung's arrival at the Tungshan Higher Primary School in Hsiang Hsiang is described by two childhood acquaintances, the brothers Siao Emi and Siao Yu, who later published their contradictory reminiscences of their schoolmate.* He had set forth at dawn, a carrying pole on his shoulder, his belongings suspended at one end and his two books, *Three Kingdoms* and *Water Margin,* balancing them at the other. After reaching Hsiang Hsiang, he walked a mile or two more to reach the school. The road wound between fields and farms; he crossed a small river by ferry, and climbed up a hill with a gravel path leading to what appeared to him enormous as a fortress, surrounded by a moat and a high brick wall. It was the Tungshan Higher Primary School. Mao crossed the stone bridge over the moat and saw before him the black lacquer doors, with children playing in the courtyard.

If Mao was afraid, he did not show it. Yet as soon as he entered the school, it was obvious he was a poor peasant. The Tungshan Higher Primary School of Hsiang Hsiang was a school for the sons of landlords and rich peasants, and the difference was striking. Mao Tsetung had worked as a poor peasant's son, and continued to look what he was, a hardy, thrifty young laborer without the air, the clothes, the habits of rich boys. He was not accompanied by a private servant to carry his luggage. He came on foot. He had only one pair of cloth shoes, and very few clothes at the end of his pole. At that time, anything smacking of manual labor, such as carrying one's luggage, even carrying a parcel, was regarded as demeaning.

Mao entered the black lacquered doors flanked by tall pedestal stones representing crouching lions. The height of the carved sym-

* Siao Yu *Mao Tsetung and I Were Beggars* (Syracuse, N.Y., 1959). Siao Emi *Mao Tsetung: His Childhood and Youth* (Bombay 1953).

bolic beasts denoted the "rank" of the board of landlords who had had the school built for their children and whose donations kept it up. These landlords of Hsiang Hsiang were wealthy; some owned islands on Lake Tungting and as much as 20,000 mous of land; they owned boats that plied on the Hsiang river as far as Shanghai; they were interested in industry, their money was invested in the Japanese- and British-owned factories of Changsha, the German-Japanese-owned coal mines of Anyuan and Pinghsiang. The school was beautiful, completely cut off from the misery of the countryside.

The children of the wealthy or the comparatively wealthy, handsome, clean, carefree and proud, stared at the "laborer" carrying his pole who now walked in. The gateman, as haughty as the "young masters" who studied inside, would not let Mao enter. Mao said to him, putting down his pole: "I have come to study at this school." The gateman started shouting, the children swarmed to the commotion; they laughed. "Look at the laborer trying to come to school." Mao refused to budge; he stood there saying: "Call the headmaster." The tumult brought out the headmaster, armed with a long pipe with a copper bowl. There is something extremely mandarin-like in the headmaster's weaponing himself with his pipe, which would not cause lethal damage but would bring enough "loss of face," should he have to use it, to make the stubborn "bandit" (as the porter apparently called Mao) withdraw in confusion.

The headmaster saw a tall young man, thin and badly dressed, with a cloth pack and a bamboo pole, like a peddler. Mao turned to him: "Please sir, allow me to study here in your school."

Even then, Mao Tsetung's personality, his extraordinary presence, seem to have wrought a change in the headmaster. "Bring him to my office," he said. He could not believe that this adolescent, a head taller and at least three years older than any other schoolchild, should now be arguing with him. He would have refused Mao's request, but another teacher named Hu intervened. Were there not, in Chinese tradition, stories of poor scholars who, like Mao, had pleaded for entrance to schools, and had turned out so brilliant as to bring luster to the establishment? Besides, Mao had a clan cousin, on his mother's side, at the school.

Mao was accepted on a temporary basis. The teacher who intervened for him offered to coach him. All his life this would happen with Mao Tsetung. People would be bowled over or violently repelled by his strength and purpose, fervor and directness, the silence and the withering flow of words, the magnetic power. No one remained indifferent. Mao paid 1,400 coppers (possibly money saved by his mother) for five months' board and lodging, and the books and material needed for study.

Within a few days, Mao Tsetung was the focus of attention; the whole school spoke of him. At first he was taunted for his poor peasant clothes and his accent (the Shaoshan and not the Hsiang Hsiang accent). The students stole his clothes, his books, accounted "bad," but later, ashamed, returned them to him. He put up with taunts and insults; in five months he won not only respect, but praise. And yet he was a difficult student, arguing with his teachers, something which was not done at this "rich" school. He was reputed bad-tempered because everything mattered to him; there was no room left for hypocrisy.

Mao Tsetung himself has told how much reading he did while at that school, but for him there was never enough, and he would sit long hours in the classroom after the others had gone, reading till he could no longer see, melting down candle ends to make new candles. He could read twice or three times faster than other students.

His teachers have left personal notes * on his ability, his singular excellence. But he was irritated by their acceptance of the obvious. "The teachers liked me . . . because I wrote good essays in the classical manner. But my mind was not on the classics." He was reading two books by the reformists Kang Yu-wei and Liang Chi-chao. "I read and reread them until I knew them by heart." Mao has left us a word picture of "one of the teachers . . . a returned student from Japan [who] wore a false queue." He was called the False Foreign Devil, and talked a great deal about Japan. Thirty years later Mao still remembered the Japanese poem the teacher quoted, a poem commemorating the victory of Japan over Russia in the war of 1904–1905. "I knew and felt the beauty of Japan, and felt something of her pride and might. . . . I did not think there was also a barbarous Japan . . ." Mao took everything seriously, and his allegiance to truth, or rather reality, drove him to enthusiastic (but temporary) devotion to many heroes. He "worshiped" Kang Yu-wei and Liang Chi-chao. Later he read of America and Washington, of Napoleon and Catherine the Great (in a book, *Great Heroes of the World*). He imbibed learning like a sponge and yearned for more; his progress was swift, too swift; at the end, the students disliked him be-

---

* On exhibit in museums. These notes date back to the years 1910 and 1911; they are not, therefore, products of hindsight.

cause he did not belong. "I felt spiritually very depressed." All they were interested in was factional snobbishness; there were three sets, upper, lower, and middle, divided according to their districts. Mao refused to take sides. "Consequently all three factions despised me."

During the winter vacation (the Chinese New Year) Mao went back to Shaoshan; his father sent him to collect money from debtors, as was the custom, before the festival. Once again there was famine in the province, so much so that the governor had been sacked in the belief (partly correct) that this would appease the angry population. Again there were uprisings. Rice was sent to Changsha, starving peasants trekked to the cities to sell their children, to beg. Mao Tse-tung, instead of collecting the debts, remitted them and went home empty-handed; and on the way back he gave his own long robe to a needy student. The reception at home, not surprisingly, must have been unpleasant. Mao does not speak of it.

He was now, at seventeen, convinced that strong men were needed to build up the nation, and in this no different from thousands of other young students. But he had no set theory, only an indignation against foreign exploitation, the heritage of his generation. He ad-mired all nation-builders — Napoleon or Washington, Han Wu-ti or Peter the Great. There was no way for him to distinguish between them at the time. To take up stray sentences which he then said — "I admire Bismarck" or "Napoleon was a truly great man" — in order to prove that Mao is "authoritarian" by nature is not to de-scribe his development. To lay stress on the "military" turn of his mind because he spoke of war and strategy is to ignore the social context of his time, a time of armed rebellion. Western history is lit-tered with martial examples to admire; Mao Tsetung deduced that military matters were as important in the West as in China. He dreamed of a way to "save the nation." The students who adhered in increasing numbers to Sun Yatsen's revolutionary Tung Meng Hui engaged in bomb-making and gun practice and dreamed no less. Young boys gravely discussed insurrection as they took walks in the wooded hills, classics under their arms. They smuggled weapons and books; they risked decapitation.

Siao Emi, the schoolmate who loaned Mao Tsetung the book *Great Heroes of the World,* recalls how Mao marked passages with circles and dots, in the Chinese manner,* and said: "We ought to

---

* The Chinese dot or put a small circle beside or under each word they wish to emphasize.

study these men, find out how to make China rich and strong, avoid becoming like India, Korea . . ." *

In the summer of 1911 Mao had ended a year at the Tungshan Higher Primary School and was becoming restless. He had learned a good deal, but now felt he was stagnating. "I am not progressing, nor really learning what I want to learn." He wanted to travel; the courses in history and geography had stimulated this desire; already he had started wandering on foot round his own district and the Hsiang Hsiang district. "I hear Changsha is a magnificent place," he told his friends, "and only 120 lis [about 36 miles] from my home." At home he spoke of travel. His father spoke of the expense. "When will you end your studies and become a scholar, and get honor for your ancestors?" he asked.

Mao's mother stood by him. At night when he read, she left warm food for him in the kitchen, mended his clothes, made him new cloth shoes. When he spoke of going to Changsha she looked at him, proud of him and loving him. She had saved a little more money and gave it to him.

Before leaving the Tungshan Higher Primary School, Mao sat for the entrance examination for its Middle School, located in the city of Changsha and catering to students who had attended the Higher Primary School. This Middle School was also built and kept in funds by wealthy Hunan landlords, and by the provincial government. Mao asked one of the teachers at the Higher Primary School to write him a letter of introduction; he was not sure he would be admitted. But he was, without difficulties, which "astonished" him. He had expected greater obstruction in the big city than in the small town; he found less. This was due to the radical atmosphere in the city of Changsha, and to his own reputation for brilliance, which had preceded him.

After the summer vacation of 1911 Mao Tsetung walked the forty miles to Changsha, and entered his first city.

Changsha, capital of Hunan province, lies on the Hsiang river in a magnificent setting of hills growing to mountains, of lush fields and dense woods. It was, like all Chinese cities, a maze of small dark houses and twisted mud lanes, yet it held fine temples and residences, parks, and great schools. It was, in the early 1900's, more than a

* The subjugation of India by Great Britain through the East India Company had a deeper effect on Chinese minds than is usually recognized by Western historians.

provincial capital, a center for intellectual radicalism. Hunan was famous for its scholars. In 1865, out of eight viceroys five were from
Hunan; all had been educated at Changsha. The endowment of
schools by guilds of merchants made Changsha a "scholastic" city.
"Subversive" material — books, pamphlets, as well as weapons —
was smuggled into Changsha by Sun Yatsen's adherents. Revolutionary associations under various names were formed by teachers
and students. Each school in that year was a small time bomb with a
short fuse; and the hunger and misery of the countryside, despite the
fertile soil, filled even "the scholars' street" with beggars and the
corpses of those who had died of starvation.

Institutes of physical culture and "self-strengthening" were the
fashion, actually they were political platforms for expression of dissent. A movement against opium smoking among the young Hunanese in the schools was part of the rejection of traditional values
and customs, also of anti-imperialism.* Mao's interest in health, in
physical culture, dates from his days in Changsha when exercise, fitness, clean living, were acts of revolt by the young generation
against the social degeneracy of their elders.

Mao Tsetung arrived at Changsha in September, a month before
the Revolution of 1911. He began his school life by reading a newspaper, *Min Li Pao,* published by Sun Yatsen's organization the Tung
Meng Hui. The Tung Meng Hui was still in Japan, where most of its
members were exiles, but their publication circulated secretly
throughout China. In this paper Mao read of an uprising which had
taken place in April in Kuangchow, of the deaths of 72 of the insur-
gents. They had been led by the same Hunanese, Huang Hsing,
whom he had admired for leading the insurrection of 1906 in
Hunan. Mao now discovered that the reformists Kang Yu-wei and
Liang Chi-chao, whose ideas he admired a few brief weeks before,
were now considered "old-fashioned," outdated by the tempestuous
course of the national revolution in the making, and vigorously attacked. Exalted by his new discovery, he wrote an article which he
posted on the school wall; this was Mao Tsetung's first *ta tze pao,* or
wall newspaper — "my first expression of a political opinion, and it
was somewhat muddled." The second *ta tze pao* we know of was
written by him in 1966, fifty-five years later.†

* Since opium had been introduced into China in vast quantities after the first
Opium War (1840).
† In his first *ta tze pao,* Mao advocated what Edgar Snow called "an absurd coa-
lition" between Sun Yatsen and Kang and Liang.

The *ta tze pao* or wall newspaper stems from an ancient Chinese tradition dating from the legendary times of the Yellow Emperor (1300 B.C.). Scholars, literati and officials, when protesting against injustice, would write an "open letter" and affix it in a public spot. In China's continuing revolution the *ta tze pao* has become a current form of expression, utilized abundantly to voice popular opinion.

The 1911 Revolution began with a mistimed dynamite blast in Wuhan on October 10. Within days the Manchu empire had collapsed and a republic had taken its place. Such was the speed of change that to many it seemed hardly credible, yet the change was irreversible.

Martial law was declared throughout the province of Hunan. A member of Sun Yatsen's Tung Meng Hui, a young teacher, came to Mao's Middle School in Changsha and made a stirring speech, explaining the aims of the Tung Meng Hui. "Not a word [from the audience] was heard as he spoke," said Mao Tsetung.

Five days later Mao Tsetung left for Wuhan to join the Republican Army, to become a soldier of the Revolution. He cut off his pigtail, then he and another student forcibly assaulted and cut off the pigtails of ten of their schoolmates who had promised to relieve themselves of these badges of slavery * but had then changed their minds. He collected money from classmates for his journey, and with other volunteers left for the "front," which meant Wuhan. They walked out of the city of Changsha on a fine late October day. Already autumn was upon the trees, and the hills glowed scarlet as the young recruit reached the city's outskirts, where he went to borrow some galoshes from a friend, a fellow student already in the Republican Army, because he had been told "the streets of Hankow † were very wet."

"I was stopped by the garrison guards . . . the soldiers had for the first time been furnished with bullets, and they were pouring into the streets." A big battle was on outside the city walls, and Mao Tsetung then saw the soldiers of the Republican Army capturing the strongpoints within the city from its Manchu garrisons. He also saw the city gates, which had been closed, stormed and taken by Chinese laborers, boatmen and coolies, who had risen to overthrow the Manchus.

He thus absorbed a lesson in the art of war he would never forget. Fascinated, he could not leave. "I re-entered the city, stood on a

---

* It was the Manchu dynastic rule which imposed the pigtail upon Chinese men. Cutting it off meant revolt, and the penalty had been decapitation.

† Hankow, one of the three cities of Wuhan.

high place and watched the battle." He then saw the revolutionary flag (a white banner with the character Han * upon it) raised over the official palace. He returned to the Middle School, since the war had now come home to him. On October 23, a new government was organized in Changsha, ostensibly representing "the Chinese people." But the landlords' and merchants' representatives in the government clashed with the representatives of the poor peasants and the workers and murdered them. This was Mao Tsetung's first direct knowledge of civil war, of class struggle, of how the fruits of victory were wrested from the laborers and coolies. "Not many days later . . . I saw their corpses lying in the streets."

Levies of the Republican "New Army" were organized in each province to fight against the remaining dynastic Manchu armies. Students were enrolled in special battalions. Instead of joining the student battalions Mao chose to become a common soldier: "I did not like the student army." It was organized by the landlords and militarists. "I considered the basis [of the student army] too confused." †This refusal was related to the massacres he had witnessed of the peasants' and workers' representatives, and to other episodes of brutality against the poor, so common in those days. Mao was already revolted by the illogic of those proclaiming freedom yet continuing to ill-treat the exploited. "I decided to join the regular army instead and help complete the revolution."

But he was nevertheless a student, a cut above the rest of the soldiery, for he could read and write. He was treated with deference by his companions, wrote their letters for them, read newspapers to them (he spent most of his seven dollars a month soldier's wage buying newspapers, and two dollars on food). He became more conscious of "class" differences, felt a beginning isolation which cut him off, by virtue of a year's schooling, from the self he had been when he carried manure to the fields. Where food was concerned he ate as the soldiers did, but was reluctant to fetch and carry his own water, and was surprised at himself. Why had he changed, and so swiftly? Why did he now think it humiliating to carry his own hot water? What was it that had made this change, so that the others also knew he was not like them, hard though he tried? Thus he studied himself,

* Han is the name the Chinese give to themselves.

† Later he was to recall that among the students joining the student battalions was Tang Sheng-chih, who was to become a warlord of Hunan; they were to meet again sixteen years later, when Tang Sheng-chih became governor of Hunan (1926–1927), and again in 1949, when a repentant Tang Sheng-chih joined Mao's government in Peking.

and later * was to write: "I might mention the changes in my own feelings. . . . I began as a student, acquired the habits of a student, surrounded by students who could neither fetch nor carry. I used to consider it undignified to do any manual labor, such as shouldering my own luggage." This transformation of feeling was a revelation to him, but he had no explanation for it until he became a Marxist. Introspection, self-criticism, became to him more than a habit, a compulsion in his long search for truth. "Having become a revolutionary I found myself in the ranks of the workers, peasants, soldiers of the revolutionary army. Gradually I became familiar with them, and they with me. Then, and only then, did a fundamental change occur in the bourgeois and petty bourgeois feelings implanted in me by the bourgeois schools. . . . This is what is meant by having one's feelings transformed, changed from those of one class into another." Because he observed this transformation in himself, Mao would endeavor, fifty years later, to obtain the same transformation in yet another generation of young people.

The complexities of Mao's adolescence — an adolescence retarded, as it is often among the peasantry, because of its exhausting physical labor — are not documented, for he kept no diary. But the extent of his preoccupation with events, this inner fury which drove him, was caused by and fed on the social turmoil in which he was plunged. He knew himself not one, but many; a sum of contradictions, more accented, more violent and highly charged than those of other young men round him. Everything for him became high-pitched, immense, intense, serious, important. He was both violent and gentle, aggressive and shy, enormously sensitive and thick-skinned, humble and proud, blistering the frivolous among his fellow students, patient, considerate with the poorest peasants, and with women. A great fear of mental and physical degradation kept him strenuously active. But there was more to him than indignation and revolt. It was a prodigious fever he suffered from, as he fashioned for himself ways of thinking and behaving, spurning self-indulgence, an ascetic figure. And in this he was part of his generation, but always with that little bit more, that longer time period, that deeper intensity, which would make him continue where others gave up.

Because he was ten before he read the Chinese classics, thirteen when two revolts and one uprising marked him deeply, sixteen when he went back to school, and at seventeen a soldier for five months

* See *Talks at Yenan Forum on Literature and Art,* May 1942. *Selected Works of Mao Tsetung* (English edition Peking 1961–1965), vol. III.

(October 1911 to February 1912), he could watch with amazement his own metamorphoses, remember distinctly how events changed him. What was truth? At the time Mao like best of all the old classical scholar Han Yu for his wild wit and furious scorn, couched in the most orthodox language. He knew the Great Doubt in the old classics, the savage and subtle innuendo — and he was voracious for vocabulary, copying and then refashioning felicitous phrases, wondering at the power of the word. Always he would be thrown back upon his search for coherence, a vision, a logic. Always he related himself not to the "elite" but to the common people. What was their place in this new world growing out of the fester of the old? Was man's fate really Heaven-determined? Or was it man himself who could fashion his own destiny?

Decades later, in the Cultural Revolution, the transformation of the "world outlook" of the student, the intellectual, by living, eating, laboring, identifying with the workers, peasants and soldiers was to be Mao's answer to his own youthful experience. This was a "long and painful struggle" and he was to repeat it many times: "It takes a very long time" — to remold one's world outlook.

Thus it was that while soldiering in this confused and doomed Revolution of 1911, Mao came across the term "socialist" for the first time in a newspaper, the *Hsiang River Daily News*. "I also discussed socialism with other students and soldiers. I read some pamphlets . . . about socialism. . . . I wrote enthusiastically to several of my classmates on this subject, but only one of them responded in agreement." "No one I have ever known," Siao Emi was to say about Mao, "hungered for so much knowledge on so many different levels." He also hungered for communication.

The 1911 Revolution swiftly sank into the morass of a power struggle. Sun Yatsen relinquished power to Yuan Shih-kai, a circumspect, double-crossing militarist * who at one time served the Manchu dynasty but was now commander-in-chief of the New Republican Army. The hopes of the people ran high, but lassitude, disillusion, cynicism, and intrigue were disrupting the great plans of reform among the intelligentsia. "Thinking the revolution over, I resigned from the army and decided to return to my books." Mao Tsetung found himself in March 1912 once again in need of a school,

---

* The term militarist is more or less interchangeable with the term warlord. In the breakup of the Manchu dynasty, military governors and commanders, with their own armies and territories, were for decades to carry on exhausting "warlord wars."

penniless, with no great endeavor except to find a way to go on studying. But he was not built for personal enterprise alone. "I say: the concept is reality, the finite is the infinite, the temporal is the intemporal, imagination is thought, I am the universe . . . the substance is the words, that which is changing is eternal," he wrote, but did not quite believe what he wrote. His whole nature was against this Taoist quietness and inward turning. But he had not yet discovered himself. He had no idea that he was uncommonly gifted.

Now he sought "a road" and found others saying to him: "Well now, what do you want to be?"

To be? To become? What did these words mean? Everyone had an idea what he wanted to be, a fatuous lavish self-portrait, softened with complacency, modest satisfaction with one's own accomplishments. Mao had no such image of himself. He did not know what he wanted, and he was eighteen years old. Listening to well-meaning advice, he scanned advertisements in the newspapers and registered for many and various schools — a soap-making school, a police school, a law school, a commercial school, each time paying a registration fee. "I did not know exactly what I wanted to do." Those around him proclaimed the "revolution" over; it had succeeded, they said. Had not the Manchus been overthrown? In a little while every problem would be solved. Mao felt puzzled and lost. Friends persuaded him to "make a career." The time for talents to be used for the salvation of China had come, and experts confirmed the virtues of soap-making (cleanliness and health), the advantages of becoming a lawyer, an official, an economist, a policeman, a trader; all these pursuits to save the nation. Mao's witty description of his trying out various schools makes fun of himself.

He sat for the examinations for the First Provincial Middle School in Changsha and passed at the head of the list of candidates. But after entering the school (and being loaned *Chronicles with Imperial Commentaries* by a helpful teacher, for his literary style had attracted this teacher's attention) he did not like it; "its curriculum was limited and its regulations objectionable." After six months "I left the school and arranged a schedule of education of my own which consisted in reading every day in the Hunan Provincial Library." Apparently reading the loaned *Chronicles* had helped him to decide that "it would be better for me to read and study alone."

In that spring of 1913 the Hunan Provincial Library in Changsha saw a tall, thin young man with a great mop of hair pacing outside its gates early in the morning, before the library opened, leaving only when the library doors closed at night. Mao sat stolidly and read the books on the shelves, one book after another, stopping only to eat two rice cakes for lunch. Thus he went on half a year. His father, however, was incensed and refused to support him unless he entered a real school. He faced his son with the despair of a parent before a hopeless offspring. Why did his son spend all day reading? The older Mao would have been pleased had his son entered a commercial school, or become a lawyer or an official . . . But to waste time just reading!

In these six months Mao laid down the foundations of an education more ample than many. He studied world geography and world history. "There for the first time I saw and studied with great interest a map of the world." He remembered everything he read and he read prodigiously fast. He read through the works of Rousseau, Spencer's logic, Montesquieu, Adam Smith and Darwin; poetry, economics, tales of ancient Greece. The world lay within his mind's grasp, and what an intricate, marvelous universe, all there for him to swallow! From then on, he would never be without books, nor spend a day without trying to learn something new. Even on the Long March he carried books with him. Even today he lives in a sprawl of books, annotating, comparing, studying.

He also read newspapers from all over China, while at the same time reading the histories of other nations. The French Revolution impressed him; he would speak of it to Couve de Murville in 1970 and surprise the French statesman with his knowledge. The mind could only be limbered by debate, contact with other minds; synthesis, cohesion came from arrangement of knowledge in categories; but which system was foolproof? Where did correct ideas come from? One's ideas changed as one's knowledge amplified; as Mao watched his own transformation, certainties laid low, new doubts arising, he realized that "knowledge is inexhaustible." There could be no end to the search, but how exciting this pilgrim's progress towards a new cosmos of wisdom, beauty and truth! All that happened, all situations and events were teaching material; life was a Long March to the discovery of the infinite. In the Changsha library Mao became a dialectician; years later Marxism would give him the answers he looked for; dialectical materialism would supply the philosophical foundation upon which he would found his vision of the world. But he would always, because of this beginning, resist dogmatism. "Although we are determined by nature, we are also part of nature. Hence, if nature has the power to determine us, we also have the power to determine nature." A seminal thought, key to the process of voluntary, self-willed direction which alone can conceive of a cultural revolution as a conscious act of change, not only of nature, but of man's very soul.

After his six months reading in the library, Mao was destitute. The guild house where he had stayed, very cheaply, during that half-year was awash with brawls between soldiers, semi-vagrants, and poor students. One night some soldiers attacked the students. "I escaped by fleeing to the toilet, where I hid till the fight was over." Mao began to scan the newspaper advertisements again, and was attracted by that of the Hunan First Normal College, or Teachers College, because tuition was so cheap. He might be suited for the career of teacher; teaching would mean access to books, constant learning as well as teaching. Teaching meant being a perpetual student as well as opening the minds of others. . . . Today Mao Tsetung says that all he wants to be known as is a teacher. But he adds that teachers must also learn from their students.

Mao was accepted at the First Normal (Teachers) College after having written an entrance examination essay. He also wrote two for friends intent on entering the same school. "I did not then think my act an immoral one, it was a matter of friendship"; but he pondered over this later, and decided it was wrong.

Hunan First Normal College in Changsha is a large and handsome building with pillars and rounded arches; it was copied from a Japanese building, in turn inspired by British colonial architecture. Nothing can be more different from the Chinese style than these paved courtyards, pillared halls and galleries. In 1913 it had 400 students; attached to it was a primary and middle school. It was partly burned in 1938 in a big fire,* but has been rebuilt since. It boasted a large auditorium holding 2,000 people, which today is exhibited to visitors because Mao held meetings there.

The entrance to the Normal College has an inscription by one of the teachers, Hsu Te-li. Hsu was to become Mao Tsetung's friend and a follower of his illustrious pupil: "Seek truth from facts," Hsu wrote; and this remains the motto of the college.

Mao Tsetung remained five years at the Changsha Normal College, from the autumn of 1913 to the spring of 1918. In these five years his political ideas took shape. He became a leader of the students, a dissenter, a "troublemaker" for some, a righter of wrongs

---

* The fire was started by Chiang Kai-shek's orders to prevent a Japanese invasion of the city, which never took place (October 1938).

for others, an incipient political and social force, and he left no one indifferent. He moved against many regulations at the college which he disagreed with. He went on campaigns to change things, fighting tradition and red tape, was nearly thrown out, reinstated on the pleas of students and professors, some of whom he had fought against. All he did was subordinate to this passion for getting things "clarified." "He never gave anyone face" was the complaint frequently heard of him. "Face," an antiquated concept, preserving a surface respect, destroyed efficiency and justice; Mao Tsetung hated its hypocrisies. He would exclaim: "Don't talk about people behind their backs, say what you have to say in front of them" — a statement now embedded in his *Selected Works* as part of the working style desirable in a Communist Party member.

In 1917, four hundred of his schoolmates chose him as a model for ethical conduct, self-control, personal courage, and ability in speaking and writing. Even his opponents, those who quarreled with him, finally gave him their respect; they even pleaded for Mao when he was threatened with expulsion after he took on the headmaster, Chang Kan, in May 1915 and tried to get him removed from his post by writing to the provincial governor. This was connected with the headmaster's refusal to allow student demonstrations against the Japanese ultimatum to China, the aggressive Twenty-one Demands.*

Mao's best friends at the college were Tsai Ho-sen (1890–1931), a young quiet Hunanese, outstanding as a scholar and like Mao ready to die for truth, and Hsu Te-li, then teacher at the Normal College and eighteen years older than Mao. Hsu Te-li (1877–1968) was of the old breed of Chinese scholar revolutionaries; his life would span three revolutions: the reformist movement of 1898 — suppressed by the Manchu Empress Dowager Tze Hsi with terrible cruelty, the 1911 Revolution of Sun Yatsen, and the Communist Revolution of 1949. He took part in all three and became his pupil's devoted follower, and a Communist, in 1927. He took part in the Long March. In 1910 he had petitioned for a parliamentary form of government, cutting the end of his finger and writing the words in his blood, an expression of sincerity and determination which during the Great Proletarian Cultural Revolution was to be emulated by many young students.

* The Twenty-one Demands, or Tanaka Memorial, of 1915 was actually an ultimatum setting out, in twenty-one clauses, the total subjugation of China's ports, cities, railroads and waterways to Japanese control under the name of "cooperation."

In February 1912 Sun Yatsen had resigned the Presidency bestowed upon him by the 1911 Revolution in favor of the militarist Yuan Shih-kai. Mao was to evaluate Sun Yatsen's character several times during the following decades, as well as meet and work with him. In 1957, for Sun's ninetieth anniversary, he wrote a commemorative statement:

"Remember his bitter struggle . . . remember the magnificent contributions he made . . . Apart from a handful of reactionaries, all modern Chinese are the heirs of Mr. Sun's revolution . . . Mr. Sun was a humble man . . . Like all great figures who have channeled the trend of events in their times, Mr. Sun had his defects [which] should be explained in terms of history. . . ." One of Sun's defects was overtrusting others. Sun trusted Yuan Shih-kai, the unscrupulous, and went south to Kuangchow, leaving Yuan in charge in the capital Peking. In the summer of 1912 Sun was to visit Peking again, for he was disturbed by reports about Yuan, now President. Huang Hsing, the Hunanese who had led the 1906 and April 1911 insurrections, was to have gone with Sun, but refused to go when two prominent revolutionaries were meantime murdered by Yuan Shih-kai. Sun went to Peking, where Yuan flattered and reassured him, and then left for Japan, while Yuan promised to "follow his instructions."

But public opinion was disturbed by the news of a six-power consortium reorganization loan offered to Yuan by the Western powers. This was actually an investment in weapons, to back Yuan as military dictator and protect foreign investments in China. Britain, France, the U.S., Japan, Germany and Russia were afraid of the new nationalism, and openly announced that they would sabotage Sun Yatsen and his Republic. Yuan was the type of ambitious and corrupt militarist, paid to keep his own people in subjection, whom they would back against Sun Yatsen.

When it was known that the internal salt taxes would be held as security for the reorganization loan (which meant foreign control of the total internal salt production) demonstrations against Yuan took place. The customs revenues were already under foreign control, and this reinforcement of imperialist exploitation, directly contrary to the spirit of the new Republic, led to clamorous protests. In April 1913 Yuan pushed the loan terms through a National Assembly packed by his own followers. Judicious assassinations cowed the assemblymen. In July 1913 Sun Yatsen asked Yuan to resign; Yuan replied by executing more of Sun's followers.

Rebellion against Yuan broke out and the whole of the Yangtze river valley smoldered with civil strife. Yuan, well supplied with foreign funds from the reorganization loan, had strongly equipped armies and defeated Sun Yatsen's hastily collected troops. Sun fled to Japan. Yuan's inauguration as chief of state by a subservient National Assembly, and the immediate recognition accorded his government by the jubilant Western powers, made Sun Yatsen's defeat appear crushing. The U.S. and other colonial powers then endeavored to popularize the idea of making Yuan emperor, but the last thing the Chinese people wanted was an emperor. Yuan's authority was contested in all the provinces. "The Revolution is not finished," said Sun Yatsen.

Thus began the warlord era, when militarists fought each other up and down the land like feudal barons in medieval Europe, and China was shredded by warlord wars. The peasants and the laborers paid for these feudal wars in grain levies and in exorbitant taxes, for armies have to be fed and paid, and only China's peasantry — 90 percent of the population — could do it. Armies also need recruits, and only the peasantry could supply them. In some areas men were press-ganged while working the fields. In Szechuan province, taxes were levied seventy years in advance.* In Hunan province, armies marched back and forth across the province for years, and ruined the countryside, which lost half its pig population in ten years. Yuan replaced the governor, Tan Yen-kai, who was pro Sun Yatsen,† by his own appointee and massed troops in Hunan, since it was the key control area for all communications to South China.

When the First World War started in Europe in August 1914, China was temporarily "vacated" by the Western powers. Japan seized the opportunity to present to Yuan in early 1915 the notorious Twenty-one Demands which substantially made of China a Japanese colony. Yuan's Western protectors were unable to counter Japan's bid for supreme power in China. Yuan, enchanted with the idea of becoming emperor, cast caution aside; the proclamation of the new dynasty in December 1915 brought uprisings in southwest China. In April 1916 Hunan and Szechuan declared their independence, and

---

* See Han Suyin *A Mortal Flower* (New York 1966) and *Birdless Summer* (New York 1968) for descriptions of taxation and extortion in the countryside of China.

† The ease and bewildering rapidity with which governors, militarists, warlords, etc., changed sides need not alarm the reader. It will be happening all through this book. Tan Yen-kai had been pro-Manchu, became pro-Sun Yatsen, then switched against Sun.

Yuan Shih-kai, abandoned by his own military, died of a heart attack in June 1916.

But Yuan's death did not stop the centrifugal forces at work in the land. No less than seven warlords were now fighting each other in Hunan, where Yuan's protégé was driven out and Tan Yen-kai came back as governor in August 1916.

Sun Yatsen returned from Japan and set up his headquarters in Kuangchow, and by July 1917 there were two governments in China: the warlord Tuan Chi-jui in Peking, successor to the late Yuan, head of an uneasy northern warlord coalition; and Sun Yatsen, with an unstable coalition of southern warlords in Kuangchow. The struggle for the domination of Hunan, the "heart" province, crossroads of the country, became particularly acute. "China is falling into chaos" was the verdict of most observers, and it looked as if partition was imminent. Tibet and Mongolia were infiltrated by Russian, British and Japanese agents. Manchuria and Shantung province were openly claimed by Japan as her "sphere of influence." Only the continuing World War in Europe prevented military intervention in China by the Western powers. Japan felt her hour had come. China was now flooded with Japanese goods.

Warlord armies were quartered in temples and schools all over Hunan. Pillage was common, hoarding of goods and grain made money worthless, the peasants starved and the townpeople rioted; students plunged into mass protest. Thus took shape another revolution, through a swift maturing of consciousness among the young. The students organized self-defense corps, trained for physical fitness (regarded as "political consciousness" at that time) and self-defense, which meant military drill. Every school had its "volunteer corps," and the Changsha Normal College was no exception. From the start Mao Tsetung took an active and swiftly a leading position in all the political activities of the student body, and that included military drill.

In 1915 he became secretary of the Students' Society at the Normal College, and created the Association for Student Self-Government, for "collective resistance" against "unreasonable" demands by the headmaster. This Association for Student Self-Government later served as a nucleus for the students' organizations of the May 4, 1919 movement in Hunan province. As he had fought against the teacher's tyranny when a child of seven, he battled now against "many regulations. . . . I agreed with very few of them. . . . Most of all I hated a compulsory course in still-life drawing. I thought it was extremely stupid."

The student association under Mao took up political causes, demonstrations against Yuan Shih-kai, against the warlords, against the Japanese Twenty-one Demands. Mao led street demonstrations by the students against the Japanese and on May 7, 1915, wrote: "To revenge this extraordinary humiliation [imposition of the Japanese ultimatum] will be up to our generation." He also organized a research department, for "social investigation," and organized student teams to visit and investigate conditions in Changsha's factories. He laid plans for liaison with other schools to promote an All-China Student Federation. And when the self-defense corps against the warlords was established, Mao became head of the college battalion in the spring of 1917. Just then scattered bands of warlord Fu Liang-tso's troops occupied the buildings of the Normal College. With some fellow students, Mao obtained a few real and some dummy rifles from a nearby police station, where he had made friends by going and talking to the policemen during street demonstrations he had led. At night he and his followers rushed the occupied college buildings, meanwhile raising a great shout: "Fu Liang-tso has run away! Kwangsi troops are here! Surrender! Surrender!" The confused troops surrendered, were disarmed, and the student self-defense corps obtained more weapons. This was Mao's first experience of a typical surprise guerilla attack; he now studied intensively the science of war.

For war was a normal, daily occurrence in warlord China, and Mao's generation saw all life as war. They had been born between two wars, had seen a revolution, and now the whole country festered with warlords.

The influence of Sun Tze's classic book *The Art of War,* written two thousand years before, extends throughout Chinese history, and also influenced Mao's generation. The book is regarded as a treatise not only on the conduct of war but also on the conduct of all affairs where rivalry occurs, negotiations with an enemy or a potential enemy, tactics and strategy in war or in peace. Chinese encyclopedias contain extensive sections devoted to the literature of war. The concept of war and peace as alternate facets of the same application of power is as old as Chinese history. Mao Tsetung studied Sun Tze, and it is not surprising that he incorporated and developed in his creative writings on war the ideas of the old master.

The notion of struggle could be applied to all situations, whether wresting a rice crop from a field, building a factory under hardship conditions, or crossing a mountain. Struggle against nature, obstacles, the elements; and the greatest, the most obstinate struggle of all, against self. This concept became embedded in the consciousness and the vocabulary of Mao's generation.

"The quality of decision is like the well-timed swoop of a falcon which enables it to strike and destroy its victim," wrote Sun Tze. "Attack the enemy where he is unprepared. Appear where you are not expected." Mao remembered and applied these dicta in the great campaigns he would conduct; meanwhile he devised small ones as head of the student corps.

He taught the students devices utilized by guerillas of the Taiping * days in the Hunan countryside — to cut the young bamboo in such a way as to leave a sharp point which would pierce the attacker's feet or hands; to scream and shout from one spot while attacking in silence from another. Thus guerilla war, peasant war, was brought into the classrooms of the Normal College by Mao Tsetung. "He took charge . . . his orders, even to the senior professors, were instantly obeyed." †

Mao now read everything concerning the campaigns then taking place in World War I in Europe. He followed Hindenburg's marches in Russia, and would mention several times in the next thirty years the commandeering of taxicabs to prevent Paris being taken. He lectured and wrote articles on strategy and tactics. But above all he took notes. He took notes on everything, and wrote his own reaction to what he noted down. A volume of Paulsen's book on logic, with 12,000 words of notes and criticism by Mao, is still on exhibit at the college today. Altogether Mao is reckoned to have written more than one million words of notes, criticism and remarks on books he read during those five years.

But his restless energy pushed him into many other activities. It was he who started, in 1917, together with Hsu Te-li, evening classes for workers and shop assistants. A building near the college was put at their disposal, how or by whom is not clear, and there is hung today the facsimile of a poster written by Mao Tsetung announcing this

* The songs and ballads of the Taiping uprising were still being sung by the Hunan peasants in Mao's youth.

† Siao San, quoted by Robert Payne (*Portrait of a Revolutionary: Mao Tsetung,* new and revised edition, New York and London 1962). Siao San is the same person as Siao Emi.

evening school, and promising that it would teach the workers culture, to read, to write and to count, free of charge.* "In our country, the situation is that most people have no opportunity for education," wrote Mao. He railed against the literary language employed by the officials, and advocated using the vernacular in these classes. "When one lectures in the literary language nobody can understand the lecture; when one writes in it, no one can read it . . . it is also impossible to do sums in it. . . . We are not wood or stone, we are men . . . so come quickly and register . . . do come and listen to some plain speech." The poster added: "You can wear any clothes you want," and "Copybooks and other material supplied free." About one hundred workers from Changsha's sweatshop factories applied. The courses were from seven to nine at night. Mao taught history and also "current affairs," read the newspapers to the workers, and made them discuss what was happening. It was through this experience that Mao Tsetung acquired his basic grounding in education techniques.

And yet Mao himself could write a beautiful, elegant literary language, as his poems prove. His essays were described as "models of style and content." But his habit of dating his work (setting the date on the end page, at the bottom) annoyed one of his teachers, Yuan Li-chin, nicknamed Yuan the Big Beard. Big Beard considered it arrogant that a mere pupil should place dates upon his work; essays were ephemeral pieces, subject to correction. He also disliked Mao's style, calling it "the work of a journalist." But for Mao each essay was a piece of his mind, ideas set in the writing, landmarks of his understanding and social action. He was keeping track not only of his own evolution but of Chinese history in the making; to date his pieces helped him to see the road he traveled. One day, overcome with anger, Big Beard tore out the last page of Mao's essay while the other students looked on. Mao Tsetung rose, seized the professor by the arm, pushed him firmly to the headmaster's room, and argued out the case. Yuan not only bore Mao no grudge, but later lent him books, gave him judicious advice on style, and pleaded for him when he was threatened with expulsion, and Mao recognized Yuan's good advice. "Thanks to Yuan the Big Beard, I can today still turn out a passable classical essay, if required."

The Normal College had a fairly extensive library where Mao gorged on books; he could be seen late at night in the classrooms,

* Seen by the author on visits to Changsha, 1966 and 1971.

still at work. Among the essays he then wrote, one on *Energy of the Mind* was much praised by Yang Chang-chi, a professor of ethics and philosophy, also a pioneer in woman's education, championing rights for women. Yang Chang-chi, who had spent ten years abroad in Britain and Japan, was a man of high moral character. He had published an article on the reform of the family and advocated the remarriage of widows, all of which was offensive to Chinese conservatism, a complete upset of the feudal-patriarchal system. Mao attributed the writing of his essay to Yang's influence. "I was then an idealist," he confesses. He also wrestled with the problem of relations in the old family system. How could there be change, revolutionary or otherwise, unless family relations were also altered? With Yang Chang-chi he would discuss these problems, centered on paternal authoritarianism in the family. Mao's essay was his first attempt at tracing consciousness, the theme of relation between mind and body, concept and material force. He would refer to it again and again throughout his life, but as a materialist his approach to mind totally changed.

Mao Tsetung's work for women's liberation is little known; yet Changsha was fertile ground for such a movement, as it boasted the best girls' school in China, the Chounan Girls Middle School, which was to produce many women revolutionaries. The participation of girl students from the schools of Changsha in the organizations that Mao would create, and subsequently in the Chinese Revolution, are of great importance to the history of the Chinese woman's liberation. One of the earliest recruits of Mao was Tsai Ho-sen's sister Tsai Chang, a vivacious, beautiful girl, still today a vigorous and active revolutionary, member of the Central Committee of the Chinese Communist Party.

"One should not stop one's pursuit of the truth until the aim is achieved . . . Ten years without an understanding of the truth are ten years without ambition"; thus wrote Mao. But only action could prove the sincerity of one's thinking, and it is action that characterizes Mao's years in Changsha. "Here I acquired my first experiences in social action."

He is remembered then as uncommonly gaunt and tall, almost emaciated, completely unaware of his good looks or his poor clothes. The photos show the large, prominent eyes, the high forehead, a calm face. He spent days and nights working, reading, training, demonstrating, debating, organizing workers' schools and students' associations. "Ten thousand years are too long, seize the day,

the hour!" He had already begun, even if he did not know it, to prepare himself physically and mentally for extreme effort. "There are
so many things to know; so many things to do." But he also listened,
intently, patiently; listened and let others speak, and he had a genius
for getting people round him involved with him in his activities. When
he listened he appeared quiet and mild, eyes fixed on the floor in intense concentration.

"Tradition can stifle what is new . . . and the ability to adapt to a
new age will be ended for China." But where was the defect in
China's history? And how could it be ended? "Understanding must
precede decision." "We must develop our physical and mental capaci-
ties to the fullest extent . . . that is why our country's three bonds,
prince and subject, father and son, husband and wife, must go, and
constitute, with religion, capitalists, and autocracy the evil demons
of the empire."

An essay Mao wrote in 1916 on physical culture was printed in
the magazine *New Youth*.* In it Mao made no distinction between
physical fitness and military training, and no one of his generation
would have done so either. Around him he could see the ravages of
ill health. Many of the students complained of nervous debility,
headache, backache, eye ache; quite a few gambled and frequented
brothels. Tuberculosis and venereal disease were common. Mao's
concern with health never left him. The well in the college courtyard
is shown to visitors; here he used to sluice himself with a pail of cold
water, summer or winter. This physical radicalism (for it went
against all accepted ideas) was a function of his political radicalism,
against the traditions of "the scholar," weak, and afraid of physical
exertion.

Many of the young Mao's ideas on how to keep fit were to be incorporated by an older Mao into the way of life promoted in today's
China. Mao asserted that external causes were to be distinguished
from internal causes of physical deterioration; physical fitness must
also be based on a change of mind, of subjective attitude; people
must *want* to be healthy before they can be. External force, the compulsory application of sport programs, will not work. "Strength depends on discipline, which depends on self-awareness," he wrote.
Mao would apply this "self-awareness," and the distinction between
internal and external causes, to revolution. Revolutions arose from
internal causes; external pressures or forces could not in themselves

* A very famous radical publication started in 1915.

make revolution. The second idea Mao promoted was that "physical education complements education in virtue and knowledge." Exactly the same idea, in almost the same words, was to be repeated during the Great Proletarian Cultural Revolution fifty years later.

It is due to Mao's early and sustained enthusiasm that sports and swimming have become an essential part of the training of every person in China. The bad habits of a beaten nation — fear of water, of air, of fatigue, fear of ghosts, of physical exertion, the use of opium, prostitution — all this Mao fought; hence his article on physical culture is a political article, and remains so in the Chinese context.

Since a good mind in a good body was an act of will, it was will which Mao strove to cultivate, and will drove him to uncommon prowess. "Energy" was in nature; one was energized by contact with her. Long walks in the hills for days, barefoot, bare-breasted to imbibe the sun, the rain. Cold swims in the rivers, the ponds. On each holiday, with or without companions, Mao would walk the land from village to village. A copy of a newspaper loaned to Mao by a teacher told a story about two students traveling across China on foot and reaching Tibet. Mao read it and was much interested; he wanted to walk "all over China"; little did he then know his wish would be fulfilled, and how.

In the summer of 1917 Mao set out across Hunan province on foot, journeying through many counties, accompanied by one of the Hsiao brothers.* In the farmhouses where they rested, receiving hospitality from the peasants, Mao inquired of conditions, of crops and rain, of rent and landlords, a peasant talking to other peasants, but also a budding social scientist and researcher. Mao kept notes of what he had been told and remembered the peasants' names. He walked over three hundred miles on this trip.

Then in the autumn of that year of 1917 Mao Tsetung founded with a friend, Ho Shu-heng,† the Hsin Min Hsueh Hui, or New People's Study Society. The significance for the Chinese Revolution to come of this society cannot be overestimated, nor what it represented as training in leadership for Mao. For about a year he had entertained the idea of organizing a society in which people would debate new ideas and create for themselves a "new" personality by discussion, debate, self-analysis and action. The idea of becoming changed by argument and debate, by contact with "reality" and by

---

* Siao Yu, author of *Mao Tsetung and I Were Beggars* (Syracuse, N.Y., 1959).
† Ho Shu-heng was to be also a founder of the Chinese Communist Party. He was executed by Chiang Kai-shek in 1935.

personal experience, he was later to expand, refine, and apply to the making of revolutionaries. "Feeling expansive and the need for a few intimate companions," he inserted an advertisement in a newspaper, signed with the pseudonym under which he wrote his articles, Twenty-eight Strokes.* In this advertisement he explained his project for the organization of a society of young men, active, resolute and patriotic. "I specified youths who were hardened and determined and ready to make sacrifices for their country."

Mao's New People's Study Society was only one of the many such student groups, but it grew into something else, the core of a political party. From the start it stipulated action as well as debate. It would not only talk revolution, but practice it, first of all revolutionizing its own members, turning them into "new men." Even if it had no political label, nor any stated aim but the pursuit of truth and knowledge and their translation into deeds, "the nucleus was formed of what later was to become a society that was to have a widespread influence on the affairs and destiny of China."

Already in creating the New People's Study Society, Mao Tsetung held the germ of the idea which would come to full blossoming at the Cultural Revolution: the conscious remolding of man and his outlook, which in turn transforms the world. Because the society was not for dilettantes, Mao made his own selections. Fifty years later, in a letter to the Red Guards during the Cultural Revolution, Mao Tsetung wrote of the necessity for "continuously and without pause revolutionizing oneself, changing oneself, criticizing oneself, seeking for one's weaknesses and correcting them." Mao had already embarked on this program for himself in 1917.

The response to his advertisement was discouraging; he received "three and a half replies": one from a young man who "was to join the Communist party and afterwards betray it"; two others from individuals who later became ultra-reactionaries. "The half reply came from a noncommittal youth named Li Li-san," with whom Mao would have an ambiguous relationship for the next fifty years. "Li listened to all I had to say and then went away without making any definite proposals himself, and our friendship never developed." Later Li Li-san was to become, in the Chinese Communist Party, an outspoken opponent of Mao's thinking and policies.†

Tsai Ho-sen, Mao Tsetung's best friend, and his sister Tsai Chang

---

* The three ideograms of his name, Mao Tsetung, are written with twenty-eight strokes of the brush.

† See chapter 10.

Mao Tsetung (above, fourth from left) with Tsai Ho-sen (next, with fur collar) and other students at the Hunan First Normal College, about 1917. Below (at right) in Shaoshan after his mother's death with (from left) his brother Mao Tse-min, his father and a clan relative.

immediately joined Mao's society. At the age of ten Tsai Chang had fled to Changsha when her father had tried to betroth her against her will. With her brother's help she entered the Chounan school and was a brilliant student. She was slim and tall, with wonderful hair; she studied physical education, a revolutionary action for a girl then.* Most of the thirteen members who made up the nucleus of Mao's society when it was formally inaugurated in 1918 had similar stories of revolt against family tradition. The society took up among other problems the oppression of women in the traditional marriage system. Its members engaged in neither flirtation nor romance. They "had no time for love or romance, considered the times too critical and the need for knowledge too urgent to discuss women or personal matters. I was not interested in women," said Mao, who had then been twenty-five years old. The program of debate, study, and social action (running night schools for workers, visiting factories, demonstrating against Japanese imperialism, writing articles, championing new ideas and the use of the vernacular) was strenuous. The manifesto of the society opposed opium smoking, gambling, drinking, concubinage, prostitution, corruption; it advocated "the reform of China and the world." Mao Tsetung said that women should be "independent persons"; man could not be free unless woman was also liberated. A new society must instill in woman a consciousness of her social and political role, equal to man's; she too must be "new." On this point, too, Mao has never wavered. Tsai Chang under Mao's and her brother's encouragement organized a Women's Work and Study Society in 1919, to send women students abroad.†

In later years all thirteen of the original members of the society were to join the Chinese Communist Party, founded in 1921. By 1919 there were eighty members, of whom over forty were to join the Party.

All these activities of Mao Tsetung's would acquire their historical significance in the massive involvement of the student population of China in the May 4, 1919 movement. Mao was already influential before the May 1919 explosion, with a considerable following not only among the intelligentsia but also among the factory workers of the city of Changsha.

* In China, where women had bound feet and were not supposed to leave the house, to study physical education was extremely progressive.
† The author had the pleasure of an interview with Madame Tsai Chang in 1956.

Mao became involved in 1918 in a Hunan branch of the Society for Work and Study in France. Started in 1903 by two Chinese scholars, one of them a French-educated biologist, by 1908 it had branches in several cities. After 1913, dismayed by the debacle of Sun Yatsen's revolution, many students and teachers went off to France under the society's auspices. Hsu Te-li started a branch of the society in Changsha and asked Mao to help him. Mao and Tsai Ho-sen helped select students to be sent to France, but Mao wanted recruiting standards changed and engaged in a combative correspondence with the headquarters of the society in Peking. Mao did not feel that aptitude for languages alone should qualify for recruitment. He urged assessment of conduct, ideals, and especially "willingness to serve the country."

It was Mao who suggested that women should also be recruited, because, he said, "women are very dependable and responsible." "More women should go away and study, thus more will be saved." "As many women as men are capable, and they have a tremendous influence on building up a society." It was through Mao's active sponsorship that Tsai Chang's Work and Study Society to send women students to France took shape. Fourteen Hunanese girls, including Tsai Chang herself and Hsiang Ching-yu, another indomitable Hunan girl who married Tsai Chang's brother Tsai Ho-sen, thus went off to France in 1919.

Mao's insistence that women were also human beings inspired him to write lengthy articles championing their cause, notably *The Women's Revolutionary Army,* in the *Hsiang Chiang Review,* which he was to found in Changsha. Its first issue was on July 14, 1919. In the third issue he appealed to women to abolish feudal morality, advocated women's suffrage, railed against the unequal demand for women's chastity — "Where are the arches of chastity to men?" *

It was as a social revolutionary if not a Marxist, a fighter against traditional oppression, a challenger of abuses, the unpaid teacher of workers and small clerks, a speaker, a debater, a writer of articles, a champion of women's rights, an ascetic athlete and a patriot that Mao Tsetung, in those five years at the Normal College, exercised a growing influence upon his contemporaries.

Throughout all these activities Mao would swim in the Hsiang river, climb the beautiful hills, walk shirtless in wind and rain, write

---

* It was the custom to erect an arch to a virtuous widow who had remained chaste all her life; also to a young girl who, once betrothed, remained unwed and virgin till her own death if her husband-to-be died before the wedding.

poetry, eat very little and that of the coarsest, depriving himself of food and clothing to pay for books. But he still had time for friendships. A number of picnics are recorded, gatherings in scenic spots, jaunts along the banks of the beautiful Hsiang river. In autumn when the orange groves glowed with heavy fruit, in summer with the smell of cassia in the air, Mao Tsetung would climb a high spot and gaze far out; at other times he would walk right round the city wall. He kept up a voluminous correspondence with hosts of friends. To save a schoolmate from an arranged marriage he exerted himself, visiting the respective families, arguing against compulsion. Much of the early poetry he then wrote has disappeared, only the printed articles remain. An enormous amount of material — speeches, debates, discussions, letters, and basketfuls of notes — has been lost. But in Changsha can still be found the letters written at the time by Mao's teachers and contemporaries.

On the evening of the autumn festival in 1917, a picnic was held by some of the college students at a famous spot on the outskirts of Changsha. As usual their conversation turned on "saving the country." Which was the best way to save the country?

"To build a large army," said one student.

"To learn science, build railways and factories," said another.

"To become a politician and sweep away corruption," said someone else.

Mao Tsetung was silent, his eyes fixed on the ground. He appeared to dream. Someone turned to him. "What do you think?"

"It takes money and influence to become a politician," Mao Tsetung replied. "As to learning science or becoming a teacher, that also requires money and influence and time. To build an army . . . what kind of an army that would not oppress the people could one build . . . unless one does like the heroes of Liang Shan-po . . ." *

At this the others laughed, and the talk turned to heroes of old.

The heroes of Liang Shan-po are the heroes of the Chinese people. In *Water Margin,* Mao's favorite book, 108 rebels, called "bandits" by the ruling power, gather in a mountain fortress to fight for justice against tyranny. By referring to them, Mao showed that he thought in terms of revolt — of fighting against the corruption and oppression round him, not joining it to reform the system. To

---

* This story, recorded by Siao Yu in *Mao Tsetung and I Were Beggars* (Syracuse, N.Y., 1959) seems accurate, though this author disagrees with the final verdict of Mr. Siao in his book.

choose, deliberately, the part of the rebel and the outcast was what he offered his friends at the picnic that night.

In his last year at the Teachers College, in March 1918, Mao Tse-tung's mother came to Changsha. Much worn, with a swollen face and a purulent cheek, she sought medical treatment. She was carried in a sedan chair all the way by a hired laborer and her second son, Mao Tse-min. In that year Mao Tse-tan, Mao's third brother, was studying at the primary school attached to the Teachers College. Treatment was of no avail; Mao's mother died in October. "More than ever" Mao lost interest in returning to his father's house; he was, however, to return briefly and to be photographed with his father and wearing a black armband.

In April 1918 Mao graduated from the college. He decided to go to Peking with a group of thirty Hunanese being sent to France by the Work and Study Society. Before leaving China they would study French at the language school in Peking. Both Tsai Ho-sen and Hsu Te-li had applied to go. Hsu Te-li, though over forty, went with the younger men as a student worker. Many of those chosen were members of the New People's Study Society. It would have been easy for Mao Tsetung to travel to France. He was certainly expected to do so. What decided him not to leave?

According to some biographers Mao was reluctant to learn a foreign language; his pronounced Hunan accent made him afraid of being laughed at. But what we know of Mao's character and ability makes this assertion hardly tenable. Mao was not self-conscious about clothes, appearance or accent. He went round in the same clothes month in and out; he had no other. His patched shoes never deterred him from calling on provincial governors or headmasters, and no one laughed at his Hunan accent.

But to sail to France was for Mao to cut himself off from the warm, exalting life, the nourishing sap he felt rise within him when he was with his people, walking in the mountains and valleys of Hunan, or going to the factories and teaching the workers at evening school. This was his strength, a strength and power undefined as yet, but real to him. He was spellbound, enthralled, unable to tear himself away from his own country. Something now told him not to go, although he himself would not be able to formulate it clearly. Later he would say that it was the needs and the exploitation of his people that had propelled him into revolution. The revolution made Mao Tsetung as much as Mao Tsetung made the revolution. But the choice was his.

We must, therefore, accept his own explanation for his staying behind. "I felt I did not know enough about my own country." In the
spring of 1919 he stood on the quay in Shanghai, tall and thin in his
threadbare, wind-blown cotton gown, and watched his friends, Tsai
Ho-sen among them, waving at him from the deck of their French
steamer. He waved back at them, then turned and walked away, to
return to his own countryside, his own province of Hunan.

3

First Trip to Peking

Mao Tsetung had spent only 160 Chinese dollars (this sum included his numerous registration fees) during his five years at the Changsha Normal College, one third on newspapers and journals. He did not ask for money from his father to go to Peking, but borrowed from friends. He went much of the way on foot, and managed to walk round Lake Tungting — at low level a circumference of 155 miles. On this trip he also did social investigation and research, for he stopped in farmhouses, earning food and lodging by lending a hand in the labor, or writing calligraphic slogans of good omen, to paste on doors at festivals. The shores of Lake Tungting belong to eleven counties; there landlords congregate, taking the fertile alluvial islands left by the sift of waters, and renting them out for rice planting to poor peasants. Of the land there, 71 percent was owned by 1.8 percent of the population, and each landlord had armed retainers. All this Mao was to note and store in his memory as he trekked onward to Peking.

When Mao arrived in Peking there were a good many Hunanese intellectuals already there. Soon he was calling on Professor Yang Chang-chi, who was overjoyed to see him. Yang had left the Changsha Normal College in 1917, having been appointed to the staff of Peking University. The Changsha schools and colleges were known for their high standards, their professors were among the best in China, and Yang was personally famous, popular as well as erudite. He had settled well in Peking, and introduced Mao Tsetung to Li Ta-chao, then university librarian at Peking University. Mao was penniless and needed a job; Yang Chang-chi asked Li Ta-chao to help him.

Mao Tsetung admired Li Ta-chao, whose articles in *New Youth* he had read; but Li Ta-chao seems at first to have paid little attention to him. A job was provided, however, that of assistant in the university library, at eight dollars a month. Could Li Ta-chao have done better for Mao? We do not know. Mao had no money; he had to live. He took the job. Anyway, a library was what he liked best. There he could read to his soul's content.

Li Ta-chao, eminent, brilliant, mercurial, was the first intellectual in China to praise the Russian Revolution of October 1917; he is described as having been the first to introduce Marxist thought to China's intelligentsia. Although young — Li Ta-chao was thirty when Mao was twenty-five — he had a great reputation for progressive ideas and personal courage. He believed that a renaissance could be achieved only by discarding the suffocating moralities and values of the past. He likened the hampering of thought which the classics imposed upon the minds of students to "bound-foot women." At first attracted by the Western liberal democratic system, he had turned away from it because of the contradiction between the pious homilies of Western democracy and its ruthless exploitation of China. He denounced the economic stranglehold of Western finance; was one of the first to write and lecture about Lenin and to translate Lenin into Chinese. He was especially impressed by Lenin's *The State and Revolution*. Like Lenin, Li Ta-chao stressed the need for arousal or "awareness" in the masses. "Education of the masses" was essential for revolutionary results of a lasting kind. Li Ta-chao wrote and talked about this a great deal, and Mao Tsetung would certainly be influenced by Li's ideas, and through Li, by Lenin to a greater extent than by any other philosopher of Communism.

It was through Li Ta-chao that Mao began to read Lenin, in Li's translations. Mao's dictum, "The people, the people alone are the motor force, the creator of universal history," is the essence of Leninism. Li predicted that "the Chinese revolution would be essentially a peasant revolution." Lenin had stated that revolution in colonial and semi-colonial countries could not be successful without the arousal and the participation of the peasantry, the "infantry" of the revolutionary process. "Go to them, educate them, make them understand that they should demand their own liberation, speak of the oppression which they have suffered, demand their release from ignorance and misery and to be masters of their own destiny," wrote Li Ta-chao. This outlines the method by which the leadership of an agrarian revolution is acquired, though it cannot be interpreted as the demand that the leadership of the revolution be agrarian. The peasantry is the "main force" of the revolution; but "leadership" is something else. Whether Li Ta-chao saw this as clearly as Mao Tse-tung was to see it we do not know. Li Ta-chao was killed in 1927,* possibly unaware that the diffident young Hunanese man who had come to him for a job would be the leader of the revolution Li Ta-chao ardently desired and died for.

The job of assistant librarian procured for Mao was a semi-job, but unemployment among the intelligentsia was rampant. "My own living conditions in Peking were quite miserable," and "in contrast the beauty of the old capital was a vivid and living compensation." "I stayed in a little room which held seven other people. When we were all packed fast on the *kang* † bed there was scarcely room enough for any of us to breathe. I used to have to warn people on each side of me when I wanted to turn over. But in the parks and the old palace grounds I saw the early northern spring. I saw the white plum blossom flower while the ice still held solid over the North Sea park. I saw the willows over the lake with the ice crystals hanging from them." Enraptured by the beauty of Peking, the poet Mao Tsetung walked for hours, exploring the enchanted city. The social investigator Mao Tsetung went to the small craftsmen's shops, to the railways workers' yard, walked to the Great Wall, round the city walls, to the Western Hills, the Marco Polo bridge, learning the city with his feet and his senses.

In the library of Peking University Mao's job consisted in fetching books required, checking the titles, writing down the names of borrowers and those who came to read newspapers or magazines. "My office was so low that people avoided me; to most of them I did not exist as a human being." It was menial work, just a little above that of a domestic. Seldom did any of the great or not so great who came there glance at his face, or talk to him. Peking University was a very highbrow, snobbish place; its intellectuals the highest intelligentsia with the greatest arrogance of all in the land. "Among those who came to read I recognized the names of famous leaders of the renaissance movement.‡ I tried to begin conversation with them on political and cultural subjects, but they were very busy men."

This job provided Mao with insight into the vanity and egotism of

* He was strangled in the wave of massacres of Communists that swept over China in that year; see chapter 8.

† *Kang* — a stone bed with fire underneath to keep it warm. Used throughout North China.

‡ The name given then to a literary movement in existence since 1907, when Lu Hsun, China's most famous revolutionary writer, was in Japan. This movement was to merge with the political and social upheavals of May 4, 1919; see chapter 4.

the intellectual who talked of humanism and socialism yet cut himself off from the wretched masses of the poor. Abstract terminology the intelligentsia dealt with skillfully, but they would never have dreamed of investigating the beggars' hovels in the filth and garbage just outside the city walls, where Mao went. Years later, when the Revolution was successful, the problem of intellectuals, of how to teach them the reality of China, would be one of the most knotty problems of all for Mao. The Chinese Revolution needed intellectuals, but they were also dangerous to it, for they would always tend to ride high above the heads of the people and to demand personal privileges as their due.

During those weeks in the library of Peking University, Mao listened to the famous and revered discourse of ways to save the country; and wondered. Sarcasm, not personal rancor, would later appraise these "talking machines" at their true worth. The fates of the brilliant ones who later gave up, gave in, became turncoats, he would describe sparingly. He was thought of as a slow-witted peasant, shouted at and ordered about; and he realized that "they [the important intelligentsia] had no time to listen to an assistant librarian speaking southern dialect. But I was not discouraged. I joined the Society of Philosophy and the Journalism Society." These gave him the right to sit in on courses at the back of the lecture rooms, coming in quietly after all the others.

Mao thus met Chen Kung-po, a fellow student then, who became a Communist but reneged and became a Chiang Kai-shek supporter; Tan Ping-shan, who became a Communist and later a member of a "third party"; Shao Piao-ping, very earnest, very excitable, somewhat anarchistic (but in those early days this tendency was easily acquired), who helped Mao greatly and was killed in 1926; Chang Kuo-tao, who became a Communist, bitterly opposed Mao during the Long March, later defected to the Kuomintang, and is now in Canada; Kang Pei-chen, who joined the Ku Klux Klan in California; Tuan Hsi-peng, later to become vice-minister of education in Chiang Kai-shek's government. Once Mao tried to talk to the famous Dr. Hu Shih, but the latter ignored him. And he met Chen Tu-hsiu, the prestigious editor of *New Youth,* the magazine which had radicalized a whole generation, the magazine Mao Tsetung read from cover to cover and for which he had already written articles under his usual pseudonym, the twenty-eight-stroke man.

Many years later, in an interview, Hu Shih would say to some American friends: "Mao Tsetung was quite remarkable. . . . All the young people then were members of a Young China Study Society * ; they were all interested in politics. Mao Tsetung was one of them. When I was at Peking University, he asked to be allowed to sit in on classes. As a prose writer, Mao was superb. No one could equal him."

Mao Tsetung read all that Li Ta-chao wrote on Marxism and joined the Marxist Study Group, founded by Li, towards the end of 1918. "Under Li Ta-chao, I developed rapidly towards Marxism." He also acknowledged his debt to Chen Tu-hsiu, who was then thirty-nine years old. "He influenced me perhaps more than anyone else." For a long time Mao Tsetung thought Chen Tu-hsiu an outstanding revolutionary. Chen was to be the first, but not the last, of Mao's disappointing experiences with "bourgeois radicals," revolutionaries and friends he would look up to and trust, and find to be unscrupulous opportunists.

Mao's personal life was changed in Peking. The puritan, the ascetic, fell in love with Yang Kai-hui, daughter of Professor Yang Chang-chi. Mao often went to visit Yang, for the old professor kept open house for the students. "He was a genuine friend to me in Peking." Yang gave him books to read, helped him to enroll in courses, and treated him with dignity, telling everyone of Mao's talents. He met Yang Kai-hui at her father's house and also at the university, where she attended courses in journalism. Yang Kai-hui, born in 1901, was beautiful, very much like Mao's mother in looks, but above all a noble and courageous girl, well read, sensitive, and profoundly devoted to ideas.

This was for both of them first love. In the New People's Study Society, "everything we did or said must have a purpose. . . . We had no time for love or romance, considered the times too critical and the need for knowledge too urgent to discuss women or personal matters. I was not interested in women." But this now changed, although "My interest in politics continued to increase."

The love of Yang Kai-hui and Mao Tsetung in Peking was "new" love, where the partners chose each other, then a daring and uncommon innovation. It remained unspoken for a good many months, since Professor Yang himself seemed unaware of it for some time. The two young people were both shy, and they had the problem which confronted many young people then. Could they, was it permissible, to enjoy love and romance when the country needed all

* A society founded by Li Ta-chao, to which Mao adhered.

their energy? This stress between duty and private affection was a deeply serious one in those days of early revolution, when high-minded young couples often voluntarily sacrificed their love for what they considered their duty. Hence they decided to wait, to be sure of themselves.

Mao also began a series of social investigations among workers on the Peking-Hankow railway. He visited them, going as far as the Chang Hsin Tien railway station, 93 miles south. Today in one of Peking's important machine plants, the February 7 plant, there are still old workers who recall how Mao Tsetung came to see them. Some of these workers became Communist trade unionists and took part in the Communist-led railway strikes of the 1920's. Some were sent to France by Mao on the work and study program after 1921.

After about six months in Peking — from November 1918 to April 1919 — Mao's Hunanese friends were ready to sail from Shanghai to France. They had studied French in Peking at the French Institute.* Mao borrowed the fare to go to Shanghai to see them off; he had only enough money to get as far as Tientsin, but borrowed ten dollars to continue the journey. On the way to Shanghai he visited (on foot) temples, scenic spots, the grave of Confucius, and climbed Mount Tai. Not far from Shanghai, at Pukou, again he was "without a copper" and without a ticket; then a thief stole his only pair of shoes. But he was again lucky, meeting outside the railway station a friend from Hunan who lent him money for a pair of new shoes and for the remaining trip to Shanghai. Having seen his friends off on their French steamer, Mao returned to Changsha. It was then April 1919.

* Also known as the Auguste Comte Institute.

4

The First Cultural Revolution— May 4, 1919

The first cultural revolution of China's twentieth century began with the May 4, 1919 movement. It has been described as a "literary renaissance," especially in the U.S., where the influence of the late Dr. Hu Shih denied its fundamentally political nature. But the changes which affected Chinese literature cannot be dissociated from the politico-social upsurges of the period. The literary revolution was part of the political process. This first cultural revolution was a precursor of the Communist Revolution, in which Mao Tsetung was to play such a leading role, and his political radicalization was hastened by it.

It was in 1915, and because of the Japanese threat,* that many radical patriotic magazines, among them *New Youth,* began publication. Dr. Hu Shih, returned from the U.S. and fresh from John Dewey's lectures, in the summer of 1917 spoke and wrote of a "literary revolution" in China, but as an isolated phenomenon, to accompany a "gradual reform" and "Westernization" of Chinese social and political structures. At the time, the question of utilizing the vernacular and abolishing the literary language was ardently debated, and Hu Shih approved of lecturing and writing in the vernacular rather than in the classical style, as this would "broaden education." But Hu Shih failed to comprehend that the fundamental question was not a change of style but a change of content and of system, a political and social revolution rather than a literary revolution alone. The debates then current concerning language and literature were symptoms of a great upheaval. Hu Shih condemned all "violence" and

* The Twenty-one Demands (Tanaka Memorial) of 1915.

"excesses" and argued that "students must study and not concern themselves . . . with political affairs." But there is no traditional separation of the "literary" from the "political" in China; * this was a purely Westernized viewpoint which Hu Shih, unconsciously perhaps, imported into a Chinese situation. He was thus out of the historical movement before it had begun, as his acrimonious correspondence with several university student associations two years before the May 4, 1919 movement testifies.

The origins of the May 4th movement are traceable to the Twenty-one Demands made by Japan upon China. During the First World War Japan sought to replace all other colonial powers in China. The Twenty-one Demands crystallized patriotic indignation among the students and the intelligentsia into a lucid, definite anti-imperialist and anti-feudal movement. The literary, political and social aspects of the movement became merged into impetuous national protest. After October 1917, the success of the Russian Revolution led to the spread of Marxism, in which Li Ta-chao was a leading figure. A nationwide boycott of Japanese imports began. Within this context the literary revolution also took place. Informing the people became an imperative duty which could only be performed by a radicalized intelligentsia using the vernacular, expressing political and social events in language intelligible to ordinary people. Already in 1917 Mao in Changsha was using the vernacular in his workers' evening classes.

National humiliation days,† anti-Japanese meetings, were held in these effervescent years from 1915 to 1919. Student orators stood on improvised platforms at street corners and explained Japanese imperialism to the crowds — and British, French, and other imperialisms. Protest sheets covered the walls, pamphlets circulated by hand. No one was interested in merely writing poems in the vernacular, as Hu Shih recommended.

Lu Hsun, the great Chinese writer, had begun a magazine called *New Life* in Japan in 1906 to urge language reform; it had not prospered because Lu Hsun's enterprise was too early; only when he returned to China and participated in the anti-imperialist movement did Lu Hsun come into the mastery of his own craft and give language reform its definite place in the literary revolution: "the propa-

* The whole of Chinese history is evidence of the close relation between politics and literary production, to a far greater extent than in any Western country.
† In both China and Japan, days of "humiliation," to commemorate defeats, were observed.

gation of political and social ideas which would unite the people against tyranny; literature not for the elite but for the masses." From then on the revolution in literature became part of the Chinese revolutionary process. Hence the Communists regard Lu Hsun as the originator of the literary and language reform, as they regard May 4, 1919, as the watershed between the old established form of literary-political dissent, with its emphasis on maintaining through reform the structures of the Chinese traditional system, and the new one, with its emphasis on the total abolition of the old.

The "literary" revolution became a nationwide complex of manifestos, demonstrations and militant action. New political terms were coined and stirred awareness of the new literature. Satirical essays constructed a new style. Repression could do little against this radicalization, which was proceeding so fast that by 1918 *New Youth* was by no means the only vanguard magazine, nor the most left-wing. "A tide of new thinking" became embodied in the New Tide Society, its members and its publications. Li Ta-chao's essays on Marxism, begun in the spring of 1912, and his translations of Lenin and Marx had set the trend of radical thought. Student societies (among them the New People's Study Society founded by Mao Tse-tung) organized centers for the production and dissemination of Marxist literature. These revolutionary groups fostered a large contingent of young intellectuals for the May 4th movement.

Mao Tsetung, twenty years later, was to identify the literary revolution with the political one, and call it China's first "cultural revolution." This "cultural revolution" remained for him a vital experience until the time came for yet another tide of renewal, fifty years later, initiated by him. No study of Mao Tsetung's development can be complete without some knowledge of the May 4th movement, Mao's role in it, and his analysis and understanding of the event which shaped China's future more definitely than anything else at that time.

Undeterred by student agitation, Japan in 1917 and 1918 gave loans of about 150 million Japanese yen to Tuan Chi-jui, then president of a coalition of warlords and militarists forming the Peking government. Tuan agreed to secret pacts and military conventions which turned North China into a Japanese satellite.

The students learned of these deals through the Soviet Union press, and demonstrations against Tuan's government occurred in May 1918. Several thousand students in Peking assembled in front of the presidential palace, demanding to know the contents of the "Sino-Japanese military mutual assistance conventions" and other pacts. The merchant guilds denounced Tuan Chi-jui, asked for a stop to the civil wars then raging in various provinces between warlords, and for resistance to Japanese encroachment upon China. In the summer of 1918 a Student Society for National Salvation was founded on an all-China basis, linking provincial student associations into united action. A section of industrialists and merchants supported the students.

In November 1918, the end of the First World War, the establishment of the League of Nations, and the declarations of Woodrow Wilson were received with great rejoicing. "The Chinese people were jubilant," writes Chow Tse-tsung.* They hoped the shameful unequal treaties imposed by the Western powers and Japan ever since 1840 (the first Opium War) would be abrogated in an equitable settlement in the peace treaty. Promises and assurances had been made to China in 1917 to obtain her entry into the war on the side of the Allies; 200,000 Chinese workers had been exported to man the depleted factories in France and to dig trenches at the front. Many intellectuals believed that the victory of the Allies was a victory of democracy over tyranny, of the rule of law over militarism, of the common people over oppressors. They thought the declared peace aims of the governments of the Allies, and Woodrow Wilson's Fourteen Points, would be translated into action. A victory parade of 60,000 took place in Peking, fireworks were exploded, and there was great hope among those who admired the Western forms of democracy that China would at last be treated fairly, and the rights she had been deprived of would be restored to her.

But when the Paris Peace Conference opened on January 18, 1919, it became evident that promises were merely vague assurances, unsubstantial words which would never see performance. The Chinese delegation, representative of the Japanese-bribed Peking government, was later reinforced, much against its will, by a "southern" delegation, sent by Sun Yatsen (who in 1918 once again briefly returned to power in Kuangchow as head of a coalition of southern militarists). The southern delegation included the brilliant Dr. Eugene Chen,† an overseas Chinese from a wealthy family in Trinidad, who managed to get a copy of the secret Lansing-Ishii agreement made between the U.S. and Japan in 1917. This agreement showed

* Chow Tse-tsung *The May Fourth Movement: Intellectual Revolution in Modern China* (Cambridge, Mass., and London 1960).
† All the information concerning Dr. Eugene Chen was obtained from his sons, Jack and Percy Chen, by the author.

that the United States had already come to an understanding with Japan concerning respective "spheres of influence" in China.

The publication of the Lansing-Ishii agreement in Chinese student newspapers revealed the duplicity of China's allies. By March 1919, rumors that the Chinese case was "hopeless" came to Peking. President Wilson, on whom the hopes of the Chinese were pinned, apparently gave in to combined European maneuvers, and China's demands for abrogation of the unequal treaties were brusquely rejected. China was to remain, as much as before the war, "everyone's colony, no one's responsibility."

Throughout these weeks of hope and expectation and shattering disillusion, merchants, shopkeepers, businessmen, students, professors kept on forming groups and associations "to obtain justice." Student organizations from all the cities sent hundreds of telegrams to the delegations in Paris. The chambers of commerce flooded the delegates with cabled exhortations. The Chinese students in France sent representatives to call upon the delegates and in the end were to picket them and prevent them from signing the treaty and "selling out" Chinese rights.

On May 3, students in Peking learned that the Paris Peace Conference granted none of the Chinese demands. On the contrary, Shantung province, Germany's previous "sphere of influence," was now given to Japan.

"We at once awoke to the fact that foreign nations were still selfish and militaristic, and that they were all great liars." "We concluded that a greater world war would come." "We must struggle." Thus spoke the students.

It was decided to hold a mass demonstration on May 7, National Humiliation Day, the anniversary of Japan's ultimatum of 1915. But the demonstration started earlier. On May 4 in Peking 3,000 students representing thirteen academic institutions circulated a manifesto written in the vernacular and marched to the house of a pro-Japanese official; the police and army, who were mobilized, arrested some and proclaimed martial law. Within the next twenty-four hours the students turned to rallying and organizing all those they could reach. Since the whole nation was shocked and indignant, a great alliance of merchants, workers, petty shopkeepers, craftsmen was formed very swiftly. And thus a massive united front was created, not only against imperialism, but against the Chinese warlords who had "sold out" the Chinese people. The newspapers and magazines printed articles in support of the students. On May 10 began a gen-

eral strike in all the schools and academic institutions. On June 2, 3
and 4, arrests of teachers and students occurred. This prompted
strikes and demonstrations on June 5, in which girls participated as
well as boys, even from primary schools.

National indignation found itself through student organizations.
Mobile groups of ten teamed to carry out street propaganda, put up
posters, direct strikes, demonstrations, and the burning of Japanese
goods found in stores. Teachers and university professors joined in
the student demonstrations. On the morning of June 6, all the business firms and factories in Shanghai went on strike. The strike
spread like a prairie fire. By noon it covered the whole city and the
suburbs. Textile plants, railways, public utility enterprises — more
than one hundred companies and factories, involving about 90,000
workers, including many women workers, shut down. Even the res-
taurants, the brothels and singsong girls' houses of Shanghai closed.
In the streets, the only activities were meetings — hundreds of students speaking to listening crowds around them — and protest
marches, banners flying, on the main roads. Even police units had
gone on sympathy strikes.

Up and down the Yangtze, river transport stopped. Labor unions,
until then proscribed, suddenly blossomed. On June 28, the date of
the signature of the peace treaty at Versailles, Chinese students,
workers, and overseas Chinese in Paris surrounded the Lutetia
Hotel, where the delegation from Peking resided, and prevented the
delegates from leaving the hotel; thus the Chinese government did
not sign the Versailles Peace Treaty. The demand for abrogation of
unequal treaties went on through the next three decades; only in
1949, thirty years later, when Mao led the Chinese Revolution to its
all-China victory, were the aims of the May 4th movement achieved
at last.

The May 1919 movement was not isolated from world events;
what went on in the USSR as well as what went on at the Paris
Peace Conference directly affected the Chinese youth revolt. In
March 1919 the Third International had held its First Congress in
Moscow, an event given much publicity in Chinese Marxist study
groups in Peking, Shanghai, and later (April) in Changsha. The First
Congress had condemned the peace conference and called for a
world revolution.

The praise of Marxism which characterized the May 4 movement,
as well as its anti-Confucianism, its demands for "democracy" and

"science," marked it as a turning point in the history of China. And truly nothing was the same afterwards. Attacks on all superstition, all tradition, went on throughout 1919. Intellectuals launched campaigns for social service; girls cut their hair short; free marriage was advocated; opium smoking, foot binding were denounced even in remote provinces. Progressive publications underwent a great expansion; more than 400 began during that spring and summer. They voiced the temper and the tone of those days: *Warm Tide, New Learning, New Voice, Awakening, New Culture, Mass Education, Upward, Strife, New Woman, Women's Bell, New China,* names evocative of this great upsurge, in which millions were becoming politicized. New books and translations, of Marxist and socialist content, were published in far larger quantities than ever before; no fewer than fifty publishers now printed translations, and translating was done at a feverish pace. All papers and magazines shifted to the vernacular, and old-type publications radically changed their editorial policies. And all this happened so swiftly, it seemed almost overnight. Everything had changed, but for years no one would be aware of the fundamental, qualitative change which had taken place.

In that April of 1919 Mao Tsetung had returned to Changsha * and immediately plunged into political agitation. He obtained a job as a lowly teacher at the Hsiu Yeh Primary School, attached to the Normal College and built within its precincts. His salary barely kept him alive. He lived on one meal of rice and broad beans a day. All through his life as a student, and now as a teacher, he saved on food to pay for books and newspapers. Political agitation left him no time for the extra coaching of wealthy students which usually formed a teacher's chief source of revenue. His greatest worry was shoes, he could not afford them. In summer he wore straw sandals as the peasants did. He had returned to Changsha with two articles by Li Ta-chao, *Victory of the Common People* and *The Triumph of Bolshevism,* and gave a lecture on "Marxism and the Revolution" under the aegis of his New People's Study Society. Mao Tsetung's popularity had grown with his return from prestigious Peking and the political excitement of the times. The students, teachers, shopkeepers, the workers of Changsha, who in 1918 already had demonstrated against Japan and carried on a very effective boycott of Japanese goods, now crowded to listen to Mao Tsetung. Mao's lecture was a great success. It ended with the assertion that only by studying

* After seeing off his friends in Shanghai, leaving for France.

Marxism could the Chinese people save themselves. In April 1919 the first Marxist study group in Hunan province was founded in Changsha.

Mao was already convinced that only a Marxist revolution could save China, although he was not yet a fully confirmed Marxist. The New People's Study Society, the Work and Study Society, the New Tide Society (Hunan Branch) all turned to the study of Marxism. It is no exaggeration to state that Mao brought Marxism to Hunan, and did all the preparatory work prior to establishment of a Communist Party branch there.

In the following weeks, Mao's influence in Changsha expanded with the anti-Japanese and anti-warlord struggle in the schools. "Hunan is the most radical province," the newspapers claimed. Mao was blacklisted by the provincial governor, Chang Ching-yao, a pro-Japanese nominee of the Peking government. Chang tried to suppress anti-Japanese activity, but the students took to the streets to lecture about "national betrayal," and such was the sway of public opinion that Chang Ching-yao dared not arrest them. Mao formed the United Students' Association of Hunan in June 1919, to link student activities to the All-China Federation of Students. While in Peking his attendance at mass meetings against the warlords in November 1918, and the student conference against Japanese encroachment in January 1919, had provided him with many interprovincial contacts. He also maintained correspondence with Hunan students in France — Tsai Ho-sen, Tsai Chang and Hsiang Ching-yu; and knew of the revolutionary groups forming there.

Twenty years later * Mao would explain the concept of the "cultural revolution," epitomized in the May 4th movement. The cultural revolution was a continuing phenomenon, the May 4th movement its beginning — "so great and so thorough a cultural revolution that it was unprecedented in Chinese history." But it was going on; it would continue as long as the Chinese Revolution itself. Thus Mao would introduce Lenin's concept of "cultural revolution" as an inseparable component of the Chinese Revolution.

---

* *On New Democracy,* January 1940. *Selected Works of Mao Tsetung* (English edition Peking 1961–1965), vol. II. See also *The May 4th Movement* and *The Orientation of the Youth Movement,* also in volume II.

It is incorrect to aver, as some scholars do, that Mao was "awakened" or "came out of obscurity" because of the May 4th movement, or that he started his career with it. His career had already started. He had been the author of one of the first anti-Japanese denunciations, on May 7, 1915, the very day the Twenty-one Demands were published.

On June 3, the United Students' Association of Hunan issued a proclamation demanding punishment of pro-Japanese politicians. Strikes of merchants, shopkeepers and workers, in which the miners of Pinghsiang and Anyuan participated, took place. The boycott spread through the schools and their faculties to countryside small towns; even schoolchildren took part. In Changsha, teams of girls inspected and searched stores for Japanese products. When these were found, they were publicly burned.

Groups of three, five or more young people would get together, pass a resolution, and go out lecturing, teaching, "arousing and awakening" the people. Mao urged them to "get organized": "Arouse the people, give them their initiative." He was beginning to learn what "the masses" meant. His style as a revolutionary was shaped then: a widespread stirring up, a multiplication of groups, societies, teams; a seeming chaos, out of which grow new ways of thought and behavior. "If we want a great union to oppose the mighty who do evil, it is necessary to have many small unions of all kinds as a base." All Mao-inspired movements have the tendency to look wildly "undirected" at the beginning, precisely because Mao feels that "directions from above" will not do; it is the people themselves who must educate themselves in doing, practicing revolution, shaping their own rules of conduct and a new order; but the leadership must keep an initiative of theoretical guidance, of ideas. The end is new cohesion and effectiveness. This is the key to the understanding of Mao's style, to "trust the people," and it began during the first cultural revolution.

Under the slogan "Use national products, resist Japanese goods," Mao addressed a rally of merchants and guilds in Changsha in July and urged them to form a committee to enforce the boycott. A "unity of all circles" association, in which workers, shopkeepers, small craftsmen and intellectuals participated was set up. He wrote numerous articles, addressed dozens of societies, committees, organizations; and began the *Hsiang River Review* (*Hsiang Chiang Pin Lun*), a weekly whose importance exceeded its short life. Founded on July 14, 1919, the weekly's manifesto was written by Mao; a week later (July 21) the first part of his article, *The Great Union of the Masses of the People,* which ran into three installments, appeared.

The Great Union of the Masses of the People contains the Mao Tsetung style and way of thinking; it proceeds methodically from the abstract theme of the power of "unity of the masses" to concrete proposals for the Chinese situation. The article urges the "union of the oppressed," union of the peasantry, of women, as well as of workers and students. The classification of the oppressed is a "united front" one rather than one based upon orthodox Marxist class analysis. Today the appeal remains substantially the same; all those who want to fight imperialism and social imperialism, the "broad masses," should form a great world common front to overthrow them. *The Great Union of the Masses* is regarded as a forerunner to the united front concept, an essential feature of Mao's revolutionary strategy.

The part played by will, option, individual consciousness, "arousal" and "awareness," which must lead to action, is expounded, but the article goes beyond individual motivation. "The greatest force is that of the union of the popular masses. . . . We are awakened, the world is ours, the nation is ours, society is ours. . . ." "We should not fear heaven, nor ghosts, nor the dead, nor bureaucrats, nor the militarists, nor the capitalists . . . we must fear nothing, but go forward together. The great union of the masses is a deluge . . . nothing can stop it, the whole world shaken by it . . . heaven and earth are aroused . . . the traitors and the wicked flee."

Mao Tsetung the Marxist would reiterate the basic theme of "the masses" throughout his life. The masses can do anything; when the masses grasp the correct idea, they transform it into an immense material force which can make heaven and earth change places. "Of all things in the world, people are the most precious . . . as long as there are people, any kind of miracle can be performed under the leadership of the Communist Party." In 1919 he wrote: "The Chinese people is not only famous for endurance and industry; it also is a people with a rich revolutionary tradition and love of freedom . . . they would never submit to a rule of the dark forces." And in 1958: "There is no difficulty in the world that they cannot overcome. I have witnessed the tremendous energy of the masses; on this foundation it is possible to accomplish any great task whatsoever."

Mao Tsetung's *Hsiang River Review* became the Hunan students' favorite weekly. From the beginning it "had a great influence on the student movement in South China." * It was quoted in the universities in Peking, in Shanghai, in Kuangchow; schoolboys volunteered to sell copies in the streets of Changsha. The articles by Mao Tsetung were popular for their vividness. He attacked every vice and

* Edgar Snow *Red Star Over China* (1937, first revised and enlarged edition New York 1968).

evil custom in society, including the oppression of women. His style was then fervid, grandiloquent; the spirit of the times was epic exaltation.

"If the peasants are not liberated, then the nation will not be liberated," Li Ta-chao had written. Marx had stated that movements of national liberation in colonial countries had their place in the socialist revolutions to come. So had Lenin.* These ideas Mao propagated in his articles. The national, patriotic features of the May 4th movement he would later incorporate in his revolutionary strategy. "Can a Communist, who is an internationalist, at the same time be a patriot? We hold that he not only can be but must be. The specific content of patriotism is determined by historical conditions. . . . In wars of national liberation, patriotism is applied internationalism." † In 1919 it was patriotism, on a national liberation surge, which led to the "great unity" of the masses; it was on this basis that Marxism progressed in China.

"The greater the oppression, the greater the resistance." This phrase, now current as a Mao quotation, is already found in 1919 in an article by Mao Tsetung in the *Hsiang River Review*. Mao spoke and wrote of the need for a cultural revolution to change society — "the only way to emancipate millions of people and their energy and to carry forward the ultimate aim of liberating the country from imperialism and all capitalists." Mao introduced the public by his writings to the Russian Revolution, the upheavals in Hungary and other parts of Europe then taking place, the possibility of the same happening in China. He gave an international dimension to the May 4th movement, an identification with all that was revolutionary in the world. And indeed the generation of May 4th did link events in China to revolution elsewhere. Beyond the scope of local events they felt the forceful, irresistible drive of world history in the making.

Mao pointed this out when he wrote and spoke against the views expounded by Bertrand Russell and John Dewey in their visit to China. Between 1919 and 1921, these two eminent men were invited by the more conservative groups in the Chinese universities to lecture and to present viewpoints to counteract the incipient Bolshevik influence. Russell and Dewey toured and lectured. They made an impression on so-called "middle of the road" liberals, es-

* V. I. Lenin *On Revolutionary Tempests in the Far East,* translated by Foreign Language Press (Peking 1967).
† *The Role of the Chinese Communist Party in the National War,* October 1938. *Selected Works of Mao Tsetung* (English edition Peking 1961–1965), vol. II.

pecially Russell, who denounced the arbitrariness of Soviet Russian methods. (He had visited Soviet Russia and was horrified by what he had seen.) But however acclaimed they were, they could not stop the urgent march of history. John Dewey's influence persisted in some circles, promoted by Hu Shih and other intellectuals. But these moderating influences had nothing to do with the irrepressible revolution. Revolution had begun but these men refused to see it. "The soft nonviolent kind of communism Russell preaches is good for capitalism, it can never achieve socialism," said Mao Tsetung, refuting Russell at a public meeting held in the auditorium of the Teachers College in December 1919.

As 1919 moved into 1920, splits, cliques, factions developed. They led to a dropping off in agitation. But subsidence did not mean a return to a previous situation. China was changed forever. "This kind of new culture movement reflects an unprecedented change among the intellectuals of China today. . . . The success of the revolution carried on by our party depends on a change of thought in China, just as the ancient book on strategy by Sun Tze says that to attack the mind is more effective than to attack a city, and as the old saying has it that a renovation of the mind is prerequisite to a revolution." Thus wrote Sun Yatsen at the time. The movement, he said, "has brought us a good east wind to move our boat forward." "This is the deluge," wrote Tsai Yuan-pei, then president of Peking University, in an article entitled *The Deluge and the Beasts*. He likened the warlords, militarists and reactionaries to beasts swept away by this deluge (the May 4th cultural revolution) now carving new channels, a new destiny for China.

Besides being involved with the May 4th movement, Mao Tsetung continued to select students for the work and study program in France. But instead of selection by intellectual ability, he recruited on the basis of ideas, enthusiasm, radicalism. He urged the formation of investigation teams among the students, to go among the people and report on actual conditions. And he began a revolt against Chang Ching-yao, the provincial governor, who seems to have been an extremely corrupt and evil man.

An article penned by Mao *On Radicalism,* calling for revolution as the only way out, made him many followers but also many enemies. The article was prompted by Bertrand Russell's lecture in Changsha in October 1919, which helped the formation of right-wing groups advocating "orderly reform." Mao stated in this article that armed struggle was the only way a revolution could succeed.

Among the enthusiasts who wrote approvingly to Mao when this article appeared was a young man named Jen Pi-shih. Born in 1904, a modest, clever, dedicated student, Jen Pi-shih would become in later years one of Mao's staunchest adherents. *On Radicalism* caused Chang Ching-yao to ban Mao's weekly in October 1919, and to disband the Student Union. Mao then led a demonstration against Chang Ching-yao, calling him a pro-Japanese traitor. He contributed articles to another student paper, *New Hunan,* which started that spring, to the newspaper *Ta Kung Pao,* to magazines. He continued his fiery denunciations of "all warlords and traitors," including of course Chang Ching-yao. *New Hunan* was suppressed in December 1919.

In the *Hsiang Chiang Review, New Hunan,* and other papers, Mao's articles covered the whole spectrum of change, of revolt against tradition and the breakthrough of a generation into a new, wide, modern world. He covered international and national events, literature, the "reorganization of thinking," vice, prostitution, arranged marriage. He proposed revolutionary solutions in a vigorous, exciting, if somewhat florid prose. The first issue of the *Hsiang River Review* contained his article *The Women's Revolutionary Army,* which evoked a tremendous response from the girls' schools and led to the establishment of "an alliance of women students" to "fight imperialism, militarism and capitalism, and all superstition." Mao called upon women to "sweep away all the goblins that destroy physical and spiritual freedom." Teng Chung-hsia, another Mao devotee at Peking University, republished an article of Mao's in which he urged that all problems be investigated before they came up for discussion or belief. "Without investigation no right to speak," * a basic tenet of Mao's, is endlessly dinned into every individual in China today. Mao wrote and published nine articles in *Ta Kung Pao* from the 16th to the 28th of November, against arranged marriage and the double standard of chastity. The suicide of a young girl, Miss Chao, who killed herself rather than be forced into an arranged marriage, horrified him. In *Advice to Boys and Girls on Marriage Problems,* he wrote: "This tragic event in the blood-filled city of Changsha should stir them to the very depths of their soul, and make them totally aware." (The word "aware," or its American counterpart "consciousness-raising," recurs often in Mao's writings of that time.)

---

* This phrase was coined by Mao in 1930. See *Oppose Book Worship,* May 1930. *Selected Readings from the Works of Mao Tsetung* (English edition Peking 1967).

Mao was never to forget that women, "who have more oppression on their backs than men, for whereas men have three mountains of exploitation, women have four, for man also exploits her," are "a tremendous potential revolutionary force." He had seen what girl students could do; had watched the lightning speed of their change; he would make of woman's emancipation a revolutionary goal. At the time of the Great Leap Forward in 1958, and again during the cultural revolution from 1966 to 1969, the reprints of his early articles on women's liberation circulated again; the role of woman in revolutionizing society would form the subject of many articles in 1970. Mao believes that man cannot be liberated unless woman is also liberated; today, untiringly, he still continues to back woman's liberation, through the continuing Revolution of China.

On May 4, 1939, Mao was to say: "On this very day, twenty years ago, a movement of great historical significance was begun in China, the May 4th movement in which the students participated. What role have the Chinese youth played since the May 4th movement? They have played the role of vanguard . . . [that is] to take the lead, to stand at the head of revolutionary ranks. . . . But this is not enough because it is not yet the main force. Who then constitutes the main force? None other than the broad masses of workers and peasants. . . . The young intellectuals and students of China must go into the midst of the masses and workers and peasants who constitute 90 percent of the population. . . . It is only if the young students and the young workers and peasants unite that they can become a powerful youth movement. . . . *The ultimate line of demarcation between the revolutionary intellectuals on the one hand and the nonrevolutionary and counterrevolutionary intellectuals on the other lies in whether they are willing to, and actually do, unite with and integrate with the masses of workers and peasants.*" And today, more than fifty years later, "integration with the masses" is the ultimate test for all intellectuals and students in the restructuring of education which is taking place in China.

But in that October 1919, the irate Hunan provincial governor called a meeting of all student representatives, some sixty of them. Mao Tsetung went with them, although he was a teacher. Governor Chang Ching-yao started by hurling abuse at the students. How dare they take up politics! Instead of studying! He also shouted at the women student representatives, threatening to "cut off their heads." One of the girls began to weep. Mao Tsetung said, loud enough to be heard: "Do not be afraid; what he says is not worth a dog's bark." (Laughter.)

In December 1919 Chang Ching-yao sent soldiers to disperse students making a bonfire of Japanese goods. Mao then wrote a manifesto calling for Chang Ching-yao's overthrow; 13,000 students signed it. He organized a march on the provincial government; wrote to Sun Yatsen in Kuangchow and to the Student Union in Peking urging denunciation of Chang Ching-yao; organized a strike of all the students in the schools of Changsha.

Chang Ching-yao, who now hated Mao so much he could neither sleep nor eat, decided to have him murdered, probably by hired thugs. The New People's Study Society had now organized an "anti-militarist League for the Reconstruction of Hunan Province," demanding autonomy — separation of Hunan from the Peking pro-Japanese government — and the ousting of the governor. Mao sponsored himself to go to Peking to denounce Chang Ching-yao, traveling as a journalist for Hunan newspapers and magazines. He arrived in Wuhan in January 1920. There he issued a statement calling for the overthrow of Chang. Reaching Peking in February, he renewed his ties with Li Ta-chao, with Professor Yang Chang-chi, with other friends. He stayed about two months in Peking, trying to get people interested in the Hunan autonomy movement. But provincial preoccupations were very secondary in Peking. By then, the May 4th movement had gone underground, was giving birth to something far more radical.

Mao's new job as a journalist kept him in funds, gave him enough to live. His friends, among them Teng Chung-hsia, with whom he had been corresponding since he left Peking, gathered round him in the room he rented in North Avenue, to the north of the city. It was a poor district, far from the university, but it was better than the accommodation he had had on his first visit. Mao continued to visit factories, the railway yards, where he discussed Marxism with the workers. He continued reading in the library of Peking University. He now read the *Communist Manifesto,* Engels, Kautsky, Kirkup's *History of Socialism*. He saw again Yang Kai-hui, and it was at that time that they decided to become engaged. Yang Kai-hui was also studying Marxism. She too had taken part in political agitation.

During Mao's absence from Changsha, however, the New People's Study Society began to split. Mao wrote to the society advising his friends to organize into small Marxist study groups; he was himself going through a time of decision and felt he could not immediately return.

Li Ta-chao now looked at the erstwhile assistant librarian with new respect. He asked Mao Tsetung to help him; Marxist study groups were not enough, there must be more. The idea of establishing a Chinese Communist Party was already in the air. Li knew that Mao Tsetung was an excellent organizer and had great influence on the students.

Mao spent these weeks in Peking making up his mind. It was a big decision he was about to take, and he studied the problem very seriously and solemnly. He read, he walked, he thought; it was not something to be undertaken without total dedication. "Once I had accepted Marxism as the correct interpretation of history, I did not afterwards waver." He would not change, once his mind was made up; and in this decision he was helped by the love of Yang Kai-hui, also to become a Party member. Together they discussed his dedication and hers. And in that bitter winter, they thought of a new spring for the world. As they pledged themselves to each other, they also pledged themselves to the Revolution.

It was clear to both of them that their lives should be together. But they also realized what this political decision they were both to make would mean: little time to love; never able to forget everything for love alone; a lifetime of hard work, revolutionary action, sacrifice, separation, possibly early and painful death. The beautiful Yang Kai-hui was just twenty years old. And then in February, after a brief illness, her father Yang Chang-chi died of pneumonia, and Yang Kai-hui and her mother left Peking to return to Changsha.

Mao Tsetung, too, now left Peking, but to go to Shanghai to see Chen Tu-hsiu, to confer with him on the organization of a Chinese Communist Party. He sold his winter clothes to pay for the train fare, arrived in Shanghai about mid-March, and there met Chen Tu-hsiu for the second time.

5

Dedication

Mao Tsetung has left us no account of his impressions of Shanghai, the biggest city in China, the one where foreign domination was only too grimly obvious through its squalid factories, its terrible slums, the poverty which surrounded those oases of luxury and wealth where foreigners lived. We can imagine his difficulty in understanding the sibilant Shanghai dialect, the anger he felt at the Sikh policemen beating up Chinese coolies, the rancor of being treated as an inferior in his own country. In later years he was to refer with searing bitterness to the conditions which were considered "normal" at the time. He himself now became a "laborer," subject to grueling exploitation. He worked in a laundry to support himself, washing, ironing and delivering linen and clothes.

There is no record of where Mao lived during these four months, but he knew the overcrowded tenements; the miseries of the overworked and hunger-driven workers were his, as he sweated in the hot steam of wooden tubs for twelve to fourteen hours a day. He delivered the clothes, bed sheets, household linen washed and ironed overnight, wrapped in white cloth to keep them clean. The houses and hotels the laundry worked for were far from the slums where the actual work was done, and a coolie was expected to pay his own transport, or else to walk. Some of the laundry workers walked over ten miles a day, dragging a handcart or staggering under piles of sheets. "The difficult part of my job is not washing but delivery. . . . Tram tickets are so expensive and most of my earnings have to be spent on them." Of the twelve to fifteen dollars a month he received as pay for this monstrous expenditure of physical energy, about eight dollars went into tram fares. He grew spectral thin; yet he continued to meet small groups, to attend secret meetings at night with Chen Tu-hsiu and other Shanghai Marxists.

In May 1920 a pre-Communist nucleus was organized in Shanghai, as well as a youth section known as the Socialist Youth Corps. The recruitment among workers was fairly successful. Mao's correspondence with Tsai Ho-sen, still in France, refers to the need for a nucleus organization.

We do not know to what extent he discussed his ideas with the then prestigious scholar and radical Chen Tu-hsiu. According to some biographers, his sole purpose in going to Shanghai to meet Chen was to get his support to oust the Hunan governor Chang Ching-yao and enlist Chen in the cause of autonomy for Hunan province. We do not know whether he still had some lingering idea of achieving this aim as well; but the lack of interest in this provincial cause both in Peking and in Shanghai must have shown him its futility.

Chen Tu-hsiu, famous then, later infamous in Communist Party annals, was the typical radical intellectual of those days of turmoil. Imprisoned for 83 days for distributing handbills on the street in June 1919, he came out of jail in September a national hero for the youth generation, declaring he had not changed his ideas. By then, the intelligentsia was splitting up into three main factions, and each of these fragmented into small groups, all of which claimed to be the answer to China's salvation. There was a very large, so-called moderate group, which represented a certain liberalism but was afraid of decisive action. A right-wing group, definitely abjuring Marxism, pledged itself to "orderly reform," without changing anything. There remained what looked like a discouraged minority of "hotheads" and "radicals"; among them Chen Tu-hsiu. But this was only the pellicle lidding reality — the reality of a whole generation of the young who had changed, and the change affected boys and girls of twelve to fifteen as well, a source of revolutionaries to be.

In Wuhan, for instance, there was Tung Pi-wu, the veteran of three revolutions. He, like Hsu Te-li, "lived through many ages in the life of China." * Born in 1886, he had become a classics scholar, had since 1911 spent every day of his life in revolutionary work, first in Sun Yatsen's organization, and later, influenced by the Russian Revolution, he also began to study Marxism. He was only one of many, older or younger, affected by these so seemingly impersonal yet so profoundly soul-moving events in which they were participating. There also was Lin Piao, only twelve in 1919, precocious, self-up-

* Said by Tung Pi-wu himself to Nym Wales (Helen Foster Snow) in 1936; see her *Red Dust* (Stanford 1952).

rooted and, like the schoolchildren of that time, also changed by the Revolution. There were others all over China — the names are thousands — and so many were to die, some others to betray. Looking further north, there was Chou En-lai, born in 1898. As students in Nankai University near Tientsin, Chou En-lai and his wife to be, Teng Ying-chao, had formed an Awakening Society, a May 4th radical group, in September 1919. The Awakening Society bore a marked resemblance to Mao's New People's Study Society. Chou En-lai wrote and published and did political work, for which he was jailed in 1920, just when Mao was going to Shanghai. In far-off Szechuan there were Chu Teh and Chen Yi. Unknown to each other, they too were "looking for a road," as Mao was. Chu Teh seemed most unlikely material for a Communist. He was born in 1886, had received some education, and enrolled in a "new learning" military academy in Yunnan in 1909. He had taken part in the 1911 Revolution. In the subsequent period of chaos, when militarists of all shades and descriptions rampaged in confused civil wars, he had become a minor militarist. Caught "in a net of warlordism," he was yet searching for truth. A friend gave him revolutionary literature to read, and Chu, by 1922, set off to study abroad and "find truth." This was to bring him to Germany, and to Communism. Chen Yi's road to the Party was similarly wayward. Of a scholar's family, he had left for France under the work and study program, and earned his living as dishwasher while studying there.

According to present-day writings, Mao Tsetung is the founder of the Chinese Communist Party. No one else is mentioned in the exhibition halls through which daily trail thousands of workers, peasants, soldiers, schoolchildren in all China's main cities. But Russian and Western sources dwell heavily on this birth as a Russian-engendered one. Which is the correct version? The CCP was a Chinese creation, but Russian encouragement cannot be denied. "The salvos of the October Revolution . . . brought us Marxism-Leninism," wrote Mao Tsetung.

Two weeks after the October Revolution (1917), Lenin had published a declaration to all countries of Asia, relinquishing unjustified privileges and territorial gains which czarist invasions had acquired. This, where China was concerned, represented a considerable amount of territory, more than 1.1 million square miles wrested by czarist expansionism in the eighteenth and nineteenth centuries. In early 1918 Chinese officials of the Peking government held talks in Moscow with the Soviet government regarding their common frontiers and previous czarist occupation of Chinese territory. These talks were suspended under pressure by the Western powers upon the northern warlord coalition. The coalition of southern warlords, which supported Sun Yatsen, was also approached by Lenin's government. Russian foreign commissar Chicherin, a brilliant, able diplomat who had met Sun in Europe in 1916 during one of Sun's travels abroad to raise funds for the Tung Meng Hui, wrote to Sun Yatsen in 1918. In July 1919 the Soviet government issued a declaration on China (the Karakhan Manifesto) declaring that "the Soviet Government has renounced the conquests made by the Czarist government which deprived China of Manchuria and other areas." Abolition of all privileges conferred by the unequal treaties and an offer of assistance to fight imperialist domination were embodied in this document.* The Karakhan declaration was ignored by the northern warlord coalition government in Peking, but was published by Sun Yatsen's southern government in Kuangchow. It had a deep effect upon the students in China. The popularity of Marxism during the May 4th movement was also due to this timely publication.

In April 1920 three members of the Communist Party of the Soviet Union arrived in Peking, where they held talks with Li Ta-chao. Their names were Voitinsky, Yang Ming-chai, and Sneevliet, alias Maring (Ma-lin).† They were all three members of the Comintern.‡ They then proceeded to Shanghai to meet Chen Tu-hsiu and other Shanghai intellectuals. It was Chen who, in May, summoned a conference and organized a "nucleus" or pre-Communist Party group. In May and again in September, the Soviet government again attempted to hold talks with the Peking government. But a China allied to the Soviet Union was intensely alarming to the colonial powers; the warlords were encouraged to expand their armies and to practice repression against "Bolshevism." The talks failed.

Mao Tsetung must have known of these Russian initiatives, of the contacts with Li Ta-chao and Chen Tu-hsiu. But there is no record of his having personally met the Russian delegation at any time, either in Peking or in Shanghai, though he was in Peking in February and in Shanghai in April and May. The odds are, however, that he did attend the May conference in Shanghai, and he seems also to

* Allen Whiting *Soviet Policies in China 1917–1924* (Stanford 1968).
† For an account of Sneevliet in China, see Dov Bing "Sneevliet and the Early Years of the CCP," *China Quarterly* no. 48 (October-December 1971).
‡ The Third Communist International, founded in 1919, known for short as Comintern.

have returned briefly to Shanghai in September to attend another, together with Tung Pi-wu. "By the summer of 1920," said Mao, "I had become in theory and to some extent in action a Marxist. And from this time I considered myself a Marxist."

In July the governor of Hunan, Chang Ching-yao, was expelled in yet another warlord war, and Mao Tsetung returned to his province. He was for a short while at home, and began recruiting for his own province's pre-Communist group among his own family, starting with his two brothers and his adopted sister. He then went back to Changsha to continue recruiting.

Because Mao was acquainted with the new headmaster of the Changsha Normal College, he obtained the post of director of the Hsiu Yeh Primary School, and also taught one class at the college. This advancement, after so many years of dire poverty, provided a salary more adequate than the previous pittance. Mao Tsetung rented a small isolated cottage outside the city, among vegetable fields, called Clear Water Pool House. The house cost twelve dollars a month rent. It was an ideal venue for secret meetings. Yang Kai-hui and her mother were now in Changsha, and that winter Mao Tsetung married Yang Kai-hui. They lived here during the year and a half that Mao was director of the Hsiu Yeh Primary School.

Once again Mao became gaunt with work, but he also knew for the first time domestic happiness with Yang Kai-hui. Those who saw Yang Kai-hui still speak of her quiet beauty, her intelligence, her devotion; she and Mao Tsetung were regarded as an "ideal" pair. She became a Communist Party member in 1922, and a leader of a youth movement in self-education. Often she left home, going on unrecorded missions to Shanghai and elsewhere for the Party. There were two sons of the marriage. One of them, Mao An-ying, born in 1929, died in November 1950 in Korea, a volunteer in the Korean war. The other, Mao An-ching, is today an accountant in a commune. Mao does not believe in promoting his relatives, and the scarcity of information, even about Yang Kai-hui, though understandable because of the dangerous secret work Party members did, is deliberate. Yang Kai-hui was arrested in the Clear Water Pool House in 1930, during the White Terror of Chiang Kai-shek, tortured and executed for refusing to denounce her husband and abjure her principles.

Among Chinese students abroad the need for a Communist Party was as evident as it was in China. Mao kept in touch with the precursor group now started in France. The French precursor Communist Party group was created by Chou En-lai. Tsai Ho-sen, his wife Hsiang Ching-yu, his sister Tsai Chang, her husband Li Fu-chun, and Chen Yi joined the French group; so did Li Li-san, the noncommittal Hunanese, and other worker-students. In Russia a pre-Communist group was formed that year by Chinese students, and another was created in Germany, to which Chu Teh, the ex-warlord from Szechuan, would adhere.

By October 1920 Mao had set up a Russian affairs study group and a work and study program for students to go to Russia, as well as a Marxist (pre-Communist) group in Changsha. Tung Pi-wu established a Marxist group in Wuhan in 1921, to which Lin Piao adhered. Others were formed in Kuangchow and Tsinan in November 1920. By April 1921 there were nine such Chinese groups: Shanghai, Peking, Changsha, Wuhan, Kuangchow, Tsinan, Paris, Berlin and Moscow, and one in Japan.

In December 1920 Mao established a Hunan branch of the Socialist Youth Corps, and by 1922 it was the largest such group in China, with 2,000 members. One of the members was Liu Shao-chi, also a Hunanese, born in 1898, who had also attended Changsha Normal College, and joined the New People's Study Society in 1919. It was through this connection that Liu Shao-chi was selected for the work and study program set up by Mao Tsetung for students to go to Russia. In the winter of 1920 he left for Vladivostok, from there to reach Moscow, where he would study, and join the Moscow precursor group of the Chinese Communist Party in 1921.

During his tenure of office the Hunan governor Chang Ching-yao had levied extortionate taxes, sold all the copper cash of the province to Japan, and issued paper money instead. Rapid inflation had resulted, and great misery for the average family. The movement for the autonomy of Hunan province was not dead; in July 1920 Mao Tsetung and Ho Shu-heng published a statement in the name of the League for the Reconstruction of Hunan Province demanding abolition of the post of military governor, the disarming and disbanding of warlords and their armies, and the establishment of a "democratic, autonomous provincial government, with elections and a constitution." The petition was signed by 377 people.

Freed of Chang Ching-yao, Mao was able to extend his activities. He was beginning to show his flair for rallying, on a very broad base, a large number of people by involvement with all kinds of issues, apparently unrelated, but actually all spelling concern with social and political change. At the end of November 1920 a new governor, Chao Heng-ti, the appointee of the new warlord in power (Tan Yen-kai, who once had been ousted as governor by Yuan Shih-kai) * assembled the heads of all Changsha schools and promised a liberal and generous policy. He swore to clean up corruption and to reform the currency. Mao Tsetung published articles in *Ta Kung Pao* urging the people of Hunan to take part in politics and make their will known. "Power comes from the people, and should be in their hands." Whether this pleased the new governor is not known; very soon Chao was to hate Mao as bitterly as his predecessor Chang had done.

Mao's most important work now was recruiting potential members for a Communist Party. In all the societies and associations he had formed since May 1919, there were members of his previous New People's Study Society, men and women he had worked with and trusted. "We must choose very carefully, reliable people, sincere comrades," wrote Mao to Tsai Ho-sen in Paris. He had been able to persuade Tan Yen-kai to preside at the opening ceremony of the Cultural Bookstore which he, with several other radicals, started in Changsha, and to dedicate a calligraphic signboard for the store. Like most Chinese militarists, Tan Yen-kai was proud of his calligraphy and pleased with the opportunity to show his erudition and "progressive" character. Because of this patronage, funds became available for the bookstore and it was held above suspicion for a while. (This illustrates another facet of Mao's character, the knack of utilizing people, all kinds of people, even the most unlikely, in pursuit of his aims. It was the same with his choice of the Clear Water Pool House — a good house, a landlord's house, hence also above suspicion.) Through the Cultural Bookstore a network passing Marxist literature throughout China's southern cities was established. By the end of the year it had half a dozen branches in Hunan besides contact with the Social Benefit Bookstore in Hupei. It acted for years as a clandestine post office and liaison center. "Education is self-education, we must provide books to stimulate self-awareness," Mao wrote. The bookstore fulfilled this aim.

Mao Tsetung and Yang Kai-hui then set on foot an education movement, starting with evening schools for laborers, craftsmen, stonemasons. Once again the scope went beyond education; the mass education movement they would propagate in 1922 would be

* See pages 45–46.

based on labor unions throughout the province, with workers' clubs and night schools. Organization depended on education, education was also organization, Mao told his friends. The work of a revolutionary was also that of a teacher; all events were lessons given by life, and analysis must be applied to all situations to elevate one's own understanding. Mao's gift of persuading and rallying others to work with him was now developing. He could delegate authority and not be niggardly in doing so, but always he would keep his aim in mind. His enemies would accuse him of making of other people and discarding them. But for Mao Tsetung what counted was the final goal of the Revolution, and if he used others, he also used himself unsparingly.

The mass education movement was an attempt at forming a broad united front, a grand alliance of the masses; it involved uniting a number of small associations and groups, guilds of stonemasons, printers, even workers in the government mint. The tenacious Mao had friends everywhere, even in government offices, and through these personal contacts he promoted political indoctrination. He wrote new educational textbooks, starting lessons with words used by miners, stonecutters, in their work. The first lesson taught the words *labor, worker, exploitation.* Arithmetic problems were based on the daily living experiences of the workers. Reading texts utilized the "one thousand word" scheme devised during the May 4, 1919 cultural revolution to teach people to read rapidly.

By 1922 there were 30,000 to 40,000 workers and small artisans in this movement. A weekly, *Labor World,* which in turn gave birth to a small monthly called *Communist Monthly,* started publication on November 7, 1920, the day Mao organized a celebration for the third anniversary of the October Revolution. "From this time on, I became more and more convinced that only mass political power, secured through mass action, could guarantee the realization of dynamic reforms." The weekly *Labor World* was suppressed after four issues. Nevertheless, a spate of Marxist publications and translations were appearing; all were on sale at the Cultural Bookstore. It is significant that Lenin's *The State and Revolution,* admired by Li Tachao and also by Mao, was carried in *Labor Monthly.* The Cultural Bookstore would usually sell 5,000 copies a week of such periodicals. *Communist Monthly* was also very popular while it lasted.

Mao was again in conflict with authority, this time with the "liberal" governor Chao Heng-ti. In 1921, workers of a cotton mill in Changsha went on strike because of the inhuman working conditions then prevalent. They struck for a ten-hour day and a day's holiday a month. Chao Heng-ti suppressed the strike; the workers were beaten up by soldiers. Chao Heng-ti then banned the student organizations and labor unions. "As soon as he got power," said Mao, "he suppressed the democratic movement with great energy." Mao Tsetung led a demonstration against the governor and the provincial parliament, "landlords and gentry appointed by the militarists." "This struggle ended in our pulling down the scrolls and banners erected in compliment to Chao, full of nonsensical and extravagant phrases."

But all Mao's activities were governed by the project which would claim his whole life, the creation of the Communist Party of China. They were the proving ground, the experimental theater for what would become the decisive political grouping in China's history.

One night in May 1921 Mao Tsetung and his friend Ho Shu-heng left Changsha secretly for Shanghai. They traveled incognito and in disguise, going as traders. The precautions they took, the secrecy surrounding their departure, were not overdone. They were the earliest to arrive of the several delegates entrusted with the founding of the Chinese Communist Party.

Those who came later, to meet in that simmering hot summer for the same purpose, were mostly young; their average age was twenty-six. Some had experience of organization, like Mao; others nothing more than a vague smattering of Marxism. Among them would be opportunists and traitors, but at that time it looked as if a single dedication animated them. They had yet to fight their first battles as Communists, and chiefly against themselves. No one could then predict the outcome, either of their purpose or of their own lives.

A few days after Mao, Tung Pi-wu arrived from Wuhan. Both Li Ta-chao and Chen Tu-hsiu also seem to have paid visits to the Shanghai organizing group during May and June, but neither was present when the Congress formally opened on the night of June 30, to start its work on July 1, 1921.

Each province where Marxist study groups had been organized sent two delegates to this First Congress. The Chinese students in Japan sent one young student, Chou Fu-hai, who was later to betray the Communist Party and join the Japanese during the Sino-Japanese war. Hupei province sent Chen Tan-chiu and Tung Pi-wu from the city of Wuhan; Shanghai delegates were Li Han-chun and Li Ta; while Chen Kung-po and Pao Hui-seng came from Kuangchow. Shantung sent Teng En-ming and Wang Chun-mei. Both Teng and

Wang were slaughtered in 1927–1928. Chang Kuo-tao, whom Mao said he had met in Peking University, and Liu Jen-chung represented Peking, and therefore the province of Hopei. The delegates from Hunan, Mao Tsetung and Ho Shu-heng, stayed all through the proceedings. If we look through the origins of these delegates, we find that Mao and Ho alone had a rural background; the others were city-bred.

Two delegates from the Comintern are said to have attended the opening of the First Congress on June 30. One was Sneevliet, alias Maring, or Ma-lin in Chinese. The other was Lizouski, a Soviet worker. Since no official history of the Chinese Revolution has yet been approved and promulgated by the Chinese Communist Party, they are not mentioned in the explanations given today; but then these explanations are regarded as nondefinitive and nonofficial. Even if two Russian delegates were present at the opening ceremony, they did not attend all of the subsequent meetings, especially when in the middle of the proceedings the venue had to be changed.

It was originally intended that Chen Tu-hsiu should be chairman of the Congress; but he remained in Kuangchow and sent messages through his representative Li Han-chun. The minutes of the First Congress have been lost. Much of what happened is obscure. An account was given by Tung Pi-wu to Nym Wales * in 1936, when both she and Edgar Snow were visiting the Chinese Communists in Yenan.

The Congress opened at the Po-Ai Girls School, situated in the French Concession and at that date, in the summer holiday, empty save for a cook-watchman. The delegates met on the second floor of the two-story building. The cook-watchman bought food and prepared meals for the guests. The cook noticed, however, that they spoke different dialects, some of which he could not understand. It was not possible to keep the goings and comings secret in spite of the precautions taken; very swiftly the secret police were alerted.

The Congress lasted four days in Shanghai,† according to Chen Tan-chiu, writing his reminiscences in the October 1936 issue of the Comintern publication. He recalled that "serious disagreement arose" between "various tendencies"; in fact, the Chinese Communist Party from its inception was far from monolithic; its delegates

---

* Nym Wales *Red Dust* (Stanford 1952).
† Four days in Shanghai, but several days more were spent in a boat on the South Lake near Shanghai.

fell roughly into three groups representing three different tendencies as to policies and methods.

One tendency, subsequently labeled the "right" wing, headed by Li Han-chun, who spoke for Chen Tu-hsiu, considered the Chinese working class "too young," "not ready," "too backward and stupid" to organize a "vanguard of the proletariat" Communist Party. Li transmitted Chen Tu-hsiu's marked aversion to the phrase "dictatorship of the proletariat." Chen's view was that it was best to organize a Marxist club for debate, and to advocate reform. Li Ta and Chen Kung-po upheld this line and voted for it. Li Ta, who seems to have withdrawn early from the Party, died of illness in Shanghai in 1968; Chen Kung-po was to become one of Chiang Kai-shek's adherents and to distinguish himself as a rabid anti-Communist.

The extreme "left" line, which would plague the young Party for years, was represented by Liu Jen-chung and Chang Kuo-tao. They had gobbled theory at the expense of common sense and realism, considered the "dictatorship of the proletariat" the immediate aim of the organization, opposed all legal forms of struggle. They advocated a "closed door policy"; that is, no united front with any other party, the creation of a sectarian, rigid, dogmatic small group relying entirely on "the Chinese proletariat" and rejecting everyone else. They denounced Sun Yatsen and his party, now renamed the Kuomintang or Nationalist Party, as "criminal" and "counterrevolutionary." Pao Hui-seng also supported these views.

It is a pity that no true record of the wrangling that went on exists; and secret police documents subsequently utilized by scholars, as well as Chang Kuo-tao's own memoirs, must be sifted with caution. No record of what Mao really said then has come down to us. All we know for certain is that he supported neither of these two lines, was inclined to a united front policy, and from the start earned the animosity of Chang Kuo-tao.

On the fourth day, as some of the delegates gathered at Li Han-chun's lodging for a group discussion, a suspicious person "in a long gown" appeared in a neighboring room. He said he had come to look for the Association of Social Organizations and its chairman, named Wan. There was no chairman by that name, and the association was three doors away. The delegates quickly left the lodging, and a few minutes later the police and nine plainclothesmen arrived. They ransacked Li Han-chun's room, but all documents had been removed. The delegates did not dare return to the Po-Ai school. They had to flee, but decided to continue the work elsewhere. How could this be done? Someone had a bright idea. They would hire a holiday boat on the South Lake, about eighty miles from Shanghai, close to the town of Chia Hsing. This was a favorite beauty spot, with soft hills and willows, a scene of great beauty where scholars often went for picnics and to sample the famous Chia Hsing wine. A summer holiday picnic was a normal pastime. To South Lake, by separate routes, the delegates went.

And there, after another several days of dispute, the extreme left line predicated by Chang Kuo-tao gained the upper hand. The resolution adopted was against collaboration with Sun Yatsen's Kuomintang and for a closed door policy, to keep membership "secret and pure." Yet the Comintern, in its Second Congress in 1920, had stated that alliance between Communist parties and "revolutionary bourgeois parties" (a term under which Sun's party figured) in a common front against imperialism was the keynote of the struggle to come. This was Lenin's thesis, repeated at the Third Congress of the Comintern in June–July 1921. At this Third Congress a thirty-seven-member Chinese delegation, including both incipient Communists and Kuomintang representatives, was present; a "temporary and vigilant" alliance with the Chinese bourgeoisie had been suggested; Lenin's words of 1912 calling Sun Yatsen's party "revolutionary although a bourgeois party" were recalled. But the young Chinese Communist Party in its First Congress voted against it, though the vote was not overwhelming.

Mao cast a contrary vote. He opposed the "erroneous, extreme left viewpoint, hostile to accepting intellectuals in the Party" which Chang Kuo-tao proposed. The term "yellow intellectual class" was then coined by Chang Kuo-tao.* This extreme left line made it difficult to extend membership in the first two years of the CCP. Mao, it is reported, also spoke against the right-wing adherents of Chen Tu-hsiu who advocated that no party should be constituted, only a debating club. In line with his article *The Great Union of the Masses of the People,* fresh from brushes in Hunan, seasoned with organizing experience, he advocated following the Leninist line, but was in the minority. Chang Kuo-tao carried the day.

The First Congress of the CCP, though it refused cooperation with Sun Yatsen's party, the Kuomintang, decided to make monthly reports to the Comintern and to send delegates to its congresses. An-

---

* At the Congress of the Peoples of the Orient, held in November 1921 in Irkutsk, then in Leningrad in January 1922, Chang Kuo-tao attended. There a common front and alliance with the Kuomintang were again proposed.

other resolution taken at the First Congress was to create a secretariat of the All-China Labor League in charge of labor. But a secretariat in charge of the peasantry was not set up till some years later, in
spite of Mao's suggestion that this should forthwith be done. The
goal set by the young immature Party was "to overthrow the capitalist classes with the revolutionary leadership of the proletariat." The
"dictatorship of the proletariat" was to be immediately adopted.
"Our party should stand up on behalf of the proletariat, and should
allow no relationship with other party or groups," said Chang Kuo-
tao. At that time there were in the whole of China fifty-seven Marxists. The largest single group was in Hunan, where there were sixteen.

Today, of that First Congress, only Mao Tsetung and Tung Pi-wu
remain. Ho Shu-heng, Wang Chun-mei, Li Han-chun, Teng En-ming
were slaughtered during the long, bloody decades of the Chinese
Revolution; Li Ta died in 1968. The others became renegades to the
Party they had helped to set up in such dramatic circumstances in
July 1921.

The Central Committee elected at the First Congress was headed
by Chen Tu-hsiu as secretary-general with Chang Kuo-tao and Li Ta
to assist him. This was the embryonic Politburo. The central headquarters of the Party would remain in Shanghai and in the French
Concession for some years. The provincial Party organizations
would receive directives from the Central Committee.

Mao Tsetung returned to Hunan at the end of July 1921. By August he had set up the first Communist trade union for workers. In
October he became secretary of the Hunan Party branch. In 1922 he
was made chairman of the Hunan branch of the All-China Labor
Federation, which was created that year, with headquarters also in
Shanghai. His own immediate family — two brothers, adopted sister, wife — swiftly followed him into the Party. All would lose their
lives for their cause.

There has been a strange reticence among some biographers to
describe Mao as a labor organizer and trade union leader. His years
of political agitation among workers from 1921 to 1925, the schools
for workers he organized, have been disregarded; the picture of a
peasant leader, organizer of rural bases and of peasant guerillas, is
the one promoted instead. Perhaps the obscurity surrounding this
phase of his activities was deliberate, as is now being said in China.
An attempt by those in opposition to him, especially Liu Shao-chi,
to present themselves as leaders of the "proletariat" in contradis-

tinction to Mao the "peasant organizer" was very evident during the early 1960's. Why Western biographers also maintain this singular omission is less comprehensible.

To build the first workers' Party cell in Hunan, Mao Tsetung went to the coal mines of Anyuan in southern Hunan, thus following the line of "the Party as the vanguard of the working class." The most famous painting in China today is of Mao Tsetung as a young man going to Anyuan. This picture was commissioned by Chiang Ching, the present wife of Chairman Mao, and is based on the recollections of the Anyuan miners themselves. A reproduction was even hung (by mistake) in the Vatican in 1969 as "a young Chinese missionary"!

The Anyuan coal mines were opened in 1898 by combined German and Japanese capital. In 1899 the Germans invested 400,000 marks to expand the coal mines; in 1913 Japanese capital led to further development. The living conditions of the workers at the Anyuan and Pinghsiang mines were typical of the exploitation of the Chinese working class. They toiled fourteen to fifteen hours a day, for which they received 26 coppers (about eight cents). Not surprisingly, the first workers' strikes in China occurred here, in April 1905 and again during the Great Hunan Famine in 1906, when three million people died. In May 1913 and October 1915 there were more strikes, also during the May 4, 1919 movement. The production of coal at Anyuan was 806,330 tons in 1920; in 1925, after the big strikes, it fell to 386,230 tons. There were twenty-four churches, of various denominations, within a four-mile radius of the mines, but only one small clinic for the 6,000 workers. Anyuan, with its appalling conditions, was an ideal base for Communist propaganda.

To Anyuan Mao went on his first visit in 1921, dressed as an intellectual in a long gown, as the painting shows; but he did not keep the gown. He lodged with a worker's family at No. 44 in Eight Corner Well Lane, and as usual took copious notes on the intimate, heart-searching, unhurried long talks which later became the technique of Communist Party political workers. For centuries the scholar had lived in a world of abstractions. Mao was the first to go down a coal mine and live the reality of a worker's life, go down the pits, walk the coal shafts, experience physically what life was like. He calculated that per month each worker produced $70 worth of coal but received only $5 in wages.

In December 1921 Mao returned again to Anyuan with his brother Mao Tse-min, whom he was training in Party work, and they lodged in a small eating house. The first Anyuan Party cell was organized in a warehouse in January 1922 in Five Happiness Lane with seven miners, five of whom would be killed before 1931. In that same January 1922 Mao went to the city of Hengyang in South Hunan and organized a Party cell there at the Third Normal School, which had affiliations with the Normal College in Changsha. The railway workers on the Kuangchow-Hankow Railway at Hengyang and at Changsha also were organized into Party cells and Communist trade unions. All together, 12,000 workers were thus enrolled.

The establishment of workers' cooperatives at Anyuan in 1922 was an initiative taken by Mao's brother Mao Tse-min, who seems to have had a financial talent. One of the hardships inflicted upon the miners was the debt load they carried when purchasing in ordinary shops and the usurious terms of loans (30 to 50 percent per month). The cooperative idea was meant to relieve this situation, to provide shops at the mine where workers could get food on credit, and even to institute a small bank with easy terms for loans. Mao Tse-min ran the cooperative, but it was difficult to maintain, as there was no capital and a total hostility from the administration.

Mao Tsetung then set up a school for Anyuan workers, as he had done in Changsha. The miners were at first reticent. What was the use of a school when they spent their lives in the pits? He then conceived the idea of a day school for the children of the miners. This had a magic effect — the miners all wanted education for their children, and there were no schools for them. Mao brought a weekly paper from the Cultural Bookstore, through the medium of this school circulated it among the miners, and established a branch bookstore. He then tried to get the men to learn reading and writing; urged them to write their own articles in their own newspaper — a suggestion which stunned the hard-driven illiterates who worked naked and had almost come to accept their half-beast condition. But the suggestion caught on, and some of the survivors are today's most brilliant high-level officials and ambassadors.

Old miners still remember how Mao talked to them, how incredible it all seemed that an "educated" young man should go down in the pits, blacken his hands, crawl through the narrow tunnels where stunted waifs of ten or twelve pushed the coal carts, sit in their hovels, take notes of what they said, then tell them to take their fate in their own hands, to become masters of their destiny.* Mao made them recall how they had risen with the peasants, in the previous

* Personal interviews with Anyuan miners, 1970.

famines, against Japanese imperialism in 1915. "History is in your hands," said Mao Tsetung. "History is yours to make." After Mao had left, his brother remained. In May 1922 a workers' club was established in Anyuan.

Mao Tsetung's activity among the Anyuan miners was based on a concept to be given nationwide propagation in the Great Proletarian Cultural Revolution: *Revolutionization of the proletariat by itself, through awareness, political education, action, organization.* Hence his action in Anyuan is a model. Both there and in Pinghsiang the workers were to become a source of future Party cadres. Mao Tsetung's stature as a leader of the proletariat, not of the peasantry alone, rests upon the work he began with the coal miners, which received no publicity in China until 1967.

The workers' club, founded to give the workers education in the form of lectures, reading newspapers, and so on, was in late summer to be put under the direction of Li Li-san, appointed by the Politburo in Shanghai. Mao's work was commended as "of great value," and Li Li-san was sent, as was later Liu Shao-chi, to reinforce this working-class nucleus of potential Communist cadres.

Li Li-san was the young Hunanese student who some years before had come to see Mao when he advertised for recruits for his New People's Study Society, and of whom Mao said: "Our friendship never developed." Li was born in the county of Liling, in Hunan, in 1899; after studying in Changsha, in 1918 he had joined classes organized in Peking by the work and study group preparing to go to France. While Mao Tsetung had elected not to leave China, Li Li-san went to France and remained till 1921, thus missing the May 4th movement. In France he adhered to the Socialist Study Group promoted by Chou En-lai, Tsai Ho-sen and Tsai Chang. In early 1922 he returned to Shanghai and was appointed to work in the All-China Labor Federation secretariat. His work in Anyuan was to cooperate with Mao.

Communists are supposed to have a dedication to a cause above private feelings. This is not always the case, for it seems that some of the intellectuals who joined the CCP never got rid of private inclinations and personal resentment. Jealousy plays a role in the emergence or attrition of personalities. Li Li-san's hostility to Mao, already in bud in 1917, developed as time went on. Perhaps Anyuan was a turning point in this respect, both for him and for Liu Shao-chi. Both were to follow policies radically different from Mao's.

Mao sent Chiang Hsien-yun, one of his recruits and a member of the Socialist Youth Corps of Hunan, to help in Anyuan when the membership of the club swelled from a few hundred to over 60 percent of the total number of workers. Mao was busy with the mass education movement, with organizing a club of railway workers at Changsha, at Hengyang. Railway workers' unions, Communist-controlled, were being set up in the north to south railways between Peking and Wuhan, and between Wuhan and Kuangchow. Mao journeyed to Liling and Pinghsiang, both mining areas, ostensibly to inspect schools (was he not a director of a school?) but actually to set up labor unions and to organize Party cells. Thus he spun a web of Party cells throughout the province in all the key industrial enterprises.

In July 1922 the Second Congress of the CCP was held in Hangchow, near Shanghai. Mao went to Shanghai, forgot the name of the place where it was to be held, could not find anyone who knew it, and thus missed the Congress. He returned to Hunan and continued his work. There were then 123 Communist Party members in Hunan, but the labor union of Anyuan miners had just been disbanded by order of Governor Chao Heng-ti, who also put a ban on railway labor unions and workers' clubs. The famous railway workers' strike was about to begin, to be followed by a strike of the Anyuan miners.

Because these strikes were Communist-inspired, great attention was paid to them at the Shanghai headquarters of the Communist Party. Liu Shao-chi was sent by the All-China Labor Federation in Shanghai, where he worked with Chang Kuo-tao, to reinforce and to direct the strike at Anyuan. Liu Shao-chi, who as we have seen had gone to Moscow in December 1920 via Vladivostok, enrolled at the Communist University for Eastern Toilers in 1921, and joined the CCP Moscow branch in the winter of 1921. In early 1922 he traveled back to China via Japan and became secretary of the All-China Labor Federation. He had no direct experience of labor organization before this first immersion in a full-blown strike at Anyuan. But due to the enormous prestige of the Soviet Union, "returned students from Russia" were held in great reverence, a reverence almost Confucian in attitude, based on the concept of a knowledge elite. This attitude would bedevil the CCP for some years.

Liu arrived in Anyuan on September 11, three days before the strike exploded on September 14. Mao Tsetung, who had begun the agitation, had drawn up thirteen articles or demands for the workers, and was now proceeding to stimulate a general strike all over Hunan in sympathy with the miners and railway workers. By November more than twenty unions had formed themselves into an association of labor unions with Mao as chairman. This was a very strong movement, which Mao would lead towards an All-Hunan Federation of Labor.

Today, at such a distance, it is difficult to tell what really happened, but obviously Liu's idea of the goals of the strike were widely different from Mao's. Liu saw it as a temporary, limited protest, useful for acquiring an improved standard of living and social benefits for a circumscribed number of coal miners. Mao saw it as a political spearhead to form a powerful base organization upon which to build the Hunan CCP branch. Nothing could be more different than the basic views of the two men as regards this single event.

Liu dismissed Mao's deputy, Chiang Hsien-yun. He and Li Li-san proceeded to lead the strike towards a negotiated agreement with the mine management. Clippings from newspapers of that time relate that Liu issued "guarantees that the strike would be peaceful." Talks with the managers resulted in a compromise agreement; Liu told the workers to give up their demands — formulated under Mao's advice — as "too drastic." The Anyuan episode looms large in the struggle between "the two lines" or two policies, between Mao's and Liu's vision of the world, which was to form the focus of the Great Proletarian Cultural Revolution, forty-odd years later.

Repression continued, however, both in the mines and on the railways after the strike had terminated on September 18. Wage increases were granted to the Anyuan miners, but after some minor and partial concessions they were rescinded and the strike leaders were expelled. However, for many years Liu Shao-chi was to base his reputation as a labor leader on the successful Anyuan strike, and a film was made in the early 1960's to extol his role as a "leader of the proletariat."

On February 7, 1923, a railway workers' strike at Chengchow on the Peking-Hankow railway was put down bloodily by the warlord Wu Pei-fu, who had also once been hailed as "liberal and progressive" until this slaughter revealed him as of the same stuff as any other tyrant. Over a hundred workers were killed or injured. In early 1923 Mao Tsetung returned to Anyuan to warn the workers that they must prepare for protracted struggle. "The bent bow must wait to be released" is the way he phrased it at the time.

In August 1923, and again in 1924, Liu was to argue that "in China's present situation, with such a childish proletariat, it will be a long time before any revolution happens, so let us not discuss it." He spoke against "this infantile disease, blind struggle . . . strikes at every occasion . . . adventurist impulses." In 1924, in his article *Save the Han Yeping Company,* Liu appealed to the workers to "keep order" and not to disrupt anything during strikes. He also dismissed 140 workers from the Anyuan workers' club for "indiscipline." Liu "only talked to the bosses . . . did not go down the pits . . . . wrote rules and regulations for us." * This is the gist of what old Anyuan workers say of Liu Shao-chi. Without trying to assess whether the strike, handled otherwise, would have led to a greater upsurge and benefited the Revolution, we may still pass a qualified judgment: that Liu was the kind of functionary who likes order and regulations, whose tendency is to compromise, and who feels that social benefits dispensed to the working class, rather than violent seizure of power, is the ideal to be achieved. Liu may have been a social reformist, but he was not a revolutionary.

In 1923 Mao Tsetung organized the first worker-peasant union at Yuehpei in Hunan; his adopted sister, Mao Tse-chien, was to work there for over two years, as also did his wife Yang Kai-hui. He recruited Anyuan workers in 1925 and sent them to train in Kuangchow at the Peasant Institute, and again in 1926.† He was to pay more visits to the Anyuan mines in September 1927, before the Autumn Harvest Uprising, when he recruited one thousand soldiers and cadres from the miners. Again in 1930, when a great wave of pessimism swept across the land in the ebb of the terrible massacres unleashed upon the Communists by the Kuomintang, he went to Anyuan.‡ "The future is bright," he said. "This put courage and patience into us. All was not lost; Chairman Mao was continuing the Revolution. So we waited and trusted."

The Self-Education College, founded in August 1922 in Changsha by Mao Tsetung, and in which Yang Kai-hui took an active part, inaugurated "a revolution in education." The teaching was directed towards "arousing awareness" or personal initiative. There were no formal classes, but many debates and seminars, with emphasis on current problems. Mao insisted on a course in hygiene — had he not even tried to do so in the Anyuan mines, lecturing the work-

* Interviews with Anyuan miners, 1968.
† See further chapters.
‡ Some say that Lin Piao accompanied Mao in 1930. But this "evidence" was produced by Red Guards, and may be incorrect.

ers on the nefariousness of gambling and dirt, and on keeping latrines clean? The college advertised for students who "wish to study
but have no resources and are against the regulations in other
schools." At its peak it had two hundred students; one of them was
Mao Tse-tan, Mao's younger brother. The whole purpose of the college actually was recruitment and training of cadres for the Communist Party; the names of the teachers are a roll call of early Hunan
Communists.

Chinese, English, mathematics, history and geography were
taught. However, the standard proved too high for the mixed lot of
factory workers, masons, carpenters, and shop salesmen as well as
ordinary students. In September 1922 a preparatory class was added
for students of junior middle school level. In April 1923 the college
began the publication of a Marxist monthly, *New Age*. Mao wrote
several articles, *Marxism and China, Against Idealism,* and *Foreign
Power, Warlordism, and Revolution.* The last was an analysis of the
Chinese situation; it predicted an "inevitable" Marxist revolution
and advocated "the unity of all progressive people." Manifestly Mao
was thinking in terms of a united front, although this had been rejected by the Party leadership. The Self-Education College was dissolved in November 1923 by the Hunan governor as a "heresy, dis-
turbing law and order." It was reborn two months later under the
innocuous name of the Hsiang Chiang Middle School.

By the end of 1922, Mao Tsetung had founded labor unions and
led strikes throughout the industrial sites of Hunan, had organized
workers' schools and Party cells, had set on foot a mass education
movement. Chao Heng-ti, the governor, had gradually worked himself into a state of apoplectic fury whenever Mao Tsetung was mentioned. On the 11th and 12th of December 1922, Mao Tsetung as
chairman of the twenty-odd Hunan labor unions called in person at
the governor's office, accompanied by some of the heads of individual labor unions. He saw Chao Heng-ti on the 13th. The interview
was a marvel of courteous acerbity. Mao Tsetung reminded Chao
Heng-ti of his promise to protect the workers "as his own children."
He quoted the classics and the provincial constitution, drawn up by
Chao Heng-ti himself. He demanded that the ban on trade unionism
be lifted, and suggested an official mediator to act as liaison and to
settle disputes.

The classic elegance of Mao's discourse left Chao Heng-ti with no
recourse but to protest his good intentions; he wanted to protect the
workers from evil influence. After the interview it is reported that

Chao Heng-ti said: "This Mao is too clever . . . he is dangerous
. . . there is not enough place in Hunan for both of us." And in
April 1923 Chao ordered Mao's arrest as a "radical . . . anarchist
. . . Communist." Mao Tsetung disappeared in the countryside, los-
ing himself among the peasants, to reappear, two weeks later, in
Shanghai.

6

The First United Front

Mao Tsetung's departure for Shanghai in 1923 coincided with the momentous decision taken by the CCP Politburo for an alliance — a united front — with the Kuomintang Party of Dr. Sun Yatsen. This was confirmed in a resolution at its Third Congress that year.

The background of the decision can be briefly retraced.

In his first visit to China in 1920, Sneevliet (alias Maring or Malin), later said to have been present at the CCP First Congress, had suggested to Chen Tu-hsiu a "grand anti-imperialist alliance to take in all classes" based on the "bloc of four classes" urged by Lenin. Trotsky had opposed Lenin on this point; Chang Kuo-tao at the First Congress also opposed a united front.

Sun Yatsen, sounded out by Chicherin and other Russian envoys,* was at first obdurate. He would have no alliance with Communism. But according to Dr. Percy Chen, the well-known lawyer now resident in Hongkong, it was his father, Dr. Eugene Chen, together with the eminent and respected scholar Dr. Liao Chung-kai, Sun Yatsen's most trusted friend, who successfully persuaded Sun Yatsen to agree to such an alliance. Sun's disheartening experiences with various warlords helped him to take this decision; since 1911 Sun had been several times at the mercy of militarists, Yuan Shih-kai among others. They would help him to power, but topple him when he did not serve their mercenary purposes. They were out for personal gain; Sun was an idealist and a selfless revolutionary.

In 1920, when Sun Yatsen was again briefly in power in Kuangchow, Eugene Chen, by now a minister in Sun's government, made several trips to Peking to conduct negotiations with the Russian ambassador Karakhan. Direct talks then took place between

---

* The Comintern envoys also contacted the powerful warlord Wu Pei-fu and even Chao Heng-ti, the reactionary governor of Hunan.

Sun Yatsen and Joffe, Lenin's envoy, in Shanghai in 1922. "Other negotiations, with the leaders of the Chinese Communist Party, were conducted by Dr. Liao Chung-kai. Thus a political alliance between Sun Yatsen's party and the Communist Party of China came into being." *

Sun Yatsen's aversion to alliance with the Russians was due to his patriotic resentment of czarist expansionism at China's expense. Czarist Russia had invaded and occupied large tracts of Chinese territory for two centuries, and participated in all the unequal treaties. "I don't believe the leopard can change his spots," said Sun; he claimed that the Russian Revolution had not altered Russian aims in Asia, despite Lenin's declaration that all unequal treaties were null and void, and that territory wrested by czarist aggression would be returned.

Czarist Russian control of Manchurian territory and of the Chinese Eastern Railway which ran through it (which it treated as an extension of the Trans-Siberian Railway) made Manchuria a Russian protectorate. Sun declared outspokenly that encroachments by czarist Russia in Sinkiang as well as Russian influence over Outer Mongolia created a vast sphere of Russian influence over "42 percent of Chinese territory."

But Sun Yatsen now realized the Russians needed a friendly China, as China needed allies in her struggle against domination by the Western powers and Japan. It was with him that the Soviet government finally decided that cooperation would be most fruitful; overtures to various warlords had proved futile. Lenin had spoken favorably of Sun Yatsen's party in 1912; Sun had cabled Lenin hailing the October Revolution of 1917. Though mistrustful of Communism, Sun was now disgusted with Western democracy. And after May 4, 1919, Sun Yatsen's opinions began to change. He read the works of Marx and Lenin. The combined persuasion of Dr. Liao Chung-kai and of Sun's own wife, the brilliant and courageous Soong Ching-ling,† finally convinced Sun of the usefulness of an alliance. He started to write down his political credo, the "Three People's Principles," now incorporating socialism in his third principle, "People's livelihood." "Nationalism, democracy, and socialism" became his new formula for the three

* Interview with Percy Chen.
† See the *Selected Works* of Madame Soong Ching-ling (in Chinese). The book of Emily Hahn, *The Soong Sisters,* does not do justice to the greatest and noblest of the three sisters. Another sister is the present wife of Chiang Kai-shek.

President Sun Yatsen with Madame Sun (Soong Ching-ling).

principles which at various times he had enunciated, but which had remained vague in content until now, revised and redefined, they began to look like a definite program. It was not until 1923, however, that this identification with socialism occurred; it was 1924 when he clearly opted for socialism.

Mao, in his historical appraisal of Sun Yatsen in 1940, was to demarcate Sun's three principles before this change of mind (called the old three principles) from their last version, or the new three principles. The last were the only ones the CCP would admit as the "Three Principles of Dr. Sun Yatsen."

"The three principles . . . as re-explained by Sun Wen * in the opening speech of the first national Congress of the Kuomintang (1924) . . . [are] the only real three principles . . . the others are not. . . . This is not a rumor spread by the Communist Party, myself and many other members of the Kuomintang, we were present at this proclamation."

Sun Yatsen encountered great opposition in his own party to this leftward switch. "If Communism is a good ally, why do members of the Kuomintang oppose the Communist Party? The reason may be that members of the Communist Party do not themselves understand what is Communism; and thus they have spoken against the Three People's Principles." Sun was obviously referring to the unflattering comments made about him and his party at the First Congress of the CCP in July 1921. "We cannot use the actions of some individuals for opposing a whole group . . . then why has this trouble arisen among our Kuomintang comrades? Because they do not realize that my third principle is a form of Communism."

This forthright endorsement, made in 1923, opened the door for the admission of Communist Party members into the Kuomintang, and for a Communist-Kuomintang alliance, which would last till 1927 and be known as the First United Front.

Sun Yatsen recalled China's grisly treatment by "Western democracy." Despite reservations about Russian ambitions, he was convinced of China's ultimate strength and power; he told his colleagues that "the Chinese people will not become satellitic to Russia." "Great revolutionary pioneer . . . our forerunner," Mao has defined Sun Yatsen's historic role. The memory of Sun Yatsen, who made the "bourgeois democratic" Revolution of 1911, continues

---

* Sun Wen is the formal name of Sun Yatsen. Most Chinese had at least two, if not more, names. This custom is now in abeyance, but many CCP members used aliases to escape identification from 1921 to 1949.

to be honored in China by the Communists, who understand his place in the history of the Revolution.

Sun Yatsen's widow, the beautiful, fearless, and noble Soong Ching-ling, is today Vice-Chairman of the People's Republic of China, and her life of dedication fits into the framework of history as a symbol of the transition from one stage of political development to the next. In this continuing process the alliance between Sun Yatsen's party, the Kuomintang,* and the CCP affords the most fascinating illustration of what was to become a basic strategy of the Chinese Communist Party under Mao Tsetung: the united front.

At the Second Congress of the CCP in 1922, which Mao had missed ("I forgot the name of the place where it was to be held, could not find any comrades, and missed it"), alliance and cooperation with the Kuomintang had again been discussed, but the majority of the delegates still remained opposed to united front strategy. But from the autumn of 1922, and throughout the next year, the violent suppression of fomented strikes, and the massacres of the railway workers on February 4, 1923, by Wu Pei-fu, had forced rethinking. The tiny Communist Party could not remain isolated. It was not growing fast, except in Hunan. Many activists were already being slaughtered.

The manifesto of the Second Congress already stated: "The Chinese Communist Party must, in the interest of the workers and the poor peasants, support the national democratic revolution, and forge a democratic united front of workers, poor peasants, and the petty bourgeoisie." But no united front policy was spelled out till the Third Congress, held in June 1923 in Kuangchow.

Coming via Shanghai to Kuangchow, Mao attended the Third Congress, where he gave a detailed report on the workers' movement in Hunan. "There must be a great revolutionary union. One cannot fight alone," Mao is reputed to have stated. At this Third Congress, however, the right wing of the CCP headed by Chen Tu-hsiu advocated virtual dissolution of the CCP. Frightened by repression, Chen suggested that the KMT make its own bourgeois revolution first, and that the CCP begin its proletarian revolution "after the historic period" of KMT rule. Chen Tu-hsiu, possessed by discouragement, told his friends that he hated "violence." The ultra-left wing, with Chang Kuo-tao, maintained that the Communist Party should be

* Also known under its usual abbreviation KMT.

free from bourgeois entanglements, and again castigated the KMT.

Mao Tsetung, together with his friend Ho Shu-heng and a young intellectual called Chu Chiu-pai,* opted for the united front, but with the Communist Party keeping its own autonomy. Mao and Chu were elected members of the Central Committee, and a majority voted for Mao's proposal. The Chen Tu-hsiu "right"-wing and Chang Kuo-tao "left"-wing theses were both criticized.

Some historians say this was due to Russian pressure. At the Comintern in Moscow, Karl Radek had scolded the Chinese delegation for its opposition to a united front. They were too theoretical, and just as the old Chinese scholars studied Confucius behind closed doors and pretended to know the world merely by reading books, they were reading Marxism but did not know how to apply it. This observation was pertinent, but it must be noted that Mao Tsetung had already indicated his option for a united front in 1922, as his articles indicate. However, he stressed that the CCP must keep its independence of action and the leadership of the working class and the peasantry in its hands. Leadership of the Revolution could not be handed over to the Kuomintang. He made this point forcefully. It agreed with the Leninist thesis on a united front. And Mao was already a Leninist.

A "united front of workers, peasants, and petty bourgeois" was the description worked out, the KMT now being identified with the petty bourgeoisie. In the petty bourgeoisie, as Mao Tsetung at the time understood it, were included merchants and traders. The policies of Mao towards merchants and traders would be to consider them useful to the Revolution; this was based on a realistic appraisal of the Chinese social context, "because of the historical necessity and current tendencies, the work of the merchants in the national revolution is more important and more urgent than the work that the rest [those other components of the petty bourgeoisie participating in the national democratic revolution] do." † They were also far more progressive than other elements of the middle class.

At the time of the Third Congress, there were only 342 Communist Party members in the whole of China.

An agreement between the CCP and the KMT was concluded at

---

* Chu Chiu-pai had joined the Moscow precursor group of the CCP in 1921. See T. A. Hsia, "Chu Chiu-pai's Autobiographical Writings" (*China Quarterly* no. 25, January-March 1966).
† Document in author's possession.

the end of 1923. In that autumn Michael Borodin, a Comintern agent, arrived in China with other Russian personnel to advise Sun Yatsen's Kuangchow government in shaping policies and institutions. The organization of a nationalist army, under officers and cadres trained by the KMT, was a top priority. The goal was to fight the warlords and to unite China. Sun Yatsen was convinced that without an army to implement the national policies of the KMT the Revolution would always be at the mercy of sundry warlords.

This development gave a great impetus to the KMT. A new hope animated its ranks, and new personages were to come into the limelight, among them Chiang Kai-shek, known at the time as a disciple of Sun Yatsen. Chiang made a good impression on Borodin, and was sent to Russia in the autumn of 1923 to study Russian military methods. He stayed in Russia five months. By June 1924 thirty Soviet instructors were attached to the newly built military academy, known as the Whangpoo Military Academy, and Chiang Kai-shek returned from Moscow to head it as director. Once again the prestige of the "Russian-returned student" label resulted in promotion to a position of influence and command.

The admission of Communists to the KMT was formally blessed by Sun himself at the First Congress of the KMT in January 1924. Li Ta-chao, China's first Marxist, was personally inducted by Sun Yatsen into the KMT. Sun insisted that Communists should be admitted without any curtailment of their activities as Communists and no one dared to contradict him openly.

Through the years, and Sun's many shifts of fortune, in and out of power, the Kuomintang had become a motley assembly of various cliques and factions, save for a handful of staunch patriots like Liao Chung-kai and his wife Ho Hsiang-ning.* Its reorganization was imperative, but was never accomplished.

One of the Communists who became a member of both parties was Mao Tsetung, who was given the task of liaison between the CCP and the KMT. To be entrusted with this important and delicate work was a tribute to his merit as organizer, recruiter, persuader, orator, and his staunch advocacy of the alliance. But the composition of the Kuomintang made it an almost impossible responsibility,

---

* Interviewed by the author in 1966 in Peking, where Madame Ho headed the Overseas Chinese Department for many years. Her son Liao Chen-chih is a prominent diplomat and expert in the Chinese Foreign Affairs Ministry. See Nym Wales *Red Dust* (Stanford 1952) for his biography.

and it became ever more difficult as the contradictions between the two parties became intractable.*

The CCP resolution on the united front was defined as cooperation — but without merging into it — with the Kuomintang; autonomy within the Kuomintang while sustaining a united front policy to attain the reunification of China as a federal republic and elimination of imperialism. Other resolutions agreed on the fundamental rights of voting, freedom of expression and reunion; an eight-hour day for workers, labor legislation, reform of education, and tax reforms.

In later years Mao would analyze what was wrong with this first united front. The strategy of a united front had been correct, but the CCP had failed to recognize that leadership must never be relinquished. "The Party . . . was in its infancy . . . inexperienced in the three basic problems of the united front, armed struggle and Party building, a party without much knowledge of China's historical and social conditions." † No other Communist Party member at the time seems to have given so much serious thought to Sun Yatsen's own program, and to the structure of the Kuomintang Party, as well as to the study of Lenin's united front techniques, as Mao did.

The resolutions of the First KMT Congress of 1924, calling for cooperation with Russia, cooperation with the CCP, and help and support to workers and peasants, the identification with "socialism," gave the KMT a much more widely based popular appeal, a refurbished, progressive, national image. Three Communists were among the twenty-four members of the Central Executive Committee of the Kuomintang — Li Ta-chao, Tan Ping-shan and Yu Shu-te — and six Communists among the alternate members, one of them Mao Tsetung. Students from the work and study programs, Communist Party members returning from France, Germany and Russia, also entered the Kuomintang as members, among them Chou En-lai in mid-1924. Chou became secretary of the military commission in the CCP Kuangchow branch, in charge of the Training Department,

---

* A note on the Kuomintang: From 1895 to 1905 Sun Yatsen's organization was known as the Hsin Chung-hui; it was after 1905 and in Japan that it was renamed the Tung Meng Hui. It became the Kuomintang (national party) in 1912, on the eve of the first elections to China's first "parliament," the National Assembly. Until 1911 it was an anti-Manchu, antidynastic alliance, vaguely democratic and republican but without a very definite program.

† *Introducing the Communist,* October 4, 1939. *Selected Works of Mao Tsetung* (English edition Peking 1961–1965), vol. II. Also *On New Democracy,* January 1940 (*ibid*).

and late in 1924 deputy director of the Political Department in Whangpoo Military Academy, where he lectured on military affairs. He was then twenty-seven years old.

In February Mao returned to Shanghai, to become secretary of the Organizing Department (Propaganda) of the Shanghai branch of the KMT, in charge of liaison. In daily contact with politicians, Mao endured from them a treatment as arrogant as that he had been subject to when assistant librarian in Peking, and sarcasm from his own comrades because he tried to do his work well under the "revolutionary" elder Hu Han-min, a great personage in the KMT. Hu Han-min had taken part in the 1911 Revolution. He was one of the editors of *Min Li Pao,* which Mao Tsetung had read in Changsha in 1911, and which had made him discard his early enthusiasm for the reformists and discover Sun Yatsen. With age Hu had become increasingly reactionary. He scorned "the peasant" Mao, who worked three months under him. Wang Ching-wei, the brilliant and ambitious opportunist, also appears to have looked down on Mao. Mao learned bitter lessons on the ambivalence of "radicals." Meanwhile, left-wingers in the CCP called him "Hu Han-min's secretary." But Mao subordinated his temper to his dedication, and went on as if he were completely insensitive. He was involved in a multiplicity of details and they drained his mind and his strength. He was appointed one of the three Communists to serve on the committee to examine and draw up the new Kuomintang Party constitution. Painstaking, he drew up a scheme for the reorganization of the Kuomintang Party structure, showing a shrewd grasp of its weaknesses.

"There are too many high-level functionaries sitting in posts in Kuangchow and doing little, whereas there are too few outside of the capital city." Where was the strength of the national movement? Among the masses; but the decisive organizations, which gave the leadership to the members, were in the cities, or at county town level, and the latter were much too remote. There was no contact between the people and the high bureaucrats who put orders on paper, orders "empty of significance." The people were enthusiastic and patriotic, but they got no real directives from the KMT. Mao even went into financial details of the organization, showing a sound knowledge of accounting and bookkeeping, possibly helped in this by his early training at home and by his brother Mao Tse-min. He tackled the work of consolidation and of training of cadres, insisted on the importance of recruiting and training cadres to work among the peasantry. It was on Mao's proposal that the Kuomintang established a Peasant Department in its Central Executive Committee. The scheme was submitted in February 1924, and by the summer the institute for training peasant cadres was working. From its inception the institute would be in Communist hands.

That Mao should be the only one out of that galaxy of intellectuals to work out a complete KMT reorganization plan is puzzling. No one else really seemed to want to do the arduous groundwork involved in such an overhaul. Liao Chung-kai praised Mao Tsetung and his "extraordinary talent" and recommended his report to Sun Yatsen. But the Kuomintang was too full of dissension and venality to be able to reform itself. By April 1924 already the first attacks against "Communist orientation" were becoming vocal. The accusation of "creating a bloc within the KMT" was launched; the alliance with Russia was not attacked, only the alliance with local Communists.

By the summer of 1924 Mao Tsetung was already overwrought and overworked and seems to have had attacks of despondency and sleeplessness. He was getting exhausted with frustration; his work, which consisted essentially of making "fire and water" coexist, was a never-ending cycle of pettiness. As the year wore on, it also became obvious that Sun Yatsen was seriously ill, and round him began the intrigues of various cliques jockeying for the succession. Mao is said to have remarked casually to a friend that the Communists were very vulnerable because they had no army, a surprising thing to say when hopes were high, when in the Whangpoo Military Academy the Russian advisers were treated with great honor, and Chou En-lai was doing his utmost to radicalize the officer cadets and appeared very successful at it.

Borodin, the Russian adviser, seems to have understood very little of the intrigues around Sun. He was almost hypnotized by Chiang Kai-shek's fluency and left-wing jargon. Chen Tu-hsiu as secretary-general of the CCP was hypnotized with "cooperation" and "unity." This self-willed intellectual, shrinking from the grossness of actual political work, afraid to displease, was not built to lead a revolutionary party in the complicated tactics of united front struggle. From Chen's point of view, was it not more reasonable to suppose these polished (if unscrupulous) gentlemen of the KMT more capable of "progress" and "enlightenment" than illiterate workers and peasants? Many of the Russian advisers at the Military Academy were fooled for a long time by Chinese courtesy, and the ability to mask thoughts and feelings under a bland, peaceful demeanor. Borodin

Mikhail Borodin, Russian adviser to the Kuomintang, speaking in Hankow, March 1927.

was apt to blame the CCP members, and especially Chou En-lai, for "pushing too hard" whenever some complaints from the Kuomintang came to him. "Unity above all" was Borodin's motto, as it was Chen Tu-hsiu's, and in the process both did forego the essential component of leadership.   .

It was on the matter of policies towards the peasantry that Mao, it is said, called on Borodin in Kuangchow in 1924. Borodin spoke no Chinese, Mao no Russian or English; if they conversed it was through an interpreter. It is possible that Borodin did not understand nor appreciate Mao Tsetung. As for Mao, he was not impressed by Borodin. "Borodin stood just a little to the right of Chen Tu-hsiu, and was ready to do everything to please the bourgeoisie, even to the disarming of the workers, which he finally ordered."

Hence 1924 was a year of great mental and physical strain for Mao. He found men of repute, men whom he had revered and respected, utterly disillusioning at close range. The admired radical Wang Ching-wei, who had thrown a bomb at the Manchu regent in 1906, and been at one time the idol of progressive students, would turn out to be an intriguer, an opportunist, a vain man with a big mouth. Hu Han-min, who also had the reputation of a revolutionary, was weak, timorous, corrupt. And then there was Chen Tu-hsiu, perhaps the greatest disillusionment of all. Mao had thought highly of him, acknowledging how much Chen had influenced him, both in personal meetings and through his *New Youth* magazine. Mao had looked up to him with all the ardor of a young man seeking a model to emulate. But affection, respect, could not blind him, as increasingly he saw Chen Tu-hsiu evade, compromise, prevaricate. To those whose dedication is revolution, there are bound to be such traumatic experiences. For them everything is measured by that supreme and rigorous passion which takes all of a man's life, the sinews of his body and the strength of his spirit, and wrings him dry and wrecks him often. All other relationships, emotions, passions, are removed from the soul's center; all must inevitably be sifted and weighed in the pitiless measure of sacrifice. For such a revolutionary there can be no loyalty, no love, except that "based on principle," which means revolution.

When Mao began to doubt Chen as a Communist, then he had to oppose him, however much it cost him in personal anguish. By the end of 1924, Mao was seeing another Chen Tu-hsiu, no longer a tower of strength but more like a weak bamboo; a vapid, arrogant, and yet pusillanimous man to whose elegant intellect workers' demonstrations, strikes, the very idea of peasant uprisings were repugnant. Chen's fear of violence was an atavistic panic, a class reaction, backed by long centuries of elitism, of the almost ineradicable superiority of scholars above manual laborers.

Mao found his relations with Chen deteriorating as Chen grew nettled, then resentful, of the younger man's arguments. Deeply sensitive in spite of his rigid control over himself, he would find the death of his affection for Chen Tu-hsiu difficult to accept for some months. But in the end he would not hesitate.*

Mao Tsetung was present at the Fourth Congress of the CCP in January 1925, contrary to reports that he did not attend because of illness. He was ill, though the cause may have been overwork, but he was there, and he gave warning that "organizationally within the CCP, and also in mass organizations, we must be prepared." For the worst. He asked for workers' and peasants' alliances, to take part in the national revolutionary movement. Resolutions to strengthen and expand peasants' and workers' unions were passed, but little was done to implement these. The complacency of the secretary-general, Chen, studiously avoiding "friction" with the Kuomintang, was unshaken. In fact, at the Congress, a tendency to speak in terms of "restraining" the peasants was evidenced in his speeches. Emphasis on the importance of the workers dominated the Congress, due to the strong representation of the "left" wing, Chang Kuo-tao, Li Li-san, in the All-China Labor Federation and in the Central Committee. Mao Tsetung seems pretty much a lone figure, and a very underestimated one, at this Congress. Dissent between himself and the "city-oriented" Communists gave rise to sharp arguing. Mao's repeated proposals that the Communist Party should train its own peasant cadres and mobilize the peasantry, that the training should be extended all over China, to provide a rear base in any province and not be confined merely to the area where the Kuomintang government held sway, were watered down in the bland rotundity of resolutions. It was not till 1926 that the CCP would organize its own Peasant Department.

At the end of January 1925, an exhausted Mao went back to his own province of Hunan. He went under an official cloud; for had he not proved "unsatisfactory" in liaison work? So write some biogra-

---

* Edgar Snow, who spent days and weeks with Mao, often told me how deeply sensitive Mao is to friendship; how often his eyes moistened when he spoke of dead comrades. "His struggles against individuals once his friends, for revolution's sake, were always intensely painful to him."

phers,* more intent on faulting Mao's performance in his impossible job than in grasping the essence of his disgust. He returned not to rest but to organize the peasantry. So secret, so quiet was he in beginning this work that for a long time nothing was known of his activities from January to August 1925. And because he was considered "right"-wing by the city-oriented leftists in the Party, he had not been re-elected to the Central Committee of the CCP.

Mao Tsetung reached Shaoshan before the Chinese New Year, and this was a family reunion. Both his wife Yang Kai-hui and his brother Mao Tse-min had been working in Shanghai also, but not with him. Yang Kai-hui did educational work, and Mao Tse-min was with the propaganda section of the CCP. Back in the old farmhouse, he read and he labored at the spring planting and sowing. His body was healed with the labor of the fields. He worked and he thought, and his thoughts were far-sighted.

He had begun to see the problem of the Chinese Revolution in the utterly concrete, down to earth, yet incomparably larger vision that was to be known as Mao Tsetung Thought, to mark his country and the history of his epoch. As he went among the peasantry, the puzzles and confusions of the slick city intellectuals fell into place. To serve a spurious "unity" in the councils of the alliance with the Kuomintang, the peasants and workers were in danger of being sacrificed. Already it had been suggested that the lowering of land tenure rents should not be left to peasant associations, but to a "collective bargaining" process. Yet all around him the reality of China was peasant revolution. How would he now proceed? Obedience to the "leadership" against what his mind and conscience cried out to him was the right course, or defiance? But never for a moment did he think of abandoning the Revolution, for that would be abandoning the peasants, the workers. He could never do it.

In February and March, the tall, thin young Mao went walking from village to village, staying with peasants in their farmhouses, working with them for his meals and lodging, in the evenings sitting with them and listening, always listening. "I have so much yet to learn from them, they know so much more than I do." † "Three old cobblers equal one Wise Man!" ‡ Once again exalted, informed, vi-

---

* See Jerome Chen *Mao and the Chinese Revolution* (New York and London 1965).
† In 1967.
‡ Reported "sayings" of Mao Tsetung; the Wise Man alluded to is the renowned strategist in the tale of the *Three Kingdoms*, Chuke Liang.

talized by this immersion in the vibrant, enormous life of the working people of China, once again, like Antaeus touching earth, Mao was filled with creative power and vision. He wrote, analyzed, investigated, planned. He went back to Changsha, and from there moved around the counties to establish peasant unions, peasant Party cells. His investigations in the countryside during the spring planting season revealed that 10 percent of the population consisted of landlords and rich peasants, 70 percent of poor peasants, and 20 percent of middle peasants. By the end of the following year, 1926, 37 out of 75 counties in Hunan had peasant unions. In the district of Hengshan, where Mao placed some of his recruits and where his adopted sister also worked for the Party, 85 percent of the peasant union membership was of poor peasant origin.

In the attic of the Mao farmhouse in Shaoshan, above his parents' bedroom, meetings were held. It was there that the first peasant Party branch was organized in August 1925. During these six months from the end of January to August, Mao elaborated a scientific investigation technique which laid the foundations for Marxist social research in China. This contribution of Mao's to the social sciences is fundamental to the creation of the new concept which today infuses China's scientific achievements. He seems to have realized how little Chinese intellectuals knew of their own country and their own people. It was not the peasants and workers alone who needed education, but also the proud and lordly "leaders," scholars, riding high over the heads of that patient immensity, the people of China. They needed to be re-educated. "Marxism is . . . the concrete analysis of concrete conditions," Lenin had said. How many Marxist intellectuals bothered to do this?

Of the thirty-two peasant cadres forming the first Party branch at Shaoshan, all were to die in the massacres of the Chiang Kai-shek terror from 1927 to 1934.* Other cadres Mao recruited during those months were to follow him to Chingkangshan, the mountain fortress where Mao was to create the first rural Red base and start the Chinese Revolution going again when, at the end of 1927, it had been almost destroyed.

In Kuangchow, the Peasant Department announced at the First Congress of the Kuomintang in 1924 had taken shape as a Peasant Institute in April 1924.

* The son of one of these is now secretary of the Shaoshan Party branch (interview 1971).

The Kuomintang Party, with its disparate composition and varied cliques, was wholly agreed on the necessity for rallying the peasantry, the "foot soldiery" of any military expedition. There had never been an overthrow of dynasty without peasant armies. It was they, the many-millioned, who made empires and destroyed them, but the power had always fallen back into the hands of the mandarinate and the landlord class, and after reforms by the new rulers — tax and rent remissions — the peasantry was again exploited. This repeated betrayal was the feudal pattern for two millennia. The KMT military unification of China would need soldiers, armies, food; only the peasantry could fulfill those needs. Chiang Kai-shek summed it up: "The task of the peasantry is to provide us with information concerning the enemy, food and comforts in our encampments, and soldiers for our armies." Not a word about the duties of the Kuomintang, once it came to power, towards the peasantry! It was taken for granted that the peasants would serve a purpose and die unprotestingly, or be beaten back into submission should they revolt. Mao Tsetung was not prepared to accept this repetition of Chinese history, but Chen Tu-hsiu was; hence Chen's reluctance to see the peasantry really armed, really taking power.

This was the heart of the matter. And yet since 1919 Lenin had stressed the importance of the peasants to the revolutions in Asia. "The national revolution in China, and the creation of the anti-imperialist front, will necessarily be followed by an agrarian revolution of the peasantry against the remnants of feudalism. The revolution can be victorious *only if it becomes possible to draw into the movement the basic masses of the Chinese population; i.e., the peasants with small holdings. . . . Thus the peasant problem becomes the central point of the entire policy of the Chinese Communist Party."* *

Far from obeying the directives of the Comintern, Chen was actually paying no attention to them where the peasantry were concerned. It is curious that this fundamental defect in Chen's leadership should already have been pointed out as early as August 1923, when an anonymous Communist Party member wrote in the Party weekly *The Guide* that the weakness of the socialist movement was "excess of urban orientation, cowardice of intellectuals who fear to leap into the mass of the people, and shortage of talented men in the local movement." (The anonymous writer sounds a little like Mao, but it is not in his character to have written this letter.)

* Comintern resolution received by the CCP before the Third Congress in 1923.

Chen Tu-hsiu had retorted: "Farmers are petty bourgeois . . . how can they accept Communism? How can a Communist movement extend itself successfully in rural China?" Peasant revolutionary excesses would "disrupt" the national revolution, bring about "splits" and "misunderstandings" with the bourgeoisie. These slurs upon peasant potential expressed the same fear as that of feudal landlords. Chang Kuo-tao also wrote that the peasantry was "conservative," "demanding only a good harvest under an emperor," and "scattered, individualistic, unreasonable." Both the "right" and "left" wings in the CCP were united in their contempt of the peasantry.

Chiang Kai-shek was well versed in the historical background of China. The military expedition to wrest China from warlord rule and to unify it under the KMT could not proceed unless the KMT had the peasants with them; this was self-evident. But already complaints of peasant "excesses" were heard among the landlords and capitalists in the KMT, for now something was happening in the countryside of the Haifeng and Lufeng counties of Kwangtung province. A peasant revolutionary movement, in which Peng Pai, whose memory is still honored, played an important part, was taking shape.

Peng Pai, surprisingly, was himself the son of a landlord and had studied in Japan. Even before he adhered to the Communist Party, Peng had already unbound his wife's feet. (The unfortunate woman was later executed by the Chiang Kai-shek regime.) When his father died, Peng Pai began to distribute his father's lands and to divest himself of property — his father owned about 1,400 tenant serfs. He went among the peasants in Haifeng county and lived with them, helping to form a peasant union in a village in Haifeng county about the same time that Mao was organizing a peasant-worker union in Hunan at Yuehpei. The peasant unions in Haifeng district grew; poor peasants and landless tenants flocked to join. Very soon they could stand up to terroristic landlords and their private armies. When some tenants were jailed because they could not pay exorbitant rent, 6,000 peasants demonstrated in front of the city magistrate's house and frightened the magistrate into releasing them. The example of Haifeng and Lufeng counties spread; landlords, alarmed, fled to Kuangchow city.

In December 1924 a warlord named Chen Chiung-ming marched against Kuangchow to oust Sun Yatsen once again. But Sun Yatsen was no longer at the mercy of a militarist coup. The Whangpoo Military Academy cadets and the workers' battalions organized by the Communists defeated Chen Chiung-ming, who fled to Hongkong. In their subsequent pursuit of his troops through the countryside, the cadets were astonished by the enthusiastic help they received from the peasantry when they crossed Haifeng county. "We had never seen such things before."

The peasants organized militia battalions, took the small towns while the landlords fled; supplied stretcher bearers for the wounded, carriers, an intelligence service. This demonstration of peasant power won admiration but increased panic; the mobilization of the peasantry, though essential for the military expedition planned, was "dangerous." If peasants were capable of such formidable initiative, they could seize power — and keep it. How was one to utilize them and then discard them? This was the task Chiang Kai-shek would perform. While despondency settled upon the big landlords of the Kuomintang, Chiang played the leftist, for he needed peasant and worker support to hoist himself to power.

Only Sun's personal prestige, by the end of 1924, was keeping the Kuomintang Party from open dissension. But Sun died of cancer in March 1925 in Peking, where he had gone for talks on a possible peaceful unification with the militarist Feng Yu-hsiang, then in power in a North China warlord coalition. No sooner was Sun dead than a covert power struggle began between Chiang Kai-shek and Wang Ching-wei, each claiming to be Sun's chosen disciple. Chiang was a poor military strategist but a master at intrigue. Wang was to be no match for him.

A Society for the Propagation of Sun Yatsenism had already been organized, with Chiang's tacit consent, within the Whangpoo Military Academy in January 1925, though it only came into the open in April. In spite of its catchy title, it was a fascist organization, enrolling cadets in the "army group" nucleus which would later form the core of Chiang Kai-shek's military dictatorship. The society clashed with a League of Military Youth organized by Chou En-lai to recruit cadets for the Communist Party. The leader of the Society for Sun Yatsenism was Tai Chi-tao, in 1919 considered "radical," but by 1925 already an extreme right-winger in the Kuomintang.

The right wing of the Kuomintang took possession of the Shanghai headquarters of its own party, and made an open bid to "cast out the Communist Party" from its position within the Kuomintang. The Central Executive Committee of the Kuomintang held a meeting which expelled 120 right-wingers from the Party, a measure to which Chiang gave his approval. This looked like a great victory for the united front and for the left. It confirmed the opinion of Borodin that Chiang was progressive. Borodin looked upon Chiang as a "left-wing hope" and treated him with friendly respect.

After Sun Yatsen's death, a triumvirate was organized to rule the Kuomintang. It was composed of Hu Han-min, Wang Ching-wei and Liao Chung-kai. On May 23, 1925, a resolution by the KMT Central Executive Committee announced the goal of a Northern Expedition — as the military campaign to reunify China was called — to be led by Chiang Kai-shek as commander-in-chief of the Nationalist armies, as well as director of the Whangpoo Academy. No compromise with the warlords was envisaged. This reinforced the popular image of a revolutionary party; it also appeared a victory for the Communists, since the resolution added that "the only government in the world with which the Kuomintang can work hand in hand is that of Soviet Russia." Borodin's prestige was enhanced, and the Kuomintang appeared to be more and more left-inclined. High-sounding declarations lulled the doubts of some Communist Party members and reinforced their desire to "cooperate."

The sudden irruption of reality in this rosy cloudland of deception was the assassination of Dr. Liao Chung-kai in August 1925, only five months after Sun's death. In China this murder is now currently ascribed to Chiang Kai-shek. Chiang was for years a member of a notorious secret society, the Ching Hong Pang, and the murder was done by two paid "dog legs" * (who were never caught). But somehow Hu Han-min's brother was implicated; and this threw suspicion on Hu Han-min. Chiang Kai-shek reacted with fury at this "betrayal of the revolution"; he arrested seventeen commanders — who also happened to be potential military rivals — and supporters of Hu Han-min, clamped military rule upon the city of Kuangchow, took over the police, and established his own control, to check a "counterrevolutionary coup." This assassination of a man known for his leftist sympathies was the first step in a deep-laid plot to wrest power.

There had been in that summer a sudden upsurge in Communist strength, in response to the killing of Chinese by British and Japanese soldiers garrisoned in Shanghai and Kuangchow. On May 15 a Chinese worker had been killed by a Japanese foreman in a textile mill in Shanghai. On May 30 the students demonstrated in the International Settlement; British soldiers fired and killed a dozen of them. In Kuangchow, on June 23, workers, students, and cadets of Whang-

* A term for paid murderers of the secret societies or of landlords' private armies.

poo demonstrated in front of Shameen, an islet on which British, French, and other European commercial firms had installed their personnel. The British fired upon the demonstrators and 56 people were killed. This gave rise to a monster protest movement throughout China. Strikes and demonstrations occurred in every city; walls were plastered with pamphlets denouncing Western imperialism. The withdrawal of all foreign troops, abolition of extra-territoriality, the return of the foreign concessions to China were demanded by the Communist-led Federation of Labor. Already in 1922, the big strikes on the mainland had been followed by a strike of 100,000 workers in the British colony of Hongkong. This time, 150,000 striking workers from Hongkong came into Kuangchow, and a strike committee was formed. Hongkong was paralyzed. The Communist labor unions found their membership growing with amazing speed; the workers organized revolutionary committees for militia, security, welfare, education and cultural activities; "power to the working class" became a daily slogan. The Communist Party all-China membership, only 995 in January 1925, was 10,000 by November, with another 9,000 members in the various Youth Corps. The All-China Labor Federation counted 540,000 members in 1925, and 1,240,000 members in May 1926. By 1927 there were to be 2.8 million members, including dock workers and handicrafts men.

It was this sudden vast increase in Communist manpower and influence, the appearance in Kuangchow of armed workers' militia in May and June 1925, which alarmed the Kuomintang right wing and precipitated the murder of Liao Chung-kai, who had sided with the workers. But this intrigue was masked by an apparent split of the Kuomintang itself into conservative and progressive factions, with the right wing apparently cast out, in exile outside Kuangchow (it was to form what became known as the Western Hills group because it held a conclave in the Western Hills near Peking). In the end there would be little difference between the two factions; both would be recuperated by the same landlord and compradore capitalist * interests. The national capitalist class and the petty bourgeoisie, fearful and leaderless, would follow where they were led by the big capital-

* The Chinese Communists distinguish between "national" capitalists, whose money and resources do not serve outside monopolies or interests, and who therefore may form part of the united front and can and must be rallied to the revolutionary cause, and "compradore" capitalists, who serve as middlemen for the invasion and exploitation of China by imperialist powers.

ists and big landlords, because no valid leadership had seized the occasion to produce a new orientation which they could follow.

It was in the middle of this tangle of intrigue and deception that Mao Tsetung returned to Kuangchow in September 1925.

Even in the Hunan countryside, the May 1925 events had roused the people. "Formerly, I had not fully realized the degree of class struggle among the peasantry." "After the May 30th movement the Hunanese peasantry became very militant . . . in a few months, more than twenty peasant unions were formed." In many areas the tenants refused to pay exorbitant rents, and beat up tax collectors. The slogan "Down with the warlords" which Mao employed in his propaganda to form peasant unions fitted in with a more positive program: land confiscation, forming a peasant militia, and anti-imperialism. The events of May 30 made it easy to explain imperialism to the peasantry, for whom foreign invasion and domination was remote, since they saw little of it. The foreigners helped the warlords; the foreigners had helped to put down the great Taiping peasant revolt; foreign bullets and money had always interfered to keep the Chinese people down. Mao described what he had seen in Shanghai — Chinese insulted on the streets, not allowed in public parks. Now the shootings which had occurred made the lesson even more vivid.

It was during this stay in Hunan that Mao Tsetung told his friends that should it become necessary, a peasant guerilla war would be the best type of war for revolutionaries. He seems to have already thought, even if only vaguely, of rural bases; on his foot treks through the provinces he reached the foothills of his future first rural base, Chingkangshan.

Rumors about the tall thin agitator who went through the Hunan countryside organizing peasant unions came to Chao Heng-ti, the governor of Hunan who had said the province was not large enough to contain both Mao Tsetung and himself, which had caused Mao to leave in 1923. Mao could trust the poor peasants, but the landlords sent out their private armies to threaten their tenants if they did not denounce Mao. A visit Mao Tsetung paid to Changsha was unfortunate; he was recognized. Now he had to go, and very quickly.

But Mao's last stay in Changsha was the occasion for a poem, *Changsha* — one of the many he wrote, one of the few that have been kept. Nothing is more beautiful to a Hunanese than the landscape of the Hsiang river in autumn, when the hills are russet and gold, and Orange Grove island, opposite Changsha city, glows like a gold nugget in the sunset. The "summer tiger" days that clamp a dripping heat upon the cities and the countryside are over, and from the Hsiang water comes a small cool breeze.

CHANGSHA

Alone, standing in autumn's chill
As the Hsiang river
Flows north past Orange Island,
I see the red-stained thousand hills
With crimson forests trooping.
On the lucid blue water a hundred barges sail,
Eagles fly above,
Fish glide in the deeps,
Under the unmoving sky, all living things strive for freedom.
I ponder, and ask the boundless earth
Who masters destiny?
In past years
I walked here with many companions,
Friends of crowded years and months of endeavor,
All of us students, all of us young,
In high assurance, strong and fearless,
Pointing the finger at all things,
Praising and condemning in our writings,
The highest in the land we counted no more than dust.
But do you remember?
How, reaching midstream, we struck the waters,
And the waves dashed against our speeding boats?

In that August there was high promise and great hope as the Communist Party swelled in numbers. The Revolution seemed very near. Mao stood, staring at the water. The Revolution would go forward, but there would be obstacles to its progress.

There is no rapture, only sober purpose in this poem. Mao Tse-tung was perhaps saying farewell to his own youth. As he slipped on foot across the hills, the autumn harvest was being reaped. Soon, armies would be trampling the winter fields.

7

The Ways Divide

When Mao got back to effervescent Kuangchow, Communist influence was at a peak. Everyone talked of the workers' battalions, of the impressive growth of the worker movement. Mao, erstwhile trade union organizer, founder of workers' evening schools and clubs, looked shunted onto a side way — peasant associations and peasant Party cells in Hunan seemed very remote and unimportant in the general excitement of the southern city, with soldiers marching, drums beating, red flags flashing everywhere.

After the May and June killings by the British and Japanese, other shooting incidents had taken place in Shanghai in September. Every bullet, every corpse brought more adherents to the Communist cause, more defiance of Western imperialism and its aggressive outlawry. The walls of Kuangchow screamed denunciations; milling crowds cheered orators at every street corner. The workers' militia drilled at dawn to the sound of trumpets; the Whangpoo cadets were acclaimed and mobbed; the excited population roared its approval of the Northern Expedition to "smash both feudalism and foreign imperialism."

But within the Kuomintang the counterrevolution was being organized. Chiang Kai-shek's rise to power had begun.

Harold R. Isaacs * describes Chiang Kai-shek as "a man whose ambition, fathered by ruthless cunning and a total lack of scruple, brought him to the center of the political scene." The adopted son of a wealthy landlord, Chiang, as a student in Japan, was inducted into the secret societies and became the protégé of Chang Ching-chiang, a banker millionaire and secret society member, with extensive

---

* Harold R. Isaacs *The Tragedy of the Chinese Revolution* (1938, second revised edition Stanford 1961).

connections with Chinese big business and foreign bankers. Through this patron, Chiang then became the "adopted grandson" of Shanghai's Al Capone, Huang Ching-yung, lord of the underworld in the French Concession of Shanghai. Chiang was then in deep financial trouble. His sponsors bailed him out, sent him to Kuangchow to become a "disciple" of Sun Yatsen and the "eyes and ears" of the Chinese secret societies there. Chiang Kai-shek reported to his Shanghai underworld friends, who sold the information to the foreign powers. Chiang, director of Whangpoo Military Academy since May 1924, was now commander-in-chief of the armies of the Kuomintang.

Chiang was far more worried about worker militancy than he was about the peasants, although the Haifeng and Lufeng experiences had disturbed him. The peasants were now dispossessing landlord families, and 70 percent of the Whangpoo cadets, and Chiang himself, belonged to landlord or rich peasant families. Thus the Whangpoo cadets were confronted with social revolution within the national war for unification of China. Some wanted to "punish" the peasants, others took the peasants' side. This caused open quarrels and even fisticuffs between the cadets. Chiang mediated, and made revolutionary speeches which greatly pleased Borodin. He was called "the red hope of the revolutionary army"; the "dark-haired darling" of Borodin. He declared he would kill his own brother should the latter "betray" the revolution. He shouted: "Long live the world revolution" and "Down with the imperialists" as heartily as any worker.

In that autumn of 1925 the Kuangchow-Hongkong Workers' Strike Committee was very powerful. Strength lay in the workers' councils, in the peasant associations (also beginning to arm themselves), in the left-wing groups of Whangpoo cadets, the League of Military Youth under Chou En-lai. "They raised the KMT nationalist leaders on their shoulders," writes Isaacs. "They were to carry Chiang to victory." Such was their power that even after Chiang began to deliver telling blows to the Communist leadership, he still had to pretend to be a radical. This appears scarcely credible, but Chiang carried it off. In this he was greatly helped by the ineffectual, flabby nonleadership of the CCP secretary general, Chen Tu-hsiu.

If Mao appeared neglected by his own party, it was not so with his membership in the KMT. He became secretary of the Propaganda Department of the Kuomintang and started a political weekly that September. The weekly was to run for eighteen months, till the spring of 1927. "I became editor of the *Political Weekly*. It later played a very active role in attacking and discrediting the right wing of the KMT led by Tai Chi-tao" (head of the Society for Sun Yat-senism). He also took charge of the Peasant Institute for training cadres, housed in a Confucian temple on the main street of Kuang-chow. He had already lectured at the institute in August 1924, invited to do so by Peng Pai, then running it. Now he called his own recruits from Hunan to come to Kuangchow for training and proceeded to renovate the teaching program. Among these recruits would be his brother Mao Tse-min.

The Peasant Institute had produced about 30 graduates during its first term (July–August 1924) and 142 in its second. All the cadres were from Kwangtung, recruited by Peng Pai from his own Haifeng and Lufeng districts. The third term was a three-month session of 114 cadres, again all from Kwangtung. The fourth term ran from May to September 1925; ten trainees were sent by Mao from Hunan, 64 were from Kwangtung.

Mao started work with the fifth term, from October 1925 to March 1926. He stipulated that the recruitment should not confine itself to Kwangtung cadres; these would prove ineffective in a northern expedition, their dialect being incomprehensible outside the province. The enrollment was now much diversified. Of 113 graduates, 41 were from Kwangtung, 44 from Hunan; others were from Fukien, Hupei, Shantung and Kwangsi.

The sixth term, from May to October 1926, was completely reorganized. Sessions were lengthened, materials and textbooks revised, the curriculum rearranged. There were fifteen teachers, able Mao recruits. The number of trainees swelled to 327; five were from Kwangtung, 36 from Hunan, 40 from Kwangsi, 27 from Hupei, 22 from Kiangsi, eight from Suiyuan, 10 from Yunnan and two from Inner Mongolia. Mao was thus building for the Communist Party a far-flung net of peasant cadres. "I established a course for this purpose [to prepare the peasant cadres for mass mobilization] which was attended by representatives of 21 different provinces and included students from Inner Mongolia."

Arrangements for students at the Peasant Institute were Spartan. Their dormitories were in the building itself, and Mao too had a room there, sparsely furnished with plank bed, table and chair, and a bamboo bookcase. The work was far more thorough and painstaking than it had been. The students attended over 250 lectures, some lasting three to four hours. Among the lecturers were Chou En-lai, on military campaigns; Peng Pai, on the peasant movement in the Haifeng and Lufeng areas and in the East river area; Teng Chung-hsia, Li Fu-chun. Mao Tsetung lectured on the problems of the Chinese peasantry, on education in the countryside, on geography. He also prepared and later lectured on material forming the subject of his *Analysis of Classes in Chinese Society,* the first essay in his *Selected Works.** Mao lectured 32 to 35 hours a week; gave students military drill, lessons in hygiene; taught them the techniques of investigation into social conditions which he had now been practicing for some years. He introduced debates, the independent study of books and articles, condensation by the students of what they read, and field teams.

"I was writing more and more, and now assuming special responsibilities in peasant work in the Communist Party." Clearly Mao Tsetung was not training peasant cadres only for the Northern Expedition, but building the nuclei of countryside Communist peasant organizations.

In January 1926 Mao presented to the Kuomintang Third Congress a report on propaganda work to be done among the peasantry, insisting that the center of the revolutionary movement was "in the countryside." Elected an alternate member of the KMT Central Executive Committee, he also moved an amendment to bring the exiled right-wing movement of the KMT under Tai Chi-tao (now dubbed the Western Hills group) under control by extending "lenient treatment and inducing them to repent." This was not dictated by benevolence; Mao argued it was better to have the right wing return so that their activities could be "checked," rather than leave them to intrigue outside the orbit of the Kuomintang. In organization and propaganda he wanted to extend the mass base, strengthen the grass roots level of the cadres among both peasants and workers. Once again his energy swept onward, became a propelling force among the people he reached. These moves, if considered in the context of the times, were those of an adroit tactician. They constituted a vigorous bid for leadership on a broad foundation. Mao's strategy was to rally as many people as possible within the revolutionary movement, including petty bourgeois members of the KMT as well as the workers and peasants, and those among the national capitalists as yet uncommitted to counterrevolution. Had he been followed in this, the CCP would have been far stronger; but Chen Tu-hsiu never saw the problem at all.

* *Selected Works of Mao Tsetung* (English edition Peking 1961–1965), vol. I.

"On the basis of my study and my work in organizing the Hunan peasants," said Mao, "I wrote two pamphlets, one called *Analysis of Classes in Chinese Society* and the other called *The Class Basis of Chao Heng-ti, and the Tasks Before Us.*" The *Analysis* is dated March 1926 *; it was the result of months of field investigations, which also served for his lectures at the Peasant Institute. Mao emphasized the strategic importance of Hunan in the campaigns to come — Hunan was the key province to conquer in the Northern Expedition, hence the work of mobilizing the Hunan peasantry was of great importance. The essay on Chao Heng-ti was a warning against "liberal" militarists who would try to join the KMT and corrupt the national movement; Chao was even then continuing his persecution of trade union leaders.

But Chen Tu-hsiu interpreted the united front relationship as: Leave the leadership to the KMT leaders.

Mao spent those months arguing, disputing, writing about the necessity of peasant mobilization, but was not listened to; Chen Tu-hsiu refused to print his *Analysis of Classes in Chinese Society* in the Communist Party journals or periodicals because he opposed the opinions advocating "a radical land policy and vigorous organization of the peasantry under the Communist Party . . . I began to disagree with Chen's right opportunist policy about this time, and we gradually drew further apart." This is Mao's reserved description of the dispute with Chen.

The substance of the matter in controversy was not only the peasant question but also the whole problem of leadership. This point is often obscured by Western writers on the subject with discussion of whether the united front alliance with the KMT should have been maintained or not. It is argued that maintenance of the united front was the fundamental error of the Communist Party. The fundamental problem was whether the Communist Party should retain the initiative, which was in its hands all the time but which was squandered by default. It was a matter of class consciousness and class stand, not of maintaining or not maintaining the united front.†

Chen was more anxious to placate and to reassure the landlords and compradores in the KMT than to proceed with the work of the Revolution. He was morally defeated even before the 1927 massa-

* It was first published in February 1926 in the *Peasant Monthly,* the magazine of the Peasant Institute in Kuangchow. It was also published in *Chinese Youth,* publication of the League of Military Youth organized by Chou En-lai in Whangpoo Academy.
† For further discussion of this fundamental problem, see part II, chapter 1.

cres began, because he refused to face the central question which Mao was now to pose: "Who is our enemy, who is our friend? He who cannot distinguish his enemies from his friends cannot be a revolutionary."

On March 13, 1926, the sixth plenum of the executive committee of the Comintern, in Moscow, was to adopt a resolution: "The most important question of the Chinese national liberation movement is the peasant question. . . . The victory of the revolutionary democratic tendency depends on the degree to which the 400 million peasants take part in the decisive revolutionary struggle together with the Chinese workers and under their leadership." This Comintern resolution is echoed in Mao's ideas and writings, though Mao's work with the peasantry antedates it. Mao Tsetung may have thought for a moment that Chen would now change, but Chen paid no attention to Comintern resolutions not to his liking. Yet by June 1926 there were nearly one million peasants organized in associations throughout China. A year later, in June 1927, there would be ten million.

In organizing the peasantry, the Mao-trained cadres of the Peasant Institute were very effective. By the next year, many of them were to die, slaughtered along with hundreds of thousands of peasants in 1927 and 1928. Mao, talking to Edgar Snow in 1936,* "did not think the counterrevolution would have been defeated in 1927 even if the Communist Party had carried out a more aggressive policy of land confiscation and created Communist armies from among the workers and peasants." But the soviets, he said, "could have got an immense start in the South, and a base in which, afterwards, they would never have been destroyed" had the policies of the CCP been for "resolute and full peasant and worker mobilization."

It was not only Chen Tu-hsiu that Mao had to do battle against. There was also the "ultra-left" group in the Party, the leaders in the All-China Federation of Labor, Chang Kuo-tao and Li Li-san.

Chang Kuo-tao argued that it was the "proletariat," the workers, who were the leadership of the Revolution, and therefore it was they and their strength alone which could win it. He persisted in his contempt for the peasantry. "The working class is strong enough . . . to make revolution alone." Mao emphasized that the working class needed allies and friends; that the semi-proletariat, the peasantry, excluding rich peasants and landlords, were its natural friends.

* Edgar Snow *Red Star Over China* (1937, first revised and enlarged edition New York 1968).

Chang despised the peasants as "backward" and "spontaneous capitalists," missing the obvious fact that a leadership also needs foot soldiery, numbers, masses, a potential of human content; it cannot fight alone. Thus, between the lethargy of Chen and the sectarian euphoria of Chang, Mao was checked and hindered in his work. Even if the Comintern and Lenin had pointed out the role of the peasant masses of Asia in the Revolution, Chang Kuo-tao and Chen Tu-hsiu, from diametrically opposite stands, chose to ignore or fear peasant mass potential; this type of "city thinking," dogmatic and unrealistic where China (with a population in which 85 percent were peasants) was concerned, was to bedevil the CCP for a long time.

As the winter of 1925 yielded to the spring of 1926, one by one the Communist positions were being eroded away. The great mass protests of 1925 throughout China had shown that it was no longer possible for foreign interests to hold China down by a show of military force, by gunboats on rivers or the shooting of demonstrators. The fear that all China would "go up in flames" and "become red" now pervaded Western business in China.

Chinese businessmen were assiduously wooed by British, American, and other financial conglomerates. There were renewed promises of taking up the question of Chinese tariff rights and extra-territoriality (clauses of the unequal treaties imposed since 1842).* The Washington conference of 1922 had promised to "look into the matter," but nothing had been done. Now a solemn declaration was issued to the Chinese merchants that tariff autonomy would be restored to China by January 1, 1930. Other lures were dangled before Chinese businessmen to wean them away from "the Reds." Suddenly British bankers and *taipans* † became "concerned" about Chinese culture. "Save the priceless heritage of China's ancient civilization," they clamored. The Western community of Shanghai even did an unprecedented thing; it actually *invited to dinner,* at the Majestic Hotel, representatives of the Shanghai Chinese business community. "The first time in history . . . any such gathering has taken place," crowed the Anglo-American-owned *China Weekly Review*. At this dinner the American chairman of Shanghai's Foreign Municipal Council begged the Chinese capitalists to join foreign interests in devising countermeasures against Bolshevism. He asked: "Why not take advantage of the extreme credulousness of the Chinese

* End of the first Opium War — the first unequal treaty imposed on China.
† Big merchant princes — a word fallen into disuse since 1949.

working classes . . . take advantage of it for their good and for ours." He suggested that the Chinese businessmen present would make better "leaders" of the Chinese society than these "mad . . . rebels." Three weeks later, again making history, three Chinese members were admitted to the all-European Shanghai Municipal Council, which ran the International Settlement.

Through businessmen, secret societies, through a thousand and one strands of guile and corruption, seduction and deceit, approaches were made to all and sundry in Kuangchow. Foreign interests were then reassured by the secret societies, many of whose members were also agents of the European police in China, that "our man" in Kuangchow would take care of the Communists when the time came. That man was Chiang Kai-shek.

And indeed, Chiang was doing his best for foreign interests and Chinese compradores and landlords. Insidiously the workers were being deprived of power. True, they were mobilized; they had armed themselves, they drilled; they worked enthusiastically. But their hours of work, conditions of work were still the same as before; apart from a few minor reforms, nothing was done to ensure security or better working conditions. Buoyed by hope, the workers suffered and sacrificed, and patiently put up with the continuing exactions. "After the Northern Expedition, all will be well." They were already being betrayed, but they did not know it. There were continual complaints from the industrialists of "excesses" by workers. The 150,000 Hongkong strikers staying in Kuangchow had to be fed and clothed. Money was short, and necessarily had to come from local capital. The customs revenues were under British control, which blocked all funds to the "Red" government in Kuangchow. To preserve "unity" the Communist labor leaders, following Chen Tu-hsiu, "restrained" the workers by a process of collective bargaining. At no time during these decisive months did the Central Committee of the CCP, led by Chen Tu-hsiu, give its own political orientation to the masses. It "restrained," "scolded," and "punished" their "excesses," and thus became an auxiliary of the counterrevolution. It did not lead, nor take bold initiatives from its position of strength.

The responsibility of Borodin for this sapping is possibly greater than appears. Borodin argued that restraint must be exercised. Things were difficult; the Communists must not "cause anxiety" to the capitalists in the KMT. There must be "unity of action" above all. . . . Thus the betrayal began.

In January 1926, to replace the murdered Liao Chung-kai, Wang Ching-wei was confirmed as head of the KMT and another triumvirate was set up, consisting of Wang Ching-wei, Chiang Kai-shek and Chiang's military superior, General Hsu Chung-chih. This was a move to curb Chiang.* But Chiang soon got rid of Hsu, with the help of the cadets and the Workers' Strike Committee, after denouncing him as a "rightist." This left a duo of Wang Ching-wei and Chiang Kai-shek. Wang Ching-wei had all the titles and civil honors, Chiang had all the military power. Less than three months later Chiang decided the time had come for the next step to weaken the more liberal wing in the KMT by getting rid of Wang Ching-wei, who stood between him and absolute power, and at the same time to deal a decisive blow to the Communist Party. This led to the famous *Chungshan* incident of March 20, 1926. Like all other landmark episodes in the story of the Chinese Revolution, it has not been completely elucidated to this day.

Borodin was away in Shanghai (his wife, Fanny Borodin, an American, had placed their children in an American school there). The Russian adviser in charge of the Navy Department of the KMT was also away. The KMT navy consisted of a few gunboats; one of them, the *Chungshan,* was in charge of a Communist, Li Chih-lung. Li Chih-lung had confronted the Society for Sun Yatsenism the year before and denounced it as anti-democratic and trying to split the united front. He had thus made himself a target for Chiang.

On March 18, Li Chih-lung received a message asking him to dispatch two gunboats, the *Chungshan* and the *Paopi,* for inspection and docking at Whangpoo dock, a mile or so from the city docks. Another message then came by telephone advising him to have the *Chungshan* ready for inspection, with full equipment.

Li Chih-lung overhauled the ships with extra combat-ready troops on board, and then telephoned Chiang Kai-shek, as he understood the orders to come from him. Chiang, later, would say that he had been warned there would be an attempt to kidnap him, and that when Li telephoned to say "The gunboats are ready" he felt his suspicions confirmed and acted "to avert disaster."

No one seemed to query the singular prescience of Chiang Kai-shek, who had *already* mustered troops and police in large numbers. These, moving with swift precision, arrested Li Chih-lung on his

* For all his play-acting, Chiang's inordinate ambition caused considerable unease among the more dedicated and upright personalities in the Kuomintang.

gunboat and forty other Communists in the city itself. The quarters of the Russian advisers in Kuangchow were surrounded, their guards disarmed. Chiang then seized and imprisoned twenty-five Communist cadres of the Whangpoo Academy, among them Chou En-lai. Before the news of these arrests could spread, the labor union headquarters were raided, leaders arrested, the Workers' Strike Committee and its pickets disarmed, and all weapons seized. Troops and police patrolled the streets, creating an atmosphere of terror; trucks rolled up and down the main thoroughfares with police and special guards armed to the eyebrows.

The other Kuomintang leaders were utterly unprepared. Li Chih-lung unwittingly implicated Wang Ching-wei, saying it was he who had ordered extra soldiers on board all the navy ships, to "prevent trouble," some weeks previously. Chiang kept the tension on with street patrols, curfews, sudden searches, all the apparatus of military intimidation. The CCP was incapable of prompt adequate action. Chang Kuo-tao clamored for an immediate rupture of the united front. This would have been disastrous, for by now the workers were disarmed, the Strike Committee paralyzed, and all the weapons in Chiang's hands. The whole of the Kuomintang would have rallied behind Chiang Kai-shek and the CCP would have been suspected of having tried (and failed) an attempted coup by gunboat.

"In view of the events, the comrades of the left should retire for a while." This resolution was passed by the KMT Central Executive Committee at an urgent meeting. Wang Ching-wei realized that Chiang wanted him out of the way; he left for Europe on a "study tour" and Chiang remained sole master.

Had the CCP then called upon the masses, rallied them — they had the means, for the press and newspapers, curiously enough, had not been occupied by Chiang's squads — had they shown mettle and courage, and refused either to submit or to run, Chiang Kai-shek might not have won this round. But Chen Tu-hsiu was petrified with fear, and kept wringing his hands and asking what to do. Borodin returned from Shanghai, and Chiang fell on his neck, sobbing that perhaps he had been a bit "excessive" but his nerves were bad; he was overworked. His life was in danger, without him the revolutionary cause could not go on; after all, there was the Northern Expedition to prepare. Borodin reprimanded the Communists, stressing they must not be "excessive" and "hasty." Chen Tu-hsiu apologized with meek alacrity; Chiang was gracious enough to accept being pacified, and now advised Chen Tu-hsiu to withdraw Chou En-lai from his post at Whangpoo, saying, "Communists take too much space there," and Chen obeyed with a profusion of apologies. Chiang was now addressed with the utmost deference by the Communist leaders, who wrote to him in deeply respectful terms as to a superior. Instead of the Communists, it was Chiang who now came forward to "explain" the situation to the workers! On May 2, he presented a report to a joint session of the two parties (KMT and CCP) entitled "The Great Union of the Workers, Peasants and Soldiers"! On May 14 martial law was declared; rumors of a "Communist coup" were floated; again the atmosphere of panic was unleashed. The workers remained disarmed; the trade unions gave no orders; the Strike Committee was helpless. In the countryside, landlords, and landlord-recruited armies, started to murder peasant union leaders.

Yet when Chiang stepped on the platform of the Third All-China Labor Federation Conference held in Kuangchow at the end of May 1926 (with Liu Shao-chi and Li Li-san in charge), which represented 400 unions and 1,240,000 workers, of whom 800,000 had taken part in more than 200 political and economic strikes in the preceding year, he sounded wholeheartedly left. "The worker-peasant masses . . . have swept away all the counterrevolutionaries and consolidated the basis of the national government. . . . From this one can see that the workers and peasants are already able to fight imperialism *with their own forces,* without reliance upon the forces of the army," said Commander-in-Chief Chiang Kai-shek, greeted with thunderous applause by the workers there. Chiang then clenched his fist and shouted: "Long live the world revolution!" To anyone versed in Chinese ways of doing things, Chiang was warning his own adherents that the workers were still too strong; the comedy must be played a little longer. As Mao Tsetung said then: "Chiang Kai-shek speaks well. Let us see which he will do." What Chiang was doing was actually very clear. He was "curbing" Communist influence.

On May 15, 1926, at the KMT Central Executive Committee plenary session, Chiang had introduced a special resolution to "readjust party affairs." It was designed to limit the role of Communists in the KMT party and its organizations. A complete list of all CCP members who were also KMT members was to be furnished to him; directing posts in the KMT should not go to Communists; all instructions issued by the CCP to its own members were to be submitted first for approval to him. The response of the CCP leadership was abject. Chiang also asked to be apprised of all messages and directives of the Comintern to the CCP. Mao was the only one present to voice dissent.

With Wang Ching-wei tactfully away on a European tour, Chiang became leader of the KMT, the army, the police; all government and party offices were subordinate to him as commander-in-chief of the Nationalist Army. He controlled finance, the arsenal, the Political Department, Whangpoo Academy. But he still needed the Communists for the Northern Expedition; without them his army would have incredible difficulties, for he could not mobilize peasants and workers. He now made a "self-criticism," invited reprimand for the "overhasty actions of his subordinates." He punished some junior officers, sacrificed a few of his old associates — such as the garrison commander of Kuangchow, whom he disliked — and with real power in hand went on to prepare his next coup.

The KMT was being transformed from a nationalist party with revolutionary elements to a counterrevolutionary instrument in the hands of a military dictator, Chiang Kai-shek. From that time Chen Tu-hsiu, in fact if not in word, abdicated leadership in the united front, the Revolution, and even the CCP. From that time the Northern Expedition to unify China was being subverted to become a military campaign to launch Chiang's rule.

For decades controversy has raged over this First United Front policy of 1924–1927. It has been asserted that Leon Trotsky, with his warnings of betrayal and his demands that the CCP "come out of the KMT" and disrupt the united front, was right, while Stalin's recommendation to preserve the united front was wrong and led to the massacres.

There is no doubt that Stalin was not only misinformed on the Chinese Revolution but never understood its complexity. The Comintern, in its resolutions and directives, would become increasingly out of touch, and especially out of time, with the situation. But this does not make Trotsky's thesis correct. The "left" of the CCP, like Chang Kuo-tao, followed Trotsky in their clamor for a rupture of the united front; but a rupture of the united front could not cure the weakness within the Communist Party; it would have meant its extermination, and Chiang would then have brought in foreign troops to "aid" in the liquidation. This would have meant the disintegration of the whole nationalist movement Sun Yatsen had given a lifetime to build up.

The substance of the matter was not the retention of the united front, but Chen Tu-hsiu's policy of capitulation, practically handing the leadership of the revolutionary movement to the counterrevolutionary leaders of the Kuomintang. The importance of this First United Front, and this first betrayal, is precisely the lesson it gave to those capable of learning it.

Trotsky's condemnation of the united front was a repudiation of Lenin's theses of "temporary alliance" with bourgeois parties. Lenin had said in 1920 that the bourgeoisie would try to seize and keep control of the national revolutionary movements. However radical they sounded, they would betray and compromise with imperialism. Hence the Communist Party must preserve its own independence and keep the leadership of the workers and peasants in its hands. This strategy of the united front only Mao Tsetung seems to have understood. Ten years later, when the Second United Front was formed, he would hammer the terrible lesson of the first into the Chinese Communist Party.

The coup of March 1926 had been reported to Moscow, but its real significance was denied or underestimated, and for this deplorable error reports minimizing its gravity, from Borodin and Chen Tu-hsiu, must also be held responsible. Borodin wrote of the "impetuosity" of the Communists. Chiang played another master stroke by sending his son, Chiang Ching-kuo, to be educated in Moscow. How could anyone then suspect him of not being pro-Communist?

Mao Tsetung was present at the combined CCP-KMT session in May where Chiang Kai-shek, through his representative there, insisted on "readjustment" of CCP-KMT relations. All the resolutions for restriction and limitation of the functioning of the CCP were passed by the KMT members. Communists lost their jobs in KMT departments. When Chiang Kai-shek's representative brought up a motion that Communist members should declare their Communist affiliations, Mao Tsetung protested. He argued that this was impossible, for in most areas in China a Communist would be arrested and executed on the spot. "This is not good for the future of the national Revolution," said Mao. He relinquished his office in the Propaganda Department of the Kuomintang. But the Peasant Institute was ignored; Mao then left for Shanghai to report to the Politburo of the CCP.

A meeting was held. Liu Shao-chi, leader in the All-China Federation of Labor, and Chang Kuo-tao were present. Liu Shao-chi said that the workers were "too backward"; that it was a great responsibility to educate the peasantry and to lead them; he implied that the working class was not ready and suffered from "infantile leftism"; he thus advocated the same policies as Chen Tu-hsiu. Chang Kuo-tao, on the other hand, maintained that the national bourgeoisie was the natural enemy of the Revolution, that a break was the only cure possible. The young CCP must release itself from the united front and fight.

Mao Tsetung started to speak of the peasants and of peasant mobilization, but was interrupted by the secretary-general, Chen Tu-hsiu. Unable to get a hearing, Mao told his friends that the only way to cure the weakness in the Communist Party was to prepare armed peasant organizations on a nationwide scale. "The peasantry is the surest ally of the proletariat," he repeated. He then went back to the Peasant Institute in Kuangchow. Li Fu-chun, married to Tsai Chang, the sister of Mao's friend Tsai Ho-shen, was then in Kuangchow as a teacher. He asked Mao to lecture to his students on the topic of the peasantry when Mao returned from Shanghai.

In July 1926 Mao again went back to Shanghai to set up, at last, the Peasant Department of the Chinese Communist Party, utilizing the cadres trained at the Peasant Institute in Kuangchow. He also went to Hunan and alerted the cadres there. In June the KMT Central Executive Committee had decided to launch the Northern Expedition; in July the mobilization of the Nationalist armies was announced. Traveling to and fro, writing articles, editorials, lecturing and mobilizing the peasant associations for the battles to come, Mao's work was the most important of all for the Revolution, but it was overshadowed by more spectacular parades, mass demonstrations of enthusiasm as the Nationalist Army set forth from the city of Kuangchow to end "feudalism and imperialism."

There is a little-known article by Mao Tsetung, written about that time, on *The Bitter Sufferings of the Peasants in the Provinces of Kiangsu and Chekiang, and Their Anti-feudal, Anti-landlord Movement,* published in November 1926 in the Communist weekly *Guide.* It was the result of investigations in the countryside conducted by Mao Tsetung when he went to Shanghai to consult the Politburo. In these field trips he took Peasant Institute trainees with him. The article was abridged from the original draft when printed; it left out the recommendation which Mao Tsetung put forward for organizing the peasantry, a "censorship" possibly imposed by Chen Tu-hsiu.

Mao wrote down in detail the situation in the various counties he visited. He related how the landlords oppressed the farmers; how Chou Shui-ping, a student of Wuhsi, returning from Japan in 1925 had tried to organize "the tenant farmers' cooperative self-help society." "The peasants followed him . . . they rose like clouds . . . with one voice demanded the reduction of rent. . . . But before the peasants had united themselves the landlords had done so. . . . The gentry and landlords of the three districts acted simultaneously." They appealed to the warlord in control of the province, Sun Chuan-fang, who executed Chou and suppressed the movement. But in 1926 again the peasants had risen to demand rent reduction, for whether the year was good or bad, landlords refused to lower rent.

In the spring of 1926 in Tzuhsi county, the landlords had refused rent reduction in spite of the drought, and the farmers rioted. "All the *lumpen proletariat* joined them very courageously," Mao wrote, alluding thus to his classification in *Analysis of Classes in Chinese Society* of the "elements" not considered worthy of Marxist classification by some of his colleagues: beggars, landless field hands, vagrants. The peasants went into the landlord houses, ate up the grain and stores, burned the police station, and shared out the weapons. "The movement was suppressed . . . the reason being that the masses did not fully organize themselves *and they did not have the proper leadership* . . . so that the movement failed when it was starting."

This article was probably meant as a warning, spelling out the course to take. The broad hint about leadership was meant to rouse his comrades in the Politburo. In vain. Chen Tu-hsiu had already adopted "limitation of peasant struggle" as his policy and in September had forbidden the formation of any peasant militia. Mao spoke of struggle, Chen propounded the formulas "Step back" and "Work for the KMT without going beyond the limits imposed by the KMT." Thus in military work, as Chou En-lai was to report, the Communists were ordered to "cooperate with the KMT" without in any way doing any political organizing for themselves within the armies preparing to set out on the military campaign to unify the country.

On July 9, 1926, the Nationalist Army left Kuangchow for the

Northern Expedition in the greatest enthusiasm. To the exultant crowds cheering the gray-clad battalions, Chiang had promised to defeat all the warlords, unify China, secure the abolition of unequal treaties and extra-territoriality, the abolition of imperialism and the achievement of "universal peace." Chiang was the man of the hour, hero of the land. This was great timing; Chiang had again wrested the initiative; the CCP appeared a captive chained to his triumph.

Within two months Kiangsi, Hunan, Hupei provinces fell to Nationalist armies. On September 12 the army of General Tang Sheng-chih, a Hunan "liberal" militarist who had rallied to Sun Yat-sen's Kuangchow government in 1923, entered Changsha. By the end of September the province was in his hands, and Tang became acting governor; the other warlords fled.

In these swift victories, it became evident that success was largely due to the organized strikes of city workers and to the peasant uprisings behind enemy lines. The fervor and self-sacrifice of the workers was unequaled; they formed militia battalions and took the warlord garrisons by surprise. The peasants in the countryside marched to seize police posts, acted as porters, couriers, guides, stretcher-bearers, fed and watered the Nationalist Army — all without pay. In Hunan, especially, where Mao Tsetung had worked so hard, the Nationalist Army was assisted by peasant self-mobilized militia which continued to expand on its own. The battles were won for the army before the battalions arrived. This massive demonstration of popular power frightened many of the officer cadets and big capitalists. Here was might and power; it could make a thoroughgoing revolution. The more victories, the more they feared for themselves.

In December 1926 Mao was back in Changsha. His presence there was of great importance, for he addressed the first Peasants' and Workers' Congress of Hunan (December 20–29, 1926), of which he had been elected chairman. At this Congress of workers and peasants, whose significance has been blurred and even ignored, Mao made a speech important in its timing and also challenging, for it went against Chen Tu-hsiu's orders.

According to a report in the Changsha newspaper dated December 29, 1926, Mao said that a great change was coming to China. Already 1,200,000 peasants had been organized; a united front of workers, peasants, traders and students was necessary. The Revolution needed a union of all revolutionary classes, but fundamentally the national revolution was a peasant revolution under the leadership of the working class, and it therefore depended on the peasantry. He then analyzed the market for the commercial trades in the countryside. He also analyzed the situation of the students and intellectuals; most of them were nonrevolutionary, some were progressive, a few were reactionary; if they wanted to make revolution they must ally themselves with workers and peasants.* We can imagine how unwelcome this speech was to Chen Tu-hsiu. But even more significant is the situation in which Mao found himself at that time.

Mao was torn between what he felt ought to be done and what he had been ordered to do. Complaints by the Kuomintang through its delegates in Moscow about "excesses" of the peasants and workers had even reached Stalin. Borodin received truculent messages from Chiang Kai-shek declaring that Hunan was "out of control" and that there would be incidents due to peasant excesses. Strict orders were given to labor unions to restrict the workers and to peasant cadres to "restrain" the peasantry in Hunan. This also was Mao's mission; he had been told to "check and thwart," to tell the Congress of peasants and workers to submit to orders. But as he faced the tremendous tide of peasant power he saw the dreadfulness of the wrong decisions and the betrayal of the Revolution they entailed. The speech he made was therefore more militant than expected by Chen Tu-hsiu.

Meanwhile Stalin, who had advocated rousing the peasants, had now been swayed; this explains a telegram from Stalin sent in October 1926, in which he enjoined "caution and restraint." Stalin, who did not know the situation, could not imagine how Chen Tu-hsiu would jump at this chance to stop effective action.

In November Stalin reversed himself. "The information we get is incorrect," he said, and a telegram was then sent which reinforced the line of peasant mobilization. In the same November the Comintern (seventh plenum) under Stalin's directive also reversed its resolution advising "restraint." But it is a pointer to the confusion and contradictoriness which existed — not to mention translation difficulties, misreporting, misinterpretation — that Chen Tu-hsiu did not show this later reversal to Mao, nor, it appears, to other members of the Politburo until much later. "No one can direct a revolution by telegraph," Stalin is reported to have said, yet this was now happening. The Comintern resolutions, Stalin's directives, came thick and fast because the CCP leadership was incapable of its own decisions. But it was also incapable of implementing those of others, and this "think-tank help" from afar added to the disaster, so much

* Documents seen by the author in Changsha museum.

so that even today the tangle has led to erroneous interpretation.* Moscow cables issued a stream of advice to the CCP, but never knew in what circumstances it would misapply. The Comintern organized committees to work on the "documentary material" and submit theses; these took time; two committees produced two divergent theses. Envoys were sent who squabbled openly and contradicted each other. And there was the time element; the situation changed so rapidly that by the time "advice" came from Moscow all was radically different. And in Moscow itself the Stalin-Trotsky struggle did not make things easier.

In the midst of this appalling muddle,† what was Mao to do? A photograph shows him at this December Peasants' and Workers' Congress singularly gaunt, standing in a loose-fitting jacket, hands on his hips. His face is not happy. All we know is that he did *not* restrain the peasants and workers at the Congress, who passed resolutions for confiscation of land from the landlords.

In the meantime, the revolutionary army swept forward to Wuhan, which fell in December. Chiang Kai-shek arrived in Changsha and delivered a speech, in his role as a "people's hero," calculated to please an audience of militant workers and banish all suspicion of himself.

"Only after imperialism is overthrown can China obtain her independence. . . . The Third International is the headquarters of the world revolution. . . . We must unite with Russia to overthrow impe-

---

* See Kostas Mavrakis, *Du Trotskyisme* (Paris 1971), pp. 151–162. It is now reported in the USSR that the Russian General Galen established a plan for the Northern Expedition and all the military operations; but neither he nor any of the other Russian advisers drew attention to the class struggle; they divided the KMT into "right" and "left" and stated that the "left," "due to the objective course of events," would "remain with the CCP." The Russian documents are interesting in that although they assess clearly most of the Chinese generals, they only mention Chiang Kai-shek favorably (the documents were prepared six months or more before Chiang's coup of March 1926). The Russians thought Chiang would be forced to keep "left" because he depended on the Kuangchow government for funds and resources. In this way they signally failed to understand the financial network of Western big business in China.

† M. N. Roy, the Comintern Indian who became a Trotskyite, and Bukharin, later to be purged by Stalin, hammered out between October and December 1926 two entirely divergent lines of action for the Chinese revolutionary situation. Tan Ping-shan, director of the CCP Labor Department, who was in Moscow as head of a delegation to the Comintern in November 1926, contradicted himself twice in his report. At one moment he was strongly urging that the peasant revolution should *not* be restricted, but later urged that it should be. Borodin emphasized that the main task was *military victory over the militarists,* and Borodin's thesis was supported. The seventh plenum of the Comintern, however, emphasized that "the party of the proletariat must put forward a *radical agrarian program* . . . or it will lose hegemony in the national revolutionary movement."

rialism. . . . The Chinese Revolution is part of the world revolution. . . . We must unite all partisans of world revolution to overthrow imperialism." Thus he spoke, and already the workers in Kuangchow were being murdered by his lieutenants.

"In Hunan I inspected peasant organizations and political conditions in five districts, Changsha, Liling, Hsiang Tan, Hungshan and Hsiang Hsiang, and made my report . . . urging the adoption of a new line in the peasant movement." This was Mao's famous *Report on an Investigation of the Peasant Movement in Hunan* * based on a five-week tour, January 4 to February 5, 1927.

Suppression of the peasants' associations had begun right after the Nationalist Army victory in Hunan at the end of September 1926. Yet the registered membership in the peasant associations had increased in two months, November and December, from one million to two million families; 54 counties out of 75 now had peasant associations. But the head of the CCP Peasant Department pelted Mao with angry telegrams urging that the "riffraff" be restrained so as not to antagonize the KMT. What were Mao's feelings as he clutched the telegrams, knew the policies wrong and heard round him the ovations of the peasantry? He could not "check and thwart." He investigated. Between December 30 and January 3 Mao spent five days in Shaoshan preparing his spirit for the great battle he would now begin.

The peasants had already started on their own to confiscate landlords' land, to punish bullies and corrupt officials; these actions, described as "atrocities" by the fleeing landlords, had the approval of Mao Tsetung. Considering what they had suffered, the peasants were remarkably fair-minded and lenient. This was revolution, and Mao Tsetung found himself on the side of the peasant masses in the midst of this tornado, this tempest, as he was to describe it, an outpouring of revolutionary energy, cosmic, elemental, irresistible; an avalanche capable of "changing heaven and earth."

All his life he would remember the impact of this extraordinary strength, "mightier than any" when once set in motion, animated by the ideas that would "teach the sun and moon to change places." Every day and night of these thirty-two days he would remember as a bone-deep experience, shaping his thoughts.

"During my recent visit to Hunan I made a firsthand investigation

* *Selected Works of Mao Tsetung* (English edition Peking 1961–1965), vol. I.

of conditions. . . . I called together fact-finding conferences in villages and county towns . . . I listened attentively . . . Many of the hows and whys of the peasant movement were the exact opposite of what the gentry in Hankow and Changsha are saying. I saw and heard of many strange things of which I had hitherto been unaware. *All talk directed against the peasant movement must be speedily set right. All the wrong measures taken by the revolutionary authorities concerning the peasant movement must be speedily changed. Only thus can the future of the Revolution be benefited. For the present upsurge of the peasant movement is a colossal event.** In a very short time . . . several hundred million peasants will rise like a mighty storm, like a hurricane, a force so swift and violent that no power, however great, will be able to hold it back. They will smash all the trammels that bind them and rush forward along the road to liberation."

Mao Tsetung went on to describe, paragraph by paragraph, all he had seen, drawing anecdotes, vivid word pictures. The development of the peasant movement fell into two periods: before September 1926 a period of organization, but from "last October to January of this year . . . of revolutionary action." This latter period did coincide with the Northern Expedition, and during it the membership in peasant associations had jumped to two million families, which meant ten million people.† "Almost half the peasants in Hunan are now organized." They were attacking the local tyrants — landlords who respected no law or common humanity, who killed, raped the daughters and wives of peasants or kidnapped them at will — "the privileges which the feudal landlords enjoyed for thousands of years are being shattered to pieces." " 'All power to the peasant associations' has become a reality. Even trifles such as a quarrel between husband and wife are brought to the peasant association." So powerful were they that small landlords sought admission to the peasant association. "Who wants your filthy money?" the poor peasants would reply, and refuse them.

But more telling is Mao's pointed remark on the reaction to all this. " 'It's terrible' or 'It's fine.' . . . When the news from the countryside reached the cities, it caused immediate uproar." Even quite revolutionary-minded people in the cities were "downhearted," said Mao, and thought that "It's terrible." But Mao asserted that it

* Emphasis not in original.
† As Mao explained, each family registered only one name.

was fine. "The great peasant masses have risen to fulfill their historic mission . . . In a few months the peasants have accomplished what Dr. Sun Yatsen wanted but failed to accomplish in the forty years he devoted to the national revolution. This is a marvelous feat . . . It's fine.

"If your revolutionary viewpoint is firmly established and if you have been to the villages and looked around, you will undoubtedly feel thrilled as never before. Countless thousands of the enslaved — the peasants — are striking down the enemies who battened on their flesh. *What the peasants are doing is absolutely right; what they are doing is fine!*

"The peasants are clear-sighted. Who is bad and who is not . . . the peasants keep clear accounts. . . . A revolution is not a dinner party, or writing an essay, or painting a picture, or doing embroidery; it cannot be so refined, so leisurely and gentle, so temperate, kind, courteous, restrained and magnanimous. *A revolution is an insurrection, an act of violence by which one class overthrows another.*" Mao made fun of those who said the peasants were going too far. "Proper limits have to be exceeded in order to right a wrong, or else the wrong cannot be righted."

Mao listed "fourteen great achievements" of the peasantry. These achievements sound very much like the suggestions and proposals which were then being made by the Comintern. Mao was proving that the peasants were indeed carrying out the agrarian revolution and doing the things they were supposed to do, according to Communist dicta. They were organizing themselves, hitting the landlords politically and economically, overthrowing feudal rule, defeating landlord armies, organizing their own self-defense, eliminating bandits, abolishing levies, and starting movements for education and co-operatives. They were also building roads and repairing embankments. And all this they were doing by their own strength, through their own organizations. Mao ended with a gibe at the Chen leadership: "To talk about 'arousing the masses of the people' day in and day out and then to be scared to death when the masses do rise — what difference is there between this and Lord Sheh's love of dragons?" This referred to a famous lord who loved dragons in paint, but when a real live dragon came to visit him, he nearly died of fear.

Back Mao went to Changsha with this piece, to find that things had very much deteriorated during the thirty-two days that he had been gone in the countryside. For now all was fear and faintheartedness. In Wuhan, where the Kuomintang government * had moved from Kuangchow, he found things highly unpleasant. This corruption of the cities under the Kuomintang we must trace briefly; for much had happened during the time Mao was away in the countryside seeing peasant power "teach the sun and moon to change places."

In Kuangchow and in other cities under the KMT, actually under Chiang Kai-shek's military control, public meetings, the press, the workers' and peasants' volunteer corps, the right to strike, were restricted in the name of "maintaining discipline to ensure the success of the Northern Expedition." All strikes were labeled "counterrevolutionary." The secret society men from Shanghai had been pouring into Kuangchow since the summer of 1926; they came by sea from Hongkong, laden with money and weapons (supplied in great part by the British and French), to destroy Communist organizations.

The secret society men formed spurious labor unions. One gang became a "policemen's union," and was then turned loose in armed attacks on the real workers' unions, a dress rehearsal for the massacres to take place the next year. The ferocity of the gangs, the cruel tortures they inflicted, gravely affected morale. More than fifty factory workers were killed in a few days, and hundreds crippled. The employers threw out the crippled workers without compensation; they were upheld by the "collective bargaining" teams instituted and accepted by the CCP Labor Department.†

In December, in a speech on the peasant question, Stalin himself had suggested the formation of elected revolutionary committees by the peasantry, to carry out the agrarian revolution. He had added, *"I know there are people in the KMT, even in the Chinese Communist Party,* who think it is impossible to have a revolution in the countryside, who are afraid that pushing the peasantry in the revolution will break the united anti-imperialist front. . . . *This is a profound error.* . . . The peasant question must be linked to the perspectives of the Chinese final aim."

---

* The Kuomintang government, previously sited in Kuangchow, installed itself in Wuhan on January 1, 1927.

† To some foreign delegates of the Third International who visited Kuangchow in January 1927 (among them J. Doriot, then a French agent of the Comintern, later a fascist) General Li Chih-seng, Chiang's henchman in command there, declared that he "loved and cherished tenderly the working class"! He was at that very moment beating, jailing and shooting them.

There is nothing in this speech of Stalin's supporting the restraint preached by Chen Tu-hsiu.

Within the KMT the power struggle between Chiang Kai-shek — assisted by the right-wingers — and a "liberal" wing, supporters of Wang Ching-wei, which was labeled the "left" Kuomintang, had now reached a climax. This "left" KMT was itself a confused amalgam; there were genuine patriots, but also many opportunists. On the whole, it had very few big landlords and businessmen. The main goal of this group was to oust Chiang from power and get Wang Ching-wei back. They represented a trend to restore civilian control of the government, in contrast to Chiang's purely military rule. This "left" KMT, now in Wuhan, sought to restrain Chiang Kai-shek, who had moved headquarters in November 1926 to Nanchang, to direct the campaigns.

Chiang had suggested that the KMT government follow him to Nanchang. This would have made it easier for him to control the civilian administration. But this was turned down, and a convention of the KMT in Wuhan in January removed Chiang Kai-shek from his party and army positions and reserved the leadership for Wang Ching-wei, who was now asked to return.

This intrigue within the KMT was generally regarded as instigated by the Communists. Chen Tu-hsiu, seconded by Borodin, pinned his hopes on Wang Ching-wei. The acting Hunan governor, General Tang Sheng-chih, was cast in the role of Chiang's rival as the military arm of the "left" KMT to continue the Northern Expedition, while Chiang Kai-shek was castigated for authoritarianism.

In the city of Wuhan the workers were jubilant. The great concentration of China's small proletariat (4 million in all, 600,000 in Wuhan) * induced a sensation of triumph in CCP members by their ardent and total support, which obscured the real issues for those who never looked beyond city walls. The "left" KMT petty bourgeois radicals, who "sounded more Red than any Communist," as Anna Louise Strong reported,† added to this general (and deceiving) impression of victory for the left-wingers. But as soon as the workers in Wuhan began to organize themselves into pickets, militia, and revolutionary committees, the traditional wail sounded — they were

---

* It is reckoned that there were at most 4 million workers in China then — 1 percent of the total population.

† Anna Louise Strong (1885–1970) in her *China's Millions* (New York 1928) gives excellent descriptions of Wuhan at that time.

"going too far," committing "excesses" — from these very men whose inflammatory speeches made screaming headlines in the press.

Again to avoid "conflict," the Communist Wuhan Labor Department set up an arbitration board which agreed "to follow tradition in fixing the working hours" and "to leave the practice of hiring and dismissing to traditional practice" as well as the treatment of apprentices, child labor, and women. The Communist Federation of Labor executive committee, with Liu Shao-chi and Li Li-san at its head, agreed to this.* The working day was twelve hours, the working week seven days; there was no compensation for accidents; children (called apprentices) went unpaid for the first five to seven years of labor.

But the political vigor of the workers created its own momentum. They demonstrated at the Hankow British Concession border; the British withdrew their gunboats; on January 4 the workers stormed the concession, removed the barricades, the barbed wire and sandbags, and took the concession back "for the country." There was no looting, no pillage, no one was killed or beaten; no houses entered. No leadership from the KMT or the Communist Party had dictated this action; it was a demonstration of working-class power. Eugene Chen, foreign minister of the Wuhan KMT government, signed the papers legalizing the return of the Hankow and Kiukiang British concessions to Chinese jurisdiction.

Chen Tu-hsiu deplored the seizure: "The foreigners might have become irritated . . ."

At Nanchang visitors, foreign and Chinese, diplomats and bankers, flowed in and out of Chiang Kai-shek's headquarters. Chiang now had access to funds and resources from the foreign powers in China and the compradores. At almost the same time that Borodin and the Russian advisers in Wuhan were saying that Chiang could not possibly turn against the national revolution because it would cut off his funds and resources, he was being amply rewarded for doing precisely that.

Soon after the takeover of the British Concession, Chiang had paid a short visit to Wuhan. Borodin took him round. Tight-lipped, Chiang inspected the city; saw the British Concession kept in order by workers' pickets; saw the workers' military training; returned in

* Liu Shao-chi, vice-chairman of the executive committee, All-China Federation of Labor, organized the Wuhan League of Labor Unions in November 1926. Li Li-san was also a member of the Communist Trade Union International. Anna Louise Strong mentions meeting him in Wuhan in 1927; see her *China's Millions* (New York 1928).

stony silence to Nanchang and announced his intention to "purify" the ranks of the KMT. All those who did not carry out the Three Principles of Sun Yatsen were to be ousted.

It was against this backdrop of confusion, intrigue, betrayal, that Mao produced his *Report on an Investigation of the Peasant Movement in Hunan*. In its passionate yet profoundly logical sweep, combining scrupulous social research and observation with an emotion almost volcanic, the report will remain one of the world's great literary documents as well as a political manifesto. In it Mao's grasp of the Chinese agrarian revolution in its political, economic, social and human dimensions appears in consummate detail. There is not only analysis, but also a plan, detailed and minute, for organization and leadership; for as Mao would say, quoting Marx: "It is not enough to study the world . . . one must change it."

What Mao's report made clear was that the peasant upsurge had coincided with his return to Hunan the previous winter and so had the membership increase. This was evidence to Chen Tu-hsiu that Mao was abetting peasant revolutionary action. He had failed to "check and thwart."

"Early next spring," Mao said (that would be February 1927), "when I reached Wuhan, an interprovincial meeting of peasants was held, and I attended it and discussed the proposals of my thesis. . . . At this meeting were Peng Pai, Fang Chih-min, and two Russian Communists . . . among others. A resolution was passed adopting my proposal for submission to the Fifth Congress of the Communist Party; the Central Committee, however, rejected it."

Mao had written: "Every revolutionary comrade and every revolutionary party will be put to the test, to be accepted or rejected as they decide. There are three alternatives. To march at their [the peasants'] head and lead them? To trail behind them, gesticulating and criticizing? Or to stand in their way and oppose them? Every Chinese is free to choose, but events will force you to make the choice *quickly*." Mao thus challenged "every comrade" to measure up to revolution.

There were more meetings at which Mao Tsetung spoke forcefully on the peasant revolution. He was supported by Tsai Ho-sen, Li Fu-chun, Peng Pai, Fang Chih-min. But Chen Tu-hsiu refused to publish or to circulate Mao's report. Thus he chose to "stand in their way and oppose them."

Yet in the same February, in Moscow, the enlarged plenum of the executive of the Comintern had once again discussed the peasant question. Mao Tsetung's report, though denied printing in the official Chinese Communist weekly, *The Guide,* was favorably received. The thesis adopted by the plenum reiterated: *The agrarian question at the present stage . . . is in acute form. . . . It is the central point of the actual situation. The class which will boldly take up this essential question and give it a radical solution . . . will direct the Revolution.*

"The might of Chinese militarism rests on foreign imperialism on the one hand, on the indigenous landlords on the other. . . . To overthrow completely the military and feudal cliques, the economic and political struggle of the peasantry *must* be developed, for it is part of the anti-imperialist struggle.

"The idea that an acute class struggle in the countryside will weaken the anti-imperialist united front is unfounded. . . . Not to boldly take up the agrarian question, not to give support . . . to the objective demands of the peasant masses will be a real danger for the revolution. . . . It would be unwise not to put *in first place* in the program of the national revolution the agrarian movement, for fear of alienating the uncertain and perfidious cooperation of a part of the capitalist class. . . . This tactic is not revolutionary proletarian politics . . . the Communist Party must not fall into this error."

Can there be any doubt but that the Comintern thesis coincided with Mao's thesis? Again, in March 1927, at a meeting of the "left" Kuomintang (with Communists present), Mao Tsetung spoke with great passion of the peasant movement; defended the peasant organizations for their direct dealing with bullies, gangsters, and bad landlords, and urged the arming of the peasantry. He once more presented his report to the Central Committee; it was rejected again, as counter to "everything that had been decided." In April, at a special commission called to "investigate" the land problem, Mao Tsetung spoke: "There is a high tide of the peasant movement, both in Hunan and in Hupei. . . . In solving the land question in China, we must first grasp reality." To people who said the peasants' actions were "illegal" he retorted: "Legal recognition of this reality will only come afterwards." He did not advocate direct confiscation of land but simply "not paying rent; this is enough." In other meetings, he reminded the political cadres active in the peasant movement that land reform was the best way to get the peasants to join in the national revolution and that "without this [land reform] the revolutionary forces would find it difficult to move."

But Mao was not through with inept and hostile bureaucracy, the last dishonorable refuge of the Chen "leadership." The special commission before which Mao spoke set up a "land survey committee," ostensibly to ascertain how land confiscation should be done, and define the difference between big landlords and small ones. Mao Tsetung, irritated by this pointless procrastination, said that "in Hunan, the peasants have already divided up the land themselves . . . the landlords are fleeing into the cities." He added, "The militarists in Hunan are also exploiters of the peasants. . . . The Nationalist government, after establishing itself in Hunan, has also not eliminated this exploitation . . . completely."

And now not only Chen Tu-hsiu but other Communists, made to face the stark facts of revolution, turned against Mao. Chang Kuo-tao found Mao Tsetung's proposals on confiscation of land of landlords over 30 mous (5 acres) but advocating "flexibility" as conditions were different in each province and locality, not thoroughgoing enough. He recommended wholesale immediate confiscation of all landlord land, big or small. Finally the land survey committee set the limit for confiscation at 500 mous (80 acres), and *only* if there were no officers from the KMT armies in the family; any land belonging to officers' families, however large, could not be touched. Since there was scarcely a landlord family who could not boast, through clan connections, of one relative, however distant, in the army, this simply meant there would be no confiscation of landlord land at all, nor any land reform.

Thus the betrayal grew.

8

The Betrayal

By the spring of 1927 the CCP-led All-China Federation of Labor was forsaking the Wuhan workers as it had done in Kuang-chow. The workers were asked sacrifices "for the sake of the revolution." They gave up their demands for an eight-hour day at the arsenal, to work thirteen to seventeen hours "because our revolutionary government is threatened." They postponed the demand for a child labor law. "I myself saw children of seven and eight working ten hours in cotton mills," writes Anna Louise Strong.* The reason for this was twofold — the pressure from the "left" Kuomintang capitalists and the economic difficulties in which the Wuhan government found itself.

On March 24, Chiang Kai-shek occupied Nanking, which he would make his capital city. He was now advancing, deliberately and slowly, upon Shanghai, symbolic city of "imperialism." In Shanghai several thousand workers had already staged an uprising in October 1926 against the local warlord Sun Chuan-fang. Chou En-lai was there to organize the workers. In February 1927 Chou had conducted a general strike with half a million workers. But the Shanghai branch of the Communist Federation of Labor was under the direction of Li Li-san, and it stuck to the principle of "unity," which was the Chen Tu-hsiu slogan. As a result Kuomintang "trade unionists" also mobilized the workers, to prepare them to receive "the heroic armies of the Northern Expedition" under Chiang Kai-shek.

No directive for combat readiness was issued by the Central Committee. Chou En-lai, however, had set up an underground city council, and also a provincial council ready to take power in a coalition if need be. He drilled the workers for armed assault. The KMT gar-

* Anna Louise Strong *China's Millions* (New York 1928).

rison commander tried to forestall Chou En-lai's bid by making preparations to surrender the Chinese part of the city to Chiang Kai-shek, and to him alone. Chou En-lai, however, prepared for the take-over of the Chinese city, and on the evening of March 20 led the workers to occupy the police headquarters, the small arsenal, and the post office. The plan involved seven surprise attacks, launched at the same time. The railroad station was also seized. This momentarily stopped Chiang's entry into the city, and gave the Communists a decisive advantage.

For three weeks the workers held the Chinese city. The foreign concessions and International Settlement were not touched by the Communists, while outside Shanghai the troops of Chiang waited. As late as March 16, 1927, the Russian advisers of the KMT still thought that "the revolutionary pressure from below is so strong that Chiang is compelled to swear allegiance to the principles of revolutionary loyalty." Rumors of a KMT-CCP rift were denied by Chen Tu-hsiu.

In late March Wang Ching-wei came back from France via Russia, where he had had lengthy talks with Russian notables. Chen Tu-hsiu went to meet him in Shanghai. On April 6 they issued a joint proclamation restating the alliance between the Wuhan KMT government and the CCP, and denouncing as "malicious rumors" all talk of a split. Wang Ching-wei also had a meeting with Chiang Kai-shek on the very same day. A sensation of optimism, of an entente, was thus created. It weakened the will to fight of the more militant workers' leaders.

Chiang Kai-shek's intermediaries were meanwhile parleying with foreign and Chinese compradore and banking firms of Shanghai, who arranged for an immediate gift to him of five million silver dollars. On April 8 Chiang met his old friends the heads of the Shanghai secret societies. These in turn met and had talks with several foreign consular officials. Arms and ammunition were moved in trucks from the foreign settlements to the gangs, and money flowed thither as well.

On April 12, six days after the meetings held "in a spirit of unity, friendship and cooperation," squads of well-armed secret society thugs went round seizing Communist-organized labor pickets and executing them. "The shooting started and did not stop for three weeks," J. B. Powell * was to record. On April 14 Chiang's army

---

* J. B. Powell *My Twenty-five Years in China* (New York 1945).

entered Shanghai and continued the butchering. Several thousand workers died, other thousands were horribly tortured. For months the daily rumble of military trucks would be heard, bringing their loads of workers to be shot. For almost two years, every weekend, the executions continued. Thus Shanghai was "saved" by Chiang Kai-shek.*

Chen Tu-hsiu, who had been wined and dined by Chiang the week before, was almost captured. He found a hiding place with a friend who smuggled him out of Shanghai. Chou En-lai, with a price on his head, managed to escape death by minutes, and to reach Wuhan in time for the Fifth Congress of the CCP, which had been scheduled for April 27.

On April 13, Chiang Kai-shek established a government in Nanking, and was immediately recognized by all the Western powers as the sole and legal government in China. There were now two KMT governments, one in Nanking and one in Wuhan, where Wang Ching-wei had been greeted enthusiastically — at the very moment the workers were being massacred in Shanghai. The Wuhan KMT government was in great disarray. There was a complete blockade by foreign gunboats, and the big businessmen and quite a few of the military were now secretly looking towards Chiang Kai-shek to "save" them as he had "saved" Shanghai. A good many of the military were ex-warlords who had rallied to the KMT cause. This had worked its corrupting effect on the Nationalist armies and their commanders. Nevertheless, the Wuhan KMT government denounced Chiang as "hired by the imperialists."

In Peking, sixty Communists and trade union leaders were arrested, including Li Ta-chao, who was strangled on April 17. The USSR embassies in Kuangchow and Peking were searched, and Russian diplomats and their wives were killed in Kuangchow. All over China now, peasants and workers were butchered by warlords and landlords. The militarists and ex-warlords of the "left" Wuhan KMT government now took their cue from Chiang Kai-shek; from sporadic killing they were to proceed to systematic massacre.

It was in this inspiring atmosphere that, "staring and trembling like a rabbit before an anaconda," † Chen Tu-hsiu convened the Fifth Congress of the CCP that April. There were eighty delegates, representing 57,967 members, and Wang Ching-wei was guest of

* A dramatic description of some of these events is found in *Man's Fate* (New York 1934) by André Malraux.
† Anna Louise Strong *China's Millions* (New York 1928).

honor. At the same time the Wuhan "left" Kuomintang also prepared to hold its own Fourth Congress.

The Congress became one massive capitulation. Chen Tu-hsiu spoke of "broadening the Revolution" (under the leadership of the KMT) before "deepening" it, which only meant once again relinquishing any attempt to deal vigorously with the situation. He now hoped the Wuhan "left" KMT would cooperate with Feng Yu-hsiang, a northern militarist reputed more democratic than others against Chiang Kai-shek, thus reverting to what the late Sun Yatsen had found so disastrous, the protection of warlord armies. The "left" KMT now saw only one recourse, to rally more militarists against Chiang under the slogan of "unification of China." However, the militarists always rallied (temporarily) to the man who had the most money and power; none of them scrupled to change sides as often as convenient, and the "left" KMT found it impossible to buy the protection of Feng Yu-hsiang, who would prove as unreliable as any other warlord. He went over (temporarily of course) to Chiang, and advised the Wuhan KMT to get rid of the Communists.

The call of "Unity above all else" became the slogan of the Fifth Congress of the CCP. Mao Tsetung was held responsible for peasant "excesses," upbraided, and denied the right to vote. Chou En-lai also was criticized for not getting the workers to disarm themselves, which had "provoked" the massacres!

The Fifth Congress * did nothing to denounce or stop the repression of workers and peasants; on the contrary, the line "was to slow down the agrarian revolution; concessions to the landlords, gentry, militarists. . . . The Central Committee made complete concessions to landlords, gentry, everyone." † "The party was still under the domination of Chen Tu-hsiu," said Mao. "Although Chiang Kai-shek had already led the counterrevolution and begun his attacks on the Communist Party in Shanghai and Nanking, Chen was still for moderation and concessions to the Wuhan KMT."

Mao Tsetung vehemently opposed the capitulation that Chen cringingly offered to the KMT, to "reassure them." It did not reassure them; they were now looking for an outlet to save themselves. Suddenly, many of these so-called radicals, whose slogans had been even more left than those of the Communists, turned against them.

---

* M. N. Roy, the Indian representative of the Comintern, who had arrived in China in March, was present at the Fifth CCP Congress. His total ignorance of Chinese conditions, and his own views, only added to the panic and confusion.

† Chu Chiu-pai's words.

As Anna Louise Strong, the American writer who visited Wuhan in those crucial days, records: "The intellectuals of the KMT had outdone the peasants and workers in the fierceness of their demands. Sun Fo, the son of Dr. Sun Yatsen by his first wife, and a typical businessman of the conservative sort, shouted: 'Kill the gentry.' Hsu Chien, elderly minister of justice, made flaming speeches more extreme in their demands than those of the Communists."

But "ultra-leftism," petty bourgeois radicalism, changes fast to ultra-reaction. This phenomenon, already described by Lenin, occurs time and again in the Chinese Revolution.

"I was very dissatisfied with the party policy then, especially towards the peasant movement," said Mao. "I think today that if the peasant movement had been more thoroughly organized and armed for a class struggle against the landlords, the soviets would have had an earlier and far more powerful development throughout the whole country, but Chen Tu-hsiu violently disagreed."

Chen Tu-hsiu later pleaded that he had merely followed instructions from the Comintern. This is not borne out by a study of the documents. Moreover, the instructions could not keep pace with the changing situation; factual details of the Chinese situation were not relayed to Moscow; and anyway, the duty of a Communist is not to "obey orders when he knows they are wrong," as Mao was to say, "but to use his own head." Mao had put the problem clearly in his essay on the peasant movement in Hunan: it was a question of *choice,* of vision and class stand, of making up one's mind. Chen and the members of the Central Committee who supported him did not refuse to choose, but they chose against the workers and peasants and clung to the property owners, the bourgeoisie and the militarists. They doomed themselves.

Through that terrible spring and summer of cowardice and betrayal, of treachery and slaughter, Borodin sat in Wuhan. Although described by Anna Louise Strong as a man who "had all the revolution at his finger tips," * he was greatly responsible, along with Chen Tu-hsiu for what ensued. Miss Strong was to meet Borodin again in 1939 in Russia, shortly before World War II, when he told her: "I was wrong, I did not understand the Chinese revolution . . . I made so many mistakes." †

Anna Louse Strong, however, says that "at that time [May 1927]

* Borodin's expertise in revolution was based upon an unsuccessful previous attempt in Mexico.
† Author's interview with Anna Louise Strong, 1962.

it was his view, and the general orthodox Communist view, that the revolution coming in China could not be a Communist revolution, or even a workers' revolution . . . but must rather be a peasants' revolution, aided and partly led by the more developed urban workers, but by no means rejecting alliance with the petty bourgeoisie." This formula, however, remained a formula, a placebo; it was Stalin's formula of 1926, but nothing had been done (save by Mao) to implement it; quite the contrary.

By the end of April the Wuhan "left" KMT had already swung far to the right; the hopes of the CCP leadership centered on Wang Ching-wei; but Wang would prove himself of the same cloth as Chiang Kai-shek, an unscrupulous opportunist.

The Comintern Indian envoy M. N. Roy, whom Mao described as a man who "stood a little to the left of Chen and Borodin, but he only just stood," was also garrulous and undisciplined. "He talked too much," said Mao. Roy was now to show Wang Ching-wei a *secret* telegram from the Comintern which outlined how the Communists were to utilize the KMT for further advance of the Communist movement. At the time Wang Ching-wei and others of the "left" were already in secret negotiations with Chiang Kai-shek. Wang Ching-wei's personal jealousy of Chiang was acute, but he was also terrified at the surge of revolution, and he was arranging, through a "mediator," a way out for himself. That mediating friend was T. V. Soong the banker, brother of the Madame Chiang Kai-shek to be, Soong Mei-ling. The resolve of Wang Ching-wei to abandon the Communists was hastened by Roy's appalling indiscretion; for in the telegram the Comintern suggested raising an army of workers and peasants. The knowledge of this document gave Wang a way out.* He would now claim there was a Communist conspiracy, and turn against the CCP.

There now began in Wuhan almost a landslide towards reaction, motivated by manic fear of real revolution. The slaughter of Shanghai was to be repeated here.

During that terrible spring thousands of petitions from peasant associations had been received by the CCP Agriculture Department, demanding clear policies, leadership, and weapons for self-defense. They had been met with harsh scolding and denunciation of "excesses." Peasants were being killed, driven from their villages; cadres and active workers were tortured and shot. But the Communist ministers of agriculture and labor ordered the disarming of the labor

* See Kostas Mavrakis *Du Trotskyisme* (Paris 1971), p. 162.

pickets and the peasants' associations, threatened the peasantry with severe punishment should it proceed against the landlords. The workers were finally disarmed by order of the All-China Labor Federation, and this order was carried out by Liu Shao-chi and Li Li-san. Liu Shao-chi in June 1927 made a report on the "successful" disarming of the workers.

In May the Chen Tu-hsiu leadership had already abandoned the workers and peasants. Two days after Chiang had started the killings in Shanghai, all over China militarists had begun their own slaughter. The slaying of peasants, the torturing, mutilating, impaling, burning of women (thousands died with breasts cut off, impaled, cut in pieces, tortured in unmentionable ways) form a nightmare recital of violence.*

Reports came pouring in, they were even printed in the *Min Kuo Jih Pao,* the republican newspaper; "of kerosene poured over peasants and burning them alive, of using red hot irons to tear their flesh." In Hupei, 4,700 peasants, including 500 women, were murdered between February and June by beheading, burying alive, strangling, burning, cutting into pieces. Never did the peasants inflict upon extortionate landlords a fraction of the horrors that were inflicted upon them.

The peasants begged for weapons; they formed militia groups and captured guns; inflexibly Chen Tu-hsiu in the name of the Central Committee called for an end to "excesses and infantile acts" and for "restoration of order," ordering the peasants and workers to surrender their weapons.

Those terrible weeks were to remain burned into Mao's consciousness; speaking of them decades later, he had tears in his eyes. Any less dedicated person would have given up or would have turned altogether bitter with the "Communism" which had given such "leadership." But Mao persisted; he and Tung Pi-wu wrote report after report on what was happening. Mao refused to give orders to disarm the peasantry, and was then accused of having instigated the "excesses."

In Changsha on May 21, to be known as "Horse Day" massacre, the KMT General Hsu Ke-hsiang put white bands round his soldiers' arms, marched them to the headquarters of the Hunan provincial labor union and of the students' and workers' associations, and

* Abundantly documented in newspapers and books of the period. Also see Harold R. Isaacs *The Tragedy of the Chinese Revolution* (1938, second revised edition Stanford 1961).

The massacres of 1927. At work here are executioners under General Li Ching-lin, Kuomintang Pacification Commissioner for Chihli and Shantung provinces.

started shooting the unarmed occupants to the cries of "Long live Chiang Kai-shek." No report of this deed was published in the press for over a month.

On the 27th of May 20,000 infuriated peasants and workers, including miners from Pinghsiang and Anyuan, marched on Changsha to avenge the massacre. It is now affirmed that Mao backed this movement. But the workers and the peasants were ordered to disarm by the Communist-led All-China Federation of Labor Unions and the All-China Peasant Association. Then they were mown down by the machine guns of the militarists. In the course of the next three months over 30,000 people were to die in the province, over 100,-000 in the year.

Every day for weeks outside the west gate of Changsha, batches of boys and girls, men and women, were marched to their death. "The soldiers amused themselves with the women, dispatching them with bullets fired upwards into the body through the vagina." Girl students who had cut their hair short were singled out for butchering.

But not all the KMT armies were counterrevolutionary. Some of the units, such as the Fourth Army, also known as the Ironsides for its outstanding performance in the Northern Expedition, were Communist-officered. However, such suspect units had been sent off to quarters near Nanchang * on the pretext of regrouping for an assault against Chiang Kai-shek, now in Nanking.

A "committee of five" with Borodin at its head was sent by the KMT executive and the Central Committee of the CCP from Wuhan to restore "order" in Hunan; it set off on its travels but could not proceed. Percy Chen, who accompanied Borodin, told me that one of the things Borodin set out to do was to try to find Mao Tsetung and order him to "stop the peasants"! But Borodin did not get far. At Yochow, a riverine city on Lake Tungting, halfway to Changsha, Borodin was courteously banqueted by the warlord in charge, then sent back to Wuhan.

In June the "left" KMT denounced its Communist ally. Decrees were issued giving protection to all who would betray Communists; peasant and worker leaders were shot; all land seized was restored to the landlords. A hundred-odd delegates of Hunan peasant associa-

* Nanchang, which had been Chiang's headquarters for some months, had been partly evacuated by Chiang troops when he marched on Nanking and Shanghai. A garrison of mixed KMT soldiers and warlord troops who had rallied to the KMT remained there.

tions, waiting for a conference in Changsha, were executed en masse. Communist schools were closed; left-wing teachers and students were burned alive.

On June 20 the Central Committee of the CCP issued a statement of eleven points, entirely giving up power and control of workers' and peasants' organizations to the KMT. Nevertheless 400 delegates of the All-China Labor Federation, also then in conference in Wuhan, were arrested. Many were jailed and some were killed. It was at this juncture that Liu Shao-chi was arrested. It seems that he then saved himself by abjuring Communism.* He spent a short time in jail reading the classics of Confucius, which were sent to him by his captors. This is regarded now as the beginning of his career as a "renegade."

Public execution of trade unionists and labor leaders enlivened the streets for weeks. The Central Committee broke up; Communists were fleeing or going in hiding everywhere.

At the time of the Horse Day massacre of May 21, Mao Tsetung had tried to hold mass meetings in Changsha to call for a punitive expedition against the militarists who had perpetrated this act. He had even called personally on General Tang Sheng-chih, the acting governor of Hunan, to ask for action against his rampaging subordinates. This was a very courageous act, as at the time no Communist dared to expose himself. He had also supported the peasants' march on Changsha of May 27. This aroused the wrath of Chen Tu-hsiu, who accused Mao of organizing the uprising and ordered him to go to Szechuan: however, Mao persuaded Chen to keep him in Hunan. Chen particularly reproached Mao for having "aided the Hunan provincial peasant association to call for the confiscation of all land belonging to big landlords." As the Terror spread, Mao Tsetung wrote bluntly: "All the peasant associations are being surrounded and the leaders killed." Wang Ching-wei blustered: "I have heard the organizers of the peasant masses say, rely on your own strength; don't trust the KMT. . . . This is disobedience . . . the people have therefore been ill-treated by counterrevolutionaries and we have not been able to save them."

Acting Governor Tang Sheng-chih issued orders for the arrest of Mao Tsetung, and the latter left Hunan along with Kuo Liang and Hsia Hsi, two of his early recruits. They hid in Wuhan for a short while, until on July 15 the "left" KMT decided to formally expel the

---

* Because of the terror and confusion in those days, this episode was not known until forty years later. See part II, chapter 5, for details.

Communist Party. Communists were ordered to give up their membership in the Party on pain of death. Execution squads rounded up and decapitated suspects throughout the cities.

On July 27, with executions going on in the streets of Wuhan, the leaders of the "left" KMT went to the Wuhan railway station to bid a courteous farewell to Borodin, who was returning — or rather, being returned — to Russia.

The hapless Borodin, accompanied by Anna Louise Strong, was driven by car by Percy Chen to safety within Russia. Their trek through North China, Mongolia, the Gobi desert, until the frontiers of China were well behind them, was no mean exploit.* But orders not to touch Borodin had been given. The journey lasted seven weeks and they finally got to Moscow. Behind them they left a Chinese Revolution almost drowned in blood, a Communist Party apparently decimated. Borodin was in despair. "It's all over," he said.

A congratulatory telegram from Chiang Kai-shek in Nanking praising its righteous and patriotic action in getting rid of Communists was received by the "left" Wuhan government. Reconciliation was effected, the Nanking and Wuhan KMT regimes "reunited." Wang Ching-wei, with a large sum of money, departed for yet another European saunter.

Tang Sheng-chih, the militarist governor of Hunan who tried to arrest Mao Tsetung, was to rally to Mao in 1949 and end his life with a sinecure. Wang Ching-wei, the brilliant "left" politician, was to end up in 1939 as a puppet of the Japanese when the latter invaded China. He accepted a post in Nanking as head of the Japanese puppet government of South China, and in China today his name has become synonymous with infamy.

* Notes and personal interview with Percy Chen, 1966, 1970.

9

The First Red Base—
The First "Left" Line

In mid-July of 1927, while the killing was in full spate, a new policy calling for uprisings in China was proposed in a resolution by the Comintern to the Chinese Communist Party. The situation had radically changed, as Stalin was to write.* Difficulties of communication, and various interpretations (including possibly translation difficulties) † rendered the directing of Chinese revolutionary movements from Russia more than precarious; hence only "guiding principles" had been issued. In 1936, Mao was to comment on this point to Edgar Snow.

"The Third International . . . is not an administrative organization, nor has it any political power beyond that of an advisory capacity. . . . Although the Communist Party of China is a member of the Comintern, still this in no sense means that Soviet China is ruled by Moscow or the Comintern . . . We are not fighting for an emancipated China to turn the country over to Moscow."

But these "guiding principles" had been made an excuse by Chen Tu-hsiu for subservience to the Kuomintang. Although Stalin later deprecated giving advice to the Chinese Communists, his suggestions did carry the force of "orders," and the orders were often ambiguous and contradictory.‡ For years psychological dependence on Moscow, a "revolution by telegraph," was to bedevil the course of the Chinese Revolution and create more tragedies.

* "Concerning Current Questions," *Inprecor,* vol. VII, no. 45 (August 4, 1927).
† See an episode described in John E. Rue *Mao Tsetung in Opposition 1927–1935* (Stanford 1966), p. 71.
‡ This is not a defense of Stalin, but there is no doubt that a close reading of all the documents must lead to an objective reassessment of his share of error and also his share of correct evaluation.

Actually, although the time for large-scale uprisings had now passed, Stalin's advice was not altogether inappropriate. It coincided with Mao's growing certainty that armed struggle was the only way out; and this was also Chou En-lai's view of the course to follow. Revolution was at a low ebb, the Party decimated, dismay and terror paramount; yet out of defeat was to be born a new strategy for victory. Seventeen days after the break with the "left" KMT government on July 15, 1927, when the latter declared the CCP outlawed, the Nanchang uprising of August 1 was launched.

A temporary Politburo had been formed; it had met on July 13 in Kiukiang with Chu Chiu-pai, a Russian-returned intellectual, in charge. A Front Committee was organized, and Chou En-lai became its secretary. It broke definitely with the old policy of cooperation with the KMT. It also started a new, military outlook among the intellectuals of the CCP. Until then indifference and disinterest in military matters was one of the handicaps of the intellectuals in the Central Committee — except for Mao Tsetung and Chou En-lai. The ease with which armed workers' pickets were sacrificed, and peasants too, was part of this class contempt for the lives of the poor, based on unconscious assumptions of their worthlessness.

The Chinese Communist Party did not have its own army but was dependent on the Kuomintang armies, in which there were units such as the Ironsides (Fourth Army) mentioned earlier, which were largely staffed by Communist cadets trained under Chou En-lai at Whangpoo. The establishment of the Front Committee, and the uprisings which followed, led to the formation of the Red Army. Yet again, for reasons which show how little the intellectuals in the CCP understood the situation, although the break with the Wuhan "left" KMT government was total, for a number of weeks the flag under which these uprisings were to take place remained the KMT flag! And because they did not understand military tactics or strategy, Chu Chiu-pai and other intellectuals now in the leadership of the CCP planned uprisings in both cities and countryside at the same time, thus dispersing the small untried forces hastily collected over a large area, and leading to their own defeat.

Not all the KMT had turned counterrevolutionary, and within the armies many units with their officers would join the Communists. As Mao Tsetung wrote in October 1928, the middle class in the KMT, the small and medium capitalists, many intellectuals, merchants, and other middle-class people, had been panicked by fear of revolution. They had followed the big landlords and compradores and thus given their adhesion to Chiang Kai-shek. "The present regime of the new warlords of the KMT remains a regime of the compradore class in the cities and the landlord class in the countryside. . . . The workers, peasants, other sections of the common people, and even the national bourgeoisie [national capitalists] have remained under counterrevolutionary rule and obtained not the slightest particle of political or economic emancipation." * This political judgment was to prove correct in the years to come, especially at the end of Chiang's rule in 1949, when the middle class rallied to the Communist Party.

The distinction between the compradore bourgeoisie, the national bourgeoisie, the petty bourgeoisie, was one of the most distinctive and useful in Mao's categories within classes. It made it possible for him to find in every class, at every stage, a layer of people who supported the Revolution, even if in a temporary, "vacillating manner." He would never crudely lump together all the "bourgeoisie," nor arbitrarily condemn anyone because of class category. It is this fine talent for lucid analysis which became a component of his ability to rally so many to his cause. Thus a portion of the KMT with, at their head, Madame Sun Yatsen (Soong Ching-ling, widow of Dr. Sun Yatsen) had disassociated themselves from Chiang Kai-shek and from the Wang Ching-wei group, and denounced the betrayal of Dr. Sun Yatsen's aims and principles, and of the Revolution. From that time on, Soong Ching-ling and many other courageous women and men, such as Ho Hsiang-ning, widow of Dr. Liao Chung-kai, represented the *revolutionary* KMT, persisted in denouncing Chiang Kai-shek (who was to become Madame Sun Yatsen's brother-in-law in December 1928 by marrying her sister Soong Mei-ling), and steadfastly refused to join in the anti-Communist wave which swept over the Kuomintang. It was therefore still possible to speak of a united front with this revolutionary KMT and its representatives whose opposition to Chiang Kai-shek's military dictatorship would last for the next decades. Perhaps this may explain why the KMT flag was kept, but it created much confusion and prevented many peasants and workers, knowing they were being slaughtered by the KMT, from joining in the risings now being organized.

The plans for insurrection were approved at a meeting of the Front Committee on July 18, 1927, in Hankow. While Chou En-lai was to lead the uprising against the city of Nanchang, Mao Tsetung,

* *Why Is It That Red Political Power Can Exist in China?*, October 5, 1928. *Selected Works of Mao Tsetung* (English edition Peking 1961–1965), vol. I.

together with Fang Chih-min and Peng Pai, would start uprisings in the countryside. These countryside insurrections were thought of as a support to the city ones, which were regarded as a priority. Mao (who only some weeks before had been upbraided for his "gunpowder" outlook when he pleaded for organized peasant uprisings) was now selected to lead the uprising in his own province of Hunan, to be coordinated with similar peasant uprisings in Kuangtung and Hupei provinces. Mao considered the countryside uprisings more important than taking cities, but he was overruled. As a result, the bulk of the existing forces loyal to the Communists was set to take Nanchang city.

On August 7, an emergency conference of the Central Committee of the CCP took place, again in Hankow. The meeting was tumultuous. Chen Tu-hsiu was deposed from his post as secretary-general; Tan Ping-shan was also held guilty for the debacle. Both had been servile and obedient towards the Kuomintang. They had given up the exercise of leadership to "the bourgeoisie of the KMT." There were only eleven members present on that occasion, but Mao told Edgar Snow that he was "active in the decision" to get Chen deposed and the leadership changed. The opportunist policy of Chen was condemned. All connections with the Wuhan KMT government were severed. The new policy of armed struggle was formulated; all this did not precede but followed the insurrection and the taking of Nanchang on August 1.

Although Chen Tu-hsiu's disastrous line was thus brought to an end, an ultra-left line of action was to develop, partly as an emotional reaction, partly because of the composition of the new Central Committee. Chang Kuo-tao, Li Li-san and Liu Shao-chi (the latter had "escaped" from jail) condemned Chen Tu-hsiu, though they had not opposed Chen before; on the contrary, they had obeyed his orders to disarm the workers.

Besides deposing Chen, resolutions at the August 7 meeting supported armed uprisings, "taking a city," and "arousal of the masses." Because of this "city-taking" outlook, the peasant uprising led by Mao would later be condemned as not having been approved by the Central Committee, and yet today it is this peasant insurrection which is regarded as the real breakthrough in Communist military and political thinking. Called the Autumn Harvest Uprising, this brief struggle was to lead to the rebirth of the decimated CCP, and to open a new road for the Chinese Revolution.

The autumn harvest season was propitious for a large-scale peasant movement because, with landlords taking the grain from the peasants for rent, taxes and usury loans, the class struggle, landlord versus tenant, especially where land confiscation had occurred, would prove extremely violent. The landlords, with private armies, with guns and whips, raided their own tenant farmers, and often executed a few to terrorize the others.

How did the Autumn Harvest Uprising begin and end? Only very briefly did Mao refer to it in 1936,* but since then details have been filled in.† Mao went to Anyuan (Chang Chia Wan) to recruit mine workers for the uprising, to build a worker-peasant force. With him was his brother Mao Tse-tan. Miners from Anyuan were to be the core of Mao's troops; these, together with peasant self-defense militia from Pinghsiang and Liling, some Nationalist Army soldiers and officers, sympathizers, some students and peasant cadres, would compose his first Red Army.

The very collection of these troops was a tour de force. The area crawled with landlord armies, warlord armies, and Kuomintang armies, all possessed with a frenzy of slaughter. The Communist recruits were a ragtag band; they had pikes and staffs, some had rifles but little ammunition. They had no uniforms. Mao himself was in cotton trousers, with a top of different color, both very patched, and straw sandals. He wound a towel round his neck and walked with the soldiers, up and down their lines. They marched from Hunan to Kiangsi and back again and fought against very heavy odds. Other peasant uprisings took place in other provinces. All were put down very quickly and the assembled forces drifted and dispersed. Mao's troops had a different fate.

"The long, open struggle for power now began," says Mao. It would last twenty-two years.

The uprising began on September 8, 1927. It ended in October. If it is hailed today as a great victory, this is not because it was a conquering feat, but because it was the first step taken by Mao Tsetung towards the creation of a new kind of revolutionary war — that of "the countryside surrounding the cities," towards the creation of a new kind of army, and towards the creation of rural bases where the Communist Party and Red Army would grow strong.

* Edgar Snow *Red Star Over China* (1937, first revised and enlarged edition New York 1968).
† Author's personal research; see the map on page 168.

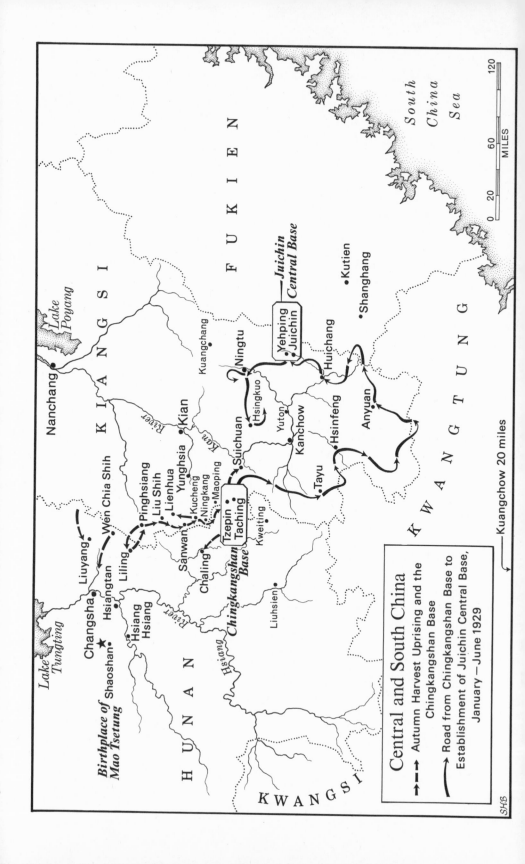

South
China
Sea

120

60

20

MILES

FUKIEN

Kutien

Shanghang

Juichin
Central Base

Yehping
Juichin

Huichang

Huichang

Kuangchang

Ningtu

Hsingkuo

Anyuan

Hsingkuo

Hsinfeng

Suichuan

Yuton

Kanchow

Tayu

KIANGSI

Lake
Poyang

Nanchang

River

Kian

Kucheng

Ningkang

Maoping

Kan

Kweiting

Pinghsiang
Liu Shih
Lienhua
Yunghsia

Sanwan

Tzepin Taching

Chingkangshan
Base

Chaling

KWANGTUNG

Kuangchow 20 miles

Liuhsien

Wen Chia Shih

Liling

Liuyang

Hsiangtan

Hsiang
Hsiang

Changsha

River

Birthplace of
Mao Tsetung Shaoshan

Lake
Tungting

HUNAN

Hsiang
River

KWANGSI

Central and South China

→ Autumn Harvest Uprising and the
Chingkangshan Base

→ Road from Chingkangshan Base to
Establishment of Juichin Central Base,
January—June 1929

SHB

The First Division of the First Peasants' and Workers' Army was the bold name Mao gave his forces. Mao Tsetung in early August urged that "the KMT flag should not be used, it confuses all." He created the flag of the Autumn Harvest Uprising, a hammer and sickle in a star (and not a plow, as has been reported). It was not until September 19 that the Politburo of the CCP finally declared that "the uprisings can under no circumstances take place under the KMT banner." Mao's flag design became, and remained, that of the Red Army until the Japanese invasion and the Second United Front.

Because the troops were so disparate, Mao had to divide them in regiments more or less according to their origin. The First Regiment of the First Peasants' and Workers' Army, vanguard in the battles to follow, was formed by the miners of Anyuan and Pinghsiang, the Second from peasant militia, the Third and Fourth from those garrison forces at Wuhan which had revolted against Wang Ching-wei and joined the Communists. These regiments totaled 8,000 men and became the First Division of the First Army.

But the confusion among the hastily assembled new leadership of the CCP almost wrecked the plans. The curious affair of a July telegram from Stalin nearly stopped the armed uprisings. This telegram was read by Chang Kuo-tao (whose Russian may not have been adequate). Chang Kuo-tao interpreted it to mean that there must be a "wait and see" policy.* But Chou En-lai disagreed with this interpretation, and went on to prepare the Nanchang uprising of August 1. It did, however, produce disunity among Party members. Another confusion centered on the vacillations of the Hunan Provincial Committee, which was supposed to prepare, in conjunction with the peasant uprisings, an assault on the city of Changsha. To this Mao was opposed, contending that the peasantry must be armed and have its own rural bases, not attack cities. As a result of this dispute the forces of Mao Tsetung carrying out the Autumn Harvest Uprising did not have any reinforcements nor support and the initial successes could not be followed up.

"This army [the one he had organized] was organized with the sanction of the Hunan Provincial Committee, but the general program of the Hunan committee and of our army was opposed by the Central Committee, which seemed to have adopted a policy of 'wait and see' rather than of active opposition." The tragic indecisions, the shift of focus, the contradictory statements, all tended to fissure the

* This was not the first instance of Stalin's reversing himself and thus causing much confusion among those who received his "advice."

small, if passionate, group of revolutionaries Mao had assembled. And when things went wrong they would bitterly shift on Mao and Chou En-lai the onus of their lack of foresight.

And then, while traveling between the Hengyang miners, where he had gone for more recruits, and the peasant militia, Mao Tsetung was captured and taken to the headquarters of the counterrevolutionary forces to be shot.

"While I was organizing the army . . . I was captured by some *mintuan* [bodies of troops formed for self-defense under command of landlords], working with the Kuomintang. . . . I was ordered to be taken to the *mintuan* headquarters, where I was to be killed. Borrowing several tens of dollars from a comrade, however, I attempted to bribe the escort to free me. The ordinary soldiers were mercenaries, with no special interest in seeing me killed, and they agreed to release me, but the subaltern in charge refused to permit it. I therefore decided to attempt to escape, but had no opportunity to do so until I was within about two hundred yards of the *mintuan* headquarters. At that point I broke loose and ran into the fields."

Mao hid in tall grass until nightfall; the search for him came so near that the searchers could almost have touched him, but he escaped. Since his shoes had been removed (preparatory to killing, a victim's shoes were always taken away, as it was feared the ghost might run after his executioner; also because shoes were a prize possession for the ordinary soldiers), his feet were badly bruised as he traveled all night across the bush-tangle of the craggy hills until a peasant sheltered him. He had seven remaining silver dollars with him and used them to buy shoes, umbrella, and food. When he reached the peasant militia, he had only a few coppers * left.

Mao rejoined his troops, and issued the Ten Articles of the Autumn Uprising. They were simple slogans, related to the situation. (1) Down with Tang Sheng-chih. (2) Down with Wang Ching-wei. (3) Down with the Hunan provincial government. (4) Down with the Kuomintang government. (5) Liquidate land tyrants and evil gentry. (6) Power to the workers and peasants and soldiers. (7) Establish the dictatorship of peasant associations. (8) Organize revolutionary committees. (9) The true revolution is a peasant revolution! (10) Long live the uprising's victory!

"The little army, leading the peasant uprising, moved southward through Hunan. It had to break its way through thousands of Kuo-

* Equivalent, more or less, to a cent for ten copper coins.

mintang troops, and fought many battles." The presence and action
of the Anyuan and Pinghsiang miners and some of the Hengyang factory workers validated Mao's claim that he was leading a worker-
peasant army. Over 30,000 peasants, armed with spears, rose in
Pinghsiang county, heartened by his presence. On September 12 the
Army took Liling county, and on the 15th the county town of Liuyang.

But there was no central direction, save "to take Changsha," and
no supporting reinforcements. The band — now four thousand
strong — walked the tiny hidden paths twisting among stark hills
and valleys, for now the fields were bare, and the gray line of ragged
men could be easily perceived against the skyline. Liuyang was besieged by KMT troops and retaken, with heavy losses for Mao's
troops. Hsia Tou-ying, a commander of KMT troops who had joined
Mao's army, deserted to the enemy with several hundred men. Discipline was poor, political training at a low level, and some of the soldiers rebelled because they were not allowed to loot. The KMT White
Terror had massacred 330,000 peasants in North Hunan by September; whole areas were bare of men; food was hard to get, and the
troops were starving. The wounded were left in the villages, but the
peasants would not always care for them, since the tortures and muti-
lations the enemy inflicted upon poor peasants were more frequent
among those who had sheltered Communists. The countryside
crawled with spies and informers, vying with each other to capture
Reds, and betrayals became common.

All the bad habits of traditional Chinese militarism infected the
small army — some of the officers shouted at and beat the soldiers
— and the confusion of contradictory orders from the Hunan Provincial Committee and the Politburo (a confusion we must get accustomed to in this story) did not make Mao's task easier. There was
not a more heteroclitic, individualistic collection of men than at that
moment in the CCP, and this fundamental diversity would continue.
What is surprising is that in spite of these disheartening factors, at this
critical juncture, instead of disbanding his very reduced forces or
marching them to join other levies engaged in city-storming, Mao
Tsetung took the momentous decision to follow his own judgment
— to forge a Red Army and to select a base in the countryside for
survival.

There can be any amount of discussion as to Mao's decision, and
the choice of the first Red base. Why did he do so? When others almost
destroyed themselves in trying to capture cities? To answer this is to

Leaders of the Autumn Harvest Uprising in the fall of 1927.
Mao Tsetung is third from the left.

reach the mechanism of Mao's thinking: Use your head coolly, relentlessly, unswayed by passion or a yearning for success. His decision corresponded to the traditional concept of peasant revolt; it was
in line with the heroes of *Water Margin* * and other popular rebels,
who went into mountain fastnesses and there existed for years, war-
ring against injustice and helped by the common people.

But there were more practical, down-to-earth reasons. Mao knew
his own province extremely well, having measured it on foot in his
long walks. When he went for a trek into the mountains near Liuyang
in January 1918, he had seen that they made an excellent hideout,
because the plication of the hill ranges, stretching into a maze of
dense forest and undergrowth, rising to rocky cliffs, boulder-strewn,
would be a nightmare for a pursuing regular army. He knew these
frowning crags held pathways crossed by smugglers and salt peddlers. From the peasants he learned that the mountains round
Chingkangshan harbored bands of rebel peasants, not only in previous centuries but even now. And he also knew that the borders between provinces were usually less patrolled by warlord armies than
the central portions; these forbidding, desolate heights would not be
claimed by the press-ganged, opium-smoking warlord soldiers. This
feature was to remain an advantage for all the subsequent Red bases;
it crystallized Mao's decision to fuse peasant tradition with present
realism. And so he took the step which in the short term saved him
and his followers, and in the long term would save the Revolution itself.

On September 20, on the sports ground of the Li Jen Middle
School, a building of some grace, at Wen Chia Shih, on the road to
the Chingkangshan massif, Mao called a meeting of his troops, now
shrunk to a thousand or so men. The decision to "go up the mountain" and to carry on with the Revolution was taken there. It is a
pity that Mao's speech at Wen Chia Shih was not recorded; for it
must have been a speech of grace and vital strength. All we know is
that at the end he shouted: "Do we dare to carry on the Revolution
or not?" And from the thousand men assembled came the answer:
"We dare!"

On September 23 the trek to the ranges began. But now a small
number of those who had shouted "We dare!" had second thoughts;
two hundred more left. Mao declared that anyone who wanted to go
home should do so, and would even be given travel money. This it-

* The famous novel of peasant revolt which had deeply influenced Mao Tsetung
in his childhood.

self was most unusual; some of the revolutionaries wanted to kill the "traitors." And so only eight hundred began to climb the treacherous, muddy foothills, trudging through the red clay soil which stuck to the soles of their straw sandals, hacking the undergrowth. They did not dare light a fire to cook rice or to warm themselves. They were hungry and they were cold. Then they reached Liu Shih, a small market town, and were attacked by a large Kuomintang force, their rear cut; but they managed to beat off the attackers, then went on to capture the small county town of Lien Hua. Here they got food and "proclaimed the Revolution." They then began to climb again, on to Sanwan.

Sanwan was a village perched precariously over a mountain stream that bubbles down to the plains. Here begin the massive mountains of Chingkangshan; a path winds up to the gorge-like access passes. What is called the "reorganization at Sanwan" of the forces Mao had under him took place from September 29 through October 3. It was Mao's first original attempt to educate what men he had left into a new force, to teach them a compelling vision which would carry them forward in a unity stronger than any enforced discipline.

Mao spoke at length. The men huddled, listening. They were in a disused temple which was their temporary refuge from the small cold rain of autumn. They were chilled and hungry, but they listened. And they were heartened and chose to go on, an act of will which committed them to the Revolution.

Here Mao began the lecture meetings he would continue all along the climbing path to the central high plateau which would become the base. For again at Kucheng in Ningkang county there would be another meeting and another talk. And there he discussed what had gone wrong with the Autumn Harvest Uprising, submitting the events to debate, to the scrutiny of his faithful band. This was the only way to grasp the initiative, he told them, to "analyse past errors," to "make the past serve the future." In 1936 he was to tell Edgar Snow very briefly that the Central Committee was practicing a "contradictory policy, consisting in neglecting military affairs and at the same time desiring an armed insurrection of the popular masses." But he did not say that the "city-taking" bent of the new leadership, their disregard of peasant power, had led to the total abandonment of himself and his band. To those who were with him at the time he said none of these things. He spoke of the ideas which had begun to germinate in him. And if it sounded extraordinary, they were all, at that moment, extraordinary men, and so he told them of high courage, and of armed struggle, land reform, and the setting up of agrarian bases, and of the countryside surrounding the cities and of conquering them. The plan for what was to become the strategy of the Revolution was created by Mao on the road to Chingkangshan.

The insurrection they had just carried out, he said, was of a kind never tried before. Many people thought that only cities mattered, but the countryside mattered because there were more people in the countryside. The countryside grew food, the cities ate it. And so the peasant was the important one, the giver of life, of food. From now on they would avoid "taking" any strongholds. The vast countryside would be theirs to roam, they would survive and create a new Red Army. Thus, even while in ascending Chingkangshan Mao was adopting a traditional feature of peasant revolt, he was at the same time transforming it by a totally new social content, of organization and ideology. A stable base in a mountain fastness would nurse their failing strength and resurrect the Chinese Revolution.

At Hsia Shui Wan, another small village, Mao made another step in the building of the Party and the Red Army. He organized the Party cell at company level, and emphasized the building of the Red Army as a political force by inaugurating a Party group in each squad, a cell in each company, and a committee in each battalion. Each committee consisted of seven to nine men, ordinary soldiers; among them one, two or three were Party members. Mao called the latter (most of them trained by him) "instructor-delegates," for they were to educate the soldiers, keep up their political consciousness and morale. They were to maintain discipline, train the Army in work among the people, in mass propaganda. Mao said that the Red Army was not only a military instrument but above all a political weapon of propaganda, agitation, seconding land reform and peasant struggles, educating the people and leading them to establish their own associations, to take power from the landlords.

Mao also created "soldiers' committees" or "soldiers' soviets" at company level to look after the welfare of the soldiers; he drew up rules — officers must never beat soldiers, they must have the same salary, and soldiers had the right of debate and of criticizing defects in officers; all army accounts were to be open to public inspection. Thus he instituted a democratic process in the Red Army, subject to Party control. He then reorganized his men into the First Regiment of the First Workers' and Peasants' Army. The regiment was divided into two battalions (the First and Third battalions) with seven companies and two detachments, one sanitary, one of surplus officers. There were too many officers in relation to ordinary soldiers. The detachment served as an officer reserve corps, whose members assumed duties as new recruits came into the Red Army after it settled in Chingkangshan.

Thus from the very start Mao was to fuse the Party and Red Army into a twin synthesis, but with the Party in ideological control; so indissolubly linked that throughout the next decades he would never envision them as separate. This essential component of his thinking, refusing the dichotomy which prevails everywhere else, had the most important consequences: Mao would always consider the Red Army as the best training ground for Party cadres, since armed struggle was the dominant factor in the Revolution in China.

Everywhere Mao's army went, meetings were held with the local inhabitants. At Sanwan, at Kucheng, the people at first fled to the mountains when the Red Army arrived. Fearful, hiding in bushes, they watched the soldiers. And this was routine; everyone fled when any soldiers came by. Mao decreed that his soldiers should never enter a house or take anything. This behavior was so unusual (soldiers looted, robbed, burned as a matter of custom) that by the third day the local people, watching from their hideouts on the slopes, filtered back. Mao talked to them, urging them to return, and distributed "some money and cloth" taken from the landlords on the way to Sanwan.* He told them that this army with its red flag was their own army, devoted to their own interests. The people were moved, and spontaneously they cooked rice and fed the soldiers, and some joined up. This was to be repeated everywhere Mao's army went.

From Hsia Shui Wan, Mao led on through the mountains, always climbing, to Hsing Chu Shan, and there laid down the first three of his famous eight rules of discipline: speak politely; buy at fair prices; return what you borrow.

These decisions were not accepted without dispute. Some of the officers, it is said, even attempted to kill him. Mao Tsetung insisted that nothing be done to them; whoever wanted to leave could do so in peace. All this had never been done before.

The peasants still remember that end of October 1927 when Mao Tsetung walked up, always up, scaling the passes of this forbidding mountain fastness, past Great Well hamlet to Tzeping, which was to

---

* Interview by author.

be his main headquarters and center of the base. He was ragged, un-
kempt, very thin, his hair very long, and his troops were in the same
sorry state. They looked terrible, like real bandits, covered in lice-
ridden rags, but they were gentle and did not take anything. The
peasants remember how Mao greeted them: "Cousin, what is your
name?" he would inquire politely. "Even the children were no longer
frightened, and the women came back and cooked for the
soldiers." *

The massive Chingkangshan is a huge natural fortress amid a
cluster of loping ranges, an amoebic spill of rocks, crags, gullies. It
is part of the Lo Hsiao range, lying between two provinces, Kiangsi
and Hunan. The massif is surrounded by plains, with very poor irrigation and poor red earth growing scant crops and a kind of oily
bush in profusion. The upper heights are densely forested; the lower
slopes are a tangle of secondary bush. Only five villages, with a total
population of under 2,000, dotted this desolate area. It is about 30
miles across from north to south and from east to west, and squats in
the midst of six counties, of which four are in Hunan province and
two in Kiangsi province. Five passes, so narrow only a few men were
needed to hold them, lead to the central weathered plateau, 5,000 to
5,600 feet high, which is a convergence of crests to form a "well"
high above the gorges twisting the folded slopes. The rock protrudes
everywhere, and the soil is thin. The inhabitants did not use the
wheel; they made fire by striking stones. They were so poor that few
had more than one pair of trousers, or one blanket per family. Most
of the men were porters and carriers for the farms in the plains
below, and all the families were Hakkas. The Hakkas, or "guest people," originally from North China,† had been pushed down by the
Mongol invasion and spread southward. Unwelcomed by the local
people, they settled in the poorest areas and on bad mountain land.
Their villages were often raided by local inhabitants and they were
at the mercy of landlords.

"A very wide rift has long existed between the native inhabitants
and the settlers [i.e., the Hakkas] whose forefathers came from the
North . . . their traditional feuds are deep-seated . . . [they] have
been oppressed by the native inhabitants in the plains." ‡ This rift

* Interview by author.
† See *Selected Works of Mao Tsetung* (English edition Peking 1961–1965), vol. I,
pp. 93–94, for comments on Hakkas, called "settlers." For a description of Hakkas,
see Han Suyin *The Crippled Tree* (New York 1965).
‡ Ibid. (*Selected Works*).

would give Mao more trouble later in Party organization. "In theory, this rift . . . ought not to extend into the exploited classes of workers and peasants, much less into the Communist Party. But it does, and it persists by force of long tradition." There would be many another theory which Mao would find inadequate to explain away practical realities; from then on his particular gift for flexible adaptation would be put to good use.

Chingkangshan was already occupied by two bands of Hakka peasants turned bandits. These were led by an ex-middle school student, Yuan Wen-tsai,* and Wang Tso, a tailor; they had 600 men and owned 120 rifles. To establish himself there, Mao Tsetung first negotiated with Yuan and Wang, and so successfully that he won not only their acceptance but incorporated them in his army of 800 men and 80 rifles. He then quartered his troops in two areas, the first in the region of the Five Wells, the second at a jutting ridge called the Nine Dragons. And thus was created the first Red base at Chingkangshan.

Chingkangshan was held that winter against the most frightful odds. The amount of persuasion, explanation, education that Mao did must have been enormous. He constantly had to repeat his three rules, also stress the equality between officers and men. "Do not kill enemy soldiers and lower rank officers," he urged. Mao Tsetung did not look down on the human material he had in hand as unsuitable, reject it a priori; he would work on it, mobilize it, educate it, make it grow. And hence he would never exclude the "lumpen proletariat," the beggars, peasants turned bandits, from this education process. This problem of consciousness-raising, mobilization of the human being, is one inherent to revolutionary action. In Western societies, to be mobilized connotes pressure because it is an external enforcement, but there is a need, a desire in man to harness his own strength and capabilities in a struggle worthwhile and enduring. All societies thrive only in the measure in which they have succeeded in inspiring individuals with worthwhile, stimulating aims; exacting sacrifice and abnegation; these aims exalt and transcend the self. And Mao, in the circumstances in which he was placed, was to develop and intensify this process, which he called political training. In doing so he became a teacher of the Revolution.

The real teacher is the mobilizer of the human spirit, who has the genius to make every sacrifice seem a worthwhile endeavor, full of meaning, linked to a wholeness inspiring and noble. And the genius

---

* Yuan Wen-tsai's widow is still alive in Maoping village, Chingkangshan.

The First Red Base — The First "Left" Line 179

of Mao Tsetung lies in this teaching. With the words "Man can change" he established a whole program of self-change, exploding the myths of helplessness, submission and despair which had fettered the millions of China. In this he trained himself in the most inauspicious circumstances, with the most incongruous and backward-seeming human material, in that bleak winter on desolate Chingkangshan.

"Because the program of the Autumn Harvest Uprising had not been sanctioned [it had been drawn up on July 18, before the August 7 meeting] * by the Central Committee; because the First Army had suffered losses, *and from the angle of the cities* the movement appeared doomed to failure. . . . I was dismissed," said Mao Tsetung. Made a scapegoat for this "failure," he was yet "feeling *certain* that we were following the correct line." †

"War was not yet made the center of gravity of the Party's work," wrote Mao in 1928. "An excessive, sectarian, inner-Party struggle . . . a serious state of extreme democratization in the Party . . . this 'left' sentiment became a left line of reckless action." The first "left" line, dating from August 1927 to the end of 1928, was to be associated with the name of Chu Chiu-pai, the young bespectacled intellectual who had become secretary-general of the Party at the August 7 meeting in Hankow. Born in 1889 in a gentry family of Kiangsu, he was essentially whimsical, erratic, though gifted. He was much influenced by Stalin's representative, some historians contend, to excuse him. But the apology is not accepted by the Chinese.‡ Chu urged a violent, almost terroristic line of "city-taking."

The results of the Autumn Harvest Uprising, which was so vehemently condemned by the leadership of the CCP, were Mao's creation of the Red base, the formation of a disciplined body of militarized teachers, and the resurrection of the Party. Without it there would have been no Chinese Revolution. The Chingkangshan Red base permitted this creation to survive and to grow, something which neither the Nanchang uprising of August 1 nor the December taking of Kuangchow could have achieved. But what Mao had done would not be recognized by his own Party leadership. He lost his place in the Central Committee as alternate member of the provisional Politburo set up on August 7. He was also deprived of membership in the

* See pages 165–166.
† Emphasis not in the original.
‡ The Chinese view has always been that the fault for erroneous lines and deviations in the Party must not be attributed to outside influence, but to those who accept it. Stalin's new representative at that time is said to have been Lominadze.

Hunan Provincial Committee. Yet he went on, convinced that his was the correct strategy.

This is not to belittle the gifted and dedicated Chou En-lai, his immense personal courage, enterprise and dedication when he led the uprisings against Nanchang, and later Swatow and Kuangchow. But the actions against the cities, however significant, were not to lead to the rebuilding of the Party and Army as interlocked essentials for the prosecution of the Chinese Revolution. "The armed struggle led by the Chinese Communist Party is a war of the peasantry under the leadership of the working class," said Mao Tsetung, and in that single sentence lay the clue to victory.

In addition to the Autumn Harvest Uprising, the city-oriented Nanchang uprising is of fundamental importance, because it was a decisive action towards the revolutionary principle of armed struggle. It involved far larger numbers of well-trained troops, yet it failed. In the failure lay a lesson which, had it been learned in time, would have spared the CCP costly mistakes. The Red Army dates its birth — August 1, 1927 — from the Nanchang insurrection, although this anniversary was not proclaimed as Red Army Day until 1932.

We have seen how Chou En-lai organized the Shanghai armed workers' squads, and was upbraided by Chen Tu-hsiu for "provoking" Chiang Kai-shek. Chou En-lai replied that these armed actions were not premature, that the CCP should concentrate on winning over the military, for without military backing, without an established base of operation, it was impossible for the young CP to assert itself as an independent party. In this way his ideas were similar to Mao's. The difference was that Chou En-lai, an intellectual from a city-based family, would also think in terms of city-taking for some time, although by 1929 he had come round to see that this policy was wrong.

Chou En-lai supported the plans for armed uprising which were the new line of action at the July meeting of the Front Committee, and on July 25 reached Nanchang city, where, incognito, he stayed at the Kiangsi Hotel in the city itself, and there contacted Chu Teh, the Szechuan ex-warlord become Communist, to plan the capture of Nanchang.

Chu Teh — we last left him when disgusted with life as a minor warlord — had given up women and opium, and gone abroad to study. He was deeply patriotic, and naturally gravitated to the Com-

munist Party, joining in 1922 in Germany on the advice of Chou
En-lai, whom he met there. He had tried, on his return in 1926, to
persuade some of the warlords of his own province to join the
Northern Expedition. Failing in this, he went to Nanchang, where he
became chief public security officer under the Kuomintang.

This is one of several reasons why Nanchang was chosen for Communist capture. Its strategic position, the fact that there were stationed in the vicinity the troops of Yeh Ting and Ho Lung, both
KMT commanders friendly to the Communists, as well as a portion
of the Communist-officered Ironsides regiment, and finally Chu
Teh's position as chief of public security at Nanchang, and also as
the city's deputy military commander, were all advantages for such
an action. Chu Teh knew all the officers on the spot, his rollicking
Szechuan manner and great gift of talk had made him highly popular with them. He would, it was thought, be able to lull them into a
false sense of security when the first assault would seize the city.

On July 26 Li Li-san, Hsu Te-li, and Nieh Jung-chen, a Communist who had joined the work and study group going to France, and
returned to enter Whangpoo Military Academy,* arrived in Nanchang. The Ironside troops were quartered close to the city; some infiltrated, wearing civilian clothes, inside its walls. Because of
Stalin's telegram, the planned insurrection was almost stopped;
Chang Kuo-tao arrived with the telegram on the morning of July 30.
But Chou En-lai refused to stop, and this decision was a breakaway
from "obedience."

The planned deception failed, and this precipitated the assault.
On August 1 the Communist-led troops attacked and seized the city,
disarming the garrison. On August 2 a mass rally was called in the
center of the city, and Chou En-lai announced the establishment of a
Kuomintang Central Revolutionary Committee with several KMT
leaders who had not defected to the counterrevolution, including
Chang Fa-kuei, a militarist then on his way to Nanchang, and Madame Sun Yatsen.

But Chiang Kai-shek rushed reinforcements to Nanchang by rail
and by water. On August 3 a withdrawal was begun. The troops
pulled out by August 5. The combined forces then moved southward
and began a long, deteriorating series of campaigns. The usual erosion took place — defections, desertions, betrayal — but a nucleus
went on, and even tried, on the way, to fulfill a revolutionary pro-

---

* Nieh was one of the Communists who taught with Chou En-lai at Whangpoo
Academy in 1926 and was arrested with him.

gram, killing landlords, proclaiming land reform, burning land titles.

Later Chu Teh was to say (to his good friend the American journalist Agnes Smedley) * that the Nanchang uprising failed because only the city people had been rallied. The insurrectionists had neglected to propagandize the countryside and to proclaim the agrarian revolution. They also failed to support the peasant uprisings (which were actually going on) in the province. "Mao Tsetung was the only leader who used armed force to help *peasant* uprisings," said Chu Teh.

But this was hindsight. Meanwhile, the now ragged troops went on pushing their way through a deserted and devastated countryside and engaging in pitched battles under harrowing conditions. They reached Swatow, a port in Fukien province, around September 23 or 24. Although ill with high fever, Chou En-lai stayed at the front line, directing the troops. But now they were vastly outnumbered, and they fell back on the Haifeng and Lufeng areas (Peng Pai's area), where peasant revolution had been so lively two years before. But now the White Terror had cut its swath of massacres. The troops starved; Chou was near death, or so it seemed, but he refused to abandon the soldiers. Thinking he would die, his comrades finally smuggled him to Hongkong with Yeh Ting and Nieh Jung-chen, while they dispersed in small groups and went into hiding, submerged in the vast ocean of fields or seeking isolated mountain villages. After two weeks in Hongkong, Chou, scarcely recovered, made his way to Shanghai. Again he was involved in insurrection there; but the workers were cowed by the violence of the repression; there was no alleyway without its spies and its killings. The Kuomintang government of Chiang Kai-shek put a price on Chou's head, and in January 1928 Chou En-lai got away to Russia. In a few months, however, he was back, and again went underground to work for the Party in Shanghai.

The subsequent years, 1928 to 1930, were to bring Chou En-lai to repudiate the city-taking military strategy. Chou contributed greatly to the new orientation and policy of the Party, though the correct strategy was to be created by Mao. Chou, like many others, was to gravitate towards Mao Tsetung. Throughout those years one of Mao's most significant victories was the fact that his ideas won over dedicated men: Chu Teh, the ex-Szechuan warlord turned Communist, a man older than Mao; Chou En-lai, the brilliant stu-

* See Agnes Smedley *Battle Hymn of China* (New York 1943) and *The Great Road* (New York 1956).

dent, organizer, a man of enormous personal bravery, charm, and intelligence; Chen Yi, the humorous Szechuan student become a Communist officer; Lin Piao, the precocious schoolboy activist, also a Whangpoo cadet, who took part in the Nanchang and Swatow uprisings; Jen Pi-shih, of great skill and valor, and so many others, men of talent and of courage; all would, sooner or later, be won over by their individual discovery of Mao's genius for revolution.

And though many were to die, and others were to be found inadequate and even opportunistic, they did, at the time, push forward the wheel of Revolution.

Life on Chingkangshan during that winter of 1927–1928 was a struggle for survival. The greatest problems were food and clothing for so many men. They could have been obtained in the way usual to marauding bands, by loot and rapine, but this Mao strictly forbade. The working out of logistics, and the expansion of his army within a framework of revolutionary action which would benefit, not prey upon, the population, led to the elaboration of new techniques, making of the Army a production corps as well as a political and military force.

His two brothers and adopted sister were with him on Chingkangshan. All three had taken part in the Autumn Harvest Uprising. In November the Red Army attacked the county of Chaling, and took its county town. Landlords were killed, and their stores and goods shared equally with the poor peasants. Land reform was proclaimed and the Red flag floated over the town. In December, it was Lung Shih in Ningkang county which was overrun. People's local governments were proclaimed in each county brought under Red rule.

Thus the six counties around the mountain base were to see the Red Army First Regiment arrive; they were to provide the food required and other necessities, but only within the limits of a redistribution of land and wealth, the agrarian revolution. Mao always deplored the first action at Chaling. For the troops were not yet sufficiently disciplined, and terrorist acts occurred in which landlords, rich peasants, and some not so rich lost their lives. It must have been difficult for half-starving men to exercise the enormous self-control required not to loot, not to kill, but to concentrate only on the houses of landlords and tyrants; not to take anything for themselves, but scrupulously to bring it to the command, for sharing with the poor peasants; to teach and educate the latter, while giving them their share from the hoarded landlord grain. Some of the poor exploited peasants were afraid to take their share of grain, at times by night bringing back to the landlord what they had received. A uniform tax of 20 percent of the crops was to replace all previous taxes and lighten the peasants' burden. Everywhere the poor peasants were to form associations, and elect at mass meetings their representatives for local government.

By February 1928 the Red Army had promoted agrarian revolution in Ningkang, Yunghsin, Chaling, Suichuan, Lienhua, Linghsien. In each a Communist Party committee had been organized. These in turn had created soviets or councils of workers, peasants and soldiers. Thus had been provided, for the base, a source of supplies and of men. The poor peasants were rallying to this new force which both protected them and improved their living conditions.

Landlords ran away, the more tyrannous were executed publicly, and poor peasants began to take heart, and now came with baskets to share the goods and the land. But the new ways and the new power were weak. The peasants were afraid of reprisals. Should the Kuomintang troops return, what would happen to them? As soon as possible, Mao organized militia and Red Guards, backed by the peasant associations among the population. These were to defend the peasantry. At the mountain base, meanwhile, he organized political and military courses for cadres and soldiers. But these could not be pushed without, also, some ordinary schooling. Learning to read and to write was hampered by a lack of teachers, of textbooks, of paper. The soldiers crouched on flat, sandy terrain and wrote with sticks on the ground.

The several hamlets that dot Chingkangshan where Mao lived, wrote, lectured, the stone he sat on, the trees he planted, his habit of watching the soldiers do their physical training, while his finger kept the book he always had in hand open at the page he was reading, are now part of the great historic legend woven round his person. It is difficult through this halo to see the greatness of the man, slogging away at what seemed a doomed adventure, his tiny handful on a stark and poor mountain, surrounded by the gathering enemy forces, so vastly superior. But Mao was flesh of the flesh, bone of the people's bone; like water underground his ideas coursed, a hidden network, through the peasantry he lived with; and they changed. The Hakka carriers of the mountain villages, going across the mountains, in and out of the plains surrounding the fortress heights, along paths known only to them and to salt smugglers, became an intelligence network and liaison for him. Salt is essential to the life of an army, and Mao's men needed salt. This organization of porters took nearly a year to fashion. Many became Red Guards, members of the village committees created by the people's councils. Today they live on a Chingkangshan transformed with schools and hospitals, Shanghai city students come to develop the land, television and electric lights, and a neat tarmac highway to bring many thousands of visitors every month.

Through that tragic winter of massacres all over China, Chingkangshan stood fast, fed itself, and fought. In January 1928 the first attack came; a warlord force to retake Ningkang was sent; it was routed. The Red Army kept Ningkang. This success heightened the prestige of the base among the population; it gave the poor peasants more confidence.

By February the troops were disciplined enough to go down to the plains to help the peasants in the early sowing and planting, and to open up some unplanted land on their own. Thus the Army began to feed itself as well. This would become a Mao concept of what a workers' and peasants' army should be, economically self-sufficient, no burden to the population. And this in China was unique, for never before had any army been a help to the peasantry. Now he kept the soldiers busy cutting wood for building and firewood, erecting huts and planting vegetables. He began a small hospital with a pharmacy storing Chinese medicinal herbs, since it was impossible to procure anything else. Elementary courses in hygiene and health were also started when in May 1928 Dr. Nelson Fu, a Methodist-trained practitioner, arrived in Chingkangshan; by November there would be sixteen "doctors" (partly trained cadres from the Army). Mao insisted that the doctors also look after the health of the local people, and shared with the peasants the very scanty medical supplies which they had brought.

All that winter Mao had been out of touch with the Politburo now underground in Shanghai. It was not until late February or March of 1928, in the midst of holding fast against a campaign launched by two warlord armies (the second attack on the base), that he learned he had been dismissed from the Central Committee as alternate member of the Politburo for his "errors" and criticized severely for what he had done, beginning with the Autumn Harvest Uprising.

The Central Committee plenum convened in November 1927 which "dismissed" Mao Tsetung, to use his own words, had rigorously condemned all that did not fit within the formulas evolved, without taking any notice of Mao's situation. All the old leaders of the CCP were damned; so were most of the leaders of the Nanchang uprising; Chou En-lai was severely censured. Apart from calling for continuous armed insurrection, confiscation of land, killing of all landlords, agrarian revolution, butchering of local bullies, and so on, the plenum announced that a "high revolutionary tide" was coming. Actually the Revolution was at a very low ebb.

Mao Tsetung at Chingkangshan was not, therefore, an undisputed chief whose authority was paramount; he was quite the contrary, a man whose ideas and policies were ignored or repudiated by his own Party leadership. He appeared, to the CCP headquarters in Shanghai, to be doing all the wrong things, leading an isolated band of guerillas in a mountain fastness, and showing "right-wing" proclivities by his moderate policies, not doing enough burning and killing.*

At no time during his stay in Chingkangshan was Mao really left in peace, whether from the warlords and the Kuomintang attacks on his base, or his own Party's stream of directives and counterdirectives and criticism. Delegates came to scold and to revoke; had he followed all the instructions and counterinstructions he received, there would not have been a Red Army and Red bases at that time, and the Revolution might have taken much longer.

But he was, luckily, in a mountain fastness; communications were slow and difficult, and he had built up, and would continue to build, an organization upon principles based on realistic appraisal of China's conditions. When told of the castigation he received, he did not show any emotion; nor did he, like some, turn against his Party or change his conviction. He went on as usual, administering, surveying, walking about, going to the villages, spending the night writing because he was so busy by day. Anyway, he was at that moment engaged in planning a counteroffensive against an attack by Kuomintang and warlord forces. And he was to win another victory.

To build broad-based organizations, to avoid extreme terrorism, was not in contradiction to the Revolution but in line with the construction necessary to carry out the Revolution. This is where Mao averred himself a Leninist, in contradistinction to the "kill all the bourgeoisie, all rich peasants and middle peasants" thesis of secretary-general Chu Chiu-pai. The policies Mao tried at Chingkangshan were "moderate," affecting only big landlords; but even then, he was

---

* This "Trotskyite" view of Mao is also found in M. N. Roy *Revolution and Counter-Revolution in China* (Calcutta 1946).

later to say, he had not drawn enough distinction between "tyrants" and big, middle, small landlords and rich peasants, though always cautious in sparing the physical lives of all but the worst. Very early he formulated the distinction between the liquidation of a class by economic and political means and the physical liquidation of human beings, which he constantly abhorred. This distinction marks him out as an extraordinary person for his time and his environment. He was thus to add a dimension of humanity to the Revolution which Stalin never possessed. But his moderation immensely displeased the Central Committee, intent on "butchering and burning" and in that way antagonizing, instead of rallying, a majority of the countryside.

Mao made the point that the peasantry must be educated and also educate itself in *class* struggle for land reform, by active and total participation in the process. It was necessary to lead peasant guerilla action against big landlords in other counties and districts, even if only for the replenishment of guns and ammunition, but this could only be done with the overwhelming support of the people. But the setting up of people's councils and other measures in Mao's land reform program were not approved by the Central Committee. In December 1927 directives had already been sent to Mao to "burn and kill" more in the countryside. The assassination in the cities of "yellow" union leaders (KMT-created labor union leaders), the robbing of banks, attacks on police stations, were all inscribed in the ultra-left policies of Chu Chiu-pai. Through a fortunate lack of liaison, however, Mao had been given till March 1928 to try out his own methods before the extreme left line caught up with him.

Mao's experiment in rural Red bases for a revolutionary Party and Army changed the history of China. There was no exact blueprint for the future; someone had to experiment, to draw the first sketches. The Chingkangshan base was such a critical test; and its success was due to Mao's refusal to accept suicidal orders and his understanding of the realities, together with a determination to make the Revolution a creative, working proposition.

Edgar Snow told me of his first impression of Mao. "It was night and I was walking back when someone (my interpreter) pointed out to me a man walking past. It was Mao Tsetung, he said. He looked like anyone else, there was nothing to distinguish him from any of the other thousands there. He walked alone, going back to his cave dwelling. A few days later I was to meet him in the daytime. It was not that he was impressive at first sight; though tall and lean, he was so quiet, taking in at first everything that was said to him, that it was only gradually I came to be more and more impressed. Here was a man with great mastery, a command of knowledge and wisdom, and talking to him one felt it. A real storehouse of knowledge and original ideas; a freedom of thought and a total lack of rigidity, surpassing anyone else.

"Talking to him one felt in the presence of a world statesman, and then one went back and one began to wonder. Here was this man living in the poorest circumstances, it seemed there was no hope for his cause, at least if one only looked at outward appearances, yet talking to him, one felt that he was the only man in China who really understood its reality. It looked as if there was a world against him, and Mao alone, yet one wanted to be on his side. He convinced; had I been Chinese, I would have joined him. After talking with him, no other way was possible than to 'see' as he saw, and to follow him."

This was almost a decade later; * but the sense of dauntlessness, of quiet endurance, already radiated from Mao in Chingkangshan; his power to make others see as he saw already proven. The Mao Tsetung of Chingkangshan saw further than any of the other revolutionaries, though he still had much to learn, as he himself said. His writings of that time link the extremely practical to the overall ground plan, meticulous detail to broad sweeping principles. And all through runs the scholarly touch, the close, cold masterly reasoning of the born scientist. For all his personal humility, Mao's writings always carry that lecture stance. It was this which probably enraged the lesser men in Party control.

Agnes Smedley, who did not like Mao, says of the Mao she met during those guerilla days; "Mao's mind perpetually wrestled with the theoretical problems of the Chinese Revolution. Sensitive and intuitive almost to the point of femininity, Mao possessed all the self-confidence and decisiveness of a pronouncedly masculine man."

This "intuitiveness" Mao would have explained easily had he been asked. He would have said that he tried to be totally integrated with his own people, and that his strength and knowledge came from them. He would say that it was they who made him, not the other way round.

In early 1928 the counterrevolution was very strong, the revolutionary forces were weak and scattered. In the cities the Communist

* In 1936, when Edgar Snow met Mao at Yenan.

Mao Tsetung in Yenan, around the time he first talked with Edgar Snow.

workers' unions had been decimated. In the countryside the peasants were cowed; yet it was here that the "foot infantry" of the Revolution could be organized. This organization needed a consolidated base, just as the course of the Revolution needed a clear political line. The definition of a rural Red base had to be worked out. It must provide the physical, geographical and economic sustenance of a political regime with an armed force as its principal support. It must be as self-sufficient as possible; it must have capabilities of defense and possibilities of expansion; it must have a sufficient population for recruitment and for economic growth; it must have leadership cadres, and institutions for education and training. The support of the people around it was its overwhelming prime condition. *It must not be an army of occupation,* but like fish in water, an army of the people.

The peasantry was the "vast paradise" in which there was great opportunity for the weak Communist party to consolidate and develop its armed strength. Mao's strategic thinking during these rigorous weeks and months at Chingkangshan meant a thorough sifting of the problems of the Chinese Revolution, and a solution. *Why Is It That Red Political Power Can Exist in China?*, written in Maoping, a hamlet of the Chingkangshan base, in October 1928, analyzes the internal political situation, and the reasons for the survival of a Red structure though surrounded by enemy forces. In his vivid descriptive *Struggle in the Chingkang Mountains* of November 1928, Mao wrote in detail of the work and the fighting, the policies of survival and build-up throughout that year at Chingkangshan.

China was not at the stage of all-out socialist revolution, but still at the stage of a bourgeois-democratic revolution, wrote Mao. This stage could only be completed under the leadership of the working class, but it did mean entirely different policies and techniques. The aims of the bourgeois-democratic revolution, which had been Sun Yatsen's aims, had been subverted by Chiang Kai-shek, but not all of the Kuomintang was with Chiang, hence the extreme left policies applied by the CCP were quite wrong; they isolated the Party and the Army from the "masses" ("cold and aloof" because of these ultra-left methods) and from a very large and possible ally, the petty bourgeoisie, as well as a section of the national capitalist class.

In these two essays of the Chingkangshan period the main ideas of Mao's strategy appear. The relation between the national and the social revolution is clearly defined in stages. The problem of leadership, of creating leadership, looms large as well as the absolute necessity of armed struggle and the building of a people's Red Army: "Without a people's army the people have nothing" is the logical conclusion. How and in what manner it will be built is of fundamental importance.

The defeat of 1927 was "a blow to the petty bourgeoisie and the national bourgeoisie as well," Mao wrote. "The national bourgeoisie had never really held power from the restrictions imposed by the reactionary policies of the big landlord class and the big bourgeoisie in power." These fine distinctions reveal that Mao was still searching for a formula to rally majorities, wresting allies from even such unlikely groups as national capitalists, and thus re-creating a sort of united front. Even if these allies were "vacillating" and the alliance temporary, they were still needed and useful. In all this Mao was displaying a subtle psychological tactic for sifting, dividing, and breaking up enemy blocs into allies, neutrals, and targets for attack.

The existence of a Red Army of adequate strength was "a necessary condition for the existence of Red political power." Again and again through the decades the supreme importance of the Red Army as a pillar of Communist power is stressed in all of Mao's work. But at all times the Army must be subordinate to the Party, framed by the Party, directed by its policies. Hence the important condition required "for the prolonged existence and development of Red political power [is] that the Communist Party organization should be strong and its policy correct."

Rebuilding the Party organizations on a mass base was a task fundamental to the strategy of power, and this was accomplished at Chingkangshan by the Red Army. It was the Red Army which cradled, protected and nourished the young Party, but it was the Party which gave the Red Army its reason for existence, and both were nurtured by the people. It was through the Red Army, carrying out the policies of the Party, that the agrarian revolution, essential for the support of the masses, could be carried out, but without the revolutionary masses, they could not exist. This complex triple relationship of masses-Party-Army forms the basis of Mao's organizational principles, and they have not varied for the last forty years.

Because of this theoretical analysis based on Chinese conditions, Mao Tsetung argued that at all times advantage must be taken of the enemy's weakness, such as inter-warlord strife, the historical weakness of provincial armed forces at borders between provinces, strife between Chiang Kai-shek and provincial warlords. The establishment of a Red rural base and its survival were unique: "It cannot

192 The Morning Deluge

occur in any imperialist country [as in Europe or the U.S. then] or in any colony under direct imperialist rule." It was due essentially to China's great unevenness of development, her disjointed state as a "semi-colonial, semi-feudal" country.

So long as splits and wars continued within the camp of the Kuomintang and the warlords in alliance with it (but often at war with it), so long could an armed regime of workers and peasants also continue to exist and develop, provided the problem of leadership was solved. On this question, Mao was ruthlessly frank, listing the opportunism, localism, "evil feudal practice of arbitrary dictation" with "no liking for the bothersome democratic system," of Party cadres. It was to provide a basic democracy in the Party, and in the Army, that Mao stressed the need for soldiers' committees, conferences of soldiers' representatives, debates and discussions.

The Chingkangshan period is thus of great importance, because Mao Tsetung wrestled with so many fundamental problems affecting the structure of a new model for the Chinese Revolution, in which recognition of the peasant component, the importance of rural bases, the strategy of the countryside surrounding the cities, the Red Army, were all his creations.

The emphasis on agrarian revolution in rural areas as an essential to the consolidation of Red power, and to the building up of an all-China Red Army, was to create a new military science, the strategy and tactics of "revolutionary people's war."

In that late February and early March of 1928, as winter still harrowed Chingkangshan and freezing rain soaked the ill-clad, ill-fed men, Mao received Ho Ting-yin, a delegate representing the South Hunan Special Party committee. This was a body set up by the Central Committee after the November plenum for the purpose of arousing insurrections in South Hunan. Ho Ting-yin came with orders to Mao to lead his small forces on an armed attempt in South Hunan, in line with the "high tide of revolution" theory evolved at the November plenum. Mao indicated that he did not think there was a "high tide," as announced by the Politburo. The time was unpropitious for such military action.

"At the same time, Ho criticized us for having leaned to the right, for having done too little burning and killing, and for having failed to carry out the so-called policy of turning the petty bourgeois into proletarians and forcing them into the revolution," wrote Mao. (Ho Ting-yin may have brought the news of Mao's expulsion from the

Central Committee, and from the Hunan Provincial Committee as well.)

Ho Ting-yin then "abolished the Front Committee," which meant that technically Mao was no longer in charge of the Red Army, and then ordered the troops to fight in South Hunan pitched battles against some large warlord troops. "Consequently the Hunan-Kiangsi border area [Chingkangshan base] was occupied by the enemy for more than a month. . . . At the end of March came the defeat in South Hunan." In these words Mao alluded to the six counties being almost totally overrun by five battalions of warlord troops under two generals (both named Yang). Thus Mao nearly lost the base he had taken all winter to build. He lost control of the troops as Ho took over. The latter carried out the "killing, burning and butchering" policy which was the line of the plenum, antagonized a great many middle peasants and small landlords, and hence the defeat, as these all turned against the Red Army.

When the troops returned from South Hunan, they too had lost a good many men; and now another campaign had to be undertaken to get rid of the occupying forces. Mao's need for men and guns, for hospital care for the wounded, was urgent. He tried all methods to win over again the hearts of the peasantry, his mass base; he set the soldiers to dig entrenchments. He was now only the secretary of the Special Committee for Chingkangshan. And then, as so often in his life, occurred an event which was to turn the tide in his favor. This was the arrival of Chu Teh.

We must now take up the tale of Chu Teh, since the withdrawal from Nanchang city in August 1927, the previous year. Chu Teh had moved southward with the other insurrectionists; the bulk of the Red troops entered Fukien province and reached the large and wealthy city of Swatow. Swatow being an overseas Chinese stronghold sympathetic to Sun Yatsen, as well as a large port, its capture would have greatly benefited the Communists. But the capture of Swatow was a transient affair; the revolutionary forces withdrew and dispersed. Chu Teh, who had been in the rear, was left with a thousand men. Pursuing evasive guerilla action, Chu Teh joined forces with an old friend of his, a Kuomintang military commander. Thus Chu Teh did not take part in the attack upon Kuangchow city, the setting up of the Kuangchow commune, and the withdrawal from Kuangchow in December, followed by a White Terror of gruesome cruelty. These three attempts to capture a city, Nanchang, Swatow, and Kuangchow, as a Communist base, and the resultant failures decimated the Red troops. Now only stubborn valor sustained them, as they withdrew and dispersed.

By joining with the Kuomintang, Chu Teh seemed to have given up his beliefs, but this was a feint, for shortly afterward (in January 1928) he left this obliging friend, renaming his army the Fourth Red Army (two regiments and one battalion), since it was the remnants of the Fourth "Ironsides" Army of the Northern Expedition, and made his way through the countryside to South Hunan. There he participated in the hapless insurrection ordered by the Hunan Special Committee, into which Mao's troops had also been drawn. The retreating Chu Teh came in contact with Mao's brother Mao Tse-tan, who was doing dangerously heroic work as liaison, and seems to have been perpetually moving about the villages of Hunan (as was Mao's adopted sister, who was butchered in Henyang, where she did underground work, by the Kuomintang in 1929).

Chu Teh's troops were in an exhausted state; they had no base, they had truly become roving guerilla bands. Although supported by the poor — even little boys from the mines of eleven and twelve were trying to join up to "kill the landlords, share the land" — Chu Teh's army was facing destruction, as every engagement cost him more men. His only course was to join Mao at Chingkangshan. This alone, had the Politburo used its brains, would have shown the importance of Mao's base.

The decision of Chu Teh to join Mao at Chingkangshan was thus partly due to an invitation from Mao, conveyed by Mao Tse-tan, and partly due to the perilous situation in which Chu Teh found himself. By the end of April, Chu had arrived in Linghsien county, at the foot of the massif. The campaign against Mao's base was in full blast. It was a combined warlord and Kuomintang operation, outnumbering Mao's depleted men by twenty to one. Chu Teh himself was in great danger, for the way up the mountain was barred by enemy troops. Most of the six counties were reoccupied by the enemy after the disastrous initiative of the "South Hunan insurrection," and a perpetual seesaw of battles round the mountain fortress took place; it was to continue, off and on, all the rest of the year. At this moment, Mao Tsetung, with the only two battalions he now had, came down from the mountain like an avalanche, in a swift and daring onslaught, hacking open a road for Chu Teh and his troops so that they could reach safety.

Visitors to Chingkangshan are shown, in Ningkang county, the plain where the historic meeting between Chu Teh and Mao Tsetung took place; at the small town of Talung, now a prosperous brigade but at that time a primitive poor village. A commemorative stone is set up on the plain where the two met, by a mountain stream. Mao was all smiles as he hugged Chu Teh. This meeting was to begin a cooperation and a legend, which would last nearly forty years, between Chu Teh and Mao Tsetung. The legend of perfect harmony was exploded during the Cultural Revolution; but it remains a fascinating human story of two human beings, with their dedication and their disagreements. We must content ourselves with imperfect knowledge, though valuable. Mao's relationships with the men round him will never be fully known; we have the right to ponder them, and the final appraisal is yet to be made. But one thing is certain, Chu Teh was never a conspirator, greedy for power. He had his defects and often acted with rashness, but he would be Mao's faithful friend too, and Mao Tsetung would never forget nor abandon him.

It is said that Chu Teh was not in agreement with Mao when he arrived, and actually had received instructions to oppose him. This may be true, but he was certainly won over by Mao's persuasive talent and sincerity of purpose, touched by the warmth with which he was received, and the personal sacrifice involved when Mao led all the men he had left to hack a way up the slopes, through enemy armies, for him. The immediate result of this merger was that, with strengthened troops, Mao and Chu Teh were able to rout the attackers and reap a brilliant victory. The aid of the population in the ravaged districts now proved itself effective; Yuan Wen-tsai, the "bandit," also joined in the battle, which was catastrophic for the two Yang warlords. This common victory soldered the alliance between Mao and Chu Teh, and between the soldiers who had endured the winter and the tired remnants who had survived so many battles against superior numbers. Chu Teh and his troops were then quartered at Maoping, and there a conference was held in May.

The Maoping conference of May 20, 1928, also called the First Congress of the Border Area (Chingkangshan), was a seminal conference, and Mao dominated it even though the news of his "expulsion" was now generally known. Chu Teh was to call it the "most important party conference after the counterrevolution began." The conference reviewed the history of the Chinese Revolution. Mao Tsetung advanced five basic points, characteristics of the Chinese revolutionary war, now in its "agrarian revolutionary war" stage.

These characteristics in turn were to determine the political and military strategy adopted. They were to be developed and expanded in a Second Congress, also held at Maoping, in October 1928.*

Because these ideas represent a total strategy for revolution, it is important for anyone who wants to understand the Revolution, and Mao, to make the effort of grasping them. And it is also important to realize that through the dreary dragging winter of bitterness and suffering on Chingkangshan, the mind of Mao Tsetung had been so active, creating an entirely new concept of revolution for China.

Mao's basic idea was that there could be no delimitation, no partition between military action and political-economic-agrarian policies in the Chinese Revolution. "Since the struggle in the Border Area is exclusively military, both the Party *and* the masses have to be placed on a war footing." Even Stalin had remarked that in China it was armed revolution against armed counterrevolution which characterized the Chinese situation (December 1927). This indivisibility of Party-Army would be a long-term phenomenon.

The five characteristics Mao brought out were:

(*1*) China was a semi-feudal, semi-colonial country with uneven development of the Revolution, few workers in coastal cities, and a vast countryside with a large population of peasants.

(*2*) China was large and had many resources, especially manpower. The masses had already proved what they were capable of in the Revolution, but the Communist leadership (meaning the Chen Tu-hsiu leadership) had followed "incorrect policies." Now a Red Army was being created (workers-peasants-soldiers). It was a people's army, absolutely essential for the Revolution. But it must be placed under the Party's control. "Our principle is that the Party commands the gun, and the gun must never be allowed to command the Party."

(*3*) The White Kuomintang regime was now strong, yet it was divided; the divisions and internal conflicts must be utilized by revolutionaries, but at the present time it was dangerous to attack it. In these words Mao showed his disagreement with the foolhardy military enterprises ordered by Chu Chiu-pai.

(*4*) The Revolution was now at a low ebb, said Mao, going directly against the "high tide" theory of the Politburo. This was a time for building up bases, educating the masses, nurturing the forces of the Revolution, and rebuilding a Party based on demo-

* A portion of Mao Tsetung's report at the second Maoping conference is incorporated in *Why Is It That Red Political Power Can Exist in China?*

cratic centralism, not a time for offensives and large-scale uprisings. The strategy and tactics of the forces must be based on the *defensive;* there must be no "military adventurism." Supplies of food, clothing, weapons, were precarious. Hence the military tactics should be:

> The enemy advances, we retreat.
> The enemy halts, we harass.
> The enemy withdraws, we attack.
> The enemy retreats, we pursue.

These were the tactics of guerilla warfare, classic tenets of revolutionary people's war.

(5) The agrarian revolution was essential if the bases (and the Red power and Army) were to survive. Therefore in building a people's army and party, prominence must be given to land reform; only through it could the ample support of the peasants be achieved, only through land reform could mass organizations be built, recruits be found, and leadership talent reared up from the masses.

Mao wrote that the revolutionary army would expand because its rank and file would come from the agrarian revolution, and because commanders and officers were at one with the men.

The *three* main rules of discipline and *eight* points for attention, or code of the Red Army, were also drawn up at the Maoping conference. They remain the cardinal principles of the Red Army today. Only six points were elaborated by Mao, points 6 and 7 were added at Lin Piao's suggestion, it is said, in the summer of 1928.*

The three main rules of discipline are:

(*1*) Obey orders in all your actions.
(*2*) Do not take a single needle or piece of thread from the masses.
(*3*) Turn in everything you have captured.

The eight points "for attention" are:

(*1*) Speak politely to the people.
(*2*) Pay fairly for what you buy.
(*3*) Return everything you borrow.
(*4*) Pay for anything you damage.

---

* This is hearsay, and is also to be found in several historical exposés in Chinese museums. But there has not been official confirmation of this point.

(5) Replace all doors and return all straw on which you sleep.*

(6) Dig latrines away from houses and fill them with earth when you leave.

(7) Do not take liberties with women.

(8) Do not ill-treat captives.

These were to be learned by heart and sung by all soldiers of the Red Army.

The first Maoping conference also decided that the Chingkang-shan base should consolidate, the six counties be retaken, then gradually expand. Mao Tsetung's policy of moderation towards middle peasants and petty merchants was accepted by the conference (though not by the Central Committee). The creation of peasant militia and Red Guards was to be carried out. It was thus a Mao program which was adopted. Mao was to develop, through this experience, the concept of "fluctuation." The area controlled by a fluctuant base might shrink or swell as it was attacked or as attacks were repelled, but the main thing was people, not territory. So long as the people were organized, and the organization held fast, the land could always be retaken.

Chu Teh was named commander-in-chief of the Red Army, now nearly 4,000 strong, and redesignated as the Fourth Red Army of Workers and Peasants. Mao Tsetung accepted the merger, becoming Party representative in the Fourth Army. They were to double in numbers when joined at the end of 1928 by other groups which had found themselves in the same predicament as Chu Teh's.

For a few short spring weeks, things became much better. The soldiers were heartened by the additional weapons, the men, and the victories. The base had enough manpower to build fortifications, dig entrenchments, and carry rice up from the plains. Chu Teh carried rice with the rest, and his pole is still shown as a museum exhibit. Medical and teaching personnel had also come in. Mao directed all political work in the Army and among the peasantry, insisting the Political Department was the "lifeline of all work in the Army." He promoted the miners from Anyuan, more politically advanced, to become political instructors and officers. An Army-Party committee was created to control the political educative process; soldiers' committees were set up throughout the newly arrived troops. "Everyone

* The Red Army borrowed doors (made of wood planks and easily unhinged) and straw to sleep on. These were returned to the peasants in the morning.

fought and everyone did political work," which broke down "military-mindedness."

"The troops were taught the history of the Revolution, of foreign aggression, methods of mass leadership and organization, how to carry on propaganda with enemy troops, singing and public speaking," Agnes Smedley writes. A special training detachment was formed consisting of some of the staunchest, most experienced miners.* Reading, writing, arithmetic were taught by officers to their men. The men sat on the ground tracing characters and figures in the dirt since there were no paper or pencils. But the most powerful educational method consisted of the conference — debate. "All rank disappeared, soldiers had full rights to free speech. . . . Not only were battles and campaigns discussed, but the individual conduct of any commander or fighter could be criticized." The inarticulate peasant thus learned to think, to express himself; he became responsible, valuing his own worth as a member of a great revolutionary company.

Besides the Red Army, Mao paid special care to the Red Guards, who now disposed of 683 rifles. They represented the guerilla peasantry, were the lookouts and watchers, meanwhile continuing their ordinary occupations. Thanks to this network, when Chingkangshan was attacked there was now warning beforehand. The local militia organized in each village supplemented the Red Army and was also a source of recruitment for it. Mao lectured on the "indissoluble link" between Party, Army, and the masses of the people. He insisted on popular representation; he would draft a detailed organic law for the people's councils established in the counties controlled by the base, to provide mass participation in their administration.

But this satisfactory state of consolidation was brief. The conflict between Mao Tsetung's line and that of the Central Committee was not at an end. Mao would not be rehabilitated till the Sixth Congress (July–September 1928); meanwhile, further irrational directives from the Central Committee and the Hunan Provincial Committee again almost destroyed what he had built.

In the next months and years Mao would be facing drastic choices: compliance with orders from above, which would mean disaster for the Revolution, or rejecting these orders, which would mean indiscipline and being censured. It was this long "tempering in ideological struggle" which he underwent which he feels is essential

---

* For instance, Keng Piao, once an Anyuan miner, who followed Mao to Chingkangshan, became ambassador to Albania, and now a Minister.

in learning to discern correct from incorrect policies. Hence far from shunning these conflicts, he would look upon them as a valuable experience, teaching patience, resilience, endurance, and firmness of purpose, indispensable adjuncts to any revolutionary's political education. Meanwhile he went on, on the one hand with the large all-encompassing vision, creating a new, grandiose blueprint for the conquest of power, on the other materializing these abstract theories in a thousand practical, down-to-earth, meticulously detailed directives and activities. Hence nothing he wrote is to be regarded as trivial; it was as essential to return straw bedding as it was to capture villages. And so, in a thousand ways, the Chinese Revolution grew in the mountains of Chingkangshan.

"In April [1928] after the whole of our army [Chu Teh's Fourth Army] arrived . . . there was still not much burning and killing, but the expropriation of the middle merchants in town and collection of compulsory contributions from the small landlords and rich peasants were now rigorously enforced. . . . This ultra-left policy of attacking the petty bourgeoisie drove most of them to the side of the landlords . . . with the result that they put on white ribbons and opposed us."

The Maoping conference of May 1928 reversed some of the highly unpopular policies which had succeeded in turning the masses against the Communists. "Thanks to these proper tactics . . . we were able to win a number of military victories and expand the people's independent regime from April to July. Although several times stronger than we, the enemy was unable to prevent the expansion . . . let alone destroy it." "We fought the enemy for four long months, daily enlarging the territory . . . deepening the agrarian revolution, extending the people's political power and expanding the Red Army and the Red Guards. This was possible because the policies of the Party organizations (local and army) in the Border Area [the Chingkangshan Base] were correct." There was a large increase in Party members in all six counties.

In the April to July series of battles, Lin Piao, then twenty-one, distinguished himself, particularly at the battle of Lungyuankou, and caught Mao's attention. The younger man seemed attracted to Mao by the latter's wide span of ideas, and his military originality. Lin Piao, too, would not always agree with Mao Tsetung; but he seemed his best pupil in military matters. On June 23, 1928, Lin Piao lured five enemy regiments in Yunghsin county into pursuing the Red forces into the mountains, then swooped upon them in a narrow place and cut them to pieces. This, called the victory of Lungyuan-kou, was to become a favorite tactic of Lin Piao's, based on Mao's military ideas.

But now, once again, the "left" line of Chu Chiu-pai interfered. "The Hunan Provincial Committee advocated three different plans within a few weeks of June and July . . . each . . . the absolutely correct policy to be carried out without the least hesitation." In June, a man called Yuan Teh-shen, representative of the Hunan Provincial Committee, arrived at the base, and approved of the measures taken to establish political power and the independent regime of Chingkangshan; that is, he approved of the Maoping conference and its results. But in July two other emissaries named Tu and Yang came, with orders for an immediate military operation to be carried out in South Hunan, leaving only 200 men and rifles at the base. "How can there be Marxism in the mountains of Chingkangshan?" they said. They found fault with everything, castigated the setup, and transmitted orders for the Army to move out of the base and advance to attack as the "absolutely correct policy." Ten days later Yuan Teh-shen returned with a letter "rebuking us at great length" and urging the Red Army to set out immediately to East, not South, Hunan, and again describing this as the "absolutely correct" policy to be carried out "without the least hesitation." "These rigid directives put us in a real dilemma. . . . Failure to comply would be tantamount to disobedience, while compliance would mean certain defeat."

Faced with these caprices of the Hunan Provincial Committee, Mao Tsetung termed both these sets of contradictory orders suicidal, and called a conference of the Party-Army committee. On July 4, at Yunghsin, where Mao was now staying, he produced a reply "in seven reasoned paragraphs" showing the dangers inherent in both these instructions, urging that the Army remain where it was.

Tu and Yang, however, went off to the headquarters of the Twenty-ninth Regiment of the Fourth Army, to persuade individual commanders to leave the base and fight in South Hunan. In this they succeeded. The Twenty-ninth Regiment, now homesick, and tired of the privations and asceticism of Chingkangshan, was persuaded to attack several county towns. They suffered very heavy losses. Yang created a rival committee and took Mao's place as secretary; at the same time the major detachment of the Red Army, which was on operations to control the counties previously overrun, was now deflected from its tasks and also ordered to go fighting in South Hunan.

In this change of plans, Chu Teh, as commander-in-chief, seems to have, possibly from a sense of loyalty, obeyed the orders of Tu and Yang from the Provincial Committee, despite Mao's protests.

The result of this disastrous South Hunan expedition was that the whole of the Fourth Red Army, except one regiment recuperating from fighting, left the base and, in August, incurred a 50 percent loss in pointless battles. The newly expanded base was left unprotected. This was "the August defeat" described in detail by Mao.* Through it, all that had been gained from April to July was again lost. The ultra-left policies were again rigorously enforced by Tu and Yang, now in control, and once more the "intermediate" classes, the petty merchants and traders, the middle peasants turned against the Red Army. Mao's patient mass work was undone once more.

Mao then attempted to bring back the remains of his army. He led some soldiers of the regiment he had left to Kweitung, in South Hunan, to catch up with the defeated main forces, rescue them, and make them return to base. On the 23rd of August he reached them, and on the 25th held a meeting. The regiments were in full mutiny; the 29th regiment wanted to go home, the 28th did not want to return, a commander defected. Mao spoke to the men, to the officers, debating with them, analyzing the cause of defeat. "We want to go home," they shouted. Mao argued with them and was able to bring many of them around. And so he led them the weary way back to Chingkangshan.

Profiting from the absence of the Red Army, "enemy units from Hunan and Kiangsi seized the opportunity to attack the Chingkang mountains on August 30. Using their points of vantage, the defending troops, numbering less than one battalion, fought back, routed the enemy and saved the base."

This was the famous battle of Huang Yang Chieh (August 30, 1928), one of the five passes into the mountain complex, which an elated Mao celebrated in a poem.† The erstwhile "bandit" forces of Yuan Wen-tsai and Wang Tso, who had remained behind, played a great part in keeping Chingkangshan against the enemy, as did the local population, who planted bamboo spikes in all the passes and fired off an old wooden cannon, making great noises with drums and howling. Mao was delighted with the victory and the valor of the Chingkangshan Hakkas, men and women. The exhausted main detachment came back, the wounded were very numerous, and again

---

* *Selected Works of Mao Tsetung* (English edition Peking 1961–1965), vol. I, p. 76.
† Poem at end of chapter.

all had to be rebuilt. The base counties had once again been overrun by looting troops on the rampage. Harvests had been burned. The population now was definitely more hostile.

Came September, autumn, and little to eat. Difficulties increased. The ultra-left line had alienated the people; the costly and stupid battles had depleted the forces. Battles were now continual between the base and the surrounding enemy, which assaulted time and again. The base needed everything, weapons, clothes, medicines. The soldiers had little to eat and wear. They got up at night to drill, in order to keep warm.

"How to fight has become the central problem in our daily life." The Red Army consisted partly of workers and peasants "and partly of lumpen proletariat" (here Mao meant the bandits Yuan and Wang, so contemptuously described by the envoys of Chu Chiu-pai). Because of incessant attacks, it was "already no easy matter to get replacements even from among them" (the lumpen proletariat). The Red Army had abolished the mercenary system, had equal distribution of oil, salt, firewood and vegetables; each company, battalion or regiment had its soldiers' committees; Party representatives were at company level — but the hardships endured were enormous. "Cold as the weather is, many of our men are still wearing only two layers of thin clothing . . . Fortunately we are inured to hardships." "From the commander of the army to the cook everyone lives on the daily food allowance of 5 cents, apart from grain." Because of the incessant battles, there were "many wounded . . . many officers and men are ill from malnutrition, exposure to cold and other causes"; and yet such was the morale that "newly captured soldiers feel that though in material life worse off in the Red Army than in the White Army, spiritually they are liberated . . . the Red Army is like a *furnace* in which all captured soldiers are melted down and transformed." Mao added that "apart from the role played by the Party, the reason why the Red Army had been able to carry on in spite of such poor material conditions and such frequent engagements" (over eighteen large and small in twelve months) "is its practice of democracy." "In China the army needs democracy as much as the people do."

More than 60 percent of the land in the border areas where the base was located belonged to the landlords — in some counties up to 80 percent. "Therefore, given this situation, it is possible to win the support of the majority for the confiscation of all the land." But there was a difficulty; that of the "intermediate class," standing between the big and middle landlords and the poor peasants. Because of the ultra-left line of complete confiscation, the intermediate class had been alienated, and a great deal of obstruction had resulted. The small landlords and rich peasants had defected to the enemy, led the KMT forces to enter and to commit atrocities. "The most difficult problem . . . is to keep a firm hold on the intermediate class — this class has attached itself almost wholly to the big landlord class, and the poor peasant class has become isolated. This is indeed a very serious problem."

Mao also pointed out that mass meetings "called on the spur of the moment" could not train the masses politically." The reason is the lack of propaganda and education concerning the new political system. The evil feudal practice of arbitrary dictation is so deeply rooted in the minds of the people and even of the ordinary Party members that it cannot be swept away at once; when anything crops up, they choose the easy way and have no liking for this bothersome democratic system . . .

"Owing to the tight enemy blockade and *our mishandling of the petty bourgeoisie,** trade has almost entirely ceased, necessities such as salt, cloth, medicines are scarce and costly, agricultural products cannot be sent out." Poor peasants were more able to bear these hardships, but not the intermediate class, and "unless a nation-wide revolutionary situation develops, the small independent Red regimes will come under great economic pressure and *it is doubtful whether they will be able to last."* †

Within the Party organization, Mao wrote, "manifestations of opportunism [in the last twelve months, since October 1927] continue to be widespread." All this made it difficult to organize a "militant Bolshevik Party." In September, after the August defeat, Mao ordered a drastic shake-up of the Party in Chingkangshan and reregistration of Communist Party members. This was the first "rectification" he had conducted at a Red base. We do not know how effective the results were. Possibly in view of having to leave the base, he now set on foot underground Party organizations and cells. The structures were the same as the visible ones, but now they could function even if the base was overrun by the Kuomintang, as indeed it would be within the next year. The second Maoping conference (October-November 1928; also called the Second Congress of the Border Area) was the occasion for a summing up of all the experiences

* From Kuomintang and warlord troops who attacked Chingkangshan.
† Emphasis not in the original.

through that grueling year. Mao could then write fully to the Central Committee, justifying all he had done. With courtesy but relentless logic, he exposed the wrongheadedness of the directives, and his indignation at the human losses incurred comes through.

Mao Tsetung emphasized the paramount importance of army-political indoctrination; a ratio of one Party member to two non-Party in the Army would now be his aim. (Today it is still the ratio in the Red Army.) By stressing the importance of the "intermediate" class, the middle peasantry, petty traders and craftsmen, he refuted the ultra-left policy of lumping them all with "landlords and rich peasants" to kill. The conference had passed resolutions on *Prohibition of Reckless Burning and Killing* and *Protection of the Interests of the Middle and Small Merchants*. This line against terrorism, against ultra-leftism, would be Mao's all through the next decades.

The land law which had been promulgated in the base territory in September was too drastic because it ordered confiscation and redistribution of all land instead of only landlord land. Mao realized this error by the year's end; he would change the law in April 1929 to "confiscate public land and the land of the landlord class." * He would also continue to make provision for the protection of merchants in county towns. The experience of Chingkangshan confirmed his natural bent for flexible practical policies based on meticulous investigation. But there was a storm of abuse against Mao not only from the provincial committee in Hunan but also the one in Kiangsi (since the base area straddled both), abuse which later was to be reiterated by the next secretary-general in charge of the Party who replaced Chu Chiu-pai in that autumn of 1928 — none other than Li Li-san. "Rifle movement," "conservatism," "peasant consciousness," "localism," "guerillaism," "alliance with bandits and lumpen proletariat" were hurled at Mao. But in spite of this his work was being highly spoken of even in Moscow at the Comintern. From July to September of 1928, the Chinese Communist Party was holding its Sixth Congress in Moscow, and Chu Chiu-pai was already out, though Mao may not have known of this till later, in November. The reason for Chu's deposition was his ultra-leftism; the Comintern had done some reappraisal of the situation.

Enemy harassment continued through September, October, November, against Chingkangshan. In October more pro-Communist groups ascended to the fortress. This time it was Peng Teh-huai who

---

* Land law of Hsingkuo county; see next chapter.

came with his troops, bringing the number to about 8,000. Peng Teh-huai was a Kuomintang officer who had revolted and joined the Communist Party in April 1928. He too had been ordered to launch insurrections in Hunan, was defeated in July, and like Chu Teh had to seek shelter in the Chingkangshan base. But now, with the bitter winter approaching, the base could not cope with this influx of men. There was simply not enough to eat. "Make revolution and eat squash!" the soldiers shouted. But even squash was difficult to get.

In early December another large enemy force of no less than eighteen regiments was launched against Chingkangshan. Grievous battles took place. It was freezing, the men were starved. They no longer even shouted, "Make revolution and eat squash!" Though Mao still insisted that the doctors of the Army should look after the population as well, there were no medicines. Some of Mao's colleagues in the twenty-four-man Border Committee he had organized in September urged abandoning the base and reverting to roving guerilla warfare. Mao still held to the notion of the base. "We hold as we always held, that it is absolutely necessary and correct to build up and expand Red political power," wrote Mao. He asked for help, some medicines, supplies, but none were forthcoming.

A conference was then held at Ningkang on January 4, 1929; at the conference it appears that it was Mao who decided that he and Chu Teh, with 4,000 men, should found another base, leaving Peng Teh-huai with 5,000 men at Chingkangshan. This is called the White Dew (Pai Lou) conference. Again Mao criticized the "roving bands" idea, and then made ready to leave Chingkangshan.

Except for a few advance squads, each soldier was issued some rounds of cartridges; the bulk of the ammunition was left on Chingkangshan. It is said that one of the first things that happened was dissension between Peng Teh-huai and the two Hakka leaders, Yuan and Wang, with whom Mao had got on rather well. But there is no real evidence that Peng Teh-huai killed them, even if this is what is now being said.* Chingkangshan was attacked again by White forces and the base almost entirely evacuated. Save for the clandestine groups (created by Mao in September 1928), the Red Guards, and the (secret) peasant militia, by March 1929 the base was no longer the vital focus it had been. But the region remained a guerilla area. It would be 1937 before Chingkangshan would be revisited by Chen Yi, to revive the Party structures there and to recruit old cadres;

* Interview, 1969. Such Red Guard and other material issued during the Great Proletarian Cultural Revolution must be handled with caution.

from this area would come fighters to staff the New Fourth Army organized to fight the Japanese invasion. Mao had indeed succeeded in forging "indissoluble links" between the people and their army, the Red Army. This was the single most important factor of the grand strategy of building rural bases which started at Chingkangshan.

As he left Chingkangshan, trudging on foot with Chu Teh and his men, the figure of Mao is already different from the energetic student, the dedicated young Communist. Already he carried with him a weight of experience, responsibility, leadership. It is as the teacher, the theoretician, as well as the administrator that we see him moving with his men, down the passes framed by their boulders, leaving Chingkangshan.

"When I say that there will soon be a high tide of revolution in China, I am emphatically not speaking of something which in the words of some people is possibly coming, something illusory, unattainable, and devoid of significance for action.

"It is like a ship far out at sea whose masthead can already be seen from the shores.

"It is like the morning sun in the east whose shimmering rays are visible from a high mountaintop.

"It is like a child about to be born moving restlessly in its mother's womb."

Moving away from Chingkangshan, southward, the soldiers did not need to ask Mao what they would do. They had been told. To make another base, to spread the Revolution.

HUANG YANG CHIEH*

At the mountain foot our banners,
On the mountain crest sound bugles and drums,
The foe round us in their thousands.
We stood fast, unmoving.

Our defense a stout wall about us,
Now our wills unite, impregnable fortress.
From Huang Yang Chieh the thunder of guns,
The enemy fades at night.

---

* Written in autumn 1928. The reference to banners at the foot of the mountain is because while the Hakkas and militia at the top were holding the passes, a small regiment left at the base, by forced marches, attacked the enemy in the rear. Thinking the armies had returned, the enemy fled after four attacks had been launched against the defenders on the crests.

10

Mao Tsetung and Li Li-san—
The Second "Left" Line

In the story of the Chinese Revolution, Mao's relentless battles for what he deemed the correct road encountered many obstacles, not the least from comrades and colleagues whose hostility to Mao can possibly be explained in a Marxist analysis by "class standpoint" — but this explanation appears simplistic to non-ideologues, for it does not convey the presence of vindictiveness or empathy, the components of love, loyalty, rivalry, resentment, ambition, which give each episode the potential of a Greek play. Becoming a Party member does not sterilize emotion, it transmutes it, makes it express itself in political language; in the end, however deep we delve, to come upon the perplexing "class imprint" answer still cannot answer all that we ask. We shall not endeavor to psychoanalyze each protagonist, but perhaps one day minute and painstaking research will tell us why Li Li-san disliked Mao Tsetung so much, why at first sight their friendship never developed.

The Mao–Li Li-san relationship is one which I find difficult to visualize as purely a political struggle, since so much of what Li Li-san did smacks of personal grudge. That Mao bore no personal resentment, sought no personal revenge, is not due to benevolence. The man had such trust in time and history to vindicate him, his inner dimension of spirit made him so different, that he probably never understood the grudge which some — especially intellectuals — seemed to bear against him. His enemies have fallen one by one, not through his actions but through their own inadequacy. Not that he does not exert himself to bring them down; for a picture of a long-suffering meek Mao, enduring all, is quite erroneous. He did bring them down, but he had an uncommon knack of doing so by being so often right that some of his haters have argued that he was simply born lucky. That he was so often, so uncannily correct in so many ways could not be forgiven him. Mao himself, once he had won, had no need to be pitiless. He destroyed his enemies' prestige and repute, showed them up, held them to ridicule. And the laughter of the audience was enough. He never felt the need to kill an adversary, it was much more satisfactory to let them live, shorn and diminished. The shallow Li Li-san would be a case study in overweening ambition, which made him join the Party, and which brought him down. There would be many others.

While Mao Tsetung and Chu Teh were trudging among the mountains of South Kiangsi in that freezing January of 1929, Li Li-san was assuming power in the Shanghai headquarters of the Central Committee. To understand how this happened we must go back a few months. The repeated reverses of the Chu Chiu-pai leadership (also known in Chinese Communist history as the "First Left Deviation") had led, in the Comintern, to dismay and alarm. Stalin in March 1928 had already asked for a special investigation. Chu Chiu-pai, Chou En-lai, and Li Li-san, members of the Chu Chiu-pai Politburo, all went to Moscow in June, and the Sixth Congress of the Chinese Communist Party was held there from July to September 1928. The policy of armed insurrection and ultra-leftist "kill and burn" was still carried out in the summer, leading to the August defeat at Chingkangshan which Mao described so vividly, despite the fact that already Chu's line was condemned in Moscow. The time factor must always be reckoned with; news of the verdict came to the Chingkangshan base only in November.

One hundred delegates, it is said, attended the Sixth Congress. Besides those mentioned above, Liu Shao-chi under the name of Tchao Kang-ming, Chang Kuo-tao, Hsiang Ying, Chou En-lai, and Tsai Ho-sen, Mao's friend from Hunan, were also in Moscow. The ones not present were Mao and Chu Teh. Li Li-san even then derided Mao. "What kind of Marxism can there be in the mountains of Chingkangshan?"

The Sixth Congress repeated the thesis that "armed struggle is the sole path to the completion of the bourgeois-democratic revolution," but the concept of Chu Chiu-pai that there was a "high tide" was repudiated. There was no revolutionary rising tide at the moment. However, one should be prepared for its coming, by organizing armed insurrection. "The direction of work should have been resolutely shifted from direct armed insurrection on a large scale to better day-to-day organization and mobilization of the masses." This condemned the South Hunan uprisings and vindicated Mao. Though the Sixth Congress in its resolutions thus upheld Mao, there was much ambiguity in the final resolutions, which allowed of various interpretations.

The issues at stake actually could only be certified correct or incorrect by trial and error, and there were several alternatives. One involved the building up of rural bases and a protracted struggle, the Mao concept; the second, a policy of continuous insurrections in both towns and countryside, the Chu Chiu-pai line, now rejected but still upheld by some at the Congress; the third, utilizing the strength built up in the countryside once again to take cities and relieve the pressure on urban Communist organizations. This third alternative was adopted by Li Li-san, although it was not thus spelled out at the Sixth Congress. "The line of the Sixth Congress was . . . basically correct." * It had defined the Chinese Revolution at that stage as still a bourgeois-democratic one; had defined the political situation as "an interval between two revolutionary high tides." It had assessed the development of the Revolution as to be "uneven." It had castigated "putschism, military adventurism and commandism, which alienate the masses."

But the Sixth Congress also had "shortcomings." It did not assess the "dual character" of the intermediate classes, the middle class or petty bourgeoisie in the cities; and it "failed to understand the importance of rural base areas." This would be the verdict of Mao at the Seventh Congress in 1945, when all historical questions would be subject to scrutiny. Because of these omissions "the 'left' ideas existing after the August 7 [1927] meeting" were not eradicated. Li Li-san was to evolve another "left" deviation.

A new Politburo was elected. Although the modest Hsiang Chung-fa, a Communist of worker origin who had been a labor organizer in Wuhan, was made secretary of the CCP, Li Li-san was to wield the power as head of the Propaganda Department. Chou En-lai was in charge of organization and Liu Shao-chi of labor, which meant trade union work in cities.

Li Li-san was six years younger than Mao. He was also from Hunan province, his father a schoolteacher. In 1919 he had gone to France in one of the work and study groups, and there met Tsai Ho-sen, Mao's long-time friend, and Chou En-lai. He had joined the

* *Selected Works of Mao Tsetung* (English edition Peking 1961–1965), vol. III, p. 182.

Communist Party branch formed there and in 1921 returned to China. In 1922 he became labor organizer at the Anyuan coal mines and director of the workers' club. At the time Mao was secretary of the Hunan Party Committee and chairman of the Hunan branch of the Labor Federation. Li went against Mao's ideas on how the Anyuan strike should be led, and associated himself with Liu Shao-chi's policies. Li continued to rise in the hierarchy as a labor organizer; he was an extremely fluent man and according to Anna Louise Strong, who met him in 1927, an eloquent speaker, one of the most prominent at the time of the united front in Wuhan. He had taken part in the Nanchang uprising in August 1927, then gone to Shanghai, and was in Moscow for the Sixth Congress.

In Moscow, where there was at the time some admiration for Mao, Li Li-san did his best to discredit him; he was responsible for the inclusion in a resolution in November 1928 of a warning against "peasant mentality" — "If the danger of peasant mentality is not corrected, the Revolution will be liquidated entirely and the party will die." As soon as he returned from Moscow he started to proclaim the danger of a shift from working-class leadership to the peasantry. This was to serve as a platform for attack against Mao Tsetung.

The Li Li-san line regarded the creation and strengthening of rural bases as a danger to the working class. To Mao there was no contradiction between proletarian leadership and peasant membership; the agrarian revolution being, as he had expounded, the necessary step in the two-stage revolution. At least 700 Anyuan workers and Shuikoushan lead miners were in his army. There were only 4 million workers in China and 500 million peasants, a proportion of less than 1 percent. Among his 4,000 Red Army men Mao had a far higher percentage in 1928, over 14 percent. While on Chingkangshan, Mao had requested the Hunan committee several times to send him more miners from Anyuan, and in December 1930 he was to go himself, again, to Anyuan to recruit miners for command posts. He had trained workers to become leaders of the peasant recruits. Peasants would also be trained to become workers in the arsenals and workshops created at the next Red base which Mao would set up. But for Li Li-san, peasants were a different breed from workers and they represented a danger to proletarian leadership.

Li Li-san's first action on his return to China was denunciation of "peasant mentality" again, as in Moscow. Peasants, he said, constituted 70 to 80 percent of the Party membership—"The peasant cannot have correct ideas regarding socialism" . . . . . . "The peasantry is petty bourgeois . . . it lacks organizational ability." This attack on "peasant consciousness" was circulated just at the time Mao Tsetung and Chu Teh were leaving the base of Chingkangshan. It had a bad effect on the rank and file of the Red Army. It was calculated to lessen Mao's prestige.

Li Li-san had been important in Communist labor organizations since 1922; as a trade unionist he knew only Party work in the cities. But when he returned to Shanghai the workers in the cities, after the terrible massacres, were cowed, and the active Communists among them decimated. Li could gather less than 4,000 workers in all China to mount strikes as a prelude to the general insurrection he contemplated. This alone should have taught Li Li-san a lesson in cool-headed calculation. In April 1927 the Party had counted nearly 58,000 members, of whom approximately 60 percent were workers; in late 1927 Party membership was down to 10,000, in 1928 up again to 40,000, but only 10 percent of these were workers. (In 1930, out of 122,318 members, only 8 percent would be workers.)

Mao Tsetung and Chu Teh, leading their 4,000 men, went through the winterbound mountains southward. Mao's plan was the building up of a new base * which would have as its foundation several scattered Communist guerilla bands in Kiangsi, in an area where the terrible exactions of the Kuomintang had effectively radicalized the peasantry. There were also commanders and officers who had taken part in the actions in Swatow and Kuangchow of the previous year now hiding with their troops in these areas. Mao Tsetung would find them and link up with them.

One pound of cooked rice, the clothes they stood in, and some rounds of ammunition were all that each of the men carried as they left the massif a week after the White Dew conference, on January 12, 1929. They went across the freezing ranges, walking by night and hiding by day. They struck at landlords and their private troops; the peasants who knew them came out to help. They revived the mass movement against landlords in several districts but were attacked and pursued; desperate battles with "enemy troops swarming against them" took place day after day. Snow fell, and as they trudged the

---

* This is now represented in China as Mao's own decision, but there may also have been an order for Mao and Chu Teh to conduct insurrection *without* the proviso of building a base; this interpretation is probably more accurate, as Li Li-san is said to have issued these orders in December 1928.

wounded left blood marks upon it. They made desperate assaults for food and were easily hunted down, as they withdrew, by their all too visible tracks. They had only thin, ragged cotton clothes, they were covered with lice; less than half the soldiers had rifles, many died of cold and exposure. There were no medicines, no fuel for cooking, no rice to eat. And yet there were recruits, for the area was ripe for revolt. Mao was emaciated, his hair grew almost to his shoulders, he wore the same straw sandals as the soldiers and he insisted, still, on keeping the three/eight rules. At home in Shaoshan he had learned to weave sandals on a wooden lathe, but now there was no straw to be had. Among the 4,000 were 100 women. The snow lay deep in treacherous pockets; the icy wind screamed about the weathered slopes; there were no pathways, and the men sheltered behind boulders. They sometimes walked two or three days without finding any hamlet that would feed them; at others they would be fed by peasants who welcomed the Red Army but had desperately little to give. They reached the outskirts of Tayu, in the tungsten-producing area, a fairly rich city, and there made a mistake; they remained too long, thus giving the enemy time to catch up and kill hundreds of them. From then on Mao avoided all the towns and cities, and hid in the countryside away from any sizable urban centers. For the next fortnight a desperate running battle through the Wuyi mountain range with its treacherous zigzag slopes took place. Carrying their sick and wounded, the Red Army loped along the border, eastward, unable to throw off the dogged troops at their heels. Again at Hsun Wu they were attacked, and crossed into Fukien, to Wuping, to shake off the enemy; then back again into Kiangsi, heading straight, it seemed, for Juichin, an important market town, but bypassing it and going on northward to Tapoti. There Mao Tsetung decided to take advantage of the terrain and to get rid of the enemy once and for all. He and Chu Teh drew up the battle plans. "Our troops discussed the plan of battle until everything was clear. They then swore to destroy the enemy or die in the attempt." * Tapoti is a shallow, basin-like valley of fields, the bed of an old clayey lake, hill-cradled, about twenty miles from Juichin. On the morning of February 10 Mao and Chu Teh prepared the ambush here. Their men hid on the many-folded hills; in the afternoon, as fog began, a feint by one of the four regiments which made up their Fourth Army lured the Kuomintang and warlord troops into the valley; the battle began at noon and went on

* Interview at Tapoti, visited by the author.

throughout the night. "It was foggy and the enemy did not know the terrain; he wasted much ammunition." Lin Piao led a small force through the night to hit the enemy at the rear, and at dawn attacked. "By noon it was over." One thousand of the 7,000 attacking troops were taken captive, including two regimental commanders, and 800 guns. It was a great victory, the first after Chingkangshan, and the decisive battle for opening up a new base.

They then captured the walled town of Ningtu in central Kiangsi and spent three days there, taking the food of the landlords and resting, calling mass meetings, opening prisons and releasing prisoners. Then they marched towards Tungku. Peasants came to help them, carried the wounded, for Tungku was under the command of a Communist, Tseng Shan, and an ex-Whangpoo cadet now turned guerilla, Lin Wen-ling. Here the peasants were enthusiastic in their welcome. Before leaving Tapoti, Mao had sent a small contingent to the Juichin post office to get the newspapers to read, a habit he would never give up. It was New Year's Eve, and the contingent surprised the local garrison, disarmed them, and ate a New Year's banquet which was ready.

Hsingkuo, a walled town twenty-five miles south of Tungku, an area of good soil and wealthy landlords, was their next target. Hsingkuo fell to them, and was joined to Tungku as a "soviet" area. Mao and Chu found that the "base" already established at Tungku was a base only in name; there had been no agrarian revolution. However, here was a central massif ringed with plains, with villages and towns, much richer and more peopled than Chingkangshan, and beautiful in spring, with bamboo and spruce and fir. At Hsingkuo they stayed and rested, deloused and bathed, continued training and teaching and drilling. At a general mass meeting held in Tungku, Mao Tse-tung spoke to the Red Army, as usual infusing hope and power, communicating his vision of a dazzling tomorrow: "A single spark can light a prairie fire; though we are weak and small today, our future is boundless." He explained the general strategy and tactics of the Revolution, the necessity for rural bases. Again they sallied forth, eastward, and now they took Changting (Tingchow), a large town on the border of Fukien province, by stratagem, luring the men of the garrison out of town and then attacking; they captured the garrison commander and a great quantity of ammunition. The battle of Tingchow was the foundation of another Red area, later consolidated into a base. There Mao changed his four regiments to three columns. Recruitment made good the losses. It was at Tingchow apparently that a messenger arrived from Shanghai with reports and documents of the Sixth Congress, and also, at the same time, a peasant messenger with a message in the lining of his jacket. This message was from Peng Teh-huai, and announced he was near Juichin, three days' march west of Tingchow, having abandoned Chingkangshan. So Mao and Chu Teh left Tingchow in April and returned to South Kiangsi, to the counties of Yutou and Hsinkuo, and there organized revolutionary committees and mass organizations, on the way to Juichin.

In this campaign to shape a new base, Mao Tsetung began to perfect "the countryside surrounding the cities" method. But his actions must have been greatly hampered by the effect of Li Li-san's denunciation of "peasant mentality." Though he received help from Tseng Shan, the several Communists commanding small agglomerations (some had participated in the putsch on Kuangchow of December 1927, others in the march on Swatow) on the whole gave him no help, and even refused to receive him. The peasants, however, were far more enthusiastic; they had been radicalized during the Northern Expedition, and massacres in this region had not been as thorough and effective as in Hunan. But they were very poor and oppressed, and this condition still existed; hence the Red Army obtained recruits — many of them under eighteen — but nothing much in the way of food or ammunition. However, the peasant families sheltered the wounded, and sometimes went without rice to feed the Red Army.

In May, Mao was to return through Tapoti, and there to hold a great popular feast, a celebration of the victory at Tapoti that February. He then gave money back to the people, three dollars per person for the food the peasants had given his army. The money came from Ningtu, where 5,000 dollars had been collected from the wealthy merchants. He distributed clothing taken from the landlords of Hsingkuo to compensate for the damage done during the battle. In 1933 Mao wrote a poem about Tapoti:

> *After the rain sunlight gleams through,*
> *Mountains and valleys melt in one azure.*
> *That year fierce was the battle,*
> *Bullet holes still scar the village walls,*
> *More lovely the hill pass they adorn.*

They now arrived at Juichin, and Peng Teh-huai was waiting for them, though not in the city. Peng Teh-huai's falling out with Yuan and Wang, the "bandit" chieftains, after Mao's departure allowed an enemy attack to succeed, and Peng lost the base.

Juichin was taken in May 1929, and it was to form the capital agglomeration of the new base, known from that time as the Central Base, or Kiangsi-Fukien Border Area.

The Anyuan and Pinghsiang miners were now organized in an engineer corps; there would be an arsenal, hospitals, schools, even a military academy of sorts. This base was far wealthier than Chingkangshan; the counties more fertile, handicrafts and trade well developed, water abundant, and the tungsten mines provided a source of income. But the organization of the base still rested on the cooperation of the peasants, its defense on the Red Army as an adequate regular force. Here, as in Chingkangshan, there would be local militia and Red Guards, mass self-defense institutions, but they were only for local self-defense. Round the Red Army and its use, the struggle between Li Li-san's "left" line and Mao Tsetung would now develop, but it would be a struggle of far more scope than merely military utilization; it also involved two different strategies of revolution.

In April, at Tingchow, another of Li Li-san's circular letters had reached Mao. The October 1928 letter, which had been an attack on the influence of "peasant mentality" in the Party, had been deleterious in its effect.* Now this second letter had been composed in February 1929; it took two months to reach Mao. Work was to be concentrated on the workers in the cities. To rebuild the Party in urban areas and to recapture working-class leadership, Mao and Chu were enjoined to abandon their efforts to create a base, fragment the Red Army into small guerilla bands, "disperse in the countryside and arouse the masses." Li Li-san also asked Mao and Chu to leave the ranks and come to Shanghai to help rebuild workers' unions in the cities. And Li advised them to postpone the land reform and redistribution, as the peasants were "not ready."

This meant undoing all that had been done between January and April. Mao had drafted the Hsinkuo land law of April 1929 to institute land reform. The Chingkangshan land law, passed in December 1928 after "one year of experience in the land struggle," contained,

* "We must make every effort to restore the Party's working-class base. . . . Peasants now constitute 70 to 80 percent of our Party membership — peasant mentality is now reflected in our Party. . . . Only a proletarian mentality can lead us into the correct revolutionary road. . . . Unless we correct [this peasant mentality] it may lead to a complete destruction of the Revolution and the Party."

said Mao, several mistakes; it did not allow for intermediate categories in the peasant economy. Mao had now revised it. On it depended the stability of the new base, both political and economic;
without a flexible, realistic agrarian revolution, Red power could not
consolidate itself, establish government and organs of mass representation, could not finance, feed, recruit a Red Army, nor develop
Party organizations in the countryside.

At Juichin in May, Mao, Chu Teh, and Peng Teh-huai seem to
have held a three-day conference. The upshot was that Mao, while
not directly contradicting Li Li-san, in reality went on organizing
the base he had in mind. That the new leadership in the Politburo
was opposed to Mao's policies and his establishing Red power was
already manifest to a good many of the local Party members, to
those commanders of guerilla bands now diminished in their own
prestige and influence, and to the Party cadres nominated by Li Li-
san. This added to Mao's difficulties. The clique spirit, currying
favor with the Central Committee by slighting or opposing Mao,
would of course occur, and with increasing frequency, during the
next year. Not only did Mao have to fight Kuomintang and warlord
armies; there would be a relentless inner-Party struggle as well.

Mao replied to Li Li-san on April 5, and would again reply in
May. He disagreed with fragmenting the Red Army into guerilla
bands. Li Li-san was confusing, he wrote, the local Red Guards,
who were the militants among the masses, with the Red Army. "This
[dispersion] is impractical . . . with small dispersed units the leadership will become weak . . . suffer defeat. The more adverse the
circumstances, the greater the need for the forces to be concentrated
and for the leadership to conduct a resolute struggle, for only thus
can we achieve internal unity against the enemy. Only in favorable
circumstances can the forces be divided, only then the leaders need
not stay with the ranks." This was a courteous way of refusing to go
to Shanghai.*

Another point at issue was "uneven development." To disperse in
order to rouse the masses everywhere, in cities and in the countryside, would not work, said Mao. It was better to select one or more
areas, and there concentrate, and build up political and military
strength.

Li Li-san actually wanted to retard the growth of the peasant

* See *On Correcting Mistaken Ideas in the Party,* December 1929, and *A Single
Spark Can Start a Prairie Fire,* January 1930, both in *Selected Works of Mao Tsetung* (English edition Peking 1961–1965), vol. I.

movement *until* the workers' movement had caught up. Both had to be simultaneous; or rather, the workers had to start first, for no agrarian revolution could succeed without the leadership of the proletariat. Thus he reasoned, forcing facts to fit dogma. Mao gave it as his opinion that "it is a mistake for any of our Party members to fear the development of the power of the peasants"; and went on to explain the structure and economics of a base, the policy of "advancing waves" to expand a base, its essential fluctuant quality. "The tactics we have worked out . . . are indeed different from any employed in ancient or modern times, in China or elsewhere." Li Li-san now accused — or rather said that "others" had accused — them of having "abandoned" the struggle in the cities. But Mao Tsetung was not to be budged, nor talked into leaving the rural base, nor was Chu Teh, and they stuck to their guns (literally speaking). Li then suggested that the Red Army go to Hunan to make insurrections. Mao pointed out that "because of the August defeat" of the previous year the mass base had been lost in Hunan, and there was no point in losing more men. Upon which Li Li-san's seconders at the base and elsewhere accused Mao of "military adventurism and banditry."

Mao now expanded the Juichin base; by fighting, expanded the Red Army, and took Kanchow; east and west, north and south, they fought. The peasants fought with "the poor man's army." In the darkness choked with tears of the great land, the Red Army brought more than hope, it brought a way out of desolation. The landlords took up to 70 percent of the crop, and lived in the cities. Mao went among the people, asking questions, setting up investigation teams in order that land reform should work better. Policies were flexible, concrete, made to fit the situation; he sought the advice of the peasants' associations formed. He was hastening to consolidate the base, and popular support, before Li Li-san thought up something else.

Li Li-san in Shanghai had in effect thought of something else. He now dreamed of a great soviet center for a soviet government in China. Perhaps remembering the previous enthusiasm in Wuhan, the large number of workers there, he thought the workers of Wuhan would rise and "smash imperialism." Gradually his daydream took the shape of "political strategy." Wuhan must be the center of a soviet government (of course run by Li Li-san). For this he would need military strength, he would need the Red Army of Mao and Chu Teh.

Because Mao Tsetung saw the disaster which Li Li-san's policies might bring about, he proceeded to a reorganization of the Red Army, apprehending that Li might seek to remove him and Chu Teh. Mao seems to have foreseen that a duel over the control of both Party and Army would develop. He now reorganized the small guerilla bands in Kiangsi already in existence before his arrival into the Third Red Army, and the guerillas from west Fukien, where he and Chu Teh had gone fighting and extended the base, into a Twelfth Red Army. To this Twelfth Army were added some Kuomintang troops who in July had mutinied against Chiang Kai-shek and came over to the Red Army. With his own Fourth Army, the 4,000 or more (with recruits) who had smashed their way from Chingkangshan, and the Third and the Twelfth, he now had three armies and about 10,000 troops.

The Fourth Army remained the center of Mao Tsetung's military strength and pillar of his power, the best training ground for officers and political education and cadres. After a term in the Fourth Army, political and military cadres would go into the other armies to train and educate, and thus assure linkage which would bring all the various contingents under control of the headquarters, under Mao's control. But resistance to this reorganization, by men such as Li Wen-ling, who had been displaced by Mao's and Chu Teh's arrival, would soon come to a head.

In June 1929 a letter from the Comintern was received by the Central Committee. While it was the first time Mao was referred to by name, and in a complimentary way, the letter was fairly uncomplimentary to Li Li-san, who had sent directives advocating a "rich peasant" line to the various bases, or "soviets," as they were called.

This Comintern letter was a slap to Li Li-san, who had written to Mao saying it was necessary to conclude an alliance with the rich peasants, and disapproving of his land law.* Mao Tsetung had previously been upbraided for *not* burning and killing enough. In order to win the intermediate class, he had in November 1928 prohibited reckless burning and killing, and decreed protection of the interests of middle and small merchants. In the Hsingkuo land law drafted in April 1929, wholesale land confiscation had been changed to "confiscate public land and the land of the landlord class only." But to spare the rich peasants did not mean to conclude an alliance with them. However, many other small guerilla areas with commanders

* The Hsingkuo land law.

owing allegiance to the Communist Party did operate under a "rich peasant" land law.

Li took no notice of this letter of the Comintern * which called alliance with the rich peasants "impermissible"; on the contrary he reaffirmed "the possibility of leading the rich peasants . . . even if tactically the poor peasant is the main force and the middle peasant his ally."

This was not at all "in line," for Stalin had now begun the drive against the kulaks, or rich peasants, in Russia. But it was not the main reason for Li Li-san's downfall. The main reason was his total loss of perspective of the Revolution. Li Li-san showed no grasp of the realities of the Chinese situation. He remained fixated on "the proletariat," never considered the revolutionary potential of the peasantry; above all, he wanted control of Mao's Red Army, but had no idea what the Red Army really was like, or what it really did. He confused leadership with membership, arousal with organization, Red Guards and militia roles with the operations of regular forces. "The principle for the Red Army is concentration, that for the Red Guards is dispersion," Mao patiently explained. And at Chingkangshan he had written: "The existence of a regular Red Army of adequate strength is a necessary condition for the existence of Red political power. . . ." "A special characteristic of the Revolution in China, a country with predominantly agricultural economy, is the use of military action to develop insurrection," but this could not be done haphazardly, by methods of "roving guerilla bands."

Unfailingly, Mao answered Li with logic and courtesy. As Li became increasingly incoherent, Mao became more coldly watchful. What he really thought of Li Li-san's mental capacity he has never told anyone. But one can guess.

Chou En-lai, who had also been at the Sixth Congress and been nominated to the Politburo with Li Li-san, Tsai Ho-sen, and others, began to point out to Li the discrepancies and irrationalities of his theses. Chou began to disagree with Li Li-san from June 1929. This disagreement reached such a pitch later that they could not meet, it is reported, without quarrels breaking out over what policies to follow.†

When the second plenum of the Sixth Congress of the Central Committee of the CCP was held that June, Li Li-san was already

---

* Letter from the Executive Committee of the (Third) Communist International to the Central Committee of the CCP on the peasant question, June 7, 1929.
† Hsu Kai-yu *Chou En-lai: China's Gray Eminence* (New York 1968).

showing signs of instability. He diverged from the Sixth Congress resolutions; whether willfully or simply because he misunderstood them, no one can say. He now changed from "dispersal" and "widespread guerilla attacks" to a city-oriented strategy, concentration of forces to attack main cities. Perhaps he thus hoped to wrest control of the armies Mao had built up. More probably he was planning to take Wuhan. The extraordinary thing is that he did not see what he was landing himself in. But now the Comintern, which was already concerned more with assuring Russia's strategic security than with any other problem, sent out a new set of directives in October, calling for an increase in activity — strikes, guerilla movements — in cities and countryside.

This directive of the Comintern was oriented towards Russian interests, not to the China situation, and was due to the Chinese Eastern Railway crisis. An attempt by the Chinese warlord government in Manchuria to take over the Chinese Eastern Railway, accompanied by raids on Soviet consulates in Manchuria and North China, had taken place. The Chinese Eastern Railway was still under Russian control.* A near war threatened and General Galen, also known as Blücher, who had been military adviser to the KMT at Whangpoo Academy in 1925 and 1926, was appointed head of the Russian Far Eastern forces.† The incident lasted about a year and ended in negotiations. Li Li-san tried to utilize this crisis in yet another effort to get Mao Tsetung's Red Army out of Mao's control and into his own hands; he called for a "nationwide upsurge" against "international imperialism and its ally Chiang Kai-shek." Li Li-san was disquietingly aware of the shift of power as Mao's base at Juichin grew and strengthened, and the Kiangsi-Fukien Border Area Independent Regime, as it was called, coalescing many small guerilla areas, was regarded now with favor and had more prestige than the Shanghai headquarters of the Politburo. With the arrival of the October Comintern letter — "strengthen and extend guerilla warfare, especially in Manchuria and in the region of Chu and Mao" — Li felt fortified. "The former strategy of avoiding taking important large cities must be changed . . . we must attack important cities and even occupy them."

At the same time, Stalin ordered a purge of "Trotskyites." Some of the Chinese students in Moscow had come back as Trotsky adher-

* In spite of the Karakhan Manifesto.
† General Galen Blücher was to perish in the Stalin purges of 1936–1937.

ents. Li Li-san sent out orders for a general purge against Trotskyist elements in the CCP.

Mao became very ill from malaria contracted in fighting, which incapacitated him from July to November 1929. Chu Teh, during Mao's illness, began to obey "central" directives and went roaming on guerrilla warfare to "arouse the masses." Carried on a stretcher, trying to get about, to go on with political work, Mao gradually got better, though off and on he was to suffer from malaria for years. Meanwhile Chu Teh suffered some losses and returned to the base. He had taken only part of the armies with him, and thus the harm done was relatively minor, but it convinced him that Li Li-san was in error. However, Chu Teh could not disobey the very definite orders given, reinforced by the Comintern.

In September 1929 the Central Committee under Li Li-san sent a directive to Mao Tsetung calling for the elimination of all nonproletarian ideas from Party organizations in the Fourth Army and the immediate establishment of a political commissariat; the Party was "still infected with nonproletarian" ideas, Trotskyites, "peasant mentality" and other such which had to be purged. The response of Mao Tsetung was the December 1929 draft of resolutions presented at a conference in Kutien, called the Ninth Congress of the Fourth Red Army Delegates and Party Workers.

The Kutien conference was to remain, for the Red Army, a historic event. The resolutions were to be republished many times in the next forty years; the last time was in 1971. They are compulsory study for every political worker and military officer in the Chinese Red Army.

Kutien is a small town ensconced in mountains, commanding a beautiful valley. In its picturesque temples and landlords' houses were quartered, for over ten days, some of the most important people in China; but there is no real report on what happened there. All we know is that the struggle between Mao Tsetung's line and the Li Li-san line was more in the open than ever; it concerned Party control over the Army, a political line versus a purely military line. Here was expounded, codified, categorized, the very reason for existence of the Red Army; here was fully set out the theme of Party control and leadership in the Army and the theme of political education and political work in and by the Army among the masses. It was the culmination of what had begun at the Autumn Harvest Uprising, had been first affirmed at the Maoping conference when Chu Teh joined Mao on Chingkangshan: the goal of "an educated, conscious revolu-

tionary army dedicated to the liberation of the country and the emancipation of our people." Mao dealt with all aspects of political education of the Army and the Party-Army relationship. Whenever a
rectification movement was held in the Army during the next four
decades, the Kutien resolutions would be the fundamental document
to be restudied.

At the Kutien conference, Mao obliquely criticized the Li Li-san
line: "Some people want to increase our political influence only by
means of roving guerilla actions, but are unwilling to undertake the
difficult task of building up base areas and establishing the people's
political power. . . .

"Some people lack the patience to carry on arduous struggles together with the masses and only want to go to the big cities to feast.
. . . The eradication of this ideology is an important objective in
the ideological struggle within the Red Army and party organizations."

*On Correcting Mistaken Ideas in the Party,** a shortened portion
of Mao's speeches at the Kutien conference, was passed as a resolution, which seems to indicate that Mao won despite bitter opposition. The full version was not made available in published form till
January 1944, in a special edition used for Party cadres in the Red
Army, during the rectification campaign in Yenan.†

The Kutien resolutions "enabled the Red Army to build itself entirely on a Marxist-Leninist basis and to eliminate all the influence
of armies of the old type. It was carried out not only in the Fourth
Army but also in all other units of the Red Army successively."

Mao Tsetung also criticized the "purely military viewpoint of
these comrades [who] regard military affairs and politics as opposed
to each other and refuse to recognize that military affairs are only
one means of accomplishing political tasks." "Some," he said, "give
military affairs a leading position over politics. . . . They think that
the task of the Red Army, like that of the White Army, is merely to
fight. They do not understand that the Chinese Red Army is an
armed body for carrying out the tasks of the revolution. . . . Besides fighting to destroy the enemy's military strength, it should
shoulder such important tasks as carrying on propaganda among the

* December 1929. *Selected Works of Mao Tsetung* (English edition Peking 1961),
vol. I.
† Three versions of the Kutien resolutions were published between 1944 and
1951 — John E. Rue *Mao Tsetung in Opposition 1927–1935* (Stanford 1966), p.
173. John Gittings also gives an account of them in his *Role of the Chinese Army*
(New York and London 1967).

masses, organizing the masses, arming them, helping them to establish revolutionary political power *and setting up Party organizations.* . . . Without these objectives, fighting loses its meaning and the Red Army loses the reason for its existence."

Mao proposed to correct subjectivism (becoming conceited when winning and dispirited when defeated), cliquism, opportunism, revolutionary impetuosity (wanting to do big things rather than "minute and detailed work among the masses"), and suggested that all this proceeded from a low political level, the mercenary mentality, the absence of trust in the masses. But it was "the Party's failure actively to attend to and discuss military work" which had led to this situation — a broadside at the Politburo in Shanghai, which never replied to reports, and sent representatives who did not know anything of the practical work done. Mao criticized those who wanted to live well ("they always hope that their unit will march into big cities . . . to enjoy themselves"); passivity, retaliation (the I'll-find-some-way-to-pay-you-back mentality), backbiting, not speaking up at meetings, malicious personal bickering, and so on.

Reinforcing the Party at company level, directing the attention of Party members to "a political and scientific spirit," to do "social and economic investigation and study," criticism and self-criticism would correct all this. The extraordinary thing about Mao, in such a forbidding environment, is that enormous faith of his that all defects can be "educated" out of a man if one is patient and relentlessly goes on educating, educating.* Besides these methods, Mao laid down new rules for admission of Party candidates, since in the bases the great majority of new Party members came from the Red Army. Hence he insisted on soldiers' committees and conferences of soldiers' representatives, which introduced democracy in the Army, as well as a new conception of discipline, not enforced, but based on ideological acceptance and comprehension. In the soldiers' conferences, "the most powerful educational method," all rank disappeared, men had full rights of free speech. "Communists must always use their heads . . . must think" would be one of Mao Tsetung's repeated dicta through the years. There were also minute and detailed paragraphs on the carrying out of the land reform *by the Army.* The agrarian revolution was fundamental to both Party and Army building; Mao

---

* But the ultra-left line would emphasize class origin irrespective of individual fitness. Later, Chang Kuo-tao, for instance, in his "purging" of "counter-revolutionaries," would "purge" anyone he suspected of "bourgeois origin."

would never tire of repeating this. Also, the Kutien conference would seek to expel from the Party those:

> Who have mistaken political attitudes.
> Who just want to eat well and live high.
> Who smoke opium and gamble.
> Who wish to get rich on foreign money.
> Who commit crimes frequently and refuse to reform.

Mao was trying to get rid of Party members who had grown corrupt; also those who wanted to get to cities and live well there; that is, the Li Li-san adherents. Hence the fight was now in the open. The Kutien conference can thus also be seen as Mao's retort to Li Li-san's call for a "purge."

On February 7, 1930, Mao Tsetung called a conference in South Kiangsi, where the question of land policy was discussed, as a continuation of the Kutien conference. Two principles were embodied by Mao in this new land law: (*1*) Take from those who have much land to help those who have little land. (*2*) Take from those who have fertile land to help those who have poor land.* He also emphasized equal shares to men and women, old and young. This land law was to meet with violent opposition and repudiation from Li Li-san's adherents, who in July 1930, when Mao was away, substituted a "rich peasant" line.

Thus Mao Tsetung neatly turned what Li Li-san had designed as a signal to his own adherents to attack Mao into an exposure of mistaken ideas in the Party. Many of the commanders and Party commissars at the base were supporters of Li, if only because against Mao's insistence on mass work and personal incorruptibility, unglamorous but solid countryside consolidation. One speculation is that Li Li-san possibly gave the order for a purge in September 1929 because he thought Mao was dead or dying, and wanted to use the occasion of a Trotskyite purge to clear out Mao's followers too. This would not be the last time Mao was reported dead; his obituary (most eulogious) would even appear in Russia. But Mao used this very "purge" of Li Li-san's to establish even more strongly his own kind of authority.

---

* The Politburo was to criticize Mao's land law in November 1931, and another land law was then fashioned, with some additions and extrapolations which brought it within the "ultra-left" line practiced between 1932 and 1934 (see next chapter).

In the spring of 1930 Li began to differ so widely from Comintern resolutions that no amount of casuistry could cover the gap; his own emotional make-up precluded self-correction. He appears to have gone from Shanghai to Wuhan to set up another organization there. He was preparing in earnest for an uprising to capture Wuhan, to turn it into the urban base, capital of a "Chinese Soviet Republic." His increasing divergences, not only with Mao Tsetung but also with Chou En-lai, only made him more intractable. He is said to have told Chou En-lai that what China needed was a Lenin; and the next day to have remarked casually that he himself was probably China's Lenin. He would look in mirrors and cultivate a Lenin stance.*

Not that Li Li-san had no support. He had. It seemed absurd to many a Party member and officer in the Red Army that "the countryside would encircle and defeat the cities." Mao was to remark then (and repeat the remark in 1969) that many people joined the Communist Party not with their souls but only organizationally; to make a career, not to serve the Revolution.

In a circular of February 26, 1930, Li proclaimed the advent of a "new revolutionary high tide." "The nationwide struggle is developing *evenly*," he wrote. Wars had broken out between Chiang Kai-shek and several warlords, and Li felt the disintegration of Chiang was near. These "contradictions" within the counterrevolutionary camp, Li felt, were decisive. He pointed to Wuhan and the cities near it as the "main objective" in the struggle, and called for a conference of delegates from all soviet areas to be held in Shanghai on May 1, 1930. He again repeated his denunciations of peasant mentality and "ascend-mountainism," but still invited Mao Tsetung and Chu Teh to come to Shanghai.

Chou En-lai was against this plan of Li's. The Sixth Congress had placed Chou in charge of organization; he was meant to reorganize the Party and link it up with a Red Army. By early 1930 there were ten Red armies scattered over China in bases or in guerilla areas, some pretty unstable, some actually more like warlord strongholds than soviet bases. The only stable, successful and expanding base was Mao's; the most impressive, the best organized Red armies were under Mao Tsetung and Chu Teh; the Fourth Red Army was a model Red Army, a fact recognized by all. Chou En-lai wrote to other Red commanders in his *Central Military Communiqué* of Jan-

* Interview with Anna Louise Strong, 1962.

uary 15, 1930 (an occasional publication to keep the various movements in touch with each other) that "in the Juichin independent regime many valuable experiences can be found . . . unique in China, never seen or heard of before in the world . . . all ought to learn from these experiences." This praise of Mao Tsetung, coming while Chou was at the Politburo in Shanghai, had a direct influence at least on the military personnel, to raise Mao's prestige. Chou also pointed out that the revolutionary tide in the cities among workers was at low level. By 1930 only 8 percent of the CCP was of worker origin.

Mao and Chu Teh ignored or did not receive the call to go to the May meeting in Shanghai. They still did not reply when it was postponed to June. Li Li-san stressed that there must be a "unified leadership" (which could only be vested in himself). He accused Mao and Chu of being "rightists" because they refused his plan to attack large cities. The Red Army (meaning principally Mao's forces) must launch attacks on big cities, in preparation for all-out state conquest, all-out attack on Chiang Kai-shek's Nanking government. Li Li-san now organized a General Front Committee, to start war preparations. He decried Mao's slow, patient build-up. "By such tactics our hair will be white before the Revolution is victorious."

Mao wrote back that the time had not come for this direct confrontation with the Kuomintang, that first a lot of hard work must be done, and that it was very dangerous to launch these insurrections against cities. Chou En-lai called Li's plan "suicidal." Li retaliated by condemning the opponents of his policy, sending some to posts known as dangerous, and in some cases even betraying one or two covertly to the KMT (according to his own confession made in Peking in 1956).

But Li Li-san was also threatened from another side. A group of Moscow-trained Chinese Communist students, later to become known as the "twenty-eight Bolsheviks" or "returned students," came back to China in the early summer of 1930. They had all studied Marxism in Russia and were "experts" in revolutionary perfection. Their leader was Chen Shao-yu, alias Wang Ming, a melancholy-looking young man, very arrogant. All were young, city-bred; none had behind him the experience in China's countryside which Mao had accumulated.

Li Li-san pushed on, hoping to achieve success and thus vindicate his "line" before the "twenty-eight Bolsheviks" caught up with him, for he was well aware that their return meant a struggle for leadership within the Party. He issued articles in *Red Flag* and other Communist publications to prove himself theoretically correct. All the emphasis was on workers' struggles and the conquest of key cities. He called Mao a pessimist, condemned again in September the idea of "the countryside surrounding the cities." But articles continued to appear praising Mao's struggle in Chingkangshan and the Central Base as a heroic epic: "Without ammunition, money or supplies they fought against the enemy many times their superior. They hid in the mountains . . . staying for months at a time without interrupting revolutionary work." *

In May 1930 Mao wrote *Oppose Book Worship,* clearly a reproof of those, like Li Li-san, who talked "nonsense" without investigating concrete situations. Surprisingly, *Oppose Book Worship* was left out of the 1951 Chinese edition and the 1961 English translation of *Selected Works of Mao Tsetung,* though published in *Selected Readings* in 1967. The reason for this omission is not known, though it is known that Mao was much criticized for writing it. But *Oppose Book Worship* is an important essay, not only on the technique of investigation, but on its essential importance. "No investigation, no right to speak," is the heading of the first paragraph.

"Unless you have investigated a problem, you will be deprived of the right to speak on it. . . . Talking nonsense solves no problems. . . . You can't solve a problem? Well, get down and investigate the present facts and its past history."

"Social investigation should be a regular part of the work of the Army. The Political Department of the Fourth Red Army prepared detailed forms covering such items as the state of the mass struggle, the condition of the enemy, the economic life of the people, the amount of land owned by each class in the rural areas. . . . Wherever the Red Army went, it first made itself familiar with the class situation in the locality and then formulated slogans suited to the needs of the masses."

This essay is constantly quoted in China today to promote the scientific objectivity, the frank speaking up, the democratic debate based on truth, which Mao Tsetung teaches the 800 million people of China. "Stress investigations! Oppose irresponsible talk!" he cried, and went on to criticize those who blindly obey directives "from a higher organ," even if the contents are incompatible with "the objective and subjective conditions of the struggle." He was against blind,

---

* These articles were signed with a pen name. Their authorship is obscure.

superficial enforcement of a directive, rigid and rigorous dogmatic application, which actually is a kind of sabotage. He was to encounter many examples of blind enforcement, and also sabotage, of his own directives.

Mao Tsetung at this time is described by Chen Chang-fong, his orderly to be, then a raw, illiterate peasant youth of fifteen, who came to serve him early in 1931. "Political Commissar Mao [he became chairman only later] would go himself, on horseback often, because of the long distances, to carry out investigations. He would come to a place, and sit down with the peasants, and throw off his cap, and start to talk with them. And they forgot who he was, so debonair he was, and so concerned with them. And they told him everything. He would stay for hours with them. He would forget time, and food, and sleep. I used to call him, to say he would be late for such and such an appointment. 'But first I must listen to this,' he would say. He would go to a meeting with an outline in his head, or already written down, with questions prepared. He would question each and every one present, and probe, and go on probing. He insisted that everyone who was engaged in political work, in administering of any kind, should do similar investigations." *

He did not believe in written reports, and sometimes would frown at them, and then go off himself to investigate. "There must be personal investigation," he said. "Marxist theory, like Party resolutions and Central Committee directives, must be tested by practice." Marxism did work; but only if one took the trouble to move one's brain, stick to principle, and modify the application in the most flexible manner.

Writing *Oppose Book Worship* may have stimulated some Party members to cudgel their brains, but Li went on with his plans. The June conference was duly called. Neither Chu nor Mao attended. There, on June 11, Li Li-san and his majority of supporters carried through the resolution for attacks on large cities by the Red Army, strikes with insurrection in the key cities. The General Front Committee reorganized the Red armies, and the Third, Fourth, and Twelfth armies under Mao and Chu Teh were grouped into the First Army Corps.

Li Li-san now saw world revolution near, China's revolution as

* Interview with Chen Chang-fong, 1971.

the spark igniting it; he saw an "even" * revolutionary high tide developing. He urged Red Army attacks and outbreaks of workers in the cities, pinpointed Wuhan as the key urban base for the proletariat; saw an immediate passage to socialist revolution without any transitional stage or period. He poured scorn on his opposition, alluding to "rightist pessimistic people" whose ideas of "localism and peasant mentality" were the most serious obstacle to Red Army expansion, and castigating the concept of using the countryside to encircle the cities as "extremely erroneous."

Battle plans were drawn in order to carry out the military actions planned by Li Li-san. All Red Army forces were placed under Chu Teh as commander-in-chief of the General Front Committee and Mao Tsetung as political commissar! This was to face Mao and Chu with an insoluble dilemma. Their nomination (in absentia) to head the very action they strenuously resisted meant insubordination if they refused (Li could blame all succeeding disasters upon them); if they obeyed, any failure would bring them discredit.

Mao and Chu held a conference in Tingchow, Fukien, where Chu Teh had been consolidating a Fukien offshoot of the base. Once again the suggestion that the Red Guards (the local peasant guerillas) should also be incorporated into Red Army units for the purpose of attack on big cities was rejected by Mao, for it meant denuding the countryside of its self-defense.

Li Li-san assumed that there would be uprisings in the countryside, mutinies in the Kuomintang, and warlord armies' strikes; he prophesied all this happening at once. "Li Li-san has gone mad," said Chou En-lai. Li demoted his opponents, among them some of the twenty-eight Bolsheviks, who had arrived in Shanghai and begun attacking him verbally. But suddenly, under pressure, Wang Ming (Chen Shao-yu), the most outstanding of the twenty-eight, gave in, apologized, and accepted Li's views (though later he was again to change). Hence in June Li Li-san appeared to have won. As Chu Teh said: "The Li Li-san line dominated the Party then . . . and was sufficiently influential to force acceptance, to some extent, in the Red Army, against the judgment of its field command. . . . Apart from Mao and myself, there was very little opposition to the Li Li-san line."

Chu was to say to Agnes Smedley that isolated in the base, he and

---

* "Even" meant similarly active in all areas of China. This was against Mao's "uneven development" idea, which stressed that not all regions were similarly prepared for uprisings.

Mao felt that perhaps Li Li-san and the Politburo in Shanghai might have more knowledge of the situation, though they were "skeptical." A civil war was raging between Chiang Kai-shek and some warlords. Perhaps Li's assessment was correct. . . . And so the troops prepared, the Red flags flew, and trumpets sounded and drums beat as the armies marched "for the Revolution." They crossed the length of Kiangsi province, and tens of thousands of peasants rose and joined the Red armies. For a while it all looked quite splendid.

Li prepared for workers' uprisings. They were to begin on a nationwide scale in mid-July. He made ready to call on November 7, the anniversary of the Russian Revolution, the first All-China Soviet Delegates Congress, to establish a national soviet government. He also set up "action committees" to carry out the details of the insurrections, and to supersede, bypass, and strip of power all other organizations in the provinces, thus taking away Mao's power in the base.

But although there were some demonstrations and strikes by workers, they did not lead to uprisings. The Kuomintang was very strong in the cities, and heads rolled, as workers were unarmed and were killed; before the strikes could be well organized, their leaders were dead.

An assault on Changsha led by Peng Teh-huai * and his Third Army Corps was at first successful; for a week the city was held.

Reluctantly, but having to obey orders, the First Army Corps of 20,000 men under Mao Tsetung and Chu Teh made haste slowly to attack Nanchang city, as ordered by Li Li-san. They reached it on July 29. It was most powerfully defended, and had big walls. Nevertheless, they took it, but only held the city for twenty-four hours. One cannot but feel that what preoccupied the commanders was not to waste human lives, not to commit a reckless victory.

It had been planned that after Nanchang and Changsha were taken, all the armies would converge on Wuhan, where it was supposed the workers would rise and take the city from within. But neither Nanchang nor Changsha had been kept. The First Army Corps and Peng's Third Army Corps were now joined. Li Li-san ordered another attack on Changsha, and at the same time on Wuhan by the Second and Fourth Army Corps under other Red commanders.

* Peng Teh-huai was in command of a Fifth Army. In June 1930 it was reorganized with the Eighth Army from a soviet area in Kiangsi into the Third Army Corps, which took Changsha. Peng, after the conference at Juichin, had been operating in a guerilla area near Chingkangshan.

Li had by now received, and suppressed, a telegram from the Comintern condemning his plans for taking cities. But this message could not be concealed indefinitely. "The Comintern does not understand the Chinese conditions and cannot lead the Chinese Revolution," declared Li Li-san. Still hypnotized by his role as the Chinese "Lenin," Li Li-san urged his revolutionaries to attack as Lenin had done prior to the eve of the October uprising in Russia in 1917, when things looked very unpromising. Letters and telegrams from Moscow urged him to abandon the capture of Wuhan. But Li Li-san paid no attention.

The second attack on Changsha was now carried out by Mao, Chu and Peng. Kuomintang forces had been dispatched to the city in great numbers. Foreign powers also helped Chiang Kai-shek. American, British, Italian and Japanese gunboats lay in the Hsiang river. They had bombarded the city while it was in Peng's hands, and hundreds of civilians were killed and wounded. Again this was repeated, but the Red troops were raked with murderous fire as well. "They fell like autumn leaves in the north wind."

Mao and Chu now took one of the most serious steps of their careers. They repudiated the Li Li-san line, and the troops were ordered by Mao to withdraw from Changsha. The other political commissars denounced them for rebellion, but the troops cursed the political commissars and obeyed Mao and Chu Teh. By this action they preserved the Red Army from destruction. After the attempt on Changsha the city was subject to the most frightful White Terror. Workers, students, anyone suspected of Communism was rounded up and killed, in the most gruesome manner, reminiscent of the terror of 1927. It was then that Yang Kai-hui, Mao's wife, who was doing underground work in Changsha, was also rounded up and executed. Mao had not seen her since 1927.

In August 1930 Chou En-lai and Chu Chiu-pai, the former "left"-liner, returned to China with specific instructions to convene the third plenum of the Sixth Congress. It was clear that Li Li-san had erred; but how much, how far, and what was the true situation? Wang Ming made things more confused by suddenly going over to Li Li-san's side. "Only those who protect militarists . . . and liquidationists, can oppose, criticize the Party for preparing armed uprisings or term these actions adventurism now," Wang Ming now said. The third plenum was held in September 1930. A new Politburo came into being, through the efforts of Chou En-lai; on it were Mao Tse-tung, Chou En-lai, Chu Teh, Jen Pi-shih. Mao and his supporters were now fully represented. In this Politburo the twenty-eight Bolsheviks were not in majority, though represented; the group would take some time and maneuver to oust Li Li-san completely.

Meanwhile, the effect of this strife between two policies was being felt at lower levels. Skirmishes between pro-Li and anti-Li factions reached the Party provincial hierarchies. The "action committee" in Kiangsi province created by Li, and supposedly in authority over the Juichin base, was rent by factional dispute, which provided excellent opportunities for counterrevolutionary penetration by KMT agents. Mao and Chu, returning with their armies from the disastrous attempt at city-taking, on their way captured the town of Kian on October 30, in accordance with Mao's idea of extending the base "in waves." In captured KMT police files at Kian, Chu Teh found evidence that certain of the Communist officers in the area whom Chu Teh and Mao had already been dealing with were actually KMT agents, of a so-called A-B group. He also found there plans for Chiang's first "annihilation campaign," soon to be launched against the base Mao and he had set up.

The A-B (Anti-Bolshevik) corps had been created by the KMT to infiltrate and penetrate the CCP and the base at Juichin. The successes of "the Red remnants" at Chingkangshan, their successes in Kiangsi and Fukien, alarmed Chiang Kai-shek. The city assaults would do more: they so frightened many warlords that they made peace with Chiang and united with him in a combined assault against the "Reds." The utilization of captured Communists who, jailed, turned renegade and went back to the Party as agents is part of the still unwritten history of the penetration of the Communist Party. The A-B group, utilizing Trotskyites, factional strife and discontent, had already set up a net of terrorism throughout the soviet areas. Among the names of Communist commanders found on lists whose families and relatives were implicated with A-B groups was that of Lin Wen-ling, who had welcomed Mao and Chu at Tungku the year before.

Mao Tsetung conducted an investigation in the districts, uncovering clan, marriage and other connections between landlord families and certain high-ranking cadres who had followed Li's "alliance with rich peasants" policies, and under pretense of obeying Li Li-san had sabotaged Mao's land policy. In certain counties one third of the Communist officials were rich peasants or landlords themselves. Evidence of business and family relations between the A-B group and some Communist officials accumulated. Mao Tsetung had already purged the Party in Chingkangshan in September 1928, expelling unsatisfactory members. Here the issue recurred, but in graver form. The dissension between the Shanghai Politburo and the base had opened the door wide for the enemy. Furthermore, some factions now proclaimed themselves "genuine" Communist groups and broke away. Other factions set up squads of murderers; three of the bodyguards of Mao and Chu Teh were killed by these squads.

In early November, large KMT forces were moving up to relieve Kian, and Mao Tsetung decided to withdraw rather than lose more men. The occupation of Kian had lasted two weeks; several hundred thousand peasants had come to see the Red Army, and there had been many recruits.

Mao was now able to find out, by checking up on land reform, where and how the land redistribution and land policy had been misapplied or not applied, or applied according to Li's action committees — for it was during Mao's absence that the action committees had abrogated his land law. "My viewpoint on the many circumstances affecting the agrarian revolution at district and village level was still muddled. . . . It was only during this investigation that I discovered that using the village as a unit in dividing land has serious consequences." But mistake or not, Mao persisted. He thus modified as he went on, restoring the ravaged areas to production.

On this occasion, however, investigation of land law application bore direct relevance to the anti-Bolshevik corps, whose members took refuge in Li Li-san's "alliance with rich peasants" land law. In late November some 4,400 suspects were arrested in one vast swoop, conducted by the Red Army under Chen Yi, the corpulent and jovial Szechuanese. In December, members of the anti-Bolshevik corps, together with some of Li Li-san's erstwhile supporters, started an armed revolt against Mao. They made a forced march to Futien and released some of the arrested officials and cadres. The provincial soviet administration in Futien was overthrown, and more than 1,800 followers of Mao were killed. Chu Teh's wife, Kang Ke-ching, was captured. They called for Mao's overthrow, set up a rival soviet government, which accused Mao of acting against the Central Committee, and asked for his liquidation. Some of Li Li-san's supporters joined them.

It was at this time that Chiang Kai-shek launched his first annihilation campaign against the Juichin base, occupying Hsingkuo and Tungku. But the Red Army was prepared; it smashed the 100,000-strong Kuomintang troops in a splendidly conducted offensive in which Mao deployed his own ideas on strategy and tactics for the first time against a large body of enemy forces.

In spite of the bitter feuding in Kiangsi, and the arrest of thousands by Mao, "neither side acted with the ruthlessness of Stalinists," writes John Rue.* Very few of Mao's opponents were shot, contrary to the legend of a "ruthless purge" having taken place. Only known agents of the KMT were liquidated; about 400 to 500 men were tried and condemned. Others were released after investigation and "education." This action, known as the Futien incident, has been much distorted, and Mao presented as having "liquidated" 5,000 men in a "power struggle."

Not only was Li Li-san now being challenged by Wang Ming and the twenty-eight Bolsheviks, he was also being challenged by other groups. Chou En-lai tried to hold the balance, to have Li Li-san's line judged equitably. "There is a tradition in the Party that stresses the importance of intra-party peace. . . . This tends to becloud the correct Party line. . . . Only by relentless struggle on behalf of the correct Party line can true unity be achieved." By these words Chou showed himself very near to Mao's conception of debate and struggle in the Party as essential to the Party's life. Chou spoke of principled struggle, but what happened now was a putsch operated by the returned-student group under Wang Ming.

Ho Meng-hsiung, a Communist Party leader, and the Wang Ming faction had both condemned Li Li-san's June 11 resolution, which had launched the city attacks. Li, with a big majority, had punished both, suspending Wang Ming for six months, taking away Ho's Party posts. Wang Ming then capitulated to Li Li-san, as we have seen, but later reversed himself. The third plenum in September revised the policies of Li Li-san. Chou made his famous Shao Shan report (Shao Shan being one of his names) criticizing the errors of Li Li-san and the Central Committee, and also criticizing Ho Meng-hsiung and Wang Ming. In December 1930 Li Li-san was called to Moscow by the Comintern, and in January 1931 Wang Ming and his twenty-seven adherents called a fourth plenum, despite opposition by Ho Meng-hsiung. They did not invite Mao Tsetung or Chu Teh, who were on the Central Committee; neither did they call for a general debate; they simply deposed Li Li-san. Ho Meng-hsiung denounced the meeting as illegal (which it was). Ho was later betrayed to the Kuomintang (some say by Wang Ming himself) and executed, together

* John E. Rue *Mao Tsetung in Opposition 1927–1935* (Stanford 1966).

with Lin Yu-nan, a relative of Lin Piao, who also had opposed the "twenty-eight." Thus the "returned students" came to power, fashioned a "provisional" Politburo and Central Committee, and proceeded to "lead" the Chinese Revolution.

11
Mao Tsetung and Wang Ming—
The Third "Left" Line

It is sometimes said by cynics that Stalin "disliked" Mao Tsetung, and personal hostility is held to be the cause of Russian-conceived policies and directives which plagued the Chinese Revolution for some years. This is hardly tenable. There is a tendency to attribute to well-planned policies what is often blind chance. The esteem in which Mao Tsetung was held by the Comintern in 1930 is undeniable. Not only from reports, which blamed Li Li-san and approved Mao even if not by name, but also from the obituary of March 1930 published about him, in which he was praised high above other leaders in the CCP. This could not have happened without Stalin's approval. It is much more likely that after 1930 Stalin lost interest in the Chinese scene, as events in Europe took up most of his attention. The Comintern was to become mainly an instrument of Soviet policy, to safeguard the Soviet Union's strategic security; Russian interests predominated, and all Communist parties in the world were expected to place Russia's welfare above everything else. The "fountainhead of socialism," the first socialist state, brooked no contradiction. The notion that there could be contradictions in socialism, both between socialist states and parties and within a socialist state itself, would not be evolved before Mao would demonstrate it and thus expand the dialectics of revolution.*

The rule of the "returned students" — the twenty-eight Bolsheviks — lasted four long, disastrous years. Not until 1945 would their line definitely be condemned.† In this historical summing up no Russian

* This would be fully elaborated in Mao's essay *On the Correct Handling of Contradictions Among the People* (February 27, 1957).
† *Appendix: Resolution on Certain Questions in the History of Our Party. Selected Works of Mao Tsetung,* vol. III, p. 177 (English edition Peking, September 1965).

is mentioned, although the returned students, led by Wang Ming, were accompanied by Pavel Mif, a teacher at the university in Moscow where they had studied, and a member of the Comintern. Pavel Mif is said to have maneuvered the student group's gain of power by the strong-arm method described. Once again the CCP follows its tradition of never blaming other than its own members, and Mif is a name forgotten in China.

After the "putsch" of January 1931, the Central Committee was reduced from 30 to 16 members, with alternates. Wang Ming (Chen Shao-yu), Po Ku (Chin Pang-hsien), Chang Wen-tien, and Shen Tse-min dominated the Politburo. The mild, inoffensive and willing Hsiang Chung-fa, personally irreproachable, was made secretary-general as a proletarian cover to the policies of the group.

The net result of the four years which followed was the loss of 90 percent of the Communist Party of China and of the Chinese Red Army; the loss of the base Mao had created and many other small bases in South China; the subjection of millions of peasants to massacres and reprisals; and a headlong flight, monstrously mismanaged, which would, however, turn into an epic: the Long March.

Very clearly, the new leadership set out to pull Mao down. "It slanderously asserted that . . . there was as yet no 'genuine' Red Army . . . and with special emphasis that the main danger . . . consisted of 'right' opportunists. . . . The new 'left' line was more determined, more theoretical, more domineering . . . than the Li Li-san line." This quotation from Mao is a cry from the heart. He could never think of the hecatombs which the returned students' wrong policies gave rise to, the purges, the massacres, and the decimation of the Party and Army without deep emotion.

In February 1931 the intra-Party struggle began; on the theoretical plane first, since the provisional Politburo was in Shanghai, and Mao Tsetung and Chu Teh were far away in the depths of Kiangsi. Wang Ming published a pamphlet, which he appears to have written either in the USSR or on his return to China, called *The Two Lines; or The Struggle for the Further Bolshevization of the Communist Party of China*. The gist of it was that the Party was not Communist enough, and that this had to be remedied. The main obstacle, as Wang Ming saw it, was "right opportunist" ideas (and ideas always mean people too) in the Party. It was actually a very direct and obvious attack on Mao.

The Shanghai abode of the Politburo was in the French Concession, and of course clandestine. But the Kuomintang secret police received the help of the foreign police in the International Settlement and the French Concession. Every week Communist workers, labor leaders, were captured and executed. There were some defections, and the defectors betrayed others. In June 1931, following the capture and execution of Ho Meng-hsiung and Lin Yu-nan, the secret police captured more Party members. Through one of them the party's secretary-general, the hapless Hsiang Chung-fa, was also betrayed and put to death.

Wang Ming became acting secretary-general without convening a plenum. But the police were not going to stop. The Politburo's hideout in Shanghai was discovered and hundreds of names were found. Hundreds were arrested in July and August; the tumbrils brought them to be shot in the waste ground reserved for such spectacles in Shanghai. The Politburo had to move; to remain was too dangerous. There was only one place where it could be safe, and that was at the base Mao Tsetung had created in South Kiangsi. But to get there would be difficult and dangerous too — in that summer of 1931, Chiang Kai-shek was launching his third and largest campaign against Mao's base. It was, however, defeated, and in September the crisis of the Japanese invasion of Manchuria preoccupied the KMT. The Politburo was able to disperse and to reach, under various names and disguises, in small groups, the Kiangsi-Fukien Border Area. Some may have gone by ship, others by land; details are not clear about this exodus. By November 1931 some had already reached the base; others would filter through during 1932.

We must now ask, who was Wang Ming? — for it is a name we shall hear often during the next decades. Born in 1907, Chen Shao-yu (Wang Ming) was a landlord's son who at the age of eighteen became a student in Shanghai University. Shanghai University was heavily politicized, and Wang Ming and many others went to Russia straight from their studies there, to attend the University for the Far East, also called Sun Yatsen University, in Moscow. He joined the CCP in Russia in November 1925 and became fluent in Russian, acting as Pavel Mif's interpreter. He may or may not have been briefly in China again in 1926 — this is uncertain. But he did return after the Sixth Congress in 1930. He had no practical experience of revolution, and does not seem to have acquired any, as he did not stay very long in China.

His friend and colleague, the one who would be identified with the Wang Ming line, was Chin Pang-hsien (alias Po Ku). He died in an airplane crash in 1946, and this has possibly saved him from execration, though he appears to have been less stubborn, less resistant to common sense, than Wang Ming. He studied English at Shanghai University and went with Wang Ming to Moscow. Chin stayed on in China till his death, whereas Wang Ming was to return to Russia in 1932 and from there "direct" the Revolution, particularly through Chin Pang-hsien.

The essential feature about Wang Ming is the contempt he had for the raw, illiterate human beings who under Mao's leadership would develop into dedicated and brilliant Party members and Red Army men. He had no idea of what the Chinese masses were like. It is doubtful that he ever knew anything about the economics of the Chinese peasantry.

Not all the group must be identified with Wang Ming's policies. Some truly changed, and in China today Wang Ming alone is held responsible for the errors of the third "left" line.

Mao's achievement in establishing, consolidating and running the Central Base must be seen in the perspective of the disasters which befell it. Its period of existence is usually divided into three stages. From February 1929, when the victory of Tapoti allowed Mao and Chu Teh a foothold in the area, till November 1930 is known as the first or the base-building stage. A judicious combination of military action and agrarian revolution took place; the military action followed the "wave" theory already delineated: withdrawal when enemy reprisals were too strong, tenacious return, swift pounces to annihilate the enemy when he was weak, tired, or withdrawing. Thus the base was gradually extended, and by 1930 seventeen counties were under Red control. Land reform, mass arousal, formation of people's associations, militia and Red Guards, Party building, intense propaganda of the peasantry . . . this pattern, already tried out at Chingkangshan, was expanded, refined, modified to local conditions, with the characteristic flexibility and imaginativeness which is Mao's style.

The capture of Kian in September 1930 provided a structure wide enough for Mao to proclaim a "provincial soviet government of the Kiangsi-Fukien base area," and set up a Central Base bureau, two months before Chiang's first large campaign against it, and before the Wang Ming group had seized power in Shanghai. On the basis of this territory a year later, in November 1931, a soviet republic was to be proclaimed. This would demote the local central bureau to secondary status, placing all organizations under the Politburo, now arrived from Shanghai.

The second phase of the Central Base, known as the period of consolidation, extends from November 1930 to November 1931. During that time Mao's work was eminently fruitful, for no one could as yet interfere too much. By the end of it the base had grown to a territory of over 19,000 square miles, with a population of 3 million people, despite two more campaigns against it by Chiang.

The base itself was a far better place than Chingkangshan. It had fertile fields and good towns; an alert peasantry, very militant — 70 percent of them were poor or landless peasants; and good rivers. The Hsingkuo land law of February 1930 was tailored to fit the area. The lower middle peasants, small landlords and rich peasants were not deprived of their livelihood. Unified taxation and an end to the excruciating feudal land rent and usury rallied popular enthusiasm for "political commissar Mao." In the cities commerce and trade were protected; merchants enjoyed security. Mao encouraged the export of tungsten from the mines of the base, which brought in revenue, and put his brother Mao Tse-min in charge. Mao Tse-min also became the head of the first people's bank in Yehping (near Juichin) in 1929. Control of the finances was thus in Mao's hands. He traveled up and down the base, supervising, investigating, and holding meetings. Chu Teh and he went forth on military expeditions in Fukien, consolidating the borders of the base and occupying strategic points.

The establishment of the "soviet republic" in November 1931 was preceded by a Comintern directive in August 1931 which stated: "A central soviet government should be formed in the shortest possible time in the most secure area." The notion was not to confine the central soviet government to a base or two, but to lay claim to a nation-wide "soviet republic"; or so it appears to have been interpreted, for this was now done. In that August-September, part of the Central Committee was already in Juichin, and a conference was held. In November the first All-China Soviet Congress elected a Central Executive Committee of 63 members and formed a government, with Juichin as its capital. This government was actually under the Party Central Committee and the Politburo, and this would lead to the subsequent downgrading of Mao Tsetung and his being shorn of power.

But in the due process of election to the central soviet government,

Mao Tsetung collected the largest number of votes and became chairman, with Chang Kuo-tao and Hsiang Ying as vice-chairmen. Wang Ming came fourth in the voting. Even so, Mao was already being somewhat circumscribed, for the two vice-chairmen were known to be opposed to his views and policies.

The soviet republic was to have a constitution, agrarian legislation, labor laws, laws on marriage and equality for women, resolutions on the Red Army, on the national minorities, and so on. The land law Mao Tsetung had drafted was now modified. Resolutions governing the Red Army were passed with drastic revision of Mao's programs, to bring them in line with the "further Bolshevization of the Party." However, due to Mao's local strength and the subtle resistance to these hazardous experiments which he was able to put up, it would not be till a year later, in August 1932, that the fully assembled Politburo would begin to make itself felt in all its "leftward" peril.

Mao Tsetung had always used the Chinese words "workers' and peasants' councils," and other titles simple to understand. But to the Bolsheviks, such terms were anathema, deviation. "General ideological poverty" together with "empiricism" and "opportunistic pragmatism" were epithets hurled at Mao's practical policies. The Bolsheviks themselves used everywhere the words "soviet" and "Bolshevik," which no one understood, especially as they were not translated but transliterated, which resulted in the Chinese "Su Wei-ai" and "Pu-Erh-Shih-wei-ke." Many people thought that Su Wei-ai was the name of a man; Kuomintang and warlords offered prizes for capture of the "Red bandit Su Wei-ai . . . dead or alive." Mao Tsetung already had a prize on his head, and so had Chu Teh and Chou En-lai. The figures kept on going higher and higher. "I'm the most expensive man in China," joked Chu Teh. Wang Ming and his wife Meng Ching-shu returned to Moscow in the winter of 1931 or early 1932, after the establishment of the "soviet republic." It was Po Ku who was left in charge to carry out the directives sent to him from Russia.

It must be noted again that September 1931 was the month in which the Japanese had invaded Manchuria. If, instead of setting up a "soviet republic" and starting to devise ways and means to "Bolshevize" the Party and to reduce Mao Tsetung, the Politburo had taken a good hard look at the Chinese situation, things might have been very different. The invasion of Manchuria had produced a nationwide shock. Patriotic Chinese everywhere, students and intellectuals, demanded resistance to Japan. Had the CCP rallied the smol-

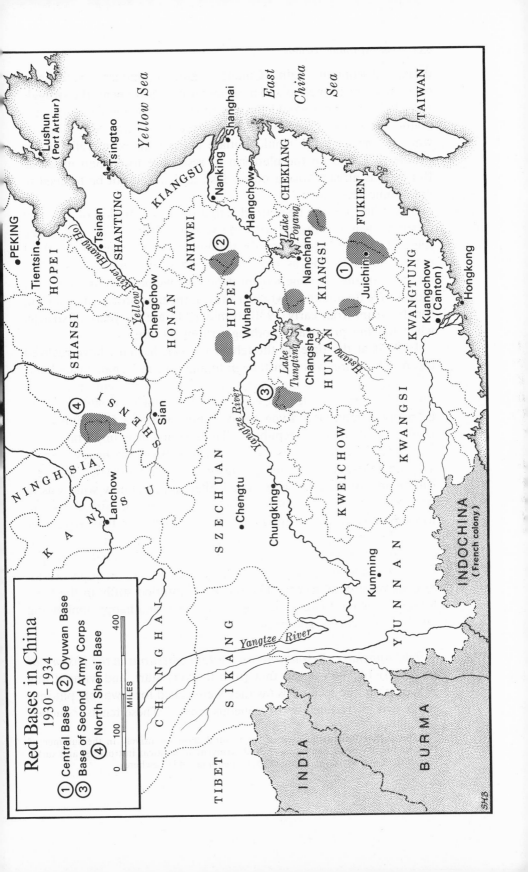

Red Bases in China
1930–1934
① Central Base
② Oyuwan Base
③ Base of Second Army Corps
④ North Shensi Base

MILES
0   100   400

PEKING
Tientsin
Lushun (Port Arthur)
Tsingtao
Tsinan
Yellow Sea
HOPEI
SHANTUNG
River (Huang Ho)
Yellow
Chengchow
HONAN
Sian
SHANSI
SHENSI
NINGHSIA
Lanchow
KANSU
Chengtu
Chungking
SZECHUAN
Yangtze River
Yangtze River
TIBET
SIKANG
CHINGHAI
KWEICHOW
Kunming
YUNNAN
INDIA
BURMA
INDOCHINA (French colony)
KWANGSI
Hsiang
HUNAN
Changsha
Lake Tungting
KWANGTUNG
Kuangchow (Canton)
Hongkong
Nanchang
KIANGSI
Juichin
Lake Poyang
FUKIEN
Nanking
Hangchow
CHEKIANG
East China Sea
TAIWAN
Shanghai
KIANGSU
ANHWEI
HUPEI
Wuhan

SHB

dering discontent with Chiang's anti-Communist campaigns, proclaimed resistance to Japan as a national movement, the struggle for power in China would have been shorter for the CCP. But the young sectarians were unable to see reality. It was Mao Tsetung who, the next spring, would initiate policies aimed at rallying the people of China on the platform of resistance to foreign invasion. But he was already losing power fast, and would not be listened to until some years later.

The other point to be noticed is that the proclamation of a "soviet republic" was not in line with the view that China was still in the stage of "bourgeois-democratic revolution" as asserted at the third plenum in 1930 and as Mao had so often expounded. In fact, it was part of this extreme leftism which we would now find fully deployed. We do not know whether Mao at the time protested against it, for the years from early 1930 to mid-1933 are his years of silence, when we find practically nothing written by him.

Even if at the time he thought it correct, he must have realized this proclamation was a mistake in timing. For in Yenan, years later, he would again make the point that the stage of revolution was not yet proletarian but "democratic-bourgeois," and he would proclaim a "people's republic." Even today, China is not a Communist republic but a "people's republic." The distinction is important.

But in those far-off days in the Central Base, the heady slogans and inflated rhetoric of the provisional Politburo carried the day. The people of the base were elated; they did not know what was in store for them. The ideological struggle which had already begun was unknown to all but the handful of men who, on that November 7, sat on a raised platform on the plain between Yehping and Juichin and watched the Red Army parade. On the ground of the parade enclosure were the words: ADVANCE IN THE BLOOD-STAINED TRACKS OF OUR MARTYRS. The red flags unfurled stiffly in the keen November wind; there were songs and dances and happy applauding crowds, and cheers and fireworks.*

The *Appendix: Resolutions on Certain Questions in the History of Our Party* of 1945 tell us that from the very start, and without any provocation, the sectarians (as they were called for a while) "put into effect two interrelated and erroneous tenets." These tenets, couched

---

* The author visited the area of the Central Base extensively in the summer of 1971 and interviewed numerous ex-Red Army men, political instructors, and survivors of the Long March at Yutou, Tapoti, Yehping, and elsewhere.

in ideological terms, aimed at wresting power from Mao. Wrenching would be a more effective word, for Mao was not a weak and puny opponent, and he fought back "on a principled basis," but with all the ability of his supple brain. As always, he had already made preparations for this onslaught. His brother Mao Tse-min held in his hands the financial structure; he would be dislodged, but it would take time. His other brother Mao Tse-tan was to help him in land reform, again an economic process. It would also take time to reach and to destroy the agrarian changes which Mao Tsetung had instituted. Mao himself was political commissar of the Red Army, and also held other posts. The two erroneous tenets would therefore have as their goals the ideological disparagement of Mao's ideas, taking away his military power and Party posts, and a purge of cadres loyal to him in the Party and in the Army. Before the First All-China Soviet Congress was convened in November 1931 this had already been plain in the pronouncements of the provisional Politburo. In the next two years these intentions would be accomplished.

Where the Red Army was concerned, Mao Tsetung had expanded the First Front Army Corps, organized in 1930 to take Changsha as Li Li-san ordered, and comprising then 20,000 men, which did not burden the population of the base. From 1930 onward a large number of eager young peasant recruits were trained, some only fifteen or sixteen years old. The Chiang Kai-shek campaigns against the base also provided a flow of recruits through desertions and defections. The policies towards captured prisoners had been defined by Mao at Chingkangshan and were strictly enforced: good treatment and political indoctrination for deserters and defectors who were ordinary soldiers or junior officers. This absence of ill-treatment, this positive benevolence, was so entirely new in China — where it was customary to torture prisoners and put them to death — that the very rumor of it brought deserters with their guns from the Kuomintang side. Some of the junior officers captured would prove useful and steady members of the Communist Party during the Long March. Some of them would bring wireless sets, and this was a great help, as the CCP was then able to link through radio with other groups scattered throughout South China.

Because of this army expansion and the swiftly growing popularity of the Communists, small guerilla bases were established in adjacent provinces; there would be twelve in all by the summer of 1932. Though some were unstable, and more like guerilla areas than bases, they did represent a rising tide of revolution. By that summer, 70

counties and 9 million people were under Red control, with ten armies of various caliber and quality. The Central Base remained the
best equipped, which was not much, until an arsenal was established
in 1931. An academy to train officers was set up, and Mao Tsetung
planned to send cadres from this academy to the other bases. This
was regarded as highly dangerous, and labeled "opportunism in
practical work" and halted by the sectarians.

Concerning the treatment of cadres, Mao Tsetung was to write in
1945 that the Wang Ming sectarians had "violated the fundamental
principle of democratic centralism, turned party discipline into mechanical regulations, fostered tendencies towards blind obedience."

It was worse than the above description would lead us to believe.
The "Bolshevization" and "strengthening of the Party at all levels"
announced by the sectarians decimated the Communist Party. This
systematic campaign involved not only punishment of many cadres,
but a terroristic so-called "counterrevolutionary" witch hunt at all
levels.

In this the two vice-chairmen, Chang Kuo-tao especially, participated. Hsiang Ying seems to have been an intelligent but rather obstinate man. The sectarians tried to make of the Futien incident of
1930, when Mao moved against the A–B group and together with
Chen Yi crushed the plot to set up another leadership, a matter for
attacking Mao Tsetung directly. Hsiang Ying was asked to investigate and appears to have turned in a report unfavorable to Mao Tsetung. However, it was not possible even then to lay conclusive
charges, as a great many of the cadres, and the Army men involved,
supported Mao's action. We must not be surprised if, from Moscow
where he lives today, Wang Ming still goes on bringing up the Futien
incident as one of the "crimes" of Mao Tsetung.

A "security" apparatus was set up by the sectarians, and acted so
thoroughly that cadres were physically liquidated on suspicion, a
practice which filled Mao with horror. He termed it impermissible,
but was not heard. After 1945, Mao Tsetung would insist that those
cadres who had been wrongfully killed should be posthumously rehabilitated. The conduct of affairs under the sectarians is so strongly
reminiscent of what happened in the USSR through the purges (and
there were already purges in the USSR in 1931) that one cannot but
feel the twenty-eight Bolsheviks were closely imitating what was
being done in Russia. It is however not possible to say they were following Russian orders; the presence and personality of Wang Ming,
back in Moscow in 1932, is enough to have motivated these

odious practices through sheer eagerness to prove to the Russians what thorough good Bolsheviks the returned students were.

The measure of failure of these unrealistic policies was the disasters they precipitated. The step-by-step wresting of power and influence from Mao was relentless. Elected chairman of the soviet government, he was still political commissar of the Red armies at the base, and secretary of the Front Committee. But in August 1932 a conference and plenum were held at Ningtu. By then most of the sectarians and their adherents had arrived. Mao Tsetung was away fighting in Fukien (yet another campaign was on, Chiang's fourth) and returned to attend this meeting. He was then divested of his posts as secretary of the Front Committee and political commissar of the Red armies at the base. His connection with the Red Army was thus severed. He remained, however, chairman of the government. But as this was entirely subject to the Politburo, he had no real voice any longer in political or military decisions.

The sectarians averred that Mao's equal distribution program to all persons, men and women, old and young, was an error. They charged that he had avoided adopting a thorough policy of "class struggle." He was soft, they said. All landlords, big or small, all rich peasants should be killed or driven off their land. Let them die of hunger. No land (or only the poorest) should be given to them to labor and to live on.

But though the sectarians refused to be "infected with reality" in Mao's felicitous phrase, the reason they could not destroy the land reform program as thoroughly as they destroyed the Party and Army was that, after all, these things take time, and the urgent necessity of being fed and feeding the troops, the need for money precisely from the very merchants and traders they tried to liquidate, slowed down this "Bolshevization."

Another reason was that they did not know the people. There is no record of their going round, as Mao did, from small village to small village, pacing the field pathways, stopping for familiar talk with the peasantry. The grass-roots cadres knew Mao, and they would obey him. Mao did not directly counter the orders given; he would proceed, as he always does, by indirection; taking up one point, then another, and showing how impracticable the decisions were; and thus finally, steadily, bringing down the theoretical edifice. But the practical demonstration of his views would not take too long to be manifest.

Although we have an absence of recorded writing from Mao during the two and a half years from the summer of 1930 till August of 1933, it is indubitable, from eyewitness reports, that he was busy writing, and making investigations. But this material went unpublished and ignored, and was probably lost with many other documents during the Long March, or left behind or burned.

It was in policies concerning the Red Army that the best examples of erroneous decisions are seen. Because Mao was not deprived of control till the end of 1932, the full force of the new line for the Army could only be applied in 1933. Already, in the resolutions passed in 1931 concerning the "Bolshevization and rebuilding" of the Red Army (it apparently was not a genuine Red Army before the twenty-eight Bolsheviks arrived), there are many pointers as to the methods by which Mao's control would be taken away. The Red Army leadership was castigated for guerilla warfare. The new line called for occupation of key points and holding them to the death, for an end to "indecisive fluctuation," for the seizure of the whole of Kiangsi province. It accused Mao of rightist opportunism for neglecting positive action, for procrastination, for being skeptical about occupying cities, for avoiding head-on confrontations. He preferred, they said, propaganda in villages to "destroying the enemy through combat," and he failed to pursue enemy forces to the end. They denounced the concept of "fluidity." All this would lead to a line of "regular warfare," or classic positional war, for which the Red Army was completely unsuited. The flexible tactics and the guerilla strategy of Mao, which spared men, collected weapons, and was maximally effective in its twin objects of political arousal of the people and social revolution, together with protracted, attritional methods of war, was to be given up entirely by the end of 1933.

But all theory must be tested in practice, and it is in war that theories are best tested. Chiang Kai-shek's campaigns would serve to illustrate the two-line struggle in a more striking manner than any other event could have done.

"Before the central leadership following the fourth plenum had time to carry through its erroneous line, the Red Army of the Central Area in Kiangsi under the correct leadership of comrade Mao Tsetung won great victories and smashed the enemy's second and third campaigns of "encirclement and suppression." *

Between 1930 and 1931 three "annihilation" campaigns were

* *Appendix: Resolution on Certain Questions in the History of Our Party. Selected Works of Mao Tsetung* (English edition Peking 1961–1965), vol. III.

launched by Chiang against the Central Base. The first campaign, as we have seen, started in October 1930,* with a force of 100,000 men. In the decisive battles of December 27, 1930, and January 1, 1931, Chiang's troops were lured deep into Red area; he lost one fifth of his men, including a top general who was killed. The Red Army numbered 20,000 men.

The second, begun in May 1931, was under the command of Ho Ying-chin, Chiang's defense minister and chief of staff, with 200,-000 men. The population and the terrain were against the KMT; the peasants and the Red Guards of the liberated areas helped the Red Army, numbering 40,000 men, which routed the armies of Ho Ying-chin. Thirty thousand prisoners were taken or came over to the Communists; there were 4,000 casualties on the Communist side.

The third campaign followed immediately upon the second. It was led by Chiang Kai-shek in person, with 300,000 men, in July 1931. Chiang set up headquarters in Nanchang; he used German and Japanese military advisers. The Communist forces maneuvered ably, gliding between the armies, cutting them off from the rear in lightning actions, covering by night unexpected distances to appear suddenly when least expected on a flank or behind the KMT divisions. Ten thousand firearms were captured, and over 20,000 men, together with their commanding officers, went over to the Communists later in the same year.

Mao Tsetung was to give, in December 1936,† a long lecture on the strategy of these first three campaigns, citing not only the military aspects but also the political situation at the time. The first campaign, he said, could have been more successful, in that a counter-offensive might have been mounted, had it not been for the disunity inside the Red Army and the split in the local Party organization (the two difficult problems created by the Li Li-san line and the A–B group). The alternation of offensive and defensive, advance and retreat, must always be kept in mind, and one must always be prepared for this alternation and not persist in offensive only. During the third campaign, the offensive was on a very large scale, and it was only by making long detours (1,000 lis or 300 miles) in order to attack the enemy at the rear that a very strong column had been crushed by weaker Red forces. "When the enemy launches a large-scale encirclement and suppression campaign, our general principle

* See chapter 10.
† See *Problems of Strategy in China's Revolutionary War. Selected Works of Mao Tsetung* (English edition Peking 1961–1965), vol. I, ch. 4.

is to lure him in deep, withdraw into the base area, and fight him there, because this is the surest method of smashing his offensive."

But we should note here that besides the military strategy involved, another factor would also predicate the success of the third campaign. This was the fact that the Japanese had attacked and invaded Manchuria in September 1931. They followed up with the total occupation of Manchuria. This in turn provoked a wave of indignation and protest within China itself against Chiang Kai-shek. "The trials and tribulations of the KMT from September 1931 to April 1932 gave the Communists a much-needed respite," writes Jerome Chen.* The defection to the Communists of 20,000 men of the KMT Twenty-sixth Route Army, with all their guns, more than a hundred pieces of artillery, and wireless sets — called the Ningtu uprising — was also a tremendous boost.

The tribulations of Chiang Kai-shek were multiple, for he now also had a full-fledged rebellion on his hands, ending with a dissident "government" proclaimed in Kuangchow. However, this revolt had already started in February 1931, and had not prevented him from mounting his second or this third campaign against the Communists; hence the excuse made by some historians that Chiang would have been militarily successful had he not stopped because of these "tribulations" is not borne out by facts. On the contrary, the invasion by Japan, (termed euphemistically the Mukden incident) was the means of a reunion between the Kuangchow dissidents and Chiang Kai-shek. Of course the dissidents had the support of that eternal peripatetician Wang Ching-wei, once again reconciled with Chiang Kai-shek. There is no evidence that the Communist triumph in the third campaign was directly due to any hasty withdrawal by Chiang. It was a straightforward military victory. Chiang did not withdraw his forces because of the Japanese; he never sent any to fight them.

By January 1932 the Japanese were also attacking Shanghai, which was bravely defended by the Nineteenth Route Army of General Tsai Ting-kai, who only a few weeks previously had been fighting in the third encirclement and suppression campaign against the Red base, under Chiang Kai-shek's orders. Chiang's reluctance to battle Japan became then very evident; he did all he could not to support (practically to sabotage) the Nineteenth Route Army's gallant efforts, which had stirred the patriotic emotions of the whole country. In order to continue his anti-Communist campaigns —

* Jerome Chen *Mao and the Chinese Revolution* (New York and London 1965), p. 171.

under the slogan "Internal pacification must come before external resistance" — Chiang Kai-shek in April 1932 ordered General Tsai Ting-kai and his Nineteenth Route Army to battle the Communists in Fukien province, with what paradoxical results we shall see.

Chiang Kai-shek then made a truce with Japan, the May 1 Tangku truce, tacitly agreeing to Japan's occupation of the three eastern provinces of Manchuria. This was to lead the following year to the establishment of a puppet state of Manchukuo, ostensibly independent, actually under Japanese control. The deposed last emperor of the Manchu dynasty, Puyi, who had been living in the Japanese Concession in Tientsin, was now made emperor of Manchukuo. Chiang meanwhile readied his fourth encirclement and suppression campaign against the Communist Central Base.

In January 1932 Mao Tsetung was urging that the Communist Party should seize the opportunity dropped into its lap, literally, by the Japanese invasion. A united front of the people of China, the "broad masses," furious with Chiang's supine attitude, and demanding resistance to Japan, was in the process of coalescing. It needed a head, a leadership. Mao Tsetung argued that this leadership should be seized by the Chinese Communist Party.

This was, said Mao, a struggle against imperialism, Japanese imperialism. Whichever party would combine the leadership of a national liberation movement together with the fulfillment of demands for social revolution, such as land reform, could win leadership of the entire nation and thus make the Revolution progress. Mao Tsetung argued that since the Revolution was still in the bourgeois-democratic stage, it was up to a united front to rally *all* the classes that wanted to resist the invader. This reasoning was sweepingly denounced by the "left" sectarians as right opportunism. They saw the whole process quite differently. The attack on China was not an attack on China; it was a preparation for a combined imperialist attack on the Soviet Union! Any sign of "nationalism" was therefore bourgeois. Only "proletarian internationalism" was the correct line. All reformist groups were enemies; Chiang Kai-shek was in league with Japan and therefore to fight him was essential. Mao tried to refute this haywire reasoning. Japan could not possibly attack anyone else before it had subdued China and turned China into its vast base to conquer the world. Hence to fight Japan was true "internationalism." This reasoning was deemed non-Marxist. "What kind of Marxism can you expect from the mountains of Kiangsi?" sneered the sectarians.

However, in April 1932, while Chiang was maneuvering for a truce with Japan, Mao Tsetung as chairman of the Chinese soviet government, Chu Teh as commander-in-chief of the Red Army, and Hsiang Ying, the vice-chairman, signed a declaration of war against Japan. This was regarded as a propaganda move abroad; and the sectarian members of the Politburo went ahead with their own logic.

A totally different military strategy was developed. The Red Army was to be expanded; it was. By the end of January 1932 it had grown to a massive 200,000 men. It was announced that "guerillaism" was now out. "It was wrong to lure the enemy in deep because we had to abandon so much territory." The sectarians argued: "Now our own state has been established and our Red Army has become a regular army. Our fight against Chiang Kai-shek has become a war between two states, between two great armies. . . . everything pertaining to guerillaism should be totally discarded." The new principles were "completely Marxist" . . . They were: Pit one against ten, pit ten against a hundred . . . exploit victories by hot pursuit," "attack on all fronts . . . seize key cities" and "strike with two fists in two directions at the same time." When the enemy attacked the methods of dealing with him were: "Engage the enemy outside the gates," "Gain mastery by striking first," "Don't let our pots and pans be smashed," "Don't give up an inch of territory," and "Divide the forces in six routes."

These quotations from the slogans show how the new strategy was to govern part of the fourth, and the fifth, defense against Chiang's campaigns. From June to October 1932 Chiang Kai-shek, who led the fourth campaign against the Communists in person, installed his headquarters in Wuhan, and first attacked the smaller bases in Central and South China. This time he used 400,000 men. He easily overran some of the smaller bases, such as the Oyuwan base under Chang Kuo-tao. Chang Kuo-tao fled westward with the bulk of the forces to set up another area on the borders of Szechuan province. He would move again when threatened by a local Szechuan warlord, avoiding battle and retreating into national minority areas deep into West Szechuan, where we shall meet him again in 1935. Only some guerilla detachments remained in the area; they were rallied by the commander, Hsu Hai-tung, who later would join up with Mao Tsetung.

Chiang also scattered a base in North Hunan-Hupei, under Ho Lung, the Kuomintang commander who had joined the Communists at the Nanchang uprising. Another column of Chiang's troops would smash the guerilla area where Peng Teh-huai now operated. Peng Teh-huai had returned in late 1930, after the fiasco of Li Li-san's "capture Wuhan" line, to the Hunan-Kiangsi border area. His base was therefore almost in the former area of the Chingkangshan mountain massif. Peng lost the territory and withdrew, to join the Central Base.

This provided the sectarians with a rival military opinion against Mao Tsetung. Peng Teh-huai agreed with them that "guerillaism" was outmoded, and that with such a large Red Army (and the Politburo called for its constant expansion throughout 1933 and early 1934), regular warfare should be engaged in. When in August 1932 at Ningtu, Mao Tsetung was finally deprived of control over the Red Army, right in the middle of the fourth campaign, both Chang Kuo-tao (who seems to have been briefly in Juichin) and Peng Teh-huai joined in criticism of Mao's military strategy. The new resolutions on the Army were now set into practice. Soldiers' conferences and soldiers' committees were done away with; they would not be restored till 1947–1948. Political education in the Army declined. Officers and privates were to be regularized, which meant different uniforms, and saluting, which Mao never bothered about. Positional warfare and trench warfare, sudden lightning attacks, were "the modern way" of fighting — "Marxist." A Military Commission was set up, to prosecute what was now called "the decisive battle between the road of revolution and the road of colonialism." A war "of short swift thrusts, blockhouse warfare, war of attrition . . . anyone who did not accept these things was to be punished, labeled an opportunist and so on and so forth. . . . [These] were the theories and practices of hotheads and ignoramuses . . . they did not have the slightest flavor of Marxism about them." Thus wrote Mao, in 1945, of this period.

The Military Commission would pass under the command of a German, Otto Braun, alias Li Teh, alias Hua Fu, alias Otto Stern, who arrived in 1933. Li Teh would have the distinction of being the only European to make the Long March. His qualifications for assuming military control were puzzling. He appears to have been a schoolteacher by profession, a member of the Comintern by conviction, a journalist occasionally, and a military strategist by virtue of having soldiered for a while and also taken some courses at the military academy in Moscow. He called on Edgar Snow in early 1933 in Tientsin, under the name of Otto Stern, journalist. He was dramatically smuggled into the base a little later. He has now written his own memoirs of those days.

The fourth campaign, which dragged on for almost nine months, was also a defeat for Chiang Kai-shek. The military line set down by the sectarians was not followed everywhere; Mao's influence would continue among some units; a commander named Lo Ming would be "struggled against" and cashiered as an "opportunist-liquidationist" and a "flightist" for having followed Mao's guerilla precepts.

Mao Tsetung was ill with malaria (he had altogether three bouts of it) and was therefore certainly not in any position to influence military events — besides having been deprived of his post with the Red Army — during the winter of 1932 and the spring of 1933. The fourth campaign was victorious, even if costly in manpower, and this seemed to prove the correctness of the new military line. It was actually due to the impetus and élan, the courage and fearlessness of the troops, much less well armed than their opponents. The losses in men were speedily made up, but new recruits are not seasoned soldiers, and this the sectarians ignored. The Red Army, they argued, could grow to "several hundred thousand" and start a nationwide insurrection.

In March and April 1933 a swift forward thrust carried the Red Army within striking distance of Changsha; but then logistics became a problem, and Chu Teh argued that Changsha could not be taken. But this seeming victory greatly exalted the Communists. Another military conference was called that April, and again Mao was criticized (in absentia).

But the expansion of the Red Army in preparation for the war "to end colonialism," the decisive stage foreseen by the provisional Politburo, needed economic support. There cannot be an army without food — what the peasant grows and supplies. Not one of the members of the Politburo could spare the time to do the laborious, boring work of economic consolidation. This was left to Mao Tsetung, who was put in charge of producing the sinews of war: food, clothing, money, and men.

In the summer of 1933, we find Mao Tsetung writing again; and it is on economic work.

The economics of the base were tied up with recruiting. Recruits could only come from the peasantry. The sectarians spoke of getting at least 500,000, if not a million, men under arms. The "regular" army would now man blockhouses, trenches, and other fortifications in "regular" warfare fashion. Peasants were set to digging and shoveling and building. This entailed a drain on field labor. The soldiers were locked in trenches and forts. All this was against Mao's ideas, which was to utilize the Red Army also as a production and work force in the fields, so that the burden on the population would be light. The intensive Army-people relationship which Mao had promoted was endangered.

At the April 1933 military conference which had criticized Mao in absentia, and started the struggle against Lo Ming because in his battles he had followed Mao's military tactics, Mao's brothers Mao Tse-min and Mao Tse-tan were also censured. Mao Tse-min was relieved of his job, as also was Mao's secretary. Mao Tse-tan was left to help Mao with land reform.

To counteract the unpopular "left" land program, which admitted of no intermediate classes and had already resulted in decline of production, Mao Tsetung organized a land investigation movement in that April of 1933, in spite of his illness. In May 1933 the policy of physical liquidation of landlords and the "tax to the limit" on rich peasants was producing poor results. Mao halted it. It antagonized the middle, yet did not fulfill the demands of the poor peasants. He then set up "experimental points," and held two more meetings on economic work in June 1933, going to villages and calling on groups of three to twenty people, asking questions, making notes, comparing reports, in fact doing what any scrupulous scientific social researcher should do. If a point was unclear, Mao would remain, stimulate a debate, and have a discussion with as many people as possible until he got to the bottom of the local problem.

All this painstaking, meticulous work would be regarded by the haughty sectarians as trivial; and there is no record of any of them doing the same. Yet this was the basis upon which Mao Tsetung set out to "verify" (which was really to mitigate) the "left" line in land reform and in economics. He said that the line practiced "was a most dangerous policy, the population will be troubled." *

In August 1933 Mao Tsetung called an economic conference for seventeen counties (the base total) for economic construction. The fifth campaign of Chiang Kai-shek had started that very month. At the conference he criticized the discrepancies between the policies urged and the goal, which was to win the war. The essence of the matter was that the enemy's campaign must be checked and the

* Interviews at Juichin Central Base by author, 1971.

enemy defeated, but the line carried out asked for an economic setup which could not sustain the war effort. There would not be such a contradiction, he maintained, if appropriate tactics and strategy were followed.* The call "Let us have a million soldiers" was devastating the countryside; it interfered with labor power needed at harvest time, as did the work on fortifications.

He was then accused of "narrow empiricism, peasant localism, and opportunistic pragmatism." Mao then withdrew to a small village where a drought had occurred and mobilized the population to dig wells, digging a well himself. At the time he repeated what he had written in 1930: "It is quite wrong to take a formalistic attitude and blindly carry out directives without discussing and examining them in the light of actual conditions."

At the end of 1933 Mao Tsetung made trips to Hsingkuo, to Shanghang. He kept moving about the base, and he visited some places, such as Yutou, where his brother had been in charge of the tungsten export, about eleven times during those four years. About a thousand cooperatives were founded to alleviate shortages in food, clothing, salt, due to enemy blockade. Mao made a report to the plenum in January 1934 on all aspects of economic work. "To conduct the task of land reform merely through the action of a few cadres," he said, "depresses the morale and the fighting spirit of the masses."

His operational principles were three: land distribution, land verification, and agricultural production. Exhaustively Mao Tsetung tackled the subject of economics, tedious to those who sail above pedestrian matters such as "oil, flour, vinegar and salt," details vital for the war effort and for the livelihood of the millions in the base. The landlord class certainly was the principal enemy of the revolution, Mao agreed, but physical extermination was not the answer. It should be used most sparingly. Only twelve "big tiger" landlords after "verification of more than three hundred families of landlords and rich peasants" had been shot in a certain area, after "mass movements in the countryside" when "for fifty-five days the masses of the whole district were set in motion." Mao indicated that the people, the poor peasants themselves, would not stand for massive liquidation.

Warning about the serious underestimation of Chiang's military ca-

* *Be Concerned with the Well-Being of the Masses, Pay Attention to Methods of Work*, January 27, 1934. *Selected Works of Mao Tsetung* (English edition Peking 1961–1965), vol. I.

pability in the fifth campaign, Mao analyzed the resources of the base, going into minute details such as the number of piculs of grain produced in certain localities, the way in which land redistribution enhanced production, the obstacles to the sorely needed good harvests. "Comrades, what is a true bastion of war? It is the masses, the millions upon millions of people who . . . support the Revolution. . . . What is the real wall of bronze? It is the people."

This was a retort to those who praised the earthwork bastions they were erecting and boasted that the base would be impregnable, with "walls of bronze and fire" around it. Alas, the wall of bronze and fire was being erected by Chiang Kai-shek round the base, to choke it off.

"Be concerned with the well-being of the masses, pay attention to methods of work." With growing anxiety as he felt the obduracy of the "ignoramuses" round about him: "Some comrades have thought it impossible to spare time for economic construction because the revolutionary war keeps people busy enough, and they have condemned anyone arguing for it as a 'right deviationist.' Comrades . . . fail to realize that without building up the economy it is impossible to secure the material prerequisites for the revolutionary war and the people will become exhausted."

Already in 1933 the food restrictions imposed by the blockade were felt, and also the shortage of textiles. No winter uniforms were made. Money dried up as trade became impossible. Just before the Long March, in October 1934, the food ration was fourteen ounces of rice per day, 60 percent of the minimum required. Cooking oil almost disappeared. Lack of salt became a great problem.

The soldiers were paid five cents * a day; officers were supposed to be paid the same, but their pay had been raised. Salt, even the minimum, would cost them twice that per day in 1934. Then it was to disappear totally. Mao organized salt-smuggling squads. Many of them were caught and tortured to death by Chiang's troops. Even the wounded in the hospital did not have salt, and saplings were cut and burned, salt recovered from the ashes, for hospital patients.†

"Salt is very dear . . . sometimes unobtainable . . . all this directly affects the life of the workers and peasants. . . . And does it not affect our basic line . . . the alliance of workers and peasants?"

Even with these urgent problems, and the tightening blockade, the sectarians "invariably attached damaging labels to all com-

* Five Chinese cents, about one and a half U.S. cents then.
† Interviews at the base by the author, 1971.

rades who, finding the erroneous line impracticable, expressed doubt about it." Doubters were treated "as if they were criminals and enemies . . . persecuted, punished, deposed . . . this resulted in the most lamentable losses inside the Party."

And yet in 1934, Wang Ming in Moscow was still to speak of the application of the left line as eminently successful; and Béla Kun, member of the Comintern, was to publish a pamphlet extolling the success of the counterrevolutionary drive throughout the Chinese soviet republic, which occupied, he wrote, one sixth of China. The Central Base was "twice the size of Holland and Belgium taken together," he wrote. The Chinese army now had 350,000 regular soldiers.*

Another opportunity would now be offered to the Communists to emerge onto a national plane, and by so doing to break Chiang's blockade of the base.

In November 1933, the Nineteenth Route Army under Tsai Ting-kai, which had stirred the whole country with its heroic resistance against the Japanese at Shanghai, revolted against Chiang Kai-shek. It had been moved to Fukien province, to "fight the Communists." Tsai Ting-kai now raised the standard of a "people's government" and opposed the authority of Chiang's Nanking government. This revolt was not unique; other warlords, such as Feng Yu-hsiang, had felt the patriotic fiber vibrate with Japanese aggression. Feng had taken up arms against the Japanese, and Chiang cut off his subsidies to stop him from fighting.

All over China massive protests, spearheaded by student groups, gave rise to demonstrations. Although for years cowed by the White Terror Chiang exercised — many students were executed, and each university had its spies — the students sent delegations to Nanking to demand resistance against Japan. Tsai Ting-kai was supported by patriotic individuals such as Eugene Chen, Sun Yatsen's former minister for foreign affairs.†

In January 1933, Mao Tsetung as chairman of the soviet central government had set out a tentative united front policy, based on resistance to Japan. If attacks against soviet areas stopped, if democratic rights were guaranteed to the people, the war against Japan vigorously prosecuted and the people armed against Japanese impe-

---

* Preface by Béla Kun to *Laws of the Chinese Soviet Republic* (New York 1934).
† General Tsai Ting-kai is, of course, now in Peking.

rialism, then the Chinese soviet government was willing to cooperate with "any armed forces" to resist Japan.

However, in 1933 the Politburo maintained that there could be no alliance with any "bourgeoisie." There could be no distinction made between compradore bourgeois, petty bourgeois, national bourgeois; all were bad, all were to be liquidated together, and this was in line with the view that there were no "intermediate" classes. In the USSR too, Stalin was against "intermediate" classes as the worst enemies of the Revolution.

By the summer of 1933, when the Fukien people's government was not yet installed but there were already signs of dissidence, contacts had been established between Tsai and the Communists and Mao had made renewed truce offers. Had the CCP leadership encouraged such contacts, and a tactical alliance, Tsai's position would have been greatly reinforced. The Communists would have immediately captured national attention. For the people were truly tired of internecine warfare. On the basis of "uniting all the people to fight Japanese imperialism" a powerful propaganda offensive against Chiang Kai-shek could have been mounted. There would have been no fifth encirclement campaign, and even if there had been, the existence of a friendly province next to them, Fukien, would have added enormously to the resources of the base and broken the blockade.

In December 1933 Mao Tsetung and Chu Teh, in the name of the Chinese soviet government, exchanged telegrams with Tsai Ting-kai. But the Politburo tarried and dallied. Wang Ming in Moscow continued to denounce the Fukien "rebels" and the people's government of Fukien. Wang Ming said of Tsai Ting-kai: "I'll shake his hand only if I can spit into his face." Moscow seems to have signified, however, through some Communists in Shanghai, that "military cooperation with Tsai" was authorized, though criticism of the "bourgeoisie" must continue. But the general impression was of reluctance to associate with the Tsai Ting-kai revolt, and no alliance was contrived.

Surprisingly, an extract of a speech by Mao on November 17, 1933, in the midst of the controversy about the desirability of an alliance with Tsai Ting-kai, appeared in the Comintern press.* In his speech Mao criticized the Party leadership for underestimating Chiang's military strength, and identified Tsai Ting-kai with the national bourgeoisie against Chiang Kai-shek as representative of the landlord compradore bourgeoisie.

* *International Press Correspondence*, vol. XIII, no. 50, p. 1124.

While this dispute within the Party about alliance with Tsai was going on, Chiang Kai-shek moved. First he managed to separate Tsai from potential allies in Hongkong and in Shanghai. Secondly he sent troops along the Kiangsi-Fukien border to separate Tsai from Communist contacts. In January 1934 he launched an offensive against Tsai in Fukien, crushing his army and destroying the people's government. Thus vanished the hopes of a united front with Tsai Ting-kai.

No wonder that in January 1934 a fierce debate between Mao Tsetung and other members of the Central Committee, in particular Po Ku, would take place. But the "line" of the January 1931 plenum, the "Bolshevik" line, was reasserted in its full fury; the slogans launched were to defend the USSR, beacon of socialism. World revolution was just round the corner and this present campaign was the decisive one. Mao asserted on the contrary that a socialist revolution would not take place until the bourgeois-democratic revolution was completed all over China. He repeated that petty and national sections of the bourgeoisie, lower and middle class, were themselves oppressed by the big bourgeoisie and imperialism. He pointed to all the splits which were occurring, the revolts against Chiang; the CCP was not taking advantage as it should of these splits and factions. One warlord plus one warlord did not make two warlords, there was always a possibility of rallying one to hit the other. "To turn the revolution into a seething surging tide all over the country it is necessary to launch a political and economic struggle for democracy involving also the urban petty bourgeoisie." He noted that in spite of their brave slogans, the "left" line had already seriously abrogated leadership even in the cities, among workers and intellectuals, sensitive spheres of the social context where CCP influence was not being built up as it should be, and all because of the neglect of this essential platform of national unity against Japan.

After the January 1934 plenum, Mao's influence was curbed even further. A seventeen-man presidium was formed out of which, at any time, a new chairman might be selected, thus imperiling Mao's position as chairman. This body was to act as a supervisory committee over Mao's actions. His training of cadres was drastically cut; he was deprived of the chairmanship of the Council of People's Commissars, the political and educational branch of the Party. He had been active in promoting a university, an academy, Lenin schools, had begun to send cadres out "in straw sandals and by night, walking the mountain paths to call on the people." It was said that the people "loved the cadres sent by Chairman Mao." This new and subtle way of keeping in touch with the people aroused fear that his popularity would be strengthened. Another of the twenty-eight bolsheviks, Chang Wen-tien, took over this job, as well as becoming secretary-general of the Party. Not a word of complaint escaped Mao, nor did he take a single action against Party unity. "The only thing to do is . . . to wait." Meanwhile he went on his inspection tours, carrying a small lantern, riding a horse. "We heard the sound of hoofs, and knew it was Chairman Mao, going his rounds by day or by night." *

Chiang's fifth military campaign started in August 1933. He consecrated to it vast funds, a new loan from the United States and Great Britain, a million troops, tanks, airplanes, the advice of German military experts, among them General von Seeckt, who came with the assent of Hitler to help Chiang Kai-shek.

The scorched earth policy of "burn, kill, destroy all" was put into practice. The total economic blockade meant not only the building of hundreds of thousands of blockhouses round the Central Base; it also meant the uprooting of thousands of villages. One million peasants were to die when Chiang cut a wide desert swath eighteen miles deep around the base.

Besides this ring of death, there was a ring of fire; all crops, trees, houses were burned. A ring of blockhouses, six miles in depth, with machine gun nests, supplemented it.

The death penalty (most horrible death, with gruesome cruelties) was provided for anyone who traded with Communists, who gave them salt or food. The secret police controlled all the schools and other public places in county towns. The system of collective responsibility, *Paochia,* by which everyone in a village was ultimately responsible if any one member helped the Reds, was enforced. Twenty-four thousand special guards were created as a supervisory body. Barbed wire was strung round all the fortifications and between to prevent any entrance or exit to the base for a depth of eighteen miles.

Because all this took time, victories could still be claimed when sorties were operated in March and April of 1934. But economically, the effects on the base were already felt by November 1933. Mao Tsetung was not impressed by the victories claimed. The loss in men and in equipment had been very heavy. The Red armies

* Interview at Yehping with peasants of those days.

"milled round and between the enemy's main forces and his block-houses"; they were reduced to passivity. "This is really the worst and the most stupid way to fight," said Mao. He had in January suggested transforming the defensive into an offensive by thrusting the "main forces of the Red Army . . . into the Kiangsu-Chekiang-Anhwei-Kiangsi region," as if to threaten the areas between the big coastal cities, a triangle of urban concentration much prized by Chiang, his vital center in fact. A push in that direction would have compelled Chiang to split his forces and give battle in areas where there were no blockhouses. "By such means we could have compelled the enemy, who was attacking southern Kiangsi and western Fukien, to turn back to defend his vital centers, broken his attack on the base area in Kiangsi, and rendered aid to the Fukien people's government." But Po Ku called this "bandit policy" and "country-side thinking." Mao had then advocated another plan, which was to move the main forces towards Hunan, driving into central Hunan, once again drawing the enemy behind them and destroying it in Hunan. This was also rejected.

In April, Suichuan, the county seat between Chingkangshan and the Central Base, and Kuangchang, on the road to Juichin, were both taken by the Kuomintang. There could not be any more "halt-ing the enemy beyond the gates." The ring tightened and the base shrank. Any sorties by the Red troops became suicidal. "We could see the corpses of our comrades strewing the plain. The summer came and the smell was very bad. We had to cross the same terrain, over and over again." * It was certainly bad for morale. Mao Tsetung wrote memoranda to the Military Commission; in vain.

Since January 1934 the Military Commission itself was split. Chou En-lai and Chu Teh were no longer happy with the military strategy evolved, although at one time they do seem to have thought that it was a workable one. Chou expostulated with Po Ku and with Otto Braun (Li Teh), but Li Teh now had too great an influence; he banged his fist on the table and was very overbearing, and there was no way to change his ideas. Back in Moscow, Wang Ming was claim-ing that the reorganization and Bolshevization of the Party and Army was a great success, and news was spread that Chiang's expe-dition had already failed and that the Red armies had won another smashing victory.

The order "Don't give up an inch of ground" was now issued as

* Interview with old Kiangsi soldiers.

the Kuomintang pressed forward into the wizened base. As a result, soldiers were literally imprisoned in the fortifications, with no rest and, towards the end, very little food or water. The ration in August and September of 1934 would fall to twelve ounces of rice per day.

On July 15 a small portion of Red troops, led by Fang Chih-min, cut its way out. Fang's columns were called the anti-Japanese vanguard; their declared aim was that they were going to the front to "fight Japan." Fang was instructed to operate a "united front" approach, should he meet with any troops prepared to accept the terms Mao had drawn up in 1933. The departure of Fang Chih-min's troops meant that a portion of the north Fukien counties, where they were quartered, was automatically abandoned. Unfortunately Fang's rear was cut, he was captured, exhibited in a cage in Changsha, and put to death. Some of his troops escaped and under Su Yu, his chief of staff, waged guerilla war on the Chekiang-Fukien border until 1938, when they joined the Communist New Fourth Army created in 1937.

German pilots bombed and strafed the base almost daily; they had one hundred and fifty planes. The Central Committee dispersed.

In August another breakthrough, by Hsiao Ke and Wang Chen, took place from the former base area of Chingkangshan; they proceeded due west, to Kweichow province. The base of Ho Lung * (north Hunan-Hupei) had been overrun in the fourth campaign, but guerilla units still remained in operation there. Ho Lung and the bulk of his forces of 20,000 men had moved to northeast Kweichow province. Wang Chen and Hsiao Ke were to join him there, and the forces merged to become the Second Front Army. Ho Lung was commander, and the political commissar was Jen Pi-shih, Mao's dedicated friend. This appointment of Jen was to be of consequence later, when Jen played a great role in persuading Ho Lung to join Mao.

The fighting at the Central Base now grew in intensity. Sometimes the soldiers went for twenty hours without any rest. Mao Tsetung had another bout of malaria, a bad one, his temperature reaching 105 degrees in August and September 1934. Just about that time Tingchow and Hsingkuo fell to the Kuomintang. Both of these places were scenes of Mao's early military triumphs in 1929, when he had been in the process of building the base.

The Central Base had now shrunk to only six counties, and the other small bases had disappeared. Very little was left of the

* See map, page 273.

"Chinese soviet republic." Or so it would appear, if one forgot the people of China.

Is there any truth in the assertion of some historians that Mao Tsetung was imprisoned, or at least under house arrest, in the summer of 1934? Most of these tales come from defectors, and defectors from the Communist Party in those years there were. They should be studied with caution, since the primary motivation of defectors is justification for their own running away. According to interviews with people at the base, including Mao's own personal bodyguard Chen Chang-fong, Mao was never a prisoner. He may have been ideologically attacked, but the rank and file knew practically nothing of the two-line struggle within the Party. Indeed, the soldiers who manned the fortifications, when they asked why the new tactics were so different, were told that they were "still Chairman Mao's tactics, but improved." This is a pointer also to Mao's great popularity. There would be many instances in the future of Mao's policies being invoked when actually the contrary was being done.

Mao Tsetung visited the fortifications on the southern line of defense in May 1934. He went to see the soldiers, advised a withdrawal from the fixed trenches, and reorganization to allow the soldiers to rest. He suggested mobile warfare as the opponent there was a warlord, Chen Chi-tang, only a late recruit of Chiang's and not inclined to lose soldiers in decisive battles. A breakthrough could have been operated from there, favorable to the whole defense. In August and September, Mao withdrew to Stone Cloud mountain and was also in Yutou. There he lay ill with malaria, quite emaciated, but dragged himself from bed to work table. Chen Chang-fong * said Mao did not complain, but set about teaching him to read. Mao wrote far into the night, and compiled a textbook for the use of cadres. Perhaps he started then on his notes for *The Chinese Revolution and the Chinese Communist Party*. But this is sheer guesswork.

"He worked so terribly hard no one could remain unmoved." His concern was very evident. Abstemious always, his frugality increased as the shortages were felt. He was brought salt, smuggled through, refused it and sent it to the hospital. He would eat only vegetables and reheated rice, and wash in cold water. It was at the Kiangsi base that, according to some witnesses, he began to suffer from the

* Personal interviews with cadres at Juichin Central Base and also with Chen Chang-fong, 1971.

acute spastic bowel condition which Edgar Snow also was to mention in Yenan. (He seems, however, to have recovered from it now.)

When his temperature reached 105 degrees, Dr. Nelson Fu came to see him. Fu had followed Mao all the way from Chingkangshan. Mao insisted that "doctors are precious, a nurse would be enough," and that Dr. Fu should not waste time on him. He also refused a chicken which Dr. Fu brought, saying that it must be shared with the soldiers. Once he upbraided the doctor for giving him too many dishes at dinner.

"Mao's uniform was the same as ours," said Chen Chang-fong. "The only difference was that the pockets on his coat always were specially large — he would put books, notebooks, and maps in them. He slept very little and was too thin. He had a small kerosene lamp, and he used it when he went on horseback to visit peasants. He would throw his cap down and sit with them, and call out: 'Old cousin, what is your name?' He often told us to observe everything, to note down what we saw. After supper he would light his lamp, open a knapsack with nine compartments which he carried always with him, and take out books and documents and work till dawn. When he left on the Long March, he did not take this knapsack with him."

"Whenever we captured a county seat or small town, Chairman Mao would send people or go himself to the local government offices and to the post office. He would get documents and archives; he would buy the newspapers and magazines and books, whatever he could get. We'd come back loaded with parcels of books and magazines and newspapers. Chairman Mao would read them, marking with a red pencil the pages he wanted to keep, so that we could clip them for him and keep them."

In 1931 Mao Tsetung had married again, a cadre called Ho Tzu-chen, a girl from a local peasant family in Kiangsi who bore him two children. There were always people coming to see him, children running in and out. "He was very patient with ordinary people; he loved to laugh and to joke with them. But he hated arrogance and complacency. He could then be very curt."

In all these years of accumulating experience, of learning how to make revolution, Mao lived and moved in a perpetual seesaw of war; how to fight, how to build; to build to fight, to fight to build. Problems of war and strategy, problems of theory, problems of economy became the links of the same process: revolution. And so though he loved people and fun, he was also often alone. He knew the solitude of one whose prescience compels a distance from his peers. During those years of vilification, his peasant patience was tested, but he never faltered. He cannot have been happy seeing everything he had built destroyed. But the depth of his feelings would not be expressed in personal grievance; they would be transmuted into a compelling historical experience. The hard lessons learned would become historical knowledge, to educate the Party in later years, so that "ignoramuses" would no longer overawe the meek, the dedicated.

As September came to the base and the leaves browned, and the failure of the military strategy became glaring, panic seems to have seized Li Teh and Chin Pang-hsien. The suggestion to abandon the base had already been made in August. And now another mistake was to be committed. Impatience. Now that there had been failure to take advantage of those occasions when the blockade could have been broken, the decision to get out of the base, abandoning it totally, was taken, according to Mao, with "unjustifiable haste." "In the circumstances then obtaining, we could well have held out for another two or three months, giving the troops some time for rest and reorganization. If that had been done, and if the leadership had been a little wiser after our breakthrough, the outcome would have been very different." *

Mao Tsetung was at Yutou, where his brother was also stationed, when Chou En-lai, Chu Teh and Chang Wen-tien † came to call on him. Chou En-lai and Chu Teh were in disagreement with the conduct of military affairs since the winter, and Mao gave it as his opinion that there should be no headlong flight; a strategic retreat must be prepared with as much meticulous care as an offensive. Another meeting was then held at Stone Cloud mountain temple, a very pretty wooden structure on a small granite boulder, overlooking the valley. It was here that the decision was made final, but Mao would have no control over the way the withdrawal would be carried out.

The decision to leave was made by Li Teh and Po Ku,‡ and Chang Wen-tien was to concur in it. It seems that as far as destination was concerned, this remained a dispute throughout the first lap of the march. Mao Tsetung linked their final goal with anti-Japanese ac-

* *Strategy in China's Revolutionary War. Selected Works of Mao Tsetung* (English edition Peking 1961–1965), vol. I.

† Some say it was Wang Chia-hsiang, not Chang Wen-tien. Both were among the "twenty-eight returned students."

‡ Po Ku is Chin Pang-hsien.

tion; this had been the proclaimed aim of the two previous break-throughs, and he opted for the slogan to be raised again. This does not appear to have been done. Mao also gave it as his opinion that a base in North China, where the Red Army would be in a strategic position, would be the best. There were students of his from the Peasant Institute in Kuangchow in the only base that was left, bar the Central Base and Ho Lung's base, and that was in North Shensi province, adjacent to Inner Mongolia. Mao also was to speak of Ninghsia as a good province for a base, with plenty of salt and natural resources.

But no decision was actually made, or rather, it seems that Li Teh again prevailed and a decision to join Ho Lung's base was drawn up. A Revolutionary Military Council was then formed, with Mao Tsetung, Chu Teh, Chou En-lai, Wang Chia-hsiang, Liu Po-cheng and the German Li Teh. One week was allowed for all preparations. Since the decision was secret, none of the rank and file, no junior officers, no political instructors, were informed. Nor, during the first few weeks, would a precise day-to-day briefing as to the plan of march be issued. Most appalling of all, no provisions for any military encounter of any importance, no briefing for battle array or for measures taken in case of attack were drawn up. This was really more like a "house-moving" than a military performance.

The Red Army divided into two large groups; the reserve, and those who were to leave. Left behind would be 30,000 soldiers, of whom 20,000 were wounded more or less seriously. Since there were about 300,000 soldiers then and only 120,000 set out, another 150,000 must either have been disbanded or dispersed as small guerilla groups in various areas which now received them.

Also left behind would be Mao Tsetung's brother Mao Tse-tan, and Chu Chiu-pai, now consumptive and ill, and many friends and adherents of Mao. All who survived the years would become members of the Central Committee at the Seventh Congress in 1945.

In March 1935, when the Kuomintang finally overran the base, Chu Chiu-pai and Mao Tse-tan were taken and executed. It is said that Chu Chiu-pai turned renegade just before his death. This was not found out until 1967, during the Cultural Revolution, when some Kuomintang documents were discovered. The imposing marble grave erected in Chu's honor in the Papaoshan cemetery in Peking, where those who have contributed to the Revolution are laid to rest, was pulled down and his remains taken away in 1968.

Mao Tse-tan's son, Mao Chu-hsiung, born in 1927, was adopted by Mao. He was to emulate his father, became a Party member in 1945, and in 1946, as a guerilla in the province of Shensi, was caught and buried alive by the Kuomintang.

Mao Tse-min, who had been in charge of the finances of the base, was among those in the departing group. He was placed in charge of transport, of archives, of the equipment, money and machinery which the Communists took with them. It is said that Mao's children by Ho Tzu-chen, who were one and two years old, were left behind with peasants, and could never be found again.

Several hundred women, teachers, cadres, nurses, started in the first lap of the exodus, but most of them had to give up or remain in hiding in friendly villages. Only thirty-five completed the journey to the end.

The marching force consisted of 120,000, of whom about 100,-000 were soldiers, and the rest cadres and others, such as stretcher-bearers and doctors. But many more started with them. According to participants, it was a veritable exodus of a whole population, with 100,000 Red Guards, militia, and peasants, afraid of being caught by the Kuomintang, following the armies; they too would be stopped during the first two weeks and compelled to return. This peasant exodus along with the Red armies happens often, and it would be seen again during the civil war. It is not surprising that it took place now, despite the secrecy with which the troops left the base. There were also 8,000 porters who started with the marchers. They too would gradually leave.

It was five o'clock on the afternoon of October 18 when Mao Tse-tung left Yutou with his personal guard and joined the vanguard of the marchers; the advance troops had left on October 16. Under cover of darkness other units from other places also left. They formed long files, processions which moved slowly out of the base, and rumors were rampant, for no one knew exactly where they were going, nor had orders been given as to resting places for the night.

The soldiers were told to put rice in their bags. They carried about three days' supply; they could take no more than two catties each.

The overwhelming impression from many interviews is of the complete bewilderment, and the walking. "We did not know where we were going, but we walked. We walked and we fought. Day and night."

Thus, as a "house removal operation," as Mao Tsetung would call it, this exodus began in panic and dismay — reflected in the lack of any practical organization, care for the soldiers, or methods for supplying information and maintaining morale. There was no winter clothing for the soldiers; they left in their summer kits. Mao Tsetung, still weak from his bouts of malaria, went like the others. His orderly relates that "we received orders to equip ourselves lightly in preparation to go to the front to fight the Japanese. Some other units apparently did not get this information; they thought they were going to open up a new base and fight landlords. Others thought they were going on a parade.

"The Chairman did not take his nine-compartment knapsack with him . . . his total personal possessions were two blankets, a worn overcoat, one woolen sweater, a broken umbrella, a bowl for eating. He took the umbrella and a small bundle of books. He told everyone to make straw sandals, light and cheap, for marching. All the way, whenever we could, we made straw sandals." The next month Mao would give his overcoat away to a wounded soldier. He took his horse with him, which he had inherited from a Kuomintang officer defeated in battle in one of the first campaigns. But most of the time he walked with the soldiers. The horse was used to carry equipment.

Some units were told to "remove telephone lines" and so they removed lengths of wires and carried them away. Paradoxically, they also took everything they could that was cumbersome, such as sewing machines, the machines from the arsenal, and furniture. The 8,000 carriers slowed down the military units.

The day the withdrawal started, a message from Moscow arrived (some say it was several days, or even a fortnight later), approving a pullout.

Later, Mao Tsetung, summing up this experience, would have this to say to those who had so violently criticized his concepts of "fluidity" of base territory, luring the enemy in, and conserving men rather than space:

"Fluidity of battle lines leads to fluidity in the size of our base areas. . . . We must base our planning on it and must not have illusions about a war of advance without any retreat. . . . We must . . . be ready to sit down as well as to march on, and always have our marching rations handy. It is only by exerting ourselves in today's fluid way of life that tomorrow we can secure relative stability, and eventually full stability.

"The exponents of the strategy of regular warfare which dominated our fifth countercampaign (1933–1934) denied this fluidity, and opposed what they called 'guerillaism.' Those comrades managed affairs as though they were the rulers of a big state, and the result was an extraordinary and immense fluidity . . . the 25,000-li Long March." *

* *Problems of Strategy in China's Revolutionary War. Selected Works of Mao Tsetung* (English edition Peking 1961), vol. I.

12

The Long March

In October 1934, the First, Third, Fifth, Eighth and Nineteenth Army Corps of the Red Army, which composed the First Front Army of the Central Base, set out on the Long March.

The First Army Corps of this vast cohort had been reorganized in June 1930 to include the Third Army under Huang Kung-lueh, the Fourth Army under Lin Piao, and the Twelfth, Twentieth, Twenty-first and Twenty-fifth armies. These six armies of the First Army Corps formed the vanguard of the immense exodus, all 7,500 miles of its trek. The Third, Fifth, Eighth, and Nineteenth followed, in that order.

The commander-in-chief of the First Front Army was Chu Teh. Was Mao Tsetung its political commissar? So it seems, although this point is obscure. At the Party conference held in August 1932 he had lost his post as political commissar. His connections with the Army were thus severed. Now, however, with the creation of the Revolutionary Military Council, he may or may not have been reinstated as commissar. In the chaotic muddle at the departure of the 120,000 from Kiangsi, it is possible this job was foisted upon him.

Peng Teh-huai was vice-commander-in-chief of this vast force, second to Chu Teh, as well as commander of the Third Army Corps; Yeh Chien-ying was chief of staff, and Liu Po-cheng, nicknamed the One-Eyed Dragon, chief of operations. There was also a corps of instructors and political cadres trained by Lin Piao at the Juichin Red Academy.

The conditions under which the Long March began could not have been worse, with totally inadequate food supplies, much cumbersome and useless baggage, no battle plans in relation to enemy troop movements. Li Teh was the man chiefly responsible for the conduct of this evacuation. Backed by Chin Pang-hsien, he overrode the opinions of other members of the Revolutionary Military Council, as he had done persistently during the fifth countercampaign.* In eight articles published under the pseudonym Hua Fu, Li Teh had rejected Mao's suggestions and Chou En-lai's. During the last four months, up till the final day of departure, peasants of the base had labored at earth fortifications and trenches; the new recruits in the Army had very poor training, severe shortages had affected their health. "Where were we going? Some were told we were going to beat the landlords and make revolution . . . We were told many different things. We did not know where we were going."

In the first stage of the Long March, from October 16, 1934, when the First Army Corps, assembled at Yutou, started marching, to January 1935, when at Tsunyi Mao Tsetung was voted into power, the Red Army sustained enormous losses. Li Teh was determined to reach another base, that of the Second Front Army under Ho Lung, previously in the Hunan-Hupei area.† Strung in four separate columns, carrying an enormous amount of goods, the ponderous, inchoate mass moved out of the base. It took a week to walk from the head of the cohort to the rear.

It appears that all that Li Teh (Hua Fu, Otto Braun) knew of military science was the straight, straight line. He drew a straight line and that was the line of march. But one important detail had been forgotten. Maps. There were no maps except the maps Mao had collected. These maps did not indicate the straight, straight roads which Li Teh wanted for marching on. The Red Army men, exhausted after months of combat, of malnutrition, lack of salt, defeats, had had no time to rest. Yet these incredible peasants and workers hurled themselves at the lines of blockhouses, machine gun nests, trenches, fortifications, barbed wire entanglements, which surrounded the Juichin base, and broke them. Nine battles were fought against one hundred regiments of the Kuomintang; 25,000 Red Army men died in the breakthrough.

During the first ten days the orders were to walk by night and rest by day; but there was no rest, as the open columns were pitilessly strafed by German-manned airplanes. The orders were changed to four hours of marching and four hours rest, day and night. But again there was no rest, for they were attacked, had no time to eat,

---

* Lin Piao, in an interview with Edgar Snow in 1936, clearly held Li Teh responsible for the debacle.

† Ho Lung's Second Front Army had already moved to Kweichow province.

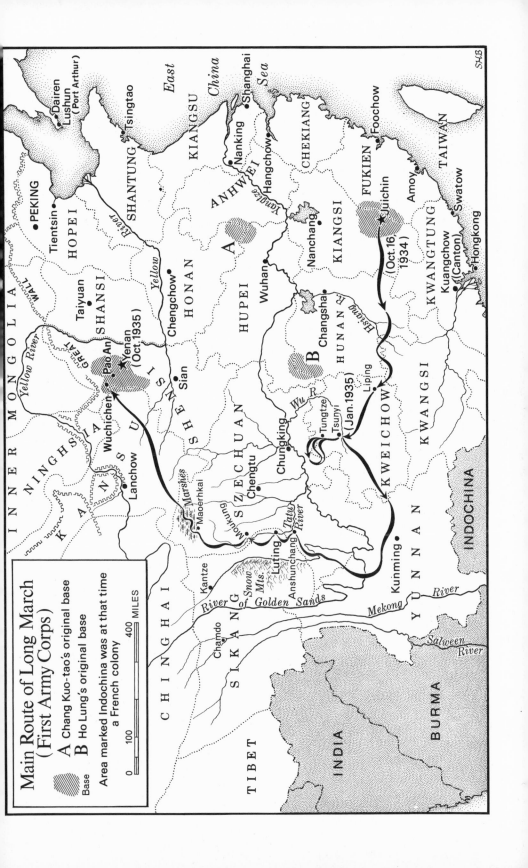

Main Route of Long March
(First Army Corps)

A Chang Kuo-tao's original base
B Ho Lung's original base

Area marked Indochina was at that time
a French colony

Base

0   100   400
MILES

to find shelter, water, before they were on the march again. "We fought every day, we were outnumbered. We could only pluck up courage, and sing: 'The Red Army fears not death, / Who fears death is not a Red Army man.'" * From the rear, from both sides as well as from the air, in front of them, the enemy attacked. "We were so tired, we strapped ourselves to trees, to our guns, we strung ourselves to each other . . . We slept standing up, we slept walking. We had only one thing in mind, sleep. But there was no sleep. The strong pulled the weak. We did not want to straggle, to be left behind. Long rows of us roped ourselves together so as to keep on the march. We called it 'sleep flying.'" *

Always going straight as a ruler, the Red Army arrived on the east bank of the Hsiang river. It had to be crossed, for now the "plan" was to march straight across Hunan and then northwest, to join the base of the Second Front Army, although by then the bulk of the Second Front Army was elsewhere.† A vast Kuomintang force barred the way, yet the river had to be forded. The Red Army waded through, the tall carrying the short; the children of twelve and thirteen who in their hundreds had come to the Army and served as orderlies, cookboys, carriers and trumpeters hitched themselves onto the veterans' shoulders.

The Red Army fought (how they fought!) with marvelous courage, stood in two columns to allow their noncombatants to use the lane between them to cross the river. There were not enough stretcher-bearers, many wounded lay in heaps dying. They stuffed cloth in their own mouths to keep from screaming. Many cadres also died, fighting side by side with the soldiers. Mao Tsetung went to the wounded, but could not do very much except cover one with his overcoat.

The battle of the Hsiang river lasted a week, with horrifying losses. The dead and the dying littered the bank. This insane attempt cost another 30,000 men. "We had to leave some of the wounded behind, there was no way to carry them. By now we had no footwear, some of us did not eat for four days; yet we fought." "I remember how it rained and it rained, we wallowed in mud, we sank in it; but we went through." According to Liu Po-cheng, by now half of the troops had been either killed or wounded grievously. But the "Head on, straight on" Li Teh would not change the orders.‡

* Interviews with Long Marchers.
† See map on page 273.
‡ Li Teh's memoirs state that there were no devastating losses in the first phase of the march. But interviews with many Long Marchers do not bear this out.

The river was crossed; on the other side the march started again. The columns sang: "Today we walk and tomorrow we walk, and where do we walk to?" The political instructors were constantly being asked: "Where are we going now?" They had to encourage the men, lead in the singsong, see the wounded were cared for, make food and rest arrangements, run up and down the units, and fight. The political instructors finally sang a reply: "We follow Chairman Mao, the end will be good."

Ahead of them was another enemy force, five or six times their number. It took them three days to advance less than two miles, fighting all the time. By then it was obvious that something was seriously wrong with the conduct of operations. Men were dropping dead from weariness, from wound infections. Yet they went on, and now they were in Kwangsi, in the region of the Miaos, a national minority.* " 'Squad leader, where are we now?' 'I don't know, comrade. Find a fellow who knows where we are.' I trotted up to a man I saw, but he did not understand me; I tried every word: Red Army, Juichin, soviet, Communist Party; I called him old cousin in three dialects. He shook his head. Then I thought: 'That's it, we're out of China, we've arrived in a foreign country where they can't even speak Chinese.' " The soldiers truly thought the Miaos were foreigners, they had not met any before. "Then Chairman Mao explained to us about the national minorities, about the Miaos. How we must respect their customs. So we talked with them by gestures.' "

The November nights were bitterly cold; the troops had no winter clothes; they trekked all night and in the morning saw "strange-looking wooden houses . . . like baskets hung in the air." On December 10, 1934, the Red Army reached Tungtao county on the border of Hunan and Kweichow; they were now only 30,000 men. "At that moment the 'left opportunists' † still wanted to join the Second Front Army under Ho Lung. A conference was then held at Tungtao. Mao Tsetung opposed this plan. He said that the First Front Army should enter Kweichow." Mao was able to sway the others at the conference, and instead of going northward, the Red Army wheeled smartly westward into Kweichow, entering the province on December 12. On December 14 another battle was fought, to occupy Li Ping county town within the Kweichow border. A meeting of the Politburo at Li Ping from December 14 to 18 was devoted to

* There are fifty-odd national minorities in China, making up 7 percent of the population.
† The sectarians, the "twenty-eight Bolsheviks."

arguing the military line to follow. The soldiers, for once, rested. They rested because, blessedly, the smothering white winter fog which wraps Kweichow and part of Szechuan from October to March was upon them; no longer were they strafed from the air.

The choice was between extermination or survival; even the stubborn Chin Pang-hsien, even straight-line Li Teh, realized it as they looked at the exhausted, overspent remnants. Two thirds of the troops had been sacrificed. "It was at this critical juncture that Chairman Mao saved the Red Army . . . saved the remaining 30,-000 from extermination," writes Liu Po-cheng, the one-eyed general in charge of operations. "Here [in Kweichow] the enemy is weak," Mao had said at Tungtao when he was able to make the change in direction effective. And he proved it almost immediately, for the Red Army had scattered warlord armies with great ease, and taken Li Ping in a day, a small victory and their first. But Li Ping was the first time they rested in two months.

Mao was able, during this brief pause at Li Ping, to carry out some regrouping; his orders were to discard all that was unnecessary on the march. Furniture, files, machines were burned or given away or buried. More would be jettisoned later. Surplus guns were given away to the villagers who came with joy to meet the Red Army; despite its losses, it was famous and well loved. Mao forbade the troops to borrow anything from the Miaos, even doors to sleep on, as they customarily did in Han villages. So the troops slept on the ground. Even though there were fish in the ponds and herds of kine, they could not have meat. The Politburo still gave the orders, but everyone turned to Mao Tsetung, for now everyone was informed through the Revolutionary Military Council of the day-to-day plan of campaign and the route.

There is very scanty material on both the Tungtao and the Li Ping conferences except for Liu Po-cheng's statement that "reorganization occurred" and a January 1936 number of the *Communist International,* Paris edition, stating: "The military errors . . . were corrected at Li Ping." The author, Chi Ping, defines two stages of the Long March: the period before the Li Ping conference, when all was confusion, and the period after it, when morale and decision returned. After Li Ping the Red Army became once again a military force capable of initiative instead of a routed mob. But this was not due to the Politburo, as the paper seems to suggest. "We all knew that Chairman Mao was again taking things in hand, and we were glad. He had a way of making even the enemy do what we wanted — he called it regaining the initiative. He would lead the enemy by the nose . . . he always did."

Now they went west, deeper into Kweichow; small towns — Chen Yuan, Shih Ping, Huang Ping — fell to them. The Red Army felt itself again; in the villages it performed theatrical sketches, dances, sang songs, once again an army with a political mission.

Now they were to cross the deep, ensconced Wu river, turbulent and savage between its high cliffs, burrowing its mountain gorges. They were still almost a hundred miles from it, but the Red Army made preparations. The soldiers were given immediate, practical slogans, and the main slogan was: "To take the warlord of Kweichow, Wang Chia-lieh, alive! Cross the Wu river!" "We made many pairs of straw sandals, we knew that we still had a long walk before us."

At Hou Chang, again dissension occurred in the Politburo. Li Teh and Chin Pang-hsien would not easily give up. They felt authority slipping from them, and even the fact that the Red Army had been saved (and this is not too strong a word) by Mao Tsetung could not dampen their resentment towards him. Hence orders given were now countered or canceled. Li Teh urged a battle plan, and again wanted to join the Second Front Army, now on the border in northeast Kweichow. This would mean turning back east. Mao Tsetung held firm for crossing the Wu river into Szechuan and again prevailed, with Lin Piao, Yeh Chien-ying, Nieh Jung-chen, as well as Chou En-lai and Chu Teh on his side. The order of the day issued by Mao was to "proceed to north Kweichow, take Tsunyi and Tungtze by surprise, and arouse the masses." Tsunyi, the second biggest city in Kweichow, was held by the warlord Wang Chia-lieh; it was on the highway to Szechuan. The Wu river curved south of it, cutting Kweichow province in two and providing a natural protection to Tsunyi. Between Tsunyi and Tungtze was a barrier of mountains, with a pass, the Loushan pass, where "one man could keep ten thousand at bay." The Wu was to be crossed, the pass captured, Tungtze and Tsunyi taken, and the way to Szechuan would be open. From January 1 to 4, 1935, the crossing of the Wu river, nearly 300 yards wide and with a flow of almost six feet per second, was attempted. "Both banks were sheer precipices. Under enemy fire the Red Army advanced. Keng Piao, the miner from Anyuan, went ahead with a small party to investigate; there was a ferry, but it was heavily guarded. The Red Army men cut bamboo, made rafts, selected eighteen swimmers; the swimmers plunged into the icy river and swam across to destroy the enemy's post on the opposite bank; meanwhile a feint attack on the ferry was carried out, to draw fire. But this plan failed. By night, we tried again; then again; finally we did cross the Wu and destroy the outposts, scaling the opposite cliff."

On January 5, Lin Piao captured Tsunyi city by a stratagem. Disguising some soldiers as warlord troops, using captives as guides, he got past the guards and fought in the city to overpower the garrison. On the 6th, Mao and the Revolutionary Politburo entered the spacious city with its beautiful carved brick portals, its park, and big walled compounds where merchants and warlords lived. Mao Tsetung came over the bridge of the small Tsunyi river and settled in the house of a minor warlord; the lower floor was occupied by a merchant of soya bean sauce. It was in this house, now famous, that the most important Tsunyi meeting took place, marking a turning point in the Long March, in Mao Tsetung's life, and in the history of the Chinese Revolution.

At Tsunyi, where I went in September 1971, the two-story house, with gracious verandas and a wide paved courtyard, where the Tsunyi conference was held, the conference room with its wood-paneled walls, the chairs and the table, have been kept exactly the way they were.*

The meeting at Tsunyi, from January 6 to 8, 1935, was called by a resolution of the Politburo. It was an enlarged meeting: besides the Politburo, "responsible comrades" from the Army and Central Committee attended. The Tsunyi decisions were not a military coup perpetrated by Mao Tsetung but a majority decision, and Chou En-lai was the decisive influence in calling it, whereas Li Teh strenuously objected, arguing that there had already been a conference at Li Ping, which had "solved all outstanding problems."

Who were the people who attended? The numbers reported vary between sixteen to eighteen; so far no one has given a complete list. We know that besides Mao Tsetung and Chou En-lai, of the military commanders Chu Teh, Yeh Chien-ying, Liu Po-cheng, Lin Piao, Peng Teh-huai and Nieh Jung-chen were there; that of the twenty-eight Bolsheviks there were at least seven or eight, including Teng Fa and Kai Feng; and that Liu Shao-chi was also present. Liu Shao-chi had left Shanghai in the autumn of 1932 for the Juichin base and become chairman of the All-China Federation of Labor in Juichin. He made the Long March until Tsunyi; and was at the time political commissar in Peng Teh-huai's Third Army Corps.

* Visit and interview with local Party and revolutionary committee members in Tsunyi.

The meeting "concentrated upon criticizing the left opportunist and adventurist line in military action." It hence defined its limitations. It would not be a full-blown ideological struggle, but would confine itself to military strategy and tactics. It was not only the present operation, the Long March, but the whole conduct of the defense against Chiang Kai-shek's fifth campaign which was called to account, for it was the defeat of the fifth countercampaign which had led to the evacuation of the base. Within the rank and file of the armies as well as among the commanders, there was resentment, argument about the defeat and the withdrawal. Why had they been defeated? Why had they built fortifications? Why had they left the base? Why had no explanation been given? Questions shelved then now returned with added virulence, and had to be answered. The appalling results of the first two and a half months, when "men died quicker than flies," had to be explained; Mao's demand since November for a change of policy had become known. There were many unit commanders overwhelmed by their own losses.

"The Tsunyi conference put an end to the Wang Ming 'left' military line; it refuted 'positional warfare,' and 'war of short swift thrusts,' the concept of 'pure defense,' and of 'not giving up an inch of ground.' It criticized the sectarianism of the 'left' line and the system of 'punishment and purges' which had wronged many comrades.

"The military leadership could not adopt the correct strategy and tactics; in spite of the bravery and skill of the Red Army, the high standard of the work in the rear, and the support of the broad masses, this was the essential reason why Chiang Kai-shek's fifth campaign could not be defeated. Instead of the strategy of active defense, or offensive defense, which Mao Tsetung had urged in view of Chiang's 'protracted war and blockhouse tactics,' there had been a 'pure defense' line, of positional defense only. The Army had been enjoined never to give up an inch of ground, the soldiers to die manning their posts rather than to retreat. 'The line of pure defense was against all the principles of strategy and tactics which had made possible, so far, the victories of the Red Army.' " *

The resolutions of the Tsunyi conference analyze how wrong it was not to employ "concentrating superior forces, selecting the enemy's weaknesses, using mobile warfare to destroy a part, or a great part of enemy strength"; in other words, using the strategy and tac-

---

* Interview at Tsunyi, September 1971.

tics laid down by Mao Tsetung and employed by him so successfully. As Mao was to say in 1936: "It was a serious mistake to meet
the vastly superior forces of Nanking [Chiang Kai-shek] in positional warfare at which the Red Army was neither technically nor
spiritually at its best."

The resolutions go on to expose exactly what Mao Tsetung later
would develop: the strategy of protracted revolutionary war when
"we do not have the support of urban proletarian uprisings and mutinies of White Army units . . . when we do not yet have airplanes,
artillery . . . when we are stlll fighting on interior lines."

The resolutions are an excellent early summary of Mao's basic
ideas on warfare, and are valuable to us because they show that
Mao's classics on war, written from 1936 to 1940, had already been
elaborated in his mind before 1935. The resolutions repeat: "We
should lure the enemy to penetrate deeply into our territory. . . .
For victory, we must not hesitate to surrender some parts of territory
. . . all this so that the Red Army can hold the initiative. . . . *All
these principles had been violated.*"

This "lecture in military strategy and tactics" delivered in Tsunyi
by Mao is in essence his theory of protracted people's war, which is
China's revolutionary war. Mao stressed the "preservation of personnel" of the Red Army, criticized the waste of human lives which had
accompanied the erroneous military line. He qualified as "opportunist tendencies" either to "overestimate the enemy's strength, inducing
us to make no further move," or "to launch attacks without any
hope of victory (for instance hopeless and unnecessary attacks on big
cities)." The failure to take advantage of contradictions in the enemy
camp was also castigated, including not aiding the Fukien Nineteenth Route Army rebellion.

It was here that he criticized the fact that the withdrawal from the
Kiangsi base had not been explained to the cadres and the officers,
and thus all had been done "like a house removal operation." And
finally, the whole conduct of the Long March until then had led to
wasting, terribly costly battles for three months which "put us almost
always in a passive position, constantly under the enemy's attack,
while quite unable to deal telling blows."

After criticizing the conduct of the defense, the meeting outlined
future strategy, and the Army and the Party's main tasks were reaffirmed. There should not be decisive battles unless the Red Army
was sure to win; there should be mobile warfare, guerilla warfare —
waiting for a favorable opportunity, luring the enemy in, causing

him to tire himself out in pursuit, inducing him to make mistakes, to reveal his weakness. There should be fluid and flexible use of territory. "The Red Army must always hold the initiative and always be in a favorable position to beat back any enemy attack. It must avoid any loss of initiative or to be placed in an unfavorable position." The appalling losses during the breakthrough from the besieged Central Base was the fault of Hua Fu (Li Teh), and Po Ku (Chin Pang-hsien). The Red Army forces were hurried off to march without preparation, their "elephantine columns" so slow they had constantly been attacked. Li Teh had stifled constructive criticism, labeled the correct suggestions "guerillaism"; Chin Pang-hsien had aided and abetted him.

Neither Li Teh nor Chin Pang-hsien accepted the criticism meted to them. Chou En-lai, who had taken the initiative in calling the meeting, took the initiative in self-criticism. Chou En-lai has never allowed considerations of his own self-esteem to stand in the way of the Revolution. This has been traduced as too ready a propensity to change sides and opinion. In reality it is a deep and humble dedication to his convictions. Chou is always the first to denounce his own mistakes. He now accused himself of having, while on the Military Commission, concurred in the wrong line, pushed the peasants to build fortifications. Had Mao's ideas been followed, the encirclement might have been beaten off and the base saved, said Chou, who then voluntarily withdrew from his post and suggested that Mao Tsetung take the leadership of the Military Commission. "He has been right all the time and we should listen to him." He moved the resolution that Mao Tsetung should take the leadership of operations.

Chang Wen-tien, one of the twenty-eight Bolsheviks, also recognized that Mao was right. Chu Teh blamed Li Teh for the losses incurred. It is not known whether the vote for Mao Tsetung was by a large or a slim majority; it probably was larger than expected because of Chou En-lai, the military commanders, who all wanted Mao Tsetung back, and some of the twenty-eight Bolsheviks group who voted for Mao.

The Tsunyi resolutions were published in a 1948 Chinese edition of Mao's *Selected Works;* they have not been reprinted publicly since. The Tsunyi conference eschewed questions of ideology, which might have brought about an undesirably prolonged session, a complicated ordeal lasting weeks, perhaps months. Thorough appraisal was postponed till seven years later, during the great Rectification campaign of 1941–1944.

The resolutions end on a note of unity, ardor, undying hope in the Revolution. "The enlarged conference . . . believes that the Chinese soviet revolution, because of its deep historical roots, cannot be destroyed or defeated." The "setback will not in the least shake our faith in the progress of the Chinese Revolution. . . . The Party has bravely exposed its own mistakes . . . it has educated itself through them." The dedication of the Red Army and the Communist Party was thus reaffirmed. Today Tsunyi, the meeting place of the conference, is one of the sacred spots of that monumental pilgrim's progress which is the Chinese Revolution.

Mao Tsetung was voted chairman of the new Revolutionary Military Council. He also became one of the secretaries of the new secretariat, with Chang Wen-tien as secretary of the Central Committee, and taking over the post of secretary-general from Chin Pang-hsien. As such Mao was still subordinate to Chang Wen-tien in the hierarchy; but he was reaffirmed as political commissar of the First Front Army. The military direction of the Long March would now be in his hands.

Mao Tsetung's long and dolorous spell in the minority seemed over; he was now the only savior and everyone knew it, including those who opposed him. Mao would say: "I have been in the minority myself. . . . The only thing for me to do at such times is . . . to wait." He would again be in the minority on further occasions. Nothing is less valid than a picture of Mao in absolute power ever since Tsunyi. "The minority is sometimes right" would be one of the tenets of the Great Proletarian Cultural Revolution. "The problem of who is right and who is wrong cannot in every case be judged by who has the majority."

On January 9 and 10, 1935, Mao Tsetung gathered the Military Commission, the instruction corps and the cadres of the Army at the elegant, monumental Catholic Church of Tsunyi; it provided a convenient hall for a large meeting. He explained the resolutions, although he gave no names and condemned no one by name. He defined the main tasks of the Red Army: to carry on propaganda among the masses, to organize and to educate them, to help them to establish a people's political government. He castigated the "purely military line," exhorted the Red Army to return to its original model, and told them the goal — "to march to the Northwest in order to fight Japan." The goal must have also been accepted at the enlarged meeting at Tsunyi, although it was not mentioned in the resolutions as published in 1948. A Tsunyi district revolutionary committee was established at a mass meeting of 10,000 on the 9th. "Only Communism can save China! Down with tyrants and evil gentry," read the slogans on the walls. The constitution of the soviet government at Juichin was again printed; a land reform movement was started in five districts and two counties round Tsunyi. Mao was photographed with the members of the revolutionary committee in Tsunyi, among them his old teacher Hsu Te-li.*

For twelve days the Army rested, reorganized. Morale was high. Mao Tsetung tightened discipline, looked into grievances. Divisions were reorganized, the arrangements of the columns of march simplified. Almost 4,000 recruits joined up. And then it was again time to move.

The "spirit of the Tsunyi conference" is said to have now permeated the 30,000 of the Red Army. Tsunyi was undoubtedly a turning point. Mao Tsetung had not moved against enemies; authority had come to him, and the initiative of power, through no trick but because his enemies had virtually destroyed the Party and Red Army. He was the only one qualified to lead.

To acquiesce is not to accept. The *political* overthrow of the "third left line" was yet to come; the sectarians were still extremely strong. Chin Pang-hsien had only made a very partial "self-criticism," but had also criticized Mao's lack of "proletarian internationalism." Liu Shao-chi, who also now criticized the "left line in the White areas" as leading to "almost 100 percent loss of cadres," had himself been found deficient in his work and enjoined to work along united front lines and arouse the students and workers in the White areas in resistance to Japan. He seems to have gone back to Northeast China from Tsunyi. The rank and file had no inkling of this intra-Party struggle; all they knew was that they were no longer in helpless flight. The Long March now became an epic, a succession of marvelous exploits, through the endurance, the courage, the unbending faith of many thousands of peasants and workers.

> *On the east, day breaks; do not*
> *Say we have started too early;*
> *For we shall cross many hills yet*
> *Before we grow old; here*
> *The land is surprising in beauty.*†

* Interviews and museum visit at Tsunyi by author, 1971.
† Poem (1934) by Mao Tsetung.

The Army set out northward "to fight Japan"; the decision ratified at Tsunyi to go northwest, actually made by Mao before the Long March, was to be carried out. They would cross Szechuan, Kansu, into Shensi province; there was a Red base in North Shensi, which was their goal.

But another struggle was to come. Chang Kuo-tao, who had now established a base in Szechuan, was a Politburo member and had been kept informed by radio of the Tsunyi conference resolutions. He sent back a radio message signifying his non-acceptance of the Tsunyi conference, though not in so many words. Nothing would ever be straightforward or plain in the course of the Chinese Revolution; nothing would ever be easy for Mao Tsetung, even when in authority. Chang Kuo-tao's long cable was couched in ideological terms; he felt that the whole policy of soviet bases was erroneous; the Long March was a great defeat; the CCP should withdraw, with its contingents, to a safe place such as Tibet or Sinkiang, and for the time being give up any attempt at struggle, as it was much too weak. He was himself organizing in his base a "soviet republic and government," and was prepared to welcome the Red Army coming from Tsunyi. This was a move to put himself in the position of chairman of the soviet republic, and to bypass or ignore the resolutions of Tsunyi.

There was a strong insistence by some members of the Politburo that a meeting with Chang Kuo-tao "to talk things over" should take place; some of them were even of the same opinion as Chang. The Red Army should "wait better days" rather than tackle the enormous military might of Japan.

In the meantime Chiang Kai-shek had not been inactive. The route northward into Szechuan was blocked with his troops; he sought to squeeze the Red Army between two rivers: the Wu, now at their back, and the Yangtze in the north, barring them from Szechuan. A pincer movement of mighty forces, his own and those of the militarists of Hunan, Yunnan, Szechuan, Kweichow and Kwangsi, was mobilized to crush the Red Army.

On January 22 the Military Council sent a radio message to Chang Kuo-tao asking him to move southward towards the Yangtze, to feint a threat to Chiang's forces, while the Red Army would attempt to enter Szechuan from the south. This would have caught Chiang's forces in a counter pincer movement and forced him to redeploy. But Chang Kuo-tao instead moved even farther north, refusing battle. This was, actually, his style of action. In 1933, when the

Oyuwan base had been overrun, Chang Kuo-tao had put up little resistance, had gone, and regrouped in Szechuan, leaving some troops in the base area. His first base in Szechuan he had also abandoned before a weak warlord attack.

The Red Army prepared to enter Szechuan by pretending not to enter it; the first principle of a successful commander being not to let the enemy know your intention. Mao made the regiments wheel and circle, adopting "sinuous lines of motion." No one could guess where their meandering course would lead them next. They launched agrarian revolutionary action, killing tyrannous landlords, burning land deeds and titles, distributing grain, opening jails, holding mass meetings with songs and dances and theatricals. Delegations of peasants came to ask the Red Army to "make a detour and come to liberate us from the landlords." Though fighting for their lives, they never forgot they were the great wind of Revolution, the educator of the people. There were no more punishments and purges, but discipline by exhortation, meetings, political sessions. A great joy buoyed up the armies; even many years later, veterans of the Long March would talk of these post-Tsunyi days with excitement. "Our hearts were light, Chairman Mao was in command. . . . He carried the Revolution's burden upon himself." And Mao wrote: "Infinite beauty lives upon the perilous peaks."

For fifteen weeks they twisted and turned and wound back on their tracks. Mao turned sharp west, crossed the Red river and went south to Tchasi in Yunnan; suddenly rushed east, crossed the Red river again, and on February 25 occupied Tungtze, attacking and capturing the famous Loushan pass in one swoop, and returned to Tsunyi on February 27. The second battle of Tsunyi was a great victory, twenty enemy regiments were destroyed.

The taking of Loushan pass was to elicit the following poem from Mao:

> *Do not say the strong pass is guarded with iron.*
> *This very day with firm step we shall cross its summit.*
> *We shall cross its summit!*
> *Here the hills are blue like the sea,*
> *And the dying sun like blood.*

It was another of these deceptive, feint-and-dart, sudden pounces which Mao learned from Sun Tze's *Art of War* and developed extensively throughout his war-strewn years.

Loushan pass, crossed by the Red Army on the Long March. Below, a Miao woman points out to the author the mountain paths through which she led the Red Army.

In March, still wheeling and circling and doubling, marching back in unexpected assaults, Mao divided his forces, sent a small contingent rushing up to the Yangtze as if about to cross it. This drew off the bulk of Chiang's armies, which they proceeded to exhaust by marching them up and down and up and down again at a rapid pace, sometimes covering over 30 miles in a day. The main force meanwhile wheeled south, smashing warlord forces, and once again crossed the Wu river southward, as if threatening the capital city of Kweichow province, Kweiyang. Chiang had installed himself in Kweiyang to direct operations. He called Yunnan troops to his aid, thus depleting the defenses of Yunnan province. As the Yunnan forces set out on the long, mountain-hacked march up to Kweichow to "protect" Chiang, another small contingent of the Red Army under Lin Piao literally ran 125 miles in three days, swooping suddenly into Yunnan itself, as if to attack Kunming, its capital. The outsmarted Chiang Kai-shek and his wife had just flown into Kunming to be sure the troops would move (warlords were wont to tarry unless supervised) when the news came: "The Red Army is arriving!" Panicky officials prepared to withdraw to Indochina; the Yunnan armies were called back. Meanwhile the bulk of the Red Army forces were crossing the Yangtze in its upper reaches, where it is called the River of Golden Sands, much farther west than they had been expected, and they were unhindered for a week. The crossing took nine days and nights, and the Kuomintang forces arrived only in the last two days. Such was the drive and imagination, the skill and elegance, the art of war of Mao Tsetung. And the Red Army laughed as the political instructors explained to them every step of what they were doing. "Chairman Mao always makes his enemies obey him."

By running 85 miles in a single day, Lin Piao and his small force also managed to return and to cross the Golden Sands river safely. Now they were in Szechuan, in another national minority region, among the Yi tribes.

"Two days after [the crossing] we reached the Yi region. . . . It was May. The fields were deserted and untilled. There were no rice fields, no farmhouses, only some rough shacks in the forest. . . . Soon after we entered a mountainous area a group of men and women in strange clothes appeared. . . . They shouted as they approached. Five tall women came out of the group, each carrying a big red cock in her arms. They approached Chairman Mao and surrounded him." Mao nodded his head, put his hands before his breast to show thankfulness. He never had a gun on him; he walked among the Yis unafraid. Some of the soldiers thought the cocks were for eating, "but we soon found out they were not. They were fighting cocks, house pets." Yi people then appeared on all the slopes, singing and welcoming; "it was a strange and moving sight that brought tears to our eyes." Again there was propaganda, theater shows and songs; about 200 men from the Kuchi-Yi tribe joined up. The Yis were "tall like the Tibetans, darkly aquiline; the younger men have smaller waists than the girls." The Red Army crossed ranges dense with camellias on the lower slopes, and went on.

A great psychological as well as physical ordeal was ahead — another river, the Tatu. Everyone was afraid of the Tatu. This was where the last of the heroic Taiping peasant rebels had been massacred in 1864. Here also enemy armies waited to pounce on them. Already Chiang had boasted that the Tatu would drown these "Red bandits" as it had drowned the last Taiping peasant rebels. The troops were apprehensive as they cut their way to the Tatu; they were quieter than usual. Above their heads the tall trees seemed suddenly threatening.

During the nearly 200-mile march between the Golden Sands and the Tatu, Mao kept up the spirits of the soldiers with droll stories, with laughter and jokes, which were repeated down the columns. He knew the soldiers' fear of becoming "water devils" — drowning — in the black swift waters of the Tatu. It was said the souls of the dead Taiping wailed here by night, lamenting their fate. "What if this happens to us?" . . . "This cannot happen to us, for we are revolutionaries. History has changed, we have changed it," Mao replied. "With Chairman Mao, even if purblind, we shall walk the straight road and not be afraid of death," the troops sang. "The past does not return," said Mao. They trusted him; for he was one of them, in comfort and discomfort, sharing every hardship, every emotion, leading them with songs and poems and laughing words. He ate the same rations and wore the same clothes; he only worked much harder; for while they slept he would sit up, by the light of a small kerosene lamp, working, planning, receiving messages, writing reports, giving orders. . . . He scarcely slept more than two or three hours at night, and not every night, during those months of the Long March.

They passed the Cool mountains, and marched 60 miles to the medieval town of Anshunchang, on the Tatu. At Anshunchang was a man-plied boat; it had to be towed by those naked rivermen whose lives were spent pulling boats against the swift current. Athwart the river, for four and a half miles against the current, the boat was pulled; it took hours, and only 50 men at a time could cross. How long would it take the Red Army? Many weeks. There was a bridge, however, across the Tatu, but over 90 miles away. Mao said: "We'll cross by boat *and* by bridge. We can do both." And he looked cheerful. "So we hacked our way another 90 miles through dense forest, while a small party of soldiers went by boat across to the other side, then, clinging to boulders along the other bank, walked along the river edge to reach the town of Luting, which had a strong garrison. Luting was at the head of the bridge on its western side. They would attack the garrison from behind while we would endeavor to cross the bridge from the east bank and do battle with the enemy from the front."

Luting bridge, over a mile long, consisted of thirteen enormous iron chains spanning the river, which 200 feet below, in the gorge it had hewn, coursed with the noise of "ten thousand racing horses." "When we arrived it was four in the afternoon. We had hacked our way through dense brush, never stopping, for three nights. We had no torches; who fell behind we could not wait for. We had run part of the way; for we knew we must take the bridge and get there in time. The fate of the whole Red Army depended on our taking the bridge.

"We had twenty-two volunteers to take Luting bridge. The Kuomintang in the garrison town of Luting had removed all the planks to the halfway point, over half a mile. They had not bothered with the other half, their own side. Our men had to cross by swinging on the iron chains, hand over hand, under heavy machine gun fire. The Kuomintang could scarcely believe their eyes. Who would have thought the Reds would insanely try to cross on the chains alone? But that is what they did. Seventeen of the first batch of 22 died, their bodies fell in the torrent, others took their place. The Red Army screamed, we all shouted, as if Heaven would tear, as one of ours got to the mid-bridge where the planks were left, uncapped a grenade, and ran and tossed it among the enemy soldiers. They set fire to the planks, but it was too late. More of our men had swung like tree apes, got to the planks; they rushed the garrison post through the flames. And suddenly there was shouting and gunfire as the small force that had crossed by boat attacked the enemy from behind. They panicked and surrendered. Thus we took Luting bridge in two hours, and the town was ours. We borrowed doors from the people; they were civil and good to us. We put the doors down on the chains, as planks, and the Red Army crossed. But our rear fought another big battle, as the Kuomintang arrived behind us. History did not repeat itself. We conquered the Tatu river. Some of the

Luting bridge over the Tatu river. Red Army men swung from the chains under fire to cross and capture it from Kuomintang troops during the Long March.

local people said the souls of the dead Taiping would no longer wail at night, they were revenged." It was May 25, 1935.*

Now they were in the high mountain ranges that run like giant stairs up and up, to Tibet; the parallel summits towered, the vast glittering ocean of icecaps of Tibet spread a marvelous, dizzying whiteness — a new world the soldiers had never dreamed of. Most of the men were southerners, or Szechuanese from the hot dank plains. They had no warm clothes. Mao told the men to boil hot chilies and ginger in water and drink it to keep warm. He climbed with them, slipping in the snow, his gray trousers wet through, his feet numb. "The snow has confiscated my feet," he said. They were to cross the great Snow mountains at 16,000 feet, many died of exposure. Hundreds fell down and never got up. Some died in the snow, and others of exhaustion and pneumonia and heart failure. A woman (there were now thirty-five of them) who had given birth to a baby and placed it in a basket on a mule's back saw the basket overturn as the mule slipped, the baby fell out and down the precipice and sank into the deep snow. No one could find it again.

The men were heavily burdened as they carried ten days' food supply and fuel. Mao told the soldiers of a mountain in Hunan called the Eight-faced, whose rocks are blue in the rain. The people say it is so high that " 'Men have to bow their heads, horses must have their saddles taken off; for it is three-foot-three from the sky.' 'How can a mountain be so high?' we asked, and Chairman Mao said: 'Are we not crossing such high mountains, and yet no one will be afraid, for the Red Army can do anything.' So we made a song about it, that the Red Army fears neither mountains nor rivers." Mao would write poems on the mountains:

> *Mountains, O mountains,*
> *I urge my swift horse, unmoving as it gallops,*
> *Lift my head, surprised that Heaven*
> *Is three-foot-three above me.*
>
> *Mountains,*
> *Untamed seas, churning tides, roll their waves,*
> *An onslaught*
> *Like a myriad steeds in the ecstasy of battle.*
>
> *Peaks,*
> *Needling blue heaven with lucid spear points,*
> *Bearing space upon their slopes.*

* Personal interview with Long Marcher, 1971.

Crossing the Snow mountains on the Long March.

In July they finally arrived at Moukung, deep in West Szechuan, where Chang Kuo-tao was established. The thousands of miles, the battles, the ambushes (for they had been ambushed by tribes, uttering war cries and rolling boulders to crush them and flinging spears) seemed over. They recalled how one-eyed Liu Po-cheng had sealed a treaty of friendship with some Yis by drinking chicken blood with their chief; how they had released from jail 200 Yis imprisoned for years because they had not supplied enough young girls for the Kuomintang. They had composed songs and made jokes, such as "catching the number 11 bus," to mean a long walk that day. Now they felt almost at the end of the journey, among comrades, fellow Red Army soldiers. For here, advancing towards them, were soldiers from the Fourth Front Army, holding large banners on which were inscribed: "Let us expand the revolutionary base of Northwest Szechuan!" Rain was pouring down. The soldiers rushed to each other's arms, embraced and wept. "We were only about twenty thousand left." *

Mao Tsetung and Chu Teh, huddled in their rags under a tarpaulin, waited for Chang Kuo-tao to appear. He came sitting on his horse and surrounded by thirty guards, all on horseback. "They were all stocky, fat men, faces red with good eating, sitting on fat, beautiful oily horses . . . we looked at them, our mouths watered . . . such beautiful horses! Chairman Mao laughed and said to us: 'Don't envy the horses!' " Mao and Chu went forward in the rain to meet Chang Kuo-tao, who did not even come halfway to them, but sat on his horse, waiting, and then "dismounted slowly."

The men who had arrived were emaciated; they crawled with lice and scabies; they were hungry and looked like a crew of beggars; but they were elated, thinking their troubles at an end. Chang stared at them and did not see their eyes, only their rags. A famine-stricken mob, some could scarcely stand up. In his memoirs, the whole of his vocabulary at this point is impregnated with paternalism. Not a word about the ordeals they had endured. The man who in 1923 had written that "peasants . . . are not interested in politics . . . only in big harvests and an emperor" now thought that with his 50,000 men, well armed and well nourished, he was far stronger than the newcomers, a scarecrow pack of 20,000 ghosts.

Since their first encounter in 1918 at Peking University, friendship had not blossomed between Chang and Mao. Chang had been to

* Interviews with Long Marchers. Official historians say there were 45,000, but this is not correct.

Russia, was an expert in Russian — had he not translated Stalin's messages in 1927? — had been a leader in the All-China Labor Federation along with Liu Shao-chi and Li Li-san, was a founding member of the CCP, member of the Politburo, vice-chairman at the Central Base. His seniority in the Party, he felt, should be duly recognized. Chang insists on the many courtesies he used; he writes that he was criticized for his formal, old-fashioned good manners * — surely an extraordinary thing to bring up at that moment. But the substance of their veiled enmity was not only personal; above all it was a question of policy and power. With military strength on his side — and the military factor weighs heavily in the Chinese context — Chang Kuo-tao felt he could impose his views; and his views, however rational they appeared, were motivated by concern for his own power base.

Two conferences were held, and many smaller meetings. Chang professed to doubt the whole course of the Revolution, did not agree with the decision to go north to fight Japan, considered the Tsunyi conference "arbitrary." Mao thought the Long March a success; Chang thought it a failure and urged a compromise solution with the Kuomintang. He wanted an entente with Chiang, incorporating the Red Army in a "national" army of Chiang; there would be, he argued, place for "national-minded officers" in Chiang's army. While negotiating the entente, a safe base had been established by him, here in West Szechuan. He suggested Mao go further inland, into Tibet or Sinkiang. The Soviet Union would help with supplies; there had been a message from the Comintern by radio suggesting the establishment of bases inland. . . .

Mao knew well what Comintern advice now meant. Since 1932 Wang Ming, back in Moscow, on the prestigious executive committee of the Comintern, had been making "revolution by telegraph." He had written, or rewritten, the reports from the base, adding his own bombast; sent "resolutions and directives" back to the base. Li Teh (Otto Braun, Hua Fu) was to be mentioned as a "correspondent of the Comintern on the Long March with the Red Army" under yet another pseudonym, M. Fred. He would write on July 20 a report which made no mention of the Tsunyi meeting or of Mao's having become chairman of the Revolutionary Military Council.

Chang's plans were contrary to Mao's. What was the purpose and aim of the Red Army, of the Communist Party, if not to promote

---

* Chang Kuo-tao's memoirs, *Ming Pao* magazine monthly, 1966–1968, Hongkong.

revolution, to fight Japan? The outlook on any event was itself a decisive factor in molding it. The Communists were confronting new, unpredictable situations. Mao maintained that a close study of the situation would reveal that it was excellent (this produced a sensation, and some guffaws, we may presume, on the part of Chang Kuo-tao).

Mao Tsetung went on, analyzing, explaining the way he saw events. The decision made to fight Japan had been correct. An anti-Japanese united front was already in potentio, among the broad masses of the people. It lacked only leadership; it would be created, but never by surrender to Chiang Kai-shek, accepting high official posts. The Communist leaders would be neutralized and massacred if they disarmed. The Long March was a success, the slogans no chimerical assertion. Chang stared at the gaunt, almost spectral Mao. "This, to speak of taking on the colossal military power of Japan!" Mao posed the question the way he had asked it of Chen Tu-hsiu, way back in 1927: "To run away, to hide, or to lead?" The leadership of the national patriotic movement *must* be the task of the Communist Party, who was alone capable of it. Chiang Kai-shek would soon find his supine acquiescence to Japanese aggression impossible — the people were against him; they wanted resistance; even warlords, even his own generals, were in revolt against him. There could be no withdrawal to await better times in the westward areas of China where the population was sparse, unable to sustain a large army, and where, above all, they could never be in touch with the large masses of the Chinese people or exercise an effective influence on events. To withdraw to Tibet or to Sinkiang was to shirk one's revolutionary duty, and to become a "warlord" preying on hostile national minorities.

The meetings at Lianghekou and Maoerhkai were extremely bitter; at one point Mao Tsetung won the majority vote for his plan. The march would be continued. It would go to North Shensi, to the small Red base there under Liu Chih-tan. This was the nearest point to counter the Japanese offensives which were developing in that direction.

Mao Tsetung would later say that the struggle with Chang Kuo-tao, which is included in the two-line struggle so perpetual within the Party, was one of the most difficult, searing episodes in his life, "the darkest moment." This shows the extent and the gravity not only of the verbal disputes, but of the danger which they ran, only avoided through a combination of firmness and diplomacy. For it was only too obvious that Chang held the upper hand where strength and fire-power were concerned, and would not hesitate to use it once he had been able to win over enough of the Politburo to his way of thinking to produce a vote against Mao Tsetung. And when we think back to the relations of the members of the Politburo with Mao, and what had happened at Tsunyi, we can see that Chang Kuo-tao had a good many high cards in his hand. Chang's arguments also would appear very tempting to many tired with the battles, the hunger, and dubious about the future. In the position they were in, the plans of Mao did appear to some too grandiose, utopian. Chang Kuo-tao tried his best to win Chu Teh to his view. Chu Teh was a Sze-chuanese; with Chu Teh and Chang Kuo-tao together, Chang would be able to rally a great many Szechuanese to his base. He already had about 35,000 Szechuan recruits among his troops. And there is nothing Szechuan people dislike more than to leave their province.

But for Mao, provincial considerations, even if they existed, were to be combated. He had been successful in mixing soldiers from many provinces together, and he continued to do so. It was a choice, he said, between abandoning the people of China, the workers and peasants, and their heroic struggle, or going on, irrespective of personal sacrifice. And Mao Tsetung's choice would be the Revolution. The dangled prospect of a comfortable "western paradise," a shelter safe from attack, the flattery of "high official posts" under Chiang, repelled him.

On August 1, 1935, the Revolutionary Military Council issued a very long, 81-article proclamation to the nation, approved by the Politburo and entitled: *Appeal to Fellow Countrymen Concerning Resistance to Japan and National Salvation.* Its appearance on Army Day, August 1, was symbolic of the determination to fight Japan; it offered a "united front" with other forces willing to resist Japanese aggression. This reaffirmed the Tsunyi decision.*

At the end of August or early September, the march resumed. The armies were to be divided in two columns: the eastern or left,

---

* It is now said that the text contains some "left opportunist" errors (dubbed "right" opportunism, in the constant paradox that what is ultra-left actually benefits reaction). The Seventh Congress of the Comintern in Moscow (July–August 1935) on August 2 approved "the initiative taken by our courageous brother Party of China in the creation of a most extensive anti-imperialist united front." Stalin, too, had now for several months been thinking of a united front against the Axis powers. But what the Russians and the Comintern meant and what Mao meant were different, as the future would show. This is probably why the August 1, 1935 proclamation is now criticized. An official Comintern declaration on united front policy would appear on August 20.

the western or right. Each column held 30,000 to 35,000 men. The right column was composed of the First and Third Army Corps of the First Front Army, together with the Fourth and Thirtieth armies of the Fourth Front Army (Chang Kuo-tao's forces). The left column was composed of the Fifth and Ninth army corps of the First Front Army, and the Thirty-first and Thirty-second armies of the Fourth Front Army. There was thus a balance of both Front armies in each column. It is not far-fetched to think this was done to effect a deliberate equilibrium, so that there would be "more unity." There were more than suspicions now that Chang Kuo-tao might attempt a military action upon the much weaker, much less well-armed First Front Army; that he might capture the Politburo and Mao, and declare himself sole leader of Party and Army. Chang Kuo-tao throughout the bitter disputes had not only affected to doubt the legality of the Tsunyi enlarged meeting, but pressed claims to becoming secretary-general of the Party. But what was even more sinister, he had refused to use his very well-equipped troops to do battle against massing Kuomintang forces in the Sungpan region northeast of his base. The Sungpan region was precisely the one that Mao Tse-tung, who was leading the right column, would have to cross. Chiang of course had guessed that Mao would attempt to go north, and he had made preparations. But the troops he had at Sungpan were not his best; these were in reserve in a second line of defense higher up in Kansu province. Chang argued that the Kuomintang were too strong, and he would not risk his troops. He does not explain how he purposed to cross, *unless* battle was given.

Heading the right column then were Mao, Chou En-lai, and most of the Politburo. Hsu Hsiang-chien, the commander of that portion of the Fourth Front Army (the bulk of it) with Chang Kuo-tao, commanded the Chang troops which were also in Mao's column. In the west column Chang Kuo-tao led, and Chu Teh and Liu Po-cheng were with him, in charge of the First Front Army elements that were included.

According to some reports, this division was planned by Chu Teh. According to others, it was Yeh Chien-ying who kept an eye on the developments, and who later was to inform Mao of Chang's plan to make a surprise attack if possible.

The Mao-led right column was to cross the Sungpan region, which Chang Kuo-tao had deemed so dangerous. In spite of the month of rest, the men were still very weak. And now they had to battle their way through. They had been quartered in an area inhabited by Tibetans; the latter had fled because of Kuomintang threats that they would be all put to death if they helped the Red Army. Mao Tsetung forbade the troops to take anything from the empty houses, and some were shot for infringing discipline. The soldiers had found fields of barley, harvested the barley for the absent villagers, piled it for them, and left money for the portions they took. "But we did not get any rice, nor meat, nor salt." Lack of salt tormented them, and they had great trouble digesting barley. A young soldier proceeded to boil some fresh pigskins he found in a house: a soup "with a wonderful smell." Bristles and all, Mao partook of this "banquet and said it was delicious . . . he had not had anything decent to eat for months." This taught the soldiers "how to boil and eat leather" when they crossed the Great Marshes.

The two columns set off, Mao aiming towards Sungpan, and reaching the Great Marshes a few days later. Chang Kuo-tao's column started west of Mao's, from the Apa region, The marshes were an enormous extent of submerged steppe, with treacherous bogs which sucked in those who stepped in them. This crossing was to be one of the most terrible experiences of the Long March.

There is great confusion about what really happened, a confusion which even the recent questioning of sixteen Long Marchers does not dispel.*

Chang Kuo-tao's version is that Mao was ahead and to the right of him and succeeded in crossing a river (the Ke Ho, a part of the Yellow river). Chang however found the river flooded, though he was in its upper reaches. At the same time Chang was being attacked by a big Kuomintang force. Chang declared the river could not be crossed, then ordered his column back south, to Apa. But this version does not explain why he also ordered the portion of his armies which were in Mao's column to turn back. Without waiting for him, writes Chang Kuo-tao, Mao, in his typical "savage" way, left by night, "sudden as the whirlwind." Chang's troops in the right column were "abandoned." There was nothing for them to do but to turn back, or be massacred by the Kuomintang. Mao Tsetung, as usual, said not a word, preferring the judgment of "the practice of revolution," which is history.

Chou En-lai told Edgar Snow that there was indeed a Kuomintang attack. This is correct, since Mao did score a victory over the Kuomintang troops at the edge of the Great Marshes at Sungpan.

* The author interviewed sixteen Long Marchers from various participating armies.

Otherwise, Chou En-lai proved as reticent as Mao. Chu Teh's wife, who was with Chu Teh in Chang Kuo-tao's column, mentions the flood which separated the columns and "forced us to spend the winter in Tibet eating horse, yak, mutton." Participants' reports shed some light. "We were in Mao Tsetung's column. Suddenly we received an order to go south again, back to Szechuan. Some of us were happy. 'We'll go back and eat good rice.' We heard that in the north there was nothing to eat. We were told that going back, we would make all Szechuan Red. So we turned back and left the column. We went back through the marshes." This is from a soldier of the Fourth Front Army who was in Mao's column. By that time, they had already crossed the Great Marshes.

Another testimony from a man of the First Front Army in Chang Kuo-tao's column: "There was no flooded river; and anyway, we had forded so many rivers we were not afraid. Yes, there were attacks, but no more than we were accustomed to. But Chang Kuo-tao would not fight. His soldiers, who were with us in the same column for over a year after we were made to turn back with them, told us: 'We have such a big army, but we never fight; even at Oyuwan we abandoned the base without any real fighting.' " The soldiers did not like this kind of "walking without aim all over the earth" without a battle.

Another, from a political instructor of the Fourth Front Army who elected to stay with Mao in the right column: "We were told: 'We go back to establish a big base in Szechuan.' . . . I was in the Fourth Front Army, but in Chairman Mao's column. When the order came, many went back but I followed Mao Tsetung."

The left column, and the larger part of the right column, all returned through the marshes to Szechuan. These who returned thus crossed the terrible marshes three times, for they would make the same journey a year later.

But another story must be mentioned. This concerns Yeh Chien-ying, then chief of staff, who was with Mao. Yeh got wind of a Chang Kuo-tao plan to get rid of Mao, not only by allowing him to fight against the massed Kuomintang forces, which were waiting for them on the other side of the marshes, but also by attacking him from behind. Whether this plan could have been carried out or not we do not know. But this might explain why Mao, "sudden as the whirlwind," decided to push forward, preferring battle with the Kuomintang to internecine war. It would also explain why Mao told Edgar Snow later that this had been one of the "darkest" moments in his life. Chang, knowing his plans discovered, then gave the orders to his soldiers to return. But he would have gone back anyway; he had no intention of fighting the Japanese or of going north. He did what he had intended to do all along — turn back.

When Chang Kuo-tao turned back, he took Chu Teh, the commander-in-chief, and Liu Po-cheng with him. Another problem, much publicized during the Great Proletarian Cultural Revolution, when these historical questions were debated by young Red Guards (sometimes with nonhistorical exaggerations) is the following. What really was Chu Teh's attitude at this critical juncture? Did he go with Chang Kuo-tao of his own free will, as Chang asserts; or was he forced to go "at gun point," as he himself told Agnes Smedley; or was he just unable to make up his mind?

Chang asserts that Chu Teh was "indignant at Mao's flight." Chu Teh's situation may perhaps be explained by the fact that he was not at all sure what he wanted to do. On the one hand, he might have been much tempted to remain in Szechuan, his own province. He would be sure to organize a successful base there, knowing the people. He may also genuinely have thought that the northward advance was an error. On the other hand, he was not the willing tool of Chang Kuo-tao, but he did not wish to see a battle between two Red armies. Chu Teh's life shows that he was brave and unafraid, but not always capable of cool, measured judgment. He had launched himself on military adventures before: at Chingkangshan and the Juichin base; he had not always seen eye to eye with Mao Tsetung. But it is certain that the man was in a great dilemma, and thought it best to avoid a bloody conflict. He was not happy during the whole year that he was with Chang Kuo-tao, and never denounced Mao Tsetung as Chang asked him to do.

The net outcome was that Mao was left with less than 8,000 men; 22,000 or more of the original column turned back. Liu Po-cheng and the Fifth and Eighth Army Corps also went with Chu Teh. "At Pahsi, where the marshes ended and we entered the steppes, higher ground with long grass, we saw our comrades from the Fourth Front Army retracing their steps, dragging themselves in long files back through the marshes. We were quite amazed. We asked Chairman Mao: 'Why are they going back?' They were shouting: 'We go back to establish a Red base in Szechuan.' But some said: 'We go back to eat good rice.' "

"Here where we were it was desolate; sightless the sky hit the long grass. There were stables with cows; the walls were of cow dung and clay. Of course Chairman Mao did not allow us to touch the cows; the people had fled, we could not take their possessions. We looked at Chairman Mao's face; we could see he was very upset as he watched our comrades filing back, weary, going back through the marshes. It seemed endless, their going away. Of course we were tempted; for in front of us were many mountains, and a big battle; and now we all knew there would be no rice to eat in the North; they just did not grow rice there, and we were Southerners, we all had dysentery; many of our comrades died of it."

"Chairman Mao said: 'Let them go.' He even told the comrades who left him to look after themselves. At Pahsi we held a big meeting and Chairman Mao asked us: 'Do you want to go back?' We looked at him; he had been with us all the time, and he had walked with us. He never used the stretcher we had prepared for him; he gave it to the wounded. We shouted: 'We never go back! We go forward with you!' So Chairman Mao said: 'The others will return. They will return to us, and we'll clear the way for them, we'll prepare the road for their return.' So we prepared for battle, and we fought very well."

This was the battle of Latzekou, the Waxy Mouth pass, a mountain pass held by 40,000 troops of Hu Tsung-nan, Chiang Kai-shek's best commander. The Red Army fought with knives and cutlasses, they hurled themselves at the cavalry, the Kansu horsemen Hu Tsung-nan used to trample them down. "We cut them to pieces. Nothing could stop us any more. We fought all night and at dawn we took the pass."

The memory of the terrible marshes is gashed in the minds of thousands of Long Marchers (over 3,000 are still alive today).* "They spread, an immense somber shoreless ocean of mud, a desert of water; swamps which sucked us down, with clumps of bushy grass here and there, and little bits of firm land; there was only one trail. Those that went forward marked it by a white rope of goat's hair. And then one day it snowed, we could not find the rope again. We moved snow with our bare hands for hours. The rope was our lifeline."

They attempted to get guides. "The local inhabitants shot at us whenever they could. But we managed to get some guides. They alone knew the way across the marshes. But they wanted meat to eat, and money. They insisted on a very high price. And they would

---

* Including members of Chang Kuo-tao's Fourth Front Army interviewed by the author.

not walk. We had to carry them in palanquins. Six men carried them; and sometimes the men stumbled. The guides knew they could ask for anything."

There was no food. Three times a day the weather changed; from pale bleak sun "like a moon" to rain to hail to snow and back again to wind; the mud froze on the men; they could not sleep; they sat back to back, in mushroom clumps, and dozed at night. They ate wild grass, weeds; discovered a small bush with some cherry-like fruit; a sweet turnip which poisoned them. They were stricken with terrible dysentery. "We ate the barley we had taken with us; it was raw, we could not digest it; it went through us and came out the same." The "little ones," the children of twelve to fifteen who went on the Long March, were wonderful. "They joined the instructors; they were always in front. They washed the sores of the men, woke at night to count the soldiers, hunted for berries, went ahead with the cadres, and stood with them singing by the path and marking the time with wood clappers. We sang? Of course we did. We sang: "Oh leather is delicious to eat." We boiled leather belts, sliced the leather up and chewed it. The water stank."

They were also shot at and ambushed, repeatedly, by Tibetans and the Kansu Hui cavalrymen who attacked them. "They came from the rear and many comrades died. We could not see the horsemen in time, especially when we reached the tall grass of the steppes. We fought, and we even captured some horses.

"Sometimes we vacillated in our minds: which death was better, poisoning, sucked in the mud, or to be shot at? We must have eaten every kind of weed or grass or root in the marshes." Their legs were covered with big gnawing ulcers. They stepped on the corpses of those who died before them. A woman who crossed the marshes three times told me: "I walked and something squeaked under my foot. I parted the dense weeds and my foot was in a dead man's face. I still dream of it."

We do not know how many died in the Great Marshes, nor how many died fighting their way out of them. "It was all one great battle, one ceaseless struggle." But there was, after Waxy Mouth pass and its battle, another mountain range, the Liupan, which Mao crossed. On the crest they found a stone inscription: "Dividing the water's crest." Here was the border between Kansu province, where they had battled the Hui horsemen, and Shensi province, their destination. On the slopes they rested a short while; it was October, very bleak and cold; around them bare bare mountains and chasms. This was the loess land, the thick yellow earth brought down by the Yellow river, folded and wrinkled, an enormous grand canyon spreading hundreds of thousands of square miles. People lived in caves scooped in the loess cliffs. "We've crossed ten provinces and we're entering the eleventh," said Mao, all smiles.

The summit passes of the Liupan are reached after six twists, by narrow paths, rock-strewn. Hence its name of Liupan — six twists. It was the 7th of October. Far out could be guessed the Great Wall, which straddled the mountains on its gigantic march to the deserts of Central Asia. Mao's happiness expressed itself in verse:

> *High is the sky and clear the clouds.*
> *The eye follows the wild goose winging southward.*
> *If we do not reach the Great Wall, we are not men.*
> *Already we count on our fingers a march of 20,000 lis.*
> *On the crest of Liupan our banners waft in the west wind.*
> *Today we hold in our hands the long rope to bind the dragon.*
> *When shall we bind fast the gray dragon?*

The gray dragon was a constellation of seven stars, representing Japan. Mao, contemplating the great stretch of North China before him, saw it already in terms of the battles to come, not as a period of rest, a haven of refuge. It was this extraordinary prescience which seemed so exaggerated to "reasonable" men; and who could have guessed that the 7,000 with him, a nothingness in the vast ocean of China, contemplating the denuded, desolate winter canyons in front of them, would indeed take on the great military power of Japan, after the murderous year they had endured? It looked like sheer rodomontade. It was history in the making.

"But we had more battles before us. For below the Liupan pass, once again, the plain was gray and brown with the cavalry of the warlord Ma Hung-kwei. We fought. Of course we won. The horses and the men screamed as we charged."

On October 20 they reached Wuchichen, a small county in North Shensi. "We arrived in the twilight. Suddenly there was the sound of gongs and drums and timbrels. . . . a crowd to welcome us, to welcome Chairman Mao. Like a small sea they came up in the darkness, crying: 'Welcome, welcome, long live Chairman Mao. Long live the Chinese Communist Party.' We wept."

The Long March was ended for the 7,000 with Mao Tsetung. In the same uniform with which he had started, tattered and thick with dirt, Mao stood, coatless. Then up came Hsu Hai-tung, commander of the Fifteenth Red Army Corps, who had been delegated to meet the Long Marchers. "Thank you for taking so much trouble to come and meet us," said Mao Tsetung. Then they were both silent, because there was too much to say.

After its arrival in Wuchichen in North Shensi, the Army took stock of its achievements. It had trudged 7,500 miles. It had crossed eighteen mountain ranges and twenty-four rivers; walked through eleven provinces; sixty-two cities and towns had been taken by assault and occupied. It had broken through ten provincial warlord armies, and fought, outmaneuvered, and beaten one million men of the Kuomintang armies of Chiang Kai-shek. It had also crossed six national minorities areas.

"Speaking of the Long March, what is its significance? We answer that the Long March is the first of its kind in the annals of history, that it is a manifesto, a propaganda force, a seeding machine. . . . It has proclaimed to the world that the Red Army is an army of heroes. It has announced to some 200 million people in eleven provinces that the road of the Red Army is their only road to liberation . . . The Long March . . . has sown many seeds which will sprout, leaf, blossom and bear fruit, and will yield a harvest in the future." *

Mao Tsetung's poem on the Long March, given to Edgar Snow in 1936, is worth quoting:

> *The Red Army fears not these prodigious distant campaigns;*
> *A thousand mountains, ten thousand rivers, they look upon*
> *   as pleasantly usual*
> *The tortuous Five ranges are but ripples they leap;*
> *The dread crests of Wumeng, mud dumps under their heels.*
> *Warm are the fog-wrapped cliffs lapped by the Golden Sands*
> *   river;*
> *Cold were the iron chains spanning the Tatu stream.*
> *How much laughter amid the unending snows of Minshan;*
> *And when the Three Armies had crossed, smiles were on all*
> *   their faces.†*

From Apa, when the columns came back, Chang Kuo-tao rode southward to Chu Kechi, a town with many Tibetan lama temples and great landlords, and there called a meeting. At the meeting,

* *On Tactics Against Japanese Imperialism*, December 27, 1935. *Selected Works of Mao Tsetung* (English edition Peking 1961–1965), vol. I.

† The "Three Armies" are the First, Second and Fourth Front armies. Mao included in his poem the two Front armies which would reach Shensi and reunite the forces in 1936.

packed with his adherents, he condemned Mao's "sudden departure" which had "broken the unity of action" of the Red Army and the Party. He says that the meeting accused Mao of "defeatism and guerillaism" (sic). Chang Kuo-tao got a subaltern to denounce the "bogus Central Committee and Politburo," product of the enlarged Tsunyi conference. He called for a plenum of all Party representatives in the whole of China to select a new Central Committee. Until the plenum was held, no orders from the "so-called Central Committee" should be obeyed. Meanwhile, a "temporary Central Committee" of which he became (reluctantly, according to his memoirs) secretary-general, was organized at Chu Kechi. A cable was sent to the North Shensi base, saying that although it was decided no longer to recognize the Central Committee with Mao, "yet military action could still be taken in concert to preserve unity." A military council, with Chu Teh as commander-in-chief and Chang Kuo-tao as chairman, became the "supreme authority over all the armies." A new soviet base (called the Szechuan-Sikang base) would now be established. A Confederacy of the National Minorities government was proclaimed as a soviet republic. Reports of these proceedings were sent to Moscow.

Thus Chang Kuo-tao tried to establish his claim to head the Chinese Communist Party. A "special independent government of the minorities" was then established by him in Kangting, capital of Sikang province, nearest to Tibet, where he now directed himself and his troops for the winter. It was an area sparsely inhabited by Tibetans and Han people, and famous only for its production of opium. The armies were an enormous burden on the population. Chang Kuo-tao was unable to turn his men into a production force. Mao Tsetung had warned him that the establishment of bases in the national minorities area was hopeless, and actually an exploiting, warlord device. The people were too few; the cultivation of land difficult, the soldiers could not communicate, did not speak the same language. A long history of oppression by the Han emperors, and by the Kuomintang, made the national minorities hostile. Chang Kuo-tao's armies survived on the sale of opium. The armies turned into a warlord army. Desertions and disease dwindled their numbers.

Mao Tsetung and the Central Committee sent telegrams exhorting Chang Kuo-tao to come to North Shensi and to join them. Then in June 1936, the Second Front Army of Ho Lung arrived in Sikang. This Second Front Army was the one which Li Teh had tried so hard to reach and merge with. It had had its own checkered career.

Ho Lung, an erstwhile Kuomintang militarist, like Peng Teh-huai, had joined the Communists and participated in the seizure of Nanchang on August 1, 1927.* He had then established a base in Northwest Hunan, his native province, later combined with another one to form the West Hunan-Hupei border area. Chiang Kai-shek had overrun it in the summer of 1934. Ho Lung withdrew to Northeast Kweichow, where he controlled about four counties, and was joined on the way by some of the guerilla troops under Hsiao Ke, Wang Chen, and Jen Pi-shih, who had broken out of the Central Base in the summer of 1934. Jen Pi-shih, who continued to be in contact with Mao, had become the political commissar of Ho Lung's Second Front Army. In the spring of 1935 the Second Front Army was driven out of its Kweichow counties and went back to Hunan; was pushed out of Hunan and, doubling back on its tracks, using much the same route as Mao Tsetung had done, went through Kweichow into Sikang, arriving at Chang Kuo-tao's base in June 1936. It was in poor shape when it arrived. "We had to give them food, clothes, everything." The scarcity felt in the base was now greatly increased by the additional burden of 20,000 Second Front Army men. Disputes arose. Jen Pi-shih then came forward with the suggestion that the armies join Mao's base in Northwest Shensi province. Chu Teh heartily concurred.

It is said also that Lin Yu-ying, Lin Piao's uncle, had been sent by Mao to Jen Pi-shih, to convey this delicate and important task in persuasion. Jen Pi-shih persuaded Ho Lung, and Chu Teh and Liu Po-cheng backed Jen Pi-shih. In July 1936 the Fourth and Second Front armies left Sikang, to walk north on their own Long March.

Nieh Jung-chen was sent by a happy Mao and Chou, with half the battle force then existing in North Shensi, to clear a way through enemy forces for the advancing armies. In October 1936, exactly a year after Mao's arrival, the reunion took place at Hui Ning, not far from Lanchow, capital city of Kansu province. The soldiers threw their arms round each other, laughing and weeping at once. "Chu Teh was thin as a ghost, but Chang Kuo-tao was fat and smooth. . . . I wonder how he kept so fat." †

Chang Kuo-tao had not given in happily. On the way, he thought up another scheme. Another wrangle took place with Chu Teh, Ho

---

* See chapter 9.

† Dr. Ma Haiteh, also known as George Hatem, an American doctor who joined the Red Army in 1936, when he was in China, a well-kept secret only lately revealed. Dr. Ma reached the North Shensi base early in 1936.

Lung, and Jen Pi-shih; Chang decided to go off to Sinkiang and establish a base there, in close proximity to the USSR. This absurdity proved him impervious to geography, logistics, or common sense. Singkiang was a great desert area, with less than five inhabjtants per square mile, strung in chains of oases. The area was quite unsuited for a base. Chang went off, crossed the Yellow river, and followed the Kansu corridor westward to Singkiang. The troops with him were cut to pieces, the worst battle occurring at the foot of the Great Wall. Only about 2,000 survived . . . to be picked up in May 1937 by Mao's rescue squads and taken back to Shensi. Chang himself once more escaped, to return to Lanchow in time to rejoin the Second Front Army trekking towards Shensi, and arrive with them at Hui Ning.

Chang Kuo-tao had destroyed his own army, and would now proceed to destroy himself politically. Like many of Mao's enemies, he worked at his own downfall by his own means. None of the commanders or units which had turned back with him were castigated; some hold very high positions today.* Mao Tsetung did not raise a finger against Chang Kuo-tao, but it is impossible for those who have failed through their own faults to forgive. In the long, protracted, blood-filled history of the Chinese Revolution, Chang Kuo-tao's place is not with those who died to serve their people, but with those who lived to betray themselves.

* For example, Li Hsien-nien, vice-premier, and Chen Chih-fang, who is ambassador to Switzerland.

PART II

1

The Yenan Period—
The Second United Front

On the Long March, Mao endured both physical hardship and mental strain. Daily staff and military conferences, marching plans for so many thousands; documents to read and decide upon, couriers galloping or running to him every hour of the day or night, urgent decisions, sudden attacks, the care of the immense cohort moving shaggily yet swiftly, enemy-surrounded, meant very little sleep, constant alertness, lucid decisions, and a mastery of the situation which no mere theory could encompass. Mao worked anywhere — on bare rock, with a wooden plank for a table; a small kerosene lamp or a candle lighted him as he pored over papers. Above him an oilcloth stretched to shield his work from the rain. He moved up and down the lines of singing men, among the disarray of sleeping soldiers lying tentless on the ground. He watched the troops wind across the mountain slopes, a giant snake procession, for fifty miles. Concerned with the numerous wounded, he would send scouts to look for native medicinal herbs. He questioned the political instructors, whom he called in conference, on the problems of each unit, rallying the weary, sending doctors, nurses, stretcher-bearers where needed. And he also delegated authority and responsibility, inciting others to initiative and selflessness, so that as the march went on, he trained and inspired scores of young men throughout the Army who would become a generation of potential leaders.*

And all this time, like the other many thousands, his body crawled with lice and other parasites; both he and Chou En-lai

* Interviews with sixteen Long Marchers, 1970–1971, and personal documents in author's files.

stuffed old newspapers (when they got any) around their feet. Physically, it was a constant misery to the almost hyper-clean Mao.

Several hundred boy "soldiers" in their early teens who made the Long March are today grown men. They remember Mao's jokes, his good humor, and the songs they sang. As the Hakkas of Chingkangshan had been for Mao a discovery, so were the national minorities, through the vast regions of West China they now crossed. He studied their manners and customs, instructed the Red Army soldiers never to retaliate, even if they were attacked by these despoiled and suspicious people. Struck by their general morbidity, one of his first decisions after the triumph of 1949 was to send the American doctor Ma Haiteh (George Hatem) to establish health programs for the national minorities.

The Long March was, for Mao Tsetung, not only a campaign but also an affirmation of his integration with the Chinese people. His grasp of the essential, his "singularly un-Napoleonic disregard for details," * kept him unclogged in mind, able to diffuse his gift of inspiring others with an almost superhuman optimism. On the march, walking with the others, he would discuss with the doctors † the impact of psychosomatic disease upon the body, how it is hope and strong motivation which make men live. For there comes a time when physical strength is not enough to sustain long and continuous effort, only spiritual exaltation can continue to make the body endure suffering and hardship. That "spirit becomes a material force" Mao was to affirm, for he himself was buoyed by unfaltering belief in the rightness of his cause. "It is possible to live on nothing but a furious hope," Robert Payne ‡ reports his saying. The poems he wrote during the Long March are among his more splendid and joyous ones; however busy and tired he was, his poet's eye raked the land, the sky; his poet's mind was stirred by beauty. He was with nature at her most elemental, loving yet fighting her; and on his shoulders, as on those of the toiler-soldiers with him, rested the destiny of China. Of this he was aware at every moment of the Long March.

Even Mao's enemies do not begrudge him admiration for his leadership during the Long March. Yet he would look upon it not as his own achievement, but a manifestation of the greatness and genius of

* A phrase of George Paloczi-Horvath, otherwise no lover of Mao Tsetung. See his *Mao Tse-tung, Emperor of the Blue Ants* (London 1962).

† Ki Peng-fei, now acting Minister for Foreign Affairs, and Dr. Nelson Fu, already referred to.

‡ Robert Payne *Portrait of a Revolutionary: Mao Tse-tung* (new and revised edition New York and London 1962).

his people. The man who counted was the poor peasant, bent over the earth he worked; the boy soldier carrying a rifle too big for him, slogging uncomplainingly on frozen feet; the mine workers become soldiers, singing while they chewed the boiled leather of harness thongs; the political instructor who pushed himself to the top of mountain passes, there to sing and call upon the wearied soldiers to walk up, for the next horizon was marvelous; the people of China, workers and poor peasants, who had followed him all the way, through Chingkangshan, through Juichin, through the Long March . . . the rank and file of the Red Army, who knew Mao Tsetung and for whom there was no other leader, who fought like heroes, and died without complaint, an army of saints destined to create a new world.

North Shensi is a desolate barrenness of windswept loess cliffs more than three thousand feet high, a fawn and gray unkemptness comparable to the Grand Canyon for grandeur, a beginning desert with scanty rain, centuries-old deforestation, tremendous dust storms whirling to veil the sun, the thick alluvial soil of the Yellow river, which meanders its sand banks for 750 miles across it. Its two million people were poor, dirty and ignorant, riddled with hunger and disease, troglodytes living in caves scooped in the loess cliffs. The ravages of invasions in centuries past had ruined the land; great peasant uprisings dating back to the Ming dynasty had been put down with ferocity, and hundreds of famines * had unpeopled it.

In 1926–1927 a small Communist nucleus had established itself in the area, with Shensi students trained in Mao Tsetung's Peasant Institute at Kuangchow. They led an insurrection, but in 1927 Chiang Kai-shek's counterrevolution had exterminated thousands of peasants and students. Within the next two years a severe famine and warlord wars brought on a general rural crisis, and the peasants rebelled again. Liu Chih-tan, one of the Whangpoo Communist cadets who survived the 1927 massacres, returned to Shensi, his native place, and organized the peasantry into guerilla bands. In 1929–1930 Liu promoted land reform, based on redistribution of big landlords' surplus lands and animals; he did not apply the "ultra-left" line followed in the Juichin base. In February 1934 the Shensi-Kansu Independent Border Region was proclaimed by Liu Chih-tan, with its capital at Pao An. Liu expanded the base and re-

* It is estimated that from the seventeenth century on there were at least three famines, big and small, every decade.

mained in control till mid-1935, despite attacks by Chiang Kai-shek's armies. He had about 5,000 men, grandly dubbed the Twenty-sixth and Twenty-seventh Red armies, and controlled about ten counties — but in the "fluctuant" manner already described.

In July 1935 another Red Army group, the Twenty-sixth Army, of about 8,000 men under Hsu Hai-tung, erstwhile commander in the Oyuwan base under Chang Kuo-tao as political commissar, arrived in the North Shensi base. Hsu had remained behind when Chang Kuo-tao left, and when Oyuwan was overrun he marched to North Shensi. Many other such groups, from small bases captured by the KMT, were making their own marches, breaking through Kuomintang cordons, marching westward and northward to reach the Shensi-Kansu (or North Shensi) base, the only one left by that autumn of 1935 — unless we count Chang Kuo-tao's "safe" base in West Szechuan.

Hsu's Twenty-fifth Army joined the Twenty-sixth and Twenty-seventh, to form a Fifteenth Red Army Corps. Hsu and Liu then had some heated disagreement on policies although it is now difficult to find out precisely what it was about. A "cadre" arrived from the (by no means extinct) "left" wing in the Central Committee. This cadre, Chang Ching-fu, nicknamed Chang the Corpulent,* cashiered Liu Chih-tan as a "right deviationist" (which meant a Mao follower in the jargon of the "left" Bolsheviks) who had not obeyed the (Wang Ming) Party line. Hsu Hai-tung sided with Fat Chang, and Liu Chih-tan was to be arrested and tried, when Mao's arrival in October restored unity. Hsu was then apprised of the Tsunyi resolutions and of his error. Mao called for a reassessment conference; the Politburo found most of the accusations against Liu Chih-tan baseless. And just in time. For the base was attacked in November by enemy forces, about 60,000 strong. The attack was repelled, and by December there was to be a lull of about four weeks before the next bout of fighting in 1936.

Within the next two years, 1936 and 1937, the situation would change radically. In December 1935 Mao's policy was still threatened, the most immediate danger being the internal struggle with Chang Kuo-tao. But Chang Kuo-tao's self-determined end was to come, and swiftly. He arrived at the North Shensi base in November or December 1936, over a year after Mao. His defection to Chiang

* Edgar Snow *Red Star Over China* (1937, first revised and enlarged edition New York 1968).

Kai-shek took place in the summer of 1938. During those months he was subjected to criticism, chiefly by Chang Wen-tien, secretary-general of the CCP, but otherwise unhindered, even being made vice-chairman and then chairman of the local government of the base, renamed the Shensi-Kansu-Ninghsia Border Region in 1936. But his opposition to Mao on the matter of a united front to fight Japan continued unabated. He built himself a secluded and pleasant pavilion on the outskirts of the city of Yenan, lectured in political science at the Resist Japan University (Kangta) * founded by Mao in 1936, and nursed his grudges till he went over to Chiang Kai-shek.

In the summer of 1938, in that compulsion to escape which seems to have been the mainspring of his actions, he fled to the arms of Chiang's secret police, was greeted with honor by Tai Li, the number one hatchet man of Chiang Kai-shek, and began working as an informer against the Communist Party.

Chang Kuo-tao's life is a curious and instructive study of an "ultra-leftist" becoming an "ultra-right-winger." Chinese Communist publications during the Great Proletarian Cultural Revolution were to assert that this is a common phenomenon — "in appearance left, in substance right." Mao Tsetung seems to have been singularly benign towards Chang Kuo-tao, sending messengers to him, even going to visit and talk with him. Mao would send back his wife and children to him in the 1950's.

A Chinese intellectual near to the Party, who was for a while under Chang Kuo-tao in the Oyuwan base, spoke to me in Hongkong of Chang's "extreme left to extreme right" switch, and related how Chang Kuo-tao in his ultra-left days conducted a purge of intellectuals in his base, proclaiming that "all intellectuals are three-day revolutionaries . . . traitors." This man, now a journalist, for years pretended not to be able to read or write, until he went to Yenan and joined Mao Tsetung. Such aberrations must be kept in mind while assessing Chang Kuo-tao's memoirs, published in Hongkong and become a source of historical material for some China-watchers.

Mao's attitude towards ideological opponents is clearly instanced in his behavior towards Chang Kuo-tao. "In dealing with comrades who have made mistakes but are conscious of them," he said . . . "we must not only watch but also help them. . . . To watch and wait for the guilty comrades to correct their mistakes is necessary; it is

* Abbreviation for Kang Jih Ta Hsueh (Resist Japan University).

Mao Tsetung with Chang Kuo-tao at Yenan, March 1938.

also necessary to help, help them to correct their mistakes. This is the only constructive attitude towards comrades." At that point, in those very years, Stalin was inaugurating massive physical purges, which were to decimate the Russian Communist Party and Army. Such purges did not occur in the Chinese Communist Party after Mao Tsetung came to power at Tsunyi in 1935.*

The flight and defection of Chang Kuo-tao put an end to one kind of opposition Mao had encountered, but this was not the end of the long ideological struggle which is the life of Mao Tsetung, of the Communist Party, which was to shape Mao the man and his thought, the Chinese Communist Party and its characteristics, and which continues unabated today.

Yet all this was but a beginning — one of the many beginnings which Mao Tsetung, walking with his people to fashion history, would make. On October 20, 1935, after reaching the Shensi-Kansu base, the Long Marchers quartered at Wayaopao, and almost immediately Mao set to work; he wrote with furious haste and speed, almost in ecstasy; he held conferences and he laid plans, but above all he wrote and he organized. For all had to be rebuilt, the Party, the Army. A new, clear program for the future was to be fashioned. The line.

Life was now somewhat easier. The Red Army dug its own caves; cool in summer, warm in winter, the new occupants lived as did the troglodyte inhabitants. Anna Louise Strong, the indefatigable American woman who kept a vigilant eye on the Revolution, extolled cave-living comforts.† At first most of the soldiers from the South could not eat the northern food; millet they had never tasted. Nor were they used to the harsh and terrible winter which now fastened upon the wild loess hills; nor to the sandstorms from the Gobi desert which engulfed the sunken valleys, blew day into a murky yellow twilight, blowing sand as far as Peking. Sleeping on a *kang* did not come easily either. Mao never got used to a *kang,* and his southern type of bed of wood with four poles and a mosquito net is shown to visitors, as are the small wooden tub in which he bathed, and Chou En-lai's long leather coat which he had worn since 1924 and which still hangs in the cave he lived in with his wife, Teng Ying-chao.

A clear and exalting vision of the work to do, which became the Yenan spirit, was here to be set down, to be expanded into a way of

* There were massive purges under the twenty-eight Bolsheviks' line between 1931 and 1934.
† Anna Louise Strong *The Chinese Conquer China* (New York 1949).

life, by Mao Tsetung. For here was time, a little time, despite harassment and desert wilderness, time giving an illusion of space. For a short while the warriors had a sensation of resting; they were only preparing for the next strenuous battles. The losses had been enormous; of fourteen bases in 1932 there remained only this one. The loss in men, in cadres, in soldiers and commanding officers, seemed to have dwindled the Communists to an easily annihilated nuisance. There were only 40,000 Communists in all China by mid-year 1937. But all figures are vague; for in these 40,000 how many would be recruits from the White areas, how many represented the Long Marchers from various bases? The Party membership was back to what it had been in 1928, whereas in 1934 it had counted 300,000 members.

Mao Tsetung had reached his full maturity of thought; he now had ideological authority, he was affluent with experience, he also had some power. But the Wang Ming faction in the Party was still very strong, biding its time. Mao set to forging a whole new Party and Army for a new stage of development of the Revolution, a stage in which the aim of the CCP was not only winning a war of liberation against Japan, but through this war to promote social and political revolution on a country-wide scale, and to *take power*.

To the preparation of this future Mao set himself, head among the stars, feet solidly planted in the Chinese earth. All those who saw him during those years in Yenan realized that he thought already in all-China terms, of nothing less than total triumph for the Chinese Revolution. And his first problem to solve, in conjunction with this total program, was the "contradiction" with Chiang Kai-shek. How would Chiang be brought to fight Japan, to accept another united front with the Communists in the name of national salvation?

The attack of October–November 1935 was ordered by Chiang Kai-shek who, well aware that Mao had escaped him, was now planning yet another annihilation campaign, and jailing and even murdering anyone determined to fight Japan. But Chiang's fatal flaw was his ultimate reliance on disparate troops and individuals. The attackers of the Red base were mixed troops of the Shansi warlord Yen Hsi-shan, of the Manchurian "Young Marshal" Chang Hsueh-liang, and of the pacification commissioner in charge of Shensi province, Yang Hu-cheng. Three divisions of the Manchurian troops of Chang Hsueh-liang were put out of commission, and numbers of Manchurian soldiers and officers captured by the Reds, in the November attack. In February 1936, Liu Chih-tan was to follow up this victory by an offensive across the Yellow river into Shansi province.* Shansi had coal and iron, and it was Liu Chih-tan's purpose to consolidate the base area and to expand it, and also to establish a strategic forward region to meet the Japanese onslaught which was sure to develop in North China. But he was killed in battle in March 1936. By all accounts a courageous and dedicated man, he was greatly mourned by the peasants of the region, and his memory is still honored in his native province.†

Once again history moved in mysterious ways, lavish in providing Mao with opportunities — or was it simply that he saw a saving grace where no one else did? The participation of the Manchurian troops of Chang Hsueh-liang in the anti-Communist assault was such an occasion. Their presence in Shensi, far from their original home, was due to the seizure of Manchuria by the Japanese in September 1931 and the conversion of the three eastern provinces, as Manchuria was known, into Manchukuo, the puppet protectorate of Japan under the ex-Manchu emperor Puyi.‡

Chang Hsueh-liang's father, the warlord Chang Tso-lin, ruler of Manchuria, had been killed by a bomb placed in his train by the Japanese in 1928. His son, known as the Young Marshal, did not resist the Japanese invasion of 1931; he left on Chiang Kai-shek's advice, and he and his armies had been quartered in the Northwest, to "fight the Reds," since 1932. This was not at all to Chang Hsueh-liang's liking. His army longed to fight the Japanese, he longed to return home. The Manchurian officers and soldiers captured by the Red Army quickly made friends with their captors; Mao Tsetung's policy of the united front against Japanese aggression was explained to them, and aroused their enthusiasm. They were well looked after, and released with gifts within weeks. By then the last thing they wanted was to fight the Red Army. Three thousand Manchurian soldiers of Chang Hsueh-liang's armies defected to the Red Army in the spring of 1936.

Through his officers, Chang Hsueh-liang heard of the Red base, was told of the honesty, the dedication, the determination to form a democratic government "with all those ready to fight Japan." This stirred his patriotism, subdued his fear of Communism. He talked to Yang Hu-cheng, the pacification commissioner, whose second wife

* Shansi province is next to Shensi province and not to be confused with it (see map, p. 273).

† Jan Myrdal *Report from a Chinese Village* (New York 1965), pp. 55–57.

‡ Interview with ex-emperor Puyi, 1960. See also *Autiobiography* of Aisin Gioro Puyi (Peking 1965).

was a left-inclined student — some even say she was a "Communist." * And wonder of wonders, his secretary, Wang Ping-nan, whose wife was German, was also a Communist.†

The pacification commissioner, ordered to smash the Reds, was reluctant to smash himself in the process. While spouting promises to Chiang Kai-shek, Chang Hsueh-liang and Yang Hu-cheng began delicate maneuvers to negotiate with the Communists. In early 1936 talks began between the Communists and Chang Hsueh-liang in Sian. Chou En-lai was placed by Mao in charge of these negotiations. Soon Communist cadres in Manchurian army uniform were going into Sian to have talks with officers of the Manchurian army and officials of the provincial government.

From Tsunyi onward, and until today, it is Chou En-lai who has been the most able executor of Mao's blueprints in internal and external policies. Today Chou enjoys immense popularity, second only to Mao, in China. He is called "the housekeeper," the one who carries out the policies.

In a speech at Wayaopao in December 1935,‡ at the end of two weeks of intense discussion in the Politburo, Mao laid down the fundamental policies of the Party for the building of a united front. Opinions on the united front were still very divided. A faction in the CCP still did not want to have anything to do with Chiang Kai-shek. They held that there could be no alliance of any kind with "the bourgeoisie." But Mao was also opposed by a numerous and growing clique who wanted to hand over the leadership (and that meant the Red Army, mainstay of revolutionary power) to Chiang Kai-shek. In this group were Chang Kuo-tao, and, surprisingly, later would be Wang Ming himself, in one of those dismaying turnabouts which discourage logic, but which happen.

"What is the basic tactical task of the Party? It is none other than to form a broad national revolutionary united front. . . . The Communist Party and the Red Army are not only acting at present as the initiators of the anti-Japanese national united front, but will inevitably become the powerful mainstay of the anti-Japanese government and anti-Japanese army, preventing the Japanese imperialists and Chiang Kai-shek from attaining their ultimate end, in their policy of

* Met by the author in 1938, in Brussels.
† Wang Ping-nan, later ambassador to Poland, was for a time in charge of talks at ambassadorial level between the People's Republic of China and the U.S. (1956–1966).
‡ *On Tactics Against Japanese Imperialism,* December 27, 1935. *Selected Works of Mao Tsetung* (English edition Peking 1961–1965), vol. I.

disrupting the national united front." The people demanded resistance to Japan — the workers, the peasants, the petty bourgeoisie. As for the national bourgeoisie, it remained vacillating. "On the one hand they dislike imperialism and on the other they fear thorough revolution." Hence it needed leadership. Only the CCP could provide it, through the tactics of the united front.

At the meeting Mao reviewed the Tsai Ting-kai fiasco of December 1933.* It had shown that the Japanese invasion was causing splits within the KMT, and now there were more splits. All these could be utilized. He attacked what he called "closed-doorism," those for whom "the forces of the revolution must be pure, absolutely pure, and the road of the revolution must be straight, absolutely straight. Nothing is correct except what is literally recorded in Holy Writ. The national bourgeoisie is entirely and eternally counterrevolutionary. Not an inch must be conceded to the rich peasants. . . . If we shake hands with Tsai Ting-kai we must call him a counterrevolutionary at the same moment. . . . Intellectuals are three-day revolutionaries . . . closed-doorism is the sole wonder-working magic, while the united front is an opportunist tactic." This was an irate and withering comment on the Wang Ming leadership, which had wrought such havoc for the CCP. Mao was sarcastically quoting back what Chang Kuo-tao and Wang Ming had been saying for a good number of years; and his audience knew it, and tittered.

"United front tactics are the only Marxist-Leninist tactics." The leadership of the war, of the united front, must remain with "the party of the proletariat," the Communist Party, although because of its weakness it needed allies to tackle the national war of resistance. And allies there were, all over China. There was already a united front of the broad masses, which was clamorous, potentially powerful; all it needed was a directing head. Chiang would no longer be able to contain the tide of public opinion demanding resistance to the invader. The slogan of Chiang, "Internal pacification before resistance to foreign invasion," no longer worked. Thus Mao gave a clear, decisive orientation to the Party for a second united front. He also delineated the policy of a "people's republic," which would now include, besides the workers and peasants and urban petty bourgeoisie, "members of all other classes who are willing to take part in the national revolution." And in this brief paragraph of his speech, the seed of the People's Republic of China was planted. "Why change the

* See pages 258–259.

'workers' and peasants' republic' [such as at Juichin] into a 'people's republic'?" asked Mao. He answered himself: "Our government represents not only the workers and peasants but the whole nation." The Japanese invasion had changed class relations in China, requiring this alteration into a people's republic. This would mean modifications in policies affecting, for instance, land reform, representation in councils, and mass associations and mass movements. The newly born formula was to be carried out into all the bases, during the war with Japan.

It was this genial adaptation, flexible and inspired, to genuine conditions, rallying the greatest number, which procured for the CCP its immense popularity during the war and made it the core of leadership of anti-Japanese resistance. Already, in December 1935, Mao was blueprinting the next ten years. Protection instead of confiscation for private property other than imperialist and feudal would rally still more of the bourgeoisie at this stage, even if their status would be altered in the next. "In the stage of democratic revolution there are limits to the struggle between labor and capital. The labor laws of the people's republic will protect the interests of the workers but will not prevent the national bourgeoisie *from making profits or developing their industrial and commercial enterprises.*" *

China was still, said Mao, at the stage of bourgeois-democratic revolution. "The change [to the socialist revolution] will come later."

On May 6, 1936, a circular telegram was sent from the Revolutionary Military Council of the Red Army to the Military Commission of Chiang's government in Nanking, asking those "Nanking gentlemen" to break with the past, stop the civil war, and form a united front against Japan. It also announced the CCP's decision of voluntary cessation of fighting against the KMT. On August 25, 1936, an open letter from the Central Committee of the CCP was addressed to the KMT Central Executive Committee in the same vein. In this letter, the CCP offered collaboration in fighting Japan and support to the Kuomintang if the latter should truly practice the Three People's Principles of Dr. Sun Yatsen and the three policies of alliance with Russia, cooperation with the CCP, and assistance to the peasants and workers which had been Sun Yatsen's cornerstone policies. "If you really do this, we shall resolutely support you and

* Marxism is . . . the concrete analysis of concrete conditions" — Mao's favorite quotation from Lenin.

are ready to form with you a solid revolutionary united front like that of the great revolutionary period of 1924–1927 against imperialism and feudal oppression, for this is the only correct way today to save the nation from subjugation and ensure its survival."

The strategy and tactics of this Second United Front were to become the main factor in the prosecution of the war, and also in the continuing revolution. But Chiang Kai-shek refused any negotiations not preceded by total submission, the total disbanding of all the Red armies or their total incorporation in his own. As Mao said: "Chiang understands power." In China, this meant an army.

In September 1936, the Central Committee of the CCP passed a resolution on "the new situation in the resistance to Japan and the national salvation movement," which repeated the offers made and elaborated a united front program. But Mao's conception of the united front was still not acceptable to all.

In Europe, the rise of Nazi Germany, and the Axis alliance between Germany, Italy, Japan, had led the USSR to the formulation of a united front policy, through the Comintern. This was proclaimed on August 20, 1935. Wang Ming, who was on the steering committee of the Comintern representing the Chinese Communist Party, reported in August 1935 that there were half a million Party members in China, a patently incorrect statement. He said, "In my opinion, and that of the entire Central Committee of the Communist Party of China, together with the soviet government of China . . . we should issue a joint appeal to the whole nation . . . to organize an All-China United People's Government of National Defense." It must also be noted that a resolution adopted on December 20, 1935, by the Central Committee at Wayaopao, indeed used similar phraseology, with Mao Tsetung dissenting. Around this sentence the two-line struggle over the strategy of the united front was to crystallize.

The formula sabotaged Mao's concept of the independence in action of the Red Army, independence of the Red base (and future bases), and initiative and leadership in the war. It encouraged Chiang Kai-shek in his pursuit of his own aims. Wang Ming was reflecting not the interests of the Chinese Revolution, but a tactic of the USSR in its own policies in both Europe and China. For the USSR was trying to win Chiang to at least a neutral posture, so that he would not join the Axis powers. Moscow knew well enough that the influential right-wing, pro-fascist cliques in Chiang's government were urging an Axis alliance. At the same time Chiang was also negotiating a nonaggression pact with the USSR which he hoped would give him leverage against Mao; he would be able either to utilize Comintern influence through Wang Ming to exert pressure on Mao, or to counter Mao's prestige in the CCP. Wang Ming still had a powerful following in the CCP, and all the press and propaganda organs of the Comintern through the world Communist parties were at his disposal. Mao was now described vaguely as a "guerilla leader," always linked with and almost always second to Chu Teh.* His brief favor at the Comintern in 1930 had been eclipsed for four years by the presence of Wang Ming.

That the conditions in which a united front would come into being meant survival or extinction for the Communist Party and the Red Army never seemed to have occurred to Wang Ming, nor that the USSR could not be the best judge of the Chinese situation. Wang Ming ignored the experience acquired during the First United Front, which had taught Mao that acceding to Chiang's demands for absolute control of the Red Army meant collective suicide. On no account would Mao allow Chiang to butcher the Communists again; yet Wang Ming's formula of unity for national defense meant precisely relinquishing leadership to Chiang Kai-shek, and this meant the armies as well. "Without a people's army the people have nothing," said Mao. And "Political power grows out of the barrel of a gun."

The control of the Red Army would always be the focus of struggle within the united front; it would be in the continuing Chinese Revolution — even today — the critical center of leadership preoccupation. There is no political leadership which does not also imply a force capable to back it, defend it and preserve its power — an army. This basic fact the propounders of a "national defense" united front under Chiang's leadership would not or could not see. Had Stalin seen it? Or was he too engrossed in Russian affairs at the time? Or were his foreign policy advisers so anxious to win over Chiang Kai-shek that they simply ignored the role of the CCP? Or, more than likely, did they believe, after the Long March, that the Mao-led Red Army was a spent force, and put back the Chinese Revolution prospects to very much later, meanwhile opting for Chiang Kai-shek?

Even though Mao seemed the unchallenged leader of the CCP

* Edgar Snow, in *Red Star Over China* (1937, first revised and enlarged edition New York 1968), was the first to give a correct perspective on Mao Tsetung's role in the Chinese Revolution. Agnes Smedley devoted most of her writings to Chu Teh.

after Tsunyi, he acquired ideological authority only locally; he had not acquired the completely unhampered exercise of power even locally. Factions both in the Party and the Army would remain. Mao has always, like Lenin, regarded intra-Party struggle as a dialectical expression of the class struggle, reflected within the Party. "Peace" within the Party, therefore, is not to be desired; there has never been an entirely monolithic Communist Party, whatever the attempts to make it so. Such monolithism would mean there was no criticism and self-criticism, no ideological education, hence no advance; for ideological struggle is a facet of progress.*

Because of this singular liveliness of the CCP at all times, unity can only be attained by ideological struggle, criticism and self-criticism, and Mao's way of handling his opposition would therefore be radically different from the Russian way. But from Moscow things may have appeared very different. Mao was but the leader of a small "peasant" faction; the Tsunyi conference was ignored; Mao was not even referred to as chairman of the Revolutionary Military Council till the end of 1938.

In the years 1936–1938, the intra-Party struggle on the question of the united front would be bitter and complex; it would become part of Mao's assertion of ideological authority. Within the Party, "closed-doorists" and "capitulationists" (i.e., the "left" and the "right") wrangled on many questions but agreed in attacking Mao's united front thesis. Wang Ming accused Mao of lacking in "proletarian internationalism" because he was not subordinating his view to the Comintern view; he derided Mao as a "chauvinist." But was it indeed not possible to be both a convinced revolutionary and a Chinese patriot? Was it true that only total subordination to Moscow's policies would work for the success of the Revolution? Some other Party leaders were plainly frightened of the bold vistas Mao unfurled, the great goal which appeared to them dangerously utopian. The CCP was much too weak, the Red Army too small and miserably ill-equipped; the Kuomintang armies were large; the Red Army would benefit in supplies, equipment and weaponry should it come under Chiang Kai-shek. How could such remnants as they had in hand, in bleak North Shensi, pretend to lead a war against Japan, capture the leadership of the whole country?

"The victory of the Chinese national liberation movement will be part of the victory of world socialism, because to defeat imperialism

* Even at the termination of the Great Proletarian Cultural Revolution, the CCP proclaimed that ideological struggle goes on within the party (April 1971).

in China means the destruction of one of its most powerful bases. If China wins its independence, the world revolution will progress very rapidly. If our country is subjugated by the enemy, we shall lose everything. For a people being deprived of its national freedom, the revolutionary task is not immediate socialism but the struggle for independence. We cannot even discuss Communism if we are robbed of a country in which to practice it." * In a felicitous sentence Mao defined the duty of every Communist to be a patriot and to fight the Japanese. "Can a Communist, who is an internationalist, at the same time be a patriot? We hold that he not only can be but must be. . . . In wars of national liberation patriotism is applied internationalism."

At the moment, in spite of appearances, Chiang Kai-shek was weak and the CCP was strong. The Long March had been a triumph, Mao insisted. A united front which demanded leadership was already in existence among the people; it was waiting for the Communist Party to lead it, and most of the people believed what the Communist Party said and no longer believed Chiang Kai-shek.

Throughout 1936, the ideological struggle over policy raged within the Party, more or less secretly. Very little of it leaked out save perhaps through Chiang's spies. Mao Tsetung even spoke in praise of some of his adversaries to Edgar Snow, who was present at the Red base at the time.† This reticence helps to confuse experts; some aver that history has been rewritten because during some years no denunciation of Wang Ming's "ultra-left" line occurred. Many years may elapse before final "historical judgment" is pronounced.

Meanwhile, the Shensi base was consolidating; the negotiations with Chang Hsueh-liang proceeded satisfactorily. Throughout that spring and summer there were meetings, friendly talks, demarcation of "buffer zones" to avoid troop clashes, transport of supplies and even gifts of weapons to the Red Army. A liaison office was established in Sian, in a German dentist's house. Students and clandestine Party members from all over China came to the liaison office and from there made contact with the Communists in North Shensi.

---

* Quoted by Edgar Snow to the author.

† "Another reason for [the Party's] invincibility lies in the extraordinary ability and courage and loyalty of the human material . . . Comrades Chu Teh, Wang Ming, Lo Fu, Chou En-lai, Po Ku, Wang Chia-hsiang, Peng Teh-huai . . . Hsiang Ying, Hsu Hai-tung, Chen Yun, Lin Piao, Chang Kuo-tao . . ." Edgar Snow *Red Star Over China* (1937, first revised and enlarged edition New York 1968), p. 449. Mao's intense wish for Party unity despite all these ideological struggles is plain in the string of names he uttered.

Chiang Kai-shek spent the summer of 1936 flying from one major city to another, giving pep talks to his commanders, urging them to "mop up Red remnants." In spite of this, such was the force of public opinion against the civil war that during that same summer Chou En-lai was able to travel to Kuomintang areas, make contacts, and hold meetings and receive enthusiastic welcome from prominent personalities, even Kuomintang Party members.*

An All-China National Salvation League was organized under Madame Sun Yatsen and Madame Ho Hsiang-ning, widow of the late Dr. Liao Chung-kai. In November 1936 Chiang arrested seven prominent leaders of the League, all well-known intellectuals. A storm of protest followed. But the obdurate Chiang knew that intellectuals and students could be shot, jailed, and coerced; he did not worry over protests. What disturbed him was reports of the goings-on in Shensi province.

His intelligence agents mentioned the visits of suspected Communists to Chang Hsueh-liang. Chang Hsueh-liang even wrote a letter to Chiang Kai-shek suggesting an end to the civil war and a united front. "It is the people's demand . . . your name as the leader of the resistance against Japan will be famous forever. . . . Don't believe only what the Japanese tell you," he added, rather insultingly. The Young Marshal had even asked the Red commander Yeh Chien-ying to dinner, had gone to see him at the base and urged him to take in hand the training and modernization of his own Manchurian armies. Students from the Japanese-occupied territory of Manchuria flooded into Sian; many went from there to the Red base, through the liaison office. The National Salvation League was also very active in the city.

Chiang decided to visit Sian in person. But in September 1936 a rebellion against him started in Kwangsi province by two militarists, Li Tsung-jen and Pai Chung-hsi, delayed him. These two warlords also proclaimed they wanted to fight Japan, and rebelled against Chiang because he refused them funds and weapons to do so. In December 1936, impelled by his mania for destroying the Reds, Chiang flew to Sian, landing there on December 7, and took up residence at the Lintung Hot Springs, former resort of a Tang dynasty emperor. On December 9, thousands of Manchurian students walked there from Sian to present him with a petition to resist Japan. They were fired upon by Chiang's personal guards. Chang Hsueh-liang rushed

* See Hsu Kai-yu *Chou En-lai: China's Gray Eminence* (New York 1968).

to the spot: "I will take personal responsibility for bringing your demands to Generalissimo Chiang." Chang Hsueh-liang had often intervened to save students from Chiang's secret police and their director, Chiang's nephew, who tortured and executed suspected Reds.

But when Chang Hsueh-liang appeared, Chiang Kai-shek scolded him like a child, recording it himself in his diary: "I severely upbraided . . . the Young Marshal." Chiang also threatened Yang Hu-cheng. The trap was then sprung. On December 12, before dawn, a subordinate of Chang Hsueh-liang's surrounded Chiang's abode with soldiers, killed his nephew, and took Chiang prisoner. It is said that this subordinate had strong Communist sympathies, and that the whole of Chiang's kidnapping was engineered by the Communists. Although there is no evidence, it is more than likely that without some "suggestions" from the Communists the Sian maneuver could not have been carried out in so masterly a fashion.

This was the famous "Sian incident," which caused enormous excitement in China and abroad. Students clamored for Chiang to be brought to public trial; some of the Manchurian officers and soldiers demanded his instant execution; in Nanking the government was stunned, immediately a power struggle began.

Mass meetings held at Pao An (capital of the Red base) demanded Chiang's public trial and execution. There were enough Communists whose relatives had been murdered by Chiang, and for whom a united front with Chiang appeared an outrageous compromise. But it is highly unlikely that the mass meetings were encouraged by Mao Tsetung, although other members of the Central Committee might have joined in the clamor for Chiang's death. Mao had already defined Japan as the principal enemy now, and not Chiang. He had made it clear that Chiang's cooperation in a united front was needed to fight Japan. It is quite certain that he never meant to kill Chiang Kai-shek.

In Nanking, the fascist defense minister Ho Ying-chin, a diehard pro-Japanese, who had long wanted to play a historic role and bring China into the Axis, threatened to bomb Sian and march armies thither — a sure way to get Chiang executed, to precipitate an all-out massacre, and to bring a massive Japanese invasion "to restore peace and order." Agnes Smedley reports that already Japanese generals had gathered in a secret conclave in Tientsin to decide whether the time was ripe for a total military occupation of China. The extreme right wing in Nanking was urging an alliance with Japan against the Communists. Meanwhile Chang Hsueh-liang issued a message to the Nanking government, and all those willing to fight Japan, with an eight-point program (which greatly resembled the Communist one). This was rejected by Ho Ying-chin.

On December 15 the USSR press condemned the detention of Chiang Kai-shek, calling it a "Japanese plot." Ho Ying-chin received a visit from the German ambassador; the Nanking regime, it was rumored, might join the Axis powers. The Moscow news release reflected the Kremlin's intense fear that this might happen. For Russia, war on two fronts has been the perennial nightmare. Edgar Snow * tells of a wire received by Mao Tsetung "from Stalin" which said: "Free Chiang at once or we shall break all connection with you." It is more probable, as Snow suggests, that the cable was from Wang Ming and not Stalin. Mao was in a great rage when he received it; he swore, stamped about, and tore up the message. But Soviet newsmen and the Soviet ambassador in China were embarrassed at the Soviet press denunciation of Chiang's arrest as a Japanese coup. "This was one of the personal experiences which would convince me that as long as Russia made Comintern policy, it would always and everywhere be made first of all in the strategic interest of the USSR as the Kremlin sees it," writes Snow.

Mao had never intended either a mass trial of Chiang Kai-shek, or his execution.† In the summer of 1936, speaking to Snow, Mao had said: "There must be a day of decision, a day when he [Chiang] must either oppose Japan or be overthrown by his subordinates. . . . This increasing pressure from his own generals and the anti-Japanese mass movement may compel Chiang to realize his mistakes. . . . We will welcome this change and cooperate wholeheartedly . . . but only Chiang can determine this for himself. The decision cannot be much longer delayed."

All Mao wanted was an occasion to persuade Chiang, if not directly, then through that most brilliant and persuasive of all Communists, Chou En-lai. The "occasion" was the Sian kidnapping. Four days after Chiang's detention, a plane brought Chou En-lai from the Red base to Sian. Chang Hsueh-liang had confiscated the airplanes and equipment accumulated by Chiang at Sian to fight the Communists; he had planned a sixth annihilation campaign.

* Edgar Snow *Random Notes on Red China* (Cambridge, Mass. 1957).
† André Migot declares that on December 15 Mao said, "This is an error, it should never have been done" (Chiang's kidnapping). Guenther Stein also says there never was a cable from Stalin to Mao about this event. (André Migot *Mao Tsetung*, Paris 1966. Guenther Stein *The Challenge of Red China*, New York and London 1945.)

Chou En-lai and Chiang Kai-shek thus found themselves face to face again, as they had in the Whangpoo Academy in 1924. What went on between them remains pure conjecture. That Mao was fully informed of the conversations is certain. Meanwhile a new Military Affairs Council was established in Sian under Chang Hsueh-liang's authority, to include "all anti-Japanese armies and representatives," including of course the Red Army. Sian began to fill up with anti-Japanese militarists, including Feng Yu-hsiang, who in 1927 had advised the Wuhan KMT to get rid of its Communists. Madame Chiang arrived, with her brother T. V. Soong and the Australian adviser to Chiang, W. H. Donald. It does seem that Chiang promised verbally to consider a united front, and said that he would be glad to be "working again together" with Chou En-lai — whatever those polite phrases might mean.

Chiang was released on Christmas Day and flew back to Nanking. But he took with him Chang Hsueh-liang, jailed and finally caused Yang Hu-cheng to be murdered in prison, together with his son. The Young Marshal remained Chiang's prisoner for thirty years, and was only recently released in Taiwan, at the age of seventy. By taking Chang Hsueh-liang with him, Chiang wanted to prevent an alliance between the Red Army and the Manchurian northeastern armies. The armies of Chang Hsueh-liang were dispersed to other areas.

On December 28, three days after Chiang's release, Mao issued a statement. In it he said that he hoped that Chiang would "keep his promises," though he had not signed any terms. "Chiang should remember that he owes his safe departure from Sian to the mediation of the Communist Party, as well as to the efforts of generals Chang and Yang, the leaders in the Sian incident." Whether Chiang intended or not to keep his promises, he certainly did not hurry to keep them. Armed clashes occurred between the KMT and the Red Army while he procrastinated. He moved ten divisions under Hu Tsung-nan, the young, fiercely fascist Kuomintang general, into Shensi province. Throughout the subsequent war with Japan, Hu Tsung-nan would keep these troops and the best equipment Chiang had to blockade the Red base.

The capture of Yenan, a key city for communications in Shensi province, had formed the focus of guerilla effort under Liu Chih-tan. In December 1936 Mao moved with troops, taking Yenan and expanding the base territory to almost 100,000 square miles. In January 1937 Yenan was declared the capital city of the Shensi-Kansu-Ninghsia Border Region; the Revolutionary Military Council and

Kuomintang troops fighting the Communists, 1936.

the Central Committee transferred thither from Pao An. The base now also straddled the borders of Ninghsia province; this ensured a permanent supply of salt from Ninghsia's famed salt deposits, and improved the strategic advantages of the base.

Had Chiang Kai-shek been able to arrange a long-term truce with the Japanese in early 1937, as he tried to do when he returned to Nanking, there would have been no united front. But the Japanese war machine could not stop. The Japanese army would not wait. The Japanese war politicians no longer trusted Chiang after the Sian talks. Neither could Chiang stop the tide of anti-Japanese feeling among the Chinese people, who now all assumed that at last he would fight the aggressors. Popular enthusiasm acclaimed his release from pure relief at the prospect of an end to the civil war. As the Chinese newspaper *Ta Kung Pao* worded it: "From now on Chinese will no longer fight Chinese."

During 1936, Chiang had tried to hasten his negotiations for a nonaggression pact with Moscow. Had the pact been concluded in the midst of his projected anti-Communist campaign against the North Shensi base, it would have meant the repudiation of the Mao leadership by the USSR. But now Chiang was reluctant to sign the pact, since it would make the Japanese even more suspicious. Until late in 1938, the Russian press and left-wing journals abroad persisted in lauding Chiang as the "leader of the resistance," and were almost tomb-silent about Mao. Mao's position as chairman of the CCP and the Revolutionary Military Council was ignored; only in late 1938 did the USSR begin to broadcast pro-Mao commentary again. Even after Chiang's release from Sian in December 1936, the Comintern was still so misinformed that *Inprecor* (the Comintern organ) wrote on January 2, 1939: "Nanking has sent troops against the rebel Chang Hsueh-liang . . . who was compelled to release Chiang Kai-shek." *

In May 1937 Mao issued a report entitled *The Tasks of the CCP in the Period of Resistance to Japan.* This document, clearly stating the course of the Chinese Revolution and the responsibility of the CCP to lead it, further developed his ideas on the united front. A concluding speech by Mao, *Win the Masses in Their Millions for the Anti-Japanese United Front,* was to stress points on which "some comrades . . . expressed different views." In one of the most signifi-

* As for Trotsky, he had denounced the CCP appeal for resistance to Japan since 1933.

cant passages, Mao says: "We are exponents of the theory of the transition of the revolution, and not of the Trotskyite theory of 'permanent revolution.' We are for the attainment of socialism by going through all the necessary stages of the democratic republic." Mao's fundamental ideas on the continuing Chinese Revolution were thus penned in the turmoil of these high-tension years of war with Japan and struggle within the Party. Mao also announced the need for "many first-rate cadres" to carry through "our great Revolution which is unprecedented in history." * If "the leadership consists of a small narrow group and if the Party leaders are petty-minded, short-sighted and incompetent," it would be impossible to carry the Revolution through. Such cadres and leaders "must be free from selfishness . . . sloth . . . sectarian arrogance. . . . To attain this aim, inner-Party democracy is essential. Let us apply democracy . . . give scope to initiative throughout the Party . . . win the masses in their millions . . . for the anti-Japanese national united front."

In that same May, while Mao was asserting this thesis, Chang Kuo-tao was to join Wang Ming in issuing speeches and an article circulating the slogan "Victory for all." Disputing Mao's views, Chang argued that it was "dishonest" not to trust Chiang Kai-shek; should there be victory in the Sino-Japanese war, it should be shared by all, *including* Chiang Kai-shek. Chang Kuo-tao rejected Mao's estimate that the united front was a part of revolutionary strategy, that the real theme and essence was class struggle and consequently the seizure of power by the Communist Party, that leadership not only of the war but also of all the classes rallied in the united front must be in the hands of the Communist Party, to prepare for the postwar era. Chang Kuo-tao now advocated, and found others to advocate, "parliamentarism" — merging of the Communist administration and Red Army with the Kuomintang administration and armies, in order to make "one government, one army, one military administration" under Chiang Kai-shek. This represented almost a death wish. Liu Shao-chi, returning to Yenan that summer, also seems to have written a pessimistic report about the outcome of the Revolution, advocating "unity" with Chiang Kai-shek.†

Mao argued that there could not possibly be any "merging" with the one-party dictatorship which was Chiang's government, which

* *Selected Works of Mao Tsetung,* vol. I, pp. 290–291 (English edition Peking 1965).

† Chang Kuo-tao, preface, *Collected Works of Liu Shao-chi* (Hongkong 1969).

gave no freedom or democracy to the people. The "capitulationists" envisioned the resistance to Japan as an alliance between two political parties, whereas Mao saw it as the arousal of the Chinese people and their mobilization in a people's war. The basic discord was, therefore, a question of "world conception or outlook" — to stand for the interests of the masses, or to act as a new power group in a power struggle, practicing compromise and "a sharing . . . of high functions and official posts."

It was all very well for the Moscow press to broadcast articles as if Chiang were the leader of Chinese resistance to Japanese invasion; it was quite understandable that Stalin, anxious about Germany, wanted to assure himself of Chiang's support, and to do nothing to strengthen the hand of the pro-Japanese clique in Chiang's government. Russian policy, pressured by the fear of war on two fronts, might placate Chiang Kai-shek, seek to draw him into a formal anti-Axis stance. But it was very different for a Chinese Communist to do so. If Stalin gave "bad advice" to the CCP, there is, on the Chinese side, silence about it. This is not only a fixed policy, but also the expression of a philosophical concept expressed by Mao — that it was internal causes which were the main factors of change, whereas external causes only set the background; they could be resisted or accepted, and the choice depended on the individuals concerned.

Mao felt free, therefore, to ignore Stalin's "advice"; he knew that Moscow was *also* negotiating with Japanese-created Manchukuo over the Chinese Eastern Railway. In Lenin's time, through the Karakhan Manifesto, the USSR had formally relinquished all rights to this railway, but the USSR had continued to hold it; in 1929 Li Lisan had called for the "masses" to arise and defend the Soviet Union, embroiled in local conflict with the Chinese troops in Manchuria who had tried to take back the railway. Now in 1937 the USSR was "selling" this very same railway to the Japanese in Manchukuo. In 1945, the USSR would take the railway back; once again they would return it, this time to the People's Republic of China in the early 1950's, and without payment.

Negotiations for a united front between the Communists and the Kuomintang began with a conference in February 1937, in which Chou En-lai played the chief role. The Communists presented a five-demand program with four conditions as basis for a united front.

The four conditions were: (*1*) The Communist-led government in

Chiang Kai-shek with Madame Chiang (Soong Mei-ling), 1937.

the Shensi-Kansu-Ninghsia base would be renamed the Government of the Special Region. (2) The Red Army would be redesignated. (It was to be named the Eighth Route Army of the Eighteenth Army Corps, under the overall direction of the KMT government.) (3) The policy of armed insurrection would be discontinued. (4) Landlords' land would no longer be confiscated.

The five demands presented at the same time were: (1) Cessation of civil war. (2) Guarantee of freedom of speech, assembly and association. (3) Convocation of an anti-Japanese people's congress. (4) Completion of preparations for resisting Japan. (5) Improvement of the living conditions of the people.

But Chiang had replied asking for: (1) *Total* integration of the Red Army and Red zones in the Nationalist army and the regular Kuomintang administration. (2) Renunciation of class struggle. (3) Stopping all doctrine and Communist propaganda "not in accord with the Three Principles of Sun Yatsen and Chinese traditions."

Negotiations dragged till September. Wang Ming in Moscow urged acceptance of the Chiang conditions. So did Chang Kuo-tao at sessions of the Central Committee in Yenan.

On July 7, 1937, the Japanese attacked a Chinese contingent at Lu Kuo Chiao bridge near Peking.* The Chinese troops resisted, and the country was electrified by the bravery of this handful of soldiers. Chiang tarried ten days before announcing an "emergency," but the Japanese attack had its own precipitating effect, both on Chiang's negotiations with Moscow and on the united front discussions with the Communists in Yenan. Between July and September, talks between the two parties became serious; Chiang could no longer dally, though still he would try to get his way. Meanwhile, within the Party, the struggle for the united front policy which would give the CCP the upper hand in the long run became more intense than ever. Mao urged the "capitulationists" once again to remember 1927, Chen Tu-hsiu's submission, the orders to surrender weapons, and the resulting massacres. "Never again . . . must this be repeated." "It goes without saying that we shall never allow Chiang Kai-shek to lay a finger on the Red Army."

In his military text *Problems of Strategy in China's Revolutionary War,* written as teaching material for new cadres and Red Army personnel, Mao made a statement crucial to the conduct of the united front. China's revolutionary war, he wrote, had passed through two

* Also known as Marco Polo bridge.

stages; the first from 1924 to 1927; the second from 1927 to 1937; now the third stage would begin, "the stage of national revolutionary war against Japan. . . . In all three of its stages this revolutionary war has been and will be fought under the leadership of the Chinese proletariat and its party, the Chinese Communist Party. . . . This war is not only the banner of China's liberation, but also has international revolutionary significance . . . in the new stage [the anti-Japanese war] *we shall lead the Chinese Revolution to its completion and exert a profound influence on the revolution in the East and in the whole world."* * These prophetic words were written in December 1936.

On July 23, 1937, two weeks after the Japanese had invaded North China, Mao delivered a most important speech entitled *Policies, Measures and Perspectives for Resisting the Japanese Invasion.* Its substance was a ten-point program: (*1*) Overthrow Japanese imperialism. (*2*) Mobilize the military strength of the whole nation. (*3*) Mobilize the people of the whole country (a point of greatest importance to Mao for protracted people's war). (*4*) Reform the government apparatus. (*5*) Adopt an anti-Japanese foreign policy. (*6*) Adopt wartime financial and economic policies. (*7*) Improve the people's livelihood. (*8*) Adopt an anti-Japanese educational policy. (*9*) Weed out traitor and pro-Japanese elements and consolidate the rear. (*10*) Achieve national unity against Japan.

On August 15 Peking and Tientsin fell to the Japanese; the provinces of Hopei and Chahar were occupied, and the Japanese began an assault on Shanghai. Chiang reluctantly had to make a declaration of war against Japan. Meanwhile, united front negotiations were locked in a frozen debate, with Chiang insisting on total control of the Red Army.

Chu Teh and Peng Teh-huai, as representatives of the Military Council, and Chou En-lai as representative of the Central Committee and the Politburo, attended the sessions of Chiang's Military Council in Nanking. By August 22, some sort of partial agreement seems to have been reached. Apparently Chu Teh and Peng Teh-huai had agreed, tacitly, to accept Chiang as supreme commander against Japan.† Chiang Kai-shek then nominated, in his role as "su-

---

* Emphasis not in original.

† During the Great Proletarian Cultural Revolution, documents and cables of the period were exhibited by some Red Guards as evidence that the Red military commanders accepted terms which Mao still persisted in refusing.

Japanese troops celebrating the occupation of Shanghai, November 1937. Below, a Shanghai suburb after heavy fighting and bombing.

preme commander," Chu Teh and Peng Teh-huai as "commanders of the Eighteenth Army Corps," which incorporated the Eighth Route Army. Some funds and equipment were granted by Chiang to this army, limited to a total of 45,000 men, in September 1937.* Chiang still refused to recognize the North Shensi base as autonomous and insisted on Kuomintang control, and he still insisted on troop integration. The nominations of Chu Teh and Peng Teh-huai were possibly meant as a step to detach them from CCP control and bring them over to a neutralized stance.

On August 23 the nonaggression pact between Chiang and the USSR was concluded, but by now it had lost its main value for Chiang; moreover, it had a clause asserting the "independence" of Outer Mongolia, which Chiang accepted but which stirred criticism in his own Kuomintang Party, never reconciled to this loss.†

Mao again outlined his ten-point program at a Politburo session, called the Lochuan meeting, in August 1937. Mao's proposals were discussed with the usual heat and intensity (Chang Kuo-tao going all out against Mao) and were finally approved. The struggle between two lines in the policies of the united front are very clear in Mao's Lochuan speech. He reiterates that the Red base or bases (later there were to be many more of them) would not be given over to Chiang's control. The preservation of the Communist Party's leadership over the Special Region (Shen-Kan-Ning Border Region) * and in the Red Army, the preservation of the Communist Party's independence and freedom of criticism in its relation with the Kuomintang . . . "these are the limits beyond which it is impermissible to go." Chiang had tried, even in that August, in spite of popular indignation, and even while the Japanese were so menacingly successful in their advance, to negotiate local truces with Japanese commanders and to make "compromises and concessions." How could anyone trust Chiang's leadership? Chiang was trying to get round certain leading commanders in the Red Army, in order to circumvent Mao's ten-point program, by offering them high ranks and ministerial posts. "The united front does not mean relinquishing the leadership, the initiative, but on the contrary taking in hand the initiative by making allies, in order to continue the Revolution."

---

* For convenience, and because historically the Chinese people identified the Eighth Route Army with the Red Army, the terms Eighth Route Army or Red Army will be used rather than Eighteenth Army Corps.

† On March 12, 1936, the USSR and Outer Mongolia had signed a protocol and defensive alliance despite a 1924 Sino-Soviet agreement recognizing Chinese sovereignty over the Mongolian area.

On September 22 a manifesto was issued by the Central Committee. This manifesto was first dated July 15, and seems to have had the approval of some "capitulationists" in the Central Committee and the Politburo; and since Mao Tsetung is reticent about it, it may have been passed over his objections.* The manifesto was endorsed by Chiang Kai-shek, and no wonder, for it is different from the ten-point program formulated by Mao. Sometimes represented as a compromise formula arrived at in view of the "grave" situation, it is a document somewhat ambiguous.

The three aims of the manifesto were: (*1*) Independence and national integrity, return to China of all sovereignty over lost territories (lost to Japan). (*2*) A democratic regime to be instituted, based on the people's rights, through a "national assembly" which would work out a Constitution. (*3*) Improvement of the life of the people, consolidation of the economy and of national defense.

In the four resolutions, the Communist Party pledged to: (*1*) Make every effort to practice the Three Principles of Dr. Sun Yat-sen. (*2*) Renounce the overthrow of the government by armed struggle, renounce the policy of soviets, stop confiscation of landlords' land. (*3*) Dissolve the actual soviet government of the base and practice democracy based on the rights of the people, so as to unify the national political system. (*4*) Disband the Red Army, and reorganize it in a national revolutionary army under direct control of the Military Affairs Commission of the national government and "ready to obey all orders to take part in resistance to foreign invasion."

The first two resolutions embodied concessions already suggested in certain of Mao's speeches and in previous letters of the Central Committee for the period of the Sino-Japanese war. The third is equivocal, though not disadvantageous; it assumes Chiang will democratize his dictatorship but makes no specific demand in that direction. The CCP had already ostensibly "dissolved" the soviet government of the base simply by renaming it, on August 10, 1936, the People's Government instead of the Workers' and Peasants' Gov-

---

* It is a feature of the intra-Party struggle in China (including the recent Great Proletarian Cultural Revolution) that so many opponents of the Mao "line" put out speeches and statements which were either attributed to his influence or considered to reflect his policy when the contrary was true. Thus even an excellent expert like John Lewis ranges the reprinting of Liu Shao-chi's *How to Be a Good Communist* in 1962 as "in line with the ideological remolding" that Mao stressed, when it was the contrary. In 1936, 1937 and 1938, as in recent years before the Cultural Revolution, the Chinese Communist Party spoke with more than one voice, and the attempt to fit all statements into one mold has given rise to erroneous interpretation.

ernment and calling for a people's republic rather than a soviet republic. The Red Army had already been renamed the Eighth Route Army and would be incorporated into Chang's Eighteenth Army Corps. The ambiguity derives from the wording in the fourth resolution, which surrendered, apparently, control of the Red Army to Chiang and accepted obedience to orders to move into the field to fight Chiang's battles. Chiang's acceptance of the "three aims and four resolutions" led, however, to his declaring war on Japan.

Immediately after the endorsement of the manifesto, the Eighth Route Army received orders to march to the Yellow river battle front. The aim was to relieve Chiang's hard-pressed forces and those of the warlord of Shansi province, Yen Hsi-shan, engaged in protecting the capital city of Taiyuan against Japanese attack. This kind of campaign was contrary to all Mao's ideas of how warfare should be carried out. It was to defend a city, and Taiyuan had no real strategic importance; it was not even an industrial city. It was evident that Chiang intended to spare his own troops while paring down the Red Army forces by throwing them time and again into positional warfare battles, for which they were ill-equipped.

The "independent, self-reliant guerilla warfare strategy and tactics" urged by Mao in the course on warfare he was at the time giving to the Red Army cadres and officers in Yenan were to become the main form of war against Japan, but they seem not to have been followed in that first compliance with the terms of the September 22 manifesto. In that great sifting of historical evidence made by the Red Guards, who searched material in the archives, during the Great Proletarian Cultural Revolution, the responsibility was to be placed on the shoulders of Peng Teh-huai and also Chu Teh. But it is difficult, in view of the good use to which this military move was put by the Red Army — building bases behind Japanese lines — to blame the decision taken. Its results were excellent for the revolutionary cause, even if the classic city-taking type of positional warfare Chiang now threw the Red Army into was murderous, facing superior Japanese firepower and massive equipment. Chiang still had ten divisions threatening the "Special Region," and the Red Army's moving in toto out of the base into a neighboring province left a big risk of having the base overrun.

Fortunately it turned out not to be so. Mao's skill at plucking advantage out of disadvantageous circumstances turned the tables on Chiang Kai-shek. Thirty years later, Mao would refuse to let Chu

Teh be criticized for having accepted this move. Simple to the bone, incapable of intrigue, not much of a theoretician, Chu Teh was a good commander, a brave and fearless man, but easily deceived. The action turned out to be one Chiang would regret bitterly having ordered.

The Eighth Route Army was made up of three divisions: the 115th division under Lin Piao and Nieh Jung-chen, the 120th under Ho Lung and Hsiao Ke, the 129th under Liu Po-chen and Hsu Hsiang-chien. The three moved to the Yellow river front, while the Kuomintang troops withdrew. The 120th and the 129th won the battle of Taiyuan by containing two successive Japanese onslaughts, which took a very heavy toll of their numbers — precisely Chiang's aim, to "win the war" against the Communists by attrition of the Red Army. In November the Japanese were to take Taiyuan.

After this bout of conventional warfare and its hard lesson, Mao's strategy would prevail: guerilla war, people's war, political arousal of the masses "in their millions," establishment of guerilla areas, later to be consolidated as bases, *behind* the Japanese lines. This would turn "the Japanese rear into a front," a front which was everywhere and nowhere, fluid, fleeting, borderless, but capturing in its web Japanese troops detailed in ever-increasing numbers to patrol, to garrison, to "pacify." It was the combined action of Japanese aggression and Red Army education of the masses which politicized the Chinese countryside in vast areas ostensibly "occupied" by the Japanese. This laid the foundation for success, not only in the war against Japan but also in the next one, the war against Chiang Kai-shek. Chiang's order to the Eighth Route Army to advance had thus made possible a spreading infiltration of China north of the Yellow river. Now each division of the Red Army fragmented into squads, teams, clusters, sometimes not more than three or four men. They insinuated into the very tissues of the Japanese-occupied areas, educating, rousing, recruiting.

In that September an operation was carried out which gave the Eighth Route Army great prestige and wiped out, in the minds of millions, the disheartening effect of successive Chinese defeats — for Chiang's battalions were crumbling on many fronts. It was the victory of the 115th division under Lin Piao and Nieh Jung-chen, at Pin Hsin Kuan, a victory in mobile warfare operations which halted the Japanese advance into Northwest China. After this battle, Mao gained the upper hand in the struggle with the Party capitulationists. Never again would he allow Chiang to try to utilize the Red Army for attrition purposes.

Japanese units moving into Northwest China during the war (1937–1945).

To "forestall capitulationist tendencies" which were "likely to appear or had appeared," as Ho Kan-chih the historian hints in his *History of the Chinese Revolution,** the Central Committee passed a resolution on September 25, 1937, concerning "the question of participation in the Kuomintang government." It asserted that the government then in existence (Chiang's) was not a government of the anti-Japanese united front, it was still the Kuomintang one-party dictatorship; hence *no Communist should participate in it lest such a step should obscure the stand of the Party and prolong the reactionary rule of the Kuomintang.*

This cleared the ambiguity of the September 22 manifesto; it implied some reproof of the acceptance by Chu Teh and Peng Teh-huai of commands bestowed upon them by Chiang Kai-shek and the military action which followed; checked a tendency (ever recurrent) to consider these appointments really significant. Chiang offered high posts to sundry commanders and also to others in the CCP leadership. The KMT secret police entertained relations, through local officials, with Communist cadres; and a place for KMT "commissars" and "instructors" in the Eighth Route Army units was openly advocated. Insidiousness was more difficult to resist than outright hostility. It must be mentioned here that the Kuomintang Party structure is modeled on the same pattern, though different in principle, as the Communist, and that both derived from the Russian. The political idiom both used, of "struggle" and "national salvation," of "cadres" and "party leadership," could at times confuse the lower levels, and the verbal resemblance increased as the united front established a foundation of common slogans.

"It is most essential to maintain absolutely independent Communist Party leadership in what was originally the Red Army and in all guerilla units, and Communists must not show any vacillation on this matter of principle." Thus ran the directive, attributed to the CC but written by Mao. He also wrote *Combat Liberalism* † in that confused period of wrangling, aimed at people "tolerant" to the point of losing all view of principle in making deals with that arch-cunning politician Chiang Kai-shek. Mao wanted to stress criticism, even of friends, when political principles were involved. The old Chinese habit of "personal relations," constantly invoked to dim the issues, must be done away with. Chiang was adept at utilizing tradi-

---

* Foreign Languages Press, Peking 1959.
† *Combat Liberalism,* is dated September 7, 1937. *Selected Works of Mao Tsetung,* vol. II (English edition Peking 1965).

tional teacher-pupil relations, Confucian emotional ties, to create a mental fuzziness in which erosion of principles could take place.

After this arduous establishment of a united front in the autumn of 1937, Mao was to be burdened with the return of Wang Ming from Moscow; a Wang Ming who still understood nothing of the Chinese situation but who now, from the ultra-leftist line of 1930–1934, had moved to the right in uncritical praise for the "leader of the resistance to Japan, Chiang Kai-shek." The return of Wang Ming to China is described in Chang Kuo-tao's memoirs. It was a gray, still autumn day. Mao, Chang Kuo-tao and some others were conferring (pleasantly) when the drone of a plane was heard. At first they thought it a Japanese bomber, but the plane was trying to land. They went to the midget airport; out of the aircraft, a Russian one, stepped Wang Ming. Mao had not been told beforehand of Wang Ming's return. Li Teh (Otto Braun) was to depart from Yenan on the same Russian plane some days later.

As soon as Wang Ming returned, he set himself up against Mao, and in December 1937 published *A Key to Solving the Present Situation,* which proposed a complete merger of the Red forces with the Kuomintang. Thus the struggle within the Party over the united front policies continued, or began all over again, if it had ever stopped. Wang Ming's adherents now re-formed their ranks. They recalled the resolution adopted on December 20, 1935, by the Central Committee (with Mao dissenting) which had used the phrase "a government of national defense"; Wang Ming sought, with his new article and with the prestige of the Comintern behind him, to widen the scope of dissent. The organizational aspect of the two-line struggle, in which key positions would be held by one or the other faction, would explain why, for so long, Mao's authority in Yenan was contested.

On September 29, 1937, in a report, *Urgent Tasks Following the Establishment of Kuomintang-Communist Cooperation,* Mao took up the question of leadership. He recalled that it was the CCP (through Mao himself) who had called for a united front as far back as 1932. The united front must be extended "to all parties and groups, people in all walks of life and all armed forces . . . a united front of all patriots." On November 12, he again spoke to activists in Yenan. The speech, now entitled *The Situation and Tasks in the Anti-Japanese War After the Fall of Shanghai and Taiyuan,* was another extensive explanation of the situation. He exposed "capitulationism" and ridiculed it. "It [the speech] met with immediate oppo-

346 *The Morning Deluge*

sition from the right opportunists in the Party, and not until the sixth plenary session of the Sixth Central Committee in October 1938 (almost a year after) was the Right deviation basically over-come," is the notice printed as footnote to this report in Mao's *Selected Works*.* This euphemism means the renewed Wang Ming op-position which was stung into open combat by Mao's hard-bitten, effective, and withering prose: ". . . We have the uneven theoretical level among Communists; the fact that many of our Party members lack the experience of cooperation between the two parties gained during the Northern Expedition; the fact that a large number of Party members are of petty bourgeois origin; the reluctance of some Party members to continue a life of bitter struggle; the tendency to-wards unprincipled accommodation with the Kuomintang in the united front; the emergence of a tendency towards a new type of warlordism in the Eighth Route Army. . . ." "We must sharply pose the problem of *who is to lead*. . . ." Thus Mao Tsetung challenged Wang Ming to a strenuous, prolonged debate, which would only be re-solved in 1945.

Historically, events went in the direction Mao had predicted. Whereas in 1937 the Red armies were weak, the cadres insufficient, and many overawed by Chiang's power and military might, by Octo-ber 1938 the situation had changed radically. Chiang had suffered defeat after defeat, losing swiftly Shanghai, Nanking, the big cities, centers of his power; all of North China. His crack regiments van-ished; his government was moved from Nanking to Wuhan in early 1938, but Wuhan was relinquished in that October; Kuangchow also fell that month. The Chiang government refugeed in Chung-king, in far-off Szechuan. Chungking would remain Chiang's capi-tal until the end of the Sino-Japanese war in 1945.

The Kuomintang was thus proved militarily useless, not only be-cause of incompetence, callous mistreatment of its soldiers — the vast majority died of malnutrition and disease, not in fighting — and corruption, but also because of Chiang's own lack of any fighting will, and his policies of deliberate retreats and withdrawals. By October 1938 the Communist armies, though still small, had be-come vitally stronger, and were fighting the Japanese with Mao-taught guerilla tactics. They had expanded, and following the plans drawn by Mao Tsetung and the Revolutionary Military Council in

* See *Selected Works of Mao Tsetung*, vol. II (English edition Peking 1965).

Japanese tanks advance under fire on Nanking, 1937. Below, Hankow
after its destruction by Japanese napalm bombs, 1938.

the summer of 1937, established guerilla areas and bases behind the enemy lines. Not Chiang but Mao was pinning down Japanese divisions; and if in Chungking the press was silent on Communist successes, it was not so in Japan, where the high military command and even the newspapers, such as the *Asahi,* began to hint at Communist prowess.

By October 1938 Chiang Kai-shek was thinking again in terms of an extended truce with Japan. German and British diplomats in China were already functioning as go-betweens. This was the time of Munich in Europe, the appeasement of Hitler by Great Britain and France, the sacrifice of Czechoslovakia. All this faced the USSR with an alarming situation. The prospect of a coalition against Russia, with France, England and Hitler on the western front, Chiang and the Japanese on the eastern front, was unpleasantly near. Moscow's attitude towards Mao changed. Russian news agencies waxed fulsome in praise of the heroic guerillas, immobilizing "vast numbers" of Japanese troops. There would not be, however, military aid from the Soviet Union to the Communist guerillas. All the military aid that came from Russia by an overland route built from 1936 to 1938 went to Chiang Kai-shek's armies. Mao was to make the point that guerilla forces arm themselves chiefly by capturing weapons from the enemy; self-replenishment is one of the abiding principles of guerilla warfare; the Red armies fought the Japanese with Japanese weapons. But the change in Moscow did produce, in the Wang Ming faction, weakening of hostility. The firm ground of the Comintern and Moscow was proving shifting sands.

By the end of 1938 many Party members who had sided with Wang Ming came over to Mao's side; among them was Liu Shao-chi, who is mentioned * by Mao specifically: "Comrade Liu Shao-chi has rightly said that if 'everything through the united front' were simply to mean through Chiang Kai-shek . . . it would mean unilateral submission." This sentence points to the ascendancy of Liu Shao-chi in the Party, an ascendancy which began when Liu decided to join Mao and to reject capitulationism. By the summer of 1938 Chang Kuo-tao had gone over to Chiang Kai-shek, and this also weakened Mao's opponents. At a talk in Lushan attended by his most trusted military officers, Mao revealed Chiang's plan (made in July 1937) to "reduce the Communist Party and Army strength by two fifths during the war." He exposed the "new types of warlordism" in the

* *The Question of Independence and Initiative Within the United Front* (November 5, 1938). *Selected Works of Mao Tsetung,* vol. II (English edition Peking 1965).

Eighth Route Army — undisciplined use of troops without reference to the Central Committee — and "individualistic heroism, taking pride in being given appointments by the Kuomintang" (this pointed to Peng Teh-huai and possibly in some measure to Chu Teh). Measures were taken to uphold the principle of "independence and initiative within the united front." The refusal to admit cadres of the Kuomintang, the rebuttal of "parliamentarism" proposed by certain Party members (which meant a system of people's representatives, but elected by KMT organizations), the correction of the tendency "towards excessive accommodation . . . in certain base areas," the re-establishment of political commissars from the Communist Party, strengthened Party unity, said Mao. "Many people *inside* and *outside* the Party . . . belittled the important strategic role of guerilla warfare and pinned their hopes on regular warfare alone." To teach guerilla war, Mao wrote in May 1938 his *Problems of Strategy in Guerilla War Against Japan* and *On Protracted War,* which together with *Problems of Strategy in China's Revolutionary War* (December 1936) are major military works which were destined to educate the Red Army and the cadres in people's war.

There was also the matter of the New Fourth Army, made up of the guerillas who had remained behind in the Central Base and in the area of Chingkangshan, and not participated in the Long March. In 1937, Chen Yi went to find them. He traveled disguised as a merchant, his corpulence and jovial wit lending itself to this role. The guerillas at first would not believe him, and nearly killed him as a traitor when they heard about a united front with Chiang. (Chen Yi was also pursued by a tiger, and hid in a cave.) He finally persuaded the guerillas to reassemble. Chiang had agreed to their presence, but stipulated that their strength remain at 15,000 and that they refrain from any expansion; they were to move to Anhwei province, and he also tried to incorporate them in his own troops. "We have taken special care not to concentrate forces regardless of circumstances which would suit the Kuomintang," wrote Mao . . . "Not to accept Kuomintang appointees . . . to be vigilant against a sudden attack by the Kuomintang. . . . Our chief purpose is to extend the ground already won and realize the positive aim of winning the masses . . . the deepest source of the immense power of war lies in the masses." But from the very start, the presence and the activities of the New Fourth Army would give Chiang much concern. They were too near the vital centers of his own influence, astride the lower reaches of the Yangtze river.

Quite openly, then, Mao was not going to obey Chiang. The united front meant united action against the Japanese, but with "independence and initiative" in Communist hands, with the leadership of the masses in Communist hands, with freedom for the expansion and spread, both in territory and in political ideology, of Communist power, with an entirely new and masterly strategy of warfare, decided by the Communists, not by Chiang. Hence, within the united front the question of seizure of power was implied; this both Mao and Chiang understood very well. The outcome would depend on Mao Tsetung, on his work of that period, his vision and grasp, and his boldness. Hence the Yenan period remains an enduring lesson in the skills of war, diplomacy and politics; for the Chinese Revolution, the foundations of its victory.

After his return from Russia in late 1937, Wang Ming held several appointments — on the Central Committee, in the Politburo, and as one of the seven Communist members of the liaison committee organized under Chou En-lai to deal with united front matters between the Kuomintang and the Communist Party. His wife, Meng Ching-shu, also on the Central Committee, became the president of Yenan Women's University. The liaison offices functioned in Sian, and also in Wuhan till it fell in October 1938; then the committee moved to Chungking along with Chiang's government. This liaison committee had a press section to deal with foreign and Chinese newsmen. Chou En-lai was chief spokesman, but Wang Ming did not refrain from issuing statements and making speeches for the Party, going counter to Central Committee resolutions when he chose.

The ideological struggle was "severe," writes the historian Hu Chiao-mu. Those responsible for "the third left line" became "rightist opportunists," "took independent action against Party rules in their work, issued statements without approval, thought the Communist army was too small . . . decided the Kuomintang should assume the leadership . . . denied the Communist Party leadership." They also looked down on guerilla warfare tactics and looked for "speedy victory," contrary to Mao's protracted war; they "believed . . . not in the masses," derided mass education and mobilization. Their slogan, "unity of action . . . a unified command, unified program, unified administration, unified discipline, unified weapons," was a pro-Chiang Kai-shek line.

Wang Ming failed, the defeats of Chiang became his own defeat;

the virulence of his faction faded, though not its long-term, protracted hostility to Mao. Mao Tsetung nailed down the leadership role the Communist Party should play in the war. In October–November 1938, at the sixth plenum of the Sixth Central Committee, he won the majority votes of the Central Committee. His three speeches * climaxed his ideological victory, the downfall of "left" and "right" factions and the rallying of the Party in unity behind Mao.

Mao would never do things by halves. He had put up with a good many insults, and now he swung back at his accusers, at the accusations of chauvinism and lack of "international proletarianism" repeatedly launched at him: "Only those who are politically muddle-headed or have ulterior motives talk nonsense about . . . our having abandoned internationalism. . . . To separate internationalist content from national form is the practice of those who do not understand the first thing about internationalism. . . ." "The victory of the Chinese national liberation movement will be part of the victory of world socialism, because to defeat imperialism in China means the destruction of one of its most powerful bases."

Revolution was not to be made by people who parroted empty slogans. These were really arrogant and slothful, for they never used their heads. Revolution was a matter of learning not only "the theory of Marx, Engel, Lenin and Stalin" but also "our historical heritage." "It is a matter of learning to *apply* the theory of Marxism-Leninism to the specific conditions of China. . . ."

"Foreign stereotypes must be abolished, there must be less singing of empty abstract tunes, and dogmatism must be laid to rest; they must be replaced by the fresh, lively Chinese style and spirit which the common people of China love." In these terms Mao announced his next battle, to restructure the Party itself.†

On November 6, Mao concluded the plenum with his analysis of the role of armed struggle and its importance for the Chinese Revolution. "The seizure of power by armed force, the settlement of the issue of war, is the central task and the highest form of revolution." Armed struggle, the direction of a revolutionary Party, and the strategy of the united front were once again asserted as the three funda-

---

* *The Role of the Chinese Communist Party in the National War; The Question of Independence and Initiative Within the United Front;* and *Problems of War and Strategy* (November 5 and 6, 1938). *Selected Works of Mao Tsetung,* vol. II.

† Emphasis not in original.

Mao Tsetung at the sixth plenary session of the Sixth Central Committee in Yenan, November 1938.

mental principles for the prosecution of revolution. They are today referred to as the "three precious things" or "three magic weapons" for revolution.

At the end of the plenum, everything had swung in Mao's favor — Chiang's fiascos, Moscow's attitude, the growing strength of the Red armies. Wang Ming had lost the battle of the united front, but it would take many more years before his influence was rooted out of the Party — as the Great Proletarian Cultural Revolution was to prove.

In 1937 the slogan of a "government of national defense" launched by Wang Ming had been taken up by the Left Writers' League, whose headquarters were in Shanghai. Four writers, of whom Chou Yang, secretary-general of the league, was to become the most notorious, promoted it in the league. This slogan had important repercussions upon the literature produced in left-wing circles. The ideological struggle in the Party was thus reflected in "two lines" in art and literature; complete clarification of these literary battles did not come until thirty years later.

The four writers, Chou Yang, Hsia Yen, Tien Han and Yang Han-sen, who echoed Wang Ming's theme, spreading the slogan "A literature of national defense," were denounced with great asperity by the famous Lu Hsun, whom Mao read and praised.

Lu Hsun, China's Gorky, became a Communist rather late in a short life. He was an intensely active, brilliant, dedicated patriot, a fiercely honest man. He had studied medicine in Japan, but turned to literature, and to the literary revolution. In the early 1930's he became a Communist. Mao admired him. They were much alike in one respect — they were artists of total integrity. There may have been correspondence between the two, though they may not have met, except perhaps briefly at Peking University in 1920. Mao Tse-tung often quoted Lu Hsun, praised his courage, studied his writings. Some of Mao's essays in the 1940's show the influence of Lu Hsun's sharp satirical style.

When the call for a united front came from Mao Tsetung in 1932 and 1933, Lu Hsun was one of the first to respond, writing and praising Mao's initiative. Lu Hsun battled fascism and reaction all his life, completely unafraid of threats, poverty or Chiang's power. He went on writing, protesting, encouraging the young. He was one of those who understood Mao's genius and vision, for at the end of the Long March, Lu Hsun sent a message to the CCP and Mao Tsetung: "The whole of the Chinese people look towards you for their salvation."

Lu Hsun took great exception to the term "literature of national defense," derided "the four guys" (as he called them) who promoted it, and launched the slogan "A literature for the revolutionary masses in resistance to Japan." Lu Hsun also denounced with pungent irony, in letters and essays, Chou Yang and Hsian Yen as "bureaucrats and officials of literature." They in turn never forgave him.*

The two slogans meant not only two different concepts of the united front but two entirely different political and ideological backgrounds for literary production. Since literature and art, in Marxist terms, are an inherent part of the superstructure (the realm of ideas, behavior, expression being inseparable from the physical base, the political, economic and social system), one slogan represented a capitulationist, "revisionist," "bourgeois" line, the other a revolutionary — Mao's — line. In 1970 and 1971 long articles were still appearing in Chinese newspapers on "the two lines in art and literature," denouncing Chou Yang and his three colleagues (all of whom had obtained high positions in the CCP) and exposing the "Wang Ming line" of the late 1930's.

What is even more thought-provoking is that the opposition to Mao should have survived, impervious to time and to the triumph of the Revolution, among the same people and for so long. There can be no understanding of the Great Proletarian Cultural Revolution without study of these problems of thirty years or more ago.

In November 1938, with a majority of the Party behind him, with Chiang proved "a big straw bag" in battle, with Chang Kuo-tao turned renegade, with Moscow eulogizing the Communist guerilla victories, Mao was able to state: "We have rejected the Kuomintang's request to appoint its members cadres of the Eighth Route Army, and have upheld the principle of the Communist Party's absolute leadership of the Eighth Route Army." The heart of the matter.

And none too soon. For in early 1939 the unstable marriage between the two parties, always under strain, suffered an increasing number of what were subduedly labeled "frictions." Chiang had al-

---

* From an interview of the author with Lu Hsun's wife, Madame Hsu Kuang-ping, July 1966. The *Selected Works of Lu Hsun* have been translated by the Foreign Lanugage Press, Peking.

ready in 1938 issued documents entitled *Methods of Dealing with the CCP* and *Methods of Restricting the Activities of the Alien Party*. Armed clashes began in April 1939. The ten divisions of Hu Tsung-nan, quartered in Shensi to keep watch over the Red base, now attacked and overran about one quarter of its territory, though this territory had been guaranteed inviolate under the administration of the Communists. Hu Tsung-nan erected rings of blockhouses and deep trenches around the base on three sides, leaving open only the side that faced the Japanese, who themselves were to start blockading the Red base in 1940.

But the struggle to establish, then to maintain, this apparently short-lived and none too successful united front is not to be validated by success in getting on with Chiang Kai-shek. This was the least of Mao's worries at any time; nor was it the purpose of the united front to placate him. The success of the united front was in obtaining, through this avowedly unstable alliance, leadership of the majority of the population. The rallying of as many of the bourgeoisie as possible, under the pressure of resistance to Japan, made the Party acceptable as a national leader; its role in the social revolution was thus enhanced. Each one saw in the CCP what he wanted to see. The policies followed during the years at Yenan would be different from those of previous Red bases. But there was never any cheating; all this was clearly spelled out; never did the Communists stoop to defining themselves as "agrarian reformists"; one has only to read Mao Tsetung's assertion that the final aim, Communism, would never be given up, to know it.*

The appraisal of the united front by some writers who judge its success or failure by the relations between the two parties, relations which deteriorated so rapidly, is therefore incorrect — this was never the objective. Only by the measure in which the Communists were able to build up their strength and win the masses through the united front can its success be judged; and in this, under Mao's leadership, the CCP was startlingly successful.

By creating this charismatic, national, immensely attractive image (and openly announcing each step) the CCP was able to build up strength and win the masses. But it is doubtful whether this success could have been achieved without the persistence, the vision and the methods of Mao Tsetung.

* "Communists will never give up their ideal of socialism and of Communism; they will reach it by going through the stage of the bourgeois-democratic revolution."

2

Profile of Yenan

The Yenan period — as the years from 1935 to 1947 were to be known — is the most important in Mao Tsetung's life. The development of his creative thinking, his methodology of revolution, his "style," his major philosophical and military works date from that time. They are the years in which he rebuilt the Chinese Communist Party and Army as revolutionary instruments with a total adaptation to the Chinese situation. The slogans of Yenan, the spirit of Yenan, the teaching and writing Mao Tsetung accomplished at Yenan, are China's renewal patterns, models not confined to a small group but known and practiced by each man, woman and child. This was the time when Mao Tsetung led his people into their own heritage, when the Thought of Mao Tsetung was first structured, became a working system, a science of revolution.

The Shensi-Kansu-Ninghsia base (known for short as Shen-Kan-Ning, or as Yenan from the name of its capital after December 1936), was more than Chingkangshan or Juichin. It was not only a Red base, with a government and social system different from Chiang's, but it became the emblem of love of country, incorruptibility, resistance to Japan, social justice. Blockade or no blockade, students and intellectuals, from 1936 on, flocked to Yenan, across Japanese-held territory, across Kuomintang barbed wire and trenches. If caught they were murdered, tortured, put in concentration camps. Yenan is 300 miles from Sian, and daily the gauntlet of secret police and the blockade was run by youngsters who left home to walk the dangerous roads to Yenan because it was the future.

Everything was lacking in 1935, when the Red Army arrived after the Long March. Devastating floods poured down the gullies of the loess cliffs, and if there was not flood there was drought. Famine stalked the land two years out of three (in 1929, 2.5 million people out of the 9 million in Shensi province died of starvation). The harvests were scanty and millet was the staple food. There were no paper, books, wood for furniture, or machinery, no industries, no resources except salt in Ninghsia — difficulties of transport made it very costly — and coal. Yet Yenan was to become the tough, secure and prestigious base where Mao trained, educated, and disciplined over a hundred thousand cadres, and an army of 2 million men was to be controlled from here. From Yenan was to issue the most formidable unity and power that China ever had. For a decade Yenan pinned down 50 percent of the Japanese armies in North China (2 million men), 80 percent of the puppet Chinese armies organized by the Japanese (another 2 million men).

The Red Army had sappers developed from the toughened miners of Anyuan and Pinghsiang who had followed Mao all through the years and the Long March (some are still with him today). Through guerilla actions and later through the friendly Manchurian officers of Chang Hsueh-liang, the Army obtained a few lathes, printing blocks, sewing machines. With these began the basic "industries" necessary for survival.

The Kuomintang started to blockade Yenan in earnest in 1939. All subsidies stopped. Attacks against the base increased in frequency throughout 1939 and 1940, to culminate in the massacre of the New Fourth Army in January 1941. After the summer of 1940, because of the ill-conceived Hundred Regiments offensive carried out by Peng Teh-huai against the Japanese, the Yenan base had to withstand rigorous blockades and reprisal attacks from both the Kuomintang and Japan. In 1941 and 1942, imitating Chiang's blockhouse tactics, the Japanese erected 7,700 fortifications and made Chinese peasants dig more than 7,000 miles of tiered trenches to surround and cut off the Red bases behind Japanese lines and the Yenan base.

The Japanese also launched a scorched-earth drive which reduced the bases in size and produced immense suffering and hardship among the people. Within a 12-mile corridor around each base, in areas known to be pro-Communist, all the men were killed, the women taken away, all the houses and crops burned. Vast tracks of land were left covered only with rubble and charred cinders. It is estimated that 30 million civilian people lost their lives through these "kill all, burn all" scorched-earth methods of the Japanese. "For a while we were reduced almost to the state of having no clothes to wear, no oil to cook with, no paper, no vegetables, no footwear for the soldiers, and in winter, no bedding for the civilian personnel."

Mao's answer was the Production Drive, launched in 1941, which transformed the base and also was to serve as a model in mass education in self-reliance. "Self-reliance" and "Get organized" were the slogans. Cotton growing was established in some of the Red bases behind the Japanese lines. Women hid the cotton harvest from the Japanese, hand-spun it at home for the Red Army. This was the first time that women had collectively and massively gone into production and were paid for their work, an economic precedent which was also a social revolution.

The machines in the spinning factories newly set up were wonders of contrivance; the belts were made of homespun soaked in resin. Factories were installed in shacks, caves, temples. Workshops for making batteries, wire, shoes, toothbrushes, soap and matches and paper were established. Paper was so scarce at first that even the rough straw paper needed for hygienic purposes was severely restricted. Production in chemicals, glass and porcelain started from a few pottery kilns; leather goods workshops were built. "Essential springs were made of coiled telephone wire looted from the Japanese, hardened and tempered by heating in a crucible with charcoal and old bones to 700 to 800 degrees Centigrade; the shop foreman who had improvised this was justly proud. He demonstrated the superiority of his telephone wire spring which, dropped from the same height, bounced higher than an imported sample," wrote Harrison Forman in his book *Report from Red China.** By 1944 there were 90 workshops employing around 20,000 men in the Yenan base, and an arsenal employing 300 men which made explosives and grenades. However, most of the firearms and ammunition continued to come from enemy sources.

A general union of workers was created in 1940; in 1943 it had 55,694 members of whom 63 percent were farm laborers, 22 percent handicraft workers and 15 percent industrial workers. By 1944 Yenan was exporting men's socks, candles, and cloth to the supposedly richer Kuomintang regions. It fed its people and it clothed them; it inspired initiative and it promoted stability. Many industries were formed with private capital and were under private management; over half were cooperatives formed with government loans as working capital.

In the Production Drive everyone was set to digging, hoeing,

* Harrison Forman *Report from Red China* (New York 1945).

planting, plowing — the Army, the cadres, the Party, the intellectuals, the officials, Mao himself. All planted and hoed, dug and spun. This "stupendous" effort, as Jerome Chen * calls it, merits study because it confirmed Mao's policies, already put into practice at the previous bases, for a materially self-supporting government administration and a Red Army which was also a production force. It turned a threatening bureaucracy of consumers into producers or part producers. During this Production Drive in Yenan we find Mao stressing using native ways and means, making do, ingenuity, initiative, frugality and economy — in short, all that is now being done on an all-China scale to make an industrial revolution with no capital but with *people,* their effort and their wisdom, their zeal and their tenacity, their awareness and their devotion to the collective.

The use of the garrisoned army battalions as a production and labor force remains a basic feature of the Red Army. In February 1971, for instance, the Army was again commended for producing 40 percent more grain in 1970 than in 1969, for running factories, workshops, plants. This tradition of the soldier being a "three in one" — a worker, a soldier, and also a peasant — was solidly implanted at Yenan, where the Army also ran cooperatives in industries. The Nanniwan valley, a bare, desolate tract, was converted by the garrisoned troops into a fertile stretch of fields. "The soldiers have on the average cultivated 18 mou [2.75 acres] per person; and they can produce or make practically everything: food (vegetables, meat, cooking oil), clothing (cotton padded clothes, woolen knitwear and footwear), shelter (cave dwellings, houses and meeting halls), articles of daily use (tables, chairs, benches, stationery) and fuel (firewood, charcoal, coal)." This was Mao's satisfied assessment in 1942, and he called upon all to do the same. In 1944 the American Dixie mission † was impressed by the rugged, successful self-sufficiency of Yenan. By then, 600,000 acres of land had been opened up, and production of cereals had doubled in the base.

In *On Financial and Economic Problems of the Border Region,* a 200-page report made in December 1944, Mao explained how "self-reliance, by making nonproducers such as civil servants, Army men, produce their own food, could cut down enormously our public expenditure." "The Kuomintang thought our difficulties insurmountable, they daily expected our collapse." But it was the KMT

* Jerome Chen *Mao and the Chinese Revolution* (New York and London 1965).
† David Barrett *Dixie Mission: The United States Army Observer Group in Yenan, 1944* (Berkeley 1970).

finances which were on the point of collapse.* "In 1941 and 1942 the supplies obtained by the Army, the organizations and the schools *through their own efforts* were actually the larger part of their total requirements." "This is a miracle never before achieved in Chinese history and forms our unshakable material foundation."

In December 1935 a land law was passed for redistribution of surplus land belonging to landlords and rich peasants, but in 1937 confiscation of land was halted and rent reduction of 25 percent or more substituted. The peasants in most cases demanded more reduction, so that sharing of the crop in kind, in the proportion of 30 to the landlord and 70 to the peasant, was followed in some base areas. Usury was also controlled, but "not to the point where the peasant would find it impossible to obtain loans" (1.5 percent per month was set as the standard interest; the rates had been 15 to 20 percent per month before the Red Army arrived). But none of this could be granted "as a favor." Mao insisted that the land reform must involve the peasantry in arousal, mobilization, formation of peasant associations to elect their own leaders, to perform rent reduction and see it enforced, though Party cadres and the local governments of the bases would help by directives and their presence. This remained the land reform policy till the end of 1946.

Mao would explain † that anti-Japanese resistance and land reform were linked; the masses who resisted Japanese aggression were also those who wanted a social revolution; the archaic, feudal land tenure could not serve as foundation for a national liberation movement. However, confiscation of landlords' land caused the flight of landlords to the cities, and was suspended. Freedom to expand production in industry and commerce was safeguarded. The number of commercial establishments in Yenan rose from 192 to 475 during those years.

The cooperative movement in agriculture began with mutual aid teams, semi-permanent, then permanent, sometimes affecting a whole village. Each locality fixed its own rules concerning working hours, accounting, remuneration (later to be known as work points). Mao insisted that women should be included in this scheme. "All women, too, should be mobilized to do a certain amount of productive work. . . . Such collective mutual-aid producers' cooperatives should be extensively and voluntarily organized in all the anti-Japanese base areas . . . there should be no constraint or forcing." Mao

* As certain American observers reported even then.
† See Guenther Stein *The Challenge of Red China* (New York 1945).

stressed the voluntary aspect; the cooperatives were still based on individual economy and were not socialism, but a step in the right direction. Twenty-four percent of the labor force was thus organized into mutual aid teams.

The amount of land under plow almost doubled in the Shen-Kan-Ning base; an agriculturally deficient area, the base became a self-sufficient production region by 1944. In 1943 the rations of an average Red Army soldier were by Chinese standards the best in China, almost 4.5 pounds of meat a month, 48 pounds of vegetables, 60 pounds of millet, with oil, fuel and salt — "The best-nourished troops I had yet seen." * Where pay was concerned, privates and officers received the same, amounting to 5 cents a day pocket money. No distinction of grades in uniform or trappings was allowed. The general health of the population was also improved, though conservatism and superstition, the lack of doctors and nurses, restricted development.

Various types of industrial cooperatives, for salt transport, credit, and handicrafts, made for secure supplies. By 1943, 137,000 women were in spinning cooperatives, 200,000 men in handicraft and transport cooperatives. The Army had its own industrial and transport cooperatives, as it would have its own food, cloth and shoe production. Under the famous New Zealander Rewi Alley, now living in Peking, the Indusco scheme was set up which established schools for technical training in various fields, such as soap-making, tanning leather, making ropes, shoes, matches, pots and pans. The base also issued its own money in 1941, since no more came from the Kuomintang after 1940.

Mao did not intend land reform and the cooperatives to remain at that "new democratic" stage. "At the moment," he said, "there cannot be a *more radical* solution to the agrarian problem; but it will become imperative one day to go further . . . but only when a truly democratic government will be in control in the whole of China. . . . However," he added, "it is not impossible that a new civil war might start when the war with Japan is ended." †

The enrollment of the population in cooperatives, associations and unions helped mass education, which was placed under the aegis of Hsu Te-li as commissioner for education. The old teacher of Mao

* Harrison Forman *Report from Red China* (New York 1945). This is corroborated by other American observers.
† Interview with Guenther Stein; see *The Challenge of Red China* (New York 1945).

at the Changsha Normal College was sixty years old in 1937. Mao wrote to him: "You were my teacher twenty years ago; you are still my teacher; you will continue to be my teacher in the future. When the Revolution failed and many members left the Party . . . you joined in the autumn of 1927. . . . You have shown . . . less fear of difficulty, and more humility in learning new things, than many younger members." *

But the base was of a forbidding poverty and backwardness. In 1936 it had a 60 percent infant mortality rate and a 1 percent literacy rate. Even in 1943 there were still a million illiterates (half the population) and 2,000 shamans (witch doctors). By 1940, 1,341 schools and 43,625 students for the 2 million people in the Shen-Kan-Ning base had been established. But the results of formal schooling were poor.† Only through the Production Drive did adult literacy classes, winter classes, self-teaching units operate. In the building of the Red Army, education was a powerful incentive (as was the fact that the families of Red Army recruits had privileges such as guaranteed team help for their fields). Recruits were taught reading and writing; because of paper shortage they often wrote in sand on the ground, and learned words by wearing paper squares showing characters on their backs as they filed one behind the other.

In October 1944 Mao wrote: "A good many vestiges of feudalism survive. . . . These are enemies inside the minds of the people . . . more difficult to combat than to fight Japanese imperialism." He advocated scattered village schools, street schools, a mass self-education drive. In 1971 this type of street school was revived and called Kangta, in memory of the Yenan period and the educational innovations of those days.

The people themselves were to be aroused to "struggle" against their own superstitions, unhygienic habits, and illiteracy. Parents were asked their advice on the study program at school, which was linked to production. Corporal punishment was forbidden. Hygiene, defense, and political education were integrated in the school courses. Each school united "practice" with "theory," which meant rearing pigs, poultry, planting trees, digging wells as part of the courses. A medical school and school of nursing were started. Mao urged the doctors to go to serve the people. "The human and animal

* Jerome Chen (editor) *Mao Papers: Anthology and Bibliography* . (New York and London 1970).

† See Peter J. Seybolt, "The Yenan Revolution in Mass Education," *China Quarterly* no. 48 (October–December 1971).

mortality rates are both very high . . . doctors should train doctors for the people. . . . [If] they do not unite with the thousand or more doctors and veterinarians of the old type . . . they will actually be helping the witch doctors."

In 1942 the administrative policies of the government of the base were organized on a system of "the three thirds" — one third of the seats in councils and committees, in labor unions, women's associations, youth corps, and other mass representation bodies being occupied by Communists, the other two thirds by "progressives" and independent members. The main object was to secure a broad base among the people and popular support. The slogan "Unified leadership and decentralized administration" defined the control exercised — overall authority and leadership were concentrated in Yenan but local originality and initiative were encouraged, a system which required a high level of political education. Throughout the far-flung territories of the bases, despite difficult communications, a single leadership prevailed and the decisions of the Party were carried through. Even if there were attempts at "independent kingdoms," they never developed into real dissidence.

The popularity of the Communist government was assured by its honesty, its integrity, the high caliber of its cadres; by fair distribution, by democratic procedure, by the security given to the population, by the abolition of extortion and the low level of taxation. This was reinforced by the help given by the Army to peasants, welfare and education movements. Army teams dug wells and ditches, helped in harvesting, substantiating the slogans "Support the Army, cherish the people," "Total integration of Army and people." In turn, this popularity eased recruiting. "The Communist government and armies are the first in modern Chinese history to have positive and widespread popular support . . . because they are genuinely of the people," wrote John Paton Davies, an American observer in November 1944, one of a score of such favorable reports on the Communist administration. The enrollment of the population in mass organizations made for democratic platforms for expression of opinion by the people, and for social change. There were associations of women, youths, peasants, workers, schoolchildren, old people; there was even an association of loafers where the loafers met, helped to criticize each other and themselves so as to "reform"!

The exaltation of the "wisdom of the people," the lists of "labor heroes," the new dignity and pride conferred on the ordinary poor peasant left memories which could not be eradicated. Suddenly the downtrodden became important, they learned the meaning of human dignity. The terrible massacres by the Japanese, the vicious oppression and ruthless killings by Kuomintang troops, in glaring contrast to the care and scrupulous democracy of the Communist Party and Red Army, turned the support of the population towards the Communists. By 1943 the peasants were hailing Mao as their "star of salvation."

Mao had come into the base after the Long March with 7,000 men; with the 5,000 already there, and Hsu Hai-tung's 3,000, a total of 15,000 men was all the base had by the end of 1935. In 1937 the Army numbered 70,000 to 80,000 men, though Chiang only supplied arms, equipment and money for 45,000 (from September 1937 to May 1939). The New Fourth Army had been limited to a 15,000 maximum. This made a total of 60,000 men for the Red Army. Yet by 1945 the Red armies numbered 910,000 men in the Communist regular forces and 2,200,000 in the militia. This enormous expansion in seven years, unfinanced by external sources, was not the burden it could have been since it was 70 percent self-sufficient. (The militia were always self-sufficient except for weapons, and constituted a feed-in reserve for the Red Army.) In this planned overall structure, almost biological in its concept, education of the Red Army was itself a means of providing cadres, leaders and instructors for mass education, thus facilitating the Revolution *and* Army recruitment.

Mao's directive, "We must spread a guerilla war over all the large areas occupied by the enemy, converting the enemy's rear into his front, and forcing him to fight ceaselessly throughout his occupied areas," was followed. To wage guerilla warfare "independently and on its own initiative" was *also* to mobilize the population, to educate it, politicize it. With its Party educators and propagandists divided and subdivided into small teams, the Party within the Army spread among the villages of China, bringing hope and militancy. Its first offensives were political, not military — propaganda, land reform, education; later came the establishment of guerilla zones, still later consolidation into bases. This step-by-step organization of the population was entirely dependent on the "fish in water" phenomenon, conditional on the support of the people. The elimination of local collaborators and bandits, collection of enemy weapons, sabotage of enemy installations became cohesive factors in which the people now took the initiative. Perhaps the most outstanding and impressive phenomenon was the gathering of intelligence by the people, as the

American observer group in Yenan found out.* Men, women and children became detectives, risking their lives to report on the enemy to the "brother Army."

The formation of bases behind Japanese lines began in 1937. After the battle of Pin Hsin Kuan (September 1937), the 115th division of Lin Piao and Nieh Jung-chen established, with the massif of Wutai mountain as center, the Shansi-Chahar-Hopei Base Area. This was to extend into central and eastern Hopei province in 1938; it spawned offshoots into the southern Hopei plains. It finally controlled a population of around 25 million living in 108 counties covering 309,000 square miles. In 1939 it spread west of Peking into Jehol, into the Liaoning province of Manchuria. This sprawl across North China was essential for long-term strategy: the access to Manchuria. Small guerilla nuclei were already implanted in Manchuria well before the civil war began in 1946.

The 129th division established the Shansi-Hopei-Shantung-Honan Base Area, with the Taihang mountains as its center. It was a very large area of two sectors, one of 85,000 square miles with 7 million inhabitants and 59 counties, and one of 122,000 square miles, 118 counties and 18 million inhabitants. The Shansi-Suiyuan base, established by the 120th division, barred the Japanese advance into Mongolia; and the Shantung base, first organized by local Communist cadres, was so successful that by 1943 the Communists controlled over half the province and there were half a million militia. Shantung army recruits were used extensively in Manchuria (almost 28 million out of Manchuria's 30 million people came originally from Shantung province).

The Central China Base Area, organized by the New Fourth Army in the lower Yangtze basin, operated in two routes, one south of the Yangtze river and the other north, in Anhwei province. The New Fourth Army was plagued with difficulties, not the least being that its second in command Hsiang Ying, vice-chairman at the Juichin base (with Chang Kuo-tao) when Mao was chairman, was one of the men who sided with Chang Kuo-tao and the "ultra-left" (which, let us not forget, became "right"!) against Mao's military ideas in Juichin. He had been left behind in 1934 when the Long March began, and proved a courageous man even if not always very

* See David Barrett *Dixie Mission: The United States Army Observer Group in Yenan, 1944* (Berkeley 1970).

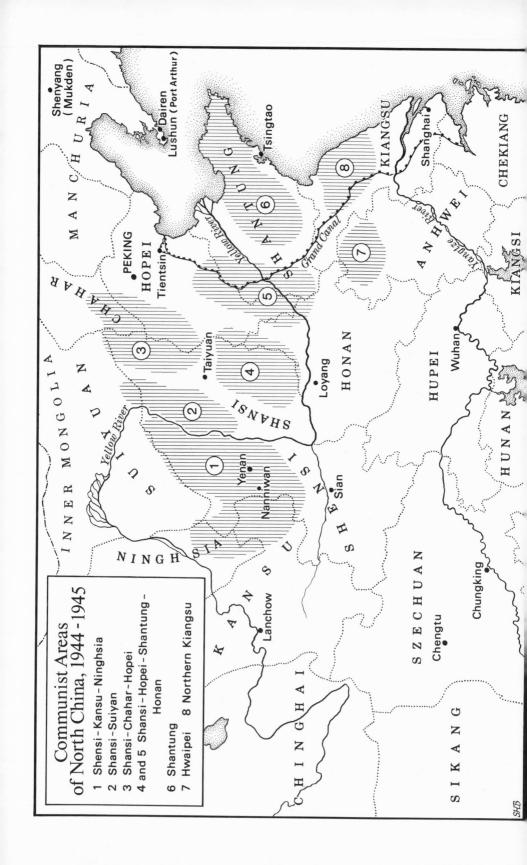

Communist Areas
of North China, 1944-1945

1 Shensi-Kansu-Ninghsia
2 Shansi-Suiyan
3 Shansi-Chahar-Hopei
4 and 5 Shansi-Hopei-Shantung-Honan
6 Shantung
7 Hwaipei   8 Northern Kiangsu

intelligent, unyielding, and somewhat inclined to stubbornness. Hsiang continued averse to Mao's suggestions, though as a good Communist he had condemned Chang Kuo-tao's defection. He differed with Mao on the conduct of operations for the New Fourth Army; thought a policy of "appeasement" of Chiang was best. Hsiang Ying's "trust" in Chiang did not save him when in January 1941 the New Fourth Army elements south of the Yangtze were ambushed by Chiang forces and 9,000 slaughtered, including Hsiang Ying. This massacre was to mark the high point of Kuomintang attacks upon the Communists during the Sino-Japanese war.

Then there were the South China bases in Kwangtung, where the movement had been strong in 1927. The Pearl river column was formed in 1941, and by 1944 10 million people were in small base areas scattered across Kwangtung and Kwangsi provinces. "Communists never die" became a saying among the South China peasants when they saw their resurrection.

In Hainan Island the entry of the Japanese in 1939 also saw the emergence of Communist guerillas, and by 1945 eight out of the 19 counties of the island were under Red control.

The physical splaying out of the bases provided a network of Communist administration, a "state within a state" effect, well before the civil war with Chiang started again. But a high political level in cadres was essential to keep this geographical sprawl united by an ideology stronger than distance or time. To this cadre training Mao devoted an enormous amount of his days and his work; for this purpose, as soon as he had reached the base after the Long March, he began writing whole courses in philosophy (dialectics), military matters (strategy and tactics), economics and politics. But to keep the Party in command of the guns meant Party cadres not only politically educated but also imbued with military knowledge. "The popularization of military knowledge is an urgent task for the Party and the whole country. I deem it imperative that we arouse interest in the study of military theory and direct the attention of the whole membership [of the Party] to the study of military matters."

Army leaders would publicly criticize themselves for misbehavior of their soldiers towards the local population, encourage the local peasantry to report misdeeds. These educational disciplines are now enshrined in the traditions of the Chinese Revolution and promote the solidarity essential to the system. The soldiers' clubs, instituted at Sanwan immediately after the Autumn Harvest Uprising, were revived during the Yenan period. They had been abolished in Juichin in 1932.

Mao Tsetung as chairman of the Revolutionary Military Council and as top man in the Politburo combined the Party-Army hierarchy in one person. This unusual combination of both military and Party strategy was to be highly successful, for Mao would now, in this backward area, forge the most efficient weapon for military and political triumph that the world has yet seen.

The effectiveness of the Red guerillas in dealing with the Japanese is evidenced by documents from the Japanese military command in China. "General Nishio's chief of staff admitted at an army briefing that the Chinese Communist forces had filled a power vacuum in northern Shansi, in Hopei, in most of Shantung and in north Kiangsu," writes Chalmers Johnson.* "The intense anti-Japanese attitude on the part of the Chinese (Communist) armies is beyond dispute." Of 15,000 engagements of the Japanese armies from 1937 to 1945, wrote the Tokyo newspaper *Asahi Shimbun,* 75 percent had been fought against the Red armies. Chalmers Johnson relates that the Bethune International Peace Hospital,† located in the Wutai base, which had 1,500 beds, could be evacuated on a half-hour's notice and was in fact evacuated twenty times. The Chinese Communists had mastered the art of creating in Japanese-occupied areas a state of constant alert and the mobilization of the population in techniques of sabotage.

From 1937 to 1945 the Red armies would fight 92,000 battles, inflict a million casualties, capture 150,000 prisoners (mostly Chinese puppets — only a few hundred Japanese were captured, most preferring to die), 320,000 rifles, 9,000 machine guns, 600 pieces of artillery; they would kill 55 high-ranking Japanese officers and suffer 400,000 casualties; all this without a single penny, bullet, or pound of food supplied by the Kuomintang after 1940.

After the fall of Wuhan in October 1938, Chiang Kai-shek settled into a tacit truce, a prolonged stalemate, with the Japanese, which lasted till 1945. For the next five and a half years action on his front would be desultory, if not make-believe, while both concentrated on attacking the Communists, almost in concert. The passage of a good

* See Chalmers Johnson *Peasant Nationalism and Communist Power: The Emergence of Revolutionary China 1937–1945* (Stanford 1962).

† So called in memory of Norman Bethune, the Canadian doctor who worked for the Red Army and died of septicemia in China in 1938.

Chu Teh (right) and Mao Tsetung in Yenan, about 1937.

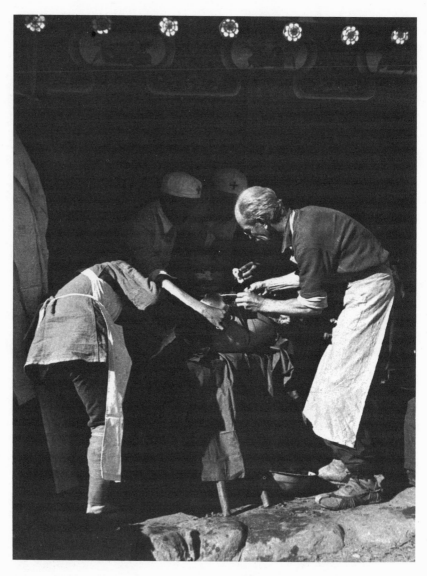

*Dr. Norman Bethune operates on a wounded soldier of the Eighth
Route Army in North China, October 1939.*

many of Chiang's troops and of some forty of his high commanders to the Japanese in 1943 and 1944 furthered this unspoken common enterprise.

But Chiang's schemes of pursuing the civil war against the Reds during the Sino-Japanese war were to fail. Strong popular support for the united front, massive indignation against him aroused by the January 1941 assault on the New Fourth Army by his troops, and Mao's skillful handling of the situation, his refusal to panic or to destroy even the fictional "united front," did exert some measure of restraint. After December 7, 1941, pressure from the United States, now involved in the war against Japan after Pearl Harbor, and Chiang's need of U.S. money also operated as a check. Local attacks on Communists continued. In 1946 Mao's nephew, the son of Mao Tse-min, was murdered, buried alive by Kuomintang agents.

In 1939 Wang Ching-wei, the erstwhile radical, had gone over to Japan, becoming head of a puppet South China government. General execration forced Chiang to condemn Wang Ching-wei, though relations between them never stopped; the Communists seized this opportunity to call for reinforcement of the united front against all such traitors. This acted as a restraint on Chiang Kai-shek. But he, Wang Ching-wei, and the Japanese were moving towards combined action against the Reds, a scheme of which Mao was aware; he warned that the danger of Chiang's capitulating to Japan had "greatly increased." Yet "in no circumstances will the Party change its united front policy for the entire period of the war of resistance against Japan," he insisted. Some Party members, infuriated by Chiang's attacks, had suggested the break-up of the united front, but Mao held firm. "Within the united front our policy must be one of independence and initiative," he said in December 1940 . . . "a policy neither all alliance and no struggle nor all struggle and no alliance, but which combines alliance and struggle. . . . In all cases we should expand . . . to reach out into all enemy-occupied areas and not be bound by the Kuomintang's restrictions . . . not . . . expect official appointments from them." This warning went unheeded by some commanders who still hankered for "official appointments" in the regular KMT army.*

In August 1940 occurred the Hundred Regiments offensive, a most controversial campaign. Chiang, understandably furious and worried over Communist Army expansion, had ordered the Eighth

---

* This represented a form of corruption of the Red Army which Mao strenuously denounced.

Chinese Communist troops in the war against Japan, 1937. Above, moving out to attack the Japanese; at right, in action.

Route Army, its commander-in-chief and second in command, Chu Teh and Peng Teh-huai, to stay north of the Yellow river, allotting them Hopei province to expand in. What sudden thrust of ambition, what spirit of recklessness induced Peng Teh-huai suddenly to switch from Mao's policy of guerilla warfare to a blitzkrieg attempt? Mao had written in *On Protracted War*,* "Our strategy should be to employ our main forces in mobile warfare over an extended shifting and indefinite front, a strategy . . . featured by swift attack and withdrawal, swift concentration and dispersal. We must avoid great decisive battles in the early stages of the war, and must first employ mobile warfare gradually to break the morale, the fighting spirit, and the military efficiency of the living forces of the enemy." The Hundred Regiments offensive was precisely the contrary.

Perhaps irritation at the elusive, slow attrition of guerilla methods, a desire to "do some real fighting," to "test Japanese strength" led to the decision which was taken by Peng without the approval of Mao Tsetung.† It may also be that the offensive was stimulated by the new Japanese anti-guerilla strategy of 1939, in which blockhouses and trenches, moats and high walls along railway tracks and highways were built to blockade and break up the Communist base areas.

On the night of August 20, 1940, 115 regiments of the Eighth Route Army attacked all the communication lines of the Japanese in North China. The railways were cut; the coal mine of Ching-hsing which the Japanese used was sabotaged; bridges and tunnels and railway stations were destroyed. Between August and December 20,000 Japanese and 18,000 puppet troops were put out of action, more than 300 miles of railway lines destroyed, 281 Japanese officers captured.

In retaliation the Japanese then had started their scorched earth policies. The Red areas behind Japanese lines were reduced by half in size and population; hardly a village was left standing in certain districts. The savagery and terror of the Japanese attacks were unprecedented, and the severe blockade of Yenan by the Japanese which ensued almost crippled the Red regime. Only

---

* May 1938. *Selected Works of Mao Tsetung* (English edition Peking 1961–1965), vol. II.

† It is reported (unofficially) that the order for the Hundred Regiments offensive was not approved by Mao but was approved by "someone" in the Politburo. This might have been Chang Wen-Tien as secretary-general. The Hundred Regiments offensive was a "huge bonfire of attacks all over the place" instead of the "concentration of a superior force" to annihilate a weaker enemy, as Mao's tactics indicated.

through the Production Drive launched by Mao was Yenan saved.

The massacre of the New Fourth Army by Chiang Kai-shek's military commanders occurred in January 1941. Chiang had ordered the New Fourth Army, which he also accused of expanding, to move and cross the river northward; Hsiang Ying obeyed Chiang's orders, sending the bulk of the troops north, leaving only 4,000 troops, 3,000 political workers, 2,000 medical personnel and their families, at headquarters. It was while this contingent of about 10,000 was leaving headquarters, inadequately protected, that it was attacked by 40,000 Kuomintang troops. Nine thousand Communists perished in a battle lasting about ten days, Hsiang Ying among them.

On January 17, 1941, the Kuomintang government in Chungking announced the dissolution of the New Fourth Army for "breach of military discipline." A wave of terror began; non-Communist progressives fled, liaison offices of the united front were closed; flare-ups between troops took place almost everywhere; it looked as if Chiang would start another "1927" massacre. . . . But Mao stuck to his united front policy, though criticizing the Kuomintang and castigating the action taken, which he said had been incited by "the pro-Japanese clique" whose "towering crimes" would be condemned by all. He did not forego the united front, in spite of divided opinion within the CCP. Had he yielded, it would have been easier for Chiang to mount a large-scale assault on Yenan, at that moment seriously enfeebled by the blockades.

Such was the indignation throughout China at this action, public opinion condemned Chiang so strongly, so much sympathy went to the Communists, that Chiang became uneasy. Even Western newsmen and diplomats criticized Chiang Kai-shek. Mao called on Chiang to "rein in on the brink of the precipice and stop your provocations," and asked once again for democratic rights for the people.

In a way, the Japanese-Chiang attacks created the conditions necessary for the success of the Production Drive *and* its concomitant mental and educational campaigns; otherwise the incentives to arouse the people might have been lacking. Even without these attacks, a pattern of material and spiritual mobilization was essential, to make cadres accept the hardships and discipline which in turn molded them into Party members.

By 1943, after two grueling years of blockade, the Production Drive had saved Yenan and the bases; the Red Army was stronger than ever; all loss of territory had been made good, and further territory liberated from the Japanese, who now could no longer maintain so many troops to garrison the vast territory, since they were engaged in war in Southeast Asia after the Pearl Harbor attack in December 1941. By 1945, ten years after the end of the Long March and Mao's arrival in North Shensi with 7,000 ragged men, there were 19 Red bases in 9 provinces, and the population under Communist administration was around 100 million people. Mao's "struggle and alliance" policies within the united front, his economic, political and military leadership, were vindicated.

3

Mao Tsetung—
The Man and the Teacher in Yenan

Mao is not an enigma. He is a fullness, a nation man, incarnating his epoch and people. The Revolution made Mao as much as Mao made the Revolution. The life of Mao is not only his life but also the representation of a period in China; of this Mao himself has always been conscious. He is a man of many contradictions: a classics scholar who swears and spits like a peasant; a health addict who keeps on chain-smoking; a being full of humor and fun who is deadly serious, candid and shrewd, naïve and nobody's fool, simple and complicated, scrutinizing and meticulous yet forgetful and negligent of personal attire; patient with the patience of a history maker, yet who will not brook a minute's delay when the time has come to act.

> *Ten thousand years are too long,*
> *Seize the day, the hour!*

In Juichin and in Yenan, Mao Tsetung continued to call on peasants. He would squat by the roadside with them, or sit under a tree, and converse for hours, or walk with them talking and waving his arms.* And at no time was he more himself than when, completely unselfconscious, he listened attentively, soaking in knowledge.

By 1935 Mao's life had become so imbricated with the Chinese Revolution that it is impossible to separate them; he is so much of a piece with his work, what he thinks and does is so much the Revolution, that to dissect him from history is to lose the dimension of his-

---

* Interview with Chen Chang-fong, 1971.

tory as well as to thin the man to a shade. The Revolution was his bone and flesh and blood, brain and power and reason for living. Edgar Snow had already observed, not only in Mao but in other revolutionaries, that childhood memories were about "I," but when revolutionary fervor took hold it was "we," and ordinary feelings, sentiments, details of personal life became faint, colorless, effaced from memory, in the passionate common enterprise which was life, all life. "We think and eat and drink and sleep revolution," a dedicated revolutionary said. "This is a world genius, he will change the world," Norman Bethune had said after meeting Mao Tsetung.* His ability to transport others into his own realm of vision was part of his charisma as a leader.

Snow described Mao in 1936 as a "gaunt, rather Lincolnesque figure." His thick black hair had grown long, but after 1940 he seems to have worn it much shorter — the same time he started putting on weight. He had large, searching eyes — his best feature — and "an intellectual face of great shrewdness . . . The story of Mao's life was a rich cross-section of a whole generation, an important guide to understanding the sources of action in China."

Snow, like so many others, was aware of Mao's personal magnetism, "a solid elemental vitality . . . the uncanny degree to which he synthesized and expressed the urgent demands of millions of Chinese . . . the simplicity and naturalness of the Chinese peasant, with a lively sense of humor and a love of rustic laughter. His laughter was even active on the subject of himself and the shortcomings of the soviets . . . He was plain-speaking and plain-living . . . he combined curious qualities of naïveté with incisive wit and worldly sophistication. . . . An omnivorous reader, a deep student of philosophy and history, a good speaker, a man with an unusual memory and extraordinary powers of concentration, an able writer, careless in his personal habits and appearance but astonishingly meticulous about details of duty, a man of tireless energy, a military and political strategist of considerable genius."

Though he could be uncommonly patient, Mao could also expose to merciless ridicule those "leaders" in the Party who with arrogance and the use of slogans overawed and misled the devoted Party cadres, "the little ones." He could rage and curse, and yet patiently explain, over and over again, the same things. He would never relent

* Papers of Dr. Norman Bethune, seen by the author in Sian, 1971.

against ideological deviations, yet would work for years with his enemies and get the better of them in the end.

There are many photographs of Mao, in patched trousers, worn and baggy jackets, pockets always deformed by books and papers. There are also many reminiscences of interviews with him, of their length — sometimes lasting all night, of Mao's untiring passion for explanation down to the last detail. He would join in the fun of parties, laugh at theatricals, in photographs he has a habit of *not* trying to occupy the center of the picture. Anna Louise Strong has left us a charming word picture of Mao dancing to a timing of his own — he is not a good dancer — of children running in and out of his cave while he worked. There is a kind of childish, impish gaiety about Mao, but it can change into deadly seriousness in a second.

Mao's political intelligence explains his command of the Communist Party, but not the real affection in which he is held by the men of the Army and the country people, wrote Edgar Snow. In speaking, he has a way of presenting a most complicated subject so that even the uneducated man can understand it. He never talks above the heads of his audience but he never talks down to them either. There is a real flow of intimacy between him and the people. He always seems to be in contact.

By 1940, a little more portly (no longer on starvation diet), his hair clipped short, he was still the mixture of peasant and intellectual, the unusual combination of real political shrewdness and earthly common sense, full of homely idioms and instances suddenly flashing into classic poetry; still the student of world events and the political analyst, hungry for knowledge. "Mao can rarely speak long without making a wisecrack or an epigram and he seems to maintain his leadership by winning all the arguments. He is very well read and an accomplished dialectician in debate. He has an interesting technique. He seldom makes a frontal attack against opposition. He delivers a blow here, another there, he outflanks his opponent's case, he breaks down its defenses one by one, until gradually he has it completely encompassed and it falls apart before a last witticism, or a telling stroke of logic." He has a lively imagination. "I remember once seeing him laugh till he wept when somebody described to him a comedy he had seen in Shanghai. It was an American movie — Charlie Chaplin in *Modern Times,*" writes Snow.

Mao's sense of humor is dialectical; he sees the obverse of any situation at once, and it is this which colors his language as it shapes his policies. It is sometimes outrageous humor; and though he hates to kill, he is lethal in mockery. And since he likes to keep his opponents about, active and in positions of usefulness (even if circumscribed in the harm they might do), life must be unpleasant to those who, brought up in the old traditions, have an inordinate amount of "face" and prefer death to being gibed at. But this is the peasant in Mao. The countryside is thus made; the village has its appointed characters, as if it needed them in a play, to act their roles; and for Mao there must be "negative characters" whose failings and errors are a reminder of the "wrong lines." He is not afraid to be disliked or hated. And although he has very sensitive, quick feelings and emotions, and especially a deep sense of friendship, yet when he despises someone it shows all the way through and all the time.

Has Mao no defects? Has he never made mistakes? He has the defects attendant upon his qualities. He is absolutely ruthless because he is dedicated, and absolutely convinced that he can convince by logic, which is not always true. He has made mistakes; he will say that at Chingkangshan the land law he passed was too harsh and had to be modified, that often he spoke too hastily, though never behind people's backs; and that, perhaps, he too often trusted others, thinking they were, as himself, animated by the singleness of one passion. But hard though we try, we cannot fault him in his grand design, and since his grand design is nearly all of himself, there is little else left to fault.

Mao is also, or rather, uniquely, an artist, an artist of Revolution, with the daemonic urge, the pitilessness towards self and towards others of the artist. As a sculptor molds stone or clay, Mao molded Revolution, working in that perpetual ecstasy which forgetting self can bring forth new beauty. More than his poems, his prose stands high in its excellence, a great clearness. His works of politics are works of art. Yet the man Mao existed also, with his child's laughter, and his keen need of friends, and never more than in Yenan. It was in Yenan, also, that Mao fell in love again.

Among the artists and intellectuals from the big cities who came to Yenan was an actress named Lan Ping (a pseudonym). Lan Ping's family name was Li. She had become a Communist Party member in 1933 and she acted in patriotic plays, refusing well-paid films, going against the Kuomintang government ban on anti-Japanese demonstrations in the theater. Lan Ping came to Yenan in 1937 and taught dramatic art at the Lu Hsun Art Academy; she joined the propa-

Mao Tsetung with Madame Mao (Chiang Ching) in Yenan.

ganda teams sent out to various parts of the countryside to put on plays for the peasantry, and she did research in the archives of the Military Commission.

It was at Yenan that Mao Tsetung met her. It may have been at the Lu Hsun Art Academy — Mao went there quite frequently. Mao's intense interest in plays, concerts, even dances, in the sober Yenan society "where he sat inconspicuously among others, enjoying himself hugely," in literature, poetry, good conversation, was of course matched by an intense interest in writers, poets and artists, especially his interest in women writers, women artists who emancipated themselves, as he felt they had struggled hard against the tradition that "actresses are all of ill-repute." The relation of art and literature to molding public opinion, as he had seen it in the May 4th movement, explains the importance he attached to these activities, as a writer and a revolutionary. In the Sinicization of Marxism-Leninism, which was what Mao performed at Yenan, art and literature too would serve the people, not copy "foreign stereotypes." Art and literature had no justification in being except to serve the revolutionary cause; the bearers of culture must serve the policies that serve the people. It was in one of these sessions that Mao met the beautiful Lan Ping, who fully understood him, and it was on this common ground of art to serve the people that they fell in love. The name Chiang Ching, which is Madame Mao's present name, was the name she took after reaching Yenan; some say Mao gave it to her.

Mao's previous wife, Ho Tzu-chen, had been married to Mao in Kiangsi in 1931. She and Mao were divorced in 1938, and Mao Tsetung married Chiang Ching in April 1939, a marriage which evoked a good deal of criticism and opposition among some Party members; it was also made the excuse for political attacks. But the marriage gave Mao great happiness and a deeper understanding of the problems of art and literature. Chiang Ching was to exercise in this sphere an abiding influence. Even though her name was not mentioned prominently for many years, and in fact she appeared to have entirely withdrawn from any public role, she has worked throughout to fulfill in the realm of art and literature the ideas of her husband, and carried out investigations and research in theater techniques, as well as doing political work among artists for many years.

Above all Mao is a teacher. It is as a "teacher," educating a party, educating an army, educating a whole people, that he dominates the Yenan scene and that his own personality is determined. It is his adapting of Communism to China, to a "land of millet and rifles," which overshadows all other aspects of Mao. "All I ever wanted to be was a teacher," Mao Tsetung said to his friend the American writer Edgar Snow in 1971. "I do not like to hear all this 'great' business, about being a great leader, great helmsman." * He had done all he could to take away the "personality cult" built around him during the GPCR.† "All I ever wanted to do really was to teach." At the Ninth Congress of the CCP in April 1969 he had looked, with that little smile he has when making a joke, at the chests of the delegates presented to him, each one adorned with a medal representing him, and then he had said, "Give me back my airplanes" — meaning that too much metal had gone into these badges of loyalty. Perhaps, as they waved the little Red book, he wondered how much teaching they still needed, wondered how many hearts, beneath those medals, were truly given to this great passion which had taken all he had, made him what he is.

Mao's philosophical texts, written in Yenan, *On Practice* and *On Contradiction,* are today Marxist classics, studied and read by every person in China, not counting millions outside China. Thirty-two years later, peasants and workers now literate apply the dialectics learned by reading Mao to their work. They learn to "think like Mao." And this embedding of dialectical materialism into the Chinese ethos is changing the Chinese mentality. From irrational, unscientific, feudal consciousness to the use of a scientific approach to phenomena is a thousand years' leap in the history of man's maturation of spirit. Scientific thought also means a new balance, new ethics, a new equilibrium of being. Professor Joseph Needham of Cambridge University has recently commented ‡ on the "extraordinary development of Marxist doctrine" in China into a "moral science," thus "tying the building of socialism to the Chinese concept of individual virtue."

Nothing is born but of necessity. It was the necessity of creating a party and an army for the Revolution, and the dearth and penury of the Yenan base, which decided Mao to rewrite, in a form accessible and luminous, illustrated by Chinese examples, the basic theories of dialectics and the theory of knowledge. It was his long and painful

* Interview by the author with Edgar Snow, June 1971.
† Abbreviation for Great Proletarian Cultural Revolution.
‡ *China* (issued by Society for Anglo-Chinese Understanding, London), November–December 1970.

apprenticeship in the Revolution which gave him the rich practical experience and taught him how to teach.*

The first requirement was for Party members to become educated in dialectics, in Marxism-Leninism. But how could this be done? In previous years Li Li-san, Wang Ming had both sneered, "How can there be Marxism in the savage mountains?" — thus reserving unto themselves all wisdom and science. True, it was hard to believe that illiterate peasants and workers would grasp the "complicated" philosophy of dialectical materialism. Who would interpret and teach them the monumental works of Marx, of Lenin, as a *living* philosophy, a code of doing and thinking immediately apprehended, something that would make the heart respond and "rub the eyes clear"? And how would they understand them and translate them into deeds without long years of education? And with all the restrictions of the material necessities, with all the fighting to do, where would they have the time for all this reading? Yet this was an absolute necessity for the Revolution. The contempt of the intellectuals for the uneducated was due to their own profound alienation from Chinese reality — perhaps they themselves did not realize their own basic repugnance to being *with* their own peasantry. But Mao had retained his strong life roots in peasant earth, merged and integrated with the peasant masses, admired their wisdom, yet at the same time he had become a scholar, a classicist, able to understand the complex subtleties of philosophy. He had grasped and used the science of dialectics as a living method, and found it worked; now he decided that he would teach this not by mechanically allotting texts out of Marx and Lenin to be read (which would confuse at least 90 percent of his students) but by Sinicizing, acculturation, transplanting these ideas and giving them a Chinese shape and contour, illustrating them with examples culled from Chinese literature and history, making them accessible and understandable by a true living interpretation, retaining their integral essence but giving them a Chinese form. Sinicization. Adaptation. Not dogma, but guide to action. And this is true creation, requiring the highest intelligence, requiring passion, experience, artistry. This is the role of the teacher, to make the substance of knowledge living and understood. It can only be done if the teacher himself knows his material thoroughly and this could only be done by Mao, because he had, by 1936, fifteen years of practice in the Chinese Revolution. Because he had been with and of the Revolu-

* As Mao explained to Edgar Snow in an interview in 1965. Interview of Snow by author, 1969.

tion every day and every hour of his life. And so Mao would never teach by rote, his language lofty and hermetic; this in itself was against Marxism, which to be the philosophy of the masses must be understood and practiced by the masses. Marxist philosophy was for the masses to live by, to live with, to transform the world; not for a dilettante elite to debate and give lofty commands.

"To apply Marxism concretely in China so that its every manifestation has an indubitably Chinese character becomes a problem which it is urgent for the whole Party to understand and solve. Foreign stereotypes must be . . . replaced by the fresh, lively Chinese style and spirit which the common people of China love. . . ."

The prospects were daunting. A low level of literacy; not more than 5 percent of the recruits for cadres and Army were even barely able to read and write in 1936. There was a lack of teachers, of books, of translations and translators for Russian texts, and almost no paper at all. Mao had seen, often he had noted, puzzlement and bewilderment among cadres "taught" Marxism-Leninism by the Party elite; the cultural background was so totally different that they felt lost.* Mao knew well by now that very few Party members, even the Moscow trainees, really *knew* what they were talking about. Did they not thus often confuse and mislead those they were supposed to enlighten and to lead?

And so Mao had not waited. As soon as he arrived in Yenan, he had started writing his teaching textbooks, both philosophical and military, *a way of thinking and a way of doing.* "Think, think, think hard, use your own head." As he had written, "No investigation, no right to speak," he now showed how knowledge is acquired. He taught the Art of Thought and the Art of War.

"Mao was an ardent student of philosophy," Snow writes. "Once . . . a visitor brought him several new books on philosophy . . . He consumed those books in three or four nights of intensive reading, during which he seemed oblivious to everything else. . . . Mao worked thirteen or fourteen hours a day, often until very late at night, frequently retiring at two or three." He worked as all creators do, with complete absorption, in a frenzy. Mao's orderly, Chai Tso-chun, tells how his famous essay *On Protracted War* was written

---

* Not only in 1937. Even fairly recently, in interviews with cadres, the author was told how few of them had really been able to master concepts of Hegel, Feuerbach, and Marx, "but when we first read Chairman Mao's texts, then they became easy for us to grasp." This acculturation problem still remains; it is only now being bridged by a thorough education process.

in 1938. For the first two days Mao did not sleep at all, even forgetting to eat, wiping his face from time to time with a moist towel. On the fifth day he was thinner, his eyes bloodshot, but went on writing. On the seventh day he was so engrossed that he did not notice the charcoal fire had burned a hole in his cloth shoes until his toes felt the pain. On the ninth day he had finished.

It was at Kangta, the famous anti-Japanese university for cadres, both "civil" and "military" — in Yenan days these were interchangeable — that Mao delivered his lectures. Kangta was set up in January 1936 directly under the Politburo; Lin Piao became its director at the age of twenty-nine. Mao paid very great attention to Kangta, for it was to be "a great nursery" for cadres. One hundred thousand of them would be trained at Kangta and its branch universities in the next seven years.

"The educational policy of the college is to cultivate a firm and correct political orientation, an industrious and simple style of work, and flexible strategy and tactics. These are the three essentials in the making of an anti-Japanese revolutionary soldier. It is in accordance with these essentials that the staff teach, and the students study." Mao wrote the Kangta motto: "United, alert, earnest and lively."

The recruiting for Kangta was done by posters; all who wanted to fight Japanese imperialism and were primary school graduates were eligible. The entrance examination was on health, cultural level, and political "seriousness." Automatically admitted to Kangta were activists, leaders in mass struggle — such as peasant leaders in land reform — and others sent by the Party from the far-flung bases. A good many students and intellectuals from the White (Kuomintang-controlled) areas also entered Kangta after 1936.

In the second semester of 1936, 1,063 cadres for the Army were formed at Kangta, and 2,764 in the first semester of 1937. From August 1937 to March 1938, 1,272 cadres for the Army came from Kangta. At the end of 1937 the rush of intellectuals, professors and students from the White areas and the Japanese-occupied areas towards Yenan altered the student composition. At the same time it gave a boost to the education level of the cadres it introduced other problems, both of political fitness and of relations among the cadres themselves. The increase in numbers led to the creation of several other academic institutions in Yenan, and to eleven branches of the original Kangta in other bases.

From May to December 1938, 5,562 young intellectuals were admitted to Kangta, and in 1939 4,900. By 1939 the students came from all regions of China, and there were also some overseas Chinese. In 1942 and 1943, however, because of changes due to the Rectification movement,* the students admitted were chiefly lower-level cadres of the Eighth Route Army whose class origin was of the poor and lower middle peasantry; soldiers and workers; in other words, the intake from intellectuals then in Yenan was cut down to permit workers and peasants to enter. The interest of this move lies in the fact that access to responsible posts was thus opened to many more toilers.

In language cogent and apt, Mao taught at Kangta his philosophical essays *On Practice* and *On Contradiction,* beginning in July and August of 1936. Certain scholars, put off by Mao's total accessibility, insist that *On Practice* and *On Contradiction* are "simplistic" and "mediocre." They are actually masterpieces of compression and clearness. Mao's aim was to popularize, so that philosophy should become "a sharp tool" in the hands of the working people, the masses, following Marx, who had said that philosophy must get out of its lofty abode in universities for the elite and must be understood and used by the working people. But in doing so, Mao actually enlarged and developed the concept of contradiction, and there is nothing simplistic in his genial rewriting of the science of dialectical thinking in "the fresh, lively Chinese style and spirit which the common people of China love," with an abundance of examples from Chinese tales and poems and classics. Mao quotes Dimitrov: "The masses cannot assimilate our decisions unless we learn to speak the language which the masses understand." Communism, to vindicate itself, must be a creative way of life, practiced by the vast majority of the people, who must think dialectically, must be able to use these scientific "Marxist-Leninist" concepts naturally, spontaneously. They must not be like Wang Ming . . . "When many scholars of Marxism-Leninism speak, they must talk about Greece. . . . They are not ashamed but proud when they understand very little or nothing about their own history. . . . For the past few decades, many *returned students* † have been making this mistake . . . all they know is to recite a stock of undigested foreign phrases. . . . They function as phonographs but forget their own responsibility *to create something new.* . . . No dishonesty or conceit whatsoever is permissible . . . [for] this process [of changing the world] has already reached a historic moment in the world and in China. . . . The epoch of

* See the next chapter.
† Emphasis not in original.

world Communism will be reached when all mankind voluntarily and consciously changes itself and the world." * Mao was himself changed by that changing world, and in turn helped to push forward the wheel of history by adding to man's consciousness, by teaching how to think, teaching others to change themselves. It is indeed remarkable that Mao had already apprehended that all mankind had already reached the threshold of a new era in raised consciousness, of which we see today many obvious manifestations.

Mao always considered *On Practice* a more important essay than *On Contradiction,* unlike Western scholars, who by now have written a good deal about *On Contradiction* but have somewhat ignored *On Practice.* Yet *On Practice* is "a mighty ideological weapon in knowledge and transformation of the world." It was delivered in about two hours of lectures when it had taken weeks to write. It was entitled *On the Relation Between Knowledge and Practice, Between Knowing and Doing.*

On Practice was a refutation of the kind of Marxism-Leninism which was being taught to the cadres by some of the "returned students." "There used to be a number of comrades in our Party who were dogmatists and . . . rejected the experience of the Chinese revolution, denying the truth that 'Marxism is not a dogma but a guide to action' and overawing people with words and phrases from Marxist works torn out of context." †

"Renegades like Wang Ming . . . refused to study the experience of the Chinese Revolution in the light of the universal truth of Marxism-Leninism . . . and overawed people with terms and expression from Marxist-Leninist works." There were others in the Party who were "empiricists," did not understand theory, or were impatient with it, saying: "We've fought our way through the Revolution, we know enough."

The refutation of apriorism is the fundamental thesis which Mao explains in *On Practice.* There is no spontaneous generation of thought, as there is no spontaneous generation of life; yet philosophical schools still assumed (in China, also in the West) that abstraction can show the process of cognition, judgment and inference. The de-

---

* In 1960 Mao told Edgar Snow that it was because of the need of the Party that he had written his essays combining the essentials of Marxism with concrete and everyday Chinese examples.

† See *Selected Works of Mao Tsetung,* vol. I, for *On Practice* and *On Contradiction* and for above quotations from the notes (English edition Peking 1961–1965).

pendence of rational knowledge upon perceptual knowledge, or the discovery of truth and reality through experiment and practice, was extremely important for the basis of scientific thinking; Mao was fighting against a solidly anchored tradition of classic philosophy through this essay; he was wrestling against feudal apriorism as well as modern metaphysics.

"Discover the truth through practice, and again through practice verify and develop the truth. . . . In endless cycles, with each cycle content of practice and knowledge rising, such is the whole of the dialectical materialist theory of knowledge."

Mao Tsetung defined the content of practice for a revolutionary, and his definition has not been changed since 1937; his three criteria of "practice in production, practice in revolutionary (class) struggle, and practice in scientific experiment" are the framework within which a revolutionary acquires his being as a revolutionary. To practice is to apply, to transform, to remold one's "world outlook through practice." The manner in which it is done is Mao's developmental application to the concrete object of the Chinese Revolution and to the target of self, for self must also be revolutionized by revolution.

Theory depends on practice; it is inconceivable, said Mao, that it should not be measured and checked by practice; in turn theory changes practice, changes methodology. Thus occurs transformation and acquisition of more knowledge. There is no inborn "wisdom" or "stupidity"; no knowledge precedent to material experience; no competence before practical doing. "The movement of change in the world of objective reality is never-ending and so is man's cognition of truth through practice. Marxism-Leninism has in no way exhausted truth but ceaselessly opens up roads to the knowledge of truth in the course of practice. Our conclusion is the concrete, historical unity of the subjective and the objective, of theory and practice, of knowing and doing."

On Contradiction was two lectures given by Mao in August 1937, and follows *On Practice* naturally. It is more attractive, particularly to intellectuals, but Mao is probably right to consider *On Practice* more important from the point of view of changing methods of work and study and cadre training, for it is basic in its rejection of idealism and apriorism, and psychologically essential, given the traditional Chinese respect for abstract pronouncements and "traditional wisdom." It was paramount in encouraging questioning, instead of submissive acceptance. Mao wanted no blind obedience, no "docile tools," but living, thinking cadres who live and think revolution, who are always asking, "Why?"

Marx had stated that "labor is . . . a process in which both man and nature participate. . . . in which man of his own accord starts, regulates, and controls the material reactions between himself and nature. . . . He opposes himself to nature as one of her own forces." We may surmise that the Long March was a tremendous practice in precisely this dialectic relation between man and nature. This interrelationship between man and nature, the essential contradiction, opposition-unity theme, finds a "major extension," says Dr. S. B. Nomoff of McGill University, Canada, "in Mao's *On Contradiction*." * This major extension is due, according to Nomoff, to the creative synthesis of certain elements of Chinese thought with Marxism-Leninism.

Because Mao understood the importance of the relation of cultural background to cognition, he chose most of his examples from ancient Chinese history and tales. "There were numerous examples of materialist dialectics in *Water Margin,* in Sun Tze's *Art of War.*" When Mao lectured on contradiction in Yenan, he also took examples from the famous novel *Dream of the Red Chamber.*† Mao's view of truth as nonstatic, nonabsolute, determined by "world outlook," by class consciousness, contains in its pursuit of reality a determination of unending practice and experimentation, unfolding new discoveries.

The unity of opposites was translated by Mao as "one divides into two," a term borrowed from Taoism, fundamental to Chinese thinking, and easily grasped by the ordinary man. As a method of analysis, "one divides into two" becomes immediately applicable by the Chinese millions. But whereas Taoism teaches nonaction as equivalent to action, Mao refuses the "harmony" concept, which had proved so stunting to Chinese scientific development. In dialectical materialism the universality of contradiction is the fundamental law of nature; Mao made it possible, by employing the sentence "One divides into two," to have this concept assimilated, both intellectually

* Paper by Dr. Nomoff in author's possession. See also *China Quarterly,* July–September 1964, p. 20. Captain Xavier Sallantin in his brilliant exposé of studies on Chinese thought (Ecole Militaire, Paris, 1971) points out that Mao's thinking is vindicated by the new discoveries of physics, of particle behavior, and certain phenomena at the electron level in biology. The creative development of *On Contradiction* derives from the practice of the Chinese Revolution as well as from China's processes of conceptualization which see all things as perpetually becoming.

† Interview with cadre who heard Mao lecture.

and emotionally, by millions of people who would have been unable otherwise to conceptualize "the unity of opposites." The phrase has now become so familiar that it is heard every day, even from children.

The flux of change, perceptible or imperceptible to human attention, is explained by the complementary of opposites, necessity for the development of contradiction, for a "becoming." As Mao states, "each of the two aspects of a contradiction, in the process of development of things, regards its opposite aspect as the condition for its existence. . . . The contradictory aspects in every process exclude each other and are opposed to each other." Such contradictory aspects are contained without exception in "the processes of all things." But whereas in Chinese dialectical thinking before Mao the balance between opposites was presumed equal, thus leading to "harmony" or confluence (the "fusion" theme, the "two merge into one" thesis, a theme which Yang Hsien-chen,* an ideological opponent of Mao, was to teach in the 1960's), Mao advances the postulate of the inherent inequality of the two aspects of a contradiction, an unbalanced state of opposites. Due to this "unevenness," the perpetual state of "becoming" is possible, the fields of force shift, the structure of contradiction becomes more complex, and change, transformation, conversion occurs.

Mao distinguishes between antagonistic and nonantagonistic particularities of contradiction; but he was to bring far more development to the distinction.† The possibility of transformation from one type of contradiction into the other was to be further amplified by him in 1957 with another philosophic essay, *On the Correct Handling of Contradictions Among the People*.

Since the opposites in a contradiction are unequal, nonidentical, and variable in more than one aspect, facet, or relationship to each other, within one and the same contradiction there are a dominant or primary aspect and a number of secondary aspects, so that "oppo-

* Yang Hsien-chen was also one of the "twenty-eight Bolsheviks." He was head of the publications department in the Comintern Far East bureau, and an accomplished Russian linguist. In 1936 he was in charge of translating Soviet works into Chinese. He may or may not have been in Yenan before 1945, but in 1949 was in Peking, became head of the China philosophy association, and began delivering lectures on Marxism-Leninism. He was vice-president of the Marx-Lenin Institute for training leading Party cadres, then its president 1957–1964, and looked upon then as a "leading ideologue," collecting some very high posts. His ideological opposition to Mao, and his refusal to place Mao's works on the compulsory study program of the institute, were revealed in the 1960's.

† See *On the Correct Handling of Contradictions Among the People* (February 27, 1957). Foreign Languages Press, Peking.

sites" become actually a multiplicity of interrelated and shifting situation aspects. The resemblance to the living cell, and to the language of nuclear biology, becomes apt for describing this "hooking" and "unhooking" type of living relation within a contradiction. Mao thus not only broke away from the "harmony" circle which fettered Chinese thought, but also from the "static absolute" which hampered the study of contradiction in Russian thought. Mao has evolved contradiction from the "linear motion" of Western dialectical thinking into a "spiral route, forever open-ended," which provides a polyvalence of possibilities; the fluctuant and unequal positions of the aspects, principal or secondary, of a contradiction providing built-in flexibility for each situation.*

Within a contradiction, opposites tend to transform into their own opposites when the contradiction is developed to the extreme, or ultimate, stage. This phenomenon of *conversion* Mao expounds with homely precepts and proverbs (a good thing can become a bad thing) and examples from Chinese legends (he might also have drawn some of them from the Long March, which started as a "bad thing" and became a memorable epic).

Thus a subtle and intricate thought motion is made accessible step by step, by the process of always keeping it "open-ended." There is no rigid, closed, hermetic circuit in Mao's thinking. We know now through molecular biology that the living protein structure exhibits a natural disymmetry and therefore a "spin," or sense of orientation or direction. Parity and complementarity are today revealed at the level of the atom, within the heart of elementary particles. The theory of fixed and immutable characteristics is negated; only the dialectic of contradiction can attempt to explain many a phenomenon in modern science, which no longer compartments energy, space, time. It is along these lines that Mao Tsetung proceeds in his extension of the theory of contradiction. His development thus also presumes antimatter, the essential inequality of energy and its various types; †
and it is this "disequilibrium" or "inequality" which is precisely the "accident" giving rise to new phenomena.

The "living application" of such concepts to the growth of peanuts, planting of cotton, running of steelworks, problems of a university department, or how to fight a war may appear baffling to Western thinking, but in reality it is the *method* of analysis and syn-

---

* See S. B. Nomoff in *China Quarterly,* July–September 1964, p. 20.
† Captain Xavier Sallantin, Seminars on the Logic of Chinese Military Thought. In author's possession. Unpublished.

thesis (which are of practical importance for the development of scientific thought and discovery) which has to be learned and applied at all levels, to all phenomena, which is so remarkable. Mao set out to teach one quarter of humanity to think in a different way, a dialectic, scientific way, about every event, situation, or problem.

Mao also spoke of the specific character (specificity) of contradiction; each required therefore its own specific treatment; each aspect also had its own particular features, again requiring a different approach. This meticulousness widens and deepens the philosophical themes, does away with mechanistic rigidity. There is also the "necessary given conditions," matrix, or background, with its own knowledge component. Without knowledge of the matrix, the specific attributes of the developmental process could not be understood.

The "war-peace" situation is ideal ground for a study of contradiction equations in all their intricacy and basic simplicity. Mao's essays on war, on strategy and tactics, cannot be treated as purely military works; they are philosophical as well as military,* grounded in the same dialectical process, in the same methodology of practice. The philosophic and military writings form a wholeness; we cannot study the one without the other.

The military thinking of Mao Tsetung, which was the application of dialectics to war, was the decisive factor for victory in the Chinese Revolution. One cannot imagine any other way in which victory might have been wrested from the "matrix" of Chinese conditions. Mao's military writings have been studied far more extensively than his philosophical essays. In Algeria, the French Army studied Mao intensively to beat the Algerians and to "reverse" the situation; but they could not operate this conversion in the contradiction, because the matrix was utterly different, they lacked the essential components of the situation — above all, the Algerian people.

Mao says himself that it was the three annihilation campaigns launched by Chiang Kai-shek against the Central Base at Juichin which taught him his strategy and tactics of war. But ultimately strategy and tactics also rest on philosophical concepts; there can be no learning by rote of such a science, unless one is a purely "mili-

---

* The chief military writings of Mao, prepared also as lectures to be given in Yenan, were *Problems of Strategy in Guerilla Revolutionary War* (December 1936), *Problems of Strategy in Guerilla War Against Japan* (May 1938), *On Protracted War* (May 1938), *Problems of War and Strategy* (November 1938). His writings on military subjects actually began in Chingkangshan, but the Yenan lectures on the art of war are far more detailed and vastly comprehensive, since they take in a great deal of history as well.

tary" expert, not a creator of strategy. The Red Army was by its very definition not purely a military but also a political instrument, whose aim was revolution. All strategy and tactics were conditioned and shaped by that goal. Hence "politics in command" was the fundamental reason for success; political leadership was essential for all enterprises.

The war against Japan was not only a war, but an example of all revolutionary wars; for, said Mao, it was the class struggle under its form of national struggle for liberation, and all such wars are part of the world socialist revolution.

"War is the highest form of struggle for resolving contradictions when they have developed to a certain stage. . . . War is the continuation of politics. . . . In this sense war is politics and war itself a political action, but war has its own particular characteristics and in this sense it cannot be equated with politics in general . . . politics is war without bloodshed while war is politics with bloodshed."

Because the study of the laws of war is a science and an art based on contradiction, the reality or matrix in which war occurs must be entirely understood; this means all political, economic, cultural, geographic and historical issues, the body of knowledge which focuses, delimits and determines the military aspect. The enemy's knowledge, his aims, also form part of this matrix. To fight Chiang one had to know Chiang; the Art of War consists not in winning battles but in winning the revolutionary war.

Revolutionary war, said Mao, is a defensive just war, never an aggressive, exploiting one. The *moral issue* — ethics — is of paramount importance. The superiority of a just, defensive war over a war of aggression is undoubted; a people with justice on its side will have the support of others in the world, those who revolt against oppression. (And this revolt is inherent in man's humanity.) There are, therefore, just wars and unjust ones. A just cause provides in itself a moral superiority. A people with justice on its side will not give up; hence the war is protracted. The aggressor would always prefer peaceful submission, but this is not available in a people's war. It is not weapons but man who in the final analysis decides the issue of the struggle, because the *initiative* rests with the defense since it rests with the people engaged in revolutionary war. The more the masses understand about the war and know the enemy, the more initiative they will display. People's war is therefore long, protracted war, waged with all the elements of the situation, of which people, the masses, thoroughly mobilized, are the mainstay.

Mao wrote and lectured copiously on strategic defensive, strategic retreat, and strategic counteroffensive; on the establishment of base areas, their relation to preceding guerilla zones, the consolidation and expansion of such bases, and the relationship between the three types of war: guerilla, mobile, positional. He wrote about the economics of a people's war, the self-reliant, self-supporting army, its leadership and administrative duties.

In all his writings, it is the role of *conscious* activity, a thorough grasp, awareness, which Mao considered essential for victory, political or military. In this he also had to counter the sectarian ideology of the Russian-trained group, who spoke of "proletarian internationalism" without reference to the concrete conditions. Mao's most illuminating remark on this subject may be again quoted: "For a people being deprived of its national freedom, the revolutionary task is not immediate socialism but the struggle for independence. We cannot even discuss Communism if we are robbed of a country in which to practice it." *

In 1946, when the Red armies were in the phase of the strategic defensive against Chiang, the preparation for going into the strategic offensive was intensive political mobilization, the mass line of education of the people, financial and economic measures, training of the Army and of the Party, study of the geographical and time elements, the build-up of bases in the countryside to achieve the "countryside surrounding the cities" principle. In this phase the mass line, achieved through land reform, was the chief condition for success. *And no elements of this phase could be skipped.*

Political and economic work took precedence over military battles; thus Mao was quite prepared to lose territory and abandon cities, because the chief thing was to economize manpower, to reassure it psychologically and save it physically, not to risk large losses in foolish onslaughts for empty "victories." The enemy armies must be drawn, sucked into a whirlpool of dissident, hostile populations politically at one with the Red Army. Their very presence and actions *aroused* hostility and *helped* the Communist armies. This technique of making the enemy serve one's own goal Mao would use over and over again.†

Decision-making, and the laws of decision, are the paramount

* Quoted by Edgar Snow, 1936.
† He also lectured on this "contradiction" many times, illustrating his talks with ferociously funny (untranslatable) thumbnail sketches of Chiang's stratagems for victory. See Edgar Snow *The Battle for Asia* (New York and London 1941).

concern of the commander. These decisions must be fully understood by the rank and file and by all the people, as many as possible; they cannot be kept as secrets nursed only in the leaders' minds. What appears to be defeat will then dishearten no one; what appears to be retreat will be a rest period safeguarding the precious element of man; these decisions entail knowledge of the enemy's mentality and of his type of decision-making. Decision-making based on the law of contradiction is also, in the final analysis, a collective phenomenon.

The concept of the *asymmetry* of contradictions — "In any contradiction the development of the contradictory aspects is uneven" — is basic. It is in war that the asymmetry between the two opposite aspects of a contradiction is most important for the outcome. This "uneven" state (for instance, a large powerful state versus a small weak one) is *not* a guarantee that the larger, better-equipped will win. "A small nation can certainly defeat a large one; a weak country can certainly defeat a strong one," Mao was to say in 1970. The outcome depends on factors which can be roused and enhanced in effect, such as the *human* factor; resolution, will, conscious mobilization, thorough knowledge of the terrain, and time. An example of this is the Vietnam war.

Mao studies the process of the *conversion* in contradiction as applied to war ("In given conditions, each of the contradictory aspects within a thing transforms itself into its opposite, changes its position to that of the opposite"). This phenomenon of transformation of one aspect of a contradiction into its opposite is the meaning of identity. It is of the very essence of dialectics. "Dialectics . . . shows how opposites can be identical . . . transforming themselves into one another . . . why the human mind should take these opposites not as dead, rigid, but as living, conditional, mobile," Lenin had said. This is crucial in a war situation; to understand the requisite action towards conversion is to hold the initiative. Mao himself would show this talent of knowing the right time when "conversion" would occur; politically he would show all his life this instinctive flair for seizing the day, the hour.

This process of conversion cannot be done unless one distinguishes the principal, or main, contradiction from the secondary. In the anti-Japanese war the principal contradiction was Japanese imperialism; hence a united front which included Chiang (but within well-defined limits) was the way of solving this principal contradiction. But in the civil war which was to follow, the principal contradiction was between the people of China, the overwhelming majority, and the Chiang Kai-shek regime, representing the compradore capitalist class, sustained by U.S. imperialism. All other contradictions became secondary to this; and it was a matter, above all, of rallying as many of the people as possible to form the broadest defense against Chiang Kai-shek; hence another kind of united front. The contradiction between Chiang's well-equipped and numerous troops with a 4.5 to 1 superiority over the Red Army was more than made up by Communist training, political consciousness, dedication, and by popular support. Nevertheless, numerical and weapon advantage could not be underestimated, and the best way to tackle it — to "convert" this contradiction — had to be studied very carefully. The method, adapted to the particular aspect of the contradiction (Chiang's forces), would be lightning attacks by concentrating superior forces to annihilate *totally* the weaker forces of the Kuomintang, without waging pitched battles against superior numbers; tiring them out in pursuit; cutting off their food supplies; sabotage, and psychological disintegration; tactics different from the guerilla war waged against Japan.

Again speaking of "reciprocal transformation" (conversion phenomenon) Mao wrote: "Some people think this is not true of certain contradictions. For instance, in the contradiction between the productive forces and the relations of production, the productive forces are the principal aspect. This is the mechanical materialist conception. . . . True the productive forces . . . generally play the principal and decisive role; but in certain conditions, such aspects as the relations of production, theory and superstructure, in turn manifest themselves in the principal and decisive role. *When it is impossible for the productive forces to develop without a change in the relations of production, then the change in the relations of production plays the principal and decisive role.* . . . While we recognize that in the general development of history the material determines the mental, and social being determines social consciousness, we also . . . and indeed must . . . recognize the *reaction of mental on material things, of social consciousness on social being, and of the superstructure on the economic base.*" * This paragraph is plangent with meaning; for it is the key to the whole process of cultural revolution (which is an idea transformation) as motive force for a material transformation (pushing the basic structures of revolution forward).

It was this consciousness-matter and matter-consciousness duality,

* Emphasis not in original.

the question of voluntarism versus material circumstances, which would in Mao's thinking become a most important factor for the solution of contradictions, for the advance of the Revolution. "Nothing in this world develops absolutely evenly; we must oppose the theory of even development or the theory of equilibrium," wrote Mao. Thus he formally destroyed statism, the "harmony" Taoist theory, and Confucianist traditionalism, and opened a new era in thinking for the Chinese people.

Another document penned by Mao must be studied in connection with his role as teacher — although all his output can be said to be teaching. It is *On New Democracy*. This is a sociohistorical document which explains the continuity of the Chinese Revolution and projects its process into the future.

On New Democracy, written at the end of 1939, was designed to clarify the issues as to where the Communist Party stood; to repudiate the Kuomintang attacks upon it as an "alien" party "not following the principles of Sun Yatsen"; to answer the "left sectarians" who wanted to break the united front with Chiang Kai-shek; to stop yet another assault upon Mao's line from the Wang Ming group. For in 1940, the unrepentant Wang Ming again took action; he republished his pamphlet on *The Two Lines* in Yenan. He was still challenging Mao's ideological leadership in the Party.

We have already seen how strongly entrenched in the Party was the Wang Ming faction. By 1940 there had been an enormous expansion of the CCP. From the 40,000 members it had counted in 1935, it had grown to 200,000 in 1938; by the end of 1940 there were 800,000 members.

That these new recruits knew absolutely nothing (or very little) of Party history, of the period antedating the Long March, is obvious. This brings us to the question of Mao's real, actual authority and power with the Party hierarchy at the time. Everyone called him Chairman Mao . . . but what was he chairman of? He was not chairman of the Border Government, nor of the Party Central Committee; he was chairman of the Military Council, and he was the top man in the Politburo but subordinate to the secretary-general of the Party, Chang Wen-tien. Hence, though unquestionably the outstanding personality in Yenan, he was bureaucratically speaking not in a position of overall power. This probably is the reason his lectures at the time were given little publicity.

The influence of the opposition to Mao was especially pronounced in the area of press and publication, normally occupied by Party intellectuals or ideologues. Edgar Snow had remarked that although Mao was a classics scholar and a prodigiously intelligent man, he deliberately kept peasant habits. I have a feeling that Mao liked to shock arrogant scholars with a display of peasant forthrightness, and this informality was not always acceptable. He had been for some years making very forthright remarks on "muddleheaded" and "sectarian" members who "overawed" simple people. Everyone knew that an accounting on the ideological plane was due sooner or later. Liu Shao-chi, who also lectured at Kangta, in 1939 is reputed to have referred rather contemptuously to *On Contradiction* to the students there. "A little less talk of contradiction . . . you should do a bit more work in the White areas," was the gist of his remarks. *On Contradiction* was not published in Yenan, in fact not published officially until the 1950's. Mao was certainly not in control of the printing presses.

When *On New Democracy* was published it was "violently criticized" by ultra-leftists in the Party. It was not welcome in Moscow either, because it introduced certain novel definitions, such as the concept of "new democracy."

In *On New Democracy* we find a very long and full explanation of what cultural revolution is. Already (January 1934) Mao had said, while in the Kiangsi base: "We have to practice a brand of democracy . . . and we must wage the cultural revolution *to arm the leaders of the masses* of workers and peasants." To look upon the process of a cultural revolution as capable of bringing forth new leadership from the masses was a tenet of Mao's thinking on revolution.

In the winter of 1939, Mao Tsetung and "several other comrades in Yenan" had prepared a history textbook for the Party called *The Chinese Revolution and the Chinese Communist Party*. This was a history of China and a history of the Chinese Revolution. It already developed the theme, to be further expanded in *On New Democracy,* of a new democratic stage and a socialist stage; both to be led by the Communist Party, "fully consolidated ideologically, politically and organizationally."

Anna Louise Strong tells of Mao's giving her his script of *The Chinese Revolution and the Chinese Communist Party* to read. She says it circulated for "over ten years" among Party members. It must have aroused, of course, a great deal of hostility from those who felt blamed in it for certain tragedies. To be thus pilloried in history is

the most unpleasant thing for a Party member; even death sometimes may seem preferable.

Mao had started the newspaper *The Communist* in October 1939
as an internal Party journal. In it he wrote: "How are we to build up
our Party today? The answer can be found by studying the Party's
history, by studying Party building in connection with the united
front and with armed struggle. . . . To sum up our eighteen years of
experience . . . and to spread this experience through the Party, so
that our Party becomes as solid as steel and avoids repeating past
mistakes . . . such is our task." Obviously the threat of a thorough
ideological struggle was there. *On New Democracy* was part of the
ideological education for such a struggle.

In *On New Democracy* Mao wrote that the democratic revolution
in China no longer involved the old category of democracy as seen
in the revolutions of the eighteenth and nineteenth centuries in Europe. "A semi-colonial country's revolution is a revolution of a new
type . . . of new democratic type. Because [such revolutions] deny
bases to imperialism, they are part of the socialist world revolution
and not part of the bourgeois-type, old democratic revolutions, as in
the West. Politically, such a new democratic revolution *always represents a struggle by a united front of several revolutionary classes*
struggling against imperialism and its satellite classes within the
country. It therefore adopts economic and social policies which differ from the old type."

However, new democratic revolutions have an ambivalent aspect.
They open the way to capitalism of a national type, because the national bourgeoisie in a semi-colonial country has some revolutionary
traits and is also included in the united front. At the same time new
democratic revolution creates conditions for socialism. It is therefore
a crossroads stage; the issue has to be decided subsequently; the revolutionary party of the proletariat must understand this dual action
and push on to socialism.

In a new democratic republic (and Mao was to assert that the
Yenan base and other Red bases already enjoyed a new democratic
type of government) the economy is also new democratic, "so that
private capital cannot control the livelihood of the people." Big
banks and big industrial and commercial enterprises are state-owned.
But small-scale private ownership is allowed.

Such a new democratic state is actually entirely in accordance
with the Three Principles of Dr. Sun Yatsen,* as embodied in the

* The Three New People's Principles; see part I, chapter 6.

First Congress of the Kuomintang in 1924, which Mao had attended. "For sixteen years the Kuomintang has betrayed this declaration [of Dr. Sun] and consequently created the grave national crisis of today." Thus neatly, Mao turned the tables on Chiang Kai-shek. It was the Communists who were practicing the Three Principles of Sun Yatsen; they were the continuators of the revolution Sun Yatsen had begun. It was the section of the Kuomintang under Chiang Kai-shek who had betrayed Sun Yatsen's ideas.

In his fundamental discussion of cultural revolution, Mao explains: "Since the May 4th movement . . . a fresh and brand-new cultural force has appeared in China. . . . A great revolution has taken place in ideological content and in form, for instance in the style of the written language. . . . A cultural revolution is the ideological reflection of the political and economic revolutions which it serves." The May 4th movement had been such a great cultural revolution — "There has never been . . . such a great and thorough-going cultural revolution since the dawn of Chinese history." A cultural revolution also has its stages; it is an inevitable accompaniment of the socio-political-economic revolution, and is essential for the *continuing revolution.*

Mao explicitly states the necessity for assimilation of new material from other cultural sources. "The new democratic culture is *national* . . . it bears the stamp of our national characteristics. It unites with the socialist and new democratic cultures of all other nations and establishes with them the relations whereby they can absorb something from each other and help each other to develop. . . . China should assimilate from foreign progressive cultures. . . . We did not sufficiently do so in the past. . . . However, we must meet these foreign materials as we do our food . . . separated into essence to be absorbed and waste matter to be discarded. . . . So-called 'wholesale Westernization' is a mistaken viewpoint. China has suffered a great deal in the past from the formalist absorption of foreign things."

Mao's "teaching" manner was very popular. "There was always much laughter." He was a brilliant speaker, interspersing his most serious political statements with anecdotes, proverbs, quotations. He would hold seminars for debate and discussion, encourage forums. Always accessible, he would spend all night explaining points which were unclear, and would be as fresh and lively at four in the morning as when he had begun twelve hours previously. But he heaped merciless taunts upon "formula Marxists"; he made every humble cadre feel intelligent, because he prodded him into thinking.

The apprehension and ire of the "formula Marxists" is under-standable. That Mao Tsetung should lecture on war was from their point of view bad enough; but that he should also lecture on Marxist philosophy was for them unbearable. Ideology is of supreme impor-tance to a revolutionary party; the ideological hostility to Mao re-mained throughout these decades; the two-line struggle in the Party is never ended. Ideological authority does not mean unhampered ex-ercise of power in the Party hierarchy. Mao had "ideological author-ity" in Yenan, but only by constant and continuous struggle on the ideological level. This makes his contribution as teacher the more significant. He was able to exercise this role, to rebuild the Party and Army along the lines he set out to do, to Sinicize and adapt Marx-ism to the concrete Chinese environment, because of the tremendous popular appeal he had in spite of the opposition, and because he was so often proved right by events.

The "crisis" within the Party, a crisis of ideological authority, once more gathered strength in 1941. It was to be resolved by the great Rectification campaign.

Since 1938 Mao had hinted several times that a great "study" drive for Party building was essential. It was necessary to reorient, correct, strengthen and stabilize the Party, especially now that it showed overwhelming expansion and consequent defects. And it was also necessary to settle some unresolved "historical questions," pend-ing since Tsunyi. A great many intellectuals were now in Yenan. In December 1939 Mao had stated the Party's need for intellectuals "who serve the working class and the peasantry; without the partici-pation of intellectuals, the Revolution cannot be victorious." But though necessary, they brought problems — problems of suspicion from the older, seasoned cadres; resentment when they saw top jobs going to intellectuals; reluctance of intellectuals to rub shoulders with peasants and soldiers; opportunism and careerism; infiltration by KMT agents. Intellectuals were almost all from the bourgeoisie; they were politically unseasoned. Mao's long-nurtured project of a wholesale "teaching" or "rectification" movement became urgently necessary. As the shortages and material difficulties temporarily added to the disunity factors, the subsequent Production Drive also created the conditions in which rectification could occur.

In June 1941 Hitler's forces invaded the USSR. This at once cleared the confusion in Communist minds arising from Stalin's non-aggression pacts with both Hitler and Japan — which Mao had de-fended. With the invasion of the Soviet Union by the Nazis, the resistance of the Chinese Communists and their war with Japan became extremely important to the USSR.

This weakened the opposition to Mao in his own Party. In December 1941 occurred Pearl Harbor. America was now in the war, and the China war theater became of enhanced importance. The primary obsession of the Americans for the next three years would be how to keep Chiang Kai-shek from making an alliance with Japan. The Chinese Communist Party and Army were now recognized as of international significance and vital to free world interests. The U.S. signified to Chiang that it would not be happy if Chiang started another anti-Communist onslaught like the one against the New Fourth Army in January 1941.

Mao's vision had now come true. Catapulted into world prominence as the main force pinning down Japanese armies, the Chinese Communist Party had to prove worthy of the next step: the conquest of power. And for this, a rectification movement in Mao's view was essential. It was *a total preparation of the Party for total victory;* reorienting its attitude to the masses, reshaping its style of work, streamlining it, throwing out opportunists, enemy agents and other "undesirables," quelling "factions," and writing Party history. It was a tremendous political education project.

To this Mao gave his attention for the next three years, preparing and then conducting the Rectification movement, the largest political teaching movement yet tried out, something that had not been done by any other Communist Party before.

4

The Rectification Movement, 1941-1944

The goal of the Rectification movement was plainly set down in a speech by Mao Tsetung: "How can we build up . . . a Chinese Communist Party . . . which is national in scale and has a broad mass character . . . No political party can possibly *lead a great revolutionary movement to victory* unless it possesses revolutionary theory and a knowledge of history and has a profound grasp of the practical movement. We can put Marxism into practice only when it is integrated with the specific characteristics of our country and has acquired a definite national form."

When Mao spoke of history, he meant not only the history of China; he meant the history of the Communist Party as well. This signified an all-out ideological struggle, pending since the Tsunyi conference.

As a young man, Mao Tsetung had shown a relentless passion for getting to the bottom of any vexing question when he had firmly seized a teacher by the arm and pushed him into the school director's office to argue out his case. Now he would put a stop to muddleheadedness and intrigue, inform the whole Party of past events, call to judgment those who had almost destroyed it, lay his case before history. He would make the past serve future victory.

Because the Rectification movement would involve each member as well as the organization as a whole, it would begin with a thorough analysis, supplemented by biographies, of each individual. A study of the composition of the Party showed that members of peasant origin still accounted for more than 60 percent, nearer to 70 percent; but there had been an influx of petty bourgeois and intellectuals from the cities and the White Kuomintang areas which would make up at least 15 percent of the 800,000 Party members. There was a tendency for the better-educated to gravitate to higher jobs, of an administrative character; this produced a good deal of friction. In certain areas revolutionary fighters of long standing found themselves ordered about by people they considered less seasoned and less worthy.

Yet a good deal of unification had been realized through cadre training in the bases themselves, at Kangta and its branches. Mao Tsetung resisted the idea of sending those with higher talent for training abroad in the USSR as had been the practice in earlier years. The Sino-Japanese war had interrupted this practice. The creation of regional bureaus whose leadership returned regularly to Yenan for reporting and consultation was designed to strengthen the administration, but it had also led to staff inflation, bureaucracy, authoritarianism, evils which Mao fought against.* Within each base there were two structures — one for the Party, one for the elected base government — with their various departments. Mass organizations under the government found themselves not guided (the Party is supposed to guide, not to execute; to suggest, not to order) but commanded. There were overlap, reduplication, a plethora of administrative personnel, and with the shortages of supplies these nonproducers had become a burden to the population. Among a minority of them the taint of corruption, opportunism, not to speak of autocratic methods, was beginning; the rapid membership expansion had included even enemy agents. A clean-up and a shake-up were necessary. The problem focused not so much on the peasants and workers in the Party, who were devoted, self-sacrificing, but did not always have the educational background to grasp the subtleties of the Marxist slogans they were asked to ingest and obey; it was mainly a problem of the superstructure, the people in a position to teach and who taught badly; it was an intellectual problem, and a problem of the intellectuals.

Many of the intellectuals who flocked to Yenan were sincere, willing, enthusiastic. Most of them came through the Rectification campaign to hold positions of trust and to do excellent revolutionary work. But there was a sizable minority which was not changed. Some of the intelligentsia had become extremely critical. They suffered from "dejection and pessimism," as the reports of the period state, because of the hardships of the blockade, the isolation, the stern military discipline, the Kuomintang attacks, and above all an incomplete understanding of the policies of the CCP. There were

* John Stewart Service *The Amerasia Papers: Some Problems in the History of U.S.-China Relations* (Berkeley 1971), pp. 167–176.

also those who expected more regard and better treatment than they received, although even in Yenan intellectuals had a higher standard of living than the average population. There was also, inherent in their upbringing, a built-in reluctance to face the hard necessities of armed struggle, of militarized life, the harsh truths of peasant China. Their addiction to liberalism, their love of gossip, their disenchantment because the long view escaped them, their muddled outlook made them easy prey to the kind of factionalism and intrigue which, in a highly ideological milieu, assumes political significance. It was a question of attitude and concepts.

The gap between old and new cadres was also difficult to bridge. There was mutual suspicion; younger and better-educated cadres were sometimes contemptuous of "old coarse" veterans, saw no reason to follow Party directives, kept aloof from the local population. Many could not speak the dialect anyway, and made no effort to learn. A small group of prominent left-wing writers erstwhile in authority in the cities found themselves neglected here, and they became even personal in their attacks, given to oblique vilification. Thus private grievances and petty grudges began to magnify, immense as a hand covering the sky, obliterating the revolutionary perspective.

But above all, they had no idea of what had happened in the Kiangsi base, or at Tsunyi; and the Wang Ming faction was certainly not going to enlighten them. On the contrary. Both Kuomintang agents and factions would thrive on rumors, restlessness, among intellectuals.

In March 1941, as a preparation to the Rectification campaign, the *Second Preface to Village Investigations,* written by Mao, was announced as a study document of the movement. There were to be eighteen such documents in all. "The only way to know conditions is to make social investigations [of] the conditions of each social class in real life . . . To do this, first direct your eyes downward, do not hold your head high and gaze at the sky." Another document was *Oppose Book Worship,* written in 1930 by Mao, which had been so opposed at the time. "Although my assertion 'No investigation, no right to speak' has been ridiculed as 'narrow empiricism,' to this day I do not regret having made it . . . I still insist that without investigation there cannot possibly be any right to speak," said Mao.

In *On Contradiction,* also for study during the Rectification movement, Mao had said: "Where our dogmatists err is . . . they do not understand that . . . we must go further and study the concrete things that have not yet been thoroughly studied or have only just emerged. Our dogmatists are lazybones. . . . They regard general truths as emerging out of the void, they turn them into purely abstract unfathomable formulas." They also taught others abstract unfathomable formulas. The documents for study Mao suggested would set a tone of scientific, objective, concrete research and investigation, meant to prevent abuse and terroristic methods. But these did happen anyway.

Two distinct trends by the leaders hostile to Mao's idea of rectification were to emerge. One was a tendency to consider rectification a mere shake-up of individual members, throwing out the unfit; this would become an ultra-left trend of trying to punish the many at mid-level or lower level rather than concentrating on the few in the leadership who were the actual target of Mao's effort. The second trend was to lag and to drag, and not accomplish what the Rectification movement had set out to do.

In *Reform Our Study,* a speech delivered in May 1941 to assembled cadres, Mao hit straight and hard and true; his words must have been a most bitter medicine for those who understood their meaning: "I propose that we should reform the method and the system of study throughout the Party." Research work was unsystematic, collected material on current conditions fragmentary and not well prepared. "We are lacking in a climate of investigation and study of objective reality." The bad style of work, with verbiage, should be corrected.

It is because of the word "style," which in Chinese is the word "wind" (*feng*) and carries with it the connotation of attitude, behavior, thought and action, that the Rectification movement is often called the "three-style rectification," style of study, style of work, and style of writing. But "style" here denotes far more than individual originality; it is the total sum of the individual and the collective Party orientation and action which is involved. Style is the outward expression of the person or the group.

Mao wanted the kind of cadres who would "use their heads," think clearly, work thoroughly and conscientiously, and also express themselves clearly and frankly. Writing well, eschewing long-winded politicalese which no one understood, meant getting rid of "empty twaddle" and jargon, the haven of those who have not understood and for whom hermetic incomprehensible slogans were a way of holding their positions without in the least knowing what real work meant. Lazybones. Hence Mao's attack on "verbiage," not only in

Reform Our Study, but again in *Rectify the Party's Style of Work* and *Oppose Stereotyped Party Writing.** He made fun of the kind of jargon which passed for political acumen, in a manner which sent his audience into fits of laughter. He derided the length of articles in the newspapers, the use of long phrases which meant precisely nothing. These two speeches are masterly essays by one who wrote clearly, thought clearly, and knew what he was doing. The last one is a classic; it would put an end — but only after the Great Proletarian Cultural Revolution twenty-five years later — to the elephantine compositions through which unfortunate Party members were supposed to wade in order to understand policy.

Mao would do battle by debate; he would win by debate; by criticism and self-criticism would the Party members, all 800,000 of them, be won over, in fair combat. In the doing they would learn and they would be changed. They would discover the new, concrete things about China which they did not know, and they would be encouraged to develop "the organ of thought," initiative and boldness. But first the "theoreticians," in academic positions of honor and respect in the various institutes, must be laid low.

"In the schools and in the education of cadres at work, teachers of philosophy do not guide students to study the logic of the Chinese Revolution; teachers of economics do not guide them to study the characteristics of the Chinese economy; teachers of military science do not guide them to study the strategy and tactics adapted to China's special features . . . *They have no intention of seeking truth from facts but only a desire to curry favor by claptrap.*"

On July 1, 1941, the Central Committee passed a resolution on "Strengthening the Party Spirit." But within the resolution, generalities replaced the whiplash sting of Mao's phrases. The resolution pointed out "tendencies" to "individualism" and to "heroism," to disobedience, independent political action, deception, the creation of cliques. A month later it issued another resolution on the necessity of "investigation and research"; this resolution did not mention Mao Tsetung by name.

In February 1942, Mao Tsetung gave another vigorous push to the movement, which seemed to be stagnating, going into the meanders of personal attacks while in some bases degenerating into "counterrevolutionary" witchhunts, with the usual propensity of the "ultra-left" to strike down a great many innocent Party members and

* Delivered at the Party School of the Central Committee, February 1 and 8, 1942.

to preserve out of harm's way the more guilty "leaders." His lectures *Rectify the Party's Style of Work* and *Oppose Stereotyped Writing* put the matter of reorientation plainly: "There is the question of thought, the question of the Party's internal and external relations, and the question of literature." The Army was not forgotten, and the Kutien resolutions of December 1929 were again circulated in January 1942. But by April 1942 the ideological study and debate ("struggle" in political parlance) had not yet got off its feet because "most branches [of the Party] have merely limited themselves to discussing the documents with the aid of documents and have not understood the spirit and substance of these."

The Rectification movement, the Production Drive, and a mass education movement among the population coincided in the same years — 1941 to 1944. This permitted integration of theory with practice, manual labor with ideological debate. It made the intellectuals really come in contact with the people providing the food and clothing for the base. It also began the "learn from the masses" movement, today the foundation of education in new China.

At the same time, reorganization of the governments in the various bases took place. The tripartite ("three thirds") system of political power, in which only one in three members of the government were Party members, broadened the mass base. Mao urged that the advice and the knowledge of individuals outside the Party be sought and listened to.

The cutting down of the bureaucracy followed naturally, in a move called "better troops and simplified administration." The suggestion was first given by Li Ting-ming, a non-Party man who had come over to the Communists because he was so indignant at Chiang Kai-shek's attack on the New Fourth Army in January 1941. Mao Tsetung welcomed it. "Our enormous war apparatus is suited to past conditions. It was then permissible and necessary . . . but men's minds are liable to be fettered by circumstance and habits from which even revolutionaries cannot always escape." They were to be unfettered now. At least 70 percent, if not more, of the cadres in the Army and administration were returned to "production," which meant to labor instead of office work. The Production Drive was ideal in creating the conditions and atmosphere in which this could be done not only without resentment but with positive glory attached to the names of those who volunteered for manual labor either temporarily or on a more or less permanent basis. Unified leadership committees were created in 1943. They seem, however, to have disappeared pretty rapidly. They were mergers of representatives from the Party, the Army and the base government mass organizations; in this way they foreshadowed the revolutionary committees with unified leadership of today. This was possibly an attempt to replace the dual and parallel organizations with a single organization, with, at its core, Party representatives to guide the executive. It is puzzling that these had apparently such a short life in Yenan. All these features of the Rectification movement were resurrected during the recent Cultural Revolution (1966–1971).

Mao's report on economic and financial problems in December 1942 laid down the principle that production determines demand; the aim of China's economic policies being the development of production, and not profit. This report was tied in with the slogans of a revived land reform campaign "to reduce rent, increase production, support the government and cherish the people in the base areas." By the end of the Rectification campaign, it could be claimed that the ideological thrust and the economic advance were inseparable, and that the latter was successful because of the former. A reanimation of motives and goals, meaningful, regenerating enthusiasm, is essential to a revolution. Mao Tsetung now performed this, not only through the Party, but also through the population of the bases. This success would give Yenan its persistent validity even today.

Success was also manifest on the field of battle. In 1942 and 1943 victories were won over the Japanese forces. It could, of course, be claimed that these victories were also due to depletion of the Japanese armies, since after December 1941 the Japanese invasion of Southeast Asia had begun and Japanese replacement troops were much fewer. The Chinese puppet troops which took their place could not make up for efficiency by numbers. But however we may argue this point, the fact remains that there were heartening Communist advances, in glaring contrast to the stalemate which continued on the Kuomintang-manned fronts. More territory and more bases were in Communist control by 1944 than in any previous year. Nineteen base areas, one million square miles in extent, were now governed by Red administrations, and almost 100 million people, 20 percent of China's population.

Two other critical platforms, known in the Communist political dictionary as "commanding heights" in the superstructure, were to be submitted to the Rectification movement. One was the realm of art and literature and artistic creation; the other, the one which formed actually the core of the two-line struggle, was the field of Party history.

Mao Tsetung's talks on literature and art, known as *Intervention at the Yenan Forum on Literature and Art,* are key pieces in policy as regards the "superstructure" of society. As important as is the material basis of a system, that ensemble of ideas, habits, attitudes, behavior, consciousness which produces, through artistic creation, a molding characteristic of a class and a system is just as important in Communist ideology. Public opinion and social action have a definite relation. In this domain, the struggle in China would be, for the next decades, prolonged, acute, and of a bitterness which only today is revealed, although it is not characterized by bloodshed, as it was in the USSR.

A forum of artists, writers and "art workers" was convened in May 1942 "to examine the relationship between work in the literary and artistic fields and revolutionary work in general." This forum Mao addressed twice, on May 2 and May 23. Visitors to Yenan are shown the modest building in which the forum was held. On May 2, eighty intellectuals attended the meeting; it began early in the morning and continued, with discussions, all day. Not only did Mao speak; he also took notes of every objection made, recorded by hand every question, especially the controversial ones, listened attentively when the intellectuals addressed the meeting to give their own points of view. This was not uncommon behavior for him; he had adopted it for all debates and seminars, and after all his lectures he used to solicit questions and the expression of personal opinion. It is a pity that a record of these discussions has not been kept.

"Some of the writers present brought books with them to prove their points. One brought *Wells World Dictionary* and read out loud the definitions of 'art' and 'literature.' There were confrontations on the meaning of these words; some stuck to Western definitions of the bourgeois culture, which were not the understanding of Chinese culture, nor of the Revolution, nor of the Chinese common people. Mao suggested smilingly to some of these writers to go down among their own people and find out what they thought about it all.

"On the 18th of May a whole day of discussion took place till late at night. They were on the five problems of art and literature which Mao Tsetung listed. The question of 'whom do we serve' was strenuously debated. On May 23 at the last meeting there was again a whole day of discussion. Many more artists and writers came than at the first two meetings. The discussions were prolonged. Mao again noted down by hand everything that was said. People there noticed one thing about him. How he saved paper. He wrote on the backs of discarded sheets. At the time, because of the great scarcity of paper, we were happy when the Japanese planes — who tried to bomb Yenan many times, and actually knocked flat 80 percent of the city, but could not knock the caves down — did some pamphlet raids; we would collect the paper and write on it. Mao Tsetung collected old envelopes, unstuck them and used them again. The forum concluded late at night, and Mao Tsetung made a final speech. That day at noon he posed for a photograph with all those who came. Mao's talks on art and literature greatly encouraged the writers, who then went among the people and started to create works of art for the people." * The song "The East Is Red" was written then.

Despite these reports of excellent results, we may doubt that *all* writers were thus affected, considering what was to happen some decades later. Mao Tsetung himself was to say that it took a very long time and was very painful for anyone to "remold his world outlook"; hence instant conversions are a little suspect.

Mao's talks at this forum are interesting because in many ways the problems evoked are still the problems of today. They deal with the alienation of the writer, the artist, from a "bourgeois" background, in the Revolution and from his own people. He evoked the "new cultural army" which the May 4th movement had brought forth; but after 1919 literature and art, even if revolutionary, had grown in cities cut off from the Red bases in the countryside, from the majority population, the peasantry. Now, in Yenan, artist and writer and the masses of the countryside had been brought together physically, yet integration of the artist with the masses was still practically nonexistent.

The five problems of the artist were class stand, attitude, audience, work and study. The audience was made up of "the workers, peasants, soldiers and revolutionary cadres in the bases"; they wanted to read books and newspapers, "those who are illiterate want to see plays and operas, look at drawing and paintings, sing songs and hear music." But writers persisted in only producing for a restricted audience, a city audience, a bourgeois audience, or for each other. "Their primary task is to understand people and know them well," but they failed to understand their own people; they failed to use "the rich, lively language of the masses." Hence they produced

* The reminiscences are from old Yenan cadres, interviewed by the author in Yenan.

insipid works which the people disliked. If they wanted to be understood and accepted they must make up their minds to undergo "a long and even painful process" of assimilation and integration called "tempering."

Mao spoke of his own tempering. He had as a student acquired the ways of a student. "I used to consider it undignified to do any manual labor, such as shouldering my own luggage. . . . At that time I felt that intellectuals were the only clean people in the world, while in comparison workers and peasants were dirty . . . But after I became a revolutionary and lived with workers and peasants and with soldiers, it was then, and only then, that I fundamentally changed the bourgeois and petty bourgeois feelings implanted in me in the bourgeois schools . . . In the last analysis, the workers and peasants were the cleanest people . . . cleaner than the bourgeois. . . . This is what is meant by a change of feelings, a change from one class to another. . . . If our writers and artists who come from the intelligentsia want their works to be well received by the masses, they must change and remold their thinking and their feelings."

Mao touched here the fundamental problem of alienation of the intellectual elite; a problem of urgency, but one which has remained, in China, a problem up to today. Only a few artistic productions bridged the gap. The Chinese opera was unchanged by the Revolution until 1964, when Mao's wife Chiang Ching at last was able to work unhindered. In the domain of art and literature, Mao's recommendations were not so well accepted as the enthusiastic paeans of praise which have issued, repeatedly, from Chinese writers, would lead us to think. The problem of artistic creation still remains the way Mao defined it. And the way to integration with the masses is long and painful indeed. Many writers never tried. Worse, perhaps, in the long run was the stranglehold on art and literature by the Left League of literocrats who, using Marxist slogans, tried to re-create a Confucian mandarinate, bureaucratic tyranny which stifled artistic function. The same writers denounced by Lu Hsun were to rise high in the hierarchy, but do nothing to change their own class stand or abrogate their own privileges. Lu Hsun had said that artists and writers in a revolution must not expect to retain their arrogance and their privileges, or even to be treated politely by the masses. "Even among comrades who have been to the front and worked for a number of years in our base areas and in the armies," it required at least eight or ten years to solve this problem of writing "for whom"; and *"This question of 'for whom' is fundamental; it is a question of prin-*

ciple," said Mao. "The life of the people is always a mine of raw materials for literature and art, materials most vital, rich and fundamental; an inexhaustible source, their only source." But "the people" meant primarily workers and peasants, not city intellectuals. How many writers would write of and for them? He criticized "copying from the ancients and the foreigners," an attitude redolent of servility, which produced "dogmatism" in art. All artists must plunge "into the heat of the struggle . . . in order to observe, experience, study and analyze all the different kinds of people, all the classes, all the masses. . . . Only then can they proceed to creative work."

No artist, no writer would quarrel with what Mao said above, on artistic creation. But a good many * will demur at the determined stance that portrayal must "lean" to drawing the heroic features of the workers, peasants and soldiers, and that there can be no vague, intermediate, indecisive, Hamletian characters held up for admiration or pity, nor any counterrevolutionary or bourgeois. Mao lived an epic, the workers and peasants had created this epic, and epics need heroes larger than life-size. He was quite right in pointing out the need for new hero figures to replace the old, for a new art and literature to describe, to convey, and to exalt the vitality of the Revolution and its many fascinating exploits.† But how was this to be done if those qualified to do it were imbued with elitism so that unconsciously, in their portrayal, they would always set a "bourgeois" in the center of the stage to display heroism? If the writer insisted on creating a Kuomintang character as lovable as a Communist one in the name of "fair play" or "artistry"? The fundamental problem was the class concept, and in this Mao's analysis is a key one for the understanding of a writer's difficulties in a Communist system. Perhaps it would need another generation, a breed of proletarian writers, intellectuals issued from the peasantry and from the workers, to create a new art and literature for their own masses. Or another Cultural Revolution. Meanwhile, the problem would remain.

Within the scope of this struggle among the intellectuals there also began a "pouring of grievances" movement, a kind of Hundred Flowers exercise, whose purpose was, of course, to strengthen the Party, to consolidate its unity and integration. Just as in the Hundred Flowers of 1956–1957, fourteen years later, some of the

---

* In Western society particularly.

† See Pingchia Kuo *China: New Age and New Outlook* (Harmondsworth, England, and Baltimore 1960).

literati, including Party members, began to challenge the principles of the leadership instead of giving constructive criticism, correcting shortcomings and criticizing errors within the limits of the system. Since the literati were also the governing officialdom in feudal and imperial days, the assumption that they would always be entitled to authority, the illusion that in revolutionary Yenan the "freedom" of "parliamentary systems" could work, would prompt some unrealistic claims. The act of "throwing oneself in the deep rich seas of the masses," as Mao recommended, spelled artistic suicide to others.

There is no doubt that some of the grievances were justified; high-handedness and bureaucratic pressure existed; nor did all artists and writers practice the virtues of patience and humility. As the Rectification movement proceeded, in the heat and fire of meetings, criticism and self-criticism (the slogan of the movement was "Unity, criticism, unity"), it was possible for lower-echelon Party members to come forward with their own grievances and suggestions. Rectification with open doors — inviting non-Party masses to criticize Party members — was also done; it has now become a tradition. All this was to teach the intellectuals the manifold complexities of a revolution. But hasty compliance does not mean change, and some of the artistic productions seem painfully forced, though there were also excellent ones.*

Rectification reached its peak in 1943. This was also the year of the dissolution of the Comintern, an event greeted with sorrowful bewilderment by many Communist parties in the world. When asked his opinion, Mao stated that it was already quite some time that the Comintern "had ceased meddling in our affairs," and that it had probably outgrown its usefulness. To Wang Ming's faction the disappearance of the Comintern was shattering.

Mao Tsetung had urged a practical program of research on Chinese economics, politics, military affairs, and history, deploring that it had not been done by the Chinese bourgeoisie although "bourgeois society in the West" had been able to undertake such research. It was therefore up to the Chinese proletariat — the Communist Party — to carry it out. A body of scholarship and critical research methods were essential to the Party if, as vanguard of the working class, it wanted to have its own sources of scientific and technological data. In 1942 the sifting of historical material began, and study of "historical questions" such as incorrect lines and devia-

---

* Such as *The White-Haired Girl, Yellow River Cantata,* books by Chao Shu-li and Chou Li-po.

tions within the Party, the Sixth Congress, the putsch organized by the twenty-eight Bolsheviks in January 1931, the Tsunyi conference. Lengthy discussions were held, "especially on the period from the beginning of 1931 to the end of 1934," as Mao requested.

In the preparatory sessions, Chou En-lai played an important role. His seniority in the Party, the trust reposed in him by all sections, his ability to hold together in unity those who otherwise might have split, his recognized selflessness, gave his words great weight. Chou had been in Chungking, in charge of the difficult task of liaison with the Kuomintang. This liaison was maintained despite difficulties such as the lodging of KMT spies in the house where Chou lodged, many restrictions, and even one murder.* It was maintained despite armed clashes between KMT and Red Army units, which never stopped.

Chou was back in Yenan in the spring and summer of 1942 to take part in the Rectification movement, chiefly in settling Party history problems. He there made a declaration entirely in favor of Mao Tsetung. "The Party's twenty-two-year history has proved that the views of Comrade Mao Tsetung were formed and maintained with historical perspective, aiming at a sustained effort for the Revolution in China. The line he took was the only correct line. . . . Comrade Mao Tsetung has integrated Communism with the movement of Chinese national liberation. . . . Because of his leadership the strength of the Party is unprecedented." †

Chou En-lai's testimony throughout the sessions rallied many of the other members of the Central Committee, even some of Wang Ming's adherents. Yet Mao noted in April 1944 that in spite of the proven success of his policies, "many Party cadres had *not yet* reached a thorough understanding of the character of the erroneous lines of the past." Intense discussions were held in the same building as the Yenan forum on art and literature. The criticism and self-criticism sessions were prolonged; Wang Ming and other "Bolsheviks" also had their say; but the "collaboration of senior cadres" of the Party heralded the victory of Mao's line. By the end of 1944 and early 1945, the struggle between the two lines concluded with the victory of Mao, and this would now be enshrined in Party history.‡

---

* At the Sian liaison office.

† Also see Hsu Kai-yu *Chou En-lai: China's Gray Eminence* (New York 1968).

‡ The settlement of these historical questions, which would confirm Mao's policies as consistently correct and condemn the Wang Ming line, would form the subject of the *Appendix: Resolution on Certain Questions in the History of Our*

Mao's policies, based upon the social sources of revolutionary power, made the mass line the most important democratic and initiative process to understand and to use. In his essay titled *Some Questions Concerning Methods of Leadership* (June 1943), Mao repeats the dialectic of the mass line. This "basic method of leadership," in which the leaders are the servants of those they lead and have to be taught by the led in order to teach them, was to be repeated for four decades; Mao in fact has never stopped repeating it. "In all the practical work of our Party, all correct leadership is necessarily 'from the masses to the masses.' This means, take the ideas of the masses (scattered and unsystematic ideas) and concentrate them (through study turn them into concentrated and systematic ideas), then go to the masses and propagate and explain these ideas until the masses embrace them as their own, and translate them into action, and test the correctness of these ideas in such action."

The idea underlying the Rectification campaign was not to purge and punish so much as to educate. The slogan was to "save the patient by expelling the disease," and self-criticism was the most vigorous and effective manner in which unity could be achieved without physical elimination. The Communist Party membership went down from 800,000 to about 763,447 and then 736,191 in the years 1941 and 1942.*

In 1944 membership went up again, to 853,420; in April 1945 it had risen to 1,211,128. Most of the new admissions were activists of the Rectification movement, peasants, workers in the cooperatives, and soldiers who had distinguished themselves in fighting and in the Production Drive. The figures of admission at Kangta also reflect this mass training of a core of proletarian members. Whereas before 1942 the intellectuals began to be admitted in a majority, after 1942 soldiers, seasoned grass-roots cadres, were admitted and promoted (though intellectuals were still admitted in considerable numbers).

Because in victory there must be justice but not vindictiveness, Mao Tsetung set down the methods of handling cases when "errors are committed." This was to leave a way out, a margin for repentance and for change. He advocated a careful attitude, so that there should be "no harm to comrades. . . . Our present task is to prepare ourselves for a still greater responsibility . . . we must pay attention

Party, penned by Mao and approved at the last plenum of the Sixth Congress of the Party in April 1945, "enabling it to attain an ideological and political unity without precedent in the history of the Communist Party of China."

* Figures from Franz Schurmann *Ideology and Organization in Communist China* (Berkeley 1968).

to work *in the big cities* and along the main lines of communication . . . *which has always been very inadequate."* This was a criticism of the work in the White areas under Liu Shao-chi, as well as a preparation for the struggle for power to come.

At the close of the campaign Mao again advocated making good use of the "organ of thought"; to move one's brains, he said, was essential. "There is all too little of this habit in our Party." *

It was in 1943 that the Thought of Mao Tsetung began to be mentioned as an entity. It would be consecrated at the Seventh Congress in April 1945. This has been termed part of a "personality cult" which began during the Rectification campaign. Mao Tsetung was unfeignedly and without any doubt tremendously popular among the people, the soldiers, the grass-roots cadres; his policies were sincerely acclaimed by them because they did correspond to their needs. "The Party only takes measures after we are sure of the approval of the majority . . . we constantly check on public opinion. . . . It is a fundamental principle of ours to keep contact with the masses and satisfy their aspirations," Mao told Guenther Stein. He also said: "You can only teach the masses what you have learned from them." Stein noticed the ease of mind, frankness, democracy in Yenan (after Rectification), in marked contrast to what he had seen in Russia. All this was the basis of Mao's popularity with "the little man," the majority of the people. It did give rise to expressions of love and respect; hence the accusation of a "personality cult."

But it is also true that Mao's opponents deliberately went overboard in fulsome praise of Mao; their laudation makes curious reading, especially after the GPCR. Mao may have considered personal charisma necessary to carry out the policies for victory he was bent on effecting. But "personality cult" is a feudal throwback which would obscure Mao's real stature and contribution to the Revolution. Hence at the moment Mao is doing all he can in order to eliminate it; the concentration must be on ideas, on the Teaching of Mao Tsetung, not on the person.

This is a very difficult notion to instill in a country where personal rule and autocratic power have been dominant for so long. It would take decades to get away from the habits of the past, and it is not

* Wang Ming was to be re-elected to the Central Committee and to the Politburo at the Seventh Congress in April 1945, next to last on the list (forty-third out of forty-four), followed by Chin Pang-hsien (Po Ku). Both were openly named as responsible for the disastrous "left" line from 1931 to 1934.

certain that even yet the habit of democratic debate is firmly established, although a beginning has been made.

The Thought of Mao Tsetung, which can be defined as Marxism-Leninism integrated with the specific characteristics of the present epoch in history, stresses the continuous production of new knowledge in contact with reality; adapts Marxism to the specifics of revolution in a country. It is a "guide to action," and in China denotes the body of theory-practice which guides the Chinese Revolution. It is axiomatic, since it is based on the mass line, that the teaching of Mao Tsetung should be widely disseminated and understood by the masses as a living, working system, not an abstract intellectual discipline. Mao Tsetung's trust in the masses and their mission to create the world and transform nature by their practice and discovery of reality is unbounded. It is this faith which underlies so many of his actions. For Mao, the Party exists to serve the people, and not for power for its own sake.

During the Rectification movement years, in spite of conflicts and blockades, the liaison offices for united front work were kept open.

On March 28, 1942, the CCP presented to the Kuomintang certain demands: recognition of the CCP as a legal party, and recognition of the liberated territories as autonomous; an agreement to expand the Eighth Route Army from three to twelve divisions, and agreement that the New Fourth Army remain south of the Yellow river. There was also a reiteration of the ten-point program as the basis for a coalition government. It can thus be claimed for the Communists that they began suggesting a "coalition" of some sort, but predicated upon reform of the Kuomintang and guarantees for the people of China, long before the episodes which were to follow in the struggle with Chiang Kai-shek for power. These demands were turned down by Chiang Kai-shek and negotiations suspended.

But the international situation had changed in favor of the Communists. With the U.S. at war with Japan and anxious to keep Chiang in the war, with Chiang dependent on U.S. money and equipment, he did not dare start a major offensive against the Communists, though storing weaponry provided by the U.S. for a final decision against Mao on the battlefield.

In Chungking, American newsmen and American embassy officials were becoming increasingly critical of Chiang Kai-shek. It was the appalling treatment of the soldiers, as well as of the population, which stirred their indignation. By 1944 the U.S. was to send General Joseph W. Stilwell to reorganize the Chiang armies in preparation for an all-out assault on Japan from the Chinese mainland. The reports that more than 50 percent of Japanese troops were pinned down by the Communists made a favorable impact upon the Americans; at the same time President Roosevelt was much perturbed by the obvious preparations for civil war that Chiang was making.

It was within this network of shifting international events and their effect in China that the Rectification movement took place, to prepare the Party for victory in the postwar period.

In 1944 Mao had warned — through Guenther Stein — of the "possibility" of civil war with Chiang. The word probability was more apt. To counter this, the Rectification movement was imperative. War there would be, and it would be merciless. Mao asked: "Shall we dare to win?" He answered the question he had asked: "Yes, we shall dare to win . . . everything." This was no less than the decision for total victory in all China. No revolution justifies itself unless its aim is to seize power. The CCP was only five years away from this goal, but no one would have thought it possible at the time, and very few could see that the Rectification movement was essential to its accomplishment.

5

The Seventh Congress, April 1945

The Seventh Congress of the CCP, held April to June 1945 at Yenan, has a place second only in importance to the Tsunyi conference. It was the conclusion of one stage of the Revolution, the beginning of another. Seventeen years had elapsed since the Sixth Congress, held in 1928 in Moscow; at that time the CCP had been a hunted, decimated, small party of survivors. In 1945 it was the second largest in the world.

The Congress, as Mao formulated it, was "a Congress of unity, a Congress of victory." The CCP had recapitulated its own history, drawn political and historical conclusions which were taught to every member, assessed its gains, castigated its errors, proclaimed its unity, the success of its Production Drive, the Rectification movement and its war against Japan; it proclaimed now its program for the future.*

The gray brick building where the Seventh Congress was held is shown to visitors to Yenan. A two-story edifice, its first floor is a large pillared hall. Here, in November 1944, Mao had received Eighth Route Army cadres of Brigade No. 359, going south to reinforce the New Fourth Army. He had told them:

> Become like a pine or a willow.
> The pine is evergreen, straight in wind or storm (the pine
>   has principle).
> The willow grows anywhere it is planted,
> In spring its branches lengthen, numberless leaves move in
>   the wind with beauty (the willow has flexibility).

* See *On Coalition Government*, April 24, 1945. *Selected Works of Mao Tsetung*, vol. III (English edition Peking 1961–1965).

Here in 1945 the Central Committee assembled. The sober platform with its long table and a dozen chairs, the wooden benches below for the members, have all been kept as they were then.

The slogan of the Rectification movement, "Persist in truth, correct your mistakes," spread under the flags hanging on every pillar. At the back of the hall the words "One heart, one virtue" (morality) were painted on the wall. Each pillar was adorned with a V for victory emblem, to emphasize the participation of the CCP and the Red Army in the World War. There were twenty-four Red flags for the twenty-four years of the CCP's existence. Upstairs were rooms for relaxing. One of them holds a pingpong table; Mao Tsetung played pingpong between sessions of the Congress. He is a good-humored, steady player, losing games with great equanimity.

It is important to assess the background of the Congress to understand Mao Tsetung's three key speeches, notably the one *On Coalition Government*.

The relations of the CCP with Chiang Kai-shek, with the United States, with the Soviet Union, and relations between the United States, the Soviet Union, and Chiang Kai-shek, were significant in shaping the speeches at the Seventh Congress, as were the strength of the Communist Party and the intentions of the Party towards seizure of power. For in April 1945 the CCP and the Red Army were not only a national force but an international one (even if this is ignored by some historians). This made the Seventh Congress a culmination, a platform of far-reaching decision. Mao Tsetung stood at the peak of his ideological authority; the Thought of Mao Tsetung was enshrined as the guiding principle of the CCP, defined as Marxism-Leninism applied to the concrete conditions of China. The Party now had 1,210,000 members, a jump of 400,000 since 1944; the Red Army counted 910,000 regular soldiers, 2,290,000 militia.

The Rectification movement had fashioned a united, disciplined party, a prodigious army, a potential government with great leadership talent, with cadres experienced in rural conditions, a core of devoted, zealous, and self-sacrificing administrators. Yenan's reputation throughout China and abroad was prestigious. "There," the peasants said, "the sun always shines." The success of the Production Drive had shown up the failure of the Kuomintang, decaying with corruption, inflation, tyranny. The CCP had evolved intelligent, flexible methods of caring for the people, with sane economic policies; Chiang's government was floundering in economic crisis and the misery of the rural population was becoming unbearable. The Communist Party had the support of the great masses of the people, not only in the liberated areas but also through China. It was the mass support which legitimized the administrations of the liberated areas, so that it was perfectly true to say that the CCP represented the Chinese masses far more than Chiang Kai-shek did.*

There was no longer any ambiguity on who had done what, nor on the central role of Mao Tsetung in achieving the present success. "The Party definitely established the leadership of comrade Mao Tsetung in the central leading body and throughout the Party." The Congress solidly endorsed the Tsunyi conference, thus legitimizing Mao's supremacy. It condemned all previous erroneous lines, the sharpest castigation being for the "particularly serious form of war-lordism" of Chang Kuo-tao and the "disastrous" failures of Wang Ming and Chin Pang-hsien, the "two dogmatists."

The resolution covering these points † ended with a note of warning; since the stage of the war of resistance against Japan was "not yet concluded, it is appropriate to postpone to a future date the drawing of conclusions on certain questions in the history of the Party *during the War of Resistance.*" Mao was fully aware that all "deviations" and opposition to his line had not been dealt with through the Rectification campaign. He knew, as the plaudits resounded, as Party members rose in ovation, as the thunder of acclamation shook the windows, that among those clapping and cheering were some who waited an opportunity to turn against him. It is said that he has a "gift for smelling out" potential opportunists, but that he usually does not act until they have had plenty of opportunity to betray themselves. There were more enemies to cope with, possibly even "nestling by his side," but the time had not come to take up the matter. In the very hours of what looked like his absolute triumph, he knew already the seed of other intra-Party struggles.

The Seventh Congress was held when both the U.S. and the USSR were already planning the postwar world. The presence since July 1944 of an American observer mission in Yenan, and the visit of numerous American officials and newsmen, had brought the CCP into the orbit of international politics.

Since Pearl Harbor, the U.S. government in its Pacific war had been concerned with the succinct problem of "keeping Chiang in the

---

* As two American observers, John Paton Davies and Major Evans Carlson, were to state.

† *Appendix: Resolution on Certain Questions in the History of Our Party*, resulting from the two-year appraisal of the history of the CCP and written by Mao (*Selected Works*, vol. III, English edition Peking 1961–1965).

war." Diplomatically, it became U.S. policy to assert that China was a "great power," in order to have China by her side as an ally in the new postwar world order. As a result, the return of territory lost to Japan, Taiwan among others, was solemnly promised at various international conferences. Chiang made full use of what he gauged as American dependence on him for the war against Japan in order to extort the maximum in money — he blandly asked for a billion dollars in 1943 — and in weapons, without trying to launch an effective military action against Japan. The U.S. government endured it stoically during 1942 and 1943; but glowing reports of the Communists and of their military successes came through. Although Chiang refused to allow newsmen to go to Yenan, the liaison office of the Communists in Chungking was popular with Americans and was a source from which facts about the Communists' war effort were gathered, as were also the Japanese intelligence reports.

It was not until June 1944, with the visit of Vice-President Henry Wallace and personal and unequivocal messages from Roosevelt to Chiang (in February and again in June), that very reluctantly Chiang Kai-shek authorized American military observers and foreign service men to be stationed at Yenan in order, as Roosevelt asked, "to collect more information on the Japanese enemy in North China and in Manchuria." During 1944 Japan launched its last and biggest military offensive after five years of stalemate with Chiang. This campaign in Central and South China was designed not against Chiang but against American air bases in South China. Chiang withdrew his troops, ordered his crack regiments not to fight the Japanese, and deliberately made things easy for the Japanese attack to proceed.

General Joseph W. ("Vinegar Joe") Stilwell, who had been sent to China expressly for the purpose of "reorganizing" Chiang's troops and making them fight, was bitterly antagonistic to Chiang. Much money had been expended in order to arm, equip and train thirty divisions. Chiang, as always, stowed away men and weapons to prepare for the only war he had ever wanted to fight, war against the Communists. The very obvious prospect of impending civil war intensely worried the U.S. government, which identified Chiang's government with China. It would mean an enormous weakening of the Pacific front if Chiang made peace with Japan. Chiang played on this American fear whenever he was refused loans or lend-lease aid; and America paid up, "to keep China in the war."

However, a spate of criticism from American newsmen and Vice-

President Wallace's visit had revealed some ugly facts about the
Chiang regime. It seems that for a short while U.S. foreign policy
makers did consider the possibility of an alternative to Chiang Kai-
shek. In July 1944 the Dixie mission, composed of some seventeen
officers of the U.S. Army and two foreign service men, arrived by
plane in Yenan. This observer group would report diligently, accurately and honestly on the Communist forces, organization, and intentions; and for this scrupulous devotion to the best interests of the
United States many of them were to lose their positions, even be attacked as "pro-Red," in that orgy of anti-Communist unreason
which seized America from 1945 on and culminated in McCarthy-
ism. But even preceding MacCarthy, only an emanation of this season of hysteria, the first manifestation of the "Cold War" psychosis
would be in the spring of 1945, when the Seventh Congress was
being held.*

The seven or more months spent by the officers and observers of
the Dixie mission in Yenan were a revelation for both sides; a revelation of friendship, good will, camaraderie between Americans and
Chinese. The Communists knew that the U.S. had urged upon
Chiang, through Stilwell and Ambassador Gauss, some basic democratic reforms. This had interested Mao; as he spoke with American
newsmen, military officers, foreign service men, in a free, warm,
happy series of interviews and informal talks, he asked many questions about American democracy and was vastly interested and also
captivated, as his interviews reveal.

So was Chou En-lai, who spent days, as Mao did, in talk with the
Americans. "For a brief period it was possible to prove to the
Chinese revolutionary movement that America stood for progress,"
wrote Theodore White, but "we cast this opportunity away." †

Leaving aside the genuine and warm friendships that members of
the Communist Party contracted with some American newsmen and
other individuals who visited Yenan — Snow, Evans Carlson, Jack
Belden, Harrison Forman among others — mutual respect, frank
speaking, and genuine appreciation for points of view so different
also emerges from the documents of the times. The author had the
pleasure of knowing personally Colonel David Barrett, head of the
Dixie mission. Barrett, John Service, John Davies were all to suffer,
some for two decades, for being members of the mission and filing

* Daniel Horowitz *Containment and Revolution* (London 1967).
† Theodore White and Annalee Jacoby *Thunder Out of China* (New York 1946),
pp. 241, 142.

The United States Dixie Mission in Yenan, 1944. Above, the banner at right of stage reads "China, America, the Soviet Union and Britain unite together"; at left, "Annihilate fascism." Below, Chou En-lai with (from right) John Service, Colonel Barrett, Lieutenant Hitch, and Ray Ludden

Above, Mao Tsetung with Chu Teh, Service and Barrett. Below, Ludden and Barrett watch Red Army soldiers working in a uniform factory at Nanniwan.

428 *The Morning Deluge*

reports which were accurate about Yenan, and thus falling foul of United States "policy" when that policy suddenly reversed itself.

The Americans in Yenan attended seminars, lectures, concerts and theaters; they walked everywhere, visited far-off bases, were shown everything. The memory of Yenan was to remain in them a wistful, nostalgic if Puritan "little heaven." They were liked, and liked the Chinese Communists.*

It was Roosevelt who had suggested to Chiang "calling in a friend," or American mediation for negotiations between Chiang and the CCP, which had actually dragged on all through the war in that curious atmosphere — no war, no peace — which was the Second United Front. To Vice-President Wallace in June 1944, who argued that the Russians had told him that Mao Tsetung and the others were not real Communists but "margarine Communists," because Communism was impossible without heavy industry, Chiang had replied, "No, no, they are real Communists. They are in fact much more Communist than the Russians."

As far as is known, the State Department at the time maintained an eminently flexible prudent position. Considering U.S. interests first, it should not make the error of thinking China was Chiang, or Chiang was China, but it never actually stated this in a forthright way. The identification of Chiang with China persisted. The self-assigned role of friendly mediator turned into something quite different, and therein lay the tragedy of those years.

The U.S. military mission to Yenan correctly appreciated that the Chinese Communists were deeply rooted among the people and could not be eradicated by annihilation campaigns. They reported on the strength and popularity of the Communists. The contrast between the young, well-fed, well-trained and well-behaved Red soldiers, and the verminous soldiers of Chiang, riddled with disease, starved, press-ganged; between the simplicity of the Communist leaders † and the gross venality of Chiang's officials, was too obvious not to impress deeply. But then along came General Patrick Hurley.

Hurley was sent as special emissary by Roosevelt to Chiang Kai-shek in September 1944, with the primary object of getting Chiang

* For entrancing accounts of the American stay in Yenan in 1944, read David Barrett *Dixie Mission: The United States Army Observer Group in Yenan, 1944* (Berkeley 1970) and John Stewart Service *The Amerasia Papers: Some Problems in the History of U.S.-China Relations* (Berkeley 1971).
† Mao Tsetung in 1944 was paid a "salary" amounting to three U.S. dollars a month.

and Stilwell to work better together. No other mission was given to him. But Stilwell was recalled — Hurley apparently supporting Chiang — in October 1944. From the start of Hurley's presence in China, whatever his self-contradictory statements and actions for the next year, he had thrown his weight on Chiang's side.

In July 1944, when the Dixie mission went to Yenan, a recommendation by the U.S. Joint Chiefs of Staff that both Nationalist and Communist forces be joined under a single command (Stilwell's) had been sent to Roosevelt; in Chungking, Ambassador Gauss broached the idea of joint operations to Chiang on September 15. Vice-President Wallace, it is said, in talks with Chiang in June, had already spoken of some sort of political coalition with the Communists. The Communists themselves could point out that throughout the years they had never refused the idea of a "democratic republic." But what they meant by a democratic republic was entirely different from Chiang's regime. Even the Communist minimum program for coalition would have ended Chiang's military dictatorship and one-party regime, and Chiang would never agree to cancel himself out. Perhaps all this increased Chiang's haste to get rid of Stilwell, who had "sympathy" for the Yenan regime. Soon after Stilwell's departure, Gauss also resigned, in November 1944. Hurley became the U.S. ambassador in Chungking (on Chiang's request to Roosevelt) on November 17. He then took upon himself the task of effecting a marriage between the Communists and Chiang Kai-shek.

Description of Hurley's physical impressiveness are many; but his was "the tragedy of a mind groping desperately at problems beyond its scope," says Theodore White. He did nothing to improve his knowledge of China; reading books or documents was beyond his weak eyes; he never took notes; relied on a chancy memory; cursed hugely, and would brook no divergence in opinion. But all this is immaterial; what is more to the point is that Hurley was so obsessed with personal prejudice that he failed to consider whether his conduct of affairs and his idiosyncrasies would be detrimental or not to the ultimate interests of the U.S., not to speak of loyal U.S. foreign service observers whose careers he savagely destroyed.

Unannounced, on November 7, Hurley landed by air in Yenan. Colonel Barrett describes Hurley's arrival "wearing enough ribbons on his chest to represent every war . . . in which the United States had ever engaged except possibly Shays' rebellion." Mao was hastily summoned to the airport by Chou En-lai, and a company of soldiers mustered for a guard of honor. Hurley "swelled up like a poisoned pup and let out an Indian warwhoop," then told Barrett he had been paid a million dollars by a certain oil company to negotiate an agreement with the Mexican government. Possibly this gave the ambassador the confidence he could negotiate anything.

Hurley spent two days in Yenan. During those two days he submitted to Mao a five-point draft which he seems to have worked out in conjunction with officials of the Kuomintang government. Mao declared bluntly that it was the Kuomintang who refused to negotiate with the Communist Party; that a coalition government had already been offered several times, but that the Kuomintang must first reform itself; Chiang did not want any reorganization. He also told Hurley that Chiang utilized the best of his armies to blockade the Communists.

The talk with Mao, and perhaps the Yenan atmosphere, seem to have given Hurley, for a short while, some lucidity. He went back to Chungking with a revised five-point agreement, which in fact he drafted himself after the Communist proposals had been submitted to him. They "did not go far enough," he said, and corrected their draft and signed the result, together with Mao. On November 10, accompanied by Chou En-lai and Barrett, Hurley flew back to Chungking. Chiang of course turned down the proposals, although they represented a moderate basis for a coalition government. Hurley himself had called them "reasonable," and in fact had signed them because he considered them "fair and just."

But Chiang answered with a counterproposal which granted nothing except a vague statement of civil liberties — "guaranteed subject only to the specific needs of security." This phrase left the issue wide open for his continued dictatorship. After Hurley became ambassador on November 17, he "increasingly inclined" to favor the Chiang side against the Communists.

Chiang prepared another draft, substantially the same as his first counterproposal but including an offer to appoint "some high-ranking officer (one only) from among the Communist forces to membership to the National Military Council." And now the pattern of interference took the place of the "mediation" which Ambassador Gauss had initiated. Hurley could not persuade Chou En-lai in Chungking to accept the Chiang counterproposals. Barrett was now charged with the unpleasant task of returning to Yenan to confer there with Mao Tsetung and persuade him to accept Chiang's terms. The interview took place on December 8, 1944, and was "stormy," and exceedingly uncomfortable for Barrett personally. After months of warm friendship and mutual trust, it must have seemed a stab in the back, rank perfidy, to Mao and to Chou that the U.S. representative in Chungking should now offer them Chiang's terms as backed by the U.S., after Hurley himself had found the Communist proposals fair and just and agreed to present them to Chiang. Mao could not understand the sudden volte-face. He kept getting angry, and calling Chiang "that turtle's egg."

"The principal point in the three terms which are offered us," said Mao in the interview . . . "is that the Communist forces must submit to 'reorganization' by the National Military Council. This means the placing of our troops completely under the control of the Generalissimo. . . . We will then be at his mercy. In return for what is tantamount to complete surrender, we are offered one membership in the National Military Council. . . . This membership means nothing." Actually the council had not met for years.

Hurley had told Chou very rudely in Chungking that before any cooperation with the Americans the Chinese Communists "must accept the Generalissimo's terms." The United States, however "offers us absolutely no guarantee of our safety under these terms," Mao said. "We cannot trust the good faith of the Generalissimo, and no one who has studied impartially the history of the relations of the Kuomintang and the Chinese Communist Party could reasonably expect us to have any confidence in him. We find the attitude of the United States somewhat puzzling," continued Mao; he was in high fury, but his statements were restrained. Hurley had come to Yenan; a five-point proposal, the basis for a coalition government, had been given to him; he had agreed the terms were "eminently fair," had even signed them on November 10. But now, thirty days later, the same Hurley asked the Communists to accept counterproposals made by Chiang which "require us to sacrifice our liberty. This is difficult for us to understand." The words "perfidious" and "treacherous," which the Communists would use later, are not too strong to describe what the Communists thought of these actions of the United States representative.

Mao reiterated that he was entirely willing to participate in a coalition government. Was this true? It probably was; because of the Dixie mission, because of the feeling which Mao Tsetung had come to in the several months that the mission had been in Yenan that with the help of the Americans, who could keep Chiang Kai-shek in check, a genuinely democratic coalition government could be made to work. Mao was prepared, as he put it "to cooperate . . . to save the situation" from impending civil war. "We do not want war . . . even for a day." But now he knew war would be inevitable, and he also realized the Americans *might* be on Chiang's side in the war.

The point is important. Before the advent of the Americans, Mao Tsetung saw no way out except seizure of power by armed struggle. With the Americans and their help,* Mao Tsetung was willing to try a peaceful coalition government; but with the proviso that Chiang must accept reforms. He had been almost persuaded that America also would insist on reforms. Had not every American he had met told him how appalled they were by Chiang's misrule? Only the U.S. could truly help China to a new democratic government, and Mao was willing then to forego armed struggle. *Perhaps* a peaceful way out could be found.

He was, understandably, extremely angry. "The U.S. believes that Chiang must be retained in power at all costs. We have no objection. . . . We are not, however, going to give up our right of self-preservation for one seat . . ." He warned that it was "useless to support Chiang Kai-shek." Mao insisted that under the five points he had proposed, and *with the help of the U.S.,* the Communists could prevent a civil war and make a coalition government work. "If the U.S. abandons us now, we shall be very sorry, but it will make no difference in our good feeling towards you. We will accept your help with gratitude any time, now or in the future. . . . If the United States does not give us one rifle or one round of ammunition . . . we shall still be friends of the United States." †

But Hurley had now gotten fixated on a "unification of the forces of China," and this unification must be under Chiang. No flexibility of any kind could be allowed. China was Chiang, Chiang was China. As he never went out to see how the people really fared under Chiang, but lived in solitary splendor, banqueted and flattered by the Chiangs, he became increasingly isolated from any advice but that of Chiang's officials.

By January 1945 the Japanese campaign had come to its end. Spent and overstretched, the Japanese withdrew; in their wake Communist guerillas sprang up. Though Chiang then assisted the Japanese with his own officers and troops, and invaded certain Red

---

* On the military side, all through 1944 and until March 1945, the U.S. had actually made promises of military cooperation with the CCP and the Red Army; and Mao had indicated that the Communists would "gladly serve . . . under a U.S. commander" against Japan.
† December 1944 interview.

bases, the cruelties of the Kuomintang caused wholesale uprisings by the mobilized population; Red Army counteroffensives took back the territories. All this Hurley ignored.

In January 1945 Hurley conceived of the idea of pressuring the Chinese Communists through Stalin to force a compromise with Chiang Kai-shek. The idea that Moscow dictated to all Communist parties in the world made him certain the CCP would also obey Moscow. From conversations in August 1944 with the Russians, Hurley had gathered that they "thought little" of the Chinese Communists, that Moscow did not support the CCP nor desire to see them in power. He too was told that the Chinese Communists were not real Communists. And he repeated it. Later, he would accuse the American foreign service men and army officers of being "Communist-inclined" because they had written favorably about people whom he himself had declared "not Communistic."

Hurley reasoned that if Mao could be made to feel "abandoned" by Moscow, he would have to agree to a compromise with Chiang. Hence Stalin must be prevailed upon to sign a treaty of friendship and alliance with Chiang Kai-shek, which would take the wind out of Mao's sails. Considerable exertions were made by the Americans to get a treaty going between Stalin and Chiang. Chiang was anxious for such an agreement. He counted on an opposition to Mao in the CCP strong enough to outvote Mao; Chiang was kept well informed on the intra-Party struggle, but he overestimated the importance of some individuals and underestimated Mao's powers of persuasion in the Party.

But now, in the U.S., the tactics of war and diplomacy began to shift. Roosevelt was engaged in active negotiations with the USSR. Doubt as to Russian reaction in case of civil war in China and, even more, Roosevelt's insistence on Russia's entering the war against Japan had led to these talks. By the end of 1944 Roosevelt considered that an alliance with the USSR for a postwar "world balance" might work to America's advantage, and China receded in importance. Militarily, also, the U.S. had concluded that Chinese forces would no longer be needed to defeat Japan, nor China be the great base from which to invade Japan, since the island-hopping strategy was successful, and later the use of the atom bomb would make it unnecessary for the U.S. to consider Chinese armies important. On the other hand, the U.S. was anxious to keep China's enormous market for itself, and its economic expansion. Hence an accommodation with the USSR on China had to be reached. This would lead to the Yalta meetings in February 1945.

In Edgar Snow's *Random Notes on Red China,* there is a hint of a "sharing" of China envisaged already by Roosevelt. Some weeks before Roosevelt's death, Snow saw the President, and in the conversation was startled by something Roosevelt said which implied that he thought of a partition of China between two "legal" governments, one in the North and one in the South. Whether this, coming after Yalta, represented a state of mind which was Roosevelt's alone or one arrived at jointly with Stalin is unclear. Thus from "mediator" to involvement to interference, bit by bit was fashioned a foreign policy towards China which would be the worst possible for the relations between the two countries. In the ensuing years of opposition to the realities of the Chinese Revolution the U.S. would waste her prestige and power until a massive accumulation of problems, the fruit of ill-conceived policies, would at last bring about a change.

The Yalta meeting of February 1945 between Roosevelt and Stalin, with Churchill a poor third, took place, while in Yenan preparations for the Seventh Congress of the Communist Party of China were being made. Was Mao Tsetung aware of the significance of Yalta? He must have noticed that Chiang was not invited, and later studied the clauses which concerned Chinese territory, bargained away by Roosevelt in his desire to have the USSR enter the war against Japan.

Stalin skillfully used Roosevelt's haunting obsession with "sparing American lives," and his trying to involve Russia in fighting Japan, to extort concessions that were not Roosevelt's to make, for these concerned Chinese territory and rights. Automatically, having made these concessions, the Americans would *have* to back Chiang Kaishek, who *agreed* to these demands in regard to China while Mao was neither consulted nor told — and would not have agreed. For if the U.S. threw its weight in favor of a Sino-Soviet pact with Chiang, surely it must appear to back Chiang to the hilt, and leave itself no alternative. This is what happened.

To enter the war against Japan, Stalin had demanded on December 14, 1944, the lease of both Port Arthur and Dairen, Chinese ports situated on Chinese territory, and the surrounding area; lease of the Chinese Eastern Railway line from Dairen to Harbin (again that famous railway!), thence northwest to Manchouli and east to Vladivostok; recognition of the status quo in Outer Mongolia (the independent republic of Outer Mongolia). On these conditions, Russia would enter the war against Japan "two or three months" after the war in Europe ended and Germany surrendered. Stalin was asking, in fact, the former rights of czarist Russia, "violated" (as he put it) by the Japanese in the war of 1904! The American negotiators managed to modify the wording to "internationalization of the ports of Dairen and the lease of Port Arthur as a naval base for the USSR; China's full sovereignty in Manchuria being retained, but the preeminent interests of the Soviet Union safeguarded." *

Two months after the Yalta conference, in April 1945, Roosevelt died. The Cold War had already begun; the premises upon which the Yalta agreement had been drawn up had already changed, for the atom bomb was being tested and the U.S. felt able to "go it alone," felt no need to share the world with anyone. The anti-Communist preparation of public opinion in the United States was immensely stepped up. Mao watched this with anxiety. He would always remember how swiftly public opinion could be manipulated. Unlike his predecessor, the new President Truman felt that a truculent attitude towards the Russians would pay off. By June 1945 there was already a categorical shift in attitude towards Russia. As for the policy towards China, Hurley seemed, in the first six months of 1945, convinced he would succeed in getting the two sides together — he was sure they were really "that near," holding the thumb and finger half an inch apart. But by "together" he meant under the supreme rule of Chiang Kai-shek.

Increasingly, Hurley urged that pressure be put on the Communists, whose strength was "exaggerated." He would not use any pressure on Chiang. American policy was "to sustain Chiang" and no one else, said Hurley. Yet as late as January 1945 the State Department had stated in a memorandum that a "government representative of the wishes of the people," and not necessarily Chiang Kai-shek's, was what the U.S. desired in China. But the State Department lagged behind the formidable imperatives of the Cold War, the ruthless calculations of profit and power. Hurley, therefore, was not the jackass some make him out to be. He was unrelentingly an imperialist. Chiang would serve America's purposes in China far better than a patriotic, strong government under Mao. The race for economic concessions in China had already begun; American company representatives flew into Chungking even before the war had ended.

* Among many others, see Herbert Feis *The China Tangle* (Princeton, N.J., 1953).

In February 1945 Hurley went to Washington and strongly recommended supporting *only* Chiang Kai-shek, with military weapons and money, opposing any other course of action. A little known memorandum of the time quoted by John Service is the following: "Hurley, Lieutenant General Wedemeyer, and Commodore Miles discussed the Chinese military problems with the Joint Chiefs of Staff on March 27 [1945]. They were all of the opinion that the *rebellion* in China could be put down by comparatively small assistance to Chiang's government." * Commodore Miles was later to head the OSS (Office of Strategic Services) in China, in close cooperation with Tai Li, Chiang's secret service director. The OSS was the parent of the CIA.

On April 1 John Service had another interview with Mao Tsetung, a few days before the Seventh Congress opened. This was his third interview; his first had been in August 1944 and the second in March 1945. Mao then told him that the people of China and of America had strong ties of sympathy, understanding and mutual interest. Both were essentially democratic and individualistic. China's great postwar need would be economic development. America and China complemented each other economically. For all these reasons there must not and could not be any conflict, estrangement or misunderstanding between the Chinese people and the American people. Mao repeated that Americans did not seem to understand the Kuomintang-Communist issue; it was not just a kind of "bickering" or legal opposition between two political parties. It was, far more, a military confrontation; and Chiang would not hesitate to massacre the Communists should they give up their armies.

Mao again offered friendship and cooperation to America in the war against Japan; he reminded Service gently that the Communists had saved many American airmen from Japanese clutches, often passing them through hostile country at the risk of their own lives. Now the Communists were even willing to place their forces under the command of an American general; they would loyally fight the common enemy. Mao said that America would win "the undying friendship" of the overwhelming majority of China's people should she decide *not* to interfere in the civil war that was looming. To interfere meant to help Chiang solely. Then America would be helping Chiang make civil war against the people of China; and this would ruin the friendship between China and America. Chou En-lai also

* John Stewart Service *The Amerasia Papers: Some Problems in the History of U.S.–China Relations* (Berkeley 1971).

urged Service to stay a few more days in Yenan; had Service done so, he would have been present at the Congress and heard some of the speeches made; but he had to leave.

Service was "Hurleyed" out of China in April 1945; Ambassador Hurley sent in a very unfavorable report on him, accusing him of pro-Communism. In June he was to be arrested in his own country in connection with "leaks" to the magazine *Amerasia*.

But even then Hurley had not been able to move the State Department — though with the fears and the pressures of the times, some quailed and caved in — to an officially adopted inflexible, help-Chiang-only policy, although the reality was that this policy was operative in substance. The principle of "flexibility" was still being advocated, but the suggestion of military cooperation with the Communists had long since vanished, leaving military cooperation with Chiang still operative. The State Department reiterated somewhat weakly the "unrepresentative" character of Chiang's government, its inefficiency and corruption. But Hurley carried on, and a growing number of rabidly anti-Communist businessmen and politicians seemed to back his policies.

It is against this background that we must analyze Mao's speech *On Coalition Government* at the Seventh Congress. The speech has the all-encompassing sweep which Mao projects in so much of his writing; the links between separate spheres of operation — military, political, economic, foreign relations — are shown very clearly. There is not a single belligerent word; but it is a speech of resolve and determination, of flexible offer to cooperate, but of inflexible principle not to disarm but to negotiate on the ten-point program set out in 1937. All this was not new; but *On Coalition Government* is also a blueprint for a new Chinese state. There is not a single word against the United States, in spite of the way in which Mao might have felt let down. He had no illusions left, but only quiet confidence. "We must exert ourselves and learn, because China depends on us for reconstruction." He expected no help from anyone.*

He repeated again that the offer made by Chiang of one post in the National Military Council meant nothing; there must be an end to one-party dictatorship and political tutelage, repeal of all laws suppressing the freedom of the people, abolition of the secret police, of the attacks and the blockade against Communist areas, recognition of the legal status of all anti-Japanese troops, and of the popu-

* *On Coalition Government*, 1945, *Selected Works of Mao Tsetung*, vol. III (English edition Peking 1961–1965).

larly elected governments in the liberated areas. Chiang's book, *China's Destiny*, had been published in 1944; it was full of Confucian precepts, and attacked the Communists as an "alien" philosophy. Mao referred to it with irony. China's two destinies were indeed plain: "Someone has written a book about one of them . . . our Congress represents China's other destiny, and we too shall write a book about it." Mao called the CCP "the center of gravity of the Chinese people's struggle to resist Japan and save the nation . . . China's center of gravity lies right here where we are, and nowhere else."

Mao Tsetung also indicated that within the Party as well as without there were people who were so wearied by war that they were ready to compromise and come to an agreement on almost any terms. The USSR, and the U.S. and Great Britain and France, were all trying to persuade the CCP to give in. But the continuation of armed attacks from the KMT throughout the years, and the blockade (which took no less than 790,000 of Chiang's men), made it impossible to come to an agreement by relinquishing the armed forces and the territories under Communist administration.

The danger of civil war was present; Chiang was indeed stepping up preparations "as soon as the forces of a certain Allied country have cleared a considerable part of the Chinese mainland of the Japanese aggressors." Obviously Mao still believed that the U.S. strategy of using China as a jumping-off base to occupy Japan held good; he did not know that the plans had changed.

The time was right for daring, but in the Party there were those who did not dare; the fear of offending both the U.S. and the USSR must have been often discussed by the faint-hearted. They had no confidence in the Chinese people, said Mao, they were "practical" men, with a fear of taking power by armed struggle. He was ready to talk peace, but not at the cost of suicide.

On foreign policy Mao had this to say: "The Communist Party of China agrees with the Atlantic Charter and with the decisions of the international conferences of Moscow, Cairo, Teheran and the Crimea [Yalta] because these decisions all contribute to the defeat of the fascist aggressors and the maintenance of world peace." The fundamental principles of the foreign policy of the Communist Party, later to become those of the People's Republic of China, were stated by Mao Tsetung at that time: "China shall establish and strengthen diplomatic relations with all countries and settle all questions of common concern, such as coordination of military operations in the war, peace conferences, trade and investment, on the basic conditions that the Japanese aggressors must be completely defeated and world peace maintained, that there must be mutual respect for national independence and equality and that there must be promotion of mutual interests and friendship between states and between peoples." In this declaration lie the five principles of peaceful existence, still the basis of China's foreign policy. This sentence implied denial of recognition of any agreement not based on "mutual interests" and "national independence and equality."

"We welcome the United Nations Conference on International Organization in San Francisco" (a delegation of the CCP was appointed to the conference and attended it, despite strenuous objections from Chiang) "in order to express the will of the Chinese people. . . . We ask the governments of all Allied countries, and of the United States and Britain in the first place, to pay serious attention to the voice of the Chinese people and *not to impair friendship with them* by pursuing foreign policies that run counter to their will . . . *We maintain that if any foreign government helps the Chinese reactionaries and opposes the Chinese people's democratic cause, it will be committing a gross mistake."* *

The United States was warned. But by that time the die was already cast.

The emergence at the Seventh Congress and the meteoric rise since 1937 of Liu Shao-chi could be looked upon as inevitable, since according to dialectics every situation is pregnant with its opposite within itself. From the time of the Seventh Congress, Liu Shao-chi would be regarded as Mao's most faithful adherent and collaborator. More puzzling is the status of "Party theoretician" he seems to have assumed so swiftly. First reports of Liu as a "philosopher of the Party" and a "rigid theologian of Marxism" appeared in the foreign press in 1948 and 1949; in the 1950's he was said to be more "Russian-oriented" than Mao, and hence more of a "Marxist." Yet his works, until then, including *Training of the Communist Party Member* (one of the documents of the Rectification campaign, to be reprinted as *How To Be a Good Communist*), are not so much theoretical as organizational theses. But whatever the reputation made or

* Emphasis not in the original.

unmade by outside observers, Liu's career between 1935 and 1945 demands scrutiny, because after Mao he was the main speaker at the Seventh Congress, although both Chou En-lai and Chu Teh also made speeches. Liu was elected vice-chairman of the Central Committee, while Mao was elected chairman.

It seems puzzling that Chou En-lai, who had done so much for the Revolution and had held so successfully so many important appointments, was not chief speaker. Chou had been engaged in the prolonged and difficult negotiations with Chiang Kai-shek — as recently as January and February 1945 — when he had reiterated the CCP demands for a coalition government. Chou had questioned Hurley as to whether the United States would give weapons to Chiang. Hurley had equivocated, saying no arms would be handed over to the troops of any *political party* (obviously he did not consider Chiang's one-party Kuomintang government a political party). Chou had been successful in rallying third party and independent personalities and even Kuomintang adherents. He had been the moving spirit behind the formation of the Democratic League, which in September 1944 signed an agreement with the CCP not to negotiate with the KMT or submit to any KMT dominance without prior consultation with the CCP. Chou "had set the pattern everywhere for a coalition government, for a national conference," according to some observers of the time. He was reaffirmed at the Seventh Congress, and became also vice-chairman.

Chang Kuo-tao has left us a clear word picture of Liu Shao-chi, whom he met in Moscow in 1922. Liu believed in organizing workers, students, women and "the poor masses" to struggle "for improvement of their livelihood." According to Chang, Liu's ideal never was revolution, but "social welfare." A striving for "legal benefits and legal activities," a liking for law and order, and rules and regulations (he was to draw a 70-point charter for industry) mark him as the opposite of Mao in his vision of how things should be done. The notion of class struggle was "repugnant" to Liu, says his friend Chang Kuo-tao. All this does not make a revolutionary. We understand better Liu's handling of the Anyuan mine strike, and his habit, as Chang says, of always having "orderly programs" ready.

In 1925, after the May 30, 1925, incident, Liu appears to have been on the point of arrest (he was at the time vice-president in the Shanghai headquarters of the All-China Federation of Labor). He fled to Changsha and hid in Mao's Cultural Bookstore. But he was

Chou En-lai with Mao Tsetung at the Seventh Congress, April 1945.

Liu Shao-chi.

442   The Morning Deluge

discovered and arrested; released, he went to Kuangchow in June 1925. In 1927, in Wuhan, Liu Shao-chi obeyed the orders given by Chen Tu-hsiu to disarm the workers, and even presented a report on this "success . . . to restore unity." He was again arrested by Wang Ching-wei, and it appears that Chen Kung-po, one of the founders of the Communist Party, who later went over to Chiang Kai-shek, got in touch with Liu when he was in jail and persuaded him to give up Communism. Liu was then given the Confucian classics to read and was "much affected." He was released, but on condition that he would be "the Kuomintang man" within the CCP. Whether this is correct or not is not known, but the personality of those who talk of this event seems to be a guarantee that something of the sort did happen.*

In 1928, after turning against Chen Tu-hsiu and denouncing his line, Liu did underground work in the Northeast and became secretary of the Party Committee in Manchuria. He also attended Comintern meetings in Russia and the Sixth Congress of the CCP, held in Moscow. The Manchurian Party Committee was arrested in 1930, but Liu escaped, and between 1931 and 1934 he was at the Central (Juichin) Base as chairman of the All-China Federation of Labor. It is said that he did not agree with the "ultra-left" line of Wang Ming. But he became a member of the provisional Politburo organized by the twenty-eight Bolsheviks, and one of the seventeen men elected to the presidium in 1934 — whose object was to check Mao's influence as chairman of the local government of the base.

In 1934 he appears to have done the first stage of the Long March, going as far as Tsunyi; from there, he went back to the White areas. He was then several times back in Yenan. Chang Kuo-tao tells of the episode in which Liu, in June 1937, wrote a "letter" criticizing everything that had been done in the Party as "left adventurist," including the First United Front. Chang seems to imply that Liu and he were of the same opinion, but without any consultation, as Liu did not go to see Chang in Yenan. The letter recommended no less than a complete abandonment of all the policies which had been followed by the CCP, and complete surrender to Chiang Kai-shek. Liu especially condemned rural bases and peasant movements, says Chang. Mao was much exercised by this and went to see Liu; then Liu withdrew the letter, went back on what he had written, and adhered to Mao's line.

* Interviews and articles in the Chinese press.

Liu returned again to work in the White areas, and with some success, after 1937; in 1938 he openly espoused Mao's line on the united front, and returned to lecture at the Yenan Marx-Lenin Institute in 1939.

And now we come to what has been called "the abjuration case." Apparently, even at this early stage, certain minor cadres had already denounced Liu as being a renegade, but these accusations went unheard. The "abjuration" case was brought out in the open for the first time on April 1, 1967, though it happened in 1936. Apparently Liu Shao-chi advised some Party members who were prisoners of the Kuomintang to renounce Communism in order to save themselves. Thus were released, among others, Peng Chen, Liu Lan-tao, An Tzu-wen, Po I-po; these and others were used by Liu to build up his own following in the Party, or, as it is now called, his own "bourgeois headquarters" in opposition to Mao's "proletarian headquarters" within the Party. This might mean that in the enormous expansion of the Party from 1938 onward, the recruits and adherents of Liu Shao-chi would be in sizable number; and although the vast majority of those recruited would know nothing of these intrigues, he would try to place his own supporters in key positions within the Party.*

Mao Tsetung was uncompromisingly against admitting anyone to the Party who had at any time abjured or reneged. A wise decision, for the policy of getting Communist prisoners to sign a paper whereby they gave up their beliefs had been practiced by Chiang since 1933 and was a way of infiltrating the Party with his own agents or potential agents. It is at the Seventh Congress that we see Liu developing, in his speech, certain articles concerning the admission of Party members which make us suspect that he was indeed trying to get people who had abjured into the organization.

In *On the Party* † Liu speaks of the "thorough ideological reform" of petty bourgeois Party members, which has "changed their former petty-bourgeois nature and imparts to them the qualities of the advanced fighters of the proletariat." This is in line with his views on human nature, but it is not Marxism. He then goes on to say that "the social origin of our party membership does not determine the character of our party, just as the social composition of the membership of the labor parties in certain European countries does not de-

---

* Interview with French Marxist-Leninists, 1969, who had held discussions in China on Liu Shao-chi. Also discussions by author in China, 1969, 1970.
† Liu's speech at the Congress.

termine their character." In the explanation of the new statutes for Party membership, more interesting phraseology comes out. Liu divides the membership into four categories, the fourth consisting of "persons who have accepted other political faiths and joined other political parties or groups." This would mean that a person who had joined the Kuomintang is eligible; rather a startling admission, considering what had happened since 1927 (it would be, of course, quite different for the period 1924 to 1927 of the First United Front). The statutes add that if a person had joined another party under coercion, he would be admitted according to his social status, and not as a person with other political affiliations; this means he might be eligible without further investigation. A former member of the Party "applying for readmission after leaving the Party must follow the procedure for the fourth category, as such a person, having displayed political vacillation, should have the recommendation of more experienced Party members." This opens the door wide for the return of abjurers. "His probationary period may generally be shortened," is added, and also that if Party connections "have been involuntarily broken off . . . he" (the Party member) "must be reinstated immediately after his application has been verified . . . he need not go through the procedure required of a new member." In this way, and in a seemingly reasonable manner, it would be entirely in the hands of Liu and his own followers, if they were in the position to decide on admissions, to admit whom they wanted. And it is certain that the cadre organization bureau was in his control. The charge that Liu built up his own headquarters in the Party does not seem therefore excessive.

Mao strenuously opposed the admission of any abjurers, saying that anyone who had reneged should never be admitted again. But Mao was never an absolute autocrat within the Party; ideological authority does not mean dictatorial power; and statesmanship is the art of getting along with opponents or future adversaries.

This thesis may provide an explanation for Liu's swift rise, and for his obvious assumption of power within the next few years, a power founded on bureaucracy within the Party. But at the Seventh Congress, Liu extolled Mao Tsetung Thought; and spoke of Mao in terms almost idolatrous; perhaps this very verbiage should make him suspect. "Long live comrade Mao Tsetung, our Party leader and the helmsman of the revolutionary struggle. . . . Using the Thought of Mao Tsetung, which unites the theories of Marxism-Leninism with the actual practice of the Chinese Revolution . . . as the guide in all

its work, our Party has formulated a revolutionary program . . .
Our party is a party that has a great leader of its own; this leader is
none else but comrade Mao Tsetung . . . who . . . has raised our
national thinking to an unprecedented height and shown to the suffering nation and people the only correct and clear road towards
complete liberation . . . the road of Mao Tsetung."

Much of this is quite true; but it simply does not sound sincere,
and we are compelled to think it was flattery, not the outpourings of
a heart full of real admiration for the undoubted achievements of
Mao. Especially as Liu's very good friend Chang Kuo-tao * writes:
"Liu was never much of an admirer of Mao" — he found him "illogical, indiscriminate . . . lacking in self-culture . . . Generally
speaking, those cadres at higher levels who are more prudent . . .
are congenial with him . . . *He does not enjoy class struggle, does
not cherish guerillaism.*" †

As the Seventh Congress proceeded to its triumphal conclusion,
Mao's warning in the *Appendix* resolution ‡ and certain turns of
phrase in his speech indicate that he was aware of the eternal anti-
thetic twin present in the Party, the two-line struggle. It was something that would always be: "one always divides into two."

The Seventh Congress was, above all, a congress of unity and of
victory. The Party stood poised, on the threshold of a new phase. In
between the sessions, carefree and jocular, Mao Tsetung, now a little
bit more fat, his hair much shorter, played Ping-Pong, joked, and
went out for walks, to talk and laugh with the peasants in the caves
just above the Central Committee building where the Congress was
taking place, and inquire of the planting and the prospects for the
harvest. In the final contest, it would be the workers and peasants of
China, and not a handful of ambitious men, who would decide the
outcome of the Revolution.

* Chang and Liu were very close friends in Shanghai in the 1920's. See the preface
by Chang Kuo-tao to the *Collected Works of Liu Shao-chi* (Hong Kong 1969).
† Italics by author.
‡ *Appendix: Resolution on Certain Questions in the History of Our Party.* Adopted
April 20, 1945, by the enlarged seventh plenary session of the Sixth Central Com-
mittee of the Communist Party of China. *Selected Works of Mao Tsetung,* vol. III
(English edition Peking 1961–1965).

6

The Conquest of Power—Prelude

"Yesterday, in a talk with two Americans who were leaving for the United States, I said that the U.S. government was trying to undermine us and this would not be permitted. We oppose the U.S. government's policy of supporting Chiang Kai-shek against the Communists. But we must draw a distinction firstly between the people of the United States and their government and secondly within the U.S. government between the policy makers and their subordinates." In these words Mao Tsetung expressed, very moderately, the conclusions to which American action had driven the Chinese Communist Party.*

The Dixie mission had gone, the last of the observers and newsmen too. Some would be arrested, and others, like Colonel Barrett, because he had recommended equipping the Communist forces, would be retired from active service. John Paton Davies, who had recommended the dispatch of the Dixie mission, was to pay dearly for writing favorable reports about Yenan.

On April 2, 1945, at a press conference in Washington convened at the State Department, Ambassador Hurley asserted that there would be no cooperation with the Chinese Communists, and praised Chiang's "democratic" government. In spite of the fact that on April 3 the State Department's paper called Chiang's government "unrepresentative," warned against the outbreak of civil war, and the unwisdom of total commitment "in any way" to Chiang's government "unless and until national political unity and stability has been achieved [and] the Chinese government [i.e., Chiang] has obtained the support of the Chinese people," Hurley did not reflect the condi-

* *The Foolish Old Man Who Removed the Mountains*, June 11, 1945. *Selected Works of Mao Tsetung*, vol. III (English edition Peking 1961–1965). This was Mao's concluding speech at the Seventh Congress.

tional and limited nature of America's support to Chiang, but flew back to throw himself, and America's military power, behind Chiang. Before leaving, Hurley promised Truman that he would bring about "unity" by the end of April.

Chiang had not been inactive. As a camouflage a People's Political Consultative Conference and National Assembly was announced; the suggestion had first been put forward by the Communists. This organization was suggested by Mao Tsetung to Hurley in January 1945, on one of Mao's many attempts to obtain negotiations on a representative basis. Mao proposed the conference should be attended by delegates of the Kuomintang, the Communists, and the Democratic League. "But Chiang retained complete control of the government and its power of ultimate decision of final responsibility," as Chou En-lai said. The National Assembly would be completely KMT-controlled and the "government would not change the reality of Chiang's personal dominance."

In July the Communists reiterated their demand for a Consultative Conference, with KMT, Communist, Democratic League representatives and independents. Now Hurley blocked this. By that time Hurley's position in China had deteriorated. Such was the popular appeal of the Communist proposal that many non-Communist leaders now criticized him.* Chiang then again played for time; he would convoke a National Assembly on November 12, to "hand state power back to the people on that date." But since the National Assembly was KMT-picked, all parties except the KMT refused to attend it. Hurley stated that Chiang was "carrying out genuine reforms," but this deceived no one, not even Hurley himself, and certainly not the hard-headed Wedemeyer, who had replaced Stilwell.

The reality was, as always, the "reorganization" of the armed forces of Yenan, the control of the Red Army. Chiang proposed that a committee of three, including one American, should be in charge of this project; but the CCP must hand over its troops before receiving "legal status," which meant it could not attend the National Assembly before disarming itself.

In July 1945 Mao warned: "The policy of the US towards China as represented by its ambassador Patrick J. Hurley is creating a civil war crisis in China. . . . If the Hurley policy of aiding and abetting the reactionary forces . . . and antagonizing the Chinese people

* See Tang Tsou *America's Failure in China* (Chicago 1963), p. 288.

continues unchanged, it will place a crushing burden on the government and people of the United States and plunge them into endless
trouble." The CCP did not want to fight, said Mao, but "the rights
the people have . . . must never be lightly given up. . . . We don't
want civil war . . . this will be a civil war forced on us." During the
Sino-Japanese war, Chiang's policy had been "to look on with folded
arms, wait for victory, conserve his forces and prepare for civil war,"
while the Chinese Communist armies fought. Now Chiang was getting ready for his kind of war, civil war, and he had dragged America, through Hurley, into backing him.

So much was to happen in August 1945, when World War II ended
and the era of atomic war began. The USSR entered the war against
Japan on August 8, Russian troops overrunning Manchuria, disarming Japanese troops, and occupying the main cities. On the 10th,
American forces in China began to help Chiang's armies recapture
the cities and lines of communication in North China. On August
11 Chiang sent a cable to Chu Teh, ordered the Communist commander-in-chief to keep the Red armies immobile, and *not* to accept
any Japanese surrenders. This was against the Potsdam declaration.*
Chu Teh, as commander-in-chief of the Resist Japan armies in the
liberated areas, had issued seven such commands and orders to advance and occupy Japanese-held territory a few hours after the
Japanese notification of surrender had been received by the USSR,
China, the U.S. and Britain.†

In reply to Chiang's order to Chu Teh, Mao Tsetung cabled a categorical no, pointing out the illegality of Chiang's order, since on
August 11 Chiang had ordered his officers to "step up the war effort
. . . push forward without the slightest relaxation," and since, according to the Potsdam declaration and the Japanese government
notification of surrender, the Red armies were just as anti-Japanese
and therefore as entitled to receive the surrenders of Japanese and
puppet troops as any other anti-Japanese armies, which also included
the Russian armies, in China only since August 8.

On August 13 Mao issued two statements. *The Situation and Our
Policy After the Victory in the War of Resistance Against Japan* was

---

* The right to disarm enemy forces and accept surrenders. Since the united front
was still in existence, technically the commander-in-chief of the Red Army had as
much right to disarm enemy forces and accept Japanese surrenders as any other
force.

† On August 10. See *Two Telegrams from the Commander-in-Chief of the 18th
Group Army to Chiang Kai-shek*, August 1945. *Selected Works of Mao Tsetung*,
vol. IV (English edition Peking 1961–1965).

a warning that Chiang was preparing to renew the civil conflict. *Now Chiang Kai-shek is Provoking Civil War* was even more outspoken and biting. "As Chiang is sharpening his swords, we must sharpen ours too."

On August 14 Chiang signed the treaty of friendship and alliance with the USSR so much desired by Hurley; on the same day General Douglas MacArthur, as U.S. supreme commander in Japan, issued the order that only Chiang's armies were recognized as the authority to accept the surrender of Japanese troops in China, and ordered the Japanese garrisons to stay put until the KMT armies arrived. "What swung the balance in favor of the Nationalist government and averted an imminent Communist victory was American assistance in expeditiously transporting the Nationalist forces by sea and air to strategic points throughout China while Japanese and puppet forces held these areas against the Communists pending the arrival of Kuomintang troops. . . . The first outlines of these military operations were laid down . . . towards the end of July." *

Chiang moved swiftly, taking over puppet troops as his own — for some of them it was only returning to their original commands. He could now play a game of high diplomacy while completing his war preparations — with which the Americans were helping him with spectacular results.

On August 19 Hurley flew back to Yenan to persuade Mao to come to Chungking for talks with Chiang Kai-shek. Chiang sent telegrams urging Mao to come, and Mao agreed on August 24. The American guaranteed his personal safety, and it was Hurley who escorted Mao back to Chungking on August 26. Chou En-lai went with him, while Liu Shao-chi remained in Yenan as acting chairman. Meanwhile, beginning on July 21, Hu Tsung-nan had suddenly attacked the Yenan base and taken a piece out of it (41 villages). Mao fought back, and the territory was recaptured on August 8.

Why did Mao go to Chungking? Because there was a great desire for peace among the war-wearied millions; because the issues were unclear to the bulk of the people in Kuomintang areas, who looked forward to the Communists bringing their efficiency and honesty and somehow changing Chiang. Because in the CCP itself the issues were not clear. Because Mao himself would rather *not* have fought; because he calculated that *even* if he had cast away all illusions, a refusal to go would have played into Chiang's hands — enabling him

---

* Tang Tsou *America's Failure in China, 1941–1950* (Chicago 1963), pp. 305, 308.

to call the Communists belligerent and rigid, determined to seek warlike solutions.

The Russians also seemed apprehensive of a conflict which might involve them, and urged unity between the KMT and CCP. Though Stalin would later, in September 1946, state that the atom bomb "is only feared by weaklings," the whipping up of anti-Russian hysteria in Europe, recent talks between British diplomats and some Nazi commanders in Western Europe, had made the USSR fearful of a surprise military attack. The Soviet Union did not have the atom bomb; it needed peace to rebuild its shattered economy. Pressure upon Mao from Russia for a "peaceful settlement" was therefore strong, but it was never a threat as some Western diplomats interpreted it. Li Li-san's return was also regarded as a "threat" to Mao; * this was typical of the Hurley type of thinking, but it is not, in a sane perspective, to be so regarded. Li Li-san had practically no following in the Party or in China.

"Some of our comrades" said Mao, "put their faith in political influence, fancying that problems can be solved merely by influence."

Which "comrades" did Mao refer to? Mao Tsetung now told his Party of his last meeting with Barrett in December 1944, a meeting which seared Barrett deeply, for he was doing what he had no heart to do. Barrett told Mao: "You should listen to Hurley and send a few men to be officials of the Kuomintang government." "If we become officials," Mao had replied, "we must be free to act . . . a coalition government must be set up on a democratic basis." And Barrett: "It will be bad if you don't." "How bad?" "First the Americans will curse you; secondly the Americans will back Chiang Kai-shek." Mao replied: "What we have now is millet plus rifles, what you have is bread plus cannon. . . . If you want to back Chiang Kai-shek, back him, back him as long as you want. But remember one thing. *To whom does China belong?* China definitely does not belong to Chiang Kai-shek, China belongs to the Chinese people." †

According to Barrett,‡ Mao said about Chiang, "that son of a turtle should have got down from his high seat long ago," and at the end of the conference said, very gently, to Barrett: "You really do want peace in China, don't you?"

* Li Li-san returned with Soviet troops arriving in Manchuria August 1945.

† *The Situation and Our Policy After the Victory in the War of Resistance Against Japan*, August 13, 1945. *Selected Works of Mao Tsetung*, vol. IV (English edition Peking 1961–1965).

‡ Personal letter to the author.

But Mao now also mentioned some "comrades" in the Party who had voiced their terror of the atom bomb. Mao quoted Mountbatten, who had said that "the worst possible mistake is to think that the atom bomb can decide the war." The comrades referred to, he went on, "are more backward than Mountbatten. . . . What influence has made these comrades look on the atom bomb as something miraculous? Bourgeois influence . . . the theory that weapons decide everything, the purely military viewpoint . . . a bureaucratic style of work divorced from the masses. . . . All the bourgeois influence in our ranks." To whom were these words addressed?

Mao went to Chungking to discuss with Chiang Kai-shek the great issues of unity and national reconstruction. Unless there was a definite way of making a coalition government work, there would be civil war; but it must not be a coalition for surrender. Mao himself had little hope; however, "it is possible that the civil war plot of the Chinese reactionaries may be frustrated. . . . We are prepared to make such concessions as are necessary and as do not damage the fundamental interests of the people." This meant drastic cuts in the size of the liberated areas and the strength of the Red Army, stopping the issue of Communist currency — issued in liberated areas since 1940 — and learning to master "all forms of legal struggle." "Without such concessions, we cannot explode the Kuomintang's civil war plot." He knew in his own heart that no matter how much he conceded, Chiang would take nothing short of complete surrender of armed power, and would break his word at the first opportunity. But "without such concessions, we cannot gain the political initiative, cannot win the sympathy of world public opinion and the middle-of-the-roaders within the country, and cannot obtain in exchange legal status for our Party and a state of peace. . . . The Soviet Union, the U.S. and Britain all disapprove of civil war in China."

Thus, having analyzed the various aspects of the contradiction, Mao, dressed in a quiet gray suit and a topee, enplaned for Chungking on August 26 with Chou En-lai, Wang Jo-fei, and Patrick Hurley.

By that time Chiang's troops had already been conveyed in U.S. planes and carried on U.S. ships to all points north, and Chiang already controlled all the big cities and lines of communication in North China as well as in the South. The Red armies, however, still had 175 medium or small cities as well as 20 percent of the rural areas of China in their hands.

"The Old Boy" as the peasants of the liberated areas affectionately called Mao Tsetung,* as he waved his topee to the crowds at Yenan, then at Chungking airport, looked again much thinner, alone and quiet. But he had made "full preparation."

Mao's arrival in Chungking was an enormous event, a triumph; his presence produced big crowds and small stampedes everywhere, despite Chiang's strict police barricades. He looked so simple, his gestures so mild; his smile was slow to come, then very gentle. He was self-effacing, so different from the boot-stamping officers and the purring officials of the Kuomintang. But there was strength behind this candor, the shrewd, cool-headed confidence of a man in time with his country and his people.

In late August 1945, at the same time Mao arrived in Chungking, 120,000 men of the Red armies, under Lin Piao with 30,000 cadres, were marching towards Manchuria with mule packs and horse packs; all the way the people helped them, streamed back with them, returning to villages wrecked by the Japanese. The troops made forty to sixty miles a day, sometimes more — a grueling trek of forced marches on foot. Since 1942 Red guerillas had been infiltrating into the northeast. These troops came mostly from North China and from Shantung province; they were at first inadequately armed, but very shortly large quantities of surrendered equipment which had belonged to 594,000 Japanese troops reappeared in the hands of the Chinese Communists.† Kuomintang historians insist that it was the Russian army who helped locally by simply allowing a takeover of supply dumps.

With these men would be organized a People's Liberation Army in Manchuria; a recruiting program in Manchuria itself would be launched, the usual process of mass mobilization, political arousal, land reform, popular government, establishment of guerila zones, then of bases in the countryside, surrounding the Chiang-held cities.

During the forty-three days that Mao stayed in Chungking, many tried to see him; hundreds of people waited to catch a glimpse of him. The liaison office, in a narrow lane in this city of staircase streets and gullies, perched on a rocky promontory like an eagle's eyrie. Mao's residence on "red cliff," with its winding pathways between two hills, saw literally thousands go back and forth, or just

---

* The term "old" indicates friendship, affection, and Mao is delighted to be called thus; it is also found in Chinese newspapers.

† F. F. Liu *A Military History of Modern China, 1924–1949* (Princeton and London 1959).

*Mao Tsetung arriving in Chungking with U.S. Ambassador
Patrick J. Hurley, August 28, 1945.*

The famous toast. Mao Tsetung and Chiang Kai-shek drink to their negotiations in Chungking.

stand, fanning themselves in the torrid noon heat, waiting for a glimpse of Mao.

Intellectuals, teachers, workers relayed his every gesture, his habits, what he ate, what he said. In the airplane Mao had written a poem. He now received poems from scholars, from admirers, and replied in kind. He was photographed toasting Chiang Kai-shek and the "success" of the negotiations. At a party he saw again the old warlord Feng Yu-hsiang, and they exchanged calligraphic scrolls. He also saw the erstwhile agriculture minister of those faraway Wuhan days, Tan Ping-shan (who had now formed a "third" party). Both remembered the massacres of 1927 but remained silent on the subject of the millions who died because of Chiang Kai-shek.

The negotiations between the Communists and Chiang Kai-shek were top secret; Chiang and his advisers were apparently cloistered with Mao, Chou En-lai and Wang Jo-fei. But the Americans were kept informed of every word, not only by the Kuomintang officials but by some of their own interpreters in attendance. The Americans were impressed by the sincerity of the Communists; in spite of their dislike of Communism they could not but respond to their skill, their businesslike ways, their realistic attitude, and above all their earnest sincerity. They reported that the Communists gave many signs of wanting to obtain a settlement.* Mao offered to withdraw all Red Army troops from the southern areas and in fact did so, withdrawing the New Fourth Army from around Nanking and other sensitive spots where their presence worried the Kuomintang officials, who looked forward to returning to the big coastal cities and their former luxury. Instead of raising their price for a settlement, the Communists now diminished the scope of their former demands. They again suggested holding a genuine Political Consultative Conference, not "hand-picked" by Chiang but with representatives from every party, to exchange views on national affairs prior to the formation of a coalition government. They were prepared to retain only 20 divisions, or 200,000 men, in their own armies, about 10 percent of what Chiang Kai-shek had in hand as his own elite central troops, not counting 3 million other troops. At that time the Red armies numbered 910,000 men, so the cut was important. Meanwhile, the extreme right-wing of the KMT clamored about Communist "insincerity," and the words "total annihilation of the Red bandits" (one of the KMT's favorite slogans) were still bandied about in Chungking.

* Tang Tsou *America's Failure in China, 1941–1950* (Chicago 1963).

Unfortunately for the chances of peace, the moderation of the Comunists, who instead of upping the ante were disposed to step down, and seemed ready to abandon the hope of gaining political power over all China and to narrow their aim to regional influence in the liberated areas of the North, was construed by certain Americans present (Hurley among them) as evidence of weakness.

The negotiations lasted forty-one days; they ended apparently on a hopeful note, with banqueting and speeches of peace. On October 10 a "summary of conversations," also known as the October 10 agreement, was issued.

Although Chiang Kai-shek agreed to bring political tutelage — which had lasted since 1928 — to a conclusion, and to reorganize the government through a Political Consultative Conference with delegates from all parties as demanded by the CCP, he refused to recognize a legal status for the CCP and the elected governments of the Communists' liberated areas. No agreement had been reached on the crucial point, the armed forces, although a maintenance of the status quo on the military fronts pending further discussions was agreed on. (Chiang attacks were going on during the talks, though limited in scope.) The "nationalization" of the armed forces was to be implemented through a committee of KMT and CCP representatives. On balance, the summary of the conference appeared hopeful. But the survey of the military actions which took place during this conference was not.

But because of the moderation of the Communists, because of Chiang's diplomatic "victory" in achieving a treaty of friendship with the USSR just before Mao's visit,* because the way the Americans and Chiang saw "strength" was to raise the price when in a strong position and not to climb down, Hurley argued that the Communists had "backed down" and were "in a position of great weakness, both militarily and politically" — he said they were "disavowed" by Stalin! This was a direct encouragement to Chiang to proceed with military action.

By mid-October, when the negotiations had ended, Chiang indeed seemed in a position of strength. With the help of the Americans, his troops had reoccupied most of the cities of the North. In Manchuria the Russians were holding the cities to turn them over to his armies, not to the Communists. The only large Manchurian city captured by the Communists would be evacuated at Russian insistence. Tsingtao

---

* Chiang even invited Mao with the Russian ambassador to dinner in order to impress Mao with his good relations with the USSR.

on the coast had become a U.S. naval base; 90,000 marines had landed in China to protect and garrison the ports, airports and communication centers for Chiang Kai-shek. A demand by Chu Teh to Hurley for 20 million dollars' aid for the Red armies to induce puppet troops to surrender had been refused, but Chiang would receive 1.5 billion dollars in equipment and loans in the course of the next two years. Hurley openly boasted that he had "helped" push Stalin into the friendship treaty with Chiang. All U.S. officials who had reported favorably on the Communists had been transferred out of the embassy in Chungking. The U.S. policy encouraged Chiang to pursue the course he had in mind and U.S. aid accelerated the outbreak of the civil conflict; for almost immediately after the Chungking negotiations, Chiang ordered an offensive against the Red areas.

But it was precisely the American help to Chiang, to place cities and coastline and key points within his power, which paradoxically helped to defeat Hurley, already in a deteriorating position in August. Hurley hoped to regain influence by the Chungking negotiations; but now the contradiction in American policy between the State Department recommendation for flexibility and "peaceful unification," and the Hurley-dominated policy of supporting exclusively the government of Chiang Kai-shek, had arrived at an impasse. The military under General Wedemeyer were supplying spectacular help to Chiang — 400,000 to 500,000 Nationalist troops were moved to new positions and American marines were occupying Peking, Tientsin, Chefoo, Changwangtao, Tsingtao, and protecting the coal mines to the north and the essential railways.

This very help proved Chiang's defeat. The Kuomintang troops behaved in such an appalling manner that by October, when Mao went back to Yenan and within only two months of the Japanese surrender, the recovered areas were seething with resentment. The Chiang occupation troops were "worse even than the Japanese," and the leading newspaper *Ta Kung Pao* appealed to the government: "Don't lose the confidence of the people *completely*. . . . An infinite number of people once rejoiced deliriously at the victory over Japan, but now all of us cannot even keep ourselves alive." *

Hurley's influence during the KMT-CCP negotiations was to stick to "overall principles" and unconditional support for the Kuomintang. No agreement of substance was reached. Meanwhile an enormous amount of sympathy for the Communists built up even in

* Tang Tsou *America's Failure in China, 1941–1950* (Chicago 1963).

Chungking — they had made concessions on many points; they were sincere; they were logical, cogent, reasonable. No one in China quibbled because the Communists could not give up their army; the Chinese were far more realistic about that point than Hurley. Also, USSR support to Chiang, which Hurley counted so much on, failed to materialize in the specific way that Hurley wanted. The Chinese Communists did not obey the Russians, and clearly played their own hand. Chiang by now was so confident of U.S. help that he had already started armed clashes with the Communists. Wedemeyer took fright. On September 14, Truman balked at all-out military assistance and made it clear that U.S. aid should not be used "for fratricidal warfare or to support an undemocratic administration." Hurley then resigned on November 27. But by that time Chiang was quite certain that should he persist in his plans the U.S. would be bound to help him more and more, and disregarding Truman's warning he established his campaign strategy, fully confident the U.S. would become more and more involved and in the end fight his war against the Communists for him.

Hurley's resignation led to the first official statement in the United States of the "Red conspiracy" theory, which was to plague the U.S. for years. Hurley blamed the failure of his policy on sabotage by the American officials who "sided with the Chinese Communist armed Party." Hurley went and General George Marshall came, and after Marshall, Leighton Stuart. But whoever the man, American policy was by now the policy of intervention in favor of Chiang Kai-shek, in the internal affairs of China, in a civil war. Despite the State Department proviso that Chiang's government should carry out reforms, the U.S. set about to back Chiang Kai-shek.

During those months Chou En-lai had long and anxious talks with the Americans, again and again stressing that this policy of unilateral military and financial aid to Chiang was jeopardizing the friendship of the Chinese people, was a deliberate encouragement to Chiang to do his worst. Chiang's reasoning was that the more the U.S. backed him, the more reluctant to see him defeated they would become. In the short term Chiang proved right.

The "weakness" of the Communists at the end of 1945, which Hurley confidently predicted would make them "knuckle down," was of course deceptive for anyone "infected with reality." Alas, the Americans did not bother with the theory of contradiction, they did not read Mao's works, or even consult their own China experts any longer, since these were all suspected of pro-Communism.

By December the Kuomintang had alienated a couple more hundreds of millions of people in areas they "liberated." "Neither military assistance nor diplomatic support could change the political ineffectiveness of the Nationalist government," writes Tang Tsou.* The confiscations, robberies, pillage, rapes, wanton murders, uncontrolled inflation, widespread terrorism and food shortages which followed the KMT troops had already produced a violent revulsion in the reconquered cities. The miasmic destruction of morale and of the stability (however precarious) of the middle class due to inflation and corruption escaped the Americans, as did the reality of Communist infiltration in the countryside. Since maps tend to emphasize cities, surrounded by the unnamed blank of the countryside, Chiang would seem to be in power for a long time. Neither he nor the American military thought in terms of people.

In Manchuria the Russian garrisons meticulously stuck to the treaty agreement with Chiang. Their withdrawal was postponed twice, at Chiang's own request. The Soviet ambassador had warned Chiang that as soon as Soviet forces withdrew from strategic points, the Chinese Communist forces had always been present to occupy them. Chiang's eldest son Chiang Ching-kuo, Russian-educated, carried out the negotiations for delayed withdrawal with Marshal Malinovsky whereby the Russians remained in Manchurian cities until March 1946, while Chiang launched a conscription drive for a million more soldiers. This cooperation had given Chiang a feeling of mastery; the Russians had allowed the airlift of one division of his troops to Manchuria, and guaranteed also the security of land transport of two more.

But from August 11 to October 10, 1945, the Communist armies had captured 220,000 puppet and Japanese troops, 197 small towns, and acquired 18,700,000 more people and 315,000 square miles. They had also been able to link up their bases in the North by a system of porters and even occasional Japanese trucks, the railroads being, metaphorically, in Chiang's hands; he was to hold the railway stations, but the rails would begin to disappear that summer.

The focus of military action shifted to Manchuria. Manchuria, with one ninth of the population and an industry which had been four times that of the rest of the country (but which now had vanished, since the Russians had stripped it of every machine in sight) was the key to the outcome of the war. General Wedemeyer recom-

* Tang Tsou *America's Failure in China, 1941–1950* (Chicago 1963), p. 312.

mended a trusteeship over Manchuria by the U.S., USSR and Great Britain. But this the Russians refused. No Americans went into garrison duty in the Manchurian cities; they would only provide, later, food and equipment by parachute to the Kuomintang garrisons which took over, when the garrisons became cut off by the "countryside surrounding the cities" tactics of the Red armies.

American "mediation" continued under General George Marshall when Hurley left. All the characteristic ambiguities of America's China policy persisted in Marshall's policy. Marshall floundered on, in a mess not of his making, bravely striving not to see the obvious. The Joint U.S. Military Advisory Group (JUSMAG) functioned, as did a program of aid and relief. But at the same time American business monopolies began a financial invasion of China to extract economic concessions from Chiang's government, and they were helped by U.S. government representatives. Chiang signed away in his smug belief that the Americans would never let him down; and that the more they paid him, the more they would *have* to fight for him.

"I was told by many people I met . . . that Chiang Kai-shek is unreliable and deceitful and that negotiations with him can lead nowhere . . . I told them that what they said was justified. . . . The Kuomintang and the Communist Party are sure to fail in their negotiations, sure to start fighting and sure to break with each other, but this is only one aspect of the matter." Thus Mao had reported on the outcome of the Chungking negotiations upon his return to Yenan, on October 17. He had spoken of the concessions made; the Communists had conceded eight liberated areas in South China to make the Kuomintang "feel easy." The Kuomintang had 263 divisions, the Communists had proposed cutting their own divisions down to 48, then 43, then to 20, though "we could form 200 divisions out of our 1,200,000 by Kuomintang standards." *

In January 1946 the People's Political Consultative Conference which the Communists had asked for at the talks, consisting of Kuomintang and Communist delegates, delegates of the Democratic League and independent parties, was at last convened. Chiang reiterated his determination to convoke a National Assembly which would

---

* Note the 300,000 increase from the 910,000 mentioned earlier. Many Kuomintang divisions were inflated, the officers reporting 10,000 men where only 6,000 at the most existed, and pocketing the difference in upkeep and salaries. *On the Chungking Negotiations*, October 17, 1945. *Selected Works of Mao Tsetung*, vol. IV.

be on his terms. Nevertheless, Marshall and Chou En-lai appeared to get on well; and for a while it looked as if a coalition government *might* come into being. The Americans clung to the hope that the Communists, though a minority in a coalition government, with Chiang still in power, might refurbish the Nationalist image, help to clean up the grosser corruption and thus render the "reformed" KMT more popular. At the same time the Communists would be taken in in another way; they might possibly be weaned away from Communism, especially if Chiang consented to offer some more high posts to certain Communists.

But by that time another headache for the Americans was beginning. It had already become obvious to some of the OSS intelligence officers in Chungking that Communist popularity was so high that free and fair elections had become a dangerous proposition. Should a truly representative National Assembly now be elected, a majority of the people would be voting for Communist representation. The political advantages of a coalition for the Communists might even offset the military disadvantages of the military self-retrenchment they suggested. Now the Truman doctrine of 1947, with its full-fledged "international Red conspiracy" theology, would not, could not, allow free elections which would bring in a Communist government; and therefore the dilemma now presented itself of how *not* to have a popularly elected National Assembly with democratically elected representatives, and yet still urge democratic reforms.

Within this Disneyland of phantasmagoric phrases designed within the limits of that all-pervading anti-Communist doctrine, Marshall and his advisers waded in a morass of ambiguous verbosity "worse than the sucking mud of the Great Marshes." It was quite impossible to arrive at anything vaguely resembling a democratic procedure, since in the very doing they would have to forego the now fixed policy of favoring Chiang at all costs. The unavoidable thus became the inevitable; the astute Chiang fully realized the mental calisthenics of his "allies." Hence it was a foregone conclusion that he would torpedo any agreement arrived it, and with impunity. "Chiang fundamentally is a gangster. You must not give way to his threats and bullying . . . then he will press his advantage," Mao had warned.* But the U.S. had let him get away with it and he would get away with a great deal more.

The People's Political Consultative Conference proceeded to

* Interview with John Service, August 23, 1944.

adopt a political program which Chiang, and some of the Americans too, regarded with trepidation and concern; it was highly unfavorable to his one-man dictatorship. It asked for a thorough reform of the one-man government, revision of the constitution, a genuine coalition through free elections.

The overriding preoccupation of the American military adviser group was now continuing to supply Chiang's armies with equipment, continuing to train 39 divisions. The war potential of Chiang was thus reinforced; he mobilized more troops; Marshall's mediation became a farce. Teams set up to inspect cease-fire violations rushed hither and thither, while mutual accusations of armed attacks rose in number and scale; whatever the rhetoric, however, the hard facts were clear. The next two years became, for U.S. interests, something very much like a wild scramble for China, hideous amidst the dreadful misery, amidst the mounting chaos. Mao Tsetung would now denounce * U.S. mediation as a smokescreen and an attempt to reduce China virtually to a U.S. colony. The impact of American goods, which now began to flood the Chiang cities, only worsened the economic situation; unsalable items and luxury leftovers came into the cities through UNRRA, and turned them into gigantic black markets. All this directly militated against the American image, aroused hostility where there had been friendship, and also contributed to sinking Chiang Kai-shek.

Chiang's secret police, aided and abetted by the American-organized OSS (later CIA), was reinforced even while Marshall spoke of "democratizing" the Kuomintang government. The police arrested liberals, members of the Democratic League, and assassinated outspoken critics even while Marshall was asking for "independent-minded personalities to serve under the Generalissimo." No middle-of-the-road party could emerge when its emergence was its condemnation. To the very end, the alternative of replacing Chiang was not seriously considered by the U.S.

Mao Tsetung was proved right, but there still lingered within the Communist Party itself people who thought it possible to come to an arrangement with Chiang. Soon after the cease-fire and truce had been arranged on January 10, the Central Committee issued a cease-fire order, hailing a "new phase of peace and democracy." In February, even as the cease-fire was being destroyed, Liu Shao-chi wrote a directive quoting again the "new phase of peace and democ-

---

* Interview with A. T. Steele, American correspondent, September 24, 1946.

racy." "The main forms of the struggle . . . have become peaceful, parliamentary forms . . ." He asked the Party "to stop assuming direct command over the Army . . . so that it may be placed under the unified command of the defense ministry. . . . We are no longer an opposition party, but a party in power . . . some of us will become officials of a central government. . . . This already happened in 1927 . . . it failed when the other side started armed action; however, this will not happen again." Where was the guarantee that the same thing would not happen again? Even Marshall would say that it was Chiang who broke the truces and cease-fires arranged, with his mania for a "definite use of force under cover of protracted negotiations."

During the six months from January to June 1946, Mao Tsetung went about quietly preparing for war. There is no word from him indicating that he engaged in the usual debate within the Central Committee against the "peace at any cost" party. In November 1945 had he not written: "Countryside civil war is already a fact. Our Party's task is to mobilize all forces."

But hope dies hard. When Chou En-lai flew back from Yenan at the end of January 1946, at the close of an apparently very successful People's Political Consultative Conference, the general feeling was still a hankering for peace. On February 28, 1946, Chou, together with Marshall and a Kuomintang general, formed the committee of three in charge of supervising the teams sent to inspect violations along the military lines. Marshall paid a visit to Yenan and was welcomed with great courtesy, whatever reservations Mao had as to his role. A song, it appears, was "composed" for the occasion. Marshall was excellently impressed; he reported on "the infectious enthusiasm" in Yenan. Asked whether he would go to Nanking to meet Chiang, Mao replied, with tongue-in-cheek modesty: "I shall go whenever Chiang asks me." With Mao's convictions, the absurdity of the situation cannot have escaped him; on the other hand he would not be the one to start the war.

In March 1946 the Kuomintang would launch a large-scale attack which effectively broke the truce and the cease-fire. "If no new development makes the Kuomintang stop its civil war quickly, the fighting in the spring of 1946 will be intense," Mao had said in December 1945.

And now he stepped up preparations. First of all, to get the support of the people. "It is . . . to defeat the Kuomintang offensive that rent reduction and production must be stepped up." A full-scale program of land reform, mass mobilization, getting the people on the Communist side, for the defense of the liberated areas. The building of stable base areas in the Northeast (Manchuria) was set out in full stage-by-stage detail. The mobilization and recruiting for the Red Army, which in that year would be renamed the People's Liberation Army, must not interfere with the planting of crops and the harvests. Great care must be taken not to recruit at all costs. City work must be reinforced. "It has become an important task . . . to take control of . . . cities and to develop their industry, commerce and finance." All qualified persons available should be used and "Party members must learn to cooperate with them and learn techniques and methods of management from them."

"Our people have now tasted democracy in the whole of North China . . . from now on, no despot can triumph any more," Chu Teh said to Anna Louise Strong. "Everything must still be considered from the standpoint of a long-term effort . . . everything must be planned on a long-term basis; thus we will be sure to win victory," wrote Mao.

If the United States and Chiang showed they could move in two directions at once, one in deeds and one in words, Mao would show a single-minded direction. "Cast away illusions, prepare for war"! It would be April 1946 before Mao would raise criticism on the danger of unprincipled compromise and "pessimism" among "certain comrades . . . who overestimated the strength of imperialism." At that point, there must have been the argument that the USSR was itself "compromising" with Chiang; were not the Russians urging prudence and conciliation? Mao tackled this problem too. It was possible for the imperialist countries and the socialist countries to reach certain compromises, but such compromises, on a state level, did "not require the people in the countries of the capitalist world to follow suit and make compromises at home." The document, not divulged at the time, was circulated only among "some leading comrades" of the Central Committee, and not made public till January 1948.

It was in August 1946, almost a year from the day that Mao Tsetung had gone to Chungking for negotiations with Chiang, and when the civil war had already started on a country-wide scale, that Mao gave to the American correspondent Anna Louise Strong the famous interview in which he called the atom bomb a "paper tiger."

The background of this interview is interesting. It was meant as much for outside consumption as for the home front. It was at a critical juncture, when Mao Tsetung was almost alone in his conviction that the Kuomintang could be defeated, that Mao chose to call all reactionaries "paper tigers."

"Of course the atom bomb is a weapon of mass slaughter, but the outcome of a war is decided by the people, not by one or two new types of weapons." Chiang and his supporters were all paper tigers . . . "In the United States there are others who are really strong . . . the American people." The interview shows that, at the time, a good many Communist Party members in the world believed an attack on the USSR imminent. This was not mere fancy. There were in the Pentagon and elsewhere hawks who clamored to finish off the Soviet Union. In the CCP too, the argument that civil war between Mao and Chiang might escalate into another world war, this time between the U.S. and USSR, must have been used very strongly. The obvious pressure by the USSR on Mao for peace with Chiang, which continued till 1949, shows this fear of war was very real in the Soviet Union. Mao's interview clearly states his own conclusion: "There will be no war between the U.S. and USSR before the U.S. has conquered or subdued the 'vast zone' of intermediate countries; i.e., the rest of the world, including the workers and democratic circles in the U.S. this talk of war concealed the real aims," said Mao, "which was world hegemony first, *before* any attack on the Soviet Union would be launched." Hence it was correct to fight Chiang. "The people of the world should unite and struggle against the attacks of the U.S. and their running dogs, only thus could a third world war be avoided. Otherwise it is unavoidable." *

Even President Truman, on August 10, would cable Chiang that the assassinations of distinguished liberals — Professor Wen I-to and his son, who were mown down by Chiang's gunmen on the doorsteps of the university — "have not been ignored . . . there is increasing belief that an attempt is being made to resort to force, military or secret police rather than democratic processes." He asserted his own "violent repugnance" to such goings-on. Chiang must have thought that Truman was deliberately playing dumb; for if the Americans did not want him to fight, why did the Americans go on giving him guns to fight with and money to pay soldiers? He therefore replied that these regrettable incidents were "mistakes by subordinates." And Truman's qualms of conscience subsided.

* *Talk with the American Correspondent Anna Louise Strong,* August 1946. *Selected Works of Mao Tsetung* (English edition Peking 1961–1965), vol. IV.

In September, Chou En-lai told Marshall that since January 13, when Chiang first broke the cease-fire, the Kuomintang had moved 180 divisions, 206 regular brigades with a strength of 1,740,000 men against the Communists. Marshall announced to Chiang in October that he would resign unless the fighting stopped; Chiang replied with a list of "evidence of Communist attacks." With the built-in resolution of the U.S. government to stick to Chiang, there could be no other solution, except war.

7

The Conquest of Power—
The Civil War and Liberation, 1946—1949

The Revolutionary Self-Defense War, as it is called in China today, started when Chiang Kai-shek launched a main offensive on all fronts, beginning with the Kiangsu-Anhwei liberated area, the previous New Fourth Army stamping ground, which was attacked by 120,000 soldiers (18 brigades). The Central Committee issued a circular on July 20, written by Mao Tsetung: *Smash Chiang Kai-shek's Offensive by a War of Self-Defense*. "We can certainly defeat Chiang Kai-shek. The whole Party should be confident of this."

Needless to say, the entire strategy was devised by Mao; throughout, with meticulous care, he would plan every military operation and go into the most minute details. Several campaigns would be fought at once, on several fronts; all China became one vast battlefield, one enormous chessboard on which the contending armies moved, wheeled, circled, fought, each with its own strategy. Mao Tsetung knew Chiang and Chiang's style of fighting; he would guess what Chiang would do months before Chiang announced his intention; hence he always could "lead him by the nose." Chiang, never a good strategist, had deteriorated. He was sure of winning, because he was sure the Americans would not let him fail.

The Communist campaigns were predicated upon the social revolution; hence we find Mao devoting as much time to writing about land reform, finance, administration and propaganda work as about purely military matters. This was especially important in newly liberated areas, such as Manchuria. "Mass work will be the center of gravity of our Party's work in the Northeast," he had written in December 1945, expounding why stable base areas should be set up, a job which might require three to four years. These bases were not to

Mao Tsetung in Yenan, 1947, during the civil war. Behind, on a horse, is Madame Chiang Ching.

be built in big cities or along main communication lines nor in regions close to these.

"The only way to study the laws governing a war situation . . . is to do some hard thinking. For what pertains to the situation as a whole is not visible to the eye . . . The problems of strategy include: Giving proper consideration to the relation between the enemy and ourselves . . . to the relation between various campaigns or between various operational stages . . . to the special features contained in the general situation . . . to the relation between front and rear . . . to the distinction as well as the connection between losses and replacements, fighting and resting, concentration and dispersion, attack and defense, advance and retreat, concealment and exposure, main attack and supplementary attack . . . protracted war and war of quick decision . . . military work and political work, between destroying the enemy and winning over the masses, fixed fronts and fluid fronts." *

By that July, Chiang had received 500 million dollars in aid and 500 million dollars' worth of equipment from the U.S. But he had cloistered his best troops in safe Manchurian cities where they would sit, imprisoned, for the next three years. He would have to supply them with a painfully inadequate railway system and now the embattled people would carry away the rails to the hills, leaving Chiang in command only of the railway stations. He had a corps of a hundred U.S. advisers, and managed to give them nervous breakdowns. He did not trust his own commanders, relied only on those "loyal" to him, would bypass the orders given and issue counter-orders, would demote or promote so that no officer felt safe to think or to act. His armies were still made up of press-ganged, starved, ill-treated peasants who were chained to each other to be sent to training camps; often they died of hunger on the way. But now these peasants knew that "life was better on the other side." Mao would lay stress on intensifying the disintegration of the Kuomintang troops by propaganda. Very shortly this would produce results. Propaganda work was carried on right through the civil war; whenever within earshot, the Communists broadcast appeals and exhortations to the Kuomintang soldiers; those captured were treated decently. Many were to join the Red forces from 1947.

Mao on his side had able commanders; but above all he had the people with him, with the Communist party. And the Party was

* *Strategy in China's Revolutionary War,* December 1936. See *Selected Military Writings of Mao Tsetung* (English edition Peking 1963).

united, disciplined, and in the vast majority, honest. Mao ordered that 1946 should be the year of "strategic defensive"; the general method of fighting would be mobile warfare. That meant letting Chiang have his victories against cities — "temporary abandonment is not only unavoidable but also necessary . . . we must use our man-power and modest resources with the utmost economy." Hence to the world looking at the maps, looking at city dots as key points, the impression was created for a whole year that Chiang was win-ning and the Communists were losing. This was quite deliberate on the part of Mao Tsetung.

During that first year of strategic defense, economics occupied much of Mao's thoughts. Production must be stepped up to become completely self-sufficient in all necessities, "and first of all in grain and cloth . . . promote the extensive planting of cotton . . . en-courage every family to spin . . . we should start to promote this even in the Northeast." The People's Liberation Army was re-minded of Mao's humorous precept of 1936: "We rely on the war industries of the imperialist countries and of our enemy . . . equipment is delivered to us by the enemy's own transport . . . this is the sober truth, not a joke." As during the Japanese war, so during the civil war; the weapons given, transported, later parachuted by U.S. forces to the Kuomintang were to find their way to the Communists, first in a trickle, later in a flood. One third of all U.S. equipment was for Chiang's armies in Manchuria; all of it was to be found in the hands of the PLA three years later.

Mao saw U.S. aid to Chiang as the main factor which stimulated civil war, and denounced it with increasing vigor, but always making a difference between the American people and those in the govern-ment who were "reactionaries." "We have only millet plus rifles to rely on, but history will finally prove that our millet plus rifles is more powerful than Chiang Kai-shek's airplanes plus tanks." Without loans or lend-lease, and with weapons picked up on the battlefield, the Communist armies would win; this would surprise not only the "imperialists," it would also greatly surprise the USSR.

The compulsions under which Russian foreign policy was acting are understandable if we refer ourselves to the well-known fear of at-tack on two fronts coupled now with the fear of atomic bombing. The experience of the war in Russia and its devastations had been a traumatic experience. It seems to have unduly dominated Russian minds — more than any consideration of the obvious necessity for the war in China. Victory for the Chinese Communist armies in

1946 looked impossible to the Russian military observers. No army could possibly win without heavy industry to produce tanks and other material of warfare. "This underestimation of Chinese strategy, and the surprise with which Moscow met the victories a year later," writes Anna Louise Strong, "seem to indicate that Russian experts had little contact with the Chinese Communist general staff." Either they had none — which is the more probable reason — or they ignored what Mao said. Russian presence in Yenan was scarce; perhaps fearful prudence dictated this omission; fear of accusation of a Russian-directed "offensive" in China (for despite Hurley's desire for Russian pressure, the U.S. government was capable of thinking in two contrary directions at once; much as some Americans wished to employ Russian pressure to mitigate Chinese Red militancy, they were also capriciously capable of discovering Russians, with snow on their boots, behind every national uprising anywhere in the world at the time).

Mao expected no aid from Russian sources; an attitude of careful neutrality was the most the Russians would give, and this was already a contribution to the Chinese war effort. Self-reliance, and people's war, would win.

Marshall departed at the end of 1946, clearly chagrined with the Chiang regime, which "had been using negotiations largely for its own purposes . . . waging war on a constantly increasing scale." His successor, Leighton Stuart, was as incapable as his predecessors of a logical policy in a hopelessly illogical position. By 1948 4.5 billion dollars would have been given to Chiang Kai-shek. By the end of 1946, demonstrations and riots against the Chiang regime were widespread in all Kuomintang-controlled cities. In the regions under Communist rule, by contrast, there was relative security and economic stability. The black market had been virtually stamped out, and production increased through land reform.

In early 1947, the riots and uprisings against Chiang began to turn into anti-American demonstrations. This was due to the obvious spectacle of American financial domination, American living standards for the very few magnates, and also the attitude of the GIs in China, who treated the Chinese people in a way only too reminiscent of previous colonial powers. The August 1946 agreement for sale of U.S. government surplus property — weapons, tanks, barbed wire, and so on — from various islands of the Pacific was called openly a fraud and a swindle in the non-Communist newspapers. A commercial treaty and a "comprehensive treaty of friendship, commerce and navigation," as well as an aviation agreement, reaffirmed special privileges for U.S. business in China and angered the Chinese, whose national pride was enhanced by the war. The exhibitionism of GIs who used to openly race rickshaw coolies like horses was followed on the streets by sullen-faced thousands. The rape in the open day of a Chinese girl student in a public park by four GIs was the spark that led to a widespread demonstration by millions of students and intellectuals.

A protest was to be handed to the United Nations on October 21, 1948, by independent liberals, alleging that the huge sums given by the U.S. only enriched corrupt bureaucrats and helped to make civil war; and that "unequal and oppressive" treaties had turned China into a U.S. colony. Thus, for Chiang's sake America forfeited the friendship of most of the Chinese people — all except a few hundred carpetbagging officials round Chiang Kai-shek. Again, Mao's prediction seemed to have come true.

And yet, by the end of 1946, it looked as if the Communists were in full retreat; only Mao would say jocularly, "We have won." Not spectacular victories in the field, but the complete attrition of Chiang's forces and their annihilation was the aim of the self-defense war. This meant "to concentrate an absolutely superior force . . . concentrate the whole or the bulk of our artillery, select one (not two) of the weak posts in the enemy's position, attack it fiercely . . . and be sure to win." He added, "Acting counter to this . . . we shall lose." Summarizing three months of war in October 1946, he pronounced it "completely successful." Of 190 brigades of the Kuomintang 25 had been wiped out and more than half of the 190 were now on garrison duty, keeping the cities they had conquered. The price had been the abandonment of a "few dozen" medium and small towns. "In any case we shall be able to recover them." This was the practice of fluidity essential in mobile warfare, and memorized by Red Army men, who sang:

> *Keep men, lose land. Land can be taken again.*
> *Keep land, lose men. Land and men both lost.*

"I have traded seventeen empty cities for sixty thousand of Chiang's troops," General Liu Po-cheng, the one-eyed dragon of the Long March (the same who had drunk chicken's blood with tribal chieftains in Szechuan to ensure a peaceful passage), said to Anna Louise Strong.

It was because of its policies of land reform and stabilization of livelihood that the Communist Party would finally win, said Mao. The peasants stood with the Party wherever land reform had been applied correctly. Although to wipe out 10,000 of the enemy, the casualties in the Red Army were 2,000 to 3,000, this price had to be paid. But as a result "70 percent of the peasants in North China were Communist-oriented" by 1947.* In May 1946 the land reform policies had been modified because of peasant demands; confiscation of the land of big landlords was begun with distribution to poor peasants, but cautiously. This had produced a upsurge of enthusiasm in newly liberated countryside areas, and recruiting for the PLA was easy.

With meticulous care, in minute detail, Mao wrote battle plan directives. This was the supreme contest, and he worked at it with all his heart and mind. Some of his military commanders appear to have recommended a reversal to guerilla warfare in the face of Chiang's "successes." Mao said the guerilla stage was past. "Apart from the fundamental political and economic contradictions which Chiang cannot resolve and which are the basic cause rendering our victory certain and Chiang's defeat inevitable, a sharp contradiction has arisen in the military sphere between Chiang's overextended battle lines and his shortage of troops . . . that is bound to be the direct cause of our victory."

Soon, Mao predicted, the People's Liberation Army would seize the strategic initiative, when "a tremendous change will surely have taken place in the relative military strength of the Kuomintang and the Communist Party." However, the war might still take a long time; every item in the situation — planning, financing, production, supplies, "unified leadership and decentralized management" — must be efficient, streamlined for a protracted conflict. Sparing men, sparing material, was essential. Morale was most important. The troops with the highest efficiency were those who had "intensified military training, production and land reform" at the same time, so that they had become "a fighting force, a work force and a production force," wrote Mao, harking back to the three-in-one combination he had promoted so vigorously in the past.

And now he would effect his boldest stroke, the deliberate abandonment of Yenan, the Red capital, itself.

In November 1946 Mao predicted that Chiang would do two

* Samuel B. Griffith II *The Chinese People's Liberation Army* (New York 1967).

things: reconvene a bogus National Assembly packed with his own hand-picked delegates, and try to capture Yenan. Chiang by then had "taken" 160 cities from the Communists. "Chiang has taken the road to ruin as soon as he makes these two moves," said Mao Tse-tung.

In early 1947 Chiang's forces and mobility were much reduced by attrition, garrisoning, and surrenders to the Communists, which began in 1946.

He thus had to abandon all-out offensives on all fronts — and there had been seven major fronts — for a concentrated offensive on one or two. His targets were now the province of Shantung and North Shensi; in a pincer movement seeking to squeeze the Communist forces in between. How deceptive the military situation was is made obvious by a three-column article by a Russian colonel which appeared in August 1947. The article deplored the loss of Yenan and explained that the Communists could not possibly win.

On November 15, 1946, Chiang reconvened a National Assembly of 2,000 hand-picked delegates, who listened while Chiang spoke. At the end Chiang would say: "Well, there is nothing to add; just pass these resolutions." The Communist delegation to the January Political Consultative Conference did not attend; Chou En-lai denounced the "one-party National Assembly." "The door of negotiation has been slammed." Chou then left for Yenan on November 19.

In February 1947 Mao issued a triumphant call, *Greet the New High Tide in the Chinese Revolution,* four weeks before abandoning Yenan to Chiang Kai-shek. He noted the anti-Chiang, anti-American demonstrations: "The policies of the U.S. and Chiang have forced all strata of Chinese people to unite." The Sino–U.S. treaty of commerce had produced malignant inflation; the national bourgeoisie was going bankrupt.

Meanwhile, in a typical maneuver to which we have already become blasé, Chiang again asked formally for "peace talks," but canceled these abruptly; all personnel of the liaison offices of the CCP were asked to leave.* Chiang then launched 230,000 troops under Hu Tsung-nan against Yenan, and 450,000 against Shantung province.

Yenan was evacuated March 16–18, 1947, a few days before Hu Tsung-nan "captured" it. Anna Louise Strong describes the exodus. The caves were emptied in rigorous order; the hospital patients, on

---

* All through the war there had also been a Kuomintang liaison office, and representative, in Yenan. He was recalled in February 1946 by Chiang.

stretchers, and equipment were carried away first. Women with babies, children, students, filed out; Mao, Chou En-lai came out last. Even the small children of Yenan knew that "cities do not matter," that it was only "pots and pans," and that the job was "to annihilate Chiang brigades, following Mao Tsetung's Thought," wrote Miss Strong.

"I spoke to Mao about the loss of Yenan. 'If you ask whether it is better to lose the city or to keep it,' he said, 'of course it is better to keep it. But if we lose it we are still all right. A people's war is not decided by taking or losing a city, but by solving the agrarian problem.' "

Hu Tsung-nan entered Yenan, and then celebrated his wedding. (He had sworn not to marry before he had captured Yenan.) Chiang got all the headlines in the newspapers round the world; but after a year of fighting he had not opened a single continuous railway line across North China. He predicted the war would be over in three months.

Mao did not leave the North Shensi base area. He remained, together with Chou En-lai, Jen Pi-shih and Wang Tung-hsing, in the base itself, among the people. From obscure villages he directed operations, sent couriers, received reports. His wife Chiang Ching accompanied him. When they remained long enough, they cultivated vegetables, hoed, and Chiang Ching had some spare clothes made by local peasant girls. Mao went under the name of Li Te-sheng, while Chou En-lai adopted the alias of Hu Pi-cheng.* A small number of bodyguards and troops went with them; they traveled fast and light. Mao had actually turned himself into a decoy for the Kuomintang's 230,000 men, who now combed the area. They were sometimes not more than a dozen miles away from the enemy, yet never once did Mao feel insecure.

The fact that Mao was among them, thumbing his nose at the adversary, present, elusive, unreachable, was known to all the inhabitants by April; it became a gorgeous joke, a real Chinese peasant joke, sublimely funny. "He is leading Hu Tsung-nan by the nose, as a peasant boy leads a water buffalo." Mao had been leading Chiang by the nose for a long time now; and Chiang was also doing precisely what Mao wanted him to do.

Mao took personal command of what he called the Northwest theater of operations, the annihilation of Hu Tsung-nan's 230,000

* Anna Louise Strong *Letter*, no. 69 (December 30, 1969). See *In His Mind a Million Bold Warriors*, *Ta Kung Pao* English edition, starting October 1971.

crack troops in the territory of the base. He led Hu a long and tiring race, making the enemy forces split, "eating them up one by one," obliging them to rush about in pursuit, keeping them marching around in circles — "unless we reduce the enemy to extreme fatigue and complete starvation we cannot win final victory." Footsore and tired, falling into ambushes, facing a hostile population, the troops of Hu Tsung-nan were decoyed by small forces, lured into gullies, trapped and cut off. "Hu came in like a fist, we forced him to open like a hand, now we cut the fingers one by one."

To facilitate carrying out the work of the Central Committee, or so it was announced, a "working party" of the Central Committee, with Liu Shao-chi as secretary, proceeded to North Shensi to "carry out tasks entrusted to it by the Central Committee," while Mao, Chou, Jen Pi-shih and Wang Tung-hsing stayed in the base. This division of the Central Committee does not appear suspect; it was a safety measure in case anything untoward happened. The working committee went to Hopei province, where there was a strong base area; the location may have been selected for the campaign to take the main cities of Hopei province, Peking and Tientsin, which would happen two years later. Chu Teh was with the working committee, which established itself in Hsipaipo village. Land reform had already been carried out in a rudimentary way. Liu Shao-chi was to take it in hand; the results would add another episode to the slow-growing story of the differences between him and Mao Tsetung.

Mao, on the run, pursued and always a little ahead, still managed to control the overall plans for the campaigns. His zigzag course through the base, now well documented, looks like a treasure hunt; * and yet all the time he was in touch, received reports, held meetings, wrote directives. Battles were fought on April 14, 1947, at Sheep and Horse river (Yang Ma Ho) and on May 4 at Pan Lung, where 6,000 Kuomintang troops were cut to pieces in a surprise attack. Pan Lung was a Kuomintang depot site; 12,000 catties (18,000 pounds) of flour, many uniforms, and ammunition were seized by the Communists. To show how safe the base was, a mass meeting was held at Chen Wu-tung, a county fair and market town, to celebrate the Pan Lung victory.

In July 1947 the Central Committee held an enlarged meeting within the North Shensi base at Hsiao Ho, with Mao presiding. Most of the political commissars of the various Red armies were there; at

* Author consulted documents and maps at the museum, Yenan, August 1971.

this meeting Mao announced the time was ripe to pass from the strategic defensive to the strategic offensive.

During this whole year of making Hu run after him, Mao was happy, confident, joyous. He chatted with the peasants in his usual way. He also spent his spare time learning "a foreign language." Unfortunately we are not told which one. "He would bring out a small stool," would sit beneath some tree, and "either study . . . or correct the writing in the guards' diaries." He had apparently persisted in teaching himself this foreign language ever since leaving Yenan, as a relaxation, "and he never dropped it."

As a result of Mao's relaxed, amused conduct of this campaign, the guards round him made a plan "to read five novels on the march, and to keep a diary." Mao sat often with Chou at the mouth of whatever cave they were temporarily living in, listened to the battery radio, and explained its workings to the assembled peasants, who looked for "the talking man inside."

Mao made the soldiers help the villagers, cut brushwood, collect water, dig wells, help with the harvesting. "The people are our wall of bronze," he said. In September 1947, he issued a statement on the strategic offensive decided in July and already being carried out. The fighting had been so far on interior lines. The price paid had been 300,000 casualties and enemy occupation of large tracts of territory, but now 1,120,000 KMT troops had been wiped out and large tracts of territory were being recovered. Now the offensive was "to fight our way to exterior lines" with the main forces and to carry the war to the Kuomintang areas themselves.

New bases would be set up in the Kuomintang areas; the enemy would be forced to spread out even more, wiping them out would continue. Another million men were being drafted by Chiang Kai-shek, but this would be of no avail. "Since its only methods of recruiting are press-ganging and hiring, to reach a million will certainly be difficult and many will desert." Besides the continuing basic strategy of concentrating superior forces to attack smaller, dispersed, tired out and isolated enemy units, the capture of medium and small cities would be on the program. It would no longer be necessary to relinquish these deliberately. "Be sure to fight no battle unprepared; fight no battle you are not sure of winning."

Replenishment in weapons and even in men would come chiefly from Kuomintang areas; the old liberated areas were not to fuel the recruiting now. Land reform, once again, was the key to success in the establishment of new bases. Thus by the process of continuous social revolution as the basis of military campaigns, Mao was absolutely sure of winning. "When he yielded Yenan, he knew he would finally take all China," wrote Anna Louise Strong.

It was three weeks after Mao had issued his *Strategy for the Second Year of the War of Liberation* * that General Wedemeyer, who despite the newspaper headlines knew the situation as a well-trained, able military man, wound up a three-month investigation he had conducted (directed by President Truman) to appraise the political, economic, psychological, and military situation. With the restraint of the professional soldier faced with inept bungling, he wrote that "the oppressive police measures, corrupt practices and maladministration of the National Government officials, the deterioration of the economy, the incompetence of the military, the loss of support from the population" were evident. The economy was actually disintegrating, said Wedemeyer, the financial situation beyond control, commodity prices increasing more swiftly than new currency could be printed. The military situation was particularly unpromising "in spite of superiority in weapons and in men."

The subsequent fiction elaborated in the United States that somehow China had been "lost" through a vast Communist conspiracy — including Americans who had tried to tell the truth — is shown for what it is by American reports such as the above. Can any people have been more consistently deluded and lied to than the American people have for two decades?

The land reform campaigns, ignored in favor of description of military campaigns, yet take up more pages in Mao's writings, and their strategy is as illuminating of the technique of revolution as the war strategy.

The modified land reform law passed in May 1946 altered the "rent reduction only" program practiced in Yenan till then. But Mao had urged great care: "It is impermissible to encroach on the land of the middle peasants. . . . Appropriate consideration in accordance with the will of the masses should be given to the ordinary rich peasants and middle and small landlords. . . . We must unite with more than 90 percent of the masses who support the reform." Likewise in the cities the petty bourgeoisie, the progressive and middle-class elements, were to be protected. There would be no change in the three thirds system of administration practiced in Yenan, how-

* September 1, 1947. *Selected Works of Mao Tsetung* (English edition Peking 1961–1965), vol. IV.

ever, "on condition that the policy of land to the tillers be carried out resolutely and unhesitatingly."

Mao drew up methods of investigation similar to those he had carried on before the Long March; they were to be taught to the cadres in the Red armies who administered land reform. He advised the cadres to have "numbers in their heads," such as percentage figures for each class, quantity of land held by each; to distinguish carefully between rich and middle peasants, and so on, "in order to draw for each locality quantitative limits and make the correct decisions." Reprints of his *Analysis of Classes in the Chinese Society* were circulated. Land reform would affect a population of 145 million people, and there should be no gross mistakes. Recruitment must leave an adequate labor force for production; army expansion was not to interfere with labor requirements. Cooperatives must be encouraged. The particular characteristics of each locality must be taken into account. "He seems throughout to have known more about China, each of its particularities, its infinite variety and details and the significance and importance of each, than any other man alive." *

In September and October 1947, several conferences on the subject of land reform as well as other matters were held at Yang Chia Kou in the county of Michih in North Shensi — a historic place with a long and glorious history of peasant revolt. Mao made another long and thorough summing up of the war, bringing it up to date. Chiang was doomed. Victory was certain for the Communists, and "it is momentous because it is occurring in the East, where one thousand million people — half of mankind — suffer under imperialist oppression." Mao reviewed his military strategy and tactics which had led to victory; and if he sounds a little pleased with himself, he certainly had a right to be. But he then went on again to land reform, and obviously he was anxious that it should not fail. He also appears to have been worried by a slackening of discipline in the armies; this was natural, since by now they were swollen with deserters from the Kuomintang and new, unseasoned recruits. The three main rules for discipline and eight points for attention (the three-eight) were again reissued to tighten control, and a rectification campaign in the Army was planned. In that October Mao issued *Manifesto of the Chinese People's Liberation Army,* an open declaration to fight to the end. He dwelt on the economic structure of the

* Interview with Mr. Rewi Alley and Dr. George Hatem, 1969, in Peking.

new China to come, "developing production, promoting economic prosperity, giving consideration to both public and private interests." He stressed the necessity of keeping a united front * of all the revolutionary classes against Chiang. "The dawn is ahead, we must exert ourselves."

But on the matter of land reform he did not have, it appears, a unified Central Committee. The American William Hinton wrote that "not only had [Mao and his supporters] to lead the people correctly but struggle with leaders at all levels including the top, who were for coexistence without struggle, for bargaining away basic strength, afraid of land reform . . . of its consequences nationally and internationally." So closely, however, did the Party keep the intra-Party struggle secret that William Hinton, himself physically involved in the land reform, was not aware of any two-line struggle until twenty years later.† Hinton seems to think that the division of the Central Committee at the time Yenan was abandoned, with a working committee under Liu Shao-chi going to North Shensi and Mao staying in the base with Chou En-lai, Jen Pi-shih, and Wang Tung-hsing, was due to divergent opinions on the conduct of the war. But it may also have been, as noted, for safety's sake.

In September 1947 a national land conference was held by Liu Shao-chi at Hsi Pai Po village, and a land law passed in October 1947 which was far more "left" than the land law of May 1946. This land law made no provision for middle peasants; hence it led to excesses. It would be December 1947 before Mao became aware of these abnormalities, and started insisting again on discrimination and careful performance. Middle peasants should not be alienated, he said. But already reports of the "terror" in some areas, due to this ultra-left kind of land reform, had circulated (Jack Belden was to report on them) in the White areas; ‡ this produced a tide of reversal against the Communists. In January 1948, in *Some Important Problems of the Party's Present Policy*, Mao spoke of those erroneous tendencies in land reform and mass movements. He was then still at Yang Chia Kou in North Shensi. The speech was a directive aimed at a high level of leadership, no less than the Central Committee — and therefore plainly meant for the working committee under Liu.

* The victory of 1949 is described as a united front of all the revolutionary classes against the compradore capitalist reactionaries and their U.S. backers.

† William Hinton *Fanshen: A Documentary of Revolution in a Chinese Village* (New York 1967). See also *China's Continuing Revolution* by William Hinton (China Policy Study Group, London, March 1969).

‡ Jack Belden *China Shakes the World* (New York 1949).

Mao spoke out against *two* divergent trends, but may have been aiming at the same people, for as we have seen, the ultra-left is objectively the right, and the two can coexist in the same person. He spoke against "some people" in the Party who "feared U.S. imperialism, feared wiping out the compradore-feudal system, feared a long-drawn-out war," but then went on to condemn the ultra-left tendency to terrorism in land reform, alienating the intermediate classes. "The interests of the poor peasant leagues must be our first concern. . . . Their forward role consists in forging *unity* with the middle peasants. . . . The slogan "The poor peasants and farm laborers conquer the country and should rule the country" is wrong; it is not the poor peasants and farm laborers alone who conquer the country . . . it is the workers, peasants — including the new rich peasants — small independent craftsmen and traders, middle and small capitalists, teachers, students, professors and ordinary intellectuals, enlightened gentry, oppressed minority nationalities and overseas Chinese, all united together under the leadership of the working class, who conquer the country and should rule the country." This united front of all these against Chiang was endangered by "adventurist left" policies of killing and brutality. Mao pointed out that the wiping out of the feudal system meant wiping out "the landlords as a class, not as individuals. . . . In accordance with the land law we must give them [the landlords] means of production and means of livelihood, but not more than [to the ordinary] peasants."

Now we know, however allusively these remarks read, because no names are mentioned, that at the time they hit a target. Liu Shao-chi was the "right" tendency in international outlook and responsible for the ultra-left in land reform. Mao sent his loyal and able friend Jen Pi-shih to Hopei to find out what was happening, Jen came back with a detailed account. On February 3, 1948, Mao sent a telegram direct to Liu Shao-chi giving directives on land reform; on February 11 he issued a severe criticism of the "left" line — *Correct the Left Errors in Land Reform Propaganda*. It was addressed to Communist news agencies and newsmen for printing reports containing "left" errors. "Rashness has been encouraged." To do everything "as the masses want it done" was not the mass line, but spontaneism, an accommodation to "wrong views existing among the masses." As a result punishment against minor cadres who had committed slight errors was much too severe, while the real incumbents, the leaders, were responsible but untouched. The slogan "Let no poor peasant remain poor and leave no landlord in possession of his property" was excessive and reeked of absolute equalitarianism. This had caused terrorism, even execution of middle peasants. All this must be changed speedily.

Hinton mentions the parallel between the "style of work" of the work teams organized by Liu Shao-chi at that time to conduct land reform investigations and that of the work teams Liu sent in 1963 to conduct a socialist education movement in the communes. The work teams Liu sent to the universities in the first weeks of the Great Proletarian Cultural Revolution in 1965 also conducted an absolute terror. "Style makes the man"; as we find Mao's style again and again in the Chinese Revolution, so do we find the hallmark and stamp of Liu in his work during the Revolution. This relationship between person and output in a cause can help solve many so-called baffling problems of understanding the Chinese Revolution; now that we must discard forever Party monolithism, now that we know the struggle between two lines is always going on in the Party, we can all the more appreciate Mao's stamina and tenacity, his endurance, and the fact that he was not, could not be, in a position to dictate. We are not surprised, then, when right in the middle of the military campaigns of the civil war we find *another* rectification movement taking place, both in the Communist Party and in the People's Liberation Army, in the winter of 1947–1948.

Mao deplored that there had been erroneous propaganda which "advocates taking account of class origin alone" and was deleterious to the forward movement of the social revolution, in consequence endangering the outcome of the civil war. Many cadres of peasant or of petty bourgeois origin were "meritorious." On February 15, Mao again wrote to the Central Committee: "Do not be impetuous. . . . The total scope of attack [for land reform] should not exceed 8 percent of the households . . . killing without discrimination is forbidden; the fewer killings the better." This is repeated, with manifest anxiety, in several different ways.

Once again an "open door" rectification is started, calling on the peasants in the peasant associations for criticism, supervision and the sifting of cadres. With the inflation in Party membership, a good many opportunists, "riffraff," again had come into the Party. The 1,211,128 of 1945 were 2,200,000 in January 1947, 2,759,457 by the end of 1947. In 1948 at midyear the 3 million mark would be reached. Due to the rectification movement, by the end of 1948 only 65,000 more cadres had been added to the Party. But some of the Kuomintang agents planted in the Party at that time would be found out only at the Great Proletarian Cultural Revolution.*

In April, in a speech to the cadres of the Shensi-Suiyuan base, Mao praised them for correcting "left" deviations, and indirectly indicated that Liu had also corrected his mistakes. By then Mao Tsetung had left the North Shensi base and had crossed the Yellow river.

It was on March 23, 1948, that together with Chou En-lai and Jen Pi-shih, and his wife Chiang Ching, Mao left for Hopei, where Liu Shao-chi, Chu Teh, and the working committee were established. When he reached Hopei three or four weeks later, he had accomplished all he had set himself to do. He had destroyed the armies of Hu Tsung-nan; yet at no time during this year of wandering about the base did Mao have more than 20,000 men. He had also concluded the first phase of the strategic offensive in the civil war, and now would come the great forward push, the magnificent design which would scatter Chiang's strength like dust. He had been able to correct a dangerous ultra-left trend and set on foot a vast rectification movement in the Party and in the Army.

In April 1948 Yenan was retaken by the People's Liberation Army, and Hu Tsung-nan and his 230,000 men consigned "to the dustbin of history."

All over the great land the armies marched, swept forward, locked in vast encounters in a war to the finish. On June 30, 1947, one field army of the PLA forced the Yellow river, crossed the Lunghai railway in August, thrust into the massive Tapieh mountain massif, a turning point for switching south, into Middle China. Three more Red armies made forward drives, cutting off large portions of Kuomintang forces in vast pincer movements and shredding their supply and communication routes. Then came the sweep downward from Manchuria, with 340,000 men, conducted by Lin Piao and Nieh Jung-chen.

In Manchuria agrarian reform had been carried out. Mass organizations and a people's government of the liberated areas of Manchuria, which rallied many local personalities, including the brother of

* Han Suyin "Interview with a Brigade Leader," *Eastern Horizon,* vol. X, no. 4. The author collected numerous stories of KMT agents being found out during the GPCR.

Chang Hsueh-liang, had been set up. Since March 1947, date of the capture of Yenan, Chiang Kai-shek's 248 regular brigades had been in swift disintegration; 227 were either at the fronts or in garrisons in cities — Chiang had no reserves left. His best troops were still locked up in Manchurian cities.

Already, at the end of 1946, half the population and 300,000 square miles of the Manchurian territory were in Communist hands. Defections of Kuomintang troops in Manchuria began later than in other areas because they were crack regiments rigorously contained in strongholds, from which they made occasional small sorties but otherwise stayed immobile. The PLA made feints, jabbing at the cities; "victories" by the Kuomintang were announced when the Communists withdrew. In December 1947, Chiang's troops were confined to a narrow corridor along cities connected by rail. When the big offensive to take the cities started at last, they were helpless.

On January 5, 1948, the Manchurian PLA armies began chewing up the remaining tenuous links around Mukden, depriving the garrison of all supplies. Mukden was sealed off. The Americans dropped food and supplies by air. Chiang fired the commander in Mukden and replaced him with General Wei Li-huang. The latter, no strategist, began increasing the Mukden garrison by pulling out troops from other Manchurian cities and airlifting them — courtesy of the U.S. — into beleaguered Mukden! This was not a very bright thing to do, for the Manchurian Red armies immediately shifted to attack the depleted cities. The PLA hacked off piecemeal bits of the reinforcements then hastily sent, like chopping off fingers of an extended hand, as Mao had described, "leaving only a useless stump."

General Wei Li-huang and General Tu Yu-ming, stalwarts of Chiang's, went over to Mao's side. Mao Tsetung now planned simultaneously two campaigns, one for taking Peking and Tientsin, and one for controlling the vast plains of the Huai Hai. On October 11 the latter was set to begin, a major and decisive military action to open up the Yangtze valley north of Nanking, Chiang's capital city, and to take it.

Mukden fell in October, and without a pause the armies swept downward in point-by-point execution, almost to the day, of Mao's plans. The armies of other Red commanders were now irresistible, winning in the west, in the center, in the east. In the Manchurian campaign Chiang lost 300,000 soldiers. "To me, the loss of the troops . . . spelled the beginning of the end," wrote U.S. General

David Barr,* Chiang's chief American adviser. "They were lost not from battle casualties but from defection," wrote U.S. ambassador Leighton Stuart.

The Peking-Tientsin campaign, guided by a special directive from Mao, would end in early 1949. The Peking commander, Fu Tso-yi, yielded gracefully, and another 200,000 Kuomintang troops were "wiped out" — went home or joined the Red armies.† Mao Tsetung entered Peking on March 25, 1949, greeted with fantastic enthusiasm by the population.

In the Huai Hai campaign, Mao cabled to the commander, Chen Yi: "You are to complete the Huai Hai campaign in two months, November and December." Nearly half a million Kuomintang troops were "wiped off the map" in this campaign. The Americans knew the troops in this area were inferior to those in Manchuria. "There is no reason to believe in their will or ability to resist an offensive," wrote the long-suffering General Barr. "And when they are gone, Nanking has no defenses worthy of the name." Only massive U.S. aid, which meant Americanization of the war, would save the situation. But by then President Truman had seen the writing on the wall. "The world's worst leadership, and many other morale-destroying factors, led to a complete loss of the will to fight," was General Barr's disconsolate verdict.

"Rest and consolidate your forces next January," Mao cabled to Chen Yi. "From March to July [1949] you will be fighting . . . to drive the enemy to points along the Yangtze river, where he will dig in. . . . By autumn your main force will probably be fighting to cross the Yangtze." It was as if he knew to the day what was going to happen. And now victory was near, much more swiftly than expected, almost too swift.

By June 1948, 800,000 Kuomintang soldiers had defected, and from July 1948 to June 1949, 700,000 more would cross over. From July 1949 to the end of the year, one million soldiers would come over to the Red armies. What could be done with them? Success itself now brought its own contradictions. Would not the overswollen Red armies decay with this stuffing of KMT soldiers, by no means politically trained?

---

* Quoted in Samuel B. Griffith II *The Chinese People's Liberation Army* (New York 1967).

† Fu Tso-yi was to become a minister in the government of Mao Tsetung in 1950, and spent peaceful days in Peking, even through the Cultural Revolution.

The People's Liberation Army enters Peking, March 1949.

Once again Mao turned to old and proved ways of doing things which implied trust in people. The democratic movement in the Army, instituted January 30, 1948, was to reinforce and restore the soldiers' committees at company level. Mao had created them on the way to Chingkangshan in 1927; they had been abolished in 1932 at Juichin.* The ablest old soldiers were turned into instructors for new recruits. "The masses of the soldiers should have the right to expose the errors and misdeeds of bad elements among the cadres." To prevent a "return to warlordism" among commanders, and "high-handedness' among political leaders, the soldiers would form committees, elect representatives to assist, but not bypass, the company leadership in managing their own food distribution and budgeting, to prevent corruption. A movement called "three checkups and three improvements" was instituted; it was a system by which the individual recruit's class origin, performance of duty and will to fight were checked, and his improvement in fighting was noted. This was a way of preventing laxity and weakening from the dilution of KMT recruits.

But another and far more difficult problem now loomed; no less than the issue of leadership itself.

It is still not clear what in fact determined what seems to have been a crisis, due to a profound divergence of opinion on the further conduct of the war, at that moment. But it was certain that a most important meeting took place in Hopei in the spring of 1948. Even the recapture of Yenan, the exhilarating triumphs on the military plane, the total annihilation of so many Kuomintang armies, do not seem to have impressed "some people." Mao's criticism of the ultra-left deviation and his launching the rectification movement brought into focus the whole issue of rectification. Mao asserted that the 1941–1944 Rectification campaign had achieved "a firmer grasp of our basic orientation, which is to unite the universal truth of Marxism with the concrete practice of the Chinese revolution." Another campaign was urgently needed before the Party took over power, in order to guarantee a continuation of success, for "many landlords, rich peasants . . . have seized the opportunity to sneak into our Party. . . . In the rural areas they control a number of Party, government and people's organizations."

In September 1948 an enlarged plenum was held in Hopei, to re-affirm "the unity of the Party." Seven members of the Politburo,

* At Yenan soldiers' clubs had been restored, but they seem to have lapsed during the civil war.

fourteen members and alternate members of the Central Committee, and ten "principal leading comrades" attended. It was then estimated that there might be five more years of fighting, surely a very conservative view. "In the coming three years we plan to admit into our forces 1,700,000 captured soldiers — estimated at 60 percent of the total we shall capture — and to mobilize 2 million peasants to join . . . Because our Party and our Army were long in a position in which we were cut apart by the enemy . . . we allowed very considerable autonomy to the leading organs of Party and Army in different areas. . . . This gave rise to certain phenomena . . . which were harmful."

The obvious tightening up of central control is here spelled out; and one does not know whether it was the land reform problem alone or linked to the problem of pushing on with the war which led up to it. "The present situation demands that our Party should do the utmost to overcome these phenomena . . . so as to bring about the transition in the form of the war. . . . For this purpose we must do everything possible to repair and to operate modern means of communications . . . to strengthen the administration of cities and industry, and to shift the center of gravity of our Party work step by step from the rural areas to the cities."

A directive called *On Strengthening the Party Committee* was penned by Mao on September 20 for the Central Committee. "The Party committee system is an important Party institution for collective leadership and preventing any individual from monopolizing the conduct of affairs." This formula of collective leadership, introduced by Mao himself then, was discussed by Mao in his interviews with Edgar Snow in 1960 and 1965. Mao affirmed that he had done this for the purpose of strengthening Party unity and democratic centralism. This collective leadership decision might enable Mao to carry out his admittedly brilliant and successful policies; but on the other hand it would, perhaps, lead to an increase, covert if not open, of Liu's influence within the Party, now that the center of gravity would shift to the cities.

We also know that in mid-1948, or slightly earlier, Stalin had through Liu Shao-chi definitely advised the Chinese Communist Party *not* to proceed onward in their military campaigns, but to leave South China to Chiang Kai-shek; not to cross the Yangtze river, but to revert to guerilla warfare.

However, the decision to cross the Yangtze river was confirmed in that autumn, and precisely at that meeting; the military operations destined to take Nanking, the Huai Hai campaigns, were drafted shortly after by Mao Tsetung.

In 1948 the cities controlled by Chiang Kai-shek experienced an increasing tempo of starvation, misery, anger, and despair. Inflation was colossal. The U.S. dollar was worth 1,800,000 Chinese dollars in April; a pound of rice cost ten million dollars, ten thousand times what it had cost three years previously. In June 1948, very reluctantly, Chiang was forced to accept Li Tsung-jen, a militarist from Kwangsi province and often his opponent, as vice-president. Li was the choice of the more "liberal" elements in the Kuomintang.

Li Tsung-jen knew the situation was desperate; so did every foreign embassy, whose reports always started with the words: "The military political and economic situation is deteriorating . . ." In August, Chiang banned all demonstrations and proclaimed "economic reform" to be performed by his son Chiang Ching-kuo. The Chinese dollar was pegged at four to the U.S. dollar; within three weeks it was at 12 million to the U.S. dollar.

Li Tsung-jen then tried to contact the Communists for peace negotiations, to save what could be saved; in this he obtained American backing. Chiang left the initiative to Li and to the Americans, thus keeping his own "face."

But after the overwhelming victories in December 1948 and the loss of Manchuria, Chiang himself had to say something. In a speech so devoid of reality as to provoke general mirth, he announced that the situation was getting better every day; but he wanted to be "generous" to his adversaries if they "sued" for peace. Mao, in a reply to this "New Year message," reviewed the successes of the People's Liberation Army, declared it now had numerical superiority, the four to one ratio at the war's beginning having vanished. He heaped scorn on Chiang's homeric absurdity and quoted the American White Paper itself, stating that the advantage was now his. He affirmed that the people of China were on the side of the CCP. And it was not a boast.

"In 1949, the Chinese People's Liberation Army will advance south of the Yangtze river. . . . In 1949 the Political Consultative Conference with no reactionaries participating . . . will be convened. . . . The People's Republic of China will be proclaimed, and the central government of the Republic will be established."

According to certain documents * there was, within the revolu-

* *Current Background,* no. 884 (U.S. Consulate, Hong Kong). Also interviews.

tionary camp, an "opposition faction" to Mao's decision to carry the revolution through to the end, organized by the "U.S.–Chiang reactionaries." It is quite true that American ambassador Leighton Stuart was desperately seeking to promote — at this late hour! — a "coalition" government. Liu Shao-chi, "an agent of the U.S.–Chiang reactionaries hidden within the Party . . . jumped forward without waiting further" — in the picturesque, literal translation style of the Chinese broadcasts. What we do know is that, possibly because the Russians continued to be so abysmally misinformed about Chinese conditions, it was not only U.S. imperialism and Chiang, but also Stalin, who concurred to try once again for "peace," and advised Mao to abstain from pushing on to final victory. There was no danger of world war now, said Stalin, but America could be "bled white" in China if the war was prolonged. Mao must not seek a quick conclusion which might bring in the Americans with massive help. But Mao had never thought, as we have seen, that the U.S. would plunge into the war with the USSR. He did not think the U.S. would go all out for Chiang. His withering denunciation of Chiang as a "war criminal," and of the U.S. as intending to turn China into a colony, was a retort to those who tried to threaten, pressure, cajole or otherwise move him. The anti-U.S. tide in China was at its height in 1948, and Mao's words found "multitudes of people . . . coming over to the revolutionary camp." Mao denounced the Sino–U.S. air transport agreement of December 20, 1946, the Sino–U.S. bilateral agreement of July 1948, as a straightforward colonial type of treaty. He announced that, come to power, the CCP would refuse to recognize any of the unequal treaties or agreements made with Chiang Kai-shek.*

On January 14, 1949, Mao published eight points as preconditions for "peace negotiations," though he knew none would ever take place. On the 21st Chiang went into retirement, leaving Li Tsung-jen to face the Communists. The negotiations, again conducted by Chou En-lai, lasted till March 1949; during that time the People's Liberation Armies rested and consolidated, on Mao's advice; this respite was exactly what they needed.

On February 8, 1949, Mao ordered the Army units to keep busy, by turning them into "a working force for production." The soldiers recuperated; hoeing and planting kept them fit, and among the people their will to fight was kept strong.

* This also would cover the treaty between the USSR and Chiang signed in August 1945.

Originally, Mao had fixed early April as the date for crossing the Yangtze; he had then advanced it to March; due to the "peace" talks, he now put it back to April and wrote: "Training and consolidation must continue; the study of policy must be stressed. . . . Preparations must be made to take over and administer large cities. . . . From now on the formula followed in the past twenty years — 'First the rural areas, then the cities' — will be reversed and changed to the formula 'First the cities, then the rural areas.' "

The Party had over 3 million members at mid-1948; it would have 4.5 million at the end of 1949. Mao again became concerned with the loss of quality in the membership and the infiltration of undesirables. The Army once again had to do political work, to reinforce Party cadres if the latter proved defective. "We are preparing to send 53,000 cadres south with the Army . . . but this is a very small number. The occupation of eight or nine provinces and scores of big cities will require a huge number of working cadres, and to solve this problem the Army must rely chiefly on itself."

And again: "The Army is a school. Our field armies . . . are equivalent to several thousand universities and secondary schools. *We have to rely chiefly on the Army to supply our working cadres. You must understand this point clearly."* * The problem of cadres was a very difficult one. Already at the second plenum of September 1945 it had been decided to enroll cadres from the big cities, where "there are many workers and intellectuals who can take part . . . and who have . . . a higher cultural level than the workers and peasants in the old liberated areas. We should make use of large numbers of working personnel from the Kuomintang's economic, financial, cultural and educational institutions, excluding the reactionary elements." Now the victories had become landslides, and the evacuation of American personnel from the large cities had begun. Chiang had only a million-odd men left in regular combat troops. Tsingtao was evacuated by the Americans in November 1948. "The march of events in China is faster than people expected. The Chinese people should quickly prepare all the necessary conditions for the establishment of a peaceful, democratic, and independent New China."

The Red armies crossed the Yangtze river on April 21; 300,000 men, using small boats, floats, rafts and junks, went across in one night. On April 25 Mao proclaimed the eight-point covenant, which formed a basis for the military takeover of all the regions of China

---

* Emphasis not in original.

pending the formation of a government. The covenant was written in his capacity as chairman of the Revolutionary Military Council, and thus in the name of the Army. The covenant promised to protect the lives and property of people irrespective of class, belief or occupation if they maintained order and cooperated; to protect all industrial, commercial, agricultural enterprises of the national capitalists, and gave other guarantees, which were scrupulously kept. It promised protection for KMT officials, save those war criminals to be impeached, such as Chiang Kai-shek. As a result of this measure almost three million officials of the Kuomintang administration were rehabilitated; they were to be paid salaries and kept alive, and many of them worked for years under the Communists. Land reform was not to be started until the PLA had arrived and had made thorough investigations. He then envisaged a period of "some years . . . maybe three or four" before land reform could be completed.

Nanking, Chiang's capital, fell on April 27, 1949. The KMT flag was pulled down and the Red flag hoisted. The citizens swarmed to acclaim the People's Liberation Army.

The speeches made by Mao in March 1949 and again in June 1949 are fundamental to the understanding of the policies of the People's Republic of China today. They are both "state of the nation" declarations, fundamental for the transition from the new democratic period to socialism. New divergences are already foreshadowed; Mao speaks of "muddleheaded" comrades who would like to rely on the bourgeoisie in the cities; who would prefer to consolidate the New Democratic period rather than go forward to the socialist stage. Once again, curiously enough, the proponent of the "go slow" theory is Liu Shao-chi, and this fact was well recognized even in 1949; Liu's speeches gave every evidence that he would "remain at the new democratic stage" and did not think it was time to carry out the transition into socialism.

In that March or April, Liu went to Tientsin to hold talks with industrial businessmen there. He promised them all help in running their industries, brushed off the demands of the workers present, and is quoted as saying, "Exploitation has its merits too." * It is not possible to verify this report, but it was currently known and widely reported in China even before the Cultural Revolution that Liu felt that production must come first, and he spoke for years of "consolidating" new democracy. He would defend himself by saying that the

---

* Interview by the author in Tientsin, 1969.

Last days of the Kuomintang. Above, street scene in Nanking as the Nationalist government fled; at right, a bank rush in Shanghai.

OVERLEAF
The People's Liberation Army arrives in Nanking, April 1949.

new democratic period was supposed to last some years; that it was Mao, not he, who had changed his time-view, but victory had come so swiftly, and the country was ripe to bursting for revolutionary change. Mao considered that the country must push on to the socialist stage, for otherwise none of the problems could be solved. It is interesting that had there been American help and financial aid, as at one time was thought, there might possibly have been a longer new democratic stage. But the necessity for pushing on was very obvious to Mao; for he who lingered at the crossroads would find the problems mounting. And so in his speeches Mao clearly states the necessity for going forward into the next stage.

In industry, Mao pointed out that China's modern industry was only 10 percent of the total value of output of the national economy and had been concentrated in the hands of "the imperialists and their lackeys, the Chinese bureaucratic capitalists." This was now to be confiscated; the state-owned sector would become dominant, and it would be "socialist, not capitalist in character." The private capitalist industry would be allowed for a while, when beneficial, "but the existence and expansion of capitalism in China will not be unrestricted and uncurbed." It would only exist within the framework of the economic policy and planning of the People's Republic, a planning directed towards socialism. "It is entirely wrong to think . . . we can discard the slogan 'Regulation of capital' . . . this is a right opportunist view."

The people's democratic dictatorship to be established meant a long-term policy of cooperation with non-Party democrats. For it was in a united front with non-Communist parties, seven in all, that the first National People's Congress would be held.

Concerning agriculture, Mao proclaimed the socialization of agriculture, step by step, but with the final aim unchanged. "Without socialization of agriculture, there can be no complete, consolidated socialism."

Now he warned: "With victory certain moods may grow . . . arrogance, the airs of a self-styled hero, inertia and unwillingness to make progress, love of pleasure and distaste for continued hard living . . . There may be some, not conquered by enemies with guns . . . but who cannot withstand sugar-coated bullets." Thus he warned against the corruption of the cities; and within two years there was to be another rectification movement.

But, he ended, "We can learn what we did not know. We are not only good at destroying the old world, we are also good at building the new."

Shanghai was captured on May 27, 1949, a month after the fall of Nanking. Wuhan was taken on May 16. Chiang fled to Chungking, then to Chengtu, then to Kuangchow, then to Hainan, and then, on December 9, to Taiwan.

On June 15 Mao addressed the new preparatory committee for the Political Consultative Conference, heir to the one which had met so briefly in January 1946. Representatives of all parties, including the "revolutionary Kuomintang," attended. Madame Soong Chingling and Madame Ho Hsiang-ning, widow of Dr. Sun Yatsen and widow of Dr. Liao Chung-kai, both attended. The former became vice-chairman of the People's Republic of China a few months later, a post she has held until today. Li Tsung-jen, Chiang's unfortunate vice-president, went in December 1948 to the United States for medical treatment and remained till 1965, when he returned to live in Peking, with his wife, and was received with honor and consideration by Mao Tsetung. He died in 1968, of cancer, in Peking.

At the Political Consultative Conference, twenty-three organizations and groups and various parties were represented. It met in Peking on September 9, 1949. Peking was to be once more the capital of China, the new China. September 9 was, almost to the day, twenty-two years since the Autumn Harvest Uprising, when Mao Tsetung had started on the way of armed struggle, started the building of an army and of Red power in the countryside, started the strategy of the countryside surrounding the cities.

On October 1, in Peking, standing on Tien An Men — the Gate of Heavenly Peace — facing south where a large portrait of Dr. Sun Yatsen was displayed, flanked by the Politburo, the members of the Central Committee, and many an ex-Kuomintang personality, Mao Tsetung spoke to the delirious and acclaiming millions milling round the great purple walls and gates of the Ming palaces of Peking.

"The Chinese people have stood up . . . nobody will insult us again. . . ."

In Mao that day, looking at the enormous crowds, hearing the ocean sound of their acclamations; that night when the fireworks threw their dazzling meteors of light above the city, there was no trace of pride, no sensation of arrogance; only a deep humility, a sense of a great work scarcely begun; all which had gone before was "but the first step . . . in a 25,000-li Long March." All the years of

Mao Tsetung proclaims the People's Republic of China, Peking, October 1, 1949. At Mao's left, Chen Yi; at far right, Chou En-lai.

struggle, the millions of dead, the sacrifices . . . all but a beginning. In front lay the future, to be built. What happened in China would transform China, but it would also transform the world. "Even if this step [winning country-wide victory] is worthy of pride, it is comparatively tiny. . . . After several decades the victory will seem only a brief prologue to a long drama . . . the road . . . will be longer, the work greater and more arduous."

And indeed, as they met that evening to sip tea and watch the fireworks, already the past was receding, receding; the future was rushing to meet Mao Tsetung and the Chinese people. Already loomed new problems, new contradictions. The United States had withdrawn from China; there had been no massive onslaught by America, but it was a defeat for the almighty power, a psychological one, and it would rankle; perhaps they would be back . . . There was, up in Moscow, the Grand Old Man of that other, that first Revolution, Stalin, with his ambiguous mind. Mao had already decided to go to see Stalin, face him with the conscience of a new world emergent, a revolution akin to the October Revolution, which had fought every inch of the way to its triumph . . . "The Chinese people have stood up . . . nobody will insult us again."

Around Mao Tsetung were his companions, those who had fought with him, and those who fought him. He knew they were not all of one mind; he knew some of them might go against him, again and yet again. As long as their opinions and their views were not harmful to the Revolution he would go on with them. But when they would be a danger to the unswerving aim of Revolution to which he had dedicated his life, then he would be implacable.

There were the people, standing, walking; millions of them, and so much to be done. True they were poor, they were backward; the country was ravaged, a spoiled ragged blanket of a country, a country full of beggars and starving people. But he had faith and trust in the people. They were the makers of history; they would rebuild, they would create prosperity, happiness. And he would be on their side, always. They were the anonymous millions who had suffered and died, all along the measureless road they had come. Never would he lord it over them. *"Serve the people."*

Perhaps then he thought again of the story he had told the Party and the Army, in Yenan, in April 1945 at the close of the Seventh Congress, when he had answered the question *Shall we dare to win?* in the affirmative. He told many stories in his colorful lectures, in his speeches, in private conversations. He loved listening to stories, too.

"An old man lived in North China long long ago. . . . His house faced south and beyond his doorway stood two great peaks . . . obstructing the way. He called his sons, and hoe in hand they began to dig up these mountains." His neighbor had laughed at the foolish old man and his tedious labor, but the foolish old man went on, replying that when he died his sons and grandsons and their sons and grandsons would continue the work, and one day the mountains would be cleared. "God was moved," said Mao Tsetung, "and sent down two angels who carried the mountains away." *

And this was the lesson. "We must persevere and work unceasingly and we too will touch God's heart. *Our God is none other than the masses of the Chinese people. If they stand up and dig together with us, why can't these two mountains* [imperialism and feudalism] *be cleared away?"*

And indeed the two mountains had now been cleared away. God's heart had been touched. But the work had only just begun. There were more mountains to clear — ignorance, poverty, the habit of tyranny . . .

And the masses would continue to be the god of Mao Tsetung. In 1949 he was fifty-four years old, and his career was only beginning; his greatest campaigns were yet to come.

* *The Foolish Old Man Who Removed the Mountains,* June 11, 1945. *Selected Works of Mao Tsetung* (English edition Peking 1961–1965), vol. III.

8

Mao Tsetung and Stalin

"Political power grows from the barrel of a gun." The triumph of the Chinese Communist Party in 1949, the protracted thirty-year conflict, had confirmed this saying; but the victory was not only a military victory, it was also a political one.

Without the people of China, and their solid support, in great majority; without land reform and social measures which assured success because they assured security in a time of chaos, the civil war might have been prolonged for many more years. Now that the battle was won, the time of building had come.

The Party had prepared for this seizure of power and this total victory since the Seventh Congress of 1945; whatever its restricted surroundings and its poverty of means, it already had remarkable methods of administration, including a foreign policy. In Yenan Mao Tsetung was already thinking in terms of all China. His interviews bear this out. His talks with personnel of the Dixie mission show him completely aware that the Communist Party is the obvious replacement for Chiang Kai-shek, either through a coalition or without it. He had already enunciated the principles upon which today's foreign policies are based.* The application may vary, but the fundamental precepts have remained the same throughout the years.

Thus the formulas of peaceful coexistence governing relations between states are expounded by Mao to Guenther Stein in 1944. They are repeated at the Seventh Congress in April 1945; again repeated in 1949 at the second plenum of the Seventh Congress. Even in Yenan a foreign affairs department was already existent, drawn from

* See *On Coalition Government, The Policy of the Chinese Communist Party, The Problems of Foreign Policy*, April 24, 1945. *Selected Works of Mao Tsetung*, vol. III (English edition Peking 1961–1965).

the members of the liaison offices functioning under Chou En-lai in Chungking, in Sian, and later in Nanking. Every base also had its personnel in charge of "external affairs," even if visitors from outside were few and far between. The presence of the Dixie mission had stimulated the need for interpreters, liaison men, all diplomats in potentio. The delegations sent to the United Nations by the Communists, in those early years, to put the case of the People's Republic of China before this body were neither without experience nor without a solid foundation of policy.

It is otiose perhaps to repeat the obvious, that contact between 1943 and 1949 was perhaps more frequent with American than with Russian personnel; and this would be true even in Manchuria, where the Russian military and diplomatic personnel adhered to the friendship and alliance pact with Chiang Kai-shek and avoided the Communists. Yet there was contact, and especially in 1948, with the Manchurian people's government, an administration similar to that established in many other Red bases, but which was to singularize itself in its far closer liaison with the USSR, for obvious geographical and later political reasons. Until the very last days of Chiang's regime, the Russians were scrupulous in fulfilling the pact; and negotiations were carried out with Chiang Kai-shek concerning Russian claims based on the Yalta agreement well into the spring of 1949. The Russian ambassador was the only diplomat who accompanied Chiang to Chengtu and to Kuangchow; he did not, however, make the trip to Taiwan island, Chiang's last refuge.

The reticence of the USSR as regards the CCP has had many and various interpretations. According to the same Guenther Stein, who traveled both to Moscow and to Yenan in 1943, Russian officials had told him that Communism was "impossible" in China. "Can you conceive of a Communist growth without a powerful heavy industry? There cannot be Communism or even socialism in a country where the industrial element and the proletariat do not form a sizable portion of the population; at the most it will be a petty bourgeois regime with some progressive tendencies." * The dearth of knowledge, both military and political, concerning real Communist strength has been analyzed by Harrison Salisbury, the able editor of the New York *Times* and renowned expert on the USSR. According to Mr. Salisbury, the great purges in the USSR had decimated the experts on China; not once, but three times, did Stalin "liquidate" those who

* Guenther Stein *The Challenge of Red China* (New York and London 1945).

really knew anything about the Chinese Revolution. The dissolution of the Comintern in 1943 had cut the last links, and certainly not promoted renewed interest in Chinese affairs. In Stalin's mind China had a low priority for many years.

But Stalin's preference for Chiang Kai-shek is not so easily explained, unless we suppose that Stalin was already a great-power chauvinist and preferred Chiang, who would not be in a position to claim back either Outer Mongolia or other interests wrested from China — with United States consent — at Yalta. This, however, supposes that Stalin already feared a strong China under a strong and powerful national leader as well as a Communist figure; and there is no indication that Stalin ever thought it possible for Mao either to win the war or to unite the country and embark on the prodigious development which the last twenty years have seen. We remain with enigmas which cannot be explained by logic, but only by the fact that Stalin, as he grew older, reverted more and more to a fixity in his opinions which influenced the whole course of Russian policies. "The Chinese have a habit of exaggerating their strength, they keep on piling figures of nonexistent armies"; "You can never believe what they say." These and other remarks by Russian diplomats and officials betrayed the already quite palpable chauvinism and racial arrogance which was to grow so fast in the USSR in the following years. The cavalier way in which, at Yalta, Stalin asked for his share of booty in China cannot have any other interpretation than this "chauvinism" which today the People's Republic of China denounces with such vigor in the present Soviet hierarchy.

Because of this defect in Russian intelligence work concerning Mao and the Chinese Communist Party — obviously they did not bother to read U.S. intelligence sources, which until 1945 accurately described the strength of the Reds — Stalin really thought Mao would lose. As late as March 1949, when the United States Army men stationed in China already had withdrawn most of their personnel, Stalin continued to direct that talks with Chiang, as the "legal government" of China, should continue. These talks affected Russian investments and companies in Sinkiang province; and the most charitable thing that can be said is that there is no difference between the extraction of concessions in China practiced at that moment by the U.S. government-allied big businesses and the Russian officials in charge of these economic talks. Even when Peking and Tientsin had been captured by the Red armies and Mao had entered the old capital (March 25, 1949) amid the most obvious enthusiasm and relief, the talks went on. Sinkiang, the western province of China, had been the object of czarist cupidity in the later nineteenth century; and the negotiations with Chiang, under the legal instrument of the friendship and alliance treaty, cannot be regarded as anything but an attempt to continue to extort as much as possible from the now beleaguered Chiang Kai-shek.

It was in April, when the People's Liberation Army crossed the Yangtze river, and when Nanking was to fall, that the press in the Soviet Union switched to calling the Kuomintang regime "reactionary." Pravda announced its fall in the autumn.

According to Vladimir Dejider,* Stalin told him that he had advised the Chinese Communists they had no prospects of victory and should join Chiang, dissolve their armies and go back to guerilla warfare. He did not elucidate the reasons he gave for this advice; we can only think it was fear of massive American involvement. Mao had disregarded this advice and pitted his acumen in foreign policy against Stalin's, and had been proved right. Stalin was to say to Kardely, the Hungarian Communist Party representative, that the Chinese had been right not to listen to his counsels. "They are beating Chiang's army . . . we were wrong." This was a very handsome admission to make; but Stalin may not have forgiven the man who had proved him wrong.

The advent of the People's Republic of China, an unexpected one, immediately threw into disarray the balance of power in the Far East which Stalin had conceived at Yalta. Everything had to be rethought. It was obvious to him, even if his meek hirelings did not dare to tell him, that the PRC was not only viable, but a government with the greatest popular backing that had ever existed in China. Any foreign policy move by the nascent power would therefore be momentous; Asia was already changed by the Chinese Revolution on October 1, 1949. What China would do would involve continuously, and in a different manner from the past, both the United States and the USSR, because both now claimed their frontiers and interests in Asia.

It is possible, though not proven, that at the momentous meeting in Hopei in the autumn of 1948 the alliance with the Soviet Union was decided upon by the assembled Central Committee of the CCP. Even had there not been American intervention on the side of Chiang Kai-shek, friendship with the Soviet Union would have been

---

* Vladimir Dejider *Tito Speaks* (London 1953), p. 331.

a necessary and strongly affirmed decision, both because of ideological affinity and of geographical proximity. The very speed with which victory had come — before the United States had time even to pull out completely, before it could get public opinion prepared for the "loss" of China, before it could adjust to the fact that this would mean reassessing all its policies in Asia — had created a vacuum, a gap which only time and patience could fill. The new Chinese government showed remarkable understanding and skill on these main issues; and that is why Mao's speech of July 1, 1949, had left the door open for the United States, so that it might study the new situation and make the adjustments which reason and good sense seemed to require. But this in no way invalidated the firm determination to seek friendship and an alliance with the USSR, if only because it was absolutely necessary to point out that any treaties made with Chiang, by Moscow, were now completely invalid.

Mao Tsetung seems to have again rightly estimated that it would take the United States some years, maybe ten or twenty, to make a change of policy; and therefore the choice of the USSR as the source of aid for the reconstruction of China was the only one left to him.

Throughout the civil war, Mao had stressed the theme of self-reliance; Anna Louise Strong had indicated that the Communists had received nothing from the Russians.* Reading back to what she wrote in 1948, one is under the impression that she, as well as Edgar Snow at about the same time, was trying to convey to American public opinion that the Chinese would have preferred establishing relations with both sides at once. But it was not their fault if they had to turn to the USSR alone. Mao stressed that "all aid," that is, from any quarter, would be welcome, but only if it did not rob the new China of its "independence of action." It was very obvious that the United States, in its full imperialist expansion then, would not fulfill these conditions; it would mean abrogating all those profitable treaties signed with Chiang and starting on a new basis. The change in Mao's view towards the United States from 1944 to 1949 is very clear; it was a change due to the transformation of the United States itself, from the image of a great democracy at the close of World War II to one of a predatory imperialism four years later. During those years Mao Tsetung became a very careful student of the American scene; he asked for books on the United States and studied them with his usual intensity.

* Anna Louise Strong *The Chinese Conquer China* (New York 1949); interview with Anna Louise Strong, 1962.

In 1944, on August 23, Mao had questioned John Stewart Service as to the nature of America's policies in the world. "Is the American government really interested in democracy — in its world future? . . . Does it want to have the government of China really representative of the people of China? . . . America has intervened in every country where her troops and supplies have gone. This intervention may not have been intended, and may not have been direct. But it has been nonetheless real."

Mao Tsetung expounded to Service, and also to other Americans, that Soviet participation in China's postwar reconstruction would depend on circumstances in the Soviet Union; evidently their priorities would be national. "We do not expect Russian help," he said. "Russia will not oppose American interests in China if they are constructive and democratic. Russia only wants a friendly and democratic China." Thus the limits of American and Russian influence in China were clearly set; in return for help, Mao offered Chinese friendship. "China must industrialize . . . We will be interested in the most rapid development of the country . . . Between the people of China and the people of the United States there are strong ties of sympathy, understanding and mutual interest. Both are essentially democratic and individualistic. Both are by nature peace-loving . . . America needs an export market for her heavy industry and specialized manufactures . . . America is not only the most suitable country to assist . . . she is also the only country fully able to participate." *

It was American policy which had changed abruptly, leaving the Communists puzzled and angry at American "perfidy." But even then Mao did not change his own foreign policy, though he condemned American imperialism — a distinction which is very clear today, even if at the time it was not clear to the U.S. State Department. One cannot reasonably expect the Chinese Communists to thank the Americans for arming their enemy, Chiang Kai-shek.

It is in this context that the famous June 30, 1949 speech of Mao, represented in the American cold war literature of those emotional days as "belligerent" and "hostile," must be reappraised as the reasonable pronouncement of a great statesman.†

The first point Mao Tsetung made was that China would not change its goal of socialism. It would not curry favor with the United States by altering the aim of its revolution. The date chosen,

* John Stewart Service *The Amerasia Papers: Some Problems in the History of U.S.-China Relations* (Berkeley 1971), pp. 167–176.

† *On the People's Democratic Dictatorship*, June 30, 1949. *Selected Works of Mao Tsetung*, vol. IV (English edition Peking 1961–1965).

July 1, 1949, was to mark the 28th anniversary of the CCP and to reaffirm this dedication.

Externally, too, China reaffirmed struggle against imperialism; for there could be no other road for the peoples of the world. "In the light of the experience accumulated, all Chinese without exception must lean either to one side, the side of imperialism, or to the side of socialism. Sitting on the fence will not do, nor is there a third road."

The phrase used, "lean to one side," was construed in the United States to mean submission to Moscow, whereas it was an affirmation that China must go socialist. Communist conviction did not, for Mao, mean blind obedience, but this distinction was not at all clear, either to the Americans or even to the Russians. Yet how often had Mao repeated: "We are Chinese first . . . We did not make the Revolution to hand the country over to Russia . . . no blind obedience." His leadership of the Revolution had proved it; but in spite of the very obvious independence of the CCP, the U.S. foreign policy makers chose to accuse the PRC for years of being a satellite of the USSR and not representative of the Chinese people.

The phrase was also an answer and a rebuff, both to those in the Party who wanted to remain in the period of "new democracy," and to those independent parties who wanted a Western democratic parliamentary form of government. The CCP, through the Political Consultative Conference, had organized the government on a coalition basis; * and proponents for a "third road," both inside the Party and also outside it, were prominent and vocal. It was therefore for the internal goal of socialism that Mao used this phrase, as well as for the definite purpose of an alliance with the USSR. "We are against no one, except the domestic and foreign reactionaries who hinder us from doing business." But the United States had shown itself an imperialist, aggressive power, bent on military interference in Asia, and this would probably continue. There could be no trafficking with imperialism, no subservience to it; hence China was on the side of all those who would struggle against imperialism and to obtain their own national independence. Even more explicitly, on June 15 Mao had said: "We proclaim to the whole world that what we oppose is exclusively the imperialist system and its plots against the Chinese people. We are willing to discuss with any foreign government the estab-

---

* The Political Consultative Conference was a democratic coalition. Of the 142 delegates of political parties who attended, 16 were from the Communist Party. The Revolutionary Committee of the Kuomintang Party, headed by Madame Sun Yatsen, had also 16, and so had the China Democratic League. There were 11 other smaller parties represented, with delegates numbering between 8 and 12 each.

lishment of diplomatic relations on the basis of the principles of equality, mutual benefit and mutual respect for territorial integrity and sovereignty, provided it is willing to sever relations with the Chinese reactionaries."

Within the next six months, twenty-six nations would recognize the People's Republic of China.

Having thus stated very clearly the position of the new China, Mao turned briskly to the only country which could help China at the time — the USSR. For China was in ruins; it was "a blanket full of holes," and it needed help urgently. To obtain this, without sacrificing independence, without giving too many concessions, was Mao's difficult task; and to this he would consecrate the winter of 1949.

The immediate effect of Mao Tsetung's victory had been to strengthen Stalin enormously. Suddenly the USSR had, on its eastern flank, a potential ally and ideological partner. And in that autumn of 1949, the Russians showed they had the atom bomb by detonating one. All over Asia, in 1947, 1948 and 1949, were born armed revolts against reoccupation of Asian territories by colonial powers — in Indonesia, in Malaya, in Indochina and the Philippines. Great Britain had been compelled to leave India. Whatever gains there had been in Europe — in Greece and in Italy — by the U.S. were offset by what was happening in Asia.

There was one area in international relations where both the USSR and the PRC would find at the time common ground for an alliance, and that was the threat of a Japan once again rearmed by the United States.

"In 1947 Japan was reduced almost to beggary; there were unemployed people anywhere; the Japanese Communist Party was becoming quite an influence . . . but in a year all had changed. The United States injected an enormous amount of money into Japan; the *Zaibatsu* [big Japanese business monopolies] sprang into life again; within a year the factories were working full time. The U.S. even subsidized the fisheries. But everything was American-controlled; for years there were American advisers in every government department. All the militarists and fascists of the war came out of jail." This graphic description by Prince Saionji to the author * gives some idea of the speed with which Japan suddenly became, in Amer-

---

* Interview in Peking, 1964, with Prince Kinkazu Saionji.

ican policy, its main base in Asia, spearhead of a possible attack against the USSR and China. The denunciation of Japanese resurgent militarism in the Soviet newspapers indicated the great disquiet of Moscow on this development.

The USSR's weakness was undeniable, especially when contrasted with the might of the United States in those years. This had dictated the overwhelmingly prudent policies followed by Stalin. The more, however, the USSR gave in, the more the United States pressed on. Stalin had not obtained a base in Turkey, promised by the Allies at Yalta; Winston Churchill made himself the spokesman of a grand alliance of the West against the USSR, advocating a partnership between Germany and France. This was tenaciously refused by de Gaulle, who thought that it would mean subjugation of France in a German-ruled Europe.* The Truman doctrine, already foreshadowed by the aggressive United States stance after Roosevelt's death, was officially confirmed in a message on March 12, 1947, a formal American declaration of the Cold War. It proclaimed that America would henceforth support any nation resisting Communism, and committed America therefore to intervention in any national liberation movement, since in all these local Communists were implicated. Just as Japan was rearmed West Germany was rearmed.

The threat against the USSR was therefore very real; the fear of nuclear attack deep and persistent. Stalin's extraordinary prudence and cautionary advice were dictated by fears for Russian security; and Mao's pursual of civil war until its complete triumph and vindication was in Russian eyes a risky gamble. But now that Mao Tsetung had won, the rearmament of Japan was a threat to be faced in common by the two countries, not by the USSR alone. It put Stalin in a far better position to counter encirclement of the USSR planned by the West.

However, if Japanese militarism was a foundation for a common accord, other problems between the two states were not. There was, for Stalin, the strategic and ideological weakness, the breach in the strong fortress of the socialist camp, opened by Titoism. The Yugoslav Communists had often been quoted as examples of "true" Communism; they were considered until 1948 the strongest supporters of the USSR. But the contradictions between socialist states and within socialism, which Mao Tsetung would study and expound so clearly in 1957, were not admitted; hence Tito's refusal to submit national

---

* His rejection of Britain's entry into the European Common Market was based on the same view.

issues to "internationalism" led to economic and military blockade of Yugoslavia by the USSR, and the utter condemnation of Tito by all Communist parties in the world, including the Chinese. Had this blockade and the damnation of Yugoslavia not occurred, one wonders whether Tito would have begun his swift slide into capitalism (for Yugoslavia is not really a consolidated socialist state). But today there is no point in such arguments, considering what is happening in the USSR itself. However, in 1948, and from Moscow, this ideo-logical break was a grave danger and a gap in the ring of strategic buffer territory which the USSR drew round itself, and thus doubly threatening. And now Stalin asked himself whether Mao Tsetung, who had exhibited such independence, would also turn out to be a Tito? In the West, many hoped so, loudly and repeatedly.

There had been, in 1945, the proclamation of Mao Tsetung Thought. Was this heresy or not? It claimed to be the concrete application of Marxism-Leninism to Chinese conditions; but curiously enough, there were others in the CCP who claimed more for Mao than Mao ever claimed for himself.

Now there are always two ways to sabotage a major argument, enterprise or thesis; one is to attack it openly, the other is to exaggerate its scope so that it is destroyed by inflation. The second way, as we have already seen, was used in a good many instances by opponents of Mao's line. Must we not, for instance, see something rather sinister in this pronouncement:

"The way taken by the Chinese people in defeating imperialism and its lackeys . . . is the way that should be taken by the peoples of the various colonial and semi-colonial countries . . . the way of Mao Tsetung." This sentence was delivered by Liu Shao-chi in an address on November 16, 1949, held for Asian and Australasian trade unionists in Peking. The Cominform, which Stalin had established in 1946 to succeed the Comintern, in its December 30, 1949, issue, made a modification in its own publications. "This path . . . of Mao Tsetung . . . *can* also become the main path of the peoples of other colonial and semi-colonial countries . . . where similar conditions prevail."

Knowing, as we do now, the divergence of opinion between Mao and Liu even at that time, it is interesting to note that the most fulsome praise and personality cult hyperbolics concerning Mao came precisely from those who, in the next twenty years, would be one by one castigated as the enemies of his line. The coincidences are remarkably frequent. In the context of the October to December 1949 period, when Mao was preparing to meet Stalin, it is impossible not to suspect Liu Shao-chi of some "dark motive," since Liu was certainly very well acquainted with Russian political thinking and with Stalin's views on anyone who deviated from his increasing absolutism. Speaking in this manner was little short of outright provocation. Was this speech, therefore, an attempt to sabotage Mao's meeting with Stalin, or was it a genuine expression of enthusiastic nationalism, exacerbated by the triumph of the Revolution? Whatever the motive, the result cannot have been to reassure Stalin that Mao was not a Tito.

Last but not least, there were the direct problems of territory and boundaries between China and the USSR — problems which Mao Tsetung would tackle most vigorously when in Moscow. We can summarize them as Sinkiang, Mongolia, and Manchuria, three territories of China in which czarist influence first, and now Soviet Russian influence, exercised themselves to a pronounced degree.

Where Mongolia was concerned, the virtual annexation of Outer Mongolia had proceeded since the 1920's. It had been reinforced in the 1930's, but the final blow had been delivered in 1945, in the treaty of friendship and alliance concluded that August with Chiang Kai-shek. The independence of Outer Mongolia had been officially recognized by Chiang as a counterpart to Soviet recognition of Chiang's regime as China's sole legal government. Of course this treaty was already invalid de facto, by the Soviet recognition on October 2 of the People's Republic of China and withdrawal of all diplomatic representation from Chiang's regime, now installed on the Chinese island of Taiwan. But the treaty had not delineated the frontiers between Outer Mongolia and Inner Mongolia, the latter a part of Chinese territory (actually the frontier demarcation would not be completed until 1963). Hence Mao's announcement, broadcast in 1948, that the Chinese Communist Party once it came to power would not recognize *any* unequal treaties, past or present, or any treaties entered into with the Chiang regime during the civil war, implicitly applied to both the United States and the USSR.

The question of Manchuria was even more sensitive. There had been the "return" to the czarist position of 1904, voiced apparently by Stalin to Averell Harriman; * there had been at Yalta the inclusion of Dairen and Lushun (Port Arthur) and the Chinese Eastern Railway as items of particular interest, to say the least, to the Soviet

* See Herbert Feis *The China Tangle* (Princeton 1953); also Tang Tsou *America's Failure in China* (Chicago 1963).

presence in Manchuria. The last time this railway was mentioned, it had been sold by the USSR to the Japanese-controlled puppet state of Manchukuo in 1935.

During the brief war with Japan that the Soviet Union carried on (August 8–15, 1945), the Russian armies had dismantled many of the Japanese-installed factories in Manchuria. In spite of the opinion of Western historians, this cannot be construed as a gesture against the CCP; there was no reason for Stalin to believe (*a*) that the Chinese People's Liberation Army would be victorious in Manchuria and (*b*) that these factories would not, on the contrary, help Chiang Kai-shek in his civil war. On the other hand, it is true the Russian armies held the Manchurian cities for Chiang Kai-shek and prolonged their stay at his request. Had they not done so, the cities would have been garrisoned by Americans, and this would have made it far more difficult for the Chinese Communists. It would also ultimately have represented a very great danger to the USSR itself.

It is therefore from another viewpoint that we must understand the Manchurian problem. There Stalin was fighting a defensive action; he needed the railway and the ports, as he told Chiang Kai-shek, to defend the Siberian provinces; with the Truman doctrine proclaimed, and the rearming of Japan, he would be very reluctant to forego this advantage.

Besides this presence of the USSR, there is also what would later be known as the Kao Kang affair, a process of internal influence, which in the next few years, would develop into something amounting to a serious danger to both ideological and national unity in China.

Kao Kang appears a complex character. A native of North Shensi, he was closely associated with Liu Chih-tan at the North Shensi base, and active in guerilla operations. He became a member of the Central Committee at the Seventh Congress in 1945, and was then sent to Manchuria along with Peng Chen and other important cadres, some 30,000 of them, and 120,000 Communist troops, to begin the infiltration of the countryside and the "countryside surrounding the cities" strategy which was so successful. Kao Kang became prominent in Manchuria after the departure of the PLA in the great campaigns of North China, secretary of the Northeast bureau, and in August 1949 chairman of the local Northeast people's government. This local government was in line with all such local governments founded in Communist-held territories. In July 1949, under the leadership of Kao Kang, a delegation of "the Manchurian

people's democratic authorities" went to Moscow to conclude a
one-year trade agreement with the USSR, *before* the People's Republic of China was formally established and while the Political Consultative Conference was still sitting in Peking.

How much suspicious dealing must we see in this? Very much, according to some students of Chinese history, and because of the fate
which befell Kao Kang in 1954, when he was accused of having
tried to turn the three eastern provinces of Manchuria into an "independent kingdom." But to interpret this trade mission as a deliberate
attempt by the Russians to utilize Kao Kang in order to detach Manchuria from the PRC is possibly presuming too much. Though we
cannot deny that a strong Russian influence within the CCP would
come to look increasingly undesirable in the years to come, we cannot classify this initial step for a trade agreement as the beginning of
a separatist stance. We do not know whether it had Mao Tsetung's
approval or not; in any case, it was only a partial treaty. Kao Kang,
however, did come back to make reports adulatory about the USSR
and to proclaim that "we must imitate the Soviet Union . . . in
every respect."

In any tale of suspense, the characters who later turn out villains
appear at intervals, one of a crowd, innocuous, even innocent; their
evil is unveiled only in a startling turnabout at the end. So, sometimes, is it in revolutionary history. Heroes acclaimed yesterday are
found wanting, and lapse into obscurity. We must mention again Peng
Teh-huai at this moment, both because of his later downfall — when
in 1959 he appears to have been transmitting information about
Chinese Central Committee decisions to Khrushchev and also in-
dulging in other inappropriate behavior — and also for his role in
the Korean war and his attempts subsequently to transform the People's Liberation Army into something closely resembling the Russian
model. In early 1949 Peng was military governor in Manchuria,
since the territory was now divided into military regions, each under
a senior commander, while liberation proceeded. It was then that he
appears to have struck up a friendship with Kao Kang, and to have
plotted with him, either then or later, for some larger role in a conspiracy designed to oust Mao, Chou, and others and to replace them.
Whatever the amount of truth in this, there can be no understanding
of what happened during and after the Korean war unless one keeps
in view the overt Russian influence in Manchuria, which was to continue till 1954.

The third problem directly concerning Chinese territory in which

Russian expansionism had been felt was Sinkiang; and Sinkiang continues to be the object of maneuvers on the part of the USSR today.

Sinkiang was consolidated against czarist encroachments by the Chinese in 1880; in 1760 it was already a recognized part of Chinese domains. The Uighurs, the majority population, had arrived only seven centuries after the Han Chinese had established the silk road and their influence on the area (135 B.C.). During the czarist annexation of Kazakh territories, tribes fleeing the Russian massacres had also entered Sinkiang; one of them, a Turkoman offshoot, the Kazakhs, had requested the Chinese emperors for protection in the eighteenth century. During the 1930's Sinkiang was held by a warlord (as were all provinces of China), Sheng Shih-tsai, whose policies hovered between alliance with Chiang Kai-shek and alliance with Moscow. Soviet strategy within the inner lands bordering its Siberian acquisitions is very poorly documented, but by 1935 Japanese intrigues in Sinkiang sought to detach the province and promote autonomous rebellions.* Sheng Shih-tsai found the Japanese invasion of China had weakened Chiang's regime so considerably that there was no counterbalance to Moscow's penetration. As a consequence of the united front, Sheng then entered into correspondence with the Communists at Yenan. A line of communication between Moscow and Yenan was established then, but as we have seen, Soviet aid went chiefly to Chiang, and there is no record of military aid from Soviet Russia to Yenan at any time during 1937–1945.† What is more significant is that Chinese Communist party members entered into the provincial administration of Sinkiang, invited to do so by Sheng Shih-tsai.

In this connection, Mao Tsetung's own brother, Mao Tse-min, was sent to Sinkiang to restructure the chaotic finances of the province and also to establish programs for development.

Mao Tse-min, under the name of Chou Ping, worked in Sinkiang from 1939 to 1942, promoting not only finances but also schools. Sheng appears also at one time to have wanted to join the CCP, but he never did.

From the early 1930's on, the Russian economic hold on Sinkiang

---

* Rebellions of national minorities, due to Han Chinese feudal exploitation and their own feudality, were not solved until the present regime would devise autonomous regimes coupled with substantial rises in standards of living, communications linkage and industrial development.

† A small gift of money is, however, mentioned by Allen Whiting and Sheng Shih-tsai in their book *Sinkiang: Pawn or Pivot* (East Lansing, Mich. 1958), which also contains controversial material on the period 1933–1945.

increased swiftly. Oil concessions, joint ventures (of stock companies) and economic loans forwarded this extension of Soviet influence. But after 1940, when the war with Germany put the USSR in a difficult position, Chiang Kai-shek's government had reasserted itself; and there appears to have been a short Russian eclipse, with transfer of authority of many concessions, and their titles, to the Nanking government. This was not of long duration; by 1945, with the treaty of friendship and alliance concluded with Chiang Kai-shek, another wave of Russian ascendancy was to begin in the province. Four years of talks and negotiations with Chiang Kai-shek would be concerned largely with the resumption of prospection, with rights for geological surveys, and other concessions in the area. It was in the midst of this that Mao Tse-min was to perish, for Sheng Shih-tsai switched his allegiance to Chiang Kai-shek. Sheng's own story * is that the Communists murdered his brother, who was Russian-educated; hence he imprisoned and later executed Mao Tse-min and other Communists. Another version, quite as unverifiable and as likely to be true, is that his Moscow-trained brother was murdered by Sheng himself, who then threw the blame on Communists and killed them, thus also working out a rapprochement with Chiang Kai-shek. With Mao Tse-min also died Chen Tan-chiu, a founder member of the CCP.

In 1948 the problem of Sinkiang was still a complex one in the relations with the new ascendant power, the CCP. In his book *Battle for Asia,†* Edgar Snow asked the question: "Is not Russia preparing to annex this territory [Sinkiang] as a buffer state?" In 1948, a national front army of "East Turkestan" was promoting a national liberation movement, seeking to make Sinkiang independent . . . and this movement was sponsored by the USSR. In 1949 the Russians reprinted the constitution of the Chinese Soviet Republic of Juichin, drawn up in November 1931.‡ In this constitution it was explicitly stated that the national minorities had the right to secede. Although Lenin had defined limits to the rights of secession, pointing out in *The National Question* that this right was subject to the overall socialist aim, a Mongolian People's Revolutionary Party had similarly been brought into being in Inner Mongolia. These movements were clearly designed to attach vast areas of recognized

---

* See Allen Whiting and Sheng Shih-tsai *Sinkiang, Pawn or Pivot* (East Lansing, Mich. 1958). The author visited Mao Tse-min's grave in Urumchi, and other areas of Sinkiang, in 1971.

† Edgar Snow *Battle for Asia* (New York and London 1941).

‡ See part I, chapter 11.

Chinese territory to the USSR. In 1949 and 1950 the liberation of Sinkiang by the PLA began, ending in 1951.

This survey gives a brief notion of some of the substantial problems which were to be discussed in the momentous meeting between Mao and Stalin in December 1949.

But besides these substantial problems bound up with national rights, sovereignty issues, national interests, and also frontiers, there was a major ideological question. The recognition of the Chinese Revolution as a revolution of the same type as the October Revolution in Russia; the recognition of the Chinese Communist Party as a legitimate, truly Communist Party.

Mao Tsetung's conversations with Stalin, we must assume, ranged not only on Mongolia, Manchuria and Sinkiang; they would also be on a high theoretical level; for Mao was the leader of a Communist Party now in power, and there was a difference between this status and that of an ordinary chief of state of any capitalist country. But what place did the Chinese Revolution hold in the view of Communist theoreticians in the USSR? Was Stalin ready to accept a dialogue as between equals, comrades in arms? How would state relations be distinguished from Party relations when the assumption of ideological authority in Moscow had led to subservience on the part of other Communist governments in power in Eastern Europe? Would Mao accept the leadership of the Soviet Union in all matters, including state affairs, in the name of ideological solidarity, of proletarian internationalism?

This question led back, finally, to the very difficult definition of the relations between Communist parties who were also national, state governments. This question Stalin had not really tackled; for in Eastern Europe, the satellite role of Communist parties even when they had formed national governments was accepted; Tito alone had stood against this continued obedience to Moscow.

That Mao Tsetung was indeed intent on establishing the Communist Party of China as genuine, and himself as the genuine leader of such a party, can be gleaned from a series of articles and broadcasts which appeared during December and January 1949–1950, that is, during Mao's visit to Moscow. Although their author, Chen Po-ta, is now surmised to be in disgrace,* and although some parts of the articles seem overdrawn, one cannot escape the conclusion that they were an attempt, which may have been approved by Mao Tsetung, to prove that his line was ideologically correct.

* Probably due to "ultra-leftism" during the GPCR.

The articles are extremely diffuse and verbose; but the aim is to prove that Mao Tsetung was not acting against Stalin's views or directives at any time. The Chinese Revolution was not only of national but also of international world order, as had been the October Revolution in 1917; the People's Republic of China was not only an anti-feudal and anti-bureaucratic regime; it was on a par with the other people's democracies established in Eastern European countries. "The Chinese people have always considered the Chinese Revolution as the continuation of the great October Revolution in new historical conditions." It was a successor come of age; not a subordinate but an equal, even if a respectful and younger one.

But there had not been for the last twenty years any ideological discussion, for Stalin, on terms of equality; the Russian party was already corrupt with a notion of infallibility; it had had its way too long, and no one had ever dared challenge it without being utterly condemned and cast out. The prestige of the Soviet Union as a state was bound up with this ideological authority; would Stalin, therefore, admit a junior partner but a potential equal?

Mao's article on Stalin's sixtieth birthday in 1939, in which he wrote, "We must learn from him [Stalin] in two respects, his theory and his work," was recalled and reprinted by Chen Po-ta in his articles; this forced the Russian press to give it coverage, which it had not done earlier. Panegyrics on Stalin, his leadership and his greatness, were not spared. The 1927 to 1930 period was lightly glanced over, and the attack was firmly centered on the period after 1930, that is, on the period when the twenty-eight returned students had been sent back to run Communist Party affairs in China.* Mao was too well aware that all reports about him from the time Wang Ming took over the Politburo had been resoundingly bad. It was necessary to set the record straight. These comrades, the articles said, had actually distorted the advice and the ideas of the great Stalin. They had not understood him. There was no reference to the Second United Front, when again Mao had rejected the Wang Ming (Moscow) definition of the united front; but the years of the Rectification movement, which were the time of the great ideological struggle against the Wang Ming line, were emphatically dwelt upon to prove that Mao's thinking was actually in accordance with Stalin's and what Stalin would have done given the same circumstances. Implying that Stalin had been consistently misinformed, the articles showed that it was Mao who had recommended Stalin's *The Foun-*

* See part I, chapters 9–11.

dations of Leninism and other works as compulsory reading matter for the CCP, whereas this had not been done by the returned students. These works of Stalin's had dealt "severe blows" to dogmatism and empiricism; Stalin's contribution to the universal application of Marxism-Leninism had been supported and spread by Mao Tsetung, who had been able to "apply Stalin's methods to the study of Stalin"; that is, "the method of *creative Marxism*." Stalin himself was quoted on the subject: "This group does not derive its direction and instructions from historical analogies and parallels, but from a study of surrounding conditions. . . . It does not base its activities on quotations . . . but on practical experience." Mao was proved a follower of Stalin all along, and no Tito.

On the controversial subject of Mao Tsetung Thought, the articles stated that this was Bolshevism linked with the practice and the special features of the Chinese Revolution, for "the experiences of the Chinese people's struggle should be noticed," sifted and analyzed to "raise what can be adopted to the level of revolutionary science and the modern struggle of the working class." This was validity through practice, adding to knowledge of revolutionary science. "Our Party unfortunately contains certain leaders who sincerely believe that it is possible to direct the Revolution in China . . . by telegraph. . . . They do not understand that the main task of leadership consists of finding out, mastering and skillfully combining the national peculiarities with the general principles of the Comintern . . . from this comes the attempt to *stereotype* the leadership for all countries." Who had said this? Stalin himself. Thus had he spoken in 1927. And thus had Mao done. He had fought against stereotypes. "All who opposed comrade Mao Tsetung were opposed to Stalin" was withering comment upon the Russian-trained "leaders" within the CCP, who had "obstructed the dissemination inside the Chinese Party" of Stalin's works.

But there is also an assertion in these articles which is puzzling: they say that Mao had no opportunity to read Stalin until after the Rectification campaign of 1942 had been launched. This is not altogether correct, since Mao seems to have quoted Stalin at least in *On New Democracy*, and that was 1940.* The bombastic assertion that Mao therefore had been able to reach the same conclusions as Stalin through "independent thinking," although quite true, was perhaps an unnecessary sting.

* *Selected Works of Mao Tsetung*, vol. II, p. 345 (English edition Peking 1961–1965).

The drift of these and other publications was to assert the validity and genuineness of the CCP, and it was therefore both as the leader of the nation, the state, and of the Communist Party that Mao went to Moscow to take up the many problems and questions that we have described.

Mao Tsetung arrived in Moscow on December 18, 1949, and the best newsmen in the world strained to catch any wisps of rumor which would uncover information about the matters discussed. But the substance of the problems which Mao Tsetung was determined to broach in his talks with Stalin is conveyed in his own words. With his usual forthrightness he said: "I have come for several weeks. . . . The length of my sojourn . . . depends on the period in which it will be possible to settle questions of interest to the Chinese People's Republic. Among them first of all are such questions as the existing treaty of friendship and alliance between China and the USSR, the question of Soviet credits to the People's Republic of China, the question of trade and a trade agreement between our countries, and others." * By then Mao Tsetung had been two weeks in Moscow, and he made no secret of the fact that he would prolong his stay until he had obtained an answer to these "questions." Such candid diplomacy and such equable, frank statements had seldom been heard from the mouth of a Communist in Moscow. They are not the words of a submissive chief of a minor party, come with reverence to the all-knowing shrine, but those of an equal head of state and head of a large Communist Party come to discuss, as an equal, with profound courtesy but with firmness, matters of great import.

The meetings between the two must have been quite extraordinary. That Mao Tsetung had made full preparation, had carefully studied Stalin, we may be quite sure. Probably he had upon him this great stillness, when he concentrated, absorbed — almost as if soaking through the pores of his skin — people, what they said, and what they were. Was Stalin aware that he had an equal, someone of his stature, before him? I think he was. Biographers of Stalin have usually been hostile; they have emphasized his cunning, his suspicion; but is it not possible to think that greatness calls forth a response in others, and that even if his mind had been prejudiced against Mao, there would be in Stalin a recognition and respect for the rich originality, the compelling honesty of Mao's mind? At least one hopes so. Stalin was capable of admitting he was wrong; he de-

* *Tass* interview, January 2, 1950.

Mao Tsetung with Bulganin and Stalin in Moscow in the winter of 1949–1950.

spised the small servile men round him, though he used them. It is not out of character to think that Mao, having listened to Stalin, seen him drink, quietly studied the setup round him, "circled round" the mind of Stalin, began to speak, and then went on. And he spoke of great ideas and of high aims, not of small objectives. He reminded Stalin of principles that, perhaps, with time and power had become obscured for the overpraised master of the Kremlin. It was on this ideological basis that he would make Stalin surrender what he had taken at Yalta. For if in terms of power Stalin was stronger, he cannot, on the other hand, have felt very easy when faced with one who could remind him so cogently of past promises, of Lenin's noble declarations; of what the USSR should mean to the world of the exploited, who were rising, who had stood up now. Mao carried on what later he would call "struggles" with Stalin (meaning ideological debates on a very high and acute level) for nine weeks. There were also banquets, and opera shows, and visits to factories and addresses and speeches; it is not known whether all the men of the Kremlin whom Mao met were impressed by him, except for Bulganin and Molotov, who openly voiced their admiration.

Stalin did not want to sign the agreements and the treaty, hence the negotiations went on; on February 7 Chou En-lai flew into Moscow, and finally the agreements were agreed and the treaty signed, to be ratified later in the year. Mao is reported to have said that Stalin still thought of Mao as "another Tito," and that it was only after the Korean war that Stalin was convinced Mao was not a Tito. Whether this is true or not we do not know; but it does lend weight to the suggestion that the talks between the two men also centered on ideology, and were possibly inconclusive. The acceptance of Mao Tsetung as a great theoretician and practitioner of Marxism-Leninism came only in 1951 and 1952.

Six agreements and a joint communiqué were the result of these weeks of negotiation; they were ratified in the autumn of 1950. They included:

(1) A treaty of friendship, alliance and mutual assistance for thirty years (instruments of ratification exchanged on September 30, 1950). By this treaty Soviet military support to the PRC was assured against attack by Japan or any other state cooperating directly or indirectly in any act of aggression with Japan. This also protected the Soviet Union from attack in the same quarter.

(2) An agreement regarding the joint administration and future

transfer of the Chinese Eastern Railway in Manchuria and the ports of Lushun and Dairen (to be returned to China by 1952). Actually, because of the Korean war, they were not returned until 1955.

(3) A Soviet grant of credits of 300 million dollars over a five-year period from January 1, 1950. The Russians also transferred "gratuitously" the property acquired from Japanese ownership in Manchuria, and also military compounds in Peking. This took place in September 1950 also.

(4) Most important was the abrogation of the treaty of friendship and alliance with Chiang Kai-shek of August 14, 1945; but the independence of Outer Mongolia was reaffirmed, and accepted by the PRC, whereas Inner Mongolia remained part of China.

(5) As for Sinkiang, joint stock companies for nonferrous and rare metals, for petroleum, were to operate for thirty years. The "national army of Turkestan," Russian-sponsored, ceased to exist. Saifuddin, a prominent Uighur and a Communist, became head of the New Sinkiang Democratic League, and is still in his post today as chairman of the revolutionary committee for the Sinkiang-Uighur autonomous region. There were also the establishment of a Sino-Soviet civil aviation joint-stock company, agreements for working conditions for Soviet experts, trade and exchange agreements, signed in March and April of 1950.

Materially, the harvest Mao reaped seemed meager, especially as regards credits; but psychologically it was large, for it was tantamount to a renunciation of the Russian sphere of influence in a wide belt of Chinese territory which had been under pressure for a hundred years. It was a halt to the relentless drive of Russian expansionism, and a reversal of Yalta.

This cannot have been easy for Stalin to accept. Although the ruble was revalued two weeks later, which cut down the aid of 300 million dollars by 20 percent, and although it appears that attempts to turn Manchuria and Sinkiang into spheres of Russian influence would only be halted temporarily, yet the treaty which Mao came back with was a great victory. It enabled the Chinese Communist Party to carry on the work of reconstruction: it gave it a voice among the socialist countries. Mao Tsetung recognized the socialist camp as headed by the USSR. "The friendship between China and the USSR," he said, was "eternal and indestructible." Although this may sound, today, naïve and optimistic, history may yet prove that in the long run Mao Tsetung was right.

The treaty was hailed as China's first equal treaty, and the Soviet

Union's unselfish, fraternal help was much praised. The weeks in Russia were to be for Mao Tsetung a period of valuable study. Perhaps he did realize then what he had already begun to think about — that it was possible to have contradictions between socialist states as well as the antagonistic contradictions between imperialism and socialism. But he could not have been aware then (it was too early) that joint-stock companies established in Eastern European countries were primarily to fuel Russian reconstruction. However, he was made acutely aware of Stalin's very real fear of schism in the socialist camp. "Agents" of imperialism were everywhere, and during the time that Mao was in Moscow, great purges went on in Eastern European countries — in Bulgaria and in Hungary, where the Hungarian Communist Party leaders were executed in that very December.

Though in September 1949 the Russians had exploded their first atom bomb, the fear of war, tiredness with war, was very evident in the USSR. Mao Tsetung would be very conscious of this too. Did he reassure Stalin with the argument that imperialism must first conquer all the "intermediate zone," the other countries in Asia, must embark first on military domination in Japan, and in Southeast Asia, before it would attack the Soviet Union? And was Korea discussed then, as is averred by certain American historians? Is it true that the Korean war was planned in Moscow that winter?

For it was only four months after Mao's return from Moscow to China that the Korean war broke out, in June 1950.

9

The Korean War

The Korean war may appear to some Americans today an incongruous chapter of unresolved perplexities. It appeared and continues to appear, to the Chinese, a continuation of the policy which dictated American interference in China, and was to dictate American involvement in Vietnam; that is, imperialism. It appeared to them a logical follow-up of the Truman doctrine, and Mao had elucidated it in his interview of 1946 with Anna Louise Strong. Just as Hurley had represented the beginning of this policy in China, Dulles was to represent its full maturity in Korea and later in Vietnam; this would continue, military involvement in Asia would continue, with the obsessive desire to stop in its tracks any national liberation movement, in the name of anti-Communism. To this America was to dedicate her manpower and resources for two decades.

The simplest and most complete explanation of the Korean war — which made normalization of relations between China and the U.S. impossible — is found in the words of Premier Chou En-lai on August 30, 1960, to Edgar Snow:

"After the liberation of China the United States government declared that it would not interfere in the internal affairs of China, and that Taiwan was China's internal affair. Dean Acheson said so in the White Paper, and it was also admitted by Truman later. As a matter of fact Taiwan was restored to the then government of China, Chiang's government, after the Japanese surrender . . .

"After war broke out in Korea in June 1950, Truman changed the policy and adopted a policy of aggression towards China. While sending troops to Korea the United States at the same time dispatched the Seventh Fleet to the Taiwan straits and exercised military control over Taiwan. Beginning from that time the U.S. started new aggression against China . . .

"Shortly afterward U.S. troops in Korea showed the intention of crossing the 38th parallel and pressing on towards the Yalu river [China's frontier], and *because of this* * the Chinese government could not but warn the U.S. government that we would not stand idly by if the U.S. troops crossed the 38th parallel and pressed on toward the Yalu river. This warning was conveyed to the U.S. through the Indian ambassador.† The U.S. government disregarded this warning and U.S. troops did indeed cross the 38th parallel and pressed on towards the Yalu river.

"The Chinese people could only take the action of volunteering support to Korea in its war of resistance. But this action was not taken until four months after the U.S. stationed its forces in the Taiwan straits and exercised military control over Taiwan, and not until U.S. troops had crossed the 38th parallel and approached the Yalu river."

In these succinct paragraphs we have the Chinese view of the Korean war, and of China's involvement in it, a most unwilling involvement, as the Chinese made no bones in proclaiming. The last thing the new government wanted was war.

Korea, once a dependency of the Chinese empire,‡ had been wrested from it by Japan in the nineteenth century, and colonized, as had been Taiwan. The Korean people never stopped their insurgency against Japan, and during the Sino-Japanese war it was from Manchurian bases, from Manchurian territory in which there are numerous Korean national minority villages, that Kim Il Sung, now president of the People's Democratic Republic of Korea (North Korea) and secretary-general of its Labor Party, waged a national liberation war against Japan.

In accordance with agreements made at Cairo and Potsdam between the Soviet Union and America, Korea was to become independent, but would be occupied "temporarily" by both U.S. and USSR forces when the latter entered the war against Japan. The temporary line of demarcation would be the 38th parallel, and Korea was to be reunited as one country through free elections held after the war.

But just as U.S.-avowed policies and agreements entered into were suddenly canceled, or ignored while the U.S. (and Great Britain, for it was Winston Churchill who struck the first note of a "worldwide

* Author's italics.
† K. M. Pannikar.
‡ No claim was made and no claim will ever be made by the PRC to Korea. Mao Tsetung never included it in any of his speeches (contrary to some reports) as part of Chinese territory.

Communist conspiracy" in his speech at Fulton, Missouri, in 1946)
went on to discard unilaterally its commitments, Korea was not to be
reunited, since obviously, had it been so, the national liberation
movement under Communist aegis would have triumphed. The prudent and even comminatory policies of the Soviet Union were once
more exampled in Korea, where Stalin gave way repeatedly.

The thesis that Stalin and Mao planned the Korean war at their
meeting is not only hardly credible; it is downright incredible. It pre-
supposes that either or both together were eager for a military show-
down. All evidence is to the contrary.

The rearming of Japan, a top priority undertaking by the Pentagon and its supreme commander on the spot, General MacArthur,
also involved Korea south of the 38th parallel, now under American military occupation. In fact the preparation of South Korea as
a bastion of America's military policies in Asia was already in evidence in 1948–1949, despite political statements to the contrary.

American troops and advisers were training and equipping a large
South Korean army, while the U.S. was resisting the reunification of
the country. Two kinds of governments had come into being on the
two sides of the "temporary" demarcation, the 38th parallel. In
North Korea, Premier Kim Il Sung was entirely in charge; from the
very beginning, although there were Russian military advisers with
the army and North Korea benefited from aid for reconstruction,
Koreans were in control of the economy, the administration, and the
army. The situation was quite different in the southern part of
Korea. MacArthur had immediately assumed supreme control and
treated South Korea as part of his Japanese imperium. "All powers
of government will be exercised under my authority . . . Persons
will obey my orders during the military control, English will be the
official language." The people's committees which had sprung up in
the wake of the anti-Japanese war were disbanded and their leaders
were jailed; Japanese police and administrators were retained and
ordered to round up Communists and "troublemakers." * But the
popular outcry against this outright colonial occupation was so intense that MacArthur had to revise, reluctantly, some of his measures. Pro-Japanese Koreans, well-known collaborators with the previous colonizer, were used instead of Japanese, but with the same
results.

Once again, it was fairly clear that free elections, which had been

* Wilfred G. Burchett *Again Korea* (New York 1968).

pledged by the United States, would have given the Communists a possible 70 to 80 percent of the votes. In December 1945 the problem of unification was discussed between the U.S. and the USSR in Moscow, and a joint commission was then established, *Tass* meanwhile explaining that the U.S. aim was to secure "a permanent division of Korea." This was a very bitter blow to the Korean people. The USSR, however, in line with its policies of prudence, compromised and accepted that reunification should be postponed. The parallel with Vietnam, where once again free elections, if held in 1956, would have given the Communists a majority and hence were prevented by the United States, is plain.

Thus the 38th parallel became frozen into a "frontier." From 1946 onward, the MacArthur administration set about establishing its own regime. Peasant associations, trade unions, youth leagues, even parties who though right-wing supported reunification were disbanded. A "government" was first created with an American, General Arnold, as chief of government and an "interim" legislative assembly, half of whose 140 members were nominated by General Arnold. By spring of 1948 Syngman Rhee had been found the best and most rabidly suitable chief of the administration to be placed in the seat of government; his accession to high office was marked by copious use of the Japanese-trained police and wholesale arrests of all liberals. "We figure that if they did a good job for the Japanese they would do a good job for us," was one of the choice comments made by an American official of those days.

The United Nations commission on Korea reported in August 1949 that 89,710 people had been arrested in the eight months prior to April 30, 1949, by the Rhee government. Chief among the crimes listed was demanding reunification of the country. Yet despite police efficiency, clubbings, assassinations, jailings, and the barring of all opposition parties, in "elections" held on May 30, 1950, Rhee's candidates got only 20 percent of the vote.

In spite of this obvious retention of South Korea as an American base, MacArthur had implicitly excluded South Korea from the American defense perimeter in his speeches. "Now the Pacific has become an Anglo-Saxon lake," he said in his usual grandiose manner, "and our line of defense runs through the chain of islands fringing the coasts of Asia. It starts from the Philippines and continues through the Ryukyu archipelago, which includes its broad main bastion Okinawa; then it bends back through Japan and the Aleutian chain to Alaska."

Secretary of State Dean Acheson had gone further, as Premier Chou En-lai pointed out. Speaking on January 12, 1950, before the National Press Club in Washington, Acheson had outlined the defense perimeter of the United States in the Pacific, excluding South Korea and Taiwan.

From the Chinese point of view, Acheson's speech was of considerable significance. The very timing precludes the hypothesis that Mao Tsetung, who was then in Moscow, would plot with Stalin for action in Korea. What the PRC was interested in was Taiwan; and Mao would not be foolish enough to entertain any proposition (supposing there had been one, which is very unlikely) for starting a war in Korea, which would jeopardize the liberation of Taiwan. Acheson's pronouncement in fact gave some hope that within a foreseeable future the United States might, grudgingly no doubt, recognize that its best interests lay in normal relations with China even under a Communist government. In fact there were indications that some officials of the State Department were encouraging a careful reappraisal of policy towards China.

The hypothesis therefore that Mao and Stalin plotted the Korean war in Moscow is untenable; the one that Stalin plotted the war is hardly likely.

The establishment of the North Atlantic Treaty Organization (NATO) in Europe, with a rearmed West Germany, was a direct threat to the Russians, and the possibility of war on two fronts, even if China were involved, and *because* of the mutual assistance treaty with China just signed in Moscow, would not be one Stalin would contemplate with great equanimity. There was nothing to gain, and much to lose, in such a gamble, and Stalin was not a gambler. Even if he was maliciously planning to involve China in war with the United States (as some cynics aver), one cannot see him taking such a big risk. The Sino-Soviet treaty of alliance specifically mentioned the resumption of aggression on the part of Japan or any other state that might collaborate in any way with Japan in acts of aggression; there was no way for Stalin to know that Japan would not be involved by the Americans in a war in Korea, if it went on long enough.

We are left with only one more hypothesis: that North Korea, on its own, invaded South Korea. In *The Hidden History of the Korean War* by I. F. Stone, the point is very clearly made that it was South Korea which started provocations, and that these provocations were encouraged by John Foster Dulles. "Peace with Russia seemed to be what Dulles feared," writes Stone. Early in March 1950, when it was suggested that Stalin and Truman should meet, Dulles denounced this as "deceptive cold war strategy."

The most suspicious event was Dulles's trip to Korea in that dramatic June of 1950; prior to it, from evidence accumulated in the press, he had "seemed to feel that something more than the Cold War was needed." He spent three days in South Korea with Syngman Rhee, returned to Tokyo on June 21 for a long meeting with MacArthur, after which, according to Associated Press dispatches, he "predicted . . . positive action by the United States to preserve peace in the Far East." The positive action that did occur was the outbreak of civil war in Korea on June 25 and the commitment of the American government — the United Nations Security Council assent being obtained with the People's Republic of China not seated and the USSR delegation not present — to armed forces by sea and ground and air, which was a large-scale intervention in the Pacific area, on June 27.

Actually the record of the Rhee administration is even more suspicious. The South Korean regime started to agitate for reunification by armed force early in 1949, almost eighteen months before the war occurred. On October 7, Rhee stated categorically to newsmen that his government troops were able to occupy Pyongyang easily, as they were "militarily prepared." From then on Rhee gave many interviews to emphasize the aim of his regime, to "regain lost territory . . . defend the national borders of Korea . . . unify South and North by our own strength." This provocative and bellicose attitude was reinforced by an agreement for joint defense and mutual assistance between the United States and Syngman Rhee, signed on January 26, 1950.

It could be argued, therefore, with far more credibility, that in spite of what President Truman, Dean Acheson, and General MacArthur were saying, the ground was being prepared for military action to be taken from South Korea. Provocations across the cease-fire line took place almost weekly, and South Korean military personnel made statements about their combat readiness. In the six months from January to June much new equipment was received from the United States.*

---

* American ships according to Stone were ready to evacuate families one week before June 25 (*The Hidden History of the Korean War*, New York and London 2nd edition 1969).

The North Korean government under Kim Il Sung was very worried; it multiplied appeals for peaceful reunification. Its own forces were equipped by the USSR and had Russian advisers; but these withdrew in June, when the war began. The North Korean government sent delegates to Rhee to plead for reunification, and on June 16 proposed that the National Assembly of South Korea join with the North Korean People's Assembly to work out a program for peaceful reunification. But on June 17 Dulles had arrived. He went straight to the 38th parallel, and was photographed there peering at maps.* "No adversary can resist you," Dulles told the troops he reviewed in a pep speech. "The time is not far off when you will be able to display your prowess."

In the early hours of June 25, while Dulles was still in Tokyo with MacArthur, Rhee's troops launched an attack, so runs the North Korean account, across the 38th parallel. John Gunther corroborates this account; he was then in Tokyo, and he was told by one of the ranking officers of General MacArthur's staff that "the South Koreans have attacked North Korea." †

The case, therefore, for supposing that it was Syngman Rhee, with the encouragement of Dulles and MacArthur, who started military provocation across the 38th parallel is much stronger than the nebulous hypothesis of plots in Moscow.

But the South Korean army, however magnificently trained and equipped by the United States, could not keep up the offensive it had begun. Within days it was in headlong flight as the North Koreans counterattacked and swept onward. For the North Koreans were also prepared, and if one wishes to be very suspicious, one might say that the North Korean troops should not have swept onward. But the demand for reunification was too strong; the people of South Korea rose to help the North Korean troops everywhere. Within six weeks it did look as if reunification would take place, but it would be achieved by Kim Il Sung's armies.

Meanwhile intervention, under the United Nations flag, had occurred, with the Security Council members stampeded (except for the courageous Yugoslavs) into voting sanctions. The North Korean armies swept far south in the peninsula, but massive American troop landings by MacArthur at Inchon reversed the tide and the North

* Wilfred G. Burchett (*Again Korea,* New York 1968) states that they were maps of actual operational plans for attack.
† See Burchett, *ibid.* Also verbal confirmation to author in meeting with John Gunther, 1954.

Korean army fell back north of the 38th parallel. Seoul, which had fallen to them, was evacuated and retaken by U.S. forces.

The decisions which would involve in the end the People's Republic of China, and make the sending of Chinese volunteers irrevocable, would be the crossing of the 38th parallel by the American and allied forces and the decision to mass for an offensive at the Yalu river, against China proper.

The Yalu river, which divides Korean from Chinese territory, is a source of hydroelectric power to both countries; because the hydroelectric stations were Japanese-installed, the Chinese supply of electricity for the factories of Manchuria came from the Korean side of the Yalu river. This was well known to the American military and State Department. They knew that any attack within a certain perimeter of the Yalu could be construed as an offensive against China, not to speak of the clear intention exhibited by MacArthur to cross the Yalu river into Manchuria.

It is not certain that the United Nations, on the day they handed over forces to a "unified command" under MacArthur, fully realized to what lengths the General would go. MacArthur had a blank check to do what he wanted, subject only to approval by the President of the United States; and Truman was as enveloped in anti-Communist hysteria as anyone else. It would only be after some months that responsibility of office and native prudence would emerge in him. Meanwhile, on July 7, an unlimited draft on American manpower to prosecute the Korean war was authorized; this not only encouraged MacArthur's plans but it seriously raised the emotional climate in the United States and created a condition in which only the testimony of all-out anti-Communism could be heard. But it must be said for Truman that even in those crisis days he wanted to localize the conflict; and thought that he could play it safely, as he had been assured by his advisers, so that neither the PRC nor the USSR would intervene. The temptation of a military victory, to recoup the galling disgrace of the fiasco in China, was also a powerful incentive in the assumptions that were made and the measures that were taken by the President at that moment.

The story of the Korean war is a story of hysterical headlines, deceitful and misleading communiqués from the supreme headquarters of General MacArthur in Tokyo, a story like that of Vietnam, which publication of the Pentagon papers finally exposed.

Whenever an armistice or cease-fire seemed possible, MacArthur would seek an extension of the conflict; and in this he showed excellent political acumen and a good knowledge of the way to stir the more unreasoning of his fellow countrymen. Had he not been checked in time, the Korean war could have developed into a full-scale conflict involving both China and the USSR.

For example, after November 5, 1950, there were moves in the United Nations for a cease-fire; America's allies were already worried over the bellicose statements of MacArthur. Also, a delegation from the People's Republic of China was due to arrive at the United Nations and to present suggestions for a cease-fire on November 24. But on that very November 24, the day the representatives of the People's Republic of China arrived in New York to participate in the Security Council debate, MacArthur launched a 100,000-man offensive towards the Yalu river, thus putting an end to all possibilities of negotiation. MacArthur had by then not only crossed the 38th parallel and driven northward, but had also made it very clear, by an ultimatum to Kim Il Sung couched in the most peremptory terms, that he was treating the North Koreans as if they had waged war against the United States, and he was to exact unconditional surrender from them. Had the Chinese not sent volunteers to North Korea, the Soviet Union would almost certainly have been involved, not only because of the treaty binding her to come to China's help, but also because her own security would then be threatened, her frontiers being contiguous to Manchuria and to North Korea.

Chinese involvement in the Korean war was due to a direct threat to China. The action taken was carefully delimited as a response to American aggression.

The start of hostilities in Korea was not expected by the Chinese. One of Mao Tsetung's first actions on his return from Moscow was the drastic reduction of the armed forces. Not only was the budget heavily weighted with expenditures for four million PLA men, but there were also four million ex-Kuomintang troops to feed, lodge, and employ, and three million ex-Kuomintang employees, all of whom had to be fed and paid. The inflation had scarcely been curbed; the country had no exports, industries were in ruin; nothing worked. All this was an unusual burden on the administration, and demobilization was the first measure taken. Hainan island, Sinkiang and Tibet remained to be liberated — Tibet by September 1950.

Except for forces on the east coast poised for the liberation of Taiwan, there were no forces in expectancy of an attack in the east or in Manchuria. Movements of units to the north in May and June, mentioned by some commentators as "preparatory" to the Korean war, were nothing of the sort. They were, as some Americans themselves aver, the return of Army units who had operated from Manchuria down to South China, and now to be demobilized. They would go back to their original provinces for assignment to state farms and PLA agricultural development areas, in Inner Mongolia, in Manchuria, and in Sinkiang. Almost two million men were thus to be shifted in the next two years.

In June 1950, major economic problems occupied the many and various sessions of the Political Consultative Conference. Mao Tsetung's speeches only a few days before the outbreak of the Korean war are blithely oblivious of any war. They speak of hope, of reconstruction; they reaffirm the liberation of Taiwan but are otherwise mainly concerned with economics, with "big reductions in army and government expenditure by the state," with the necessity, urged by him so many times, of turning soldiers into "productive workers." The first outline of the first five-year plan was to be drafted; there were to be great irrigation projects and afforestation. The resolution on army demobilization, and the movement of soldiers to their original provinces or recruitment areas for conversion to production, all took place in June. The resolution was passed on June 24, and on June 25 the Korean war broke out.

The problem of Taiwan still remained, and units still remained poised on the coast of Fukien to liberate Taiwan. There is no reason to suppose it could not be taken in an amphibious operation comparable to the one which had secured Hainan island. But no precipitate move was made. Some fanciful writers have stated that the troops training to seize Taiwan all came down with schistosomiasis while learning to swim in the rivers of South China, hence the operation was postponed. In any case, the Korean war put a stop to the operation in June, and for a very good reason. For on June 27, along with the decision to employ U.S. ground, air and naval forces in Korea, also came the naval deployment of the Seventh Fleet to the straits of Taiwan, although Taiwan had nothing to do with Korea and was Chinese territory, and China was not involved in the Korean civil war. Yet the decision by the Americans to use the Seventh Fleet on the shores of South China was taken on the very day it was decided to send U.S. and U.N. forces to Korea, and it was taken "to prevent any attack on Formosa [*sic*]."

Taiwan (Formosa) was thus linked arbitrarily to the Korean conflict by the United States, and therefore, since Taiwan was Chinese territory, it immediately involved the People's Republic in a military confrontation with the United States. This was great military provocation, but the Chinese kept cool, though protesting vigorously. They saw it as a continuation of the military interference which had occurred in China during the civil war with Chiang Kai-shek. It was also exactly the opposite of all that had been authoritatively affirmed as United States policy by Dean Acheson supported by the United States President that January. Could self-contradictoriness go further?

And thus Taiwan as well as South Korea was placed within the U.S. defense perimeter in Asia and turned into an American base against China.

The protection of Chiang Kai-shek, as a puppet regime, to become the "sole representative" of the "Republic of China" was confirmed, and this grotesque farce would last two decades.

Yet, as Chou En-lai pointed out in 1960, it was four months before China would be provoked into sending volunteers to Korea, and then only after the U.S. military announced their intention of crossing the frontier and proceeded to a massive buildup of forces to carry out this plan.

The vigorous verbal reactions to the Seventh Fleet patrols throughout the summer left no one in doubt. Both Mao Tsetung and Chou En-lai proclaimed in public meetings their determination to liberate Taiwan, for this was part of China and China's domestic affair. But the theme of Taiwan's liberation was now linked to the theme of a wider struggle, against imperialism in Asia, and particularly its armed intervention in Korea. No surprise therefore if Chairman Mao's *Imperialism and All Reactionaries Are Paper Tigers* interview of 1946 was reprinted in July. When heads became cooler in the United States, the injustice done to the People's Republic of China would become increasingly evident, even in conservative circles.

Mr. McGeorge Bundy, in a Rand report in 1960 commissioned by the U.S. Air Force, was to conclude that China had neither planned the Korean war nor intervened under Russian pressure, but had assumed from the statements and actions of General MacArthur that the U.S. intended to invade the territory of China. General MacArthur himself was to reaffirm, in that same year, that such had been his intention, and that it remained his "unfulfilled ambition."

Allen Whiting, in *China Crosses the Yalu*,* points out: "There is

* Allen Whiting *China Crosses the Yalu* (Stanford 1960).

no agreement nor any direct evidence on the degree to which Communist China participated in the planning, even if the North Korean attack was planned and directed by the Soviet Union." Mr. Whiting appears convinced that the USSR got the North Korean government to instigate the Korean war, but a search through his facts does not validate what remains an assumption.

The proponents of the "Russia-instigated" theory are also divided on the reasons for this alleged Russian plan: some say the Russians were "testing American strength everywhere, in Iran in 1946, in Berlin in 1948." This is distortion, to say the least; for Iran was a withdrawal on the part of Stalin, and only by a blockade of some sectors of Berlin did he try to evict the forces of his erstwhile allies from the city, an attempt which failed. Berlin was to remain an unsettled problem for many years; it does not stand up to scrutiny as an attempt to test American strength by a military show of force. The consistent denial of the agreements made with the USSR by the United States would then also come within the range of aggressive and provocative action, and of this there were plenty of instances in the Cold War. Another line of reasoning is to say that Russia egged on North Korea to attack precisely in order to get the Chinese involved, so that there would be no possibility that the PRC would normalize relations with the United States. This is based on alleged remarks made by Khrushchev, expatiating on the great difficulties Mao had in his talks with Stalin. It supposes that Stalin foresaw massive U.S. action in crossing the 38th parallel, foresaw that MacArthur would deliberately — as he did — try to attack China, foresaw that the Seventh Fleet would be sent to the Taiwan straits, in spite of the statements made by Truman, Acheson and MacArthur in January, all three having excluded both South Korea and Taiwan from the U.S. frontiers in Asia. All this makes Stalin almost a seer.

From the beginning, the Chinese view of the Korean war was that it would be a protracted war. Throughout the summer they dropped cautious but multiple hints about the necessity for political mobilization and arousal and for making long-term plans. Utmost solidarity was shown and pledged very early to the Korean people in their struggles for liberation. "The American imperialists . . . will strengthen their aggressive forces," the Chinese warned in July. By July 26 the invading troops were clearly going to be reinforced, and they warned that Korea would be made "a foothold of aggression for the United States," obviously for war on the Chinese mainland later. Chou En-lai warned that the People's Republic would not tolerate invasion, nor "supinely tolerate seeing their neighbors savagely invaded by imperialism." He reiterated that Taiwan would surely be liberated.

Troop movements took place, northward, in July and in August; they were to assure protection of the frontier. The papers printed maps of Korea, and the Yalu river was described. Besides the denunciation of American aggressiveness by Mao Tsetung on June 28, and the launching of the slogan "We shall surely liberate Taiwan," it is said that many thoughtful articles on protracted war were penned by him at the time. He seems to have also written that American imperialist strategy was "to invade Taiwan, Vietnam, and the Philippines" as well as Korea, as this phrase was abundantly quoted. Protracted war, people's war, would be a long-term struggle in Asia, and the editorials and radio broadcasts thus conveyed a larger picture of the Asian struggle for liberation. For indeed Asia was witnessing a massive return of colonial domination, with the British back in Malaysia, the French fighting in Indochina, and the Dutch in Indonesia. In the Philippines, too, there was an uprising of the Huks and a national liberation movement. American policy was now to back the colonial powers; thus Dulles was to pledge massive American aid to the French in their colonial war against Vietnamese people. French military sources today state that their war in Indochina would have ended two years sooner had not the U.S. insisted on its continuation.

There can be no more uncomfortable experience for a U.S. State Department official today than to read the statements of Dulles, Robertson, U.N. representative Warren Austin, Secretary of the Navy Francis P. Matthews, and other hawks of the Korean war period, calling for all-out preventive war, for war to compel cooperation for peace, and so on.

At the end of July, MacArthur flew from Tokyo to Taiwan for forty-eight hours with Chiang Kai-shek. The meeting was pleasant for both, and a joint communiqué was issued. Chiang followed up with a call for an anti-Communist grand alliance in Asia. In August tension rose sharply. The USSR delegate at the U.N. Security Council, Yakov Malik, who had been absent for seven months from the U.N., returned as president and put forward a conciliatory proposal — that PRC delegates as well as representatives of "the Korean people" should attend the U.N. session to discuss the Korean question, and also a cease-fire and withdrawal of all foreign troops.

This was countered by a belligerent speech by Warren Austin on

August 10, stating that the goal of the U.N. was "a unified Korea." A week later he was calling for "total victory" over North Korea and unification under U.N. auspices.

Once again the Russian policy of overall prudence expressed itself; the initial hard verbal stance had a soft core which showed very quickly. Malik did not insist on the legitimate seating rights of the PRC in the U.N., did not bring up the subject of expelling the Chiang "representative," tacitly admitted a permanent division of Korea by speaking of "two governmental camps, North and South." This disappointed the North Koreans. The Chinese were far more principled. They continued to call Syngman Rhee's government a "puppet regime." Because of this soft stance, Russian responsibility for the continuation of the Korean war, even if involuntary, exists.

The "style" of Yakov Malik at the United Nations would be repeated many times; at first it was not understood as an overall policy. But it is much clearer now. Even as early as 1950 there was already, on the part of the USSR, an attempt to impose solutions in local conflicts, solutions worked out by the USSR and in the perspective of her own strategic security or interests; solutions which would not be discussed with and would not respect the wishes or rights of the nations involved in the conflict, but would serve as bargaining counters with the United States. This "superpower" stance was already present in Malik's speeches in that August and September. It disappointed the Chinese as well as the North Koreans, although not a word was said and Malik's speech was lauded in the Chinese press.

But such a speech, such flexibility, was a signal: it did probably encourage, even if indirectly, the more bellicose among the U.S. military and State Department officials, who now realized that the USSR would certainly *not* interfere should the 38th parallel be crossed by the U.S.–U.N. forces and North Korea invaded. And so it was.

By mid-August, and while fighting was going on in South Korea, Chou En-lai was holding talks with India and other nations, searching for a negotiated settlement of the war. But the basis of the negotiated settlement suggested was very clearly different from the Russian one. On August 11, a comfort mission was sent to North Korea, and expressions of solidarity increased. But still nothing was said of military intervention; a campaign throughout the nation to inform the people of what was happening emphasized resistance and defense, and especially the inalienable right of the PRC to liberate Taiwan. But already, in hope of an imminent American invasion of China, many of the 800,000 or more Chiang adherents, secret police and Blueshirts * left in China were starting sabotage actions, and the PLA was busy from August to October against armed gangs which tried to spread terror in some provinces. Mobilization of the people was, however, primarily for construction and not for military activity.

In September the North Korean divisions were pushed back towards the 38th parallel and MacArthur made clear his intention to cross it.

This seems to have been foreseen in late August by Chou En-lai, who had cabled to the United Nations: "Korea is China's neighbor. The Chinese people cannot but be concerned about solution of the Korean question. . . . It must and can be settled peacefully." Now the worry became very pronounced, and on September 25 the Chinese issued a warning which was of great importance. General Nieh Jung-chen, at that time acting chief of staff, in a quiet and unexcited manner told K. M. Pannikar (the Indian delegation had been active in seeking a cease-fire in Korea) that the PRC would not sit back with folded hands and let the Americans come to the Chinese border. "We know what we are in for. The American bombers, they can destroy our industries, but at all costs American aggression has to be stopped." We may take it that he was repeating the words of Chairman Mao Tsetung.

On October 1 MacArthur called upon General Kim Il Sung to *surrender unconditionally*. In Peking, Mao Tsetung called on "the people of China and the world" to be on the alert to "defeat any provocation by U.S. imperialism." The Chinese waited; their response would be tailored to American military steps taken towards their own borders. Chou En-lai denounced imperialist aggression and warned the U.S. to stop advancing. Throughout September more hints had appeared in various Chinese publications that the Koreans should envisage a protracted war with full political mobilization of the population, for this would achieve the *political objective* of reunification by politically directed means. So far, however, the North Korean forces had fought a regular war because they had been equipped for it by the Russians. They were thus somewhat handicapped by their very training in this respect, although their leader Kim Il Sung had successfully led a guerilla war against Japan

* A fascist secret organization once controlled by Tai Li, hatchet man of Chiang Kai-shek and head of his secret police.

previously and guerillas would spring to action soon. But now with the massive involvement of American forces in the war — there would be up to 440,000 men — this kind of regular warfare was a handicap to the small nation of 11 million people in the North.

Chou En-lai had reiterated in September: "The Chinese people are determined to liberate Taiwan. . . . The Korean people can surely overcome their many difficulties and obtain final victory on the principle of persistent, long-term resistance. . . . The Chinese people absolutely will not tolerate foreign aggression [on their own territory], nor will they supinely tolerate seeing their neighbors being savagely invaded by imperialists." On October 2 Chou En-lai informed Pannikar that "should the U.S. troops invade North Korean territory," China would be forced to enter the war. The same warning was repeated through embassies in Moscow, Stockholm and other capitals. President Truman thought it was a bluff, and decided that Pannikar was too pro-Chinese and not an impartial observer. The directive sent by Truman to MacArthur on September 27 had assured the General that he could conduct operations north of the 38th parallel provided "there has been no entry into North Korea by major Soviet or Chinese communist forces, no announcement of intended entry, nor a threat to counter our operations militarily in North Korea." Precisely such a warning had been issued twice by China's premier and chief of staff, and twice discounted.

The United Nations had now been pressured into a resolution calling for a unified, independent and democratic government in the sovereign state of Korea, thus justifying MacArthur's invasion of North Korea. The danger of a mighty base complex consisting of Japan, Korea and Taiwan in a triangle of forces threatening China, was now very clear to the Chinese. On October 15 MacArthur assured Truman at a meeting in the Pacific (the Wake island meeting) that the Chinese would *not* intervene. On October 19 U.S. forces entered Pyongyang, capital of North Korea. Before October 19 the frontier territory bordering the Yalu had been declared by Truman out of bounds to U.S. and U.N. troops, but not to South Korean troops. This was Truman's first attempt to avoid direct confrontation. But five days later, on October 24, MacArthur took it upon himself to lift this restriction and ordered all U.N. forces to advance to the Yalu river. Repeatedly he declared that there were no Chinese units. Actually, the first Chinese people's volunteers had crossed on October 16, had been seen by the Americans on the 18th, but they

U.S. troops at the Yalu river, Korea 1950.

Chinese troops on a road in Kaesong during the armistice talks, Korea 1951.

were not "discovered" till October 31.* Some writers on the Korean war think that this timing was deliberate on MacArthur's part, so as to precipitate a confrontation and bypass an order to withdraw; for between October 16 and October 29 MacArthur was mounting a massive offensive to cross the Yalu. The tide now turned. Between October 29 and 31 the Chinese volunteers, and North Korean troops were to inflict devastating losses on South Korean troops, repeatedly punching in weak spots and forcing the U.N. and U.S. forces to withdraw.

By that November, as the tide began to roll back, the demand at the U.N. for negotiations and for a cease-fire grew stronger. A marked lull in the fighting then occurred, the Chinese volunteers disengaging and withdrawing in order to give an opportunity for a truce and cessation of military action. This was not propitious for MacArthur's plans. His headquarters "did its best to picture this continued swift withdrawal as infused with aggressive intent," writes I. F. Stone.† United States forces began to exhibit reliance on massive air strikes; heavy bombers carried out raids within Manchuria and on the frontier. In London and in Paris questions were raised as to the role of MacArthur and his objectives.

MacArthur then mounted another offensive towards the Yalu. This was a most publicized offensive; he postponed it (with fanfare) from November 15 to November 24, the day PRC delegates General Wu Hsiu-chuan and Chiao Kuan-hua arrived at the United Nations. Thus any hope of constructive talks leading to a cease-fire were obliterated.

But contradictions now began to show up in Truman's entourage; some civilians denounced MacArthur; the Wisconsin Mikado, they said, had assured the President that the Chinese would not come in. By this November offensive MacArthur was going against the Wake island decisions.

On November 26 the offensive was smashed; the North Koreans and Chinese people's volunteers counterattacked along the entire front. MacArthur now called for Chiang's troops to be thrown into the war, but the United Nations refused their consent. Through December, MacArthur, as he retreated farther and farther, and often without combat, kept calling for more troops and for permission to

---

* They were, however, very small in number, sent to protect the hydroelectric installations.

† I. F. Stone *The Hidden History of the Korean War* (New York and London 2nd edition 1969).

destroy "sanctuaries" in Manchuria. He was trying, and did succeed, to create another panic. Dispatches from his Tokyo headquarters mentioned vast hordes of Communist Chinese pouring forth in a torrent. He demanded an extension of the war to China, otherwise he would evacuate Korea. There is no doubt that some units, especially the South Korean troops, now that they encountered a reinforced opposition, fought poorly. The tactics of North Korean and Chinese units of biting great chunks out of the line, of chopping up units and annihilating them, produced a terror out of proportion to the losses. There were more casualties from the headlong retreat, the savage selfishness of units who fought each other for the trucks to leave in (often only the G.I.'s would thus benefit), and the guerilla action than from actual encounters. It was a morale-stricken army which in December was re-formed in another line north of Seoul.

On December 14 the General Assembly of the United Nations passed a resolution sponsored by thirteen nations for a cease-fire. The Chinese delegation had now been able to put forth its proposals. The speech, called "truculent," was actually eminently reasonable. It supported the North Korean demand for withdrawal of all foreign troops, demanded American withdrawal from Taiwan, and made its claim to its rightful seat in the United Nations.

On January 1 an offensive by the North Koreans was reported. It breached the new line at Seoul, which collapsed; a further retreat took place. According to I. F. Stone * there was no offensive and the retreat was a planned one. "Their only thought was to get away, to put miles between them and the fearful army that was at their heels," wrote U.S. General Matthew B. Ridgway of his own troops. Meanwhile the Chinese U.N. speech, reiterating that China wanted peace and not war, had impressed a good many delegates. Chinese action to lessen tension had been taken prior to it, with the release of a hundred U.S. and South Korean prisoners and the offer to release a thousand more. MacArthur continued to justify his retreat with news of hordes pouring again. Actually there had been a withdrawal of the Chinese volunteers and North Koreans, for another lull to take place, another peace effort. Truman, however, was pressured by a clamor of senators demanding that the atom bomb be used on China as the only way to "end the war." But the British prime minister, Clement Attlee, flew to the United States to speak to the President, which seems to have been some-

* Stone *op. cit.*

General Wu Hsiu-chuan and (extreme left, behind him) Chiao Kuan-hua of the People's Republic of China at the United Nations, November 27, 1950. In the center, Kenneth Younger, United Kingdom; at right, John Foster Dulles, United States.

what effective. In January 1951 a cease-fire committee went into action. This did not please MacArthur or the hawks. If peace broke out, could the U.N. condemn the Chinese as aggressors? A resolution in that vein brought up in November was now pressed through; during the second half of January the U.S. utilized its Marshall foreign aid programs, threats, even declared it would withdraw from the U.N. unless the latter condemned Peking. On January 30, 1951, China was branded an aggressor by the Political and Security committee of the U.N. and the General Assembly ratified this the next day.

Thus the retreat — more or less deliberate, for there were no Chinese hordes, none crossed the 38th parallel, and pretty soon cynical newsmen would be asking how many hordes there were to a platoon of volunteers — provoked a stampede and hysteria which reaped the political goal desired. The U.S.–U.N. armies now reoccupied Seoul. However, Truman had set limits to MacArthur's paranoia; he would not be allowed to bomb Manchurian bases, nor to utilize Chiang Kai-shek's forces.

On March 13, aware there were now serious indications of a cease-fire, MacArthur again ordered some forces to cross the 38th parallel, then issued his own "political statement" for a truce, in an effort to bring back to himself the power of decision-making in Korea. Truman once again gave in, and in April the bulk of the forces once more crossed the parallel. Misjudging Truman, Mac-Arthur went on systematically to defy him, communicating over the President's head with Republican leader Joseph W. Martin, endorsing the use of Chiang Kai-shek's forces for the Korean war. This was too much. On April 11 MacArthur was dismissed by President Truman. It was then obvious that the United States would *not* attack the PRC, though it would still seek a local military victory in Korea, for a defeat was too humiliating for such a great power.

The Korean war would continue for two more years, though it was really fought to a stalemate around the 38th parallel by the summer of 1951.

During the first four months that the Chinese volunteers were in Korea, up to January 1951, they appear to have been armed with Chinese weapons, cast-off Japanese weapons and American weapons. * The strategy and tactics were of mobile warfare, following Mao

* Captured during the civil war with Chiang Kai-shek.

Tsetung's teachings. Guerilla harassment was also successful, pinning down, according to American sources, nearly 30 percent of U.S. troops in Korea; and these guerillas were the Korean people, both North and South. By mid-January more than twenty incidents caused by guerillas occurred every day, and this political mobilization of the population was very important.

But by April 1951 a change was occurring, with important repercussions later, within the People's Liberation Army in China itself. This was a switchover which occurred over that spring and summer from mobile to positional warfare, with trenches dug, positions held, tunnel warfare against airplane bombing, and World War I human wave type of assault. This change is supposed to be due to the type of warfare the Americans were waging; but was no doubt also impelled by the type of weapons and equipment, requiring skilled and "regular" technical army personnel, which now came in massively from the USSR. The Chinese now also acquired an air force, to fight the vastly superior U.S. air force. Here, therefore, weapons seem to have compelled, for use to maximal effect, a change of tactics, and this is puzzling. It could not have been done unless Peng Teh-huai, who was in command of the volunteers from October 1950, had deliberately opted for this change.

All reports praise the high morale, courage, and combat efficiency of the volunteers; but in the next two years many were to die and be replaced by less well-trained volunteers, so that the tendency to train highly efficient and skilled personnel in small groups increased. In April 1951 Peng was to launch a large offensive, a week after Mac-Arthur had been dismissed. This was the beginning of the change from one kind of warfare to another, the beginning of utilization of Soviet weaponry; it is rumored that Mao Tsetung was against the offensive launched, and the decision was Peng's alone.

By now, because of the ferocity of the American bombing, there was also a large refugee problem; of the 11 million in North Korea, almost 2 million had been pushed by obliteration bombings to flee southward.

Yet by all acounts the Chinese were aware of negotiations by France and Great Britain during February and March, pressing the U.S. for a formal declaration of war aims, and of Truman's increasing irritation with MacArthur. On March 12 an article had appeared in the New York *Times. U.N. Dropping Idea of Unifying Korea by Military Force. Diplomats say U.S. taking position task will end round 38th line* were the headlines. However, the commanders in the field insisted on a military victory, and the Truman administration too could not afford to withdraw on a defeat; such was the great military prestige of the Chinese volunteers whose advent had turned the tide that all over Asia there were most favorable comments on their heroism. Did all this go to Peng Teh-huai's head, or is there reason to suspect that deliberately the Russians encouraged a prolongation of the war? Peng had now most friendly relations with Russian personnel, and the routing of supplies to Korea through Manchuria was to increase greatly in volume after the summer of 1951.

A week after MacArthur's dismissal came Peng Teh-huai's famous offensives, with the proclaimed aim of "pushing the imperialists to the sea." The fighting that followed was entirely different from the Mao style. The battles see-sawed, but the result was a prolonged stalemate. Heavy casualties were inflicted on both sides.

Peng Teh-huai, already a "professional" soldier, impatient with political precepts, and who had earlier proved his insubordination, was to evolve into an opponent of Mao's military principles. He would emerge from the Korean war as a "hero," and later as minister of defense would start "professionalizing" the People's Liberation Army, following the Soviet model and becoming reliant on Soviet weaponry to a very high degree. Thus, in a few short years, the quality of the People's Liberation Army would be changed. Political instruction would be at a minimum, technical modernization emphasized. This would lead, later, to a bitter struggle between two sides in the Red Army leadership, and ultimately to the downfall of Peng Teh-huai.*

Because Mao Tsetung's "tit for tat" line of struggle, which was most economical of men and material and also left far more room for diplomatic maneuver, was not heeded, China became very dependent upon the USSR for the next two years, through the flow of military supplies for the Korean war. This at first might not have appeared a burden, until suddenly, when Sino-Soviet relations deteriorated, the truth was out. A large part of overall Soviet loans to China for reconstruction were used up in the Korean war. In 1962 Khrushchev demanded immediate repayment for these supplies, and this caused much hardship in China. However, everything was repaid. "The Korean people carried by far the heaviest burden and sustained by far the greatest losses. The Chinese people too

---

* It must be noted that differences in Army policy were not the only cause of Peng Teh-huai's downfall.

made great sacrifices and incurred vast military expenses . . . even the war materiel supplied to China in the war to resist U.S. aggression and aid Korea has not been given gratis." *

It is possible then to suspect that the lengthening of the Korean war was due, on the part of the Russians, to a desire to see China tied up in debt and dependent upon them. If so, the operation was quite successful. Not only did it increase dependence in a material way, it also was to leave many ideological problems, involving such men as Peng Teh-huai and Kao Kang, which would not be easily solved.

America's disengagement from Asia, which might have happened — although with Dulles and the Truman doctrine, this is very doubtful — would have meant more concentration against Eastern Europe and consequent pressure on the USSR at its more vulnerable flank. This was dreaded by Moscow. Some cynics have even felt that the withdrawal of the Soviet delegation from the U.N. on the ground that it would not stay while the Chiang delegation was seated (it returned after seven months despite the same delegation's presence) was a deliberate move *not* to block by its veto the U.N. resolution which made the Korean war possible. But this may be assuming too much.†

During 1951 and 1952 the Soviet newspaper *Pravda* mightily strove to call the Chinese people's volunteers the PLA, writing that Mao had planned and timed the military campaigns. The Korean war also won for the CCP and for Chairman Mao ideological recognition in the USSR, where Mao's works were now extolled. Mao himself would say, much later, that the Chinese action in Korea had convinced Stalin that there was no Tito in China and that China stood solidly in defense of the socialist camp.

In 1963, when the Sino-Soviet ideological dispute was acute, the *Comment on the Open Letter of the Central Committee of the CPSU — Two Different Lines on the Question of War and Peace,‡* probably penned by Mao Tsetung himself, had this to say: "The leaders of the CPSU . . . accuse us of hoping for a 'head-on clash' between the Soviet Union and the U.S. . . . Our answer is no, friends, the Chinese Communist Party is firmly opposed to a head-on clash . . . and not in words only. In deeds too it has worked hard to

* Letter of the CCP Central Committee to the CPSU Central Committee, February 29, 1964.
† Edgar Snow *The Other Side of the River: Red China Today* (New York 1962); also interview with Edgar Snow.
‡ November 19, 1963.

avert direct armed conflict between them. Examples of this are the Korean war against U.S. aggression, in which we fought side by side with Korean comrades. We ourselves preferred to shoulder the heavy sacrifice necessary . . . and stood in the first line of defense of the socialist camp so that the Soviet Union might stay in the second line."

The inference is that if China had not intervened, but allowed and even lured the enemy deep into Manchuria, and onward, the Soviet Union would have been compelled to come into the war and clash with the United States.

The Korean war also had the result of turning America's hatred upon China; Russia had been the enemy number one until then; from then onward America became obsessed with "Red China," who now occupied first place as "the enemy." American policy for the next twenty years would be colored by the Korean episode.

On the other hand, the U.S. could have stopped the war in June 1951, had it not been that the build-up of men and weapons was too high, and the desire for a military victory too urgent. On June 23, two days before the first anniversary of the Korean war, Malik proposed cease-fire talks as preliminary to a peaceful settlement in Korea. The Malik offer was already a victory for Truman, since Truman had made precisely such an offer shortly before. (1) The fighting must stop. (2) Concrete steps must be taken to ensure it would not return. (3) There must be an end to "aggression."

The North Korean and the Chinese political conditions, formulated in November 1950, were thus bypassed by the USSR. The Chinese had asked for withdrawal of all foreign troops from Korea, return of Taiwan to China and an end to U.S. interference in China's domestic affairs, seating of the PRC in the U.N. as the legitimate government of China. Malik's proposal allowed the U.S. to go on recognizing Chiang Kai-shek as the "legitimate government of China," a policy affirmed by Dean Rusk on May 18 — "The Peking regime does not represent the people of China," said Rusk. It allowed the Seventh Fleet to go on patrolling the South China coast, and Taiwan to remain within the perimeter of U.S. defense. It also legitimized indirectly the 38th parallel and allowed U.S. forces to remain in South Korea, where they still are today.

Meanwhile Chiang Kai-shek and Syngman Rhee had both secured for themselves cover within the perimeter of U.S. defense; the U.S. security treaty with Japan was drafted and signed.

But by 1952, with mounting casualties in an endless war — "What

are we here for anyway?" asked the U.S. soldiers — a growing weariness among the American people manifested itself. The statement
made by some rejoicing big businesses that "Korea has been a bless-
ing. There had to be a Korea either here or some place in the
world." no longer sounded acceptable. In May 1951 the forthright General Omar Bradley had testified, "Red China is not the
powerful nation seeking to dominate the world," and called the
Korean war "the wrong war, at the wrong place, at the wrong time,
and with the wrong enemy."

In March 1953 Josef Stalin died. Again, some historians maintain
that he had kept the war going, since an armistice was made three
months after his demise. But it was the U.S. military who kept the
war going because they needed a military victory and it was American public opinion which slowly ground the Korean war to a halt.
The deadly and inconclusive fighting came to an end at Panmunjon
at 10 A.M. on July 27, 1953. It had cost the U.S. over 300,000
casualties.

At Panmunjon today the demilitarized zone, 2.5 miles wide on either side of the 38th parallel, still exists. The talks are still going on,
twenty-one years later.

On October 26, 1971, twenty-one years almost to the day when
Chinese volunteers came to North Korea, the People's Republic of
China was at last restored its legitimate seating in the United Nations
General Assembly and Security Council, and Chiang's representa-
tives were at last expelled.

That this "conversion of contradiction" could occur *without a war*
was due to Mao Tsetung, to his consummate patience, vision and
effort. And to his often repeated belief that the forces of history
were bound to bring the two peoples together again in friendship. It
was due to his clearly stated principle of peaceful coexistence, stated
in 1944 and in 1949, and carried out the years through.

During these twenty years another war, the Vietnam war, would
be fought by the United States with direct American involvement on
the Asian mainland. It would spread to Laos and to Cambodia.
Once again, China had nothing to do with creating this war, and
did not provoke it, but the bogey of a "red China" seeking to
engulf all her neighbors had been used to justify the costly and
absurd military presence of American armies to the American people, and the appalling sufferings inflicted upon the peoples of Indochina. And now the lie has proved itself a lie.

During those two decades the people of China, under the leadership of Mao Tsetung, had carried on the construction of New China. They had rebuilt their country, had learned new ways of thought and behavior, and made "heaven and earth change places." They had won by hard work the respect and admiration of the world's peoples; they had carried out another cultural revolution, and fulfilled the dream that socialism would not be a tyranny but a true liberation. The Chinese people had indeed removed the mountains of ignorance, exploitation and misery from their own shoulders.

The story of how this was done is one which will be unfolded in the second volume. The name of Mao Tsetung, in these twenty years, had become a household word, a word known throughout the world. "There is no conflict of basic interest between the peoples of China and the United States and friendship will eventually prevail," Chou En-lai had said to Edgar Snow in 1960. In this he was quoting Mao Tsetung. And this sentence would apply not only to the American people, but also to all the other peoples of the world.

Second and last volume in preparation.

Picture Credits

INDEX